Jazz The First 100 Years

Jazz The First 100 Years

Henry Martin   RUTGERS UNIVERSITY

Keith Waters   UNIVERSITY OF COLORADO

SCHIRMER
THOMSON LEARNING

Australia ■ Canada ■ Mexico ■ Singapore ■ Spain ■ United Kingdom ■ United States

Editorial Director: Clark G. Baxter
Assistant Editor: Jennifer Ellis
Editorial Assistant: Jonathan Katz
Executive Marketing Manager: Diane McOscar
Marketing Assistant: Kasia Zagorski
Project Manager: Dianne Jensis Toop
Senior Print/Media Buyer: Karen Hunt
Permissions Editor: Stephanie Keough-Hedges
Production Service: Ideas to Images

Photo Researcher: Roberta Broyer
Copy Editor: Molly Roth
Proofreader: Elizabeth von Radics Editorial Services
Autographer: Ernie Mansfield, Mansfield Music-Graphics
Cover and Interior Designer: Gary Palmatier, Ideas to Images
Cover Image: Vasily Kandinsky, *Composition 8*
Cover Printer: Transcontinental Printing
Compositor: Robaire Ream, Ideas to Images
Printer: Transcontinental Printing

Printed in Canada

3   4   5   6   7   05   04   03   02

ISBN 0-02-864789-0

Wadsworth/Thomson Learning
10 Davis Drive
Belmont, CA 94002-3098
USA

For more information about our products, contact us:
Thomson Learning Academic Resource Center
1-800-423-0563
http://www.wadsworth.com

International Headquarters
Thomson Learning
International Division
290 Harbor Drive, 2nd Floor
Stamford, CT 06902-7477
USA

U.K./Europe/Middle East/South Africa
Thomson Learning
Berkshire House
168-173 High Holborn
London WC1V 7AA
United Kingdom

Asia
Thomson Learning
60 Albert Street, #15-01
Albert Complex
Singapore 189969

Canada
Nelson Thomson Learning
1120 Birchmount Road
Toronto, Ontario M1K 5G4
Canada

For Barbara and Gene

BRIEF OVERVIEW

CONTENTS

Courtesy Frank Driggs Collection

CHAPTER **5**

The Swing Era 102

Courtesy Frank Driggs Collection

CHAPTER **7**

The Bebop Era 170

CHAPTER **9**

The Sixties Avant-Garde 238

CHAPTER *11*

Jazz-Rock, Jazz-Funk Fusion 292

CHAPTER **12**

Jazz Since the 1980s

322

Copyright © Bettmann/CORBIS

PREFACE

WE WROTE *JAZZ: THE FIRST 100 YEARS* to provide college students with a text that presents a fresh overview of jazz history and focuses greater attention on jazz since 1970, a period often slighted in previous surveys. We have also tried to stimulate fresh thinking about the jazz canon by including on the accompanying two-CD set recordings that complement more than duplicate the selections available on the *Smithsonian Collection of Classic Jazz*. In addition to the book's primary concern—the development of jazz and its most important artists— our text relates the music to relevant aspects of social and intellectual history, including the Harlem Renaissance. Finally, we try to include the most up-to-date information possible, taking advantage of the fine scholarly work on jazz that has appeared during the past several years.

Our chronological presentation of jazz history preserves the customary divisions of the music into stylistic periods, because we feel that this is the clearest method of introducing the material to the student. Nonetheless, throughout the text we acknowledge the arbitrariness of the stylistic divisions and emphasize that many (if not most) artists have produced significant work beyond the era in which they first came to public attention.

As with any history, we sometimes must stray outside the time frame of a given era to complete the narrative of an important figure. For the most part, however, an artist is generally treated in the era in which he or she exerted the most influence. The two main exceptions to this practice are Miles Davis and Duke Ellington. Although Ellington was prominent and influential throughout his career, he played an especially important role in early jazz and the swing era (Chapters 4 and 5). Davis exerted considerable influence on the disparate styles of 1950s cool jazz, 1960s mainstream jazz, and 1970s jazz-rock, so his story is related in Chapters 8, 10, and 11. King Oliver's Creole Jazz Band, which is usually treated as representative of New Orleans jazz, is covered in Chapter 3 on Chicago jazz; this is because Oliver achieved his greatest success in Chicago and because the text flows naturally into the story of Oliver's second cornetist, Louis Armstrong, and his consequent rise to stardom.

Features

▶ We offer a two-CD set with a variety of jazz recordings from 1917 to 1999.

▶ An ⏺ Audio Primer CD, prepared by the authors, is included with every copy of the text. This CD demonstrates basic musical concepts (scales, syncopation, blues, rhythm changes, inside/outside playing, and so forth) as well as the instruments of jazz (the four principal saxophones, trumpet and trombone with different mutes, electric and acoustic guitars, the different sounds of the drum set, and so on). Where appropriate, the definitions of key terms in the text refer to the ⏺ Audio Primer CD so that the student can hear what is being defined.

▶ Listening Guides for each CD track appear in the text, with detailed CD timings keyed to events in the music and the work's overall form.

▶ The book features a historical focus on the evolution of significant trends, key figures, and the changing role of instrumental and improvisational style. It also includes relevant ideas in twentieth-century U.S. social and intellectual history, including the Harlem Renaissance and the countercultural movements of the 1960s. Many issues related to contemporary U.S. political and social history appear in the photographs and their captions.

▶ We include a balanced and nuanced view of jazz since 1960. One-third of our book chronicles jazz since 1960, detailing significant trends and performers of the 1960s through the 1990s.

▶ Current scholarly and critical work is reflected throughout. The text takes into account some of the groundbreaking jazz research of the previous two decades. The presentation attempts to illuminate and amplify current historical and musical controversies rather than assert unqualified truths.

▶ Questions at the end of each chapter are given for class discussion or assignments.

▶ Key terms are listed at the end of each chapter.

▶ The book includes a glossary containing definitions presented in the text.

▶ There are endnotes to each chapter, a recommended discography, and a bibliography listing extensive sources for further listening, study, and research.

▶ We offer access to a Web site with a link to the electronic instructor's manual. The manual contains suggestions for additional recordings to play in class and information about other important artists relevant to each chapter. The Web site also includes notes to the additional recordings and will include updated information as it becomes available.

ACCOMPANYING TWO-CD SET

The recordings selected for the CDs attempt to give a general overview of jazz in the twentieth century. We could not include all of the many important artists in a brief two-CD presentation, of course, but the selections nevertheless sample a broad cross-section of significant jazz artists and styles. The text includes Listening Guides for each track, which readers may refer to while working through the material. These Listening Guides contain commentary highlighting aspects of form, instrumentation, and improvisation. In choosing our selections, we followed these criteria:

▶ The recordings should be representative of the artists' work generally.

▶ The recordings should be well known, unless there is reason to include something more obscure.

▶ Excerpting should be minimal.

▶ The choice and arrangement of the selections should work aesthetically. We hope that students will enjoy listening to the CDs for pleasure rather than just focusing on each selection as it is discussed in the text.

▶ The recordings generally avoid duplicating the selections contained in the *Smithsonian Collection of Classic Jazz (SCCJ)*. Some of the material posted on our book's Web site references the *SCCJ* for instructors who wish to supplement the material on our accompanying CDs. (Although the *SCCJ* is out of print at the time of this writing, we expect it to be available again soon.)

USING THE TEXT

The text is divided into twelve chapters; for a one-semester class, an instructor should cover approximately one chapter per week. There is certainly more material in the book than can be discussed or listened to in class under this schedule, so we hope that students will find our work a useful guide for further exploration of the music. Within each chapter the material is organized through main headings and subordinate headings, which should help the instructor maximize the use of class time and (in smaller classes) coordinate discussion according to the most important topics.

The text can also support a two-semester class. Instructors may wish to finish with Chapter 7 in the first semester; in this case the first semester presents jazz from 1900 to 1950, and the second semester covers jazz from 1950 to 2000. The text is suitable for a variety of classroom formats, from large lecture courses to smaller classes that encourage more student participation. Because the book combines a historical narrative with broader summaries of stylistic features, the instructor is free to use and shape the given material. Instructors of lecture classes may concentrate on the larger-scale overview, highlighting key performers and examining developments in instrumental and improvisational styles. Instructors of smaller classes may spend more time discussing controversies and historical developments.

MUSICAL ANALYSES AND TRANSCRIPTIONS

Although the book contains several musical analyses and notated transcriptions, students do not need to be able to read musical notation to learn from *Jazz: The First 100 Years*. Because the analytical portions are separated from the main text, the instructor can choose whether to assign this material, depending on the interests of the students and purposes of the class. Music majors or advanced students might profit from working through some of the analyses, whereas the general student need focus only on the text and Listening Guides.

Acknowledgments

Jazz: The First 100 Years began as an expanded second edition of Martin's *Enjoying Jazz* (Schirmer Books, 1986) but quickly developed into a comprehensive jazz history text. Readers of *Enjoying Jazz* will recognize some of its analyses, which have been transferred and reworked here. Some of the transcriptions of improvised solos from *Enjoying Jazz* appear as well, although new material has been added.

Schirmer Books guided the original composition of the manuscript. The staff at Schirmer was a pleasure to work with in the planning stages of the project. After preliminary discussions with Maribeth Payne, Jill Leckta helped us formulate and refine the original concept. In addition to Jill's suggestions, Schirmer engaged several anonymous readers to critique our first proposals. They offered excellent suggestions for improving basic layout and coverage. We thank Maribeth, Jill, and the original readers.

Richard Carlin, former music editor of Schirmer Books, supervised the initial composition of the manuscript with experience and tact. His many suggestions were perceptive and timely, contributing greatly to the book's overall content and final form.

The environment and support provided by the Special Interest Group in Jazz (SMT-Jz) of the Society for Music Theory have helped make this book a reality. Many thanks to the members of SMT-Jz who encouraged us to pursue this project and offered suggestions throughout the composition of the manuscript.

Once a draft of the manuscript was complete, we turned it over to our research assistant, Javier Gonzalez, who worked tirelessly, checking discographical and biographical information. Javier's background is in both historiography—he has a master's degree in Jazz History and Research from Rutgers University–Newark— and in jazz performance. His insight, suggestions, and corrections were invaluable. Naturally, any remaining errors are the authors' responsibility. We hope that any such errors will be corrected as new information becomes available and as jazz scholarship continues to separate fact from legend. We plan to include updated and corrected information in future editions of this book and will post important emendations to the book's Web site.

In late 1999 the music textbook division of Schirmer transferred to Wadsworth, which has overseen the final stages of manuscript revision and production. Clark Baxter, editorial director for the humanities at Wadsworth, showed professional insight in suggesting ways in which the book could be improved and made more accessible to a wider audience. We are especially indebted to him for formulating the idea of the ⓐ Audio Primer CD, which we expect to be quite helpful to instructors in the classroom. His colleagues reviewed and edited the final manuscript in detail to make sure it was consistent and balanced and suggested numerous improvements. We owe them a tremendous debt for their tireless work in uncovering the photographs, sheet music covers, and other pictorial material used in the text. Clark's commentary for all the pictures provides an important dimension to the book, particularly by placing the development of jazz within the larger context of U.S. social and political history.

For the ⓐ Audio Primer CD, many thanks to the excellent Denver-based musicians who agreed to perform on it. They include Rich Chiaraluce, Mark Harris, Bill Kopper, Ron Miles, Todd Reid, and Ken Walker. We also would like to thank our assistant engineers, Ty Blosser, Jerry Wright, and John Romero. A special thanks to Joe Hall, who was the principal engineer as well as trombonist.

We thank Tom Laskey of Sony Music Special Projects, who worked with us on the production of the two historical CDs. Tom's patience in locating the best possible audio sources for each selection was admirable. The engineer who helped assemble the CDs from the various audio sources was Charles LaPierre of SoundByte Productions in New York.

We would also like to thank the readers engaged by Wadsworth to critique the manuscript. From David Joyner, professor of music, North Texas University; Wallace J. Rave, associate professor of music, Arizona State University; and David Schmalenberger, professor of music, University of Minnesota–Duluth, we gained excellent insights and suggestions. Thanks to Dianne Toop, Pamela Suwinsky, and Stephen Rapley of Wadsworth, who oversaw the details of final design and production.

The striking cover and interior design is the work of Gary Palmatier of Ideas to Images, the company that produced the final book. Molly Roth did the meticulous copy editing. Molly caught many inconsistencies and played a pivotal role in clarifying and focusing our prose. We thank her profusely. The beautiful music examples were prepared by Ernie Mansfield of Mansfield Music-Graphics. The comprehensive index was prepared by Edwin Durbin.

We are proud to include personal statements by composer Maria Schneider and conductor/producer Robert Sadin, who commented on musical passages for this book in response to written queries. For the time they spent on their informative analyses, we are especially thankful.

Our historical and analytical insights are profoundly indebted to the explosion of recent first-rate scholarly and critical studies on jazz. Many have proven invaluable, including (but not limited to) Lewis Porter's excellent studies of Lester Young and John Coltrane, Mark Tucker's work on Duke Ellington, Scott DeVeaux's writings on bebop, Stuart Nicholson's book on jazz-rock fusion, and Enrico Merlin's material on Miles Davis's electric period. We would like to thank Tom Riis for his input on late-nineteenth-century American music in general. Bill Kirchner offered excellent advice in the early stages of the process, as did Greg Dyes, formerly of the University of Colorado, and Michael Fitzgerald. Carl Woideck suggested several improvements and clarifications, for which we are grateful. Brian Fores's unpublished master's thesis on John Zorn contributed material not available elsewhere. John Galm provided excellent insights into the retention of African music in the United States and helped us clarify the summary of African music in Chapter 1.

The graduate students in the master's degree program in Jazz History and Research at Rutgers University–Newark read earlier drafts of many sections and provided valuable feedback; we thank them for their time and comments. We particularly acknowledge the staff of the Institute of Jazz Studies at Rutgers University–Newark: Dan Morgenstern, Ed Berger, Don Luck, and Vince Pelote were extremely generous with their time and advice.

We thank the University of Colorado at Boulder for providing a Graduate Committee on the Arts and Humanities grant to Keith Waters, which provided travel funds for research. A sabbatical for Henry Martin from Rutgers University–Newark in fall 1999 was extremely helpful in the final stages of composition.

Finally, we would especially like to acknowledge the personal and endless support of Barbara Fiorella and Gene Hayworth. Each managed to deal with the authors' individual whims, predilections, peccadilloes, and other personal idiosyncrasies with humor, support, and continuing encouragement. The term *significant other* is clumsy, but for each of us there truly is no one more significant. We are extraordinarily fortunate to have our lives so enriched. We dedicate this book to Barbara and Gene.

ABOUT THE AUTHORS

Henry Martin

Henry Martin is associate professor of music at Rutgers University–Newark. With a Ph.D. from Princeton University and degrees from the University of Michigan and Oberlin Conservatory, he has pursued a dual career as a composer-pianist and as a music theorist specializing in jazz and the Western tonal tradition. His compositions have won several awards, including the 1998 Barlow Endowment International Composition Competition and the National Composers Competition sponsored by the League of Composers–International Society for Contemporary Music, and are published by Margun Music (distributed by Shawnee Press).

Martin teaches in the master's degree program in Jazz History and Research at Rutgers–Newark, the country's only program granting a degree in jazz scholarship. He is associate editor of the *Annual Review of Jazz Studies,* which is published by Scarecrow Press and the Rutgers Institute of Jazz Studies. His book *Charlie Parker and Thematic Improvisation* was published by Scarecrow Press in 1996. *Enjoying Jazz* was published by Schirmer Books in 1986. He has published numerous articles on music theory in such journals as *Perspectives of New Music* and *In Theory Only.* He is also the founder and chair of the Jazz Special Interest Group, an organization of music theorists devoted to advancing scholarship in jazz theory.

Keith Waters

Keith Waters is assistant professor of music theory at the University of Colorado at Boulder. He received a Ph.D. in music theory from the Eastman School of Music, an master of music degree in jazz piano from the New England Conservatory of Music, and a bachelor of music degree in applied piano from the University of North Carolina–Greensboro. He has published articles on topics related to jazz analysis and pedagogy, as well as on twentieth-century composer Arthur Honegger.

As a jazz pianist, Waters has performed in concerts, jazz festivals, and clubs throughout the United States, Europe, and in Russia, appearing in such venues as the Blue Note and the Village Corner, in New York, and Blues Alley and the Kennedy Center, in Washington, D.C. He has performed in concert with numerous jazz artists, including James Moody, Bobby Hutcherson, Eddie Harris, Chris Connor, Sheila Jordan, Keter Betts, Buck Hill, and Meredith D'Ambrosia. He has recorded for VSOP Records, and his playing has been featured in *Jazz Player* magazine.

The authors welcome suggestions for subsequent editions. Comments may be posted to the book's Web site at *www.wadsworth.com* or e-mailed to the authors directly:

Henry Martin   martinh@andromeda.rutgers.edu

Keith Waters   watersk@stripe.colorado.edu

Jazz
The First 100 Years

This tattered sheet music cover of "Dawn of the Century," published in 1900, celebrates the birth of the twentieth century with the latest inventions, many American. The artist implies that Americans will continue to invent, and the evolution of jazz proved him correct. Notice the variety of inventions shown here . . . and the number that are not shown.

ROOTS

1

WHAT IS JAZZ? It seems proper to begin a book on the history of jazz by defining it, but this is a famous dead end: Entire articles have been written on the futility of pinning down the precise meaning of jazz. Proposed definitions have failed either because they are too restrictive—overlooking a lot of music we think of as jazz—or too inclusive—calling virtually any kind of music "jazz."

Jazz is difficult to define, in part, because of its complex history, for jazz has African, European, and even Caribbean roots. Although the precise contributions of various cultures and subcultures remain controversial, without their blending, jazz would not have come into being. This much is clear: Jazz arose not in Africa, not in Europe, and not in the Caribbean, but in the United States, thanks to the importation of nonnative musical elements into the dominant European culture of U.S. society.

Because African and European cultures have contributed the most to jazz, we begin with a brief examination of these cultures and the elements that they contributed. More specifically, we discuss the following:

- Genres of folk and popular music from the African tradition, including
  - ▶ Spirituals
  - ▶ Early African-American folk songs

- European culture, including
  - ▶ Tonality
  - ▶ Instruments
  - ▶ Marches and other important genres

- The rise of minstrelsy and its stereotypes of African-American music

- Ragtime

- The blues

Ragtime and the **blues** are the direct predecessors of jazz.

3

African-American Music in the Nineteenth Century

To **transcribe** a piece of music is to write in standard, European musical notation what the listener, or transcriber, hears. The transcriber's notated version is called the **transcription.** Transcriptions of the same piece of music can vary widely, depending on the quality of the original sound source, the skill of the transcriber, and what the transcriber chooses to include in the notation. (See the box, "The problem of Transcribing African-American Music.")

The story of African-American music in the nineteenth century can be told only partially. It is the story of the stevedores on the wharves of Savannah, the tobacco pickers in the Piedmont of North Carolina, the cotton pickers on the plantations of rural Alabama, the worshipers at the camp meetings in Kentucky, the Methodist ministers of Philadelphia, the oarsmen of the Sea Islands in South Carolina, the dance hall performers of New York, the riverboat minstrels on the Mississippi, and the conservatory-trained musicians of Boston. Most of their music was not written down but transmitted orally from musician to musician. Except for a few collections of transcriptions, the only tangible sources of information are diaries, letters, newspapers, and novels, as well as paintings and pictures—but these do not always depict African-American music clearly or reliably.

From *Cabin and Plantation Songs* as sung by students of the Hampton Normal and Agricultural Institute of Virginia—now Hampton Sydney University—and published by G. P. Putnam's Sons in 1875 at the height of Reconstruction following the Civil War. To raise money for their college, the Hampton students toured the country with this booklet. In his introduction, Thomas P. Fenner, head of Hampton's music department, noted that although "slave music is … rapidly passing away, [i]t may be that this people who have developed such a wonderful musical sense in their degradation will, in their maturity, produce a composer who could bring a music of the future out of this music of the past." Note the use of black dialect in the lyrics, a feature of much African-American music of the time.

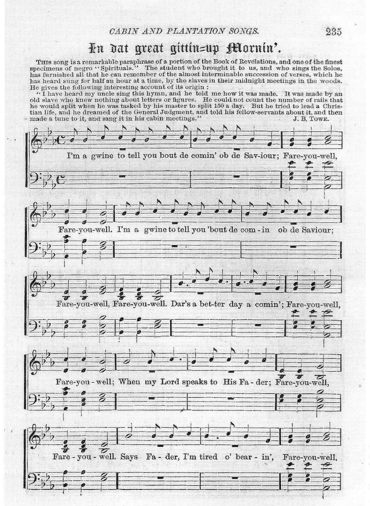

Courtesy Morgan Collection

SOURCES OF MUSICAL DIVERSITY

Countless, mostly nameless, individuals contributed to a rich African-American musical heritage before, during, and after the Civil War. This diverse musical culture varied over time and from region to region. There were clear musical differences between the North and South; among the East, Midwest, and West; between urban and rural areas; and before and after the Civil War. Despite these distinctions, the African-American heritage provided a foundation for jazz when it began to develop around the end of the nineteenth and the beginning of the twentieth centuries.

Much of this musical heritage emerged from African music and culture. The earliest slaves came to the New World in the beginning of the seventeenth century, and the tyranny of slavery continued for more than two hundred years. Uprooted from their homelands, especially from the rain forests of the west coast of Africa—including Senegal, the Guinea coast, and the Niger delta—the slaves witnessed the destruction of their family institutions and the elimination of their well-defined social structures. Nonetheless, many West-African musical traditions persevered and ultimately blended with American and Western-European traditions.

Geography strongly influenced the degree to which African slaves preserved their musical traditions. In regions where whites lived separately from African Americans, slaves tended to retain their African traditions. For example, the relative inaccessibility of the coastal Sea Islands of Georgia and South Carolina allowed the resident Gullah blacks to preserve several musical as well as linguistic elements from African culture, some of which survive to this day. But in the northeastern United States, where farms were relatively small and the number of slaves fewer, blacks and whites often interacted. As blacks in the North converted to Christianity and gained literacy and early emancipation, they preserved their African traditions less distinctly. In contrast, larger plantations in the Southeast, dependent as they were on large numbers of slaves who lived together in separate quarters, made it possible for some African traditions to survive more intact. Furthermore, many owners encouraged slaves to perform their music as well as learn European musical styles.

THE PRESERVATION OF AFRICAN TRADITIONS

When we look at the preservation of African musical traits in the New World, several questions arise: What characteristics of African music took root on American soil? How were they preserved, and how were they adapted? More specifically, which of these elements influenced jazz?

The tribes from western, sub-Saharan Africa, which contributed most of the slaves to the New World, exhibited numerous and varying musical cultures in the eighteenth and nineteenth centuries. These cultures were not studied much at the time, but we can assume that the same musically significant traits that exist today in these regions also characterized African music in the eighteenth and nineteenth centuries and therefore must have been part of the musical culture of U.S. slaves. As such, we need to examine twentieth-century African musical cultures to see which African musical features likely contributed to jazz.

Above all, African music today plays an important social function: It accompanies work, forms an essential part of religious and social events, and is often accompanied by dance. Thus African music is highly functional. There are six characteristics shared by the various tribes that distinguish their functional music cultures from the European tradition:

Call-and-response is a musical procedure in which a single voice or instrument states a melodic phrase—the *call*—and a group of voices or instruments follows with a responding or completing phrase—the *response*.

Syncopation is the unexpected accenting of a "weaker" melody note or offbeat. Syncopation displaces the accent, or emphasis, from an expected to an unexpected position. For example, because the first and third beats are usually emphasized in each bar of a 4/4 piece, then emphasizing the second beat would be syncopation. In general, syncopation involves unexpected accents occurring within a regular pulse stream. For an illustration, see Music Example 1-3, third measure, and listen to Track 4 of the Audio Primer CD. The Joplin phrase is played first as it was written (with syncopation), then without.

Meter in music is a rhythmic pattern arising from regular groupings of two or three beats. These define, respectively, duple or triple meter. Most music has meter.

Cross-rhythms refer to the performance of simultaneous and contrasting rhythms, such as patterns with duple and triple groupings. By superimposing one rhythmic pattern on another, we create a cross-rhythm.

Originally derived from African religious practice, a **ring shout** is a rhythmic dance performed in a circular figure. Worshipers moved counterclockwise while singing spirituals and accompanying themselves by clapping and stamping. The worshipers ingeniously circumvented the prohibition against dancing—strictly speaking, to lift and cross the feet—by shuffling. Some historians describe the ring shout

1. *Metronomic sense.* African musicians tend to maintain a steady, underlying pulse throughout a performance. The regularity of the beat can be compared to a metronome, a mechanical device that enables musicians to maintain a steady beat while practicing. The dancers' motions generally show the pulse.

2. *Overlapping call-and-response.* In call-and-response, a solo vocalist sings one line (often improvised), then a group responds. In African traditions, the group response tends to overlap the original solo part.

3. *Off-beat phrasing of melodic accents.* This is the unexpected accenting of "weaker" notes within the melody, or what many scholars describe as *syncopation.*

4. *Dominance of percussion.* In African music, percussion instruments are plentiful and used more widely than melodic ones, with some exceptions. The melodic instruments themselves are sometimes played percussively.

5. *Singing that stresses nasal textures, with bending of pitches and colorful effects.* (This will be described more completely later in this chapter.) These effects are sometimes used to imply more than one musical part (for example, a change between falsetto and natural voice).

6. *Polyrhythm.* This is an intricate web of rhythms heard among the different parts.

Although the first five attributes of African music are fairly straightforward, polyrhythm is more complex. The rhythmic layering of the different instruments in an African ensemble is typically founded on a single ground beat, usually in duple or triple meter. Africans themselves often think of their music's rhythm as projected along a time line in which patterns may be based on large numbers of beats, perhaps as many as twelve. In addition, many of the rhythms arising from this layering can seem independent though they are not played separately. Thus African music is often described as rhythmically polyphonic.

We assume that these traits were true of African music in the eighteenth and nineteeth centuries; certainly, many of these elements appear in African-American music today. Religious and secular music retained the metronomic sense. Call-and-response patterns, nearly universal in West-African culture, formed the basis of work songs and **spirituals** in the United States and became a significant component of blues and jazz. African-American music in the nineteenth century retained the offbeat phrasing of melodic accents, a key characteristic that became part of the jazz tradition.

African slaves brought their tradition of drumming to the United States. Slave owners, however, suspected that the drums allowed slaves to communicate over long distances. Moreover, drumming and dancing were forbidden by Methodists and Baptists, the Protestant denominations that most actively worked to convert slaves to Christianity. Hence, throughout most if not all of the American South, slave owners outlawed drums and thus eliminated an important percussive element of West-African music.

Lacking drums, the slaves adapted in ingenious ways. They used stringed instruments in a percussive manner. They added percussion by clapping and stamping, for example, when performing the "ring shout" in religious worship. Finally, "patting juba" (clapping, stamping, and slapping thighs) provided percussive dance accompaniment, frequently without any other instruments.

The survival of rhythmic polyphony is more difficult to trace. In African music, percussion parts are typically played on different drums and rattles, each with its own rhythm, creating a complex overlay of contrasting patterns. Mostly because of the proscription against drums, though, African Americans did not retain this practice in the United States. Instead, they expressed percussive rhythm in syncopated melodies and cross-rhythms, the legacy of African rhythmic complexity in African-American music.

Clearly, rhythm played a prominent role in defining the African musical aesthetic. Hence, it became crucial in shaping the African-American musical aesthetic as well. In discussing the relationship between West-African and African-American music, one writer states:

> The approach to metrical organization with cross-rhythms as the norm, the percussive technique of playing any instrument resulting in an abundance of qualitative accents, the density of musical activity, the inclusion of the environmental factors as part of the musical event, the propensity for certain "buzzylike" musical timbres—all these are African features which have been consistently maintained in Afro-American music.[1]

European Music in the Nineteenth Century

The European tradition remains embedded in jazz. Indeed, throughout jazz history the precise mix of European and African elements often characterized the specific jazz substyle from the earliest days on. Here we look at the three main contributions of European music to jazz: instrumentation, form, and harmony.

INSTRUMENTATION, FORM, AND HARMONY

Many elements of the European tradition contributed to the formation of early jazz. The instruments of early jazz are virtually all European. The *front line* and rhythm section of a typical early jazz band included the following:

MELODY	RHYTHM
Trumpet or cornet	Piano (melodic also)
Clarinet	String bass or tuba
Trombone	Guitar or banjo
	Drums

The saxophone was not commonly heard in early jazz. The banjo, which lost favor in subsequent jazz styles, was common in early jazz and has African roots, although its specific origins are controversial.

Despite the prominence of rhythm as a key ingredient of African music, the basic instruments of the jazz drum set—snare drum, bass drum, and cymbals—are those of the European marching band. Pioneering drummers in early jazz bands created the drum set by arranging these instruments so that one person could play them all at once. Modern additions to the basic drum set—gongs, wind chimes, hand drums, and so on—come from cultures the world over.

as contributing the essence of African song, dance, and spirit to African-American music.

Polyphony describes music with at least two distinct and simultaneous melodic lines. Another name for a polyphonic texture is *counterpoint*.

The **front line** described the lead (melody) instruments in early jazz bands and usually included trumpet (or cornet), trombone, and clarinet. The saxophone came later to jazz.

The **rhythm section** in early jazz bands included three or four players on drums, bass or tuba, and one or more chordal instruments (piano, banjo, or guitar). To hear a modern rhythm section, listen to Tracks 44 and 45 of the Audio Primer CD. Track 44 has bass and drums; Track 45 adds the piano.

Obbligato is a term borrowed from classical music to describe a complementary melodic part played along with the main melody as a necessary, or expected, addition. In early jazz obbligato parts were often florid, usually played by the clarinet, and sometimes improvised. To hear an obbligato-like clarinet melody, listen to Track 21 of the Audio Primer CD.

Like an obbligato, a **counter-melody** is a secondary melody that accompanies the main melody. A countermelody is generally heard in the trombone or a lower voice, has fewer notes than the obbligato, and is often improvised. To hear a countermelody, refer to Track 7 of the Audio Primer CD. The piano enters in the middle register with a countermelody.

AABA song form comprises an eight-bar theme (A) played twice. A contrasting melody (B) follows, also usually eight bars long, before the A theme returns. Quite often the second and third A sections will vary slightly. In the **ABAC song form**, each section is, again, usually eight bars. Musicians often speak of the "first half" of the tune (AB) and the "second half" (AC).

The European marching or brass band also contributed instrumentation that served as a model for many early jazz bands, and that we hear in the basic textural layout of the cornet (or trumpet) lead melody, trombone countermelody, and clarinet obbligato.

In addition to instrumentation, the most significant European contributions to jazz are its form—that is, the basic layout of the music—and harmony. Early jazz is characterized by forms that maintain the eight-, sixteen-, and thirty-two–bar symmetrical sections of European popular song and marches. These symmetrical forms provide large-scale paths through the music and tell us where we are in the composition. We discuss the march form, which can be heard in the important pre-jazz style known as ragtime, later in this chapter.

European song form became especially prominent as jazz matured through the 1920s. Two basic formats, AABA and ABAC, have been mainstays of the music ever since. In each of these forms, the A section is often called the *head*, and the B section the *bridge*. (Two older terms for the B section, *channel* and *release*, are now uncommon.) We shall point out examples of these forms later when we analyze specific pieces.

We can think of form as large-scale rhythm, because it marks off periods of time. In general, there are several different levels of rhythmic activity in a jazz piece, from the note-to-note progression to the overall form of a work. Examining these levels clarifies the mixture of the African and European traditions:

▶ At the note-to-note level, we hear clear African influences: accents fall in unexpected places, the music shows syncopated movement, and unusual vocal and instrumental timbres are evident.

▶ At the level of meter and phrase, we hear both European and African tendencies. The harmonic flow is European in origin, yet the syncopation, cross-rhythms, and call-and-response forms are largely of African origins.

▶ Finally, at the level of form, the European influence is strongest in such features as sectional structure, tonality, and instrumentation.

European harmony is based on chords built on triads that define musical keys. And it is this European model that defines much of jazz form and its use of harmony. (See the box "Roman Numerals Designate the Harmonies Relative to the Key" for an illustration. Also, listen to Track 2 of the Audio Primer CD.)

Roman Numerals Designate the Harmonies Relative to the Key

In the key of C major, the C major triad is a tonic or I chord.

In the key of G, the same C major triad is a subdominant IV chord.

In most jazzlike **textures,** the melody is an overlay, that is, it plays on top of the harmony. The accompanying rhythm instruments (piano, banjo, or guitar) provide the backup chords to the primary melodic instruments (cornet or trumpet, trombone, clarinet, or saxophone). The chordal element of jazz is so pervasive that a system of slash notation describing chords has become standard in most jazz styles. See Music Example 1-1 for an illustration of this notation. (Listen to Track 3 of the 🅟 Audio Primer CD to hear a melody played without chords, then with chords.)

Music Example 1-1
Slash notation.

WRITTEN VERSUS HEAD ARRANGEMENTS

Jazz groups with large numbers of players usually require arrangements. Arrangers are responsible for the final sound of a band, because they work up all the elements required for a performance: form, chord voicings, introductions, codas, and so on. The arranger provides the players with the written music, called *parts,* which they may practice at rehearsal. This concept of musical performance comes largely from the European tradition.

The arranger usually provides the rhythm players with *slash notation* in written arrangements, but he or she may specify the parts more precisely when necessary. Arrangers often use slash notation to designate passages of improvisation, usually for the soloists.

One alternative to the written arrangement is the *head arrangement,* that is, a musical plan and form worked up by the players themselves, who create their own parts. Less common than the traditional written arrangement, especially for larger groups, the head arrangement relates conceptually more to the African tradition than to the European. Head arrangements were probably common in jazz through the late 1930s, because there was little turnover in band personnel and players had more time to rehearse. Since then, written arrangements became standard.

A constant dialogue between the written (European) and improvised (African) traditions runs throughout jazz history. Whereas the African musical tradition was oral, jazz band members performing written arrangements must be able to read their parts. Some jazz players learned to play "by ear" but then joined bands for which they needed to learn to read music. Such stories are especially common in early jazz.

An **arranger** plans the form of a band's performance and often notates the parts for the different instruments. See *head arrangement,* below.

Slash notation is a type of jazz and popular-music notation that tells the player the harmonies or chords. Each slash in a measure denotes a beat. The arranger places chords over the slashes in order to show the beats on which the harmonies change. (Music Examples 1-1 and 1-6 provide illustrations.)

A **head arrangement** is a musical plan and form worked up orally by the players themselves in rehearsal or on the bandstand.

Early African-American Music

Throughout the eighteenth and nineteenth centuries, African-American music drew on both European and African characteristics and appeared in both sacred and secular settings. This music was communal and woven into the daily rituals of life. The notion of the professional musician was largely unknown (a characteristic typical of folk music), as was the separation between performer and audience that we know today.

Although the music that evolved was rooted in the African tradition, it soon took on European elements. Slaves who were called on as musicians to entertain whites at dances and balls came to know the European tradition. Classified advertisements in newspapers of the period referred to slaves as highly skilled players on European instruments. An advertisement from as early as 1766 called attention to a slave proficient on the French horn; other advertisements announced slaves' skills on the violin or fife.

Contemporary descriptions of the gatherings of the slaves on Sundays and holidays in New Orleans' Place Congo (now called Louis Armstrong Park) reveal the mix of African and European instruments. The ban on drumming throughout much of the South was relaxed for these weekly performances. Performers used the long drums of the Congo, the *ndungu,* as well as other drums struck by hands, feet, or sticks; gourds filled with pebbles or grains of corn; and scrapers made from the jawbones of oxen, horses, or mules. Other instruments included a derivative of the African thumb piano, or *mbira,* which had several reeds stretched across a wooden board, and the four-string banjo, an instrument imported by West-African slaves from Senegambia. One writer imagines the unique mix:

> The tremendous creative energies released when Kongo-derived traditions combined in New Orleans with those from the equally sophisticated Malian, Nigerian, and Cameroonian traditional civilizations must have been amazing. That does not even take into account the final fillip: the blending of it all with the equally complex mix of musics—French, Spanish, English—in that culturally strategic city.[2]

Today we know very little about African-American music before the eighteenth and early nineteenth centuries. Songs and instrumental pieces passed from one individual to another almost completely through an oral tradition in which performers played by ear. Over many years, as one person taught another, this music and its performance undoubtedly underwent gradual stylistic changes. Unfortunately, these changes have been lost to historians because there is little or no hard evidence to help them document the music's development in any detail.

The Problem of Transcribing African-American Music

Contemporary transcriptions of nineteenth-century African-American folk music emerged in the second half of the century. Three white scholars collaborated in 1867 to produce the first published collection, *Slave Songs of the United States.* As an early attempt to apply the European notational system to performance practices of African-American music, the plight of the transcribers shows the gap between European practices and those derived from African musical traditions.

The early transcribers frankly admitted to the difficulty of notating African-American music. Lucy McKim Garrison pointed to the problem of accurately rendering the vocal effects and the rhythmic qualities: "It is difficult to express the entire character of these negro ballads by mere musical notes and signs. The odd turns made in the throat, and the curious rhythmic effect produced by single voices chiming in at different irregular intervals, seem almost as impossible to place on the score as the singing of birds or the tones of an Aeolian Harp."*

Garrison's comments describe a number of performance practices. The technique

---
* William Francis Allen, Charles Pickard Ware, and Lucy McKim Garrison, *Slave Songs of the United States* (New York: Peter Smith, 1951; reprint, Mineola, NY: Dover, 1995), vi.

of vocal ornamentation, referred to by some writers as "trimming" and what Garrison calls "the odd turns made in the throat," points to a flexibility of interpretation and perhaps even alterations in vocal timbre. Garrison also describes the overlapping call-and-response pattern: the "curious rhythmic effects produced by single voices chiming in at different irregular intervals." Although the transcriptions in the book suggest single-line melodies, Garrison implies that non-unison singing occurred in the original performances that either could not be or were not notated.

Another transcriber discusses the inability of the European notational system

CHRISTIANITY, THE RING SHOUT, AND WORK SONGS

As African Americans converted to Christianity, they learned Protestant hymns and other religious songs that introduced them to the melodic, formal, and harmonic elements of European music. African-American religious music took on the practice of "lining out" psalms, a European tradition in which a leader read or chanted the psalm verse one or two lines at a time, and the congregation sang back the lines, often elaborating on the original tune. Introduced in New England in the mid-seventeenth century, the practice eventually took root in the rural South and West. Interestingly, although a European tradition, the practice closely resembled the call-and-response patterns of African music.

The first all-black churches appear to have developed near the end of the 1700s, and hymns and spirituals replaced the tradition of "lining out" psalms. The first independent hymnal, *A Collection of Spiritual Songs and Hymns Selected from Various Authors by Richard Allen, African Minister,* was printed in 1801. Choirs or congregations sang the spirituals in the call-and-response form, alternating solo verses with refrain lines. Hymns and spirituals spread not only through church worship but also through open-air camp meetings, where often thousands gathered to worship for days at a time.

Observers at the camp meetings and churches described the use of the West-African ring shout, which persisted in Christian ecstatic rituals in the Deep South. One writer witnessed a ring shout in Florida during the 1870s or 1880s:

> The shouters, formed in a ring, men and women alternating, their bodies close together, moved round and round on shuffling feet that never left the floor. With the heel of the right foot they pounded out the fundamental beat of the dance and with their hands clapped out the varying rhythmical accents of the chant; for the music was, in fact, an African chant and the shout an African dance, [a] whole pagan rite transplanted and adapted to Christian worship. Round and round the

to represent other African-derived performance practices: "Tones are frequently employed which we have no musical characters to represent. Such, for example, is that which I have indicated as nearly as possible by the flat seventh.... The tones are variable in pitch, ranging through an entire octave on different occasions, according to the inspiration of the singer."[†]

The last sentence points to an important feature of the music—an emphasis on improvisation, in which pitch choices may be made or altered "according to the inspiration of the singer."

Transcriptions are at best only an approximation of actual practice. In 1899, Jeanette Robinson Murphy noted that she had followed "old ex-slaves, who have passed away in their tasks, listened to their crooning in their cabins, in the fields, and especially in their meeting houses, and again and again they assured me the tunes they sang came from Africa."

She noted, for example, that in certain collections of transcriptions, nothing indicated to the singer

> that he must make his voice exceedingly nasal and undulating, that around every prominent note he must place a variety of small notes, called "trimmings," and he must sing notes not found in our scale; that he must on no account leave one note until he has the next one well

under control. He might be tempted ... to take breath whenever he came to the end of a line or verse! But ... he should carry over his breath from line to line and from verse to verse, even at the risk of bursting a blood vessel. He must often drop from a high note to a very low one, he must be very careful to divide many of his monosyllabic words into syllables.... He must intersperse his singing with peculiar humming sounds.... [‡]

Murphy has described here many of the vocal elements commonly heard in blues singing.

† Quoted in Eileen Southern, *Music of Black Americans,* 2d ed. (New York: Norton, 1971), 192.

‡ Jeanette Robinson Murphy's 1899 article, "The Survival of African Music in America," reprinted in *The Negro and His Folk-Lore,* ed. Bruce Jackson (Austin: University of Texas Press, 1967).

ring would go. One, two, three, four, five hours, the very monotony of sound and motion inducing an ecstatic frenzy.[3]

Sterling Stuckey has argued that the ring shout was one of the most significant and powerful elements of African culture to be retained in America.[4] In nineteenth-century New Orleans, accounts of voodoo ceremonies—a religion of Dahomean origin—similarly describe a circle dance. Such dances, especially the ring shout, clearly preserved several African musical elements and indicate a nineteenth-century link to jazz, from the "rhythms and blue tonality, through the falsetto break and the call-and-response pattern, to the songs of allusion and even the motions of the African dance."[5]

In rural areas, nonreligious music included occasional songs, field hollers, and work songs. Occasional songs accompanied various aspects of slave life, such as playing games or celebrating holidays. Work songs—nearly universal in African culture—accompanied different types of labor. Field laborers picked tobacco or cotton, threshed rice, husked corn, or harvested sugar cane to the sound of work songs. Up and down the eastern seaboard and on the Ohio and Mississippi rivers, stevedores loaded and unloaded boats and oarsmen rowed in unison to work songs. These songs enabled laborers to synchronize their tasks and movements to the call-and-response pattern. A group leader sang out the main phrases, while the rest of the workers responded together in time with their work. Field hollers were both a form of song and a means of communication; in half-sung, half-shouted language, the worker called for water or asked for help across large distances in the cotton fields. (See the box "The Problem of Transcribing African-American Music.")

BLUE NOTES AND SYNCOPATION

William Francis Allen, one of the transcribers of *Slave Songs of the United States,* recognized that African-American musicians "seem not infrequently to strike sounds that cannot be precisely represented by the gamut [scale]."[6] To the transcribers' perplexity, the singers used pitches *between* the natural and flatted versions of the third and seventh scale degrees, pitches not heard in the equal-tempered European system. In general, these pitches are often called "neutral" thirds and sevenths; in African-American practice, they are called **blue notes**. (For more, see the box, "The Blues Scale.")

Nearly all types of African-American music used these blue notes—work songs, field hollers, ballads, spirituals, and hymns—yet historians still debate their origin and performance. Among the most intriguing theories is that African slaves manipulated their traditional and largely pentatonic melodies to fit the seven-note diatonic Western scale by adding blue notes. Again, there is no way to prove whether such a process occurred or not. Still, the ethnomusicologist A. M. Jones noted that he "never heard an African sing the third and seventh degrees of a major scale in tune. . . . Aural impressions so plainly verify the widespread use of the two 'blue' notes among Africans in Africa."[7] However, because Jones mostly discusses music of East and Central Africa, which are regions outside the primary homelands of the American slaves, the lines from Africa to America are not completely clear.[8] Bruno Nettl, a well-known ethnomusicologist, asserts that neutral thirds and sevenths are pervasive in "primitive" music everywhere and that blue notes "probably cannot be traced to Africa."[9] Scholars may never settle this issue conclusively.

The Blues Scale

The use of blue notes in African-American music is complex.* Some scholars have suggested that blue notes refer to pitch inflections or slurred pitches rather than discrete pitches. For example, Gilbert Chase writes that "it is not the flatted third [or any other lowered interval of the scale] as such, but rather this ambivalent, this *worried* or slurred tone that constitutes the true 'blue note.'"† Others suggest the presence of a **blues scale,** which incorporates natural as well as "neutral" thirds and sevenths:

Sometimes, the blues scale has incorporated other pitches. For example, the jazz style that evolved in the 1940s, bebop, features extensive use of a flatted fifth, which can take on the quality of a blue note. More generally, it is possible to inflect any note of the scale in such a way that it becomes a blue note, but the blue third and seventh are by far the most pervasive.

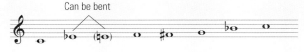

Can be bent

---

* For this and the following points, we are particularly indebted to William Tallmadge's article "Blue Notes and Blue Tonality," *The Black Perspective in Music* 12, no. 2 (1984): 155–64.

† Gilbert Chase, *America's Music: From the Pilgrims to the Present*, 2d ed. rev. (New York: McGraw-Hill, 1966), 453.

A few of the transcriptions in *Slave Songs of the United States* show both natural and flatted thirds and sevenths in the same composition. The transcribers offer one song in a major key and an alternative version in a minor key, showing a further variability between major/minor thirds and sevenths. Even so, most songs appeared notated in a major key with many of their melodies emphasizing the pentatonic scale, which is found in folk music around the world.

The opening lines of the spiritual "Nobody Knows the Trouble I've Had" are built entirely on the B♭ pentatonic scale (See Music Examples 1-2 and 1-3).

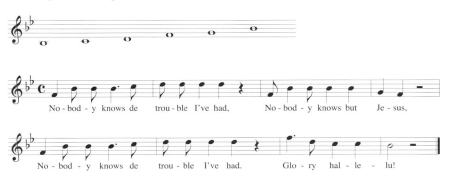

Music Example 1-2
The B♭ pentatonic scale.

Music Example 1-3
Measures 1–8 from "Nobody Knows the Trouble I've Had."

Notice that this spiritual features syncopation: The pattern eighth note–quarter note–eighth note (♪ ♩ ♪) occurs at the beginning of the third measure. Moreover, in practice the first, second, and fifth measures may also be performed with the same syncopated rhythm. In effect, this pattern enables the performer to avoid emphasizing the second beat.

A similar syncopation pattern (transcribed below) occurs in a satirical song from Louisiana, within the notated beat, as a sixteenth-eighth-sixteenth–note rhythm.

The title of the song—"Musieu Bainjo" ("Mister Banjo")—suggests an association between syncopation and banjo playing.

Whatever the origins of these kinds of syncopation, minstrel songs adopted them, and they gradually became signature elements of the rhythmic language of ragtime at the turn of the twentieth century. In 1913, the composer Nathaniel Dett identified the sixteenth-eighth-sixteenth figure as a prominent characteristic of antebellum African-American music but lamented its later use as overly caricatured.[10]

Minstrelsy

African-American folk music joined with the dominant European musical culture around the middle of the nineteenth century in the minstrel show—a hodgepodge of songs, comic sketches, dances, and melodrama. **Minstrelsy** was especially significant as the first distinctively U.S. musical genre, reflecting a decisive blend of the European and African-American traditions.

Minstrel shows became a widespread form of entertainment in the United States between 1845 and 1900, especially in the emerging frontier. Initially, minstrel shows were performed by white troupes in blackface. But beginning in 1865, authentic black companies toured the United States and Europe, with the performers still appearing in blackface because audiences expected it.

An early photograph of a minstrel from *Brainard's Ragtime Collection*, published in 1899.

Courtesy Morgan Collection

On the one hand, minstrel shows were overtly derogatory, based on negative stereotypes of black characters, such as the city slicker, sometimes called the "Zip Coon," or the lazy, shiftless Jim Crow. On the other hand, the success of this entertainment showed white America's deep fascination with African-American culture and allowed blacks the possibility of careers as professional entertainers.

Minstrel shows featured instruments that blacks played in the South—the banjo, tambourines, and bone-clappers. These instruments constituted American music's first rhythm section—the constant underlying beat that was derived from the African tradition and has given jazz and American popular music much of its characteristic sound. Nevertheless, it is difficult to gauge whether the music in minstrelsy was authentically African American or was as caricatured as the minstrel figures themselves. Historian Thomas Riis notes:

> Trying to imagine sounds heard long ago, with only verbal descriptions to go on, obviously presents problems. We can be sure, however, that where black performers and composers were active a strand of authenticity resided. The vigorous, unsentimental tunes of 1840s minstrelsy, only rarely identified with known black composers, present persistent syncopations, asymmetrical note groups, and the call-and-response pattern. These features all point to the retention of African elements, although the evidence for direct African provenance is slim.
>
> The presence on the minstrel stage of African and Afro-American instruments—drums and banjos—and of strong black characters drawn from American folklore—John Henry and his kin—confirms a unique black influence, in comparison with other ethnic groups, on the development of minstrelsy.[11]

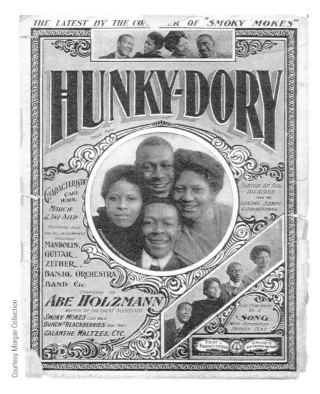

Courtesy Morgan Collection

This 1900 cover of "Hunky-Dory" is unusual in its treatment of the minstrel performers. Although we do not learn the names of these artists, we see them portrayed as people, not stereotypes. Notice that the cover is as stuffed with visual information as many contemporary Web splash screens are.

This picture of a black debutante on the cover of the Sunday Musical Supplement of the *Denver Times*, March 24, 1901, appears to be an unusual item for the time. As we shall see, whereas photos of white composers and performers invariably appeared on sheet music covers, not until the 1950s did photos of black or female composers regularly appear as well.

One of the most famous minstrel figures was James Bland (1854–1911), a black performer who gained international fame in minstrelsy and who composed several famous songs, including "Carry Me Back to Old Virginny" and "Oh, Dem Golden Slippers." Many of the most famous songs of the first professional U.S. songwriter, Stephen Foster (1826–1864)—including "Old Folks at Home" ("Swanee River"), "Old Black Joe," and "My Old Kentucky Home"—were minstrel-type songs that incorporated black dialect.

Despite the initial exclusion of blacks from minstrelsy and the later pejorative portrayals of blacks, minstrel shows introduced many whites to black music; provided employment for black actors, dancers, and musicians; and helped popularize various black dances. Among the most memorable dances was the cakewalk, which achieved considerable popularity with whites. Bert Williams, a well-known black entertainer and dancer in the early twentieth century, taught the dance to Edward VII of England.

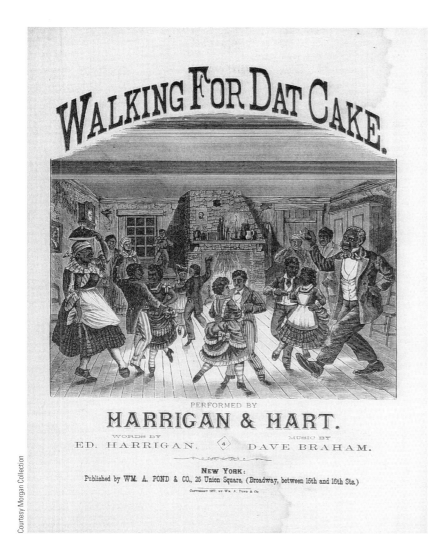

Published in 1877, this sheet music is an early reference to the cakewalk. Here is a portion of the lyrics:

*Twas down at Aunty Jackson's,
there was a big reception
Of high-tone colored people
full of sweet affection.
Such singing and such dancing,
we made the ceiling shake,
The cream of all the evening
was a'walking for dat cake.*

Notice that although the art is not that skillful, it appears to be an honest attempt to capture the dance without undue caricature.

In the late nineteenth century, minstrelsy was replaced by vaudeville, a touring entertainment form similar to minstrelsy but without self-contained troupes. Vaudeville often included much ethnic humor, which we would now regard as offensive, but its stereotyping of African Americans was less overt than in minstrelsy. Great vaudeville performers, such as the blues singer Bessie Smith (discussed later in this chapter), helped popularize jazz in its early years.

Urban musical theater also developed out of minstrelsy. Turn-of-the-century New York developed a flourishing black theater community that included the composers Bob Cole, James Weldon Johnson, Ernest Hogan, and Will Marion Cook. They built many of their works on African-American themes, and their songs served as important precursors to classic ragtime. With the decline of minstrelsy, many composers turned to ragtime and vaudeville. Yet the composers just listed also continued to work in black musical theater and greatly contributed to the rising consciousness regarding African-American culture.

The **cakewalk** was more an exhibition than a dance. At the end of the evening, the most talented couple won a cake—hence the dance's name. Some believed the exaggerated walking step was an imitation of the way members of white "high society" comported themselves.

Ragtime

The 1893 World's Fair in Chicago marked the beginning of the popular fascination with ragtime. For the first time, thousands of Americans heard a new type of music associated with black, itinerant piano players. Adapting African polyrhythms to piano, these players developed the use of syncopation that would become one of ragtime's central features. "Syncopation," Irving Berlin maintained, "is nothing but another name for ragtime."[12] As a sober observer of the London *Times* said, "In American slang to 'rag' a melody is to syncopate a normally regular tune."[13] The traditional ragtime piano figures, which often pivot around fixed notes, may have been taken from banjo playing. In time, Scott Joplin and other ragtime composers would formalize the genre to create the works we now call "classic ragtime."

Beginning in the 1890s and lasting two decades, ragtime swept the nation. The success of ragtime was unparalleled. It was especially significant because, for the first time, a specifically black musical genre entered and dominated the U.S. mainstream. The music was not only wildly popular, it was also commercially successful. Entrepreneurial fortunes were made, as publishing houses for ragtime compositions sprang up throughout U.S. towns and cities. The first manual of ragtime performance, *Ben Harney's Ragtime Instructor,* appeared in 1897. Two years later "Maple Leaf Rag"—Scott Joplin's second published rag—became the most celebrated ragtime composition for piano.

During its heyday, however, ragtime was not strictly associated with piano music. Early ragtime probably derived from songs taken from minstrel shows and urban musical theater. Although many of these songs were unsyncopated, the early ragtime pianists worked up arrangements for solo piano or for piano and voice. The syncopated manner in which these songs were performed came to be described as ragtime.

Although the idea of "ragging" melodies was first associated with songs and solo piano, ragtime was quickly taken up by bands. In the late nineteenth century, brass bands were extremely common throughout the country and sometimes acted as a

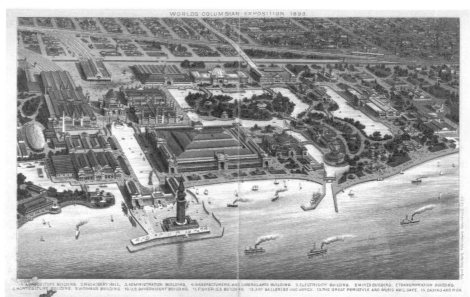

A bird's eye view of the World's Columbian Exposition, May 1 to October 31, 1893, Jackson Park, Chicago, Illinois—where many Americans first heard ragtime. The Chicago Exposition occupied 664 acres, with a frontage of 1½ miles on Lake Michigan, and cost an estimated $25 million to build, an enormous amount of money at a time when many workers earned $1 a day or less.

Courtesy Morgan Collection

locality's cultural focus. A small city might have three or four bands; an average town usually had at least one. In larger cities, such as New Orleans, there were numerous bands, both black and white, that competed through concerts, funerals, dances, parades, and other venues. The southern black bands served as training ensembles for many early jazz musicians and often performed marches from the white repertory (see Chapter 2). As ragtime grew in popularity, the practice of ragging marches—especially those by John Philip Sousa—became common. (Sousa, the country's premier march composer, was himself a champion of ragtime and included it in his band concerts.) The sectional design and the key relationships of classic ragtime were taken from marches, and many ragtime composers, including Scott Joplin, named some of their rags "marches" or indicated "march tempo" as the speed and rhythm of a work.

Proficient ragtime pianists were expected to improvise ragtime versions of popular songs, and in the Ragtime Championship of the World Competition, held in New York in 1900, the three semifinalists were required to improvise a version of the popular period piece "All Coons Look Alike to Me." (This song is not as racist as its title suggests. It is sung by a black woman lamenting the loss of her lover; because other black men do not interest her, they all "look alike.")

Ragtime versions of other types of music were also popular. *Ben Harney's Ragtime Instructor* included syncopated versions of hymns and folksongs. Patriotic songs were not immune; several pianists featured syncopated versions of "The Star-Spangled Banner" in their repertories. In another practice, called "ragging the classics," performers created ragtime renditions of classical compositions—Felix Mendelssohn's "Wedding March" was a particular favorite.

These practices show that ragtime began as an *improvised* music—a style of performance—and later became a written art form. The early players improvised, but the masters of classic ragtime worked over their pieces with much attention to compositional detail. Aside from Scott Joplin, whose life and work we shall examine closely, the finest classic ragtime composers included James Scott, Joseph Lamb, and Artie Matthews.

SCOTT JOPLIN

The solo piano rags of Scott Joplin became the pinnacle of the classic ragtime canon. Born in Texarkana, Texas, in 1868, Joplin worked as an itinerant musician in the Mississippi valley during his teens, settled in Sedalia, Missouri, in 1895, then relocated in St. Louis. In 1907 he moved to New York, where he died in 1917.

The success of "Maple Leaf Rag" allowed the composer to live comfortably after its publication in 1899 by John Stark, a music store owner trying to capitalize on the rising popularity of ragtime. Remarkably, Stark offered Joplin a publishing contract for "Maple Leaf" that included a penny royalty for each copy

A well-known photograph of Scott Joplin, c. 1900, dressed to reflect the respectability that he sought for his music.

Courtesy Frank Driggs Collection

Chicago Syncopations
By Axel W. Christensen

A picture of John Stark from an article that appeared in *Melody, A Monthly Magazine for Lovers of Popular Music,* October 1918. The writer reported, "It was [Stark] who discovered Scott Joplin, who put on paper for the first time the genius of that wonderful composer of classic ragtime." In fact, Stark was not Joplin's first publisher.

Courtesy Morgan Collection

sold. This was a generous arrangement at the time: Although such contracts are commonplace now, a fair agreement between a white publisher and a black artist was virtually unheard of in the 1890s. The fame Joplin achieved through "Maple Leaf" increased the sales of his other rags. Joplin's music returned to vogue in the 1970s with the success of the movie *The Sting*, which featured several of Joplin's rags, including "The Entertainer."

Joplin sought to elevate ragtime to an art form. His earliest training included the study of European harmony. Later, his published ragtime compositions artfully combined the African-American tradition with techniques, forms, and principles derived from European music.

In addition to writing piano rags, Joplin incorporated ragtime within larger, more classically oriented musical forms, including the ballet *Ragtime Dance* and two operas. The first of these operas, *A Guest of Honor,* is now lost. Joplin financed a performance of the second, *Treemonisha,* in 1915, but it was unsuccessful. These works anticipated later attempts to merge European classical forms with jazz, as we shall see with the works of jazzmen James P. Johnson and Duke Ellington.

JAMES SCOTT

Often considered second only to Scott Joplin as a classic rag composer, James Scott (1886–1938) was born in the small town of Neosho, Missouri, where he began studying piano as a child. His talent and dedication transcended the early absence of a piano in his home, and his study included sight-reading. By the time he was a teenager, he was living in Carthage, Missouri, and "plugging" songs for a living. *Plugging a song* meant to promote it by performing it for potential buyers. He published his first rag, "A Summer Breeze—March and Two Step," when he was seventeen.

*A **song plugger** performed a song, usually at a music store, in the hope that patrons would like it enough to buy the sheet music.*

Scott later established a relationship with John Stark, Scott Joplin's publisher, and continued to write exceptional rags, including "Frog Legs Rag" (1906), "Ragtime Oriole" (1911), and "Don't Jazz Me—Rag (I'm Music)" (1921). Note that this third title speaks of Scott's antipathy to the rapidly rising popularity of jazz. Scott eventually moved to Kansas City in 1914, where he became a music teacher, a theater organist, and eventually a band leader.

The opening of Scott's "Troubadour Rag" (1919) shows the use of dotted rhythms, a feature of late ragtime that is a link to early jazz styles (see Music Example 1-4).

Music Example 1-4
James Scott, "Troubadour Rag."

JOSEPH LAMB

Originally from Montclair, New Jersey, Joseph Lamb (1887–1960) was a white composer fortunate enough to meet Scott Joplin in New York in 1907. Joplin took an interest in the younger man's work and helped him secure a publishing agreement with Stark. Among Lamb's finest rags are "Ethiopia Rag" (1909) and "Ragtime Nightingale" (1915). The latter is especially striking: a lush, romantic composition with a rich harmonic conception.

ARTIE MATTHEWS

Artie Matthews (1888–1959) worked for the Stark Publishing Company, where he published his own material and worked up arrangements for composers unable to notate their own pieces. He is best remembered for a series of "Pastime" rags, numbered 1 to 5, which are daring in their use of unusual musical materials. "Pastime Rag No. 4" (1920) uses "wrong note" cluster harmonies in the right hand. "Pastime Rag No. 5" (1918), published before No. 4, shows the dotted-rhythm influence of late ragtime.

RAGTIME'S RELATIONSHIP TO JAZZ

Was ragtime just another name for early jazz? The boundaries between them were certainly never fixed. Whatever their differences, ragtime and early jazz mightily influenced each other during the early twentieth century, as the following timeline shows.

1885(?)–1900	*1900–1917*	*1917–1930*
Ragtime developing (almost entirely improvised)	**Ragtime flourishing** (written and improvised)	**Ragtime quickly declining**
	Jazz developing (largely improvised)	**Jazz flourishing** (largely improvised, also written)

Although the ragtimers must have improvised to some extent, evidence is generally lacking; in recorded ragtime, multiple strains often repeat their melodies verbatim. In part, this may have been because fairly well-known ensembles were the first to record and were expected to perform a "straight" version—the version they had made popular. More informal ragtime was surely improvised at least in part, because so many of its practitioners played by ear.

As further evidence of the ragtime-jazz symbiosis, both forms were persistently associated with dancing. Published ragtime pieces frequently listed dances for the work: the cakewalk, the two-step, the slow drag, and the march. From this we can argue that jazz not only replaced ragtime but also *became* early jazz at a later stage. We can also argue the other side—that ragtime and jazz were distinct. According to this reasoning, a stricter, more vertical sense of rhythm characterized ragtime performance, while jazz rhythm was looser and more fluid. Furthermore, jazz incorporated more improvisation as a matter of course. Without further evidence, the debate remains open.

After 1913, jazz—or at least the use of the term—began to gain in popularity over ragtime. The work of the classic ragtime composers showed a shift toward simpler, sometimes fewer, syncopations. The use of dotted rhythms became commonplace, bringing about what the scholar Edward A. Berlin described as the "erosion" of classic ragtime.[14]

Berlin offers three hypotheses for this new rhythmic convention of dotted rhythms:

1. Composers were reflecting the performance practice of pianists, who were already interpreting eighth notes (♪ ♪) as dotted eighth–sixteenth notes (♪. ♪).

2. Composers were looking for ways to replace the outmoded and hackneyed rhythmic figures of ragtime.

3. Ragtime composers were writing music to accompany new dances, such as the fox-trot and the turkey trot, which came to prominence after 1910.

Whatever their origins, the use of dotted rhythms provided one of the links from ragtime to the more fluid rhythmic language of early jazz. Recordings of jazz-oriented

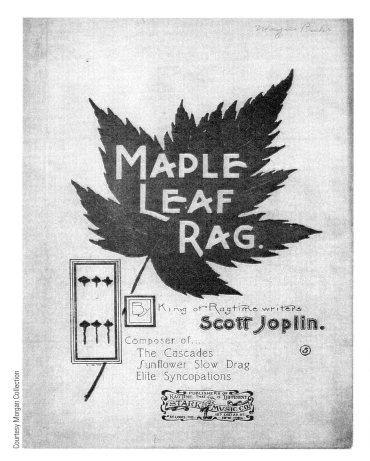

Courtesy Morgan Collection

An early edition of "Maple Leaf Rag" by Scott Joplin, the "King of Ragtime writers," published in 1899. The sheet music cover advertises more recent Joplin rags. Notice that the Stark Music Co. bills itself as "publishers of ragtime that is different" but does not show a picture of "King" Joplin on the cover—a cautious omission that was to continue for the next several decades.

treatments of ragtime compositions—such as Jelly Roll Morton's interpretation of Joplin's "Maple Leaf Rag"—made clear the practice of "swinging" the eighth notes, that is, playing them either as dotted eighth–sixteenth notes or as triplets, as suggested in Music Example 1-5.

Music Example 1-5
Swinging the eighth notes.

The decline of ragtime paralleled, or gave rise to, early jazz styles that made greater use of these looser rhythms.

Additionally, the style of solo jazz piano known as "stride" evolved directly from ragtime. Stride pianists used left-hand techniques similar to those of ragtime but treated the melodic right hand in a freer manner with added blues elements (as we shall see in Chapter 4). Pianists James P. Johnson, Fats Waller, Count Basie, and Duke Ellington were brought up in this style of piano playing, which owes its origins to ragtime, but which clearly became part of the jazz tradition.

"Pork and Beans"

CD **1**   Track **1**

Earl Fuller's Rector Novelty Orchestra: "Pork and Beans" (Luckey Roberts). Columbia A-2370,
New York, July 19, 1917. Nat Harris, violin, director; Bill Scotti, alto saxophone; Phil Bardi, Jack Harris,
Frank Copie, violins; Babe Fuller, piano; George Hamilton Green, xylophone; Paul Farmer, drums.

Luckey Roberts (1887–1968) was one of the prominent Harlem stride pianists, a movement to be
discussed in Chapter 4. "Pork and Beans," a rag published in 1913, was the first composition of the
Harlem pianists to appear in print and achieve popularity. As originally published, the arrangement is
said to have been a simplification of Roberts's own virtuosic performances. It is an ingenious rag,
with infectious spirit, excellent melodic invention, and a highly original harmonic progression in its trio.

The Earl Fuller Orchestra was in residence at Rector's, an expensive and fashionable Manhattan
nightclub in the 1910s. Earl Fuller himself was an important star of ragtime and novelty music and one
of Columbia Record's best-selling artists.

Typical of band recordings of rags at this time, this performance by the Earl Fuller Orchestra is
delightful—rhythmically sharp and exact with all the parts well played. We hear a violin and xylophone
largely carrying the lead melody. Interesting counterpoint and snappy percussion occur throughout. Notice
that all the strains are in C minor or C major. Roberts omits the typical modulation to the subdominant for
the trio, probably because the harmonic adventurousness of the C section itself provides sufficient variety.
Thus the usual modulation not only is unnecessary but might clutter the overall harmonic plan.

Introduction—4 bars

0:00   Count the pulse throughout the piece in a moderate two beats to the bar. The performance in
octaves of the first two bars is typical of ragtime style and sets up the key of the piece, C minor.

0:03   We hear a piano doubling the violin and supplying chords in the last two bars.

A strain (C minor)—16 bars, repeated

0:05   The solo violin carries the lead, sometimes doubled by the xylophone, which at other times plays
in counterpoint. Listen for the syncopated snare drum in the background. An uncredited trombone
player or the alto saxophone fills with longer notes in the mid-lower register.

0:23   Repeat

B strain (C minor)—18 bars as 8 + 10

0:42   The contrasting B strain is an irregular eighteen bars. The irregularity is produced by an extra two-
bar repeat of the B strain's two-bar basic melodic idea in bars 5 and 6 of the second ten bars.
During the basic two-bar melodic idea, the trombone provides a descending idea in counterpoint.
Though this idea is brief, it can be considered a *countermelody*. (Listen to the 🅿 Audio Primer
CD, Track 7, for a demonstration of countermelody.)

Return of the A strain—16 bars

1:02   The A section repeats, but this time it plays through only once.

C strain as trio—16 bars as 8 + 8

1:20   In the C strain (trio), the most
famous section of the piece,
the music is in C major rather
than C minor. The harmonic
progression is

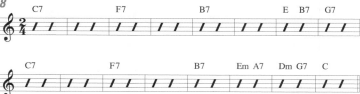

The distant harmonic progression to B7 is incorporated quite smoothly. Extra syncopated percussion—probably a woodblock—adds rhythmic lift.

D strain—16 bars as 8 + 8

1:38   The D strain acts as a bridge between the two C strain statements, much as the B strain functioned between the A strain statements. The woodblock stops during the D strain presentation.

C strain—16 bars as 8 + 8, repeated

1:56   Return to the C strain, but without the woodblock the first time. Instead, the xylophone provides an extra and insistent counterpoint.

2:14   The woodblock adds rhythmic lift the second time through.

D strain—16 bars as 8 + 8

2:32   Return to the D strain as a bridge.

C strain—16 bars as 8 + 8, with a one-bar tag

2:50   A last, climactic presentation of the C strain.

3:08   A short tag adds a sense of finality.

Courtesy Morgan Collection

A cubist cover for "Pork and Beans" (CD 1, Track 1). The famous Armory Show, which opened in New York City in 1913, introduced cubism to shocked U.S. audiences and was to have an enormous impact on U.S. visual art—including advertising. Notice the change in the artistic style from that of the opening page of this chapter.

The Blues

The addition of blues to ragtime created jazz. More precisely, ragtime—both in its classic piano form and in songs and marches "ragged" by ensembles—gradually metamorphosed into jazz. It did so through an internal evolution alongside the infusion of the blues. Because the addition of this final ingredient was so significant, some claim that to improvise with authority and passion in the jazz tradition requires the ability to play the blues well.

An active musical genre to this day, the blues has roots in the nineteenth century. By the 1870s and 1880s, the diverse, formerly African slaves living in the United States had become African Americans and, thanks to emancipation, were now free citizens. The blues—from spirituals and work songs, through hollers and shouts—jumped out to celebrate black entrance into a world less repressive, less harsh, and more optimistic—but also far more uncertain, still tragic, and full of deprivation. The unique character of the blues projected sadness, guilt, and sometimes despair, but also humor and bawdiness. Ironically, the blues could express joy, although this was less characteristic of the form as a whole.

The origins of the blues can be traced to the African-American secular and sacred music of the late nineteenth century. However, the classic form of the genre coalesced from its various antecedents rather suddenly at the dawn of the twentieth century; not until shortly after 1900 do examples of **blues forms** or written descriptions of what sounds to our ears like the blues surface. The classic blues featured an AAB lyric pattern that fit regular chord changes:

The blues is a lowdown, achin' heart disease,
The blues is a lowdown, achin' heart disease,
It's like consumption, killin' you by degrees.[15]

Where and how was the blues first performed? The music was originally vocal, usually accompanied by guitar, piano, or harmonica (although instrumentalists also played the blues). In the country blues tradition, singers often accompanied themselves. Groups of performers would gather informally in what were known as "jook joints," "barrelhouses," "honky-tonks," or "chock houses." These were simple, wooden structures with a bar for drinking, perhaps a floor for dancing, and a few stools and tables. The "bandstand" might consist of a battered piano in the corner— used not only for the blues, but also for ragtime. The musicians themselves were often nonprofessionals who substituted improvised, homemade instruments for the real thing: A washboard played with thimble became a snare drum, a jug blown on became a bass. The audience added clapping, call-and-response lines, and encouragement. From such humble beginnings grew what was to become one of the greatest and most influential folk traditions of the United States.

While local variations and styles of the blues proliferated throughout the country, the Mississippi Delta and Texas spawned the greatest number of early blues singers. As first performed by these folk artists, the blues was free in form, befitting its origins in the African-American vernacular tradition. Many of the early blues singers sang about a life of pain and despair and of the need to endure. Indeed, the great authority of their performances arose from vivid descriptions of tragic hardship yielding to the necessity of song. Among the great country blues performers were Charley Patton and Robert Johnson. See the box "Pioneers of the Delta Blues" for more on these artists.

Pioneers of the Delta Blues

The Mississippi Delta was a particularly fertile area for growing cotton (thus supporting large plantations worked primarily by African Americans)—and creating blues music. In the early twentieth century, several extremely talented performers surfaced in this region, each influencing the other. Thanks to the popularity of blues on records, we can hear many of these performers today.

Among the pioneers was Charley Patton, a singer and guitarist who played with a bottleneck slide—the glass neck of a liquor bottle run across the fret board to give a sliding or whining sound. Patton's intense vocal style and original songs were widely copied.

A younger guitarist than Patton and more popular among blues revivalists and rock and roll musicians is Robert Johnson. He also grew up in the Delta region and was said to have made a "pact with the devil" to learn to play the blues. He authored many songs that have become rock favorites, including "Love in Vain" and "Crossroads." In the 1990s, Johnson's complete recordings, reissued on CD, sold more than a quarter million copies, much to the surprise of the music industry. Clearly, Johnson's music holds strong appeal for a new generation of listeners.

Courtesy Morgan Collection

A disproportionately small number of women worked as instrumentalists—as opposed to vocalists—in early jazz. Still, several women published successfully—among them, Nellie W. Stokes (here, 1906), Adaline Shepherd, and Charlotte Blake.

Gertrude "Ma" Rainey

Ma Rainey (1886–1939) worked in minstrel shows with her husband Will. She went on to record prolifically in the 1920s, often with jazz musicians rather than to her own accompaniment in the country blues manner. Compared to her protégé, Bessie Smith, Rainey was fairly limited in technique; her vocal lines were often quite similar to one another. Nonetheless, she bridged country blues and the classic blues with performances that were effective in their deeply felt honesty.

Unfortunately, the earliest recordings of the blues were not made in any quantity until the 1920s. By then, the country blues form had acquired the professional sound of the classic blues as heard in the work of such artists as the incomparable Bessie Smith. Many of the best-known blues performers from the 1920s got their start in vaudeville, where most of the blues singers were women. These performers often recorded with jazz musicians, although blues singers were soon to be differentiated from jazz singers as such. Still, through their recordings, we can view the blues as the first jazz vocal style. One of the earliest of the important blues singers to record was Gertrude "Ma" Rainey, although she did not make the first blues record. (See the box "Gertrude 'Ma' Rainey.")

Mamie Smith made the first blues recording, "Crazy Blues," for OKeh/Phonola records in 1920. Within a few weeks, it sold more than 75,000 copies in Harlem alone and precipitated the blues craze and a demand for music by and for blacks. *Variety* magazine noted that "colored singers and playing artists are riding to fame and fortune with the current popular demand for 'blues' disk recordings."

> A **race record** was a recording, usually of jazz or blues and typically performed by and marketed to African Americans.

These special recordings, known as *race records,* targeted black audiences that had expanded in the black neighborhoods of urban centers, particularly New York. Throughout the twenties, recording companies such as OKeh, Paramount, and Vocalion released numerous blues and blues-oriented vocal music.

Until the end of the twenties at least, many great jazz musicians worked as accompanists for the blues singers. Record companies called on cornetists such as Louis Armstrong and Joe Smith, pianists such as Fletcher Henderson and James P. Johnson, and many others to make blues recordings. Later, the Dixieland style adapted various blues vocal techniques. Certainly, the interaction between the instrumentalists and singers on these early blues recordings brought to bear the blues influence on instrumental jazz even more closely.

Ultimately, we can trace the story of the blues from its country origins in field hollers, spirituals, and folk ballads, to the jook joints, circuses, minstrel shows, and vaudeville stages, and finally to the center of U.S. songwriting in New York's Tin Pan Alley. No other artist more embodied the professional emergence of the blues thran the composer and collector of several important blues compositions, W. C. Handy.

W. C. HANDY

As a youngster, William Christopher Handy (1873–1958) was lucky to receive a solid education in his hometown of Florence, Alabama. Discouraged from pursuing music by his father, who was a minister, Handy felt that "becoming a musician would be

Courtesy Morgan Collection

Composer W. C. Handy published this 1916 edition of "Saint Louis Blues." Unlike most composers of the time, Handy retained copyright and started his own publishing company. Notice that the music hall performer (later, the recording artist) was invariably pictured on early sheet music. The cityscape in the background is Saint Louis; notice the riverboat approaching the bridge. The large cube in the foreground is a bale of cotton among cotton plants.

like selling my soul to the devil."[16] Nonetheless, music became his overwhelming interest. He learned some formal music theory and soon was playing with various bands despite plans to attend college. In an important early job, he became a soloist with Mahara's Minstrels in 1896, a group he would later direct. He then organized his own bands.

Handy moved to New York with his Orchestra of Memphis, where the group made a recording in 1917. Among his early records was "Livery Stable Blues." Upon arriving in New York, Handy worked to popularize the blues and devoted himself to the cause of black music and its recognition. Although he eventually became known as the "Father of the Blues," this was an overstatement. However, he did compose the most famous blues tune of all, "St. Louis Blues" (1914), as well as "Beale Street Blues" (1916) and "Memphis Blues" (1912). With such works, the various forms of the blues became fairly standardized, and as such provided an interesting contrast to the looser performance practices of the original country blues.

BLUES FORM

It is difficult to ascertain precisely how country blues influenced early jazz. Jazz evolved as a more instrumental music. Instruments such as the cornet, trombone, and clarinet preferred the "flat side" of the key range (that is, F, B♭, and E♭). Country blues was more vocal. Its most common instrument was the guitar, and guitarists naturally preferred sharp keys, such as G, D, or A, which fit the open strings of the instrument well. With such disparate preferences, how much or how often did these two genres interact during the formative years of jazz? *Exactly* how blues catalyzed the earliest forms of jazz and ragtime remains controversial and is not likely to be settled, because all the forms were predominantly oral between about 1890 and 1910. However, the influence of blues is clear.

Because folk musicians often perform very informally, simplifying the harmony, embellishing the melody, and freely interpolating extra bars, country blues exhibited great flexibility of form. Once we reach the classic blues of the 1920s, however, we can represent the blues form as a single twelve-bar **chorus** with a strict basic harmonic progression. Within this framework of standard chord changes (Music Example 1-6a), we can construct many variants (Music Example 1-6b). Blues forms can occur in minor keys as well. Listen to Track 11 of the Audio Primer for a demonstration of blues changes.

Music Example 1-6
Classic blues form with a single 12-bar chorus and a strict harmonic progression.

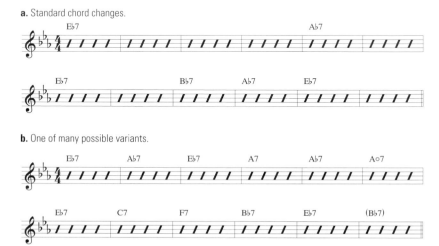

a. Standard chord changes.

b. One of many possible variants.

Sometimes a verse introduces the chorus, much like the verse in a Tin Pan Alley song. The lyric, too, follows a sharply defined format. In AAB form, each A and B usually encompasses four of the twelve bars. This form is ideal for improvisation, because the singer can think ahead for a rhyming third phrase during the repetition of the first. Adding to the ease of improvisation, each A and B phrase usually falls within the first two or three bars of each four-bar phrase. The concluding part of each phrase can be filled with a response from the instrumental accompaniment while the singer ponders the next phrase.

> A. *I was with you, ba-by, when you did not have a dime.*
> A. *I was with you, ba-by, when you did not have a dime.*
> B. *Now since you've got plenty mon-ey, you have brought your good gal down.*

BESSIE SMITH

In the early 1920s, before microphones, blues singers establishing their reputations needed volume and projection. Of all the fine blues singers of this period, the greatest was Bessie Smith (1894–1937). She is probably the most beloved of all classic blues singers. The richness and breadth of her tone are evident even on her oldest recordings.

Ma Rainey's greatest protégé, Smith was a member of Rainey's Rabbit Foot Minstrels and frequently appeared in traveling vaudeville shows before embarking on a solo career. Her first blues recordings for Columbia, "Down-Hearted Blues" and "Gulf Coast Blues," were hits in 1923, but by the end of the decade her

An elegant publicity portrait of Bessie Smith (CD 1, Track 2) at about age thirty. Later images of Smith showed her dressed more flamboyantly, in keeping with her vocal power and musical standing as "Empress of the Blues."

"Back Water Blues"
CD 1 Track 2

Bessie Smith and James P. Johnson: "Back Water Blues" (Smith). Columbia 14195-D, New York, February 17, 1927. Smith, vocal; Johnson, piano.

James P. Johnson was Bessie Smith's favorite accompanist. Their superb performance of "Back Water Blues" is one of their finest joint efforts. The form and performance of the piece could not be simpler, but the power of the expression is clear throughout. Johnson's accompaniment provides a steady and beautifully wrought commentary to Smith's story.

After a two-bar introduction, the song unfolds in seven choruses of twelve-bar blues. Practice counting the twelve-bar choruses, with four beats to the bar, in order to determine where each chorus begins and ends.

Introduction—2 bars

0:00 Count this piece in a moderate four beats to the bar. Johnson provides a rolling introductory vamp before Smith comes in for her first chorus.

1st chorus

0:04 Smith's phrases generally fill the first two bars of each four-bar phrase. Johnson fills the remaining two bars. The first chorus sets the scene with its depiction of five days of rain.

2nd chorus

0:32 The song turns more personal. Note the despair of the line "Can't even get outta my door."

3rd chorus

1:00 The story continues with the description of the boat picking up Smith with her clothes to escape the flood.

4th chorus

1:28 A return to the nature description of the first chorus.

1:34 Note how Johnson's expressive bass answers Smith's phrases.

5th chorus

1:54 A return to the personal as Smith looks down on her flooded house.

6th chorus

2:21 "The blues" calls Smith to reflect on her loss.

7th chorus

2:49 Complete despair: Smith "can't move no more." Johnson ends the piece without a tag or any extra musical statement.

popularity waned as classic blues vocalists found themselves less in demand. Almost forgotten, she began to work in minor musical shows that toured the country. She was on such a tour when she died in a car crash in Clarksdale, Mississippi. With Smith's work we can begin to detect the qualities that later differentiated the jazz, pop, and blues vocal idioms.

CHARACTERISTICS OF EARLY JAZZ SINGING

In the performance of "Back Water Blues," we can point to three features of Bessie Smith's style that will remain characteristic of subsequent jazz singing:

1. Loosely constructed phrasing

2. Offbeat, syncopated placement of notes and lyrics

3. Use of slides, blue notes, and other vocal embellishments

First, in jazz singing, the phrasing of the song must be loose. For example, sometimes the phrase may begin on the downbeat, while at other times it may begin as a pickup, that is, at the end of the preceding bar. This practice of varying the placement of the phrase relative to the beat gives a free quality to the performance and contrasts with the on-the-beat feel of nonjazz singing. In later styles, beginning in the 1930s, such singers as Billie Holiday delayed the placement of the melody as much as a full bar. Slight delays and embellishments, as heard in Smith, are typical of 1920s blues singing.

Second, jazz and blues singing is characterized by the offbeat, syncopated placement of important notes and their lyrics. Jazz singing epitomizes the freedom of loose phrasing allied with inventive syncopation.

Third, jazz and blues singers use slides, blue notes, and other melodic pitch inflections and ornaments. Although these features appear in all popular singing, they are especially prominent in the blues. In general, constant modification and the embellishment of various phrases play important roles in distinguishing jazz and blues singing from pop singing, which is usually less ornamental.

With the popularization of the blues in the 1920s, composers began to write songs in the twelve-bar blues style. For example, during the swing era, blues pianists of the South and Southwest developed a driving style of piano playing called boogie woogie that became extremely popular throughout the country. Such important songs as "In the Mood" (Garland) and "One O'Clock Jump" (Basie) were in fact blues tunes with riffs based on the melodic figures of the boogie-woogie pianists. Later, in such songs as "Rock Around the Clock" (Freedman-DeKnight) and "Blue Suede Shoes" (Perkins), we can hear blues harmony, form, and phrasing. These features of early rock offer evidence of its evolution from the blues and R&B (rhythm and blues).

In addition to the standard twelve-bar blues form, by far the most common in jazz, there are eight- and sixteen-bar forms whose harmonic structures are somewhat more unpredictable. Although modern composers have written blues tunes with highly irregular structures, much classic blues retains the simpler twelve-bar, rhyming lyric structure.

With ragtime's popularity waning in the late teens and the blues thriving as a separate genre, the necessary conditions were in place for jazz to become the primary musical medium of popular culture. The next two chapters examine this breakthrough, which largely takes place during the late teens and 1920s and is fully completed by the 1930s.

Questions and Topics for Discussion

1. How do the European and African musical traditions differ? Contrast both musical and cultural qualities.

2. In what ways was ragtime fresh and innovative?

3. What are some of the characteristics of the blues? How do these characteristics relate to the African tradition?

4. What are the important differences between blues and ragtime?

5. In what ways can ragtime be seen as a blend of the African and European traditions?

Key Terms

AABA song form
ABAC song form
Arranger
Blue note
Blues
Blues form
Blues scale
Cakewalk
Call-and-response
Chorus
Countermelody
Cross-rhythms
Front line
Head arrangement
Meter
Metronomic sense
Minstrelsy
Obbligato
Polyphony
Race Record
Ragtime
Rhythm section
Ring shout
Slash notation
Song plugger
Spiritual
Syncopation
Texture
Transcribe
Transcription

At the same time that jazz was developing, the United States, led by President Woodrow Wilson, entered World War I (1914–1918) to "make the world safe for democracy." This sheet music cover (1917) captures the dominant artistic style and ardent patriotism of the early 1900s.

EARLY JAZZ AND NEW ORLEANS JAZZ

2

IN THIS CHAPTER, we explore the first appearances of a music much like ragtime but still called jazz. As argued in Chapter 1, no clear line of demarcation marked the change from ragtime to jazz; rather, a gradual transformation occurred during the second decade of the twentieth century. Despite controversies surrounding the origins of jazz, which this chapter considers, the city of New Orleans figures prominently in any discussion of the music's early history. After we discuss the emergence of various jazz-based styles in New Orleans and other areas of the country, we shall consider changes in the use of instruments. Much of what made early jazz exciting was the innovative way players approached traditional instruments, producing effects that were considered tawdry by traditionalists but brilliant and creative by early jazz fans.

The Shift from Ragtime to Jazz

New Orleans is popularly considered the birthplace of jazz, but the entire picture is much more complex and has produced a significant and ongoing controversy among historians. Some contend that jazz crystallized in New Orleans. Other scholars argue that jazzlike styles were evolving throughout the country but New Orleans musicians were the first to break through with the **Dixieland** style. Because this style and its star players were subsequently so widely imitated, New Orleans–style Dixieland came to be defined as jazz in the 1920s. Thus, while some historians define early New Orleans style as the beginning of jazz, others define it as the first jazz style to achieve national prominence.

Both positions are partially true. During the teens and twenties, in a decisive step toward the emergence of jazz, some prominent New Orleans musicians and therefore jazz styles moved to Chicago. But jazz styles also developed in other urban centers such as New York and Kansas City. In fact, jazz styles developed wherever musicians, encouraged by the spontaneous performance practices of ragtime and turn-of-the-century popular music, took jazzlike liberties.

For example, in his groundbreaking study *Early Jazz*, Gunther Schuller interviews George Morrison, an African-American violinist who discusses playing jazz in Denver, Colorado, around 1920. Morrison mentions Benny Goodman (not the famous clarinetist), a musician who "was a violinist and he improvised just [as] I did on the violin. And we had piano players who improvised on the piano. That's what we did up in those mining towns."[1] This and other examples show that improvisation did not proceed from the New Orleans tradition alone.

Even the origins of the word *jazz* are murky. The word first appeared in print in 1913 in the baseball column of a San Francisco newspaper, where it seems to have meant "pep" or "energy." The word gained currency by 1917, especially after the first recording labeled as jazz (from the Original Dixieland Jazz Band—to be discussed shortly). Its variable spelling was noted by a writer for the *New York Sun* in 1917:

> Variously spelled Jas, Jass, Jaz, Jasz, and Jascz. The word is African in origin. It is common on the Gold Coast of Africa and in the hinterland of Cape Coast Castle. . . . Jazz is based on the savage musican's wonderful gift for progressive retarding and acceleration guided by his sense of "swing."[2]

In fact, the etymology of the word *jazz* is even more obscure than the writer suggests. Some have pointed to a French origin from the verb *jaser,* which means to chatter or gossip; others have said that the word is a synonym for sexual intercourse. It is unlikely that the origins of its name will ever be precisely determined.

Use of the term *jazz* was controversial when it was fairly new. In 1924 Meyer Davis, a radio broadcaster, held a contest to rename *jazz*; out of 70,000 suggestions, the winner was *syncopep*,[3] which obviously did not catch on. Other attempts to revise the name or concept also failed. Thus, the term *jazz* remains with us today.

The boundaries between ragtime and jazz were considerably blurred between 1910 and 1920. A lack of agreement over the meanings of both terms added to the confusion. Historians such as Lawrence Gushee have suggested that their usage was regional. To the New Orleans musicians who were performing before 1920, jazz was nothing more than "just a fashionable, Northern name for New Orleans instrumental ragtime."[4] For example, one of the leading early jazz saxophonists from New Orleans, Sidney Bechet, consistently used the term *ragtime* throughout his life to refer to the type of music he played.

Musicians performed and wrote compositions that highlighted the ambiguity of the ragtime-to-jazz shift. Older New Orleans musicians played "jazz" based on the formal structure of ragtime. For example, the majority of Jelly Roll Morton's works maintained a ragtime architecture: multiple sixteen-bar strains, with the trio (the C section) modulating to the subdominant. Many of the works played by King Oliver's Creole Jazz Band, the first important New Orleans group to record, also follow ragtime form. The stride pianists also maintained a close connection to the ragtime form and much of its performance practice (see Chapter 4).

In time, musicians began moving away from the ragtime format. Instead of relying on multiple sixteen-bar strains, they took the popular songs that emerged

The cover of the *Gem Dance Folio* from 1920 displays photographs of the composers of 1919's hit songs. Notice that *jazz* is in quotes, indicating that the word was not yet in common usage. Notice, too, that this cover is integrated by race and gender. Interestingly, we have forgotten the names of most of these composers, but not Clarence Williams (shown bottom right), the composer of "Texas Moaner Blues" (CD 1, Track 3), discussed in this chapter.

from publishing houses, record companies, and musical theater and used them as vehicles for jazz—casting them primarily in a thirty-two–bar AABA format. In addition, Morton, like many of the New Orleans and Chicago musicians, made the twelve-bar blues a staple of the repertory. Jazz musicians such as Louis Armstrong and Fletcher Henderson accompanied blues singers on recordings as well. Lawrence Gushee summarizes these changes:

> Also obvious in the years after World War I was a shift from tunes with many articulated sections (several strains differing in character and often in key, along with introductions, transitions, interludes, codas) to the verse-chorus format, with the verse often disappearing in instrumental performance. The older pieces were routines that had to be played as such; the newer ones were repetitions of a chord progression that cried out for elaboration and enlivening through ingenious arrangement or solo extemporization.[5]

Despite the practice of improvisation in urban areas throughout the country, jazz musicians from New Orleans were especially skilled in "elaboration" or "extemporization." At the same time, these black pioneers incorporated elements of the blues tradition in their treatment of ragtime forms. The next section describes the fertile musical environment of New Orleans, the "Crescent City."

New Orleans

By all accounts, music was omnipresent in New Orleans during the first two decades of the twentieth century. Anecdotes and remembrances by those who were present describe a constant flood of outdoor and indoor social events, nearly all of which required music. Groups such as the Eagle Band, the Magnolia Band, the Imperial Band, the Superior Band, and the Olympia Band supplied music for nighttime dancing and often performed on horse-drawn wagons during the day to advertise an upcoming dance that night. Sit-down orchestras such as John Robichaux's nine-piece band performed sophisticated scottisches and quadrilles for dancing. The legendary red-light district of Storyville, the section of town set off for legalized prostitution in 1897, flourished until its closing by the U.S. Navy Department in 1917. Storyville's bordellos provided steady employment for pianists. The bars and sporting houses of "the District," as Storyville was known to musicians, hired dozens of bands. Clarinetist Louis "Big Eye" Nelson recalled that the four saloons on the corner of Iberville and Franklin had eight bands among them, and the saloons "changed bands like you change underclothes."[6]

Another participant, bassist Pops Foster, described the explosive musical activity in the city:

> There were always twenty-five or thirty bands going around New Orleans. There was all kinds of work for musicians from birthday parties to funerals. Out at the lake [Lake Ponchartrain] they had some bands in the day and others at night; Milneberg was really jumping. There were a lot of string trios around playing street corners, fish frys, lawn parties, and private parties. The piano players like Drag Nasty, Black Pete, Sore Dick and Tony Jackson were playing the whorehouses. In the District there were the cabarets, Rece's, Fewclothes, Huntz & Nagels, and Billy Phillips who had the best bands. Some bands played dances in mild dairy stables and the bigger name ones played the dance halls like the Tuxedo Dance Hall, Masonic Hall, Globes Hall, and the Funky Butt Hall. The bands played picnics out at the lake; they played excursions on the riverboats and for the trains. The restaurants like Galatoires on Dauphine Street had bands. On Chartres Street there was Jackson Square Gardens where they had two or three bands going. There were tonks like Real Tom Anderson's at Rampart and Canal, and Tom Anderson's Annex at Iberville and Basin Street. Out in the country, like Breakaway, Louisiana, or Bay St. Louis, Mississippi, you played dances, fairs, picnics, and barbecues. We had plenty of fun together and there was music everywhere.[7]

Enshrined in the history of New Orleans jazz are the brass bands. They played for street parades, carnivals, lawn parties, and picnics. Although they emerged out of the tradition of military march music performed by reading musicians, these bands altered this tradition in significant ways. Whereas typical marches such as John Philip Sousa's "Washington Post March" were written in 6/8 and performed as written, a tradition developed of "ragging" (syncopating) the marches, or performing them in a ragtime 2/4 meter and improvising. Edmond Hall, who began playing around 1915, stated that "in the very early days of brass bands, in the '90s and even before, the music was mostly written—I mean in the kind of band my father played in. As time went on, there was more improvising."[8]

The influence of brass bands and early jazz dance bands was probably reciprocal. Historian William J. Shafer suggests that the brass band influenced jazz bands in three ways: repertory, instrumentation, and technique. More specifically, the roles of the instruments in the brass band, in which the cornet performs the melody, the clarinet plays piccolo-like elaborations, and the trombone provides an independent voice of harmony notes and glissandi, suggest an origin for the front line of Dixieland instrumentation.[9]

The jazz bands also probably influenced the brass bands. Brass bands most likely made their styles hotter by adopting the improvised syncopated style of the dance bands. At any rate, the relationship between jazz and brass bands is difficult to disentangle, because many of the same musicians played for both groups. The street brass bands provided the training ground for early jazz musicians: Joe Oliver was part of the Onward Brass Band, while Louis Armstrong was a member of the Tuxedo Brass Band. Jelly Roll Morton, although better known as a pianist and composer, claimed to have organized brass bands and to have played both trombone and drums.

In their role in New Orleans funerals, brass bands made a prominent contribution to jazz lore. New Orleans had numerous fraternal organizations—clubs, lodges, and benevolent associations—that would pay for the funeral of one of its members and provide a band to accompany the funeral procession to and from the burial site, which was often a mausoleum because the swampy Louisiana ground did not permit burial under the ground. Band members usually earned between $2.00 and $2.50 a funeral. On the way to the burial, accompanying the casket, the band played dirges. But returning from the graveyard after the burial, the band would unmuffle the drum and launch into up-tempo, jazzlike popular compositions.

One of New Orleans's most renowned drummers, Baby Dodds, described this tradition:

> Of course we played other numbers coming back from funerals. We'd play the same popular numbers that we used to play with dance bands. And the purpose was this: As the family and people went to the graveyard to bury one of their loved ones, we'd play a funeral march. It was pretty sad, and it put a feeling of weeping in their hearts and minds and when they left there we didn't want them to hear that going home. It became a tradition to play jazzy numbers going back to make the relatives and friends cast off their sadness. And the people along the streets used to dance to the music. I used to follow those parades myself, long before I ever thought of becoming a drummer. The jazz played after New Orleans funerals didn't show any lack of respect for the person being buried. It rather showed their people that we wanted them to be happy.[10]

WHY DID JAZZ ARISE IN NEW ORLEANS?

Two general theories have arisen to explain the origins of jazz in New Orleans. The "uptown/downtown" theory holds that the mixing of uptown-dwelling black musicians with downtown-dwelling Creoles of Color created a catalyst for New Orleans jazz.

Creoles of Color were people of mixed black-and-white ancestry who throughout the nineteenth century enjoyed a privileged status over the blacks. These Creoles of Color (as distinguished from the Creoles who were French-speaking people of white ancestry) formed a professional, skilled class and were usually well educated. Some Creoles of Color even owned slaves. Most of the Creoles of Color lived in downtown New Orleans, in what is now known as the French Quarter. By comparison, the blacks of New Orleans lived uptown above

Canal Street and were primarily unskilled workers. Throughout the 1880s, however, the whites enacted increasingly restrictive legislation against the Creoles of Color and gradually reduced their status. By 1894 the segregation code removed the final legal distinctions between Creoles of Color and blacks. From that point on, Creoles of Color were to be segregated along with blacks.

The "uptown/downtown" theory, then, maintains that jazz emerged out of the musical chemistry between Creoles of Color and blacks after 1894. While the musicians among the downtown Creoles of Color were conservatory-trained in the European classical tradition, with many of them playing in the French opera orchestras of New Orleans, the uptown black musicians received far less musical training. Because the black musicians often did not read music, they relied on memorization and, significantly, improvisation. The Creoles of Color thus performed in a more refined, sophisticated style (sometimes called "sweet" or "dicty" by the musicians), while the black musicians played in a rougher, improvised style (called "hot" or "ratty"). **New Orleans jazz** arose from the combination of the European musical tradition from the Creoles of Color and the African tradition from the black musicians.

> **Creoles of Color** were people of mixed black and white ancestry. Until the late nineteenth century, they enjoyed more freedom and were better educated than the general black population. Musicians from this group generally had classical training and could read musical scores.

A second theory suggests that the rougher improvised music gradually *replaced* that of the more refined style. According to this "generational" theory, an earlier generation of reading Creole musicians, such as the clarinetists Lorenzo Tio and Alphonse Picou and the trumpeter Manuel Perez, taught and were followed by a newer generation of musicians who played in a hotter style. The novelty of ragtime and changes in social dance styles brought about a demand for this style, which evolved into jazz. As more jobs of this type became available for musicians, even the trained Creole musicians who could read music were forced reluctantly to switch to the more popular (and lucrative) style. Some Creole musicians born after the 1894 segregation laws, such as Sidney Bechet, were not primarily reading musicians and performed only in the rougher style.

Another layer of complexity in the development of New Orleans style is the probable influence of Caribbean music. Jelly Roll Morton, whose work we discuss shortly, spoke often of the "Spanish tinge," a basic Latin rhythm that he applied to several compositions. Apart from such works, some of the syncopated patterns associated with early jazz may have originated in the Caribbean. For example, the musicologist Christopher Washburne identifies Caribbean *clave* rhythmic patterns in early jazz: "The frequency of these rhythms in early jazz suggests that the Caribbean influence was so tied to its developmental stages that the rhythms became part of the rhythmic foundation of jazz."[11]

CHARLES "BUDDY" BOLDEN

Interestingly, many of the New Orleans musicians attributed the genesis of the rougher, improvised style to a single person: black cornetist Charles "Buddy" Bolden. For instance, see how one musician wistfully described the generational change between the older music readers and the younger improvisers of his time:

> Bolden cause all that.... He cause these younger Creoles, men like [Sidney] Bechet and [Freddie] Keppard, to have a different style altogether from the old heads like [Lorenzo] Tio and [Manuel] Perez. I don't know how they do it.... Can't tell you what's there on the paper, but just play the hell out of it.[12]

Courtesy Frank Driggs Collection

Buddy Bolden and his band, c. 1900. L to r: Jimmie Johnson, bass; Buddy Bolden, cornet; Brock Mumford, guitar; Willie Cornish, valve trombone; Frank Lewis, clarinet; Willie Warner, clarinet. This famous photograph has been the subject of controversy with various writers claiming that some of the players are holding their instruments incorrectly. Musicians have been known to do this as a practical joke.

Bolden was born in 1877. A plasterer by trade, he formed a band around 1895 that performed throughout New Orleans in the saloons of Storyville, in the dance halls, and in the parks. Said to be heard for several miles, the volume of Bolden's horn was legendary. Cornetist Peter Bocage claimed that Bolden "was powerful. Plenty of power. He had a good style in the blues and all that stuff."[13] By 1901 Bolden's band included cornet, clarinet, valve trombone, guitar, double bass, and drums. He developed as a player through the 1890s and achieved his greatest influence around 1905, leading a band that performed in numerous venues throughout New Orleans. Bolden was a heavy drinker, and his bouts of insanity led to his institutionalization in 1907. He died in a state institution in Jackson, Louisiana, in 1931.

Bolden's style of improvisation was based on "ragging" the melodies. As Wallace Collins noted, "He'd take one note [of the original] and put two or three to it."[14] This technique is similar to what clarinetist Alphonse Picou described when he said that the rising jazz style was made up of "additions to the bars—doubling up on notes—playing eight or sixteen for one."[15] Further, Bolden was particularly remembered for playing the blues, and henceforth this folk idiom, imported from the Mississippi Delta, became a primary source for New Orleans musicians. Blues then became closely allied with jazz and the jazz repertory. Clarinetist Louis "Big Eye" Nelson even averred that blues "is what cause the fellows to start jazzing."[16]

Was Bolden the first New Orleans jazz musician, the first "hot" jazz cornetist? That is probably impossible to answer. Banjoist Johnny St. Cyr claimed that Bolden inserted the same "hot lick" in each of his compositions but that other bands, such as the Golden Rule Band, were playing in a hotter style. Clearly Bolden's six-piece band, along with his use of a ragged, improvised style and reliance on the blues, strongly influenced an emerging New Orleans jazz style, instrumentation, and repertory. Even so, it was probably the next generation of musicians, those born around 1890, who solidified the New Orleans jazz style. According to Jelly Roll Morton, cornetist Freddie Keppard formed the "first Dixieland combination" in 1908 when Keppard rearranged his band, dropping violin, bass, and guitar and adding pianist Bud Christian to the already-present Dee Dee Chandler on drums, Edward Vincent on trombone, George Bacquet on clarinet, and Keppard on cornet.

SIDNEY BECHET

Although many, if not most, of the early woodwind players played clarinet, the saxophone did appear during the early jazz period. Sidney Bechet (1897–1959) began as a clarinetist, but he took on the soprano saxophone as his primary instrument and became one of its early virtuoso soloists.

Vibrato is a method of varying the pitch frequency of a note, producing a wavering sound.

Bechet's style on both clarinet and soprano saxophone was unique and unforgettable. The sound was rich and woody, modulated by a quick and surprisingly wide **vibrato.** On the clarinet, Bechet tended to be demure, while on the soprano sax he was more experimental and freewheeling. On either instrument, the opulence of tone and passionate vibrato combine to create an intense expressiveness that made him one of the two or three most important and renowned soloists of the 1920s. Furthermore, Bechet insisted on equal time for the clarinet, refusing to let the trumpet keep the lion's share of attention in the Dixieland ensemble.

Bechet was possibly the first jazz musician to be recognized as first-rate by the musical establishment. In one of the most famous pronouncements in jazz history, the Swiss conductor Ernest Ansermet hailed a 1919 performance of Bechet in Europe by referring to him as an "artist of genius."[17] Some historians interpret Ansermet's recognition of Bechet as evidence that Europeans accorded jazz respectability before Americans at home. The actual story is more complex, because numerous U.S. critics throughout the 1920s wrote of the greatness of jazz. Still, the Ansermet review is significant because it came from one of the most important musicians in Europe and probably represented the first praise for high artistic quality in a jazz performance and a jazz musician.

Returning to the United States in the early 1920s, Bechet recorded important records with Louis Armstrong in groups organized by the pianist-composer and music publisher Clarence Williams (c. 1893–1965). While Bechet was more established than Armstrong, the latter's emerging excellence created a tension in the band that led to such fine recordings as "Mandy, Make up Your Mind" (1924) and two versions of "Cake Walking Babies (from Home)" (1924 and 1925).

Courtesy Morgan Collection

Clarence Williams

Jazz Performance Terms

A **break** occurs when the band stops playing for a short period of time—usually one or two bars—to feature a soloist. When the band or rhythm section punctuates beats, it is said to be playing in **stop time.** Often a band will play in stop time while the soloist improvises breaks during and between the band's chords.

(Listen to Tracks 46 and 48 of the 🅿 Audio Primer CD to hear breaks and stop time.)

A **tag** is a short, codalike section added to the end of a composition to give it closure.

Musicians play **staccato** when they play short notes with distinct spaces between them. The opposite of staccato is **legato,** in which the notes are connected smoothly.

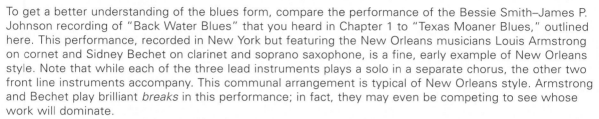

L I S T E N I N G   G U I D E

"Texas Moaner Blues"
CD **1** Track **3**

Clarence Williams' Blue Five: "Texas Moaner Blues" (Williams-Barnes). OKeh 8171.
New York, October 17, 1924. Louis Armstrong, cornet; Charlie Irvis, trombone; Sidney Bechet,
clarinet and soprano saxophone; Clarence Williams, piano; Buddy Christian, banjo.

To get a better understanding of the blues form, compare the performance of the Bessie Smith–James P. Johnson recording of "Back Water Blues" that you heard in Chapter 1 to "Texas Moaner Blues," outlined here. This performance, recorded in New York but featuring the New Orleans musicians Louis Armstrong on cornet and Sidney Bechet on clarinet and soprano saxophone, is a fine, early example of New Orleans style. Note that while each of the three lead instruments plays a solo in a separate chorus, the other two front line instruments accompany. This communal arrangement is typical of New Orleans style. Armstrong and Bechet play brilliant *breaks* in this performance; in fact, they may even be competing to see whose work will dominate.

In the arrangement of "Texan Moaner Blues," we hear five blues choruses followed by a two-bar tag. As with the earlier listening examples, practice counting the twelve-bar choruses so you can tell where each begins and ends.

1st Chorus

0:00   The group launches into the tune without introduction or preparation. Armstrong, on cornet, plays the lead melody. Bechet, on clarinet, embellishes in the higher register, and Irvis constructs a counterpoint in the lower register. This arrangement is a hallmark of New Orleans Dixieland style. The Armstrong lead generally occupies the first two bars of each four-bar unit. In the first four-bar unit, he answers himself, while in the second four-bar unit, he allows Bechet and Irvis to frame the response. In the third four-bar unit, Armstrong also answers himself.

2nd Chorus

0:37   Irvis trombone is featured on the lead. This chorus largely repeats the melody as heard in the first chorus. Armstrong and Bechet provide a background, sometimes with held notes, other times with answering figures.

0:56   During the second four-bar unit, Bechet plays a break for the last two bars.

3rd Chorus

1:14   Armstrong cornet is featured on the lead.

1:32   In the last two bars of the second four-bar unit, Armstrong has a break, which parallels Bechet's in the second chorus.

4th Chorus

1:50   Bechet switches to soprano saxophone for his solo. Note the bent notes and slurred notes contrasting with other runs played *staccato* (with very short notes).

2:08   His break in the last two bars of the second four-bar unit is spectacular, spanning two octaves on the instrument before a beautiful, bluesy slurring of the phrase. Armstrong and Irvis accompany Bechet with answering figures and held notes.

5th Chorus

2:26   The cornet lead returns with a planned ensemble passage. Bechet returns to clarinet for the remainder of the performance. The cornet and trombone begin with a passage in sixths in *stop time*. Stop time occurs through the remainder of the chorus as well.

Tag—2 bars

3:01   Bechet gets a solo break for a tag added to the fifth chorus.

Bechet continued to record prolifically for the remainder of his long career, often superbly. By virtually all accounts, he was egocentric and difficult to work with. Possibly for this reason, he had difficulty establishing a long-lived working band with a standard identity that could amass a substantial and unified body of work. Further, like Jelly Roll Morton, Bechet was one of the great individualists in early jazz—not easily pigeonholed and often just slightly out of the mainstream. For example, he refused to move with the tide when big-band music began to dominate in the 1930s. He nevertheless continued to make excellent recordings, even into the 1950s. His autobiography, *Treat It Gentle,* was published posthumously in 1960 and remains one of the most perceptive of jazz memoirs.

JELLY ROLL MORTON

One of the most influential of New Orleans musicians was a pianist and composer-arranger named Lemott Ferdinand Joseph "Jelly Roll" Morton (1890–1941). A pool hustler, braggart, and "ladies' man," he often made a living from gambling and pimping, which were far more lucrative than playing the piano. From 1907 to 1923, he traveled around the country, leading bands and playing solo gigs (jobs), often remaining for a few months in each city. Bumming around Texas, Mississippi, Oklahoma, and Arkansas, he reached Chicago by 1914. From late 1917 to 1922 he worked on the west coast, but he returned to Chicago and settled there in 1922. (See the box *"Jelly's Last Jam"* for a note on a recent interpretation of Morton's life.)

Jelly Roll Morton (CD 1, Track 4), the self-styled "inventor" of jazz, pictured here c. 1923. Morton was one of the most significant composer-arrangers and pianists to have emerged from New Orleans.

Morton cut classic recordings in Chicago over the next several years, including superb piano solos and the best-arranged ensemble numbers of early jazz. In his ensemble work, principally with the Red Hot Peppers recordings of the mid-1920s, Morton shows a deft awareness of the balance between improvisation and worked-out arrangement. In this regard, Morton was undoubtedly the finest composer-arranger in early jazz and remains among the best in jazz to this day.

The wide variety of music Morton played points to the complexity of early jazz evolution. In a series of interviews recorded by the folklorist Alan Lomax in 1938, Morton discussed playing not only rags, blues, and stomps but also selections from light opera, popular songs, and dances such as quadrilles. Morton also claimed to have invented jazz in 1902. While this is an exaggeration, Morton's performance on a series of recordings produced by Alan Lomax for the Library of Congress provides convincing evidence that he was part of the cutting edge of ragtime and protojazz musicians.[18] He was likely one of the first musicians to loosen up the stricter rhythms of ragtime. Morton played with an orchestral conception—his left-hand lines often sounded more like the trombone part in the brass band than like simple piano accompaniment.

Like James P. Johnson, to be discussed in Chapter 4, Jelly Roll Morton was among the first pianists to transform the traditional ragtime figures into a more linear jazz style. His informal performances of "Maple Leaf Rag" (from the Library of Congress recordings) demonstrate the liberties most early improvising pianists took with written compositions. These performances also reveal the close relationship between ragtime and early jazz.

Morton's early solo recordings for Gennett between 1923 and 1924 remain classics, equal in quality to the famous sides he soon recorded with the Red Hot Peppers. Throughout the 1920s, he recorded voluminously, both solos and small-band arrangements. During the 1930s, unable or unwilling to update his style to swing, he commanded less and less attention. When he died in 1941, relatively few people remembered him.

Significantly different from the Harlem stride piano style (see Chapter 4), Morton's performances are less virtuosic and often include his so-called Spanish tinge. Such works represent the first recorded example of the fusion of Latin music and jazz.

Jelly's Last Jam

As one of the great characters in jazz history, Morton inspired a controversial Broadway show in the mid-1990s called *Jelly's Last Jam*. The show dramatized Morton's background as a Creole of Color who sought to deny the importance of his black heritage.

It is in fact true that Morton took pains to emphasize his French ancestry, but *Jelly's Last Jam* displayed an anachronistic understanding of the complexities of racial relations.

One of the greatest musicians in jazz history was reduced to a bigoted stereotype on the basis of late–twentieth-century attitudes and ethnic pride. While the difficulties of racial issues in jazz are dramatized by Morton's multiethnic background, his contribution to jazz must be considered on its own merits and in its own time period. We shall briefly explore issues of race and authenticity in jazz in future chapters.

L I S T E N I N G　　G U I D E

"The Chant"
CD **1** Track **4**

Jelly Roll Morton's Red Hot Peppers: "The Chant"—Take 3 (Morton). Victor 1649.
Chicago, September 15, 1926. George Mitchell, cornet; Edward "Kid" Ory, trombone;
Omer Simeon, clarinet; Ferdinand "Jelly Roll" Morton, piano, arranger, leader;
John St. Cyr, banjo; John Lindsay, bass; Andrew Hilaire, drums.

This remarkable piece—one of Morton's classic Red Hot Peppers recordings—employs an unusual structure, in which the first section features a military figure with unusual syncopation, harmonization, and instrumentation. Later sections develop both eight-bar phrases and the twelve-bar blues format.

In contrast to the Smith and Bechet performances heard earlier in this chapter, the blues choruses in "The Chant" are not wistful and despairing but instead offer examples of the paradoxically joyful blues.

Section A—8 bars as 4 + 4, repeated; tonality of D♭ and D major

0:00　Count the pulse for this piece either in a fast four to the bar, or moderate two to the bar. The work opens with the cornet and clarinet playing an almost military figure as shown here:[19]

Note the complex syncopation and unusual grouping of the cornet and clarinet in overlapping sixths. The D♭ major tonality of this opening contrasts with the highly unusual D major of the last 4 bars played by the entire group.

0:08　Repeat.

Section B—8 bars, repeated; tonality of B♭ major

0:16　After the stop time presentation of the first section, this section moves into a steadier rhythm. The clarinet glides between notes, much like the Bechet performance discussed earlier. The trombone plays some glissandos, typical of what is sometimes called *tailgate* trombone.

0:24　Repeat.

Section A—8 bars

0:31　Section A repeats, this time played only once.

Section C—12 bars; A♭ blues, repeated

0:39　We hear an abrupt change to an A♭ blues. Without steady rhythm, we hear a kind of stop time performance.

0:51　The section repeats. The cornet plays the lead. The clarinet figure could be termed an obbligato, with its repeated and rapid arpeggios.

Section D—16 bars; A♭ major

1:02　A new section appears with a bluesy lead figure in the cornet.

　　　　The four-bar units of this sixteen-bar section add up to a miniature AABA form.

　　　　There is a cornet break in the B part.

Section D—16 bars; clarinet solo

1:18　Section D now provides the backdrop for a clarinet solo. The miniature AABA follows the format of the first D section.

1:26   But Simeon's clarinet now takes a virtuoso break in the B part.

Section E—12-bar blues

1:34   The ensemble improvises a twelve-bar A♭ blues in New Orleans style with all the instruments improvising together.

Section E—12-bar blues

1:45   Banjo solo.

1:55   Band enters with a syncopated figure during the last two bars. This figure will return at the end of each solo to "announce" the next solo.

Section E—12-bar blues, clarinet solo

1:57   Simeon displays much characteristic slurring and sliding in his solo.

2:07   The band answers with the same syncopated figure in measures 11–12 to introduce the cornet solo.

Section E—12-bar blues, muted trumpet solo

2:08   The muted cornet offers a new timbre.

2:18   The band answers with the same syncopated figure in measures 11–12 to introduce the trombone solo.

Section E—12-bar blues, trombone solo

2:20   Trombone solo.

2:30   Again, the band answers with the same figure during the last two bars of the solo to set up the piano.

Section E—12-bar blues, piano solo

2:32   Morton's solo includes the march bass in the left hand taken from ragtime. He is accompanied by drums alone.

2:41   The band enters with the syncopated figure during the last two bars for the final climactic *out-choruses*.

Section E—12-bar blues, full band, 2 choruses

2:43   The performance ends with the full band performing two improvised choruses.

3:07   A seven-beat tag rounds out the performance.

The Evolution of the Jazz Band

An **out-chorus,** sometimes called a **shout chorus,** is the final, usually highly exuberant, chorus of a jazz performance.

Jazz ensembles evolved from different types of groups, including dance bands, brass bands, and string bands. As pointed out in Chapter 1, numerous ensembles featured three horns—usually trumpet, trombone, and clarinet—and three rhythm players—drums, bass, or tuba—and a chordal instrument—piano, banjo, or guitar. Naturally there were exceptions. For example, King Oliver's Creole Jazz Band featured the two cornets of Oliver and Louis Armstrong. And even though we associate the tuba with the bass voice in early jazz, the string bass was also common because it blended better with the violins of the New Orleans string bands. We even see a string bass in the only extant picture of the Buddy Bolden group (page 41).

By the end of the late 1920s, some dance bands had as many as twelve or more players. Saxophones became common in these larger bands. In fact, the use of the saxophone in jazz in the late 1920s was an adaptation of its presence in earlier dance bands.

The early jazz style with the standard six- or seven-piece ensemble was called Dixieland, making clear its New Orleans origins. Although earlier prejazz bands probably featured melodies played in unison, perhaps by clarinet and violin, the jazz style moved toward polyphonic improvisation, in which the horns improvised simultaneously, creating an intricate web of rhythmic and melodic activity.

As defined in Chapter 1, *polyphony* describes distinct, simultaneous parts. Applying the term to the sound of the New Orleans ensemble, however, would be slightly inaccurate. Normally, *polyphony* refers to equally important parts or melodies, but in New Orleans style the lead cornet dominates the ensemble texture while the other instruments play parts similar to accompaniments.

The ensemble frequently used the technique of breaks, in which the band stopped and allowed a soloist to play alone in time. In his discussions of jazz, Jelly Roll Morton made it clear how important breaks were: "[W]ithout breaks and without clean breaks and without beautiful ideas in breaks, you don't even need to think about doing anything else, you haven't got a jazz band and you can't play jazz."[20]

Breaks not only featured soloists but also provided textural relief from the busy sound of collective improvisation. As the soloists' improvisational prowess increased through the 1920s, collective improvisation became less frequent, especially in the highly competitive urban musical centers of Chicago and New York.

It is important to distinguish our current conception of spontaneous improvisation from what occurred in early jazz. Listening to alternate takes of early jazz recordings confirms that "improvised" solos were in fact often worked out and repeated from take to take. Soloists most likely duplicated their efforts in live performance as well. Nonetheless, as the twenties proceeded, improvisation as we understand it was typically associated with "hot" style and became more often the norm. Hot soloists even played with more commercial orchestras, such as Louis Armstrong's performances with Erskine Tate, or Bix Beiderbecke's performances with Paul Whiteman.

The 1920s also show a general shift from melodic to harmonic improvisation. At the beginning of the decade, so-called improvised solos often closely adhered to the melody of the composition, embellishing it occasionally. By the end of the decade, soloists were developing improvisational methods that reflected the harmonic framework of the composition. The development of individual soloists and their improvisational expertise gradually shifted the focus of jazz away from ensemble playing to music that heightened the importance of the individual soloist. As the jazz historian Martin Williams wrote, this made jazz "a soloist's art."[21]

The Advent of Jazz Recording

Recording was the decisive step toward national prominence for artists and the popularizing of their work. Recordings are also the most important evidence to be examined by historians trying to present a coherent picture of the story of jazz. Yet, because bands that were physically present near the recording centers of New York and Chicago would naturally have had the opportunity to record first, such recordings taken out of context may present historians with a distorted view of how early jazz crystallized.

Until 1925, recordings were made acoustically instead of electrically. Musicians played into a large horn with a tapered end that connected to a cutting stylus. This stylus cut a groove into wax that covered a disc or cylinder. With this somewhat crude process, sound reproduction often suffered. Yet, we must be thankful for the recordings we have. Jazz is the first musical genre to be so documented in its entirety.

The placement of the musicians also affected recording balances. For example, louder instruments needed to be located farther away from the recording apparatus so as not to overpower the softer instruments. According to some sources, the drums had to be placed at a distance because their dynamic range upset the acoustic recording devices. However, the recordings of James Reese Europe, whom we shall discuss shortly, featured a reasonable drum sound as far back as 1914, and drums were recorded with considerable presence in 1919.

By 1925, the advent of electric recording had improved sound fidelity. This method used microphones to capture the sound. At the standard speed of 78 rpm (revolutions per minute), recordings were normally about three minutes long for each song and remained so until long-playing records (LPs with 33⅓ rpm) appeared in the late 1940s.

Changes from ragtime to jazz appeared on recordings beginning around 1914. James Reese Europe's Society Orchestra, based in New York, performed music influenced by ragtime. Europe's orchestra accompanied the dance team of Irene and Vernon Castle, who demonstrated several new dances—the fox-trot, tango, and maxixe. Europe's 1914 recordings feature ragtime numbers, often played with violin lead, that seem worked out and well planned. By the time of Europe's 1919 recordings of the 369th Infantry ("Hell Fighters") Band, improvised breaks within the multiple-strain compositions show the growing influence of the New Orleans style and recall Morton's comment about breaks being a defining quality of jazz.

Edison first patented his phonograph in 1877 as an "Improvement in Speaking Machines" and later realized its advantages for music. In this advertisement from 1904, notice (at the base of the horn) the revolving metal cylinder that carried the recorded sound.

THE FIRST JAZZ RECORDING

According to anecdotal legend, cornetist Freddie Keppard was the first New Orleans jazz musician given the opportunity to record. He turned down the offer for fear that others would steal his music. Nevertheless, in early 1917 when Victor Records released the first jazz record with Nick LaRocca, white cornetist and bandleader of the Original Dixieland Jazz Band (ODJB), Keppard's influence on LaRocca was clear. The ODJB recorded two pieces, "Livery Stable Blues" and "Dixie(land) Jass Band One Step." These included humorous barnyard effects, with clarinetist Larry Shields crowing and cornetist Nick LaRocca imitating a horse's whinny. A white band from New Orleans, the ODJB had achieved popularity performing at Schiller's Cafe in Chicago and Reisenweber's Restaurant in New York. The group, which included Shields, LaRocca, Tony Sbarbaro on drums, Eddie Edwards on trombone, and Henry Ragas on piano, brought the New Orleans style to national prominence. The brash and energetic barnyard effects of these pieces also made jazz synonymous with novelty or slapstick music.

After the ODJB's appearance at Reisenweber's, the band recorded prolifically through 1923 and helped spread the jazz craze outside the United States. They

The Original Dixieland Jazz Band (ODJB) formed in 1916 and published this song in 1921. Notice the billing that the band gives itself and the instrumentation. Sheet music promoted a star or band by featuring their publicity photographs.

appeared in London in 1919—even performing for the royal family—then afterward in Paris. During the mid-1920s, the group broke up, but they later tried a comeback in 1936. Although they made several recordings for Victor, they never fully reestablished themselves.

Part of the novelty of early jazz bands, such as the ODJB, rested with the public's perception of a performance built on completely spontaneous improvisation. Bands played up their inability to read music and increased the mystique of the new music. For example, LaRocca quipped, "I don't know how many pianists we tried before we found one who couldn't read music."[22] Despite the band's pose of musical naiveté, they played repeated sections of compositions virtually note for note. A comparison of alternative versions of the same compositions reveals that the ODJB consistently played the same memorized arrangements for years.

Even James Reese Europe's orchestra maintained a pose of musical illiteracy, despite the fact that they were all highly trained players. As William Howland Kenney points out:

> Orchestra leader James Reese Europe, in order to maintain the illusion of the "naturally gifted" black musician, would rehearse his band on stock arrangements, leave the scores behind, and, when taking requests for these thoroughly rehearsed tunes, ask customers to whistle a few bars, and then "confer" with the musicians "in order to work it out with the boys."[23]

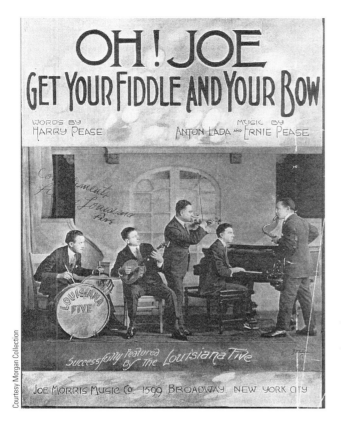

Courtesy Morgan Collection

The Louisana Five, pictured here, made their first jazz disc for Emerson in New York, around December 1918. This song was their last recording and was done with Lyric Records about September 1920. Notice the presence of the violin and banjo. Compare the instrumentation to the more familiar makeup of the Original Dixieland Jazz Band shown on the facing page.

In the early 1920s, numerous white bands in the tradition of the ODJB—such as the Louisiana Five, the Original New Orleans Jazz Band (with pianist Jimmy Durante), and the New Orleans Rhythm Kings (NORK)—issued recordings with the spirit and the instrumentation of the ODJB. Many of these sides helped establish the Dixieland repertory. "Tin Roof Blues," recorded by the NORK for Gennett on March 13, 1923, is an early example of the excellence of some of these white groups. The rise of dance as a social craze augmented Dixieland's popularity and brought about a proliferation of jazz-influenced dance-band records by small groups as well as hotel-ballroom orchestras.

The year 1923, a seminal time for instrumental jazz recording, witnessed releases by King Oliver's Creole Jazz Band (with Louis Armstrong)—the first recordings by a black Chicago jazz band. Gennett Records was setting out to enlarge their catalog of race records, and Oliver's band traveled from Chicago to Richmond, Indiana, to record nine numbers. (Drummer Baby Dodds later recalled that the band recorded all nine tunes in one day because none of them had a place to stay in Richmond.) That same year, Jelly Roll Morton produced the first interracial jazz recording by recording with the New Orleans Rhythm Kings. The band recorded several of Morton's own pieces, including "Wolverine Blues" and "Mr. Jelly Lord."

These early recordings led to the wide dissemination of jazz on a national scale and allowed musicians anywhere to imitate the solo and ensemble styles of New

This 1911 advertisement for different models of the Victor-Victrola appeared in an issue of the *Literary Digest,* which tells us something about who Victor thought purchased phonographs. Inventor Emile Berliner used a 7-inch diameter disc (rather than Edison's cylinder) and, together with Eldridge Johnson, formed the Victor Talking Machine Co., later to become RCA Victor with its famous *Nipper* logo. Notice the prices and consider how they compare with the price of a CD player.

Courtesy Morgan Collection

Orleans. Aspiring jazz musicians could now imitate not only the players they heard in their community but also the players heard on recordings; as a result, records helped to break down or soften regional differences in jazz. Dispersed through phonograph players, jukeboxes, and eventually radio broadcasts, jazz became a nationwide phenomenon. Throughout the decade, the music evolved rapidly through both live performances and countless recordings.

Early Jazz Instruments and Their Players

The development of the standard Dixieland ensemble—front line: cornet/trumpet, trombone, and clarinet; rhythm: piano/banjo, bass, and drums—was one of the key contributions of New Orleans jazz. Moreover, thanks to the talents of individual musicians, the role of each instrument grew and changed. The removal of the violin, which sometimes played in unison with the clarinet, allowed for the simultaneous improvisation of the front line instrumentation. The piano could be used in indoor performances, but outdoor performances usually required a guitar or banjo. By about 1915 the banjo eclipsed the guitar as the accompanying string rhythm instrument.

CORNET

The cornet in early jazz bands usually carried the melody. In addition, the cornet adapted to jazz by incorporating techniques such as *glissandos,* "half-valve effects," and the use of a variety of *mutes* and stopping devices. How a player combined these effects helped define the specific attributes of that player's style. Although originally one of the primary jazz horns, the cornet was eclipsed during the 1920s by its close relative, the trumpet.

Because the cornet was the principal lead instrument of the New Orleans style, many cornet players became bandleaders. For example, Manuel Perez (1871–1946) led the Onward Brass Band and Imperial Orchestra from 1903 to 1930. He was known not as a hot player but as a "military man [who] played on a Sousa kick," and "a great street-parade trumpet player."[24] Unfortunately, Perez and many of the other early players never recorded during the peak of their popularity.

Freddie Keppard (c.1890–1933) was another important player who went un-recorded during his prime performing years. Leader of the Olympia Orchestra around 1906, he was considered one of the best New Orleans cornetists. Mutt Carey claimed that Keppard had "New Orleans all sewed up."[25] He became established as a New Orleans musician during the years 1906–1914, then spent years on the road and performed in vaudeville. He finally settled in Chicago in the 1920s. Rumored to have turned down the first opportunity to record, Keppard eventually recorded in Chicago in 1926. By then, Keppard's health was in decline and his best playing lay behind him. Recordings such as his "Stockyards Strut" give evidence of crisp staccato playing strongly influenced by ragtime.

Buddy Petit (1897–1931) was yet another legendary player who never recorded. Despite gigs with Jelly Roll Morton in California and a few other tours, he was primarily a New Orleans player who remained mostly in that area.

TROMBONE

The instrumental technique of the trombone underwent rapid developments through the end of the 1920s. Well suited to jazz phrasing, the instrument allowed the chromatic motion of blue notes and bent notes. In the traditional collective improvisational style of New Orleans, the trombone would play countermelodies, bass pitches, and harmony, often sliding from one pitch to the next. The New Orleans style of playing with chromatic glissandos was known as **tailgate trombone,** because the trombonist played in the back—the tailgate—of the wagon that the band drove around in to advertise that night's dance. Among the prominent early New Orleans trombonists were Kid Ory (1890–1973) and Honore Dutrey (c. 1887–1935). The latter's performance of "Snake Rag," recorded with King Oliver's Creole Jazz Band, provides a clear example of tailgate trombone playing. Listen to Track 25 of the 🅟 Audio Primer CD for an example of tailgate trombone.

CLARINET

Although the earlier New Orleans Creole clarinetists Lorenzo Tio, Sr., (1866–1920), Lorenzo Tio, Jr., (1893–1933), and Alphonse Picou (1878–1961) were known as readers rather than improvisers, they taught many of the first generation of jazz clarinetists, including Sidney Bechet, Omer Simeon (1902–1959), Barney Bigard (1906–1980), and Albert Nicholas (1900–1973). These players developed a generally

A **glissando** is a technique whereby the notes are slurred directly from one to another, producing a continuous rise or fall in pitch.

Mutes are devices played in or over the bells of brass instruments to alter their tone. Different mutes create different kinds of effects, but a muted horn will usually be less brilliant than an "open" one. Listen to the 🅟 Audio Primer CD, Tracks 13, 14, 15, 23, and 24, for muted brass sounds.

less trained and more blues-based style of playing that became part of the New Orleans tradition. Most of the musicians played the standard B♭ clarinet, although some players, such as George Lewis (1900–1968) preferred the E♭ soprano clarinet favored by some of the older clarinetists.

Two of the most important New Orleans clarinetists who moved to Chicago were Johnny Dodds (1892–1940) and Jimmie Noone (1895–1944). Dodds was part of King Oliver's band at the Lincoln Gardens. Dodds played and recorded not only with Oliver but also with many of the famous New Orleans players in Chicago, including Freddie Keppard, Armstrong's Hot Five and Seven, and Jelly Roll Morton. Although occasionally marred by technical flaws, Dodds's blues-inspired playing was highly emotional and characterized by a vibrato slightly below pitch. A more technically proficient player, Jimmie Noone had studied in New Orleans with Lorenzo Tio, Jr., and probably Sidney Bechet, then toured with Freddie Keppard's band. While in Chicago, Noone had also taken classical training with Franz Schoepp, and Noone developed a sound technique in every register of the instrument. He had a strong influence on later clarinetists; the great swing-era player Benny Goodman singled Noone out as an important predecessor. Listen to Tracks 20 and 21 of the 🎧 Audio Primer CD for examples of the clarinet.

BASS/TUBA

A bass instrument was commonly used in ragtime groups as early as the 1890s. In these groups, players often doubled on tuba and string bass, using tuba for marching band and bass for "sit-down" groups. Discographies often refer to a "brass bass." This instrument could be a tuba, sousaphone, or helicon—these last two being variations on the tuba. Curiously, the only known photograph of Buddy Bolden's band (see page 41) shows a string bass player. Initially the bass was bowed, not plucked, because the bowed bass was typical of New Orleans string bands. In general, the bass provided the basic harmonic accompaniment of roots and fifths of chords. The New Orleans bassists played usually on the first and third beats or the 4/4 meter but occasionally marked all four beats or used stop time. Note that a bass was not always used in the early bands; for example, in several King Oliver and Armstrong recordings, the piano and banjo supply the bass notes.

BANJO/GUITAR

As with the bass, the banjo was primarily an accompanying rather than a solo instrument. The player strummed usually every four beats or else syncopated the meter by playing on beats 2 and 4 of the bar. Sometimes a more involved accompaniment (eighth-note triplets, for example) was played.

DRUMS

The drum set evolved when players organized a variety of marching band instruments so that they could be played by a single seated percussionist. Early on some players used a foot pedal with a drum almost twice the size of bass drums used today. The bass drum marked the first and third beats of a 4/4 measure (sometimes all four beats), which coincided rhythmically with bass or tuba. For sound effects, woodblocks and cowbells were attached to the bass drum. In addition, there were tom-toms, cymbals controlled by a foot pedal, and a snare drum mounted on a stand directly in front the player. A suspended cymbal was used for highlighting and accents; a common ending of compositions involved quickly dampening this cymbal. The hi-hat—two parallel cymbals that closed by means of a foot pedal—was not used until the 1930s. Usually a drummer used drumsticks, although such players as Zutty Singleton (1898–1975) recorded with brushes in the late 1920s. Singleton's accompaniment patterns often stressed the second and fourth beat on temple blocks or woodblocks. (Prior to the mid-1920s, drummers sometime recorded with just woodblocks and cymbals because the vibrations of the bass drum could potentially knock the needle off its groove during acoustical recording.)

Ragtime drumming was often indebted to military patterns, and such patterns were taken over by the early jazz drummers. These techniques can be heard in early recordings by Tony Sbarbaro (1897–1969) with the Original Dixieland Jazz Band. One technique was known as "double drumming," in which the snare was placed at an angle to the bass drum, so that the player could hit the bass drum first, then quickly hit the snare. In early jazz style, as typified by Baby Dodds (1898–1959) and Zutty Singleton, the drummer often improvised patterns to correspond with the soloist, with beat divisions of eighth notes and triplets. Listen to Tracks 26–35 of the 🅟 Audio Primer CD to hear the different drums and cymbals.

PIANO

In a jazz band, the piano supplied accompaniment, chords, and backup rhythm. Because it was self-contained, it also appeared in a wide range of other milieus, from the staid Victorian living room to the brothel. As such the piano—a one-person entertainment system—was perhaps the most important instrument of the early twentieth century.

Many of the early jazz band pianists also worked as solo entertainers in bars, brothels, restaurants, and at New York "rent parties" (see Chapter 4 on stride piano). So-called piano professors entertained the clientele and sometimes pimped for the women in brothels.

Among the many interesting and unsung pianists associated with the New Orleans tradition was Lil Hardin (1898–1971), who played with King Oliver (discussed shortly) and Louis Armstrong, whom she married. Although not remembered for her work as a solo pianist, she occasionally showed herself to be a superb accompanist, as during the clarinet-piano duo with Johnny Dodds in Hardin's own composition "Sweet Lovin' Man." Hardin herself recalled that her role was not as a soloist:

> It wasn't the style during the King Oliver days for the pianist to play many solos.... Sometimes I'd get the urge to run up and down the piano and make a few runs and things, and Joe [Oliver] would turn around and look at me and say, "We have a clarinet in the band."[26]

The Exodus from New Orleans

During the late teens, many of the best New Orleans musicians began leaving the city. It has been traditionally thought that the 1917 closing of Storyville, the well-known red-light district, cut down employment opportunities for New Orleans musicians, thus causing their departure, but this factor has probably been overstated. In fact, many musicians left earlier. In 1914, the Original Creole Band, which included Freddie Keppard on cornet, Bill Johnson on bass, and George Bacquet on clarinet, played Los Angeles and for the next four years was booked on vaudeville circuits throughout the country. Similarly, Sidney Bechet first left New Orleans in 1914, playing "dances, shows, one-night stands, and dime stores all over Texas with pianist/composer Clarence Williams"[27] before moving on to Chicago, New York, and Paris. Jelly Roll Morton, as we saw earlier, spent much time in California before moving to Chicago. Others stayed closer, departing the city for brief periods of time. Players could work the Midwestern towns up the Mississippi by playing on the riverboat lines.

Musicians were probably drawn away from New Orleans by the allure of the road or the steadier employment conditions in bigger cities. The trombonist Kid Ory, whose New Orleans band had included many of the top musicians in the city (such as Louis Armstrong, King Oliver, Jimmie Noone, and Johnny Dodds), left for Los Angeles in 1919. (Ory's 1922 Los Angeles recording as the leader of Spikes' Seven Pods of Pepper was the first record cut by a black New Orleans band.) Additionally, white bands such as the Brown Brothers, the New Orleans Rhythm Kings, and the Original Dixieland Jazz Band caught the spotlight of national recognition after leaving New Orleans.

Chicago had the strongest pull. Joe "King" Oliver moved to the city in 1918, bringing with him such first-rate New Orleans musicians as trombonist Honore Dutrey, drummer Baby Dodds, and clarinetist Johnny Dodds. In 1922 Oliver sent for Louis Armstrong to come up from New Orleans to join the band, and in Chicago Oliver's Creole Jazz Band became the leading exponent of the New Orleans jazz tradition. (Because the Creole Jazz Band flourished in Chicago and helped launch the career of Louis Armstrong, we shall discuss the band in the following chapter rather than here).

Other players who had left New Orleans earlier eventually migrated to Chicago. Freddie Keppard came through Chicago in 1918, and Kid Ory left Los Angeles to join King Oliver's Dixie Syncopators in 1924.

Many New Orleans musicians, of course, chose to stay in the Crescent City. Some, like cornetist Chris Kelly, never recorded. Kelly was legendary during the twenties for his blues playing and his rendition of "Careless Love," which, it was claimed, moved men to tears and women to tear off their clothes. Other musicians who remained did record. Oscar "Papa" Celestin and his Original Tuxedo Jazz Orchestra was recorded by OKeh Records in 1925. Celestin's career lasted from 1910 to his death in 1954; his New Orleans bands included many of the finest musicians in the city, including Mutt Carey, Louis Armstrong, and Alphonse Picou. In 1927, Columbia recorded Sam Morgan's Jazz Band in New Orleans. Many of Morgan's musicians were born around 1890; because they never left the city, their recording preserves a New Orleans sound perhaps purer than those of players who made their mark outside New Orleans. Nevertheless, the two saxophones in the group indicate a change in group instrumentation that was taking place throughout the twenties, and Morgan's loose-swinging group is aided by the virile four-to-the-bar bass playing of Sidney Brown.

Listeners and critics normally refer to the music associated with New Orleans—that is, small instrumental groups marked by collective improvisation—as New Orleans jazz or traditional jazz. The term *Dixieland jazz* is also used, although this term is now often used to refer to music performed by white musicians. Throughout the 1920s and 1930s, New Orleans jazz was eclipsed by later developments, which altered the musical style and instrumentation, although some of its repertory, such as Jelly Roll Morton's "King Porter Stomp," was retained.

The 1940s saw a revival of New Orleans jazz and the discovery (or rediscovery) of many of the original players. In conducting research for their 1939 book *Jazzmen,* Bill Russell and Fred Ramsey were directed by Louis Armstrong to trumpeter Bunk Johnson. Johnson had traveled and played throughout New Orleans during the first three decades of the century, but because of dental problems he had stopped performing in 1934 and worked as a field laborer. After his rediscovery, Johnson recorded throughout the 1940s. He claimed that he had originally played with Buddy Bolden in 1895, but these claims have now been called into question. With the New Orleans revival, several of the players present in New Orleans during the inception of jazz—including Jimmie Noone, Baby Dodds, and Sidney Bechet—enjoyed a "second career" of performing and recording.

New Orleans jazz is still played today. There are entire newspapers devoted to New Orleans jazz, and numerous players specializing in the style continue to find work. In 1961, Preservation Hall was established in New Orleans to help focus attention on the contributions of the city to the founding of jazz. The Preservation Hall Jazz Band continues to tour worldwide and is probably the most prominent ensemble devoted to keeping the New Orleans tradition alive.

Questions and Topics for Discussion

1. How did ragtime and the blues each contribute to the formation of early jazz?

2. Should ragtime be considered an early form of jazz or a distinct genre of music? Cite arguments for both positions.

3. Was jazz born in New Orleans, or was the New Orleans style the first jazz style to capture wide attention?

4. Compare and contrast the two theories regarding the Creole participation in the creation of New Orleans style.

5. How did recording influence the early history of jazz?

Key Terms

Bass/tuba

Banjo

Break

Clarinet

Cornet

Creoles of Color

Dixieland

Drums

Glissando

Guitar

Legato

Mute

New Orleans jazz

Out-chorus (Shout chorus)

Piano

Staccato

Stop time

Tag

Tailgate trombone

Trombone

Vibrato

Sung with Great Success by *Alma Gluck*

Carry me Back to Old Virginny

by

James A. Bland

Small Orchestra and Piano .25 *net*　　Full Orchestra and Piano .35 *net*
Song and Chorus .60　　Piano Solo .50
Duet for Soprano and Tenor (with Violin Obbligato) .60

Boston: Oliver Ditson Company
New York: Chas. H. Ditson & Co.　Chicago: Lyon & Healy
PRINTED IN U. S. A.

A 1920 edition of "Carry Me Back to Old Virginny,"
written by the black composer James A. Bland and
first published in 1906, testifies to its enduring
popularity. As many African Americans migrated to
Chicago and other Northern cities in search of better
jobs and opportunities, this idealized image of a
peaceful, close-knit family captured the nostalgia that
they felt for their homes and a pastoral way of life.

JAZZ IN CHICAGO

3

THE NEW ORLEANS style discussed in Chapter 2 flourished in Chicago during the late teens and early twenties of the twentieth century, when many of the New Orleans musicians relocated to the Windy City. Among the most famous were King Oliver and Louis Armstrong, both of whom had a major and lasting impact on jazz history. In this chapter, we examine the emergence of the New Orleans musicians to national recognition in the 1920s as well as a style that has been called "Chicago jazz"—and the important players who created it.

The Migration North

Around the time of World War I, New Orleans jazz musicians migrated north as part of a much larger trend known as the Great Migration. The most important reason that blacks chose to abandon life in the rural South was probably the availability of city jobs that paid a fair wage. For example, Henry Ford had invented the automobile assembly line in 1914 and needed workers to manufacture the first mass-produced automobile—his Model T. Fords. He guaranteed $5.00 a day—an astonishing wage at the time. As a result of opportunities like this, nearly half a million blacks moved from the South to the North between 1916 and 1919, the largest internal migration in the history of the United States.

Between 1910 and 1920, more than 65,000 blacks emigrated from the southern states of Louisiana, Mississippi, Alabama, Arkansas, and Texas to Chicago alone. Most northern cities developed black sections, because whites refused to have blacks as neighbors. The presence of blacks and black neighborhoods changed the urban entertainment industry across the country. In Chicago, for example, the entertainment community responded enthusiastically to the resulting demand for black music: Cabarets and nightclubs sprang up along the South Side and created a glittering urban nightlife full of music for listening and, especially, dancing.

The newly transplanted black population could spend an evening seeing floor shows, dancing, and hearing live music at any number of dance halls. Chicago's so-called black-and-tan clubs allowed more interracial mingling than the clubs in New York did. Whites could take in the night life, and—important to the development of **Chicago jazz**—white musicians could hear the black bands. South Side clubs such as the Elite #1 held up to 400 customers. According to one newspaper account, "The entertainers and the orchestra always hit it up pretty lively during evening hours."[1]

In 1914 the Dreamland Cafe opened with a capacity of 800 people. Even larger was the Royal Gardens Cafe, later renamed the Lincoln Gardens, on Thirty-First Street. This club, where King Oliver's Creole Jazz Band performed nightly, sported a huge spotlighted mirror ball suspended from the ceiling and reflecting glittering light over the dancers. Other clubs that hosted live music during the 1920s include the Plantation Cafe, allegedly controlled by the Capone syndicate, and the Sunset Cafe, just across the street from the Plantation.

The enactment in 1919 of the Prohibition Amendment to the Constitution, which outlawed the sale of alcoholic beverages throughout the country, encouraged the connections between the nightlife and the underworld. Because Chicago was one of the principal centers of organized crime in the 1920s, Prohibition did little to curtail the nightlife or the consumption of alcohol in South Side bars and cabarets. Instead, organized crime expanded its smuggling and distribution networks to satisfy the demand for liquor. Despite alcohol's illegality, it was easily available in nightclubs, cabarets, and *speakeasies*, in which most of the jazz players of the time found ready employment.

Chicago's many performance opportunities attracted New Orleans musicians. Through extended engagements at cabarets and dance halls, they transplanted their music to a much more sophisticated venue. No longer were the musicians playing for street parades, fish fries, and the small saloons and wooden dance halls of New Orleans. Abandoning the open-air, folksy quality of New Orleans music, they adapted to the urbane musical professionalism of Chicago. The extended engagements and higher level of musical competition produced two important results:

▶ The creation of distinct ensembles with their own characteristic arrangements

▶ The development of individual, improvisational skill

The competition on the Chicago scene required a higher level of virtuosity from the players than before. Up-tempo compositions were expected. Banjoist Johnny St. Cyr recalled that "the Chicago bands played only fast tempo . . . the fastest numbers played by old New Orleans bands were slower than . . . the Chicago tempo."[2] In the push for moral respectability in Prohibition-era Chicago, organizations such as the Juvenile Protection Agency urged that fast tempos would eliminate "immoral," slower dances like the toddle and the shimmy. As such, even the more respectable "sweet" white dance orchestras cultivated brisk tempos.

A **speakeasy** was a Prohibition-era nightclub in which liquor was sold illegally.

Sweet bands played less syncopated, slower pieces, such as ballads and popular songs. **Hot bands** featured faster tempos and dramatic solo and group performances, usually with more improvisation than sweet bands had.

King Oliver and the Creole Jazz Band

Joe Oliver's arrival on the scene in 1918 brought the flourishing of New Orleans music in Chicago to a climax. In 1920, he put together his own band, which played in California before returning to Chicago in 1922 and beginning an extended engagement at the Lincoln Gardens in June. His band, billed as King Oliver's Creole Jazz Band, featured first-rank New Orleans players—Johnny Dodds on clarinet, his brother Baby Dodds on drums, Honore Dutrey on trombone, and Bill Johnson on double bass and banjo. The pianist, Lil Hardin, was from Memphis, Tennessee. Oliver augmented his own cornet when he sent for cornetist Louis Armstrong a month into the Lincoln Gardens engagement. The popularity and success of the group earned Oliver the nickname "King."

The band recorded prodigiously—forty-three sides for the OKeh, Columbia, Gennett, and Paramount labels in 1923 alone. These recordings are important because they are some of the earliest and best works in the history of jazz. In the studio the group could omit the popular hits audiences demanded from the bandstand and record only their specialty numbers. Although today we assume that a band records its specialties, in the 1920s bands did not always have that freedom. During much of that era, record companies required bands to record the most

Joe "King" Oliver and his Creole Jazz Band (CD 1, Track 5) pose in their studio in Chicago, c. 1922. The band, which had a life span of just four years, was one of the most influential early jazz bands, and it became the launching pad for Louis Armstrong's brilliant career. Left to right, the members are Johnny Dodds, clarinet; Baby Dodds, drums; Honore Dutrey, trombone; Louis Armstrong, second cornet; King Oliver, lead cornet; Lil Hardin, piano; and Bill Johnson, banjo.

popular songs of the day as determined by sheet music sales, requests, and dance fads. Thus Oliver's importance in early jazz stems in part from his ability to record his most significant (hot) repertory.

Some of Oliver's numbers were recorded more than once, either on the same recording date or at one of the later sessions. The band twice recorded "Snake Rag," "Working Man Blues," "Riverside Blues," and "Dippermouth Blues," as well as recording three versions of "Mabel's Dream." These were mostly original compositions by Oliver, Armstrong, and Hardin but also included works by the New Orleans musicians A. J. Piron and Alphonse Picou. The group also recorded New Orleans standards such as "High Society," originally made famous by Picou's clarinet performance of the florid piccolo part in the trio section.

Oliver's fine personal performances greatly influenced the jazz cornet style of the times. He altered the sound of his instrument with mutes, often creating a wah-wah effect. In addition to mutes, he used cups and glasses to change the horn's tone. When Louis Armstrong joined them, the group became renowned for the breaks both cornetists seemingly improvised. According to a famous anecdote, Oliver in fact would silently finger the upcoming break so Armstrong could play along with him "spontaneously."

The group performed in a tightly knit fashion, with collective improvisation among the melody instruments. They recorded a roughly even number of fast three-strain rag-format compositions, medium popular songs with a verse-and-chorus format, and slow blues tunes. Lawrence Gushee found that Oliver's group played in three principal tempos, reflecting these three compositional types:[3]

1. Fast/ragtime tempo at about quarter note at 196–212 beats per minute

2. Medium/pop song tempo at 144–180 beats per minute

3. Slow/blues tempo at about 108–128 beats per minute

The recordings are probably at best only an approximation of the group's live performance. For example, Baby Dodds was required to keep time on woodblocks instead of playing his usual drums. Certainly the three- to four-minute length of the recordings did little to capture the group's live sound—one listener described a live performance of "High Society" that ran to forty minutes! While such reports are likely exaggerated, the band's live improvisations must have lasted longer than what we hear on their recordings. It is unfortunate that we cannot hear precisely how they did it.

Through their recordings and live performances, the group was profoundly influential, with a highly integrated ensemble sound that was more than the sum of its parts. Hoping to become jazz musicians, white teenagers were sometimes permitted into the clubs and became infatuated by the level of musicianship. Banjoist Eddie Condon attested to the powerful influence of the band when he and cornetist Jimmy McPartland heard them at the Lincoln Gardens: "Oliver and Louis [Armstrong] would roll on and on, piling up choruses, with the rhythm section building the beat until the whole thing got inside your head and blew your brains out.... McPartland and I were immobilized; the music poured into us like daylight running down a dark hole."[4]

The degree to which Oliver's band kept intact a "pure" New Orleans style of playing is controversial. Although many considered the Creole Jazz Band the leading exponent of New Orleans–style jazz, at least one observer suggested that Oliver's playing had altered by adapting to the more refined requirements of Chicago audiences. Edmond Souchon, a guitarist and writer on New Orleans jazz, had heard Oliver play both in New Orleans and later in Chicago. After hearing Oliver's band in 1924, Souchon noted a change:

> He was now "King," the most important personage in the jazz world, surrounded by his own handpicked galaxy of sidemen.... By the time Oliver had reached Chicago and the peak of his popularity, his sound was not the same. It was a different band, a different and more polished Oliver, an Oliver who had completely lost his New Orleans sound.[5]

While Souchon's opinion can be questioned, it seems reasonable that Oliver's style evolved to some extent while he worked in Chicago. Moreover, Souchon may have heard Oliver late in 1924, after the departure of the entire Creole Jazz Band. Bill Johnson, Dutrey, and the Dodds brothers had already left the previous year, while Louis Armstrong and Lil Hardin left in the middle of 1924. Most likely, Souchon was describing Oliver's performance with a group later to be called the Dixie Syncopators, a ten-piece band with a reed section of two to three saxophones and arrangements that reflected a smoother and more refined commercial dance-band sound. The group, also called the Savannah Syncopators, included several New Orleans veterans— Kid Ory, Barney Bigard, Albert Nicholas, Paul Barbarin, and Bud Scott—but their sound and style were more modern overall than that of the earlier Oliver group. Their version of "Sugar Foot Stomp," recorded in 1926 for the Vocalion label, was a remake of "Dippermouth Blues," a work earlier recorded by Oliver's Creole Jazz Band.

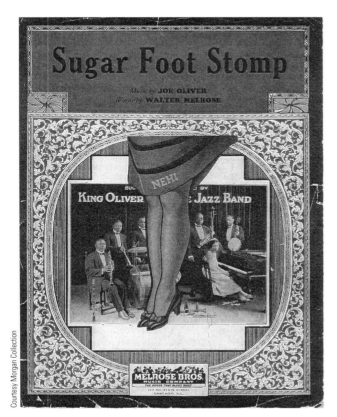

Courtesy Morgan Collection

Published 1926 in Chicago, this sheet music for "Sugar Foot Stomp" by Joe Oliver and performed by King Oliver's Creole Jazz Band advertises Nehi stockings for women. Using the same daguerreotype as the studio portrait, but with the advertisement obscuring two members of the band—one of them the young Louis Armstrong—this image may represent the one and only time that Lil Hardin upstaged her famous husband.

The Syncopators held the gig at the Plantation Cafe until the club was bombed in 1927, a victim of gangster violence. After a two-week stint at the Savoy in New York, the band broke up, but Oliver remained in the city. Ailing, with gum problems that affected his playing, he continued to record and play as a leader, but his final recording took place on February 18, 1931. Despite his success in Chicago during the 1920s, Oliver's popularity had waned. After touring with a ten- and eleven-piece band for the next five years, he worked as a pool hall janitor in Savannah, Georgia, and died there of a stroke in 1938.

The late-1920s recordings of King Oliver show the trend toward more arranged jazz, a trend that had progressed through the decade. Louis Armstrong and, more conspicuously, the large New York ensembles of Fletcher Henderson and Duke Ellington continued to challenge the freewheeling New Orleans style. We shall look at these developments, which paved the way for the big band craze of the 1930s, in the next chapter.

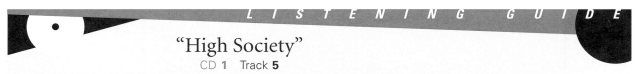

L I S T E N I N G   G U I D E

"High Society"
CD **1** Track **5**

King Oliver's Jazz Band: "High Society Rag" (King Oliver's Jazz Band). OKeh 4933. Chicago, June 22, 1923.
Joe Oliver, cornet, leader; Louis Armstrong, cornet; Honore Dutrey, trombone; Johnny Dodds, clarinet;
Lillian Hardin, piano; Arthur "Bud" Scott, banjo; Warren "Baby" Dodds, drums.

"High Society" became one of the best-known New Orleans jazz vehicles and is typical of the Oliver band in its 1923 period. The original 78-rpm OKeh issue of "High Society" lists the band as composers, but according to Lawrence Gushee, a copyrighted version of the march by Yale student Porter Steele antedates the recording by about twenty-two years.[6]

The New Orleans style is apt to sound cluttered or even a little chaotic at first because of the thickness of the sound, the exuberance of its hot style, and the technical limitations of acoustic recording in the early 1920s. After listening several times, however, you will hear the three or four principal instrumental parts of the ensemble as well as their distinct functions within the dense texture more clearly:

▶ The cornet carries the main melody. In Oliver's band, Armstrong (playing second cornet) either harmonized the lead or added a countermelody.

▶ The trombone plays a countermelody (defined in Chapter 1) below the cornets, much like a melodic bass line.

▶ The clarinet plays an obbligato (defined in Chapter 1) above the cornets. The obbligato, which usually contained more notes than the cornet parts, was often virtuosic.

Introduction—4 bars

0:00   The pulse throughout the piece should be counted in a medium-tempo march beat with two beats to the bar. The first two notes of the piece indicate the basic beat. The introduction sets up the key of B♭ major.

A strain—16 bars as 8 + 8, repeated

0:05   The band plays the sixteen-bar A strain in B♭ major twice. The cornet carries the lead, while the clarinet provides a higher obbligato part. The trombone provides lower-register counterpoint.

0:13   In the second eight-bar phrase of the strain, the tonality shifts to the relative minor, G minor, as a contrast to the B♭ major.

B strain—16 bars as 8 + 8, repeated

0:41   The contrasting B strain begins on the dominant harmony as a seventh chord, which is characteristic of many rags. The group improvisation continues with the cornet carrying the lead and the trombone and clarinet providing accompanying parts.

Interlude—4 bars

1:17   The interlude introduces the trio and modulates to the subdominant key (E♭ major).

C strain as trio—16 bars, repeated

1:21   Armstrong, playing second cornet, takes the lead for the trio's C strain, harmonized by the clarinet in its lower register. The trombone and Oliver rest. The calmer, more melodic texture of the trio is characteristic of marches in general. Simplifying the texture here creates an effective contrast with the A and B strains.

1:37   The last two bars of the sixteen-bar strain are a break for clarinetist Dodds on a B♭7 chord to return to the top of the trio. The second time through the C strain contains harmonic and melodic modifications that resolve the strain to E♭ major as a tonic I chord.

Interlude—16 bars

1:56   Oliver reenters to begin a dramatic interlude, which serves to separate the statements of the trio. A shift to the relative minor, C minor, heightens the drama. This shift to C minor parallels the focus on the relative minor heard in the piece's A section. Oliver reenters with the lead at this point, although the instruments often play together in octaves and unison. The return to E♭ major occurs only at the very end of the interlude.

C strain—16 bars, repeated

2:15   A reprise of the trio as out-chorus, this time incorporating the famous clarinet obbligato, shown here in a transcription by Lewis Porter.[7]

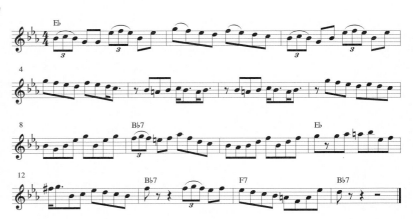

2:33   Performers repeat the strain and move into a two-bar tag. While obbligatos in New Orleans style are often improvised, important and well-known lines can become fixed and repeated from performance to performance.

Tag—2 bars

2:50   Proceeding directly into the tag from the out-chorus without interrupting the rhythm maintains the momentum of the whole performance and provides an exhilarating conclusion.

Reviewing the New Orleans jazz we have heard so far, we find the following characteristics:

- ▶ Typical instrumentation of one or two cornets, clarinet, trombone, piano, banjo, and drums

- ▶ Improvised ensemble sections with the first cornet taking the lead and the other instruments providing countermelodies and accompaniments

- ▶ Hot style with exuberant performances by all the musicians

- ▶ A driving 4/4 meter, with emphasis on the beat

- ▶ Simple rhythm-section parts with all the rhythm instruments articulating the beat

Chicago became a hotbed of jazz thanks to the regular performances of groups like King Oliver's. But even as Oliver was enjoying great popularity, the New Orleans ensemble style was rapidly becoming passé as innovators began to claim attention. The most important of these was Oliver's former student, Louis Armstrong. In turn he influenced a group of young, white, Midwestern jazz fans who converged on the city. One of them, Bix Beiderbecke, was a cornet player with a distinctive, bell-like tone that would help him become a jazz legend. Beiderbecke and Armstrong were the two most important cornet players of the 1920s.

Louis Armstrong

Louis Armstrong was born in New Orleans on August 4, 1901 (not July 4, 1900, as Armstrong himself thought) and spent an impoverished childhood first with his mother, Mayann, then, from age thirteen, at the Colored Waifs' Home where he played cornet in the band. He soon befriended Joe Oliver, who became his mentor, and later replaced him in the Kid Ory group when Oliver left New Orleans for Chicago in 1918. Armstrong continued to develop alongside his mentor after joining the Creole Jazz Band in Chicago in 1922, but by 1924 it was clear that Armstrong was ready to direct his own career:

> I never did try to overblow Joe at any time when I played with him. It wasn't any showoff thing like a youngster probably would do today. He still played whatever part he had played, and I always played "pretty" under him. Until I left Joe, I never did tear out. Finally, I thought it was about time to move along, and he thought so, too.[8]

Once Armstrong left Oliver, he played a brief stint at the Dreamland Cafe with Ollie Powers, a vocalist and drummer. Then late in the summer of 1924, Armstrong left for New York to take over (as cornet) the third trumpet chair in Fletcher Henderson's band. This second apprenticeship with Henderson on the East Coast earned Armstrong growing national attention as the leading hot cornet player in the country. After a year with the Henderson band, Armstrong returned to play at Dreamland in Chicago in 1925. The pace of Armstrong's performing and celebrity increased: He played movie houses with the Erskine Tate Orchestra early in the evening before moving to Dreamland for late-night sets.

Louis Armstrong's Hot Five,
Exclusive Okeh Record Artists

Copyright © CORBIS

Louis Armstrong and His Hot Five, left to right: Johnny St. Cyr, (banjo), Edward "Kid" Ory (trombone), Louis Armstrong (trumpet), Johnny Dodds (clarinet), and Lillian Hardin (piano) in New Orleans. (All on CD 1, Track 6 except Kid Ory, who can be heard on CD 1, Track 4.) Lillian Hardin, now married to Armstrong, encouraged the trumpeter to take charge of his own career. Note the serious demeanor of Armstrong, seen here at about age 24. Within a few years, he would become the ebullient entertainer with the winning smile, trumpet in hand, and trademark handkerchief.

Armstrong began recording under his own name almost immediately after returning to Chicago. Interestingly, the groups he recorded with were not working bands but were put together for the recording sessions. With these recordings Armstrong departed from the collective improvisation of the New Orleans style, as heard in the Creole Jazz Band, altering it to feature a succession of solos with his own work as the climax. In other words, Armstrong redefined jazz as an art in which individual solos played a greater role than in the original New Orleans style.

The first recordings of Louis Armstrong and His Hot Five, one of the groups assembled for recording, were cut on November 12, 1925, for OKeh Records. In addition to Armstrong on cornet and Hardin on piano, the musicians included the New Orleans players Johnny St. Cyr on banjo, Johnny Dodds on clarinet, and Kid Ory on trombone. By this time the Dixieland format was becoming quaintly archaic, but Armstrong continued to play cornet and use the plunger in the style of Joe Oliver.

The same band recorded again the following year on February 26. This session included "Heebie Jeebies," a vocal number for Armstrong in which he sang "scat"—nonsense—syllables over the chord changes. While probably untrue, jazz mythology claims that Armstrong was forced to make up the syllables when his lyric sheet dropped to the floor.

An important, forward-looking recording that showcases Armstrong's emerging solo virtuosity is "Cornet Chop Suey" (1926). In this vibrant, well-balanced performance, Armstrong shines through from beginning to end, with an apt mixture of the improvised and what was likely planned. His playing here anticipates much of the swing-era phrasing to follow in the 1930s. Thus, in these recordings Armstrong remained part of the band, acknowledging the communal, polyphony-based

The **plunger** is a type of mute derived from a plumber's sink plunger. The rubber cup of the plunger is held against the bell of the instrument and manipulated with the left hand to alter horn's tone quality.

Scat singing is a jazz vocal style in which the soloist improvises using made-up or "nonsense" syllables.

New Orleans jazz idea, but at the same time he loosened and heated up jazz phrasing through virtuosic brilliance and unprecedented technical command. Jazz would never be the same.

ARMSTRONG'S CLASSIC STYLE

Not only did Armstrong revolutionize cornet playing, but he also stands as the single most powerful, individual, and influential voice in early jazz. Although Armstrong's playing was deliberately restrained in his 1923 recordings with Oliver, his later recordings attained ever higher levels of musical, artistic, and technical advancements as the decade progressed.

Around 1927 or 1928, Armstrong switched from cornet to the more brilliant and penetrating trumpet, which helped showcase his newfound virtuosity. He extended the upper register of the instrument, cultivating a three-octave range with dazzling technical proficiency. Armstrong's playing showed an inventive improvisational skill, and his ability to create coherent musical relationships conveyed a dramatic depth and pacing. Why was Armstrong's the most powerful individual voice in early jazz? Among the most important factors were the following:

1. Instrumental virtuosity: Armstrong was head and shoulders above other trumpeters technically.

2. Emphasis on logical, brilliant solo improvisation: He was able to create coherent musical relationships and convey them with dramatic depth and pacing.

3. More than his peers, Armstrong had an ability to generate swing in his playing. He did this through the following techniques:

    ▶ Unequal eighth-note rhythms that implied an underlying 2 + 1 triplet organization

    ▶ Unexpected accents that were largely off the beat within the melodic line

    ▶ Control over placement of the notes just before or after the beat

    ▶ **Terminal vibrato** to add excitement and "movement" to notes at the ends of phrases

Armstrong had an overwhelming influence on his contemporaries. Max Kaminsky captured something of Armstrong's effect:

> I felt as if I had stared into the sun's eye. All I could think of doing was to run away and hide till the blindness left me.... Above all—above all the electrifying tone, the magnificence of his ideas and the rightness of his harmonic sense, his superb technique, his power and ideas, his hotness and intensity, his complete mastery of his horn—above all this, he had the swing. No one knew what swing was till Louis came along.[9]

On returning to Chicago, Armstrong began a musical association with pianist Earl Hines that would have lasting repercussions. Armstrong had met Hines shortly after the pianist had gone from Pittsburgh to Chicago in 1924; by mid-1926 both men were doubling in Carroll Dickerson's Band at the Sunset Cafe and in Erskine Tate's orchestra at the Vendome Theater. In Hines, Armstrong found a peer. Both had developed a level of musical virtuosity far above their contemporaries; both soloists were willing to take improvisational chances. Hines was an easterner who had trained in the classics and absorbed stride and blues-based piano. Armstrong's roots were more casual, grounded in the predominantly oral tradition of New Orleans and the King Oliver band. Together, they created a combination that produced some of the era's most exciting jazz records. Eventually, Armstrong accepted the leadership of Dickerson's band and made Hines the musical director.

ARMSTRONG IN CHICAGO AND HIS LATER CAREER

Hines and Armstrong first recorded together in 1927, but their primary collaborations came the following year. In the meantime Armstrong continued to use pianist Lil Hardin for the most important records of that year. His band the Hot Seven, which was the Hot Five augmented by Pete Briggs on tuba and Baby Dodds on drums, went into the studio on May 7, 1927, and again on May 13 in a session that included "S. O. L. Blues." Later that year, Armstrong recorded nine sides with the Hot Five in September and December. The latter session is especially notable for the versions of "Savoy Blues," "Struttin' with Some Barbecue," and "Hotter Than That." These recordings also marked a switch to the new technique and increased fidelity of electrical recording. Hines, meanwhile, had recently joined Jimmie Noone's five-piece band at the Apex Club; he would later record with Noone in spring 1928.

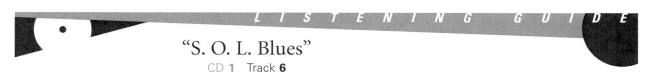

L I S T E N I N G   G U I D E

"S. O. L. Blues"
CD **1** Track **6**

Louis Armstrong and His Hot Seven: "S. O. L. Blues" (Armstrong). Columbia 35661. Chicago, May 13, 1927.
Louis Armstrong, cornet, vocal, leader; John Thomas, trombone; Johnny Dodds, clarinet; Lillian (Hardin)
Armstrong, piano; Johnny St. Cyr, banjo; Pete Briggs, tuba; Baby Dodds, drums.

Although not released until some years later, "S. O. L. Blues" is one of the many fine recordings Armstrong made in the 1920s. Armstrong's horn solo in this piece is famous for its unique combination of logic and impetuousness. In another solo, we hear Armstrong's inimitable vocal style, which unites scat with a loose phrasing style. Armstrong's vocal style had a notable impact on later jazz singers.

"S. O. L. Blues" was rerecorded by the same band the following day, probably because of the objectionable thrust of Armstrong's lyric and the imperfect ensemble on the coda. The remake, "Gully Low Blues," was taken at a slightly faster tempo in order to accommodate an extra chorus of Armstrong's vocal. Of even greater interest in the rerecording is the close degree to which both Dodds and Armstrong duplicate their previous solos. This example shows how improvisation of 1920s jazz recordings was in many cases planned in considerable detail.

Introduction—4 bars

0:00   Armstrong kicks off the performance with an in-tempo solo much like a solo break.
The tempo should be felt as a fast four beats or a slower two beats to the bar.

A section—8 bars, repeated

0:04   In typical New Orleans fashion, the trumpet has the lead, with the clarinet and trombone accompanying.

0:11   Bars 7 and 8 of the A section are a break for Armstrong before the section repeats.

B section—6 bars + clarinet break and changing tempo

0:23 Dodds clarinet solo. The B section alludes to ragtime form by beginning with a dominant harmony as a seventh chord.

0:30 At bar 7, Dodds begins a clarinet break that will change tempo into a slow blues.

C section—12-bar blues at new tempo

0:34 Dodds blues clarinet solo. The slow blues tempo is a surprise. Dodds's solo is especially expressive, with numerous slides and blues turns.

C section—2nd blues chorus

1:00 Armstrong's vocal. While not exactly a scat vocal, Armstrong takes liberties with the lyrics and melodic lines. The "S. O. L." of the title is said to refer to a scatological expression commonly used to denote being "outa luck."

C section—3rd blues chorus

1:26 A second clarinet solo for Dodds, who this time creates a contrast by focusing on the lower register.

C section—4th blues chorus

1:52 A famous solo by Armstrong. He begins each of his phrases by holding a high concert B♭, then proceeds from the note, each time in a different and highly original manner.

2:11 His last high B♭ is held longer to provide a climactic statement.
The solo thus combines logical variation with intense emotional projection.

C section—out-chorus + tag

2:20 The entire band provides a climactic blues out-chorus.

2:46 The three horns play a short tag before a cymbal crash cut-off.

We can summarize the Chicago-style features of "S. O. L. Blues" as follows:

▶ Typical instrumentation of trumpet, clarinet, trombone, banjo, piano, and drums (with tuba included)

▶ Group improvisation in which the trumpet carries the lead accompanied by trombone and clarinet countermelodies

▶ Horn solos accompanied by the rhythm section

▶ Use of call-and-response

▶ Frequent use of expressive blues elements: slurs, slides, blue notes, and so on

▶ Use of instrumental breaks

The 1928 collaborations between Hines and Armstrong spotlighted the two as the leading jazz instrumentalists of the day. Working primarily within a six-piece format, the group included alumni from the Carroll Dickerson Savoy Orchestra: Fred Robinson on trombone, Jimmy Strong on clarinet, Mancy Carr (not "Cara," as seen in old discographies) on banjo, and Zutty Singleton on drums. Their June–

July recordings in summer 1928 were released as *Louis Armstrong and His Hot Five,* the last of Armstrong's Hot Five recordings. With Hines and the Dickerson musicians, though, this set clearly showed Armstrong's departure from the New Orleans format of the earlier Hot Five and Hot Seven records. Dickerson's band at the Savoy were using the arrangements of Bill Challis, Don Redman, and Fletcher Henderson, and these Hot Five recordings revealed more of the small big-band format than the collective improvisational Dixieland style. Furthermore, Armstrong by now had switched to trumpet permanently, imparting an even greater brilliance and flair to these sides.

The same group recorded again in December, 1928; the records were released as *Louis Armstrong and His Orchestra.* Armstrong sang on "Basin Street Blues," which, while not a blues composition, would become a Dixieland standard. Several cuts from the sessions included Don Redman on saxophone, who had played with Armstrong in Fletcher Henderson's band in New York. Redman arranged "No One Else but You" and "Save It Pretty Mama." Alex Hill wrote and arranged "Beau Koo Jack," another superb number. Thus we see, in the evolution of Armstrong through the 1920s, an increasing focus on arrangement and larger ensembles. From the evenly distributed, collective improvisation of King Oliver—the essence, perhaps, of New Orleans style—we have seen an evolution through an increasing emphasis on solo playing to well-arranged works in which Armstrong is featured.

Yet it was perhaps a mere duo performance that precisely captured the improvisational art of the music and forecasted the direction in which jazz would eventually turn. Amid the six- and seven-piece groups, Armstrong and Hines found time to record "Weather Bird," a three-strain composition written by King Oliver. Armstrong had recorded the tune with Oliver and the Creole Jazz Band in 1923 as "Weather Bird Rag," but now the duo version saw Armstrong and Hines take great improvisational liberties with the tune, engaging in fanciful flights, harmonic departures—a sort of cat-and-mouse improvisation that was both playful and ingenious. The two players kept the three-strain framework of Oliver's original version but expanded it to A1 B1 B2 A2 C1 C2 C3 A1 coda.

Hines and Armstrong parted ways in early 1929, shortly after these sessions were concluded. Hines went on to establish a major career as both soloist and bandleader (see Chapter 6). Armstrong struck out for New York with Dickerson's band, landing a gig at Connie's Inn for himself, and for the band a role on Broadway in *Hot Chocolates,* a show with music by Fats Waller and Andy Razaf. Armstrong's great success at singing "Ain't Misbehavin'," which would become one of Razaf and Waller's most popular songs, hinted at a gradual transformation of the traditional New Orleans jazz cornetist into an internationally famous entertainer.

Armstrong's manager, Joe Glaser, helped to cultivate Armstrong's persona as an entertainer. By the end of the 1930s, Armstrong was appearing in feature films and would become the first black to have a major radio show.

As the swing era dawned in the 1930s, Armstrong spent more and more time fronting big bands as the feature attraction. His many superb performances included solo features on "Stardust" and "When It's Sleepy Time Down South," both from 1931. "Sleepy Time" became a trademark Armstrong number. Also noteworthy were the driving virtuosity of "Swing That Music" from 1936—in which Armstrong hits dozens of concert high Cs before a final flourish to high E♭—and the high-spirited chart "Jubilee" from 1938.

Trombone Technique

Trombone technique had greatly advanced since the days of the New Orleans tailgaters. One of the earliest trombonists to attain a high level of virtuosity was Miff Mole (1898–1961), whose recordings with Red Nichols had a profound effect on later trombonists. Jack Teagarden (1905–1964), originally from Vernon, Texas, arrived in New York in the late twenties. With his rich full-toned sound and his relaxed virtuosity, Teagarden became one of the finest trombonists in jazz. During the New Orleans revival, he worked frequently with Armstrong.

When the big-band era began to wane during World War II, Armstrong was well positioned to appear again with smaller groups. This profile fit his early work as a New Orleans Dixieland cornetist, so he was able to take full advantage of the New Orleans revival in the 1940s. He played with a group known as the All Stars, which included a reunion with Earl Hines as well as the fine trombonist Jack Teagarden. (See the box "Trombone Technique.")

By the 1950s, Armstrong's career had peaked, but he continued to work as hard as ever. When Armstrong became an ambassador for U. S. goodwill during the cold war with the Soviet Union, the State Department sponsored many of his tours. In 1959, Armstrong suffered a heart attack, which forced him to cut back his performances—especially the physically exhausting, bravura trumpet playing he was known for in the 1930s and 1940s. Despite declining health, he continued working through the 1960s, though featured more as a singer than as a trumpeter. In fact, he played gigs right through 1971, the year he died on July 6.

Armstrong was a musical revolutionary in his youth and one of the two or three most important jazzmen ever. He also became a preeminent figure in twentieth-century popular culture. Amazingly, Armstrong had a Top 10 record in every decade from the 1920s to the 1960s—a span of fifty years.

The Chicagoans and Bix Beiderbecke

Transplanted black New Orleans players in Chicago gave early jazz its strongest impetus, but the music soon attracted white musicians as well. During the twenties, as Chicago-based white players flocked to clubs such as the Lincoln Gardens to hear their idols Oliver and Armstrong play, the city provided a training ground for musicians cultivating a Chicago style. Listening to the original New Orleans players, a second generation of jazz instrumentalists fashioned their own improvisational and group styles. These players are collectively know as the "Chicagoans" and epitomize what has been called "Chicago jazz."

These musicians included native Chicagoans as well as players from other parts of the country, drawn by the magnetic pull of Chicago's jazz world. While Eddie Condon, Elmer Schoebel, Wild Bill Davison, Bix Beiderbecke, Hoagy Carmichael, Rod Cless, and Frank Trumbauer were born in the Midwest outside Chicago, many of them subsequently became associated with and made their careers in the city.

The relatively affluent suburb of Austin, on the Far West Side of Chicago, fostered the most influential group of musicians. Collectively known as the Austin High Gang, the players included Jimmy McPartland on cornet, his brother Richard McPartland on guitar, Bud Freeman on tenor saxophone, Frank Teschemacher on clarinet, Dave North on piano, and Jimmy Lannigan on bass. It is primarily this group, together with banjoist Eddie Condon, drummer Dave Tough, and William "Red" McKenzie, who became the self-styled "Chicagoans." Although the Austin High Gang's most significant performing and recording would take place after the twenties and in New York, the group helped to articulate and define the notion of Chicago jazz.

Before hearing Oliver and Armstrong, the Chicagoans had learned from the recordings of the white sweet dance bands and the Original Dixieland Jazz Band (ODJB). A more significant influence was the New Orleans Rhythm Kings (NORK), a white band made up of New Orleans and midwestern musicians (introduced in Chapter 2). Although, to a certain extent, the Rhythm Kings based their instrumentation and repertory on the ODJB's performances, they were somewhat more successful transforming the ragtime syncopations of the ODJB into a looser, more swinging approach. The NORK's extended engagement at the Friar's Inn in Chicago allowed teenage Chicagoans to hear them; their records, originally released under the name *Friar's Society Orchestra,* exercised enormous influence on fledgling Chicago jazzmen.

Cornetist Jimmy McPartland described how they learned from the NORK:

> What we used to do was put the record on—one of the Rhythm Kings', naturally—play a few bars, and then all get our notes. We'd have to tune our instruments up to the record machine, to the pitch, and go ahead with a few notes. Then stop! A few more bars of the record, each guy would pick out his notes and boom! we would go on and play it. Two bars, or four bars, or eight—we would get in on each phrase and then play it all.... It was a funny way to learn, but in three or four weeks we could finally play one tune all the way through—"Farewell Blues." Boy, that was our tune.[10]

Possibly the deepest influence on the Chicagoans came from a cornet player born in Iowa in 1903, who received his earliest musical experiences in Chicago—Leon Bix Beiderbecke. In contrast to the virtuosic flamboyance of Louis Armstrong, Beiderbecke had developed a style marked by introspection and refinement. Contemporaries strove to pinpoint Beiderbecke's restrained and uniquely lyrical sound: Mezz Mezzrow stated that every note sounded "like a pearl" and stood out "sharp as a rifle crack." Hoagy Carmichael described it as a mallet hitting a chime; to Eddie Condon, Bix's sound came out "like a girl saying yes."[11]

Bested only by Armstrong, Bix Beiderbecke was the second leading voice on the cornet during the twenties. Whereas Armstrong used differing timbres, a wider range, and consistent vibrato as expressive devices, Beiderbecke's sound had a more even timbre, a narrower range, and a straight tone, with only occasional vibrato. Beiderbecke's unique tone color resulted partly from unusual trumpet fingerings, in which higher **partials** were sounded in a lower overtone series. He also emphasized the ninths and thirteenths of the chords in his playing.

Although often associated with Chicago, Beiderbecke actually performed there infrequently. He began playing cornet in his hometown of Davenport. With the exception of a few piano lessons, he was largely self-taught as a musician and learned by playing along with recordings of the Original Dixieland Jazz Band. His parents, unhappy about his jazz playing, sent him to Lake Forest Military Academy outside Chicago in 1921. But Beiderbecke's gigs and frequent trips into the city in order to

Bix Beiderbecke's Solo on "Jazz Me Blues"

"Jazz Me Blues" (CD 1, Track 7) opens with a motivic lick composed of two notes a minor third apart:*

No blue notes appear in the first two bars, however; the first blue note, an E♭, occurs at the downbeat of measure 6. Moreover, Beiderbecke does not concentrate on a single opening motive, but instead, without overtly repeating any single idea, he opens new paths gradually from phrase to phrase.

> A **motive** or **motivic material** is a short melodic fragment that is used as the basis for improvisation or development.

While unfolding the melodic phrases, Beiderbecke discreetly refers to the original song in measure 9. This reference fits the solo perfectly, is wholly contained within the logic of the phrase sequence, and does not interrupt the melodic development for the sake of a gratuitous quotation. In avoiding obvious motivic repetition, some other means becomes necessary to provide coherence. That is, to be truly convincing, the solo must move from pitch to pitch, each new note and phrase progressing from the previous in such a manner that clumsy and unintentional continuations do not jolt the listener. An important technique for providing coherence, heard in almost all tonal music, is *voice leading*, based on a principle of step connection.

> **Voice leading** is a means of making logical melodic and harmonic sequences within an improvised solo.
> **Step connection,** a key element in voice leading, is the principal means of stringing together the melodic and harmonic elements. The steps are often based on the scale determined by the key of the piece.

In step connection, pitches are thought to proceed naturally to other pitches a half or whole step away in the associated

scale of the harmony. This principle is derived from the natural tendency for sung melodies to proceed mostly, though not exclusively, by step. (For example, the melodies in Gregorian chant, one of the oldest European musical traditions, proceed largely by step.)

Pitches that have no stepwise connection to succeeding pitches are often considered to be left "hanging." In a solo or melody that employs classical voice leading, few if any pitches are left hanging for long. In particular, chord tones—pitches that are included in the prevailing harmony—are often followed in the next chord change by stepwise related chord tones.

The actual solo is shown on line (c), while the voices are schematized on lines (a) and (b). In the schematic presentation,

*Transcription and analysis by Henry Martin.

the relative importance of a pitch is shown by the type of note value, namely (in decreasing importance), half notes, quarter notes, filled-in note heads (without stems), and eighth notes.

The first two bars consist of the pitches A and F#, which are members of the prevailing D7 chord harmony. Each pitch forms the beginning of a voice. In measure 3, the F# proceeds to the F of the G7 chord, while the A continues, or is "prolonged." The idea behind prolongation is that the feeling or effect of the same pitch is continued through a new harmony or harmonies.

> A **prolonged note** is a note held across a harmonic change. More abstractly, we conceive of notes that are not actually being played as holding through chord changes to connect stepwise to later notes in a solo. Prolongation helps build continuity in a solo.

Note that no pitches are left hanging for long—instead, all new voices are absorbed quickly into previous voices, and there is a tendency for most voices to move downward.

There is a "principal voice," shown in half notes on line (a), that continues through the whole solo with an initial dip in measure 7 to A♭. In measure 9 the voice begins again on A, which is prolonged from measure 9 to measure 18, where it proceeds to A♭, and finally (in a skip) to F in measures 19–20.

The voice-leading line, A–G–F, prominently occurs in both halves of the solo but is reharmonized in the second half. This reharmonization prepares the extended *cadence* of the second half of the piece.

> A **cadence** is the closing strain of a phrase, section, or movement. It can also be used to describe a common closing chord progression.

In the final cadence, derived from the blues, the flatted third proceeds to the tonic pitch in a manner that suggests a replacement of the normal second degree to first degree cadence common in European tonal harmony. Certain melodic skips, like the flatted third to the tonic, because they occur so frequently in jazz, are often equivalent to normal step motion in the European harmonic tradition:

which is ideally balanced between skips and steps.

"Jazz Me Blues" exhibits an ingenious use of voice leading, providing the listener with a sense of coherence in lieu of obvious motivic development. An impression of clear voice leading is often obtained from a work when its overall development is smooth and no pitches seem out of place.

Every aspect of Beiderbecke's performance contributes to the overall effect of the melodic line he improvises. His liquid tone rolls effortlessly and confidently from phrase to phrase: the high F in measure 7 is articulated perfectly with just the right amount of emphasis. The final F of the solo is so satisfying because it is prepared both by the syncopation of the preceding phrase and by the voice-leading lines stretching through the entire solo.

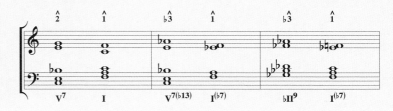

Another subtle aspect of "Jazz Me Blues" may be described as the unique identity of each voice; that is, no melodic continuation is ever duplicated. For example, A and A♭ are a pair of pitches that often occur contiguously throughout the solo, but their rhythmic and motivic environment is constantly fresh. This feature is echoed in the melody line itself,

Beiderbecke's slight accent on this pitch and his continuation of it for seven full beats close out the solo without showiness. Combining perfect structural balance, thoughtfulness, and cool emotional projection, Beiderbecke's "Jazz Me Blues" is one of the great cornet solos of the 1920s. See the Listening Guide on "Jazz Me Blues" for more on this fine piece.

hear the NORK created an alarming truancy rate, and he was expelled from the academy the following year. His dismissal freed him to become a full-time professional musician; he played gigs on an excursion steamer in Lake Michigan, at fraternity parties on campuses, and throughout the Midwest with a group of players who gradually became known as the Wolverines.

In February 1924, like Oliver's Creole Jazz Band the year before, Beiderbecke and the Wolverines travelled to Gennett Records' studio to make their first recording. The session yielded "Fidgety Feet" and "Jazz Me Blues." Few solos rank higher than Beiderbecke's "Jazz Me Blues" for their elegance and simplicity (see the

MODERN MUSIC AND ITS MAKERS

BIX BEIDERBECKE

The well-known Bix Beiderbecke (CD 1, Track 7) portrait from The Wolverines' publicity photograph of 1923

Courtesy Frank Driggs Collection

box "Bix Beiderbecke's Solo on 'Jazz Me Blues.'"). Not even a single note could be changed without detracting from the lyrical quality of its melodic line. The technical performance was exquisite and confident, yet it also expressed a cool reticence captured by no other major trumpet player except possibly Miles Davis some thirty years later.

The Wolverines recorded later that year, eighteen sides in all. "Tiger Rag" and "Royal Garden Blues" had been recorded earlier by the ODJB and the NORK, but Bix's playing was becoming tinged with the blues he had undoubtedly been hearing from King Oliver and Louis Armstrong. "Big Boy" captured Beiderbecke's piano playing.

Beiderbecke was beginning to create an impact on the jazz world. Cornetist Red Nichols reproduced Beiderbecke's solo from "Jazz Me Blues" verbatim on a dance-band arrangement. Rex Stewart also recorded some of Beiderbecke's solos note-for-note. Jimmy McPartland knew Beiderbecke's solos well enough that McPartland left his Austin High group, the Blue Friars, to take over Beiderbecke's chair when Beiderbecke left the Wolverines.

When Beiderbecke left the Wolverines, he headed back to the Midwest from Manhattan, where the group had been playing. He picked up some jobs with Jean

Goldkette, a Detroit-based bandleader, and in 1925 joined one of Goldkette's bands in St. Louis, under the leadership of Frankie Trumbauer. In the company of high-caliber musicians such as Trumbauer, who played C-melody saxophone, and Pee Wee Russell on clarinet, Beiderbecke's playing deepened. His reading improved; he played piano more frequently. Frankie Trumbauer (1901–1956) was an important white jazz player of the 1920s and one of few who played the C-melody saxophone. He became closely associated with Beiderbecke and significantly influenced Lester Young, the swing saxophone great.

Although the Goldkette group was a dance band, Beiderbecke experimented with their arrangements by introducing some of the harmonic procedures of French impressionism—often to the chagrin of the ballroom manager. Beiderbecke did no recording during this time but instead played gigs, did jam sessions, and indulged his legendary drinking habit.

In 1926, Trumbauer and Beiderbecke graduated to Goldkette's first-string New York band, which recorded prolifically for the next year or so. The next year, Bix also began to record with an orchestra under the direction of Trumbauer that mostly included members of the Goldkette band. After the latter group folded in September 1927, both Beiderbecke and Trumbauer, along with the arranger Bill Challis, moved to the famous Paul Whiteman band, Beiderbecke's last major ensemble. Unfortunately, the recordings made with the large Whiteman band contain only brief cornet solos by Beiderbecke.

Beiderbecke's recordings of 1927 made a lasting impact. His solo on "Singin' the Blues," recorded with Trumbauer's band, was imitated widely by other players. Challis's arrangement on "Ostrich Walk" showed Beiderbecke to great advantage; this number by the Original Dixieland Jazz Band was remarkable for the way it mixed written material for the saxophones with the spontaneity of the Dixieland ensemble. Beiderbecke's fine up-tempo work on "Clarinet Marmalade," also from the ODJB repertory, was satisfyingly precise.

Beiderbecke also recorded as band leader—under the name of Bix and His Gang—including rerecordings of the Wolverines' "Royal Garden Blues" and "Jazz Me Blues." A unique item in the Beiderbecke catalog that was recorded by the artist himself is his solo piano composition, "In a Mist." This piece reflects the hazy harmonic texture of French impressionism, especially the use of *whole-tone scales* and dominant ninth, sharp eleventh chords. Challis notated "In a Mist," along with Beiderbecke's other piano works "Candlelights," "Flashes," and "In the Dark," and published them as a piano suite.

Beiderbecke's drinking caused a rapid deterioration in his health, and he died in 1931 at age twenty-eight. Although largely unknown to the general public, Beiderbecke's legacy among musicians was profound. Other cornetists such as Jimmy McPartland, Red Nichols, Rex Stewart, and Bobby Hackett directly imitated Beiderbecke's playing. His improvisations, which emphasized diatonic pitches and upper chordal extensions such as ninths and thirteenths, affected musicians of all instruments. His melodic ideas seemed to grow logically and organically from one into the other, giving the impression of improvisation as a unified whole—what Lester Young later referred to as "telling stories." To many who idealized his brief life, he served as the tragic hero of the jazz age, a romantic symbol of the Roaring Twenties, and became the model for Dorothy Baker's novel *Young Man With a Horn*.

The **whole-tone scale** was common among French composers such as Claude Debussy. It consists only of whole steps, thus making it impossible to form major or minor triads. A whole-tone scale is created by starting on a note and proceeding up or down by whole step only. There are only two whole-tone scales: C–D–E–F#–G#–Bb and Db–Eb–F–G–A–B. They have no notes in common. Listen to Track 1 of the Audio Primer CD; the whole-tone scale is the fifth scale played.

L I S T E N I N G   G U I D E

"Jazz Me Blues"

CD **1** Track **7**

Wolverine Orchestra: "Jazz Me Blues" (Delaney). Gennett 5408. February 18, 1924. Bix Beiderbecke, cornet;
Al Gande, trombone; Jimmy Hartwell, clarinet and alto saxophone; George Johnson, tenor saxophone;
Dick Voynow, piano; Bob Gillette, banjo; Min Leibrook, tuba; Vic Moore, drums.

Melody A section—Whole band, 8 bars, repeated

0:00   Count this piece in a moderate four beats or slow two beats to the bar. There is no introduction: The band begins right on the first part of the song. In standard Dixieland fashion, Beiderbecke has the lead on cornet while the other musicians harmonize and create countermelodies.

0:11   The eight-bar melody is repeated.

Interlude—4 bars

0:21   A four-bar interlude introduces the next section of the song. The entire band continues to play. The use of the interlude recalls the ragtime and march forms often found in early jazz.

Melody B section—20 bars as 8 + 12

0:27   The B section of the song functions as a chorus in a verse-chorus format.

0:35   Measures 7–8 of the form are a break for clarinetist Hartwell.

0:37   After 8 bars the form repeats but is extended to create a slightly irregular twelve-bar second "half."

0:43   Hartwell's solo breaks (measures 5–8 of this half) are part of a call-and-response with the band.

Return to the A section of the melody—8 bars, repeated

0:54   Reprise of A section by whole band.

Interlude—4 bars

1:15   Repeat of the earlier interlude. This time it sets up Beiderbecke's cornet solo.

Beiderbecke cornet solo on B section melody—20 bars

1:20   Beiderbecke's cornet solo on the B-section of the original melody. This famous early solo of Beiderbecke's with the Wolverines was admired for its effortless perfection and melodic beauty. Note that Beiderbecke's breaks occur in the same places that the clarinet breaks did in the first rendition of the B section. (See the box on Beiderbecke's solo for a detailed analysis of its structure.)

Repeat of B-section melody—20 bars

1:47   Repeat of the B-section melody, this time by the entire band.

1:56   There is a solo trombone break in measures 7–8.

2:04   You can hear short trombone breaks in measures 5–8 of the second half of the B section. The format of this section parallels that of the first B section, where the clarinet provided the solo breaks.

Repeat of B-section melody—20 bars + 1-bar tag

2:15   Final performance of the B-section melody by the entire band.

2:24   In measures 7–8 of the first half, the banjo gets the solo break (playing unusual augmented triads that are surprisingly dissonant in this context).

2:32   The tenor saxophone in measures 5–8 of the second half gets the solo breaks. Thus, the tune's arrangement allows the band to showcase its front line players with short solos and its star, Beiderbecke, with an entire chorus.

2:43   A short one-bar tag closes the tune.

"Jazz Me Blues" is an excellent example of the genius of Bix Beiderbecke. His performance is both a brilliant solo on its own terms and representative of certain aspects of his general style:

▶ Concentration on the middle register

▶ A lyrical, mellow tone

▶ Rhythmic variety

▶ Extreme subtlety of melodic continuation

▶ Restrained use of blue notes

▶ Small but compelling emotional compass

▶ Little use of vibrato

▶ "Inside" playing

Beiderbecke seemed to synthesize all that Chicago had to offer New Orleans bands and styles in the twenties. He merged the tradition of the white New Orleans bands such as the ODJB and the NORK with the emerging solo emphasis pioneered by Armstrong in the context of larger bands. He helped to solidify a Dixieland repertory, a group sound, and an improvisational style that the Chicagoans kept alive for the next several decades. Hundreds of later bands maintained the Dixieland tradition, and it continues to this day.

Jazz musicians are said to be playing **inside** when their melodic lines favor the principal notes of the harmonies. The more players depart from the notes of the harmonies, the more they are said to be playing **outside.** (These terms are most commonly associated with modern jazz. Listen to Track 8 of the 🅟 Audio Primer CD for an example.)

Questions and Topics for Discussion

1. In what ways can Chicago be considered the center of jazz in the early 1920s? What was Chicago's relationship to New Orleans?

2. What are the key stylistic components of the early New Orleans jazz ensemble as typified by King Oliver's Creole Jazz Band? Discuss instrumentation, repertory, and the role of each instrument within the ensemble.

3. How did Louis Armstrong revolutionize the role of the soloist in jazz? What are key aspects of his style?

4. How did Armstrong's approach to music change in the 1930s? Discuss his relationship to the larger world of popular culture.

5. How does Bix Beiderbecke's style compare with Armstrong's?

6. With which important bands did Beiderbecke perform?

Key Terms

Cadence

Chicago jazz

Hot band

Inside playing

Motive (motivic material)

Outside playing

Partials

Plunger

Prolonged note

Scat singing

Speakeasy

Step connection

Sweet band

Terminal vibrato

Voice leading

Whole-tone scale

EVERYBODY WANTS A KEY TO MY CELLAR

Prohibition, which made the sale and public consumption of alcohol illegal throughout the United States, began on January 16, 1920. But Americans bought liquor illegally from smugglers and gangsters, hid it in their cellars, made their own "bathtub gin," and headed to speakeasies to enjoy lively jazz bands. Notice that the cover of this sheet music, published in 1919 in anticipation of Prohibition, features black and white hands.

NEW YORK IN THE 1920s

WHILE THE NEW ORLEANS jazz diaspora were revolutionizing music in Chicago, a vibrant black population in New York—centering on the neighborhood of Harlem—was helping to make jazz an important cultural force and the voice of a new, educated black class. The earliest manifestations of New York jazz were in the society and military bands, such as those of James Reese Europe—bands that were identified with syncopation and the new ballroom dance music. Meanwhile, stride pianists such as James P. Johnson and Fats Waller introduced jazz rhythms to Broadway shows and laid the foundation for swing and subsequent jazz piano styles. Bandleaders such as Fletcher Henderson codified new arranging techniques and instrumentation that planted the seeds for the big-band jazz of the 1930s. One of these bandleaders was a young pianist originally from Washington, D.C.—Duke Ellington. Achieving national prominence while in residence at Harlem's Cotton Club in the late 1920s, Ellington would become one of the most important bandleaders and composers in the history of jazz.

After World War I, jazz in New York flourished. The "hot," improvisational New Orleans–Chicago school strongly influenced the New York musicians. Even so, New York eventually became the center of jazz largely through the innovations of Henderson, Ellington, and the stride pianists. Moreover, it was the work of these artists that helped set the stage for swing music in the 1930s.

The Harlem Renaissance

By the end of the 1920s, New York—already the media and entertainment capital of the country—had become the leading center of jazz, a position it still occupies today. If bands or artists were to have a national presence, then they needed to gain acceptance and promotion in New York. The major figures of New Orleans—Louis Armstrong, King Oliver, Jelly Roll Morton—eventually came to the Big Apple. Bix Beiderbecke spent his last productive years in the city with Paul Whiteman's band, and many of the Chicagoans earned their reputation in Manhattan. New York had become the center of the music publishing industry, which was concentrated in the district known as Tin Pan Alley.

Tin Pan Alley pioneered mass-marketing and aggressive sales techniques in the popular music industry, techniques that still define the business in this country today. The district eventually consolidated on West Twenty-Eighth Street in Manhattan. As part of their sales strategy, Tin Pan Alley promoters actively plugged songs by hiring pianists to play, sing, and hawk the latest tunes at the publishers' offices. Customers would wander down the street, in and out of the publishing offices, in search of the sheet music for songs that caught their ears. In the days before air conditioning,

Published in 1932 in New York, this sheet music aptly captures the energy and high style of the Harlem Renaissance that attracted so many to its nightlife. Patrons, black and white, came to listen and dance to the great jazz bands.

publishing companies kept the windows and doors open during the warm months—the sounds of all the song pluggers playing simultaneously led to a street cacaphony that sounded like the banging of tin pans.

Many musicians—from George Gershwin to Fletcher Henderson—got their start as song pluggers playing and singing the constant stream of newly written popular songs that flowed from Tin Pan Alley. New York had become the heart of the nation's recording industry, and jazz musicians such as cornetist Red Nichols and guitarist Eddie Lang earned much of their living from playing in studios.

From 1917, when the Original Dixieland Jazz Band performed at New York's Reisenweber's Restaurant, to 1931, when Duke Ellington gave his last performance at Harlem's Cotton Club, jazz had matured. The ODJB's success in New York owed much to its onstage antics and comical barnyard effects, and in the public's eye jazz was synonymous with novelty and slapstick. Duke Ellington described this public perception of jazz in his early years:

> When I began my work, jazz was a stunt, something different. Not everybody cared for jazz and those that did felt it wasn't the real thing unless they were given a shock sensation of loudness or unpredictability along with the music.[1]

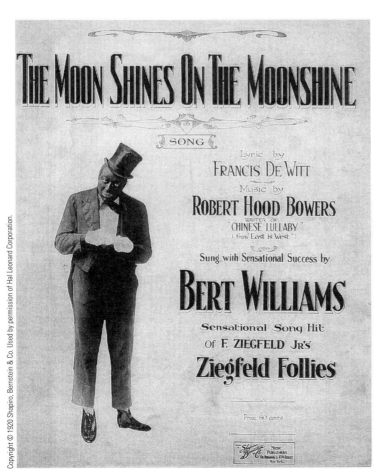

Bert Williams in prescribed vaudevillian blackface appears on the cover of this sheet music published in 1920 for Broadway's *Ziegfeld Follies*. "Moonshine" is home-brewed liquor.

Throughout the 1920s, Ellington and many others helped to change this perception. Although the music continued to develop as entertainment, particularly as dance music, players improved technically. Jazz earned a seal of approval from important musicians in Europe. European composers—including Maurice Ravel, Darius Milhaud, Ernst Krenek, and Arthur Honegger—incorporated jazz elements into their orchestral concert works. Promoters and practitioners, both in Europe and in the United States, began to present jazz as serious and sophisticated entertainment rather than as the comical stepchild of vaudeville.

In New York's African-American community, the growing acceptance of jazz paralleled the rise of the **Harlem Renaissance**.[2] Harlem in the 1920s became the central locale for black artists, writers, and musicians and the engine of a self-confident black artistic consciousness. The primary shapers of the Harlem Renaissance "aspired to high culture as opposed to that of the common man, which they hoped to mine for novels, plays, and symphonies."[3] For example, writers Langston Hughes and Zora Neal Hurston, painter Aaron Douglas, and composer William Grant Still gravitated to Harlem as the primary center of African-American culture.

As pianist Eubie Blake pointed out, music was central to the Harlem Renaissance.[4] Historians often date the beginning of the Harlem Renaissance from the opening of

Noble Sissle appears on the cover of his composition published in London, 1929. Noble Sissle and Eubie Blake wrote the first all-black Broadway musical, *Shuffle Along*, a huge success of 1921.

Noble Sissle and Eubie Blake's show *Shuffle Along*, which opened in 1921 and ran to 504 performances. Other shows quickly followed, including Maceo Pinkard's *Liza* (1922) and James P. Johnson's *Runnin' Wild* (1923). Black musical theater on Broadway flourished during the 1920s—from two to five productions were initiated each year.

For many of the key figures of the Harlem Renaissance, the concert stage was the appropriate place for musical performance. Singers Marian Anderson and Paul Robeson performed spirituals in concert; the National Association of Negro Musicians initiated concerts and recitals. As early as 1918 Will Marion Cook had taken his Southern Syncopated Orchestra, which included Sidney Bechet, to play concert venues in England, and during the twenties and thirties Cook became a pivotal figure in establishing recital performances for African-American performers and composers. Black classical composers sought to incorporate African-American music into larger concert forms. William Grant Still stated that his role was "to elevate Negro musical idioms to a position of dignity and effectiveness in the field of symphonic and operatic music."[5] Such values exercised a powerful impact on many of the Harlem jazz players, particularly James P. Johnson and Duke Ellington, who themselves later merged jazz into concert music and classical forms.

James Johnson (CD 1, Tracks 2 and 8).

On the back of sheet music, Warner Bros. & Vitaphone Singing & Talking Pictures advertised theme songs. Resident orchestras in theaters showing silent films played theme songs during particular sequences. The success of a theme song directly influenced the success of the film and vice versa. The Warner brothers joined with Vitaphone Singing & Talking Pictures to produce short films that connected a projector to a phonograph for accompanying sound. Using a technically more sophisticated version in 1927, Warner Bros. produced the first "talkie"— *The Jazz Singer*. Although they hailed it as the first full-length sound picture, it was actually a mostly silent film with Al Jolson song sequences. The first all-singing film was *Broadway Melody* (1929).

By the 1930s, jazz had become a mainstream entertainment and a gradually integrating force in U.S. culture. Although jazz was performed by black and white artists to black and white audiences, white acceptance of the work of black composers was gradual in the United States. Notice that for the successful Fats Waller composition, "Keepin' Out Of Mischief Now," the cover of the British edition carried a picture of Fats Waller, but the U.S. edition did not.

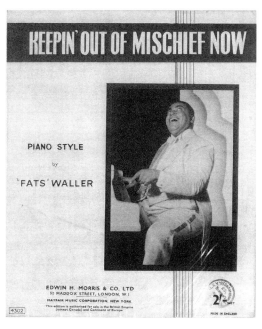

Courtesy Morgan Collection

Harlem and jazz were inextricably bound. The Harlem-based jazz musicians Duke Ellington and Fletcher Henderson became the two primary black bandleaders, developing their bands through nightly performances at all-white nightclubs. White musicians such as Artie Shaw, Benny Goodman, and Paul Whiteman frequented these clubs, and classical composers such as Darius Milhaud and Aaron Copland heard the bands and listened closely.

In addition to nightclub performances, "rent parties" allowed many of the Harlem jazz pianists to develop their technique. These were "funky, down-home affairs," writes Samuel Floyd:

A **rent party** was an informal gathering held to raise money for rent or groceries. At these parties, musicians would often gather and perform, sometimes in competition with one another.

> As far as creativity is concerned, such affairs served as the proving ground for the pianists. Dominating this creative world were James P. Johnson, Willie "The Lion" Smith, Thomas "Fats" Waller, Luckey Roberts, and Duke Ellington. It was in this world that these and other musicians honed their artistic tools and worked out their ideas for presentation in the world of show business.[6]

The elevation of jazz's status during the 1920s—and its increased popular appeal—owed a particular debt to the energies of several white musicians and composers. Paul Whiteman became the most successful American bandleader during this period, in part by incorporating jazz elements within an orchestral format. Whiteman's recordings of "Whispering" and "Japanese Sandman" from 1920, the year he came to New York, sold more than a million copies. He referred to his music as "symphonic syncopation" and devised lush, colorful, and complicated arrangements, often more suitable for listening than for dancing. Whiteman's renown led to his label, "King of Jazz," and in 1930 he appeared in a film by that name.

As he put it, Whiteman was attempting "to make a lady out of jazz" when he took jazz out of the nightclub and into the concert hall. His most celebrated concert took place in New York's Aeolian Hall on February 12, 1924. Entitled "An Experiment in Modern Music," the concert's grand finale featured the premiere of George Gershwin's *Rhapsody in Blue,* which Whiteman had commissioned. The composer appeared as the piano soloist. With its opening chromatic slide for clarinet, its use of blue notes, and its syncopated rhythms, *Rhapsody in Blue* placed on the concert stage the devices and rhetoric of jazz that Gershwin had enthusiastically absorbed from black Harlem musicians.

Whiteman had commissioned *Rhapsody in Blue* after hearing Gershwin's earlier jazz-influenced work, the one-act opera *Blue Monday.* Gershwin was an important composer of popular song and musical theater prior to *Rhapsody in Blue.* After its success, however, he turned his energy to jazz-based concert works and became increasingly preoccupied with the integration of jazz and classical music. He subsequently composed several important concert works with jazz elements, including *Concerto in F* (1925). The second of his *Preludes for Piano* (1926) and the orchestral work *An American in Paris* (1928) employ the twelve-bar blues structure. Gershwin's most ambitious work was his folk opera *Porgy and Bess* (1935), based on a drama about black Americans and infused with elements of jazz and the blues. It is arguably the best twentieth-century American opera written. Because of the general popularity of his tunes, their syncopated melodies, and their numerous performances by jazz musicians, Gershwin has been called "The Jazz Composer."

The Harlem Renaissance and coinciding rise of jazz in New York City during the 1920s contributed to the spirit of excitement and creativity that was essential if jazz were to change from a curiosity to a phenomenon. Many musicians helped secure jazz as a music of cultural and artistic significance. Among them was a group of pianists known as the "Harlem Stride" school.

Harlem Stride Piano

Around World War I, New York became the center of a type of piano playing that developed out of ragtime but took on techniques that led to a high degree of virtuosity. This early jazz style, called *stride piano,* evolved at the same time that the musical developments in New Orleans and Chicago did. It embodies the transition of jazz from ragtime; indeed, stride energized ragtime with greater flash, speed, incorporation of blues elements, and sometimes improvisational variations (often planned). The development of ragtime into stride parallels the hectic pace of U.S. life during and after World War I, with stride's energy mimicking the speed of the assembly line, the automobile, the telephone, and the airplane.

Fundamentally, stride playing described the left hand "striding" up and down the keyboard, with a bass note or octave played on the first and third beats of the 4/4 measure, alternating with a midrange chord on the second and fourth beats. Various stride players cultivated their own flashy techniques and trademarks as well. At rent parties in Harlem, at the Jungles Casino on West Sixty-Second Street, in the piano competitions known as "cutting contests," pianists James P. Johnson, Luckey Roberts, Willie "The Lion" Smith, and Richard "Abba Labba" McLean emerged as the best players in the highly competitive New York world. Scholars sometimes call this stride style the "eastern" school to distinguish it from midwestern styles, but the regional influences overlap so that we cannot always distinguish them. In any event, while centered in Harlem, stride piano boasted fine players working throughout the Northeast and as far south as Washington, D.C.

Stride piano is a school of jazz piano playing derived from ragtime. With greater speed and virtuosity than ragtime, stride combines a left-hand accompaniment of alternating bass notes and chords (march bass) with a tugging right hand that seems to pull at the left-hand rhythm to impart swing.

Piano Rolls

Piano rolls were cylinders of rolled paper punched with holes. When fed through a properly equipped **player piano**, the holes activated hammers that played the piano automatically. Many of the great pianists of the teens and twenties recorded piano rolls, including James P. Johnson, Eubie Blake, Fats Waller, and George Gershwin. The rolls, however, could not reproduce dynamics and phrasing adequately, and tempo depended on how fast the roll was fed through the piano. Hence, the "recordings" of piano rolls are not accurate guides to players' styles. In the last several years, the use of electronic technology has vastly improved the performance of piano rolls, and remarkably lifelike versions of piano-roll performances by George Gershwin, for example, are now available.

Harlem stride linked ragtime to swing by featuring elements of both; its melodies floated effortlessly between angular ragtime rhythms and smooth swing. Even the music of later Harlem pianists, such as Fats Waller, continued to exhibit connections to ragtime in both melodic style and left-hand rhythm. Stride bass formed the basis for many solo jazz piano styles.

The stride pianists took their repertory from reworkings of popular show tunes and traditional ragtime pieces, as well as classical compositions played in a ragtime style. In addition, several prominent stride pianists began composing their own works.

EUBIE BLAKE

Eubie Blake (1883–1983), who began his career playing piano in Baltimore's bars and brothels (what used to be called the red-light district), recorded in 1917 a version of his brilliant "Charleston Rag" on a piano roll. (A recording of the piece, issued as "Sounds of Africa," followed in 1921.) Blake later claimed that he wrote the work, which was extremely forward looking, in 1899. If so, it would be evidence of a jazz style emerging on the East Coast around the same time as New Orleans jazz.

Blake was an important pianist and composer who, with lyricist Noble Sissle, wrote the most successful black musical of the 1920s, *Shuffle Along* (1921). The same year that Blake recorded his piano roll of "Charleston Rag" (1917), James P. Johnson issued piano rolls of his compositions "Caprice Rag" and "Stop It." Johnson would take the ragtime-stride style to a new level. (See the box "Piano Rolls" for more on this technology.)

JAMES P. JOHNSON

James P. Johnson was born in 1894 in New Brunswick, New Jersey, and raised in Jersey City and New York. Though essentially a stride and popular composer-pianist, he had a strong classical background and always remained interested in concert music. Most of his life was spent working in Atlantic City, New York, and other cities along the East Coast, although he also toured extensively on the vaudeville circuit and even played in England.

Known as the "Father of Stride Piano," Johnson developed his style from playing dance music at clubs in the Jungles, the black section of New York's Hell's Kitchen in the West Sixties. At the Jungles Casino he played for transplanted southern workers, many of them black merchant seamen from Savannah and Charleston; those from the Georgia Sea Islands were called "Gullahs" and "Geechies." These patrons demanded the country dances they had heard growing up in the South, and this provided the origin for one of Johnson's most famous compositions:

> The Gullahs would start out early in the evening dancing two-steps, waltzes, schottisches; but as the night wore on and the liquor began to work, they would start improvising their own steps and that was when they wanted us to get-in-the-alley, real lowdown. Those big Charleston, South Carolina, bruisers would grab a girl from the bar and stomp-it-down as the piano player swung into the gut-bucketiest music he could.
>
> It was from the improvised dance steps that the Charleston dance originated. All the older folks remember it became a rage during the 1920s and all it really amounted to was a variation of a cotillion step brought to the North by the Geechies. There were many variations danced at the Casino and this usually caused the piano player to make up his own musical variation to fit the dancing. One of James P. Johnson's variations was later published as a number called "The Charleston."[7]

Johnson wrote "Charleston" for the Broadway musical *Runnin' Wild*. His playing and compositions became celebrated for the way they combined ragtime with elements of blues and jazz.

Johnson's most famous stride composition was "Carolina Shout," which appeared on piano roll twice in the teens. Johnson first recorded it to disc in 1921. "Carolina Shout" served as a test piece for players attempting virtuosic stride; in fact, the young Duke Ellington claimed to learn the style by slowing down the player-piano mechanism of "Carolina Shout" and fitting his fingers to the rising and falling keys. Johnson also recorded "Harlem Strut" and "Keep off the Grass" in 1921, works that contain similar virtuosic devices, as does his 1930 recording of "You've Got to Be Modernistic." Johnson's technique and inventiveness were prodigious. His playing

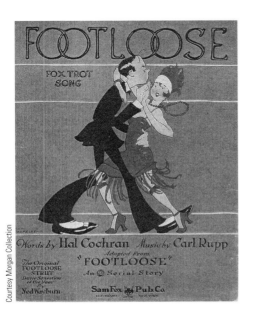

Courtesy Morgan Collection

The Roaring Twenties was a time of dance crazes. The Charleston and lindy hop were significant, but most of the dances were short-lived—including the "Footloose" strut from 1925. On the back of the sheet music for "Footloose" are the diagram and instructions for "How to Dance It." Ned Wayburn, the choreographer, appears to have given this eccentric creation his most sober attentions.

seemed to absorb all the tricks of the other piano "ticklers," from Eubie Blake to Luckey Roberts. Johnson discussed his musical growth in a later interview:

> I was starting to develop a good technique. I was born with absolute pitch and could catch a key that a player was using and copy it, even Luckey's. I played rags very accurately and brilliantly—running chromatic octaves and glissandos up and down with both hands. It made a terrific effect.
>
> I did double glissandos straight and backhand, glissandos in sixths and double tremolos. These would run other ticklers out of the place at cutting sessions. They wouldn't play after me. I would put these tricks in on the breaks and I could think of a trick a minute. I was playing a lot of piano then, traveling around and listening to every good player I could. I'd steal their breaks and style and practice them until I had them perfect.[8]

Johnson did more than just play brilliant solo piano. He also recorded with blues singers Bessie Smith (see Chapter 1) and Ethel Waters, and he composed his first Broadway musical, *Runnin' Wild*, in 1923. The musical was a hit with 213 performances, and Johnson continued to compose music for the stage through 1947. A true child of the Harlem Renaissance, he began composing large-scale concert works that placed elements of jazz and African-American music in classical forms and models. For example, *Yamekraw* (1927) was written for piano and orchestra and premiered at Carnegie Hall with Fats Waller as the soloist. Other orchestral works include his *Harlem Symphony* (1932), which concludes with a variation on the hymn "I Want Jesus to Walk with Me," and a piano concerto entitled *Jassamine* (1934). He suffered several strokes in the 1940s but continued to play and record up to a final recording with Sidney Bechet in 1950. A stroke in 1951 left him unable to play, and he died in 1955.

Back-beat (or **change-step**) is a stride piano technique in which the performer breaks up the regular striding left hand with its unyielding alternation of bass note and mid-register chord— that is, 1-2-1-2 ("1" refers to a bass note and "2" refers to a chord). Instead, the left hand plays a more complex pattern such as 1-1-2-1/1-2-1-2 or 1-2-2-1/2-2-1-2/1-2-1-2, which is called a back-beat (not to be confused with a drummer's "backbeat," as defined later in this book). Listen to Track 5 of the 🅐 Audio Primer CD to hear an example. James P. Johnson used this technique more often than the other stride pianists did.

L I S T E N I N G   G U I D E

"You've Got to Be Modernistic"

CD **1**   Track **8**

James P. Johnson: "You've Got to Be Modernistic" (Johnson). Brunswick 4762.
New York, January 21, 1930. James P. Johnson, piano.

"Modernistic" is a brilliant example of a Broadway-style popular song adapted to a stride piano interpretation. It shows Johnson's piano virtuosity at its best. The word *modernistic* in the title refers to the use of augmented chords. Probably inspired by the French Impressionist composers Debussy and Ravel as well as the works of Gershwin, this harmonic color became popular in the 1920s.

"Modernistic" shows how the stride players often "improvised" variations during the C strain—that is, they played variations that often were planned in advance, especially for recordings. Although we cannot be certain, the C strain variations of Johnson's "Modernistic" do sound planned; they are very exciting and build to an exhilarating finish.

Introduction—4 bars

0:00   Throughout the piece, count the pulse in a moderate two beats or fast four beats to the bar. The introduction features the "modernistic" augmented chords.

A strain (A♭ major)—16 bars, repeated

0:04   A strain repeats for the first time.

0:10
and
0:16
The A strain features breaks from the rhythm in measures 7–8 and measures 13–14, which bring back the augmented chords.

0:20   Repeat

B strain—16 bars as 8 + 8, repeated

0:35   The contrasting B strain begins with a descending chromatic series of chords. Here the regular stride rhythm is broken up by rhythmic material that alternates the hands. The contrast to the A section is not only melodic but also rhythmic.

0:51   On the repeat of the B section, the first eight bars are played with a lighter texture.

Return of the A strain—16 bars

1:06   The A section is reprised. The return of the left-hand stride brings a wonderful rhythmic lift. This time the section is played through only once and the right hand is an octave higher.

Interlude—4 bars

1:21   The interlude section again features prominent augmented chords as a modulation to the subdominant, D♭ major.

C strain—16 bars as 8 + 8

1:25   The C strain is a trio, in which the rocking rhythm—interrupted by the interlude—returns. The first time through the C strain is a "head," in which the basic melodic idea is presented. It features a repeating harmonic pattern, not unlike Jelly Roll Morton's "King Porter Stomp," that allows for improvised variation. Interestingly, "King Porter" is in the same keys, A♭ to D♭ major.

C strain, 2nd chorus

1:41   Johnson begins the second C strain with the first of a series of variations. Here, he moves to the higher register.

C strain, 3rd chorus

1:56   In the third chorus, the left hand takes the lead with a repeating bass figure. The right hand continues the rhythm with chords on the second and fourth beats of the bar.

C strain, 4th chorus

2:11   A return to the right-hand lead with an exciting rhythmic riff.

2:20
and
2:23
At measures 10 and 13 of the chorus, the left hand creates a "back-beat" or "change-step" by disrupting the 1-2-1-2 flow of the bass-treble alternation. This technique is difficult at such a whirlwind tempo and enhances the rhythmic interest of the piece.

C strain, 5th chorus

2:26   In the fifth chorus, the right hand moves into the higher register again with a neighbor-note figuration, that is, a melodic pattern that keeps returning to the same note through step-wise motion.

C strain, 6th chorus

2:42   The sixth chorus features sustained right-hand chords.

2:47   During this chorus, measures 7–8 feature a delightful passage with chromatic chords that recall the chromaticism of the opening sections of the piece.

C strain, 7th chorus

2:57   Here, the right hand plays an exciting repeating chord riff in a way that parallels the left hand in the third chorus. The chorus, and performance, end directly without a tag.

FATS WALLER

James P. Johnson's student, Thomas "Fats" Waller (1904–1943), went on to even greater fame and renown than Johnson himself. Although Waller became better known as a humorous entertainer, his virtuosity on the piano was unparalleled. Before meeting Johnson, Waller had been at age fifteen the organist at Harlem's Lincoln Theatre. Under Johnson's tutelage he began to excel as a stride pianist. With the help of his mentor, he established himself in the New York musical world and began to record piano rolls in 1922. The same year he recorded for OKeh Records, doing two sides as a piano soloist and working with blues singers Sara Martin and Alberta Hunter.

Like Johnson, Waller was a fine songwriter who wrote such classics as "Squeeze Me," "Honeysuckle Rose," "Black and Blue," and "Ain't Misbehavin'." Also like Johnson, Waller composed for the Broadway stage, working with lyricist Andy Razaf on the 1928 musical *Keep Shufflin'* as well as *Hot Chocolates* (1929), which had Louis Armstrong as a singer and soloist.

Waller was the first important jazz musician to record on the pipe organ, an instrument not especially disposed to the sharp attacks of jazz phrasing. Despite his unparalleled keyboard prowess, Waller ultimately succeeded in the public eye as a popular singer and entertainer: His witty asides often called attention to the emptiness of the disposable pop songs he was increasingly called on to play.

Nevertheless, Waller's solo piano recordings are among the high points of stride piano. The piano works written and recorded between 1929 and 1934—"Handful of Keys," "Smashing Thirds," "Numb Fumblin'," "Valentine Stomp," "Viper's Drag," "Alligator Crawl," and "Clothes Line Ballet"—keep alive many of Johnson's techniques while projecting an eloquent swing regardless of tempo. Waller's harmonic palette was somewhat more advanced than Johnson's. In addition to alternating octaves with mid-range chords in the left hand, Waller also made frequent use of left-hand tenths. Waller's hands were huge: Pianist George Shearing compared shaking hands with Waller to "grabbing a bunch of bananas."[9]

"Handful of Keys" is a tour de force of effortless up-tempo stride playing, and it became a test piece for other stride pianists. It most particularly recalls James P. Johnson and classic stride, while at the same time blending it with the looser feel of swing. The piece connects to the ragtime tradition as well because of

▶ The marchlike form with a trio in the subdominant key

▶ The composed rather than improvised character of the sectional melodies

▶ The stride accompaniment

The striding left hand racing along at such a fast tempo testifies to Waller's technique and the virtuosity of Harlem stride style itself.

Many pianists from the heyday of stride piano kept the tradition alive well past the twenties and thirties. In addition to Johnson and Waller, Willie "The Lion" Smith and Luckey Roberts continued to perpetuate the Harlem solo piano style. Eubie Blake, already discussed as an important predecessor to Johnson and Waller as both pianist and composer, enjoyed a comeback in 1969 at the age of eighty-six. Stride piano was the developmental core in the playing of such pianists as Duke Ellington, Earl Hines, Teddy Wilson, Count Basie, and Art Tatum, although these players quickly departed from a pure stride style. Still, later pianists—Johnny Guarnieri, Ralph Sutton, Dick Wellstood, and Dave McKenna—studied and kept alive the Harlem piano tradition.

Beginnings of the Big Bands

In earlier chapters, we discussed the New Orleans and Chicago traditions in which groups tended to be roughly five to seven players. In such groups, the front line combination of cornet, trombone, and clarinet featured one instrument per function: cornet (or trumpet) with the lead, trombone with a lower counterpoint or countermelody, and clarinet with an upper obbligato.

The big band featured a *section* of instruments for each instrument in the New Orleans–style band: a section of trumpets, a section of trombones, and a section of reeds (as saxophones or clarinets). In general, the use of sections required either written or head arrangements worked out in rehearsal, because it was difficult to be completely spontaneous with a larger number of players.

The evolution of the early big band is a matter of some controversy in jazz history. Who was the first bandleader to use a saxophone section? Recent scholarship suggests that the Art Hickman band, a San Francisco–based group, may have been the first to use two saxophones as a "proto-reed section" in 1919.[10] Bands led by Paul Whiteman and Fletcher Henderson continued to pioneer band division into four sections (trumpets, trombones, reeds, and rhythm), but the early history of the big band remains murky. Although the actual course of innovation remains unclear, it is likely that the major New York–based groups, such as the Whiteman and Henderson ensembles, solidified the use of big-band sectional formulas and textures for the 1930s.

FLETCHER HENDERSON

Fletcher Henderson arrived in New York in 1920. The twenty-two-year-old came from Atlanta, where he had received a degree in chemistry from Atlanta University and began to work as a song plugger for the Pace-Handy Music Company, one of the first and most successful black publishing companies. When Pace left Handy to form

Courtesy Frank Driggs Collection

Fletcher Henderson with his band in New York, 1924. Left to right: Howard Scott, Coleman Hawkins, Louis Armstrong, Charlie Dixon, Henderson, Kaiser Marshall, Buster Bailey, Elmer Chambers, Charlie Green, Bob Escudero, Don Redman. (Except for Henderson and Bailey, the band includes different personnel on CD 1, Track 10.) Coleman Hawkins went on to form his own groups (CD 1, Track 15).

Black Swan Records, Henderson moved as well and began playing piano and forming bands for the new company. As the blues phenomenon hit its peak, Henderson recorded with dozens of blues singers, including Bessie Smith, Ma Rainey, and Ethel Waters. Henderson's recordings with Ethel Waters became the best-sellers of the Black Swan catalog. Touring with Waters, Henderson at one point unsuccessfully tried to lure Louis Armstrong into Waters's band.

In the meantime, Henderson had formed his own band and played at the Club Alabam for half a year before moving in 1924 to the Roseland Ballroom at Broadway and Fifty-First Street. The Roseland maintained a whites-only policy for clientele but had recently decided to feature both white and black bands after the success of A. J. Piron's group from New Orleans. With arranger and reed player Don Redman as musical director, Henderson's band developed a repertory that alternated written ensemble sections with the improvised solos of saxophonist Coleman Hawkins and cornetist Joe Smith.

Shortly after the band opened at Roseland in 1924, Louis Armstrong left Chicago to join Henderson as third trumpet and the featured "hot" soloist. Armstrong's technique, sound, and ideas had developed rapidly in his preceding two years with King Oliver, and his solo style and rhythmic sense revolutionized the Henderson band's playing. The group's somewhat stiff staccato rhythms loosened into Armstrong's more swinging, propulsive, and smooth style, which affected the sound of the soloists as well as the entire ensemble. Their recordings of "Shanghai Shuffle," "Go 'Long Mule," and "TNT" reveal some of the energy that Armstrong introduced. At the same time, New Orleans clarinetist Buster Bailey left King Oliver's band and joined Henderson, creating a reed section of three players; the addition of trombonist Charlie Green to the trumpets gave the band a total of four brass players.

With these instrumental forces, arranger Don Redman began to create many of the techniques that would be used by bands for years for follow. In some cases, Redman altered preexisting stock arrangements to improve them. Redman's arrangements and modifications not only heightened the distinction between improvised and written sections but also made skillful use of the contrast between brasses and reeds. Redman alternated brass and reed sections in call-and-response fashion, or he set one section to play background figures behind another. Henderson's recording of "Alabamy Bound" contained another characteristic device of Redman's, the clarinet trio.

The high point of Redman's work for Henderson during this period was his arrangement of "Copenhagen." Working from a stock arrangement, Redman transformed the original into a highly effective vehicle for the band. The written portions alternate sections of the full ensemble, trumpet trio, and clarinet trio. When Armstrong solos over a twelve-bar blues structure, he works within the New Orleans style of collective improvisation but also has a forward-looking rhythm section accompaniment. The three-minute composition is a tour de force in which Redman seems to summarize the collective developments in jazz while predicting its future direction.

As a hot jazz dance band, Henderson's group earned increasing popularity. "Sugar Foot Stomp," a reworking of King Oliver's "Dippermouth Blues," became a popular hit. In 1925 the trade publication *Orchestra World* crowned Henderson "king" of the black orchestra leaders. Even after Armstrong left the band and returned to Chicago, the band continued to develop and mature. It hosted an arsenal of top-notch soloists, including saxophonist Coleman Hawkins, trumpeter Rex Stewart, and trombonist Jimmy Harrison.

A **stock arrangement** or **stock** was an arrangement created and sold by a publishing company to bandleaders. In some cases, stock arrangements were generic and unimaginative; other times, the arrangements were quite effective. Bands performed stock arrangements in order to keep up with the latest hit songs. They would either play them as given or modify them to work with their bands' individual styles.

In 1927, however, Don Redman left to become the arranger for McKinney's Cotton Pickers. Henderson then began arranging for his group, turning out excellent charts that highlighted the band's capabilities. Some, such as his arrangement of Jelly Roll Morton's "King Porter Stomp," were based on riff ideas that the band contributed.

The Henderson band featured other writers and soloists who would become important in jazz. Alto saxophonist Benny Carter began contributing arrangements in 1930. Carter would go on to become one of the finest arrangers in jazz as well as a premier saxophone stylist. Trombone technique was advancing as well, as various players became more proficient as soloists. Jimmy Harrison (1900–1931), for example, who recorded with the Fletcher Henderson Orchestra, earned the nickname "Father of Swing Trombone."

Ultimately, Henderson could not sustain his band. He lost many of his players to other groups and, because of his poor management skills, was often unable to pay those who remained. Many band members were heavy drinkers, which contributed to a general decline in quality; they were, in Duke Ellington's words, "probably one of the partyingest bands that ever was."[11] Financial difficulties forced Henderson to sell his arrangements. In 1934 Benny Goodman bought many of them; ironically, Goodman, as a successful white bandleader, brought Henderson's music to more people than Henderson himself ever had. Henderson became the staff arranger for Goodman between 1939 and 1941 but returned to lead his own bands until his death in 1950.

Historically, Henderson's band of the 1920s and early thirties formed a crucial link to the succeeding swing era. With its careful chemistry of ensemble passages and solo playing, the group played a fundamental role in the development of the big band. Moreover, Henderson's ensemble writing was often written to sound like the hot solo improvisations it surrounded, bringing about a swinging style of ensemble playing. This would soon become the signature sound of the big bands as they jumped to unprecedented popularity in the 1930s.

DUKE ELLINGTON'S EARLY CAREER

When Duke Ellington originally put together a big band in New York, he modeled it on Henderson's successful group.[12] Although Henderson's band was much better known during the 1920s, Ellington's unique combination of musicianship, compositional skill, professional savvy, and aristocratic persona eventually made him perhaps the most celebrated bandleader and composer in the history of jazz.

Born in Washington, D.C., on April 29, 1899, Edward Kennedy Ellington began studying piano at the age of seven. As a teenager, he developed an interest in stride piano and began to perform publicly. During this period, he earned the nickname "Duke" for his aristocratic deportment and tasteful dressing. In places like Washington's Howard Theater, Ellington could have heard such groups as James Reese Europe's Clef Club

A **riff** is a short melodic idea, usually one to two bars in length, that is repeated as the core idea of a musical passage. Sometimes, the different band sections will trade riffs in a call-and-response format. Usually rhythmic and simple, the riff also can provide a swinging background for an improvising soloist. Listen to Track 49 of the Audio Primer CD to hear a trumpet playing a background riff in a small-group context to back up the tenor soloist.

Courtesy Morgan Collection

In Duke Ellington (CD 1, Tracks 9 and 14) the black performer's progression from minstrel buffoon to serious artist became complete—as we see here in a publicity photograph of the elegant Ellington at about age 30.

Orchestra and Will Marion Cook and his Southern Syncopated Orchestra (with Sidney Bechet on saxophone), stride pianists such as Luckey Roberts, and the musical revues of Eubie Blake and Noble Sissle. The Howard Theater also held performances of concert music, some of which drew on themes from the history of African Americans. These performances likely provided an early prototype for Ellington's later extended compositions—*Symphony in Black* and *Black, Brown, and Beige*—which dealt with similar themes. After high school, Ellington formed his own band in Washington, the Duke's Serenaders.

Initially Ellington moved to New York to play with Wilbur Sweatman's vaudeville act in March 1923. Gigs were scarce at first. Ellington remained briefly before returning to Washington, but later that year he moved permanently to New York with his Washington band—Sonny Greer on drums, Otto Hardwick on saxophone, Elmer Snowden on banjo, and Arthur Whetsol on trumpet. Their band, the Washingtonians, became regular performers at the Hollywood Cafe. Though Snowden initially led the band, Ellington replaced him as leader early in 1924, and the Hollywood Cafe changed its name to the more down-home Kentucky Club.

During their earliest days, the Washingtonians represented a typical downtown dance band that was probably more sweet than hot. However, one change in the band's personnel had far-reaching consequences—the addition of cornetist Bubber Miley. Not only was Miley a hot player, but his use of the plunger mute and the straight mute created a "growling" style of playing that entirely altered the sound of the band. Miley became the featured soloist of the band. "Our band changed its character when Bubber came in," Ellington acknowledged. "He used to growl all night long, playing gutbucket on his horn. That was when we decided to forget all about the sweet music."[13]

Although not particularly distinctive, the Washingtonian's earliest recordings do capture Miley's "gutbucket" sound. In works such as "Choo Choo (I Gotta Hurry

Bubber Miley and Joe "Tricky Sam" Nanton

Bubber Miley (1903–1932) was the cornerstone of Duke Ellington's early band. Miley's mute playing, which incorporated both the straight and cup varieties, owed a debt to King Oliver as well as to the New York–based cornetist Johnny Dunn. The growling sound formed the basis of Ellington's "jungle effects," a key feature of the band's Cotton Club performances that was adopted by subsequent Ellington trumpeters and trombonists. Ellington historian Mark Tucker suggests that "Miley's power comes not from volume or speed but from his subtle coloring of individual notes and his ability to create and sustain a mood. . . . Miley was a different kind of hot trumpeter from the brilliant and rhythmically daring Armstrong."[*]

In the second half of the 1920s, trombone players cultivated a solo approach over the polyphonic role they had played earlier. With the Ellington band, Joe "Tricky Sam" Nanton (1904–1946) adapted Miley's plunger-and-growl technique to the trombone. (Listen to Track 24 of the Audio Primer CD for an example of plunger-and-growl technique on the trombone.) The duet between Nanton and Juan Tizol (1900–1984) in Ellington's 1931 recording of "Creole Rhapsody" is probably the earliest recorded trombone duet in jazz.

*Mark Tucker, *Ellington: The Early Years* (Urbana, IL: University of Illinois Press, 1991), 148.

The Cotton Club—at Lenox Avenue and 142nd Street in Harlem—was famous for its extravagant floor shows. *Rhyth-mania*, with dances by Clarence Robinson, was one of them.

Home)" and "Rainy Nights" (both from 1924), Miley uses the cup mute and his left hand to alter the sound of the instrument.

The "growling" style of brass playing was not restricted to the cornet: As the group gradually expanded to a ten-piece group during its four-year tenure at the Kentucky Club, trombonists Charles Irvis and, later, Joe "Tricky Sam" Nanton cultivated the "gutbucket" sound on their instruments. Other additions to the group were Harry Carney on baritone saxophone, Rudy Jackson on clarinet and tenor saxophone, Wellman Braud on bass, and Fred Guy on banjo. (See the box "Bubber Miley and Joe 'Tricky Sam' Nanton" for more on these players.)

Throughout his career, Ellington melded his players' individual sounds with the color of the entire band. Each musician contributed to the group's distinctive timbre, enhanced by Ellington's own stride-based piano style. Many of the band's

PRIX : 4 FR.
(FOREIGN 5 FR.)

3ᵉ ANNÉE
NUMÉRO 21

JAZZ HOT

JIMMY LUNCEFORD
ET SON ORCHESTRE
AUQUEL CE NUMÉRO EST CONSACRÉ

INTERNATIONAL REVIEW OF JAZZ MUSIC
REVUE INTERNATIONALE DE LA MUSIQUE DE JAZZ
NOVEMBRE-DÉCEMBRE 1937
DERNIÈRE MINUTE
Concert BENNY CARTER, le Vendredi 17 Décembre, à 21 heures, Salle de l'École Normale de Musique

Jimmie Lunceford on the cover of a French magazine announcing a forthcoming concert. Lunceford and his band played at Harlem's Savoy Ballroom, which occupied the second floor of a building that ran the entire block of Lenox Avenue from 140th to 141st Streets. As the place where everyone went to dance, it was one of the earliest integrated clubs.

Courtesy Morgan Collection

compositions were clearly collaborative efforts. "East St. Louis Toodle-oo," "Creole Love Call," and "Black and Tan Fantasy" are among Ellington's early masterpieces, relying on the blues for form or feeling and featuring Miley and Nanton.

Under the management of Irving Mills, Ellington and the band enjoyed increasing prestige. Mills began touting Ellington as the leader of the "foremost dance band in America."[14] Mills's hyperbole soon proved true. After the band moved from the Kentucky Club to Harlem's Cotton Club in 1927, Ellington quickly became one of the leading national jazz figures. At the Cotton Club the band played music for dancing, vocalists, and elaborate floor shows to a well-heeled after-theater crowd.

With a ride from Broadway to Harlem, patrons could feel the slightly risky thrill of enjoying black entertainment in a black neighborhood while remaining part of an all-white audience. The club's jungle decor enhanced the exotic atmosphere, and the band exploited the brass section's growl techniques to create the jungle sound in compositions such as "East St. Louis Toodle-oo," "The Mooche," "Jungle Nights in Harlem," and "Echoes of the Jungle."

In addition to nightly performances at the Cotton Club, Mills generated high-visibility appearances for the band: backing Ziegfeld's *Show Girl,* accompanying French singer Maurice Chevalier at the Fulton Theatre, performing in films, and playing on radio broadcasts. The popular response to a 1930 broadcast of Ellington's composition "Dreamy Blues" led Mills to retitle the song and provide a lyric for what would become one of Ellington's most famous compositions, "Mood Indigo." With the addition of Barney Bigard on clarinet, Johnny Hodges on saxophone, Freddie Jenkins on trumpet, Juan Tizol on trombone, and—replacing Bubber Miley—Cootie Williams on trumpet, the band now had twelve players.

The band's four years at the Cotton Club served as "a prolonged workshop period."[15] Nightly performances for thirty-eight months allowed Ellington the freedom to develop the band's musical identity, to highlight the individual players, and—most important—to experiment with unusual instrumental combinations and colors. Ellington began to create larger extended compositions. Shortly before their tenure ended at the Cotton Club in 1931, Ellington recorded two versions of "Creole Rhapsody," a composition that took up two sides of a 78-rpm record. This was a substantial departure from the standard three-minute, one-sided jazz record. The six-minute extended composition operated as a suite in miniature, making use of tempo changes and passages in free tempo, and heralding an important, new compositional direction for Ellington. In later years, Ellington would write several suites.

In the heady atmosphere of the Harlem Renaissance, Ellington's manager Mills sought to portray Ellington not merely as a bandleader and songwriter but as "a great musician who was making a lasting contribution to American music."[16] Ellington's work was taking on elements of "mood" or "character" pieces, many with African-American themes. As Ellington noted,

> Our aim as a dance orchestra is not so much to reproduce "hot" or "jazz" music as to describe emotions, moods, and activities which have a wide range, leading from the very gay to the somber.... Every one of my song titles is taken principally from the life of Harlem.... [I look] to the everyday life and customs of the Negro to supply my inspiration.[17]

Ellington's big band was an expression of his artistic vision. He composed original works that drew on the individual skills of his musicians. Band members felt that they were given an opportunity to express their own talents while playing Ellington's unique music. Unlike other bands, members would often work with Ellington for years, sometimes decades, enabling them to absorb his style as he continued to develop. As we shall see in the following chapter, as composer, spokesperson, and bandleader, Ellington would be a central force in the ongoing evolution of jazz as a serious art form.

A musical form of the classical European tradition, the **suite** most often denotes a piece containing several sections, each with distinctive melodies and moods. The sections may or may not be related thematically. Often, composers will extract the most popular or most effective sections from extended works, such as opera and ballets, to create a suite for concert performance.

L I S T E N I N G   G U I D E

"The Mooche"
CD **1** Track **9**

Duke Ellington and His Cotton Club Orchestra: "The Mooche" (Ellington-Mills). Victor 38034.
New York, October 30, 1928. Duke Ellington, arranger, piano, leader; Arthur Whetsol, Freddy Jenkins,
trumpets; Joe Nanton, trombone; Johnny Hodges, clarinet, alto saxophone; Harry Carney, clarinet,
baritone saxophone; Barney Bigard, clarinet, tenor saxophone; Fred Guy, banjo;
Lonnie Johnson, guitar; Wellman Braud, tuba; Sonny Greer, drums.

Jazz frequently relies on the "head-solos-head" format. However, like Jelly Roll Morton, Ellington insisted on a refreshingly different approach. In arranging an AABA song for a band it is often difficult to vary the "head-solos-head" pattern creatively and still fashion a workable, uncontrived arrangement. Ellington and Morton circumvented this problem by composing *and* arranging the material. Particularly in extended works such as "The Mooche," they conceived the arrangement as an intrinsic part of the composition. Ellington's "The Mooche" is a fine example of his late-1920s style, complete with the "jungle" sounds made famous during his residency at the Cotton Club.

Introduction—4 bars in C minor

0:00   Count the piece in a moderate four beats to the bar. The introduction alternates two chords, the tonic I chord (C minor), with a ♭II7 chord as an altered dominant (D♭9(#11)). Each harmony lasts four beats. The percussionist accompanies on temple blocks. The exotic, foreboding quality of the introduction forecasts the pseudo-African tone that pervades the piece.

Section A—8 bars, repeated in C minor

0:08   Section A is an eight-bar melody, repeated, played by a clarinet trio, a common ensemble instrumentation in the 1920s. The harmonic rhythm changes to eight beats (a chord change every two bars): C minor–B9–D♭9(#11)–C minor. This encircling of the C minor tonic is an original and effective chord progression and contributes to the exotic quality of the piece as a whole.

Repeat.

0:23   Trumpeter Arthur Whetsol plays instrumental fills, some of which use the "growling" tone for which the band was famous. He uses a mute, which, when manipulated with his left hand, creates the "wah-wah" effect.

Section B—8 bars, beginning in C minor

0:39   The clarinet trio that continues section B serves as a transition and modulation to E♭ major, the relative major of C minor. Note the bluesy inflections on the held-out clarinet notes. Whetsol continues his muted-trumpet answers to the clarinet phrases.

Section C1—12-bar blues in E♭ major

0:55   The full band takes up the melody for a new section, a twelve-bar blues in E♭ major.

Section D1—12-bar blues in E♭ minor

1:18   The twelve-bar blues idea continues with a new melody played by a clarinet solo in the low register. The E♭ minor key—the parallel minor to E♭ major—extends the principle of sections in both major and minor. Note the effective tone color contrast to the full band in the previous section.

Section D2—12-bar blues in E♭ minor

1:42   In call-and-response, Whetsol plays a second chorus of twelve-bar blues with answering licks from saxophonist Johnny Hodges. The trumpet melody emphasizes blue notes. As with the clarinet in the previous section, this solo seems to be composed, not improvised. The saxophone answers are "freer" and probably at least partially improvised.

Section C2—12-bar blues in E♭ major

2:06 Johnny Hodges extends his answering functions from the previous section into a solo, as the mood returns to E♭ major. It seems likely that this solo is at least partially improvised. The return to the parallel major key also serves as a bridge to C minor, the relative minor of E♭ major, in the next section.

Transition—4 bars in C minor

2:31 The introduction is reprised as a transition.

Section A reprise—8 bars in C minor, repeated

2:39 Section A returns with the clarinet trio, answered by trumpeter Whetsol.

2:56 Repeat.

Section B reprise—8 bars in C minor

3:12 The section B reprise has the clarinet trio an octave lower than it was in Section B previously. Whetsol continues to answer the clarinets, then adds a short cadenza on the final chord.

The overall form of "The Mooche" can be summarized by the following schema:

A B	C1	D1 D2	C2	A B
C minor	E♭ major	E♭ minor	E♭ major	C minor
8-bar units	12-bar blues	12-bar blues	12-bar blues	8-bar units

"The Mooche" has a kind of "arch form," a symmetrical structure that builds to the middle (the D1 D2 E♭ minor blues), then reverses to end with the beginning. Very little of this arrangement features solo improvisation; rather, the formal sections engage the players in a series of calls-and-responses between either the brass or reed section and the soloist, or soloist and soloist. In Chapter 5 we shall examine another Ellington arch form with "Sepia Panorama."

Questions and Topics for Discussion

1. How did the center of jazz shift from Chicago to New York in the later 1920s?

2. How did the Harlem Renaissance contribute to the growing sense of black history and accomplishments?

3. In what ways can stride piano be considered a jazz style growing out of ragtime? Who were the best-known stride pianists of the 1920s?

4. What leaders and arrangers contributed to the foundations of big-band style in the 1920s? What were some of the stylistic features of 1920s big-band writing?

5. Describe Duke Ellington's early career. What were some of the characteristics of Ellington's music that distinguished his works from those of the other big bands?

Key Terms

Back-beat (change-step)

Harlem Renaissance

Piano rolls

Player piano

Rent party

Riff

Stock arrangement (stock)

Stride piano

Suite

THERE IS NO DEPRESSION IN HEAVEN—IT'S ON EARTH!
RESPECTFULLY DEDICATED TO GREATER AMERICA, AND THE NATIONS OF THE WORLD.
C. A. MULLINER, THE KING OF THE SHEET MUSIC BUSINESS, HAS-UP-TO-HIS-FORTIETH ANNIVERSARY, PUBLISHED OVER FORTY SONGS.

THE BIGGEST HIT
EVER PUBLISHED
IN
AMERICA!
Every Home Should Have a Copy of this Great Song.

THE CAUSE OF THE GREAT
DEPRESSION IN THE TIMES

Words and Music
-BY-
C. A. MULLINER

50¢

THE MUSIC MAN.

PUBLISHED BY THE
C. A. MULLINER MUSIC PUB. CO.,
WILLIAMSPORT, PA.

In 1929 the U.S. stock market crashed and ushered in the Great Depression. Farmers lost their land, businesses failed, and 25 percent of men were out of work. This song, published in 1932, was not "the biggest hit ever published in America," perhaps because of the lyrics, which although accurate, didn't really sing: "Now what's the cause of all this rage, Lack of confidence at this stage; You would sell but we can't buy, wages were low and goods were high."

THE SWING ERA

FROM ROUGHLY 1935 TO 1945, "swing" dominated the popular music of the United States, the only time that any type of jazz achieved such mainstream success. Adoring fans idolized the top players and made the most successful bandleaders rich. The big-band era had arrived.

This chapter presents the **big bands** in the context of their time. After examining the growth of the territory bands, we shall turn to three of the most influential big bands: the Count Basie Orchestra from Kansas City and the Benny Goodman and Duke Ellington bands from New York. Although Goodman achieved the greatest mainstream success, Basie and Ellington contributed key elements to the big-band style and enjoyed long and influential careers.

A **territory band** played and toured a region around a major city that served as a home base.

Overview: A Decade of Swing

Swing music was a phenomenon. Between 1935 and 1945 it became the popular music of a generation. Speaking for the generation who came to adolescence between the beginning of the Great Depression and the end of World War II, James Lincoln Collier remembers the following:

> Swing was theirs alone. Dancing to swing was central to their courtship style. Young people danced—at first the fox-trot, then the so-called jitterbug dances which arose in the mid- to late-1930s—in huge, often elaborate dance palaces, in hotel restaurants and ballrooms, in high school gyms and, perhaps most of all, in living rooms to swing music from radios and record players. By means of the new

"portable" radios their music went with them everywhere: on woodland picnics, to beaches, summer houses, skating ponds, big city parks. These people not only danced to swing, they ate to it, drank to it, necked to it, talked to it, and frequently just listened to it. It was everywhere.[1]

As Ivie Anderson sang in Duke Ellington's band, "It Don't Mean a Thing (If It Ain't Got That Swing)." In the early 1930s when the song was released, however, *swing* was only an insider's term. Duke Ellington even had to explain in 1933 that his orchestra and a few others "exploited a style known as 'swing' which is Harlem for rhythm."[2] Within a few years, though, the term—and the music—dominated popular culture.

Swing is the generic term used for the jazz and much of the popular music of the mid-1930s through the mid-1940s.

As the 1930s progressed, more people had access to the music. Radios, increasingly more affordable, broadcast the big bands from ballrooms and hotels in the major cities. In 1930 only one-third of U.S. households had radios; by 1935 two-thirds of all homes had them. Similarly, the number of jukeboxes jumped from 25,000

This cover of Jolly Time Popcorn sheet music—written for a 1930 radio commercial—offered a comforting image of the simple life and an American variation on the familiar formula for true contentment: "a jug of wine, a loaf of bread, and thou." The popcorn came in two varieties, with hulls and without.

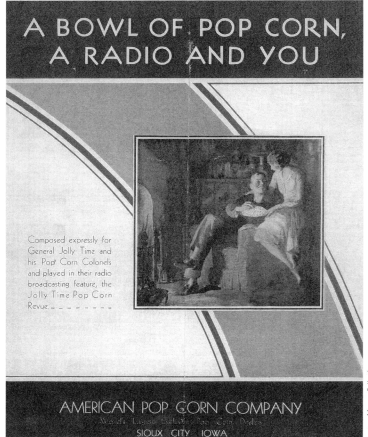

in 1933 to 300,000 in 1939. The dramatic growth of the record and radio industries changed popular music forever. No longer did people have to sing or play an instrument in order to enjoy music whenever they wished. Furthermore, musical success came from the numbers of records sold, not just prestigious live engagements.

It is impossible to sort out all the reasons why both white and black audiences demanded to hear, more than any other style, the hot jazz music of the 1920s pioneered by black bands. At the beginning of the 1930s, Duke Ellington and Fletcher Henderson, with their enlarged bands, were becoming the primary interpreters of swing music; many of the white bands, such as the Guy Lombardo band, played in a sentimental, sweet style. We should not carry this divided view of white and black bands too far, though. The repertory of the black bands was never exclusively hot jazz: Some of their arrangements qualified as sweet music, and Ellington's Cotton Club revues and Jimmie Lunceford's shows always included novelty and show numbers. By the same token, some white bands of the early 1930s used elements of jazz: In particular, the Casa Loma Orchestra, popular on college campuses, mixed

Courtesy Morgan Collection

Fletcher Henderson (CD 1, Track 10), pictured on the cover of this sheet music, created memorable arrangements for Benny Goodman and helped spur his popularity.

Paul Whiteman and his band, who had appeared in the 1930 Universal film *King of Jazz,* featured another dance fad called "Crazy Walk" in 1933; it did not endure.

raucous up-tempo works with sentimental waltzes. Thus, while the black bands featured more hot music than the white bands did, all the bands featured wide variety in their repertories—it was necessary in order to survive.

By the middle of the decade, Benny Goodman became known as the "King of Swing" after rising to dizzying heights of success playing many of Fletcher Henderson's arrangements. Goodman's success was contagious. By the end of the 1930s, there were more than 200 name bands, each with star soloists. Often the prominent soloists, having begun their careers in other bands, went on to lead their own groups. Clarinetist Goodman, trumpeters Harry James and Bunny Berrigan, trombonists Jack Teagarden and Tommy Dorsey, drummer Gene Krupa, and pianists Duke Ellington and Count Basie all formed their own bands, and each had a distinctive sound:

> You could hear all types of swing bands: the hard-driving swing of Benny Goodman, the relaxed swing of Jimmie Lunceford, the forceful dixieland of Bob Crosby, the simple, riff-filled swing of Count Basie, the highly developed swing of Duke Ellington, and the very commercial swing of Glenn Miller.[3]

When we listen today to the music that the swing bands played in their heyday, we would not consider much of it to be jazz. Continuing a trend from the 1920s, bands often avoided outright improvisation. Some bands worked out the solo (or improvisational) sections in advance and played them identically night after night—often because listeners expected the same improvisations they heard on the recordings. Many of the bands continued to churn out sentimental ballads along with up-tempo swing. And almost all of the bands had singers—invariably called "girl" singers and "boy" singers, whatever their age—and vocal music constituted a sizeable portion of any band's song list. Many of the singers who later became famous on their own began their careers singing with swing bands: for example, Frank Sinatra got his start with the bands of Harry James and Tommy Dorsey, Peggy Lee with Benny Goodman.

The swing boom continued unabated through the early 1940s but began to decline during World War II. Gasoline rationing and the shortage of tires made trips difficult to schedule or prohibitively expensive for bands that needed to travel extensively for live performances. Many of the singers who began with the bands gained more success on their own. The decline of nightlife made it more expensive to spotlight the bands. At the end of 1946, eight of the most famous groups disbanded either temporarily or permanently, including those of Benny Goodman, Jack Teagarden, Harry James, Woody Herman, Tommy Dorsey, and Benny Carter. The swing boom thus came to an end.

Beyond the societal upheavals that hastened the end of the swing era, swing itself was largely exhausted as a jazz style—the public wanted something new. While it lasted, swing defined a golden age of jazz, a time when great musicians and first-rate bands produced outstanding music and brought jazz its greatest popular acclaim.

The Big Band in the Swing Era

INSTRUMENTATION, TECHNIQUE, AND ARRANGEMENT

The dance orchestra and large jazz ensemble became all but synonymous during the swing era. The lindy hop—also called the jitterbug—was a frenetic and virtuosic dance that required an up-tempo, hot jazz sound. As discussed in Chapter 4, the big band evolved for the most part from the dance orchestra, but during the 1920s the hot rhythm and improvisation of the Dixieland jazz players gradually transformed these orchestras. We have seen how bandleader Fletcher Henderson and his talented arranger, Don Redman, began to develop the big-band style. Other popular bands, such as the relatively mainstream Jean Goldkette and Paul Whiteman orchestras, incorporated jazz improvisation and spread the influence of large bands. These groups, along with the band of Art Hickman, spurred the development of the big band into an ensemble using four instrumental divisions. The four divisions or "sections" of instruments in a typical big band are

A **section** of a big band is a group of related instruments; three trumpets and three trombones might form the brass section.

▶ Trumpets (listen to Tracks 12–15 of the Audio Primer CD for an example)

▶ Trombones (with trumpets and trombones grouped together as the "brass") (Tracks 22–25 of the Audio Primer CD)

Big-Band Terms

A band's **library** or **book** is its collection of arrangements or pieces. These are usually songs but may also include larger-scale works. A library is necessary for big bands, but smaller groups may also have one.

Musicians with good **intonation** are said to be playing "in tune." That is, the players know how to make small adjustments in the pitch of their instruments as they play, so that they match the pitches of the other players in the section.

Balance refers to the ability of a section to blend. In a well-balanced section, none of the players will be too soft or too loud relative to the others.

An often-heard term for each part in a section is **chair,** as in first trumpet chair, first trombone chair, and so on.

The player who usually takes the melody or top part in a section is called the **lead player** of the section. That is, the lead player occupies the first chair of the section. Within a given section, the lead player will usually be slightly louder than the other players in a correct balance.

A band depends in particular on the lead chair or first trumpet player of the trumpet section. The **lead trumpet** must be a dominating player, capable of precision, power, and control of the high register.

The **jazz chair** of a section may be a player hired especially for improvisational fluency. For example, Bix Beiderbecke occupied the jazz trumpet chair in the Paul Whiteman band, as did Bubber Miley in the Ellington band.

A player who is not a lead player or featured soloist is usually called a **sideman.**

▶ Woodwinds, usually called "reeds" (saxophones and related instruments) (Tracks 16–21 of the Audio Primer CD)

▶ The rhythm section, frequently consisting of piano, bass, drums, and guitar (Tracks 26–43 of the Audio Primer CD)

The demands on the musicians playing in a big band differed significantly from those placed on small-group players. The extensive "library" or "book" of arrangements that all big bands developed required that the musicians be skilled in reading parts. Playing with a big-band section required musicians to blend with similar instruments, that is, to play together with precision and constant attention to intonation and balance. (See the box "Big-Band Terms.")

Big-band arrangements formed the basis of the swing-era repertory. The most creative arrangers of the period—including Don Redman, Duke Ellington, Fletcher Henderson, Eddie Sauter, Sy Oliver, and Benny Carter—successfully and creatively balanced written ensemble sections with sections for improvised solos that showed off the star players in the bands. These arrangers skillfully used the band's various resources, for example, by setting off the brass section from the reed section or writing a brass or reed accompaniment behind the soloist.

One characteristic technique that arrangers used involved the antiphonal alternation of different sections of the band. An example of this occurs in Fletcher Henderson's celebrated 1935 arrangement of Jelly Roll Morton's "King Porter Stomp" (see Music Example 5-1).[4] Notice how the arranger gives the figure to the brass in the pickup and measures 2 and 4, and to the reeds in measures 1, 3, and 5. This

Antiphony is the trading of melodic figures between two different sections of the band; it is a more formal musical term for **call-and-response** (see Chapter 1). Antiphony implies an equal division of the musical forces rather than an answering response to a leading call. Listen to Track 47 of the Audio Primer CD: The trumpet and saxophone, by trading twos, engage in a form of antiphony.

typical passing back and forth of the figure between brass and reeds continues the use of the call-and-response patterns we first saw applied to vocal music. Henderson's "Down South Camp Meeting" also illustrates antiphony (see the Listening Guide).

Music Example 5-1
From the Fletcher Henderson arrangement of "King Porter Stomp."

Henderson created an especially fine composition and arrangement in "Down South Camp Meeting," which, like "King Porter Stomp," later became a huge hit for Benny Goodman.

"Down South Camp Meeting"
CD **1** Track **10**

Fletcher Henderson and His Orchestra: "Down South Camp Meeting" (Henderson).
Decca 213. New York, September 12, 1934. Fletcher Henderson, arrangement, piano, leader;
Henry Allen, Irving Randolph, Russell Smith, trumpets; Keg Johnson, Claude Jones, trombones;
Buster Bailey, clarinet; Hilton Jefferson, Russell Procope, clarinet, alto saxophone; Ben Webster,
tenor saxophone; Lawrence Lucie, guitar; Elmer James, bass; Walter Johnson, drums.

In "Down South Camp Meeting," which predates the more famous versions by Goodman, we can hear many of the swing-style techniques discussed in this chapter. Note that there is little solo improvisation in the arrangement, only one twenty-four–bar solo by trumpeter Henry Allen. The focus instead is on the composition and arrangement.

Introduction—4 bars

0:00   Count this piece as either a fast four beats to the bar or a moderate two beats to the bar. The introduction features a syncopated figure played by the entire ensemble; the prevailing harmony is G7 (extended to the 13th), which as a dominant sets up section A in C major.

A section—8 bars as 4 + 4 in C major

0:05   The saxophone section has the syncopated melody, sustained notes that are attacked just before the beat. We can hear in the lead saxophone that the second-to-last note of each four-bar unit is a blue third, which contributes a hot, blues-tinged quality typical of up-tempo swing pieces. In the fourth bar of each four-bar unit, the brass answer antiphonally.

B section—8 bars as 4 + 4 in A minor

0:14   In the contrasting B section, brass and saxophones reverse roles: The brass take the lead, while the saxophones answer. The downbeat note of the lead trumpet in each four-bar unit is the blue fifth, E♭, of A minor. Thus, the blue third (E♭) of C major in the A section is reinterpreted as the blue fifth (E♭) of A minor in the B section. The relative minor, A minor, offers a tonal contrast to C major.

A section—8 bars as 4 + 4

0:23   The A section returns with minor embellishments to the principal melody.

ABA trumpet solo as 8 + 8 + 8

0:32   The ABA framework just presented serves as a background for a Henry Allen trumpet solo. The saxophones sustain chords as an accompaniment.

0:42   Allen alludes to the original melodic idea of the B section in the B section of his solo.

0:52   Return to A section of the solo.

Transition—8 bars

1:01   In this transitional and modulating section, hear the antiphonal saxophone and trumpet solos. Saxophones and trombones accompany with sustained chords, which crescendo as they are held. The harmonic progression features a circle of fifths of dominant chords: C7, F7, B♭7, and E♭7, each held for two bars. The chord progression serves to set up A♭ major for the following section.

C section—CCDC as 8 + 8 + 4 + 8

1:10   The C section is analogous to the trio in the older ragtime-, march-influenced jazz of the 1920s. Here, though, the key is not the subdominant, but the distant key of A♭ major, or ♭VI relative to the opening key of C major. The saxophones have the melody for the most part. The C section (first eight bars) features a swinging tune with an E♭7 (V7) chord for the first four bars resolving to an A♭ (I) chord for the second four bars. We can hear the use of C♭, or the blue third of A♭ major as a key part of the tune.

1:29   The bridge of the C section, D, is an irregular four bars and is syncopated to provide a contrast to the relative rhythmic regularity of the C section's main theme, which contains many on-the-beat and accented quarter notes.

1:33   The return of the C section's main theme is modified in order to create a more conclusive cadence.

C section repeated—CCDC as 8 + 8 + 4 + 8

1:43   The brass take the melody for the first two C sections. There are some modifications and embellishments to the C theme, which we first heard in the saxophones.

2:02   The saxophones take the bridging D theme, which is also modified from its first presentation. These small changes indicate the care Henderson took to enhance the effectiveness of the arrangement.

2:06   Return to C section.

Transition—4 bars

2:15   An antiphonal transitional section on an A♭7 chord sets up the following section, a second "trio" in D♭ major. Note the call-and-response between the brass and reeds (with lead clarinet).

E section—8 bars, played 4 times

2:19   A new timbre complements a new melody and key: The melody is in the saxophones, but with a clarinet lead in a fairly low register. The first note of the lead clarinet is F♭, the blue third of D♭ major. Thus, Henderson continues the idea of featuring blue notes as key elements of his themes.

     The section is played four times.

2:39 and **2:48**   The third and fourth times, the reeds play an octave higher.

     The brass answer the short phrases in the reeds antiphonally.

Tag—1 bar

2:56   A short tag consisting of rising tutti chords—syncopated off the beat—extends the E section by a bar.

One of the many reasons why big bands enjoyed such popularity was their focus on the hit songs of the day. The bands developed a symbiotic relationship with the publishers of Tin Pan Alley and would vie to be the first to perform and record the best new songs. Similarly, the publishers would try to interest the most popular bands in their latest efforts. The result was a steady stream of hit songs that the public enjoyed and their favorite bands personalized. For an extremely popular song, different groups would compete with arrangements that varied from quite similar to distinctive.

During the course of writing a chart, arrangers often took liberties with the melodic and rhythmic structure of the original song and reworked it into swing style. Frequently they syncopated melodies to give them the rhythmic character of an improvised jazz solo. This swing-style melody made the transitions from written sections to improvised-solo sections more seamless.

Territory bands and the groups in and around Kansas City favored the head arrangement (first discussed in Chapter 1). Fashioned by ear during rehearsal or performance, band members worked out their own parts or suggested parts to each other. These arrangements were often simple and riff-oriented, lacking the variety of textures available to arrangers working with printed scores.

THE CHANGING ROLE OF THE RHYTHM SECTION

The rhythm section largely generated the hard-driving swing that propelled the ensemble and improvised sections of the bands. In the big-band era, expectations of the rhythm section—bass, drums, piano, and guitar—changed. Responding to innovations in the design of instruments and changes in musical taste, these instruments performed differently during the swing era than before. During the 1920s either the tuba or the string bass provided the rhythmic underpinning for the band, but the bass gradually superseded the tuba. In addition, the bass or tuba player was expected to play either on beats 1 and 3 or on all four beats of the measure. By the mid- to late-1930s, however, the bass player often played consistently on all four beats, creating the walking bass sound. The four-beat walking bass then freed the pianist from a timekeeping role. Pianists could play fewer notes and were able to accompany soloists by playing syncopated chordal figures.

The drummer's role changed considerably after the hi-hat became a part of the drummer's set. Instead of keeping the pulse in the bass drum, swing drummers such as Walter Johnson of Fletcher Henderson's band and Jo Jones of Count Basie's band used the hi-hat to create a more subtle propulsion that could drive an entire big band. The hi-hat, introduced in 1927, consisted of two face-to-face cymbals that the drummer controlled with a foot pedal. The pedal closed the cymbals with a "chick" sound. (Listen to Track 31 of the 🎧 Audio Primer CD to hear this sound; Track 32 shows a swing beat played on the hi-hat.) Drummers learned to keep the pulse on the hi-hat. Often the drummer would close the pedal on beats 2 and 4, slightly accenting these beats in relation to the first and third beats. In addition, by the mid- to late-1930s, many drummers used the bass drum on all four beats, as exemplified by Gene Krupa's work with Benny Goodman, especially on what Goodman called his up-tempo "killer-diller" numbers.

By the end of the twenties, the guitar gradually replaced the banjo in the rhythm section. Eddie Lang (1902–1933) was an important player who helped create this change. A Philadelphia-born guitarist, he contributed to the important Beiderbecke-Trumbauer recordings and recorded with Red Nichols, Jean Goldkette, and Paul Whiteman, as well as with violinist Joe Venuti. Advances in recording technology and the use of the arched-top guitar allowed the instrument to be audible in recordings and performances. With his single-line solos, Lang helped define guitar as a solo instrument. He used rich harmonies in accompaniments, often by alternating single notes with chords.

As the swing era evolved, guitarists began to play four chords to the measure, giving a slight accent to the second and fourth beats. The introduction in 1936 of the electric guitar allowed the guitarist to be heard in a large group. The electric guitar also enabled the performer to take on an improvisational role in a large ensemble rather than merely providing accompaniment. (The various sounds of the acoustic guitar and electric guitar can be heard on Tracks 36–42 of the 🎧 Audio Primer CD.)

In performing a **walking bass,** the bassist articulates all four beats in a 4/4 bar. The bass lines often follow simple scale patterns, avoiding too many disruptive leaps between notes. The walking bass is common in jazz, heard in all styles since becoming firmly established during the swing era. Listen to Track 43 of the 🎧 Audio Primer CD to hear a walking bass.

Territory Bands

The rise of swing took place gradually over time and space. While New York bands of the late 1920s and early 1930s were developing the swing style, many of the midwestern and southwestern territory bands were contributing to its evolution as well. From St. Louis to Denver, between Texas and Nebraska, in towns such as Omaha, Oklahoma City, and Salina, territory bands abounded. Centering themselves on a regional capital, the territory bands toured their regions and played dance halls and theaters for one-night or multiweek engagements. Many of the bands covered a lot of territory:

> Jumps of 800 or 1,000 miles between engagements were not uncommon, and, among the less affluent orchestras, these trips were made by passenger car, with perhaps a truck carrying the instruments and arrangements, if any. Accounts of panic trips, with twelve musicians crammed into a single automobile, and a man or two hanging onto the running board or fender, are encountered in interviews dealing with the Depression years.[5]

Many of the territory-band members were not music readers. Players and soloists relied on head arrangements and their own improvisational skills. The territory bands had rivalries, some friendly and some not, and legendary "battles of the bands" in the dance halls show a fierce competitive spirit that helped improve the bands' sounds. Importantly, many of the significant players of the swing era—Coleman Hawkins, Ben Webster, Herschel Evans, Lester Young, Buster Smith, and Count Basie—received their earliest training in these bands.

Alfonso Trent, Terence T. Holder and His Clouds of Joy, and Troy Floyd were three of the leading Texas-based territory bands. Floyd's orchestra, which consisted of two trumpets, one trombone, three saxophones, and a rhythm section of banjo, piano, and drums, made some rare recordings in 1928 and 1929. Two of them,

Territory bands proliferated as they responded to local popular demand generated by radio. Among them were Art Landry and His Call of the North Orchestra, Gage Brewer's Versatile Radio Orchestra— which "delighted thousands during the International Petroleum Exposition at Tulsa in 1936"—and Whitey Kaufman's Original Pennsylvania Serenaders.

"Dreamland Blues" and "Shadowland Blues," were head arrangements and revealed the popularity of blues in Texas. The George Morrison Orchestra played most of the dance hall engagements in Denver, Colorado. Among Morrison's sidemen were several players who would later become important bandleaders themselves, including Andy Kirk and Jimmie Lunceford.

THE ORIGINAL BLUE DEVILS

In Oklahoma City, Walter Page's Original Blue Devils emerged in 1925 and within the next five years became one of the most respected territory bands. The group relentlessly recruited many of the best players; at different times Page's bands featured tenor saxophonist Lester Young, bassist Walter Page, trumpeter Hot Lips Page, trombonist/guitarist Eddie Durham, pianist Bill (Count) Basie, and vocalist Jimmy Rushing. In the battles of the bands, Page's group competed fiercely. Rival bandleader Jesse Stone described an upset he received at the hands of the Blue Devils:

> The biggest upset we ever had in our life . . . happened to be in Sioux City, Iowa. . . . and it was a battle of bands between Page and Jesse Stone. We got up on the stand first because we were considered like a house band there. We played there regularly. Well, we started out with some of our light things, little ballads. And the guys [the Blue Devils] hit right off the reel, *wham*, and they didn't let up all night long. They had a tough band.
>
> They were just sharper, cleaner, more powerful, and they had more material, which was an upset to us because we had five arrangers, including myself. How could anybody have more material than we had? We had a book about that thick, you know, all arrangements. These guys came in with *three* books. Three books the same thickness.[6]

Unlike many regional bands, Walter Page's Blue Devils were fully developed musicians who could read scores. They also competed with the Bennie Moten band out of Kansas City. When the Blue Devils outplayed Moten's band, Moten solved the problem by hiring the star players of the Blue Devils. Basie, Jimmy Rushing, and several others joined the more lucrative Moten band. Following a disastrous tour that left them stranded in West Virginia, the rest of the Blue Devils then joined Moten in Kansas City, forming the nucleus of what would later become the Count Basie Band. But the Blue Devils' relocation into Kansas City was part of a larger trend. During the Great Depression, dance jobs for the territory bands dwindled, and many of the players made their way to Kansas City.

KANSAS CITY

As William Saunders recalled, in discussing the Kansas City scene in the late 1920s:

> We listened. We didn't have radios or television to interrupt us. . . . That developed the Kansas City style because you would hear in a cluster and the style just developed between your ideas coming in here from Texas and Oklahoma and possibly Nebraska and Colorado, and there's a fusion of all those ideas together, and over a period of years and a period of sessions it became obvious as the Kansas City style.[7]

In all the Midwest, only Kansas City seemed immune to the Depression. Music flourished. In 1935 there were more than three hundred Kansas City clubs with live music. Jam sessions took place nightly; musicians spoke of leaving a session and returning several hours later to find the band still jamming on the same tune. Like the gunfighters of the old West—or stride pianists at the rent parties of New York— the local Kansas City musicians issued challenges to well-known players, such as Coleman Hawkins and Cootie Williams, who were passing through town. According to legend, musical battles sometimes lasted twelve hours. Listeners could go to the Sunset Club and hear blues singer Big Joe Turner and pianist Pete Johnson, Count Basie's band at the Reno Club, and the arrangements of pianist Mary Lou Williams with Andy Kirk's Twelve Clouds of Joy.

In part, corruption in city government protected Kansas City from the Depression. Between 1926 and 1939, city alderman Tom Pendergast and his machine dominated the city; Pendergast made certain that gambling, liquor, and prostitution were readily available. Although Pendergast had no interest in music himself, his practices allowed nightlife and live music to flourish. In this way, Kansas City maintained a relative affluence while the rest of the country suffered the ravages of the Depression.

Kansas City bands had several features that set them apart from the bands of the urban Northeast. In contrast to the complex arrangements of the eastern bands, Kansas City bands tended to feature head arrangements. The twelve-bar blues was a staple of their repertory. Kansas City players developed riff compositions based on simple melodic ideas, and horn players often spontaneously composed riffs to play behind other soloists.

One Kansas City band that achieved national recognition was Andy Kirk's Twelve Clouds of Joy. Like most of the bands of the swing era, they played both hot and sweet jazz. Originally from Dallas, the band migrated to Kansas City after dismissing its prior leader, Terrence Holder, in 1928. Led by Kirk, who played bass saxophone and tuba, the band featured the pianist Mary Lou Williams, an accomplished musician who created many of the arrangements for the band. The Clouds of Joy first recorded in 1929 but scored a string of hits for the Decca label between 1936 and 1945, including "Until the Real Thing Comes Along."

© Bettmann/CORBIS

MARY LOU WILLIAMS AND THE CLOUDS OF JOY

Mary Lou Williams (1910–1981) was a remarkably fine pianist and composer, a superb musician who emerged from the swing era with a unique career. She remains not only one of the most important women in jazz history, but one of the very few women of her time able to develop a notable career in jazz at all. Prominent as both a pianist and an arranger-composer, she was the person primarily responsible for the sound of the Andy Kirk band and its hits in the 1930s. Although she left the band in 1942, she continued to provide excellent arrangements for the major band leaders of the era: Duke Ellington, Benny Goodman, Earl Hines, and Tommy Dorsey.

The remarkable career of pianist, composer, and arranger Mary Lou Williams (CD 1, Track 11) spanned five decades.

In addition to creating musical arrangements, Williams built a strong career in composition. The New York Philharmonic performed part of her *Zodiac Suite* in 1946. Though her work reflects mostly the late 1920s and the swing era, Williams befriended many of the jazz modernists in the 1940s and absorbed aspects of their style. As such she continued to develop as both a composer and a pianist, eventually writing bebop-style arrangements for the Dizzy Gillespie band. In the 1950s, her strong religious interests led her to compose many sacred works. She remained active through the 1970s, eventually teaching at Duke University.

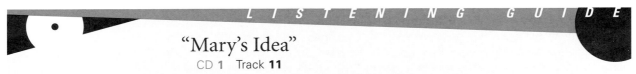

L I S T E N I N G   G U I D E

"Mary's Idea"
CD **1** Track **11**

Andy Kirk and His Twelve Clouds of Joy: "Mary's Idea" (Williams). Decca 2326. New York, December 6, 1938. Andy Kirk, director; Harry Lawson, Clarence Trice, Earl Thomson, trumpets; Ted Donnelly, Henry Wells, trombone; John Harrington, clarinet, alto and baritone saxophones; John Williams, alto and baritone saxophones; Earl Miller, alto saxophone; Dick Wilson, tenor saxophone; Mary Lou Williams, arrangement, piano; Ted Robinson, guitar; Booker Collins, bass; Ben Thigpen, drums.

"Mary's Idea" is just one of the many superb charts Mary Lou Williams wrote for the Andy Kirk band. In them, she deftly combines a solid understanding of swing-era conventions with sufficient experimental curiosity to produce works of uncommon interest and effectiveness.

Introduction—4 bars

0:00 The four-bar introduction consists of a vamping figure in the saxophones, doubled by the bass and piano. The vamping figure is atypically chromatic, incorporating the half steps surrounding the fifth scale degree, B♭ (as can be seen in the music example below). The drummer provides a clear example of a swing beat on the hi-hat cymbals; you can hear the foot pedal closing the cymbals on the second and fourth beats of each bar.

A section—8 bars, repeated

0:06 The brass enter with a theme in counterpoint to the saxophone vamp. Note how well the different sections combine in counterpoint:

The trumpet melody is almost entirely off the beat, while the saxophone vamp mixes on- and off-beat notes.

0:15 The saxophones answer the brass in the last two bars of the A section (first time).

B section—Bridge, 8 bars

0:29 The saxophones take over the lead for the first four bars of the bridge.

0:35 The last four bars are a trombone solo, which provides further textural contrast and variety.

A section—8 bars

0:41 The A section returns with brass lead and saxophone vamp. The music is modified in both brass and reeds to create a more definitive cadence.

0:50 The lead trumpet, in particular, moves down to the tonic through the blue third, G♭.

AA—16 bars as 8 + 8, trumpet solo

0:51 An improvised trumpet solo over the A-section material.

1:01 The saxophones answer at the end of the first eight bars.

1:13 The entire band answers at the end of the second eight bars.

BA—16 bars as 8 + 8, piano solo

1:15 Williams takes over the solo at the B-section bridge and continues on to the final A section. Her spare melodic style contrasts the busy virtuosity we heard in the stride stylists. Nevertheless, you can detect a remnant of the stride left hand, which occasionally follows the march-bass pattern. Her right-hand melody is elegant, with occasional blues licks fitted in.

1:32 She finishes her solo with runs of syncopated virtuosity.

1:36 In the last two bars of the section, the saxophones usher in the clarinet solo.

C section—14 bars as 8 + 6, clarinet solo

1:38 The clarinet solos over a new harmonic progression. The combination of muted brass and clarinet is quite refined and attractive. The final two bars are elided into a break that develops into an interlude.

Interlude—5 bars

1:59 The complex syncopation of the interlude imposes a 3/4 rhythmic pattern on the 4/4 bars. The section ultimately can be measured as five 4/4 bars, but this is only clear after the next section, a climax, has begun. This is one of Williams's fine experimental twists.

AA—16 bars as 8 + 8, climactic development

2:06 The climax features extensive syncopation over the final four bars of the eight-bar unit. There is again the implication of a 3/4 pattern imposed on the 4/4 meter. On the whole, the section develops material from the opening A section.

2:18 These eight bars, a wonderful and experimental development of the opening idea, repeat.

B section—8 bars

2:29 A trombone solo for the first four bars of the B section provides a satisfying release from the dislocating syncopation of the preceding section.

2:35 The whole band enters for the second half in a crescendo leading to the last A section statement.

A section—6 bars

2:40 A reprise of the A section as first heard. The "missing" two bars that would complete an eight-bar section are elided into the coda to become its beginning.

Coda—8 bars

2:49 The opening vamp begins the coda and continues for four bars.

2:55 The last four bars transform the opening material into a final cadence.

The young Count Basie (CD 1, Track 12) on a one-cent publicity postcard from Music Corporation of America.

Count Basie

By 1932 Moten's band included many of the finest players in Kansas City. Bennie Moten was already well established. Ten years earlier, he had with his six-piece group recorded several blues numbers, including "Elephant's Wobble" and "Crawdad Blues." The size of the band grew along with its national reputation, and the group's final recording session of 1932 featured three trumpets, two trombones, three saxophones, and four rhythm section players. An accomplished pianist himself, Moten hired Bill Basie as a second pianist. Basie and trombonist/guitarist Eddie Durham contributed arrangements, such as "Toby," "Moten Swing," and "Prince of Wails," which featured fine solos by Ben Webster, Lips Page, and Bill Basie. "Prince of Wails" is an especially interesting virtuoso number that shows off Basie's northeastern roots in stride piano. Moten's death in 1935 left one of the most important bands in Kansas City without a leader, and the job fell to Bill Basie.

Basie's band gained a national reputation as an outfit capable of playing swing with equal measures of drive and relaxation. Additionally, it was remarkably long-lived; Basie managed to keep his group together until his death in 1984, and it continued to perform under different leaders afterward. Led by Basie's nearly imperceptible cues and nods at the piano, the band played with incredible rhythmic drive and exuberance. The band's book was based on blues and riff compositions— a legacy of their origin as a territory band. Basie became famous for his understated solos, a few well-placed chords or a simple repeated lick that propelled the band. Like a finely calibrated machine, the band's infectious swing drove such compositions as "Jumpin' at the Woodside" and Basie's signature song, "One O'Clock Jump."

Basie was born in Red Bank, New Jersey, in 1904. He learned many of his piano skills by hearing Fats Waller play piano and organ in Harlem, and made his living touring the Theatre Owners Booking Association (TOBA), the largest black vaudeville circuit. In 1927, while touring with Gonzelle White, the show broke up and left Basie stranded in Kansas City. He remained in town and worked with the Blue Devils and Moten's band. After Moten's death, Basie's nine-piece Barons of Rhythm picked up Moten's engagement at the Reno Club and played for floor shows and dancing every night from nine until four or five the next morning.

The band's break came when record producer John Hammond heard the band broadcast from the Reno Club over an experimental shortwave radio station, W9XBY. Hammond went to Kansas City in 1936 and was overwhelmed. He later wrote:

> Basie became almost a religion with me and I started writing about the band in *Down Beat* and *Melody Maker*.... (M)y first night at the Reno in May, 1936, still stands out as the most exciting musical experience I can remember. The Basie band seemed to have all the virtues of a small combo, with inspired soloists, complete relaxation, plus the drive and dynamics of a disciplined large orchestra.[8]

Hammond convinced the Music Corporation of America (MCA), a major white booking agency, to sign the band that fall. The band expanded to thirteen players (five brass, four saxes, and four rhythm), making it the size of the popular Benny Goodman big band and allowing the group to play theaters and dance halls. The big band issued its first recordings for the Decca label in 1937.

Much of their appeal came from the exuberant drive of the rhythm section. The combination of Basie on piano, Walter Page on bass, Jo Jones on drums, and Freddie Green on guitar drove the band brilliantly, at all tempos and levels of volume and

The advent of radio spread the sounds of jazz around the country. This advertisement for the Philco radio appeared in 1936 on the back of *Etude Magazine*. Notice the prices—from $20 to $600.

energy. Though rooted in Harlem stride piano, Basie developed a freer, less cluttered, more up-to-date accompaniment style. Page's walking bass and Freddie Green's regular guitar strumming worked with Jo Jones's timekeeping on the hi-hat and stated all four beats to the measure. Pianist Teddy Wilson wrote:

> The Basie rhythm section was a completely new sound at the time. Musicians took a great deal of notice of it.... Jo Jones was playing with open cymbals, not choking them like other drummers, plus a very light bass drum and his particular use of the sock [hi-hat] cymbal.... [Walter Page] created quite a stir among the bass players with his use of the G string—the high string on the bass violin—in a 4/4 rhythm, playing very high notes with... sparkling crisp chime-like notes from Basie's piano.[9]

Unfettered by the more complicated arrangements of the urban Northeast bands, the band's top-flight soloists had ample freedom. Lester Young's light tenor sound provided a wonderfully cool pastel contrast to the red-hot swing of the band in recordings such as "Lester Leaps In" and "Roseland Shuffle." Herschel Evans provided a contrast to Young's airy sound. A veteran of the territory band of Troy Floyd and Bennie Moten, Evans's tenor style derived from Coleman Hawkins's brash and vibrato-laden sound. Young and Evans developed a friendly rivalry, and their contrasting styles play to excellent advantage in Basie's recording of "Swinging the Blues."

"Shoe Shine Boy"

CD **1**   Track **12**

Jones-Smith Incorporated: "Shoe Shine Boy" (Cahn-Chaplin). Vocalion 3441.
Chicago, November 9, 1936. Carl Smith, trumpet; Lester Young, tenor saxophone;
Count Basie, piano, leader; Walter Page, bass; Jo Jones, drums.

Basie's small-group ensemble recorded "Shoe Shine Boy" under the name Jones-Smith Incorporated because of record company agreements. It is one of the most famous examples of Kansas City small-group jazz in the swing era. We shall return to the performance in Chapter 6, where we discuss Lester Young's well-known saxophone solo in greater detail.

Introduction—8 bars, repeated

0:00   Basie developed a trademark of opening his tunes with a swing vamp of four or eight bars. Here the eight-bar idea, repeated, serves as an introduction to his own piano solo. Basie's Shoe Shine vamp is shown here.

Although the striding bass is evident in the left hand, it is not really an example of stride piano, because the right-hand figuration incorporates a light swing riff, which is not a characteristic of stride. This open, lighter sound is more typical of swing-era piano styles, which sometimes kept the striding left hand but featured airier right-hand playing. The sometimes-striding left hand became known as "swing bass."

0:07   Repeat.

AABA—Basie piano solo, 1 chorus

0:14   Basie presents the thematic structure of the piece, a thirty-two–bar structure, which is a close variant of the chord progression known as "rhythm changes." The lightness of Basie's touch and ideas is reminiscent of Mary Lou Williams's solo in "Mary's Idea." Jones enters with a swing beat on the hi-hat.

0:22   Basie's second A section states the main idea of the original melody, which is never given in its entirety in the performance.

0:29   B section.

0:35   The seventh bar of the bridge features a descending whole-tone run.

AABA, repeated—Lester Young tenor solo—2 choruses

0:44   Young's two-chorus tenor solo was one of the most famous of the swing era. He develops the solo using melodic formulas, which we shall examine in Chapter 6.

1:15   Second chorus.

AABA—Smith trumpet solo, 1 chorus

1:45   Trumpeter Carl Smith plays one chorus with his trumpet muted. This third consecutive improvised solo shows that the performance is not projecting a complex arrangement but instead is simulating a jam-session atmosphere with loose, freewheeling solos and ideas. Smith begins in the high register with a syncopated lick that emphasizes the blue third (A♭) and blue seventh (E♭) of the key of F.

1:53   The second time through the A section provides contrast by avoiding emphasis of these notes.

2:01– 2:03   The repeated high A quarter notes at the start of the B section bridge are echoed by the repeated C notes comprising most of his final A section. These repeated-note ideas are foreshadowed earlier in the solo.

AA—2-bar breaks

2:16   The band alternates two-bar solo breaks in this order: Basie piano, Young tenor saxophone, Smith trumpet, Basie piano, Young tenor, Smith trumpet, Basie piano, Young tenor. Note that because *three* players each take two bars, the music is unevenly distributed through the sixteen-bar AA. The use of alternating solo breaks here is called *trading twos.* More common than trading twos is *trading fours,* with each soloist getting four bars of improvisation. *Trading eights* is also sometimes heard. The technique of trading solos is often used to create climaxes in performance.

B section—drum solo

2:32   An eight-bar Jo Jones drum solo. Basie articulates the chord changes to provide a sense of the bridge harmony through the drum solo.

A section—whole ensemble

2:40   An exciting out-chorus with the whole ensemble improvising. Smith provides a lead riff reminiscent of the beginning of his solo; Young complements with a countermelody.

Coda—10 bars

2:47   To wrap up the performance, a coda features four two-bar breaks by (in order) Basie, Young, Jones, and Page, and then the whole ensemble in a two-bar cadence.

Jazz Performance Terms

Rhythm changes are the harmonies of the George and Ira Gershwin song "I Got Rhythm" (1930). (The final two-bar tag of the original song is omitted, so that a symmetrical thirty-two-bar AABA plan results.) The bridge in rhythm changes consists of two-bar harmonies following a circle-of-fifths pattern that returns to the tonic. For example, if rhythm changes are performed in B♭, then the harmonies of the eight-bar bridge are D7 (two bars), G7 (two bars), C7 (two bars), and F7 (two bars). The F7, as the dominant of the tonic B♭, leads back to the A section. Extremely popular since the 1930s, rhythm changes are still commonly used by jazz musicians for improvisation and composition. Listen to Track 10 of the Audio Primer CD for an example of rhythm changes.

Trading twos, trading fours, or **trading eights** are improvisational formats in jazz, common since the swing era. In trading fours, for example, each soloist improvises for four bars before the next soloist takes over for four bars. Any number of soloists may participate, but most typically two to four. Trading solos is often used to create climactic moments in performances. Listen to Track 47 of the Audio Primer CD to hear an example of trading twos.

A prime example of small-group swing style, "Shoe Shine Boy" (see Listening Guide) highlights some of the features that made the Basie band unique:

▶ Emphasis on up-tempo jazz and improvisation instead of sweet dance music

▶ Fine balance between ensemble tightness and uninhibited swinging solos

▶ First-rate personnel, including some of the finest improvisers of the day

▶ Relaxed, understated atmosphere that provides the soloists with the opportunity to develop ideas against a relatively free backdrop

The Basie band continued to record into the 1940s despite the loss of many of its key players. Herschel Evans died in 1939; Lester Young left Basie the following year to form his own group. Walter Page and Jo Jones, two of the mainstays of the rhythm section, also left. Nevertheless, the band continued to thrive and maintained strong soloists: tenor player Don Byas filled Lester Young's chair. Tenor player Illinois Jacquet, a former member of Lionel Hampton's band, and trombonist J. J. Johnson both joined the band in 1945. Although the band broke up temporarily in 1950, Basie reformed the group, and the band's subsequent arrangements were penned by many of the best arrangers in the business, such as Neal Hefti—known for "Li'l Darlin'" and "Girl Talk"—as well as Thad Jones, Benny Carter, and Quincy Jones.

For the remainder of his career, Basie continued to tour with his group—including visits to Europe and Japan—and record. One highly acclaimed piece is his live recording with Frank Sinatra at the Sands hotel in Las Vegas, in which Basie gives many of Sinatra's most familiar songs a hard-edged, brilliant swing without commercial compromises. Basie's health began to deteriorate in the 1970s when he suffered a heart attack, but he continued to perform. In the early 1980s, he began working with Albert Murray on his autobiography, *Good Morning Blues,* which was published in 1985. After Basie's death, his band continued to tour and perform under the leadership of Thad Jones, then later under Frank Foster.

Basie's legacy is undiminished. Having perhaps the most easily imitated piano style in jazz, his work continues to inspire. Ironically, the Basie style is so familiar that other pianists cannot appropriate it without sounding clichéd. For example, Basie-style performances sometimes include a signature ending in which the band breaks for three light chords in the upper register of the piano, a trademark not unlike the piano vamps that opened his arrangements in the 1930s.

Fans will always revere Basie's music for its joy, its swing, and its exemplary balance between freewheeling improvisation and classic arranging. As Basie himself put it at eighty years old, "The main thing for me is the music. That's what excites me. That's what keeps me going. The music and people having a good time listening to it. People dancing or just patting their feet."[10]

Benny Goodman—King of Swing

For many people, the name Benny Goodman is synonymous with swing. His record sales and performances helped usher in the swing craze of the 1930s; for more than a decade, the "King of Swing" enjoyed incredible heights of popularity. Members of his band became near cult figures. With his flashy playing and ever-present grin, Gene Krupa, Goodman's drummer, was a popular idol; trumpeter Harry James, who is featured in Goodman's recording of "Ridin' High," was one of the best-known

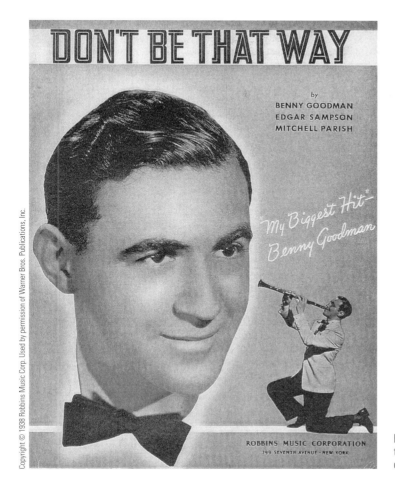

Benny Goodman (CD 1, Track 13), the "King of Swing," on the cover of one of his hit songs from 1938.

brass players of the period; pianist Teddy Wilson became one of the era's most emulated pianists; and Lionel Hampton helped to popularize the vibraphone as a jazz instrument.

Although Goodman's dance band was a big band, Goodman also developed the idea of a "band within a band" that featured a small group—first a trio, then a quartet—for performances that incorporated more improvisation than the big band did. Although interracial bands had recorded prior to Goodman's band, Goodman's small group—with black musicians Teddy Wilson and Lionel Hampton—was the first important interracial band to perform live concerts.

Goodman was born on May 30, 1909, to an extremely poor immigrant family in Chicago. Coming of age in the early 1920s, Goodman associated with a group of inner-city musicians from the gritty and mostly poor immigrant sections of the city. Of these players, Benny Goodman and Gene Krupa would become leading performers during the subsequent swing era. Other inner-city Chicago players included Muggsy Spanier, Art Hodes, Mezz Mezzrow, Floyd O'Brien, Volly de Faut, Joe Sullivan, Vic Berton, and Joe Marsala.

Goodman began learning the clarinet at age ten when he played with a boy's band at a local synagogue. Eventually he developed a prodigious technical foundation on the instrument while studying with Franz Shoepp, one of the preeminent classical clarinet teachers in the country at the time. Shoepp's students included not only performers with the Chicago Symphony but also jazz players Buster Bailey and Jimmie Noone. A child prodigy, Goodman gave his first public performance in 1921, imitating clarinetist Ted Lewis; soon after, he started playing dances with members of the Austin High Gang (see Chapter 3).

In 1925 Goodman joined Ben Pollack's band and in 1928 made his way to New York. He was not only an excellent sight-reader but also a strong, hot improviser, and he developed a busy career playing in studio recordings, radio broadcasts, and pit bands on Broadway. As a studio sideman, Goodman made nearly 500 recordings between 1929 and 1934. Although these were not all jazz recordings, he did cut sides with jazz players Red Nichols, Bix Beiderbecke, Jack Teagarden, and Fats Waller. He also played on two numbers, "Your Mother's Son-in-Law" and "Riffin' the Scotch," notable for being the first, if tentative, recordings of singer Billie Holiday.

In 1934 Goodman formed his own big band, which featured vocalist Helen Ward. The radio series "Let's Dance" hired them as the hot band, allowing Goodman to purchase top-flight arrangements. For example, Fletcher Henderson provided the charts for "Sometimes I'm Happy," Jelly Roll Morton's "King Porter Stomp," and "Down South Camp Meeting." Edgar Sampson, the arranger for Chick Webb's band, contributed "Don't Be That Way" and "Stompin' at the Savoy." While he was getting his big band off the ground, Goodman jammed with pianist Teddy Wilson at a private party; this led to a recording with Wilson and drummer Gene Krupa of four sides: "After You've Gone," "Body and Soul," "Who," and "Someday Sweetheart." In addition to the three highly individual musical personalities, the lack of a bass pegged the sound of the group. Wilson's swing-bass left hand coupled with Krupa's drumming provided the group's rhythmic backbone. The Goodman trio (and later quartet) recordings were among the key small-group recordings of the 1930s.

A hard-working musician and perfectionist, Goodman maintained exacting standards for the band. His extensive rehearsals required, as Goodman stated, "good musicians, a blend of tone, and uniform phrasing."[11] During his career, he earned a reputation as an unyielding taskmaster. He became infamous for what musicians called "the Goodman ray"—a hostile glare so unnerving that it drove some of his musicians to quit the band. Nevertheless, the rigorous musicianship he required of the band helped Goodman rise to the top of the competitive music business.

When the "Let's Dance" show ended in May 1935, Goodman took his band on the road heading west. The group's reception was decidedly lukewarm in many towns, particularly in Denver, Colorado, but the group had a triumphant performance at the Palomar Ballroom in Los Angeles on August 21. According to Goodman, the band began by playing their more conservative and commercial arrangements to a listless and unresponsive crowd. Once the group launched into their hot repertory, though, the audience came alive. As Goodman told it:

> To our complete amazement, half of the crowd stopped dancing and came surging around the stand. It was the first experience we had with that kind of attention, and it certainly was a kick. That was the moment that decided things for me. After travelling three thousand miles, we finally found people who were up on what we were trying to do, prepared to take our music the way we wanted to play it. That first big roar from the crowd was one of the sweetest sounds I ever heard in my life—and from that time on the night kept getting bigger and bigger, as we played about every good number in our book.[12]

Goodman soon realized that the difference in time zones between California and New York helped account for his overwhelming success. On his radio broadcasts from the East Coast, Goodman reserved his hot numbers until later in the evening, and these exciting swing arrangements reached California during prime time and thrilled younger listeners.

In the years following the success at the Palomar Ballroom performance, Goodman's fame reached phenomenal heights. Goodman added West Coast vibraphonist Lionel Hampton to his trio, and the quartet recorded the song "Moonglow," which became a hit. The CBS radio broadcast "Camel Caravan" hired the Goodman band, and a wildly enthusiastic audience applauded his 1937 performances at New York's Paramount.

Goodman's celebrated Carnegie Hall performance the following year brought together his big band, his small group, and guest stars from Duke Ellington's and Count Basie's bands. This concert contained one of Goodman's most famous numbers, "Sing, Sing, Sing," a minor-key composition that featured Gene Krupa in a series of drum solos and included a duet with Goodman on clarinet and Krupa on tom-toms. Goodman hired only the strongest players and improvisers, and at one time or another his band featured many of the important players of the swing era, including trumpeters Bunny Berrigan and Harry James as well as pianists Jess Stacy and Mel Powell. At the request of John Hammond, Goodman took on guitarist Charlie Christian in 1939. During Christian's all-too-brief career (see Chapter 6), he was one of the leading improvisers of the period and revolutionized jazz guitar playing.

In the early 1940s, Eddie Sauter wrote arrangements for the Goodman group, earning it the nickname the "Sauter band" for some of the most ambitious jazz arrangements of the era, such as "Benny Rides Again" and "Clarinet à la King." The

The all-women band—in this case, Ina Ray Hutton and Her Melodears—was still a novelty in 1934, when this song was published.

pianist Mel Powell also contributed arrangements. After 1942, when Sauter left, Goodman tried to stave off the downturn in swing-band popularity by returning to a simpler style, but to no avail. Semiretirement followed in 1946 while he considered what to do next.

The bebop revolution—a modern jazz development of the early 1940s—intrigued Goodman. Despite occasional negative comments on the style, he admired the work of saxophonist Wardell Gray and trumpeter Fats Navarro. In 1948 Goodman experimented, first with a seven-piece group, then with a bebop-styled big band. Goodman produced some interesting work, including a Chico O'Farrill arrangement of "Undercurrent Blues." Ultimately, though, Goodman remained most at home in the swing style of his youth and early maturity. When his fans did not respond positively to his experimentation, Goodman ended his flirtation with bebop in 1949. For the remainder of his long life, Goodman led small groups ensconced in swing and, occasionally, big bands assembled for specific events.

There is no question that Goodman set clarinet style in the 1930s. It has been said that his perfect conception of swing style on the clarinet made him a difficult act for other players to follow. Hence, after Goodman, the clarinet declined as an instrument of modern jazz; only in recent years has its popularity begun to recover. That Goodman was the consummate swing stylist was perhaps best shown by his difficulties adapting to bebop.

Goodman continued to perform until his death in 1986. He undertook several overseas tours, playing in the Far East and South America, and appeared as a highly regarded "exhibit" at the United States pavilion of the Brussels World's Fair in 1958. During the height of the cold war in 1962, he traveled to the Soviet Union. With his classical training, he maintained a remarkably high degree of commitment to musicianship and clarinet technique, and he frequently performed classical works as well as jazz. For example, he recorded and performed works by Mozart, Debussy, and Stravinsky, and he commissioned works by classical contemporary composers Béla Bartók, Aaron Copland, and Paul Hindemith.

L I S T E N I N G   G U I D E

"Avalon"

CD **1** Track **13**

The Benny Goodman Quartet: "Avalon" (Jolson-Rose). Victor 25644. July 30, 1937, Hollywood, California.
Benny Goodman, clarinet; Lionel Hampton, vibraphone; Teddy Wilson, piano; Gene Krupa, drums.

The Benny Goodman Quartet was created by adding vibraphonist Lionel Hampton to the preexisting Goodman trio. Featured with the Goodman big band, the quartet was one of the acclaimed small jazz groups of the 1930s. Their recording of "Avalon" is typical of the impeccable and stylish swing performances associated with Goodman throughout his career. Here we examine "Avalon" as a whole; a more detailed discussion of Goodman's solo appears in Chapter 6.

Introduction—4 bars, vibraphone solo

0:00   Count "Avalon" in a moderate two beats or a fast four beats to the bar. Hampton begins with an up-tempo solo that ushers in the main melody. He first outlines the tonic chord with added sixth for two bars ($E^\flat 6$), then moves to a dominant seventh chord with an augmented fifth ($B^\flat 7^{(\#5)}$) for the last two bars.

Head AA'BC chorus—32 bars, Goodman lead

0:04 Main presentation of the melody. Rather than an AABA form with a well-defined bridge, "Avalon" has a more irregular form, although still comprising the conventional thirty-two bars. Examining it in eight-bar blocks reveals something like an AA'BC form with each main phrase occupying eight bars. The A and A' sections have the same harmonic structure, four bars of V7 to four bars of I.

0:19 The B section, beginning on the dominant seventh of the ii chord (C7), thus feels like a bridge.

0:27 The C section begins on the tonic, unlike the A and A' sections. All four sections develop the opening thematic idea, which begins in half notes after a quarter-note pickup.

1 AA'BC chorus—Wilson piano solo

0:35 Wilson plays his solo in the classic piano swing style he epitomized. You can hear occasional march-bass motions in the left hand, but rendered now as the lighter "swing bass" we heard from Count Basie in "Shoe Shine Boy." Here, Wilson's right hand develops light swing figuration.

0:51 A particularly nice harmonic moment comes at the beginning of the B section. Rather than move to the C7 chord (as in the Head Chorus section), Wilson substitutes a D♭ chord at the top of the C section and, moving through F minor, reaches the C7 chord by the fourth bar of the section. At the end of Wilson's solo, a drum fill by Krupa introduces Goodman's clarinet solo.

1 AA'BC chorus—Goodman clarinet solo

1:06 Goodman's style epitomized swing for clarinet, much as Wilson's style did for piano. This elegant clarinet solo is analyzed in detail in Chapter 6. For now, notice its balance and apparent effortlessness. For Goodman's solo, both Wilson and Hampton add accompanying chords.

1 AA'BC chorus—Hampton vibraphone solo

1:39 Hampton begins his solo with an arpeggio-like reference to the original melody.

This textural idea is repeated at the top of the A' section, but with emphasis on the E♭ tonic note even though it does not fit the harmony of B♭7 (V7). Wilson, meanwhile, accompanies with a light swing bass in both hands: bass note in the left (on beats one and three) with chord in the right (on beats two and four).

Out-chorus AA—Arranged ensemble

2:10 The climax of the performance arrives as an ingenious arranged-ensemble figure. Goodman and Hampton play a syncopated chromatic scale in descending minor triads that creates a cross-rhythm with the underlying swing bass as maintained by Wilson. The figure lasts four bars, with Krupa accenting the descending scale. The second four bars of the A section (on the E♭ tonic) feature a call-and-response figure on G♭–F–E♭.

2:18 The whole eight-bar unit then repeats.

Out-chorus B—Goodman clarinet solo

2:26 For the B section, Goodman improvises a lead line, while Hampton improvises a countermelody. Note the increased intensity and energy as the band drives to the conclusion of the piece.

Out-chorus C—8 bars, return to the arranged ensemble

2:35 For the final eight bars, the band returns to syncopated, descending minor triads. This time, instead of continuing through four bars, the band extends the figure through the entire eight bars of the section to create an unexpected, highly satisfying conclusion.

Ellington After the Cotton Club

Duke Ellington may have been dismayed during the mid-1930s when the commercial success of such leaders as Benny Goodman and Glenn Miller eclipsed the popularity of his own band. But Ellington's perseverance paid off. When he died in 1974, it was as one of the world's preeminent jazz artists. The recipient of numerous musical and international honors, Ellington served for many as the most important figure in the history of jazz.

Ellington's artistry was wide-ranging. Known for his prodigious output of music, his command of arranging and orchestration detail, and his expansive musical creativity, Ellington established his excellence while crisscrossing the globe under a hectic and seemingly incessant touring schedule. As the title to one laudatory biography concluded, Ellington was "beyond category."[13] As such, his work is difficult to summarize. Nonetheless, we can identify four categories:

1. Popular songs such as "Satin Doll" and "Don't Get Around Much Anymore"

2. Big-band arrangements

3. Feature compositions for particular members of the band

4. Extended concert works

After leaving the Cotton Club, Ellington began to tour widely. The band traveled to Europe in 1932, playing to enthusiastic crowds and attracting critical attention in the British press. Moreover, during the 1930s, he became increasingly successful as a composer writing in the American popular song tradition—usually thirty-two–bar AABA compositions. "Sophisticated Lady," first recorded in 1933, was unusual in that the A sections of the composition (measures 1–16 and 25–32) were in the key of A♭, while the B section or bridge (measures 17–24) was a half-step away in the key of G major. The song became a classic, and others followed. "In a Sentimental Mood" became more known in Benny Goodman's rendition. "Prelude to a Kiss," with its sinuous chromatic melody, was first recorded as an instrumental and played by two of the principal soloists of the group, trombonist Lawrence Brown and saxophonist Johnny Hodges.

Following the death of his mother, with whom he was extremely close, Ellington in 1937 wrote the extended musical composition "Reminiscing in Tempo," his longest, most ambitious work to date. Thirteen minutes long, the piece covered four record sides. Critical reaction to the composition was more negative than positive, but Ellington had shown growth as a composer. In particular, the work is remarkably sparing in its use of thematic material, restricting itself largely to two principal thematic ideas, their accompaniments, and transitions, which Ellington develops deftly. The work also uses unusual phrase lengths of seven, ten, and fourteen measures and requires little improvisation. Another extended work from 1937 was "Crescendo in Blue" and "Diminuendo in Blue," companion pieces occupying both sides of a 78-rpm record. Again, these longer works, rooted in the blues form and tradition, use little improvisation.

BUILDING ON THE BAND

Because Ellington was determined to build upon the strengths of the individual band members, much of the band's distinctive character came from its players. During the 1930s, Ellington's compositions grew out of an occasional whole-band collaboration. Ellington noted in 1937 that some of his works were composed "almost by unanimous inspiration while the orchestra was gathered together for a practice session. New ideas are merged at each meeting, and each man contributes to the offerings of the other."[14] This tendency to borrow ideas from his sidemen led to the infamous remark by trombonist Lawrence Brown, "Duke, I don't consider you a composer. You are a compiler."[15] Brown was going too far, of course—he claimed to have written the A section of "Sophisticated Lady" even as Ellington worked assiduously at this composition. The remark reveals the tensions that can develop in a band when creativity among all the players is constantly encouraged.

As part of his desire to work with his band's strengths, Ellington wrote with particular players in mind. This important aspect of his compositions and his sound emphasized the talents and characteristic styles of his band members. A number of Ellington's compositions thus were inspired by and showcased individuals from the band. "Echoes of Harlem," for example, featured Cootie Williams, the trumpeter who replaced Bubber Miley in 1929. Ellington also displayed Williams's multifaceted playing in the celebrated "Concerto for Cootie," a three-themed work on which Williams played open trumpet, muted trumpet, and growl trumpet (listen to Track 24 of the Audio Primer CD to hear a brass growl on trombone). The first theme of "Concerto for Cootie" was later given lyrics and retitled "Do Nothin' Till You Hear From Me," which became a hit song in 1943. Ellington's work provided the perfect vehicle for his players; commentators noted that his sidemen often faltered in their playing and careers once they left the band.

"Clarinet Lament," based on the harmonic progression of the standard song "Basin Street Blues," exhibited the playing of Ellington's New Orleans–born clarinetist Barney Bigard. For trumpeter Rex Stewart, who left Fletcher Henderson to play with Ellington from 1934 to 1943, Ellington wrote "Boy Meets Horn." And with his trombonist from San Juan, Puerto Rico—Juan Tizol—Ellington co-composed the exotic Latin-tinged song "Caravan." In this work, drummer Sonny Greer introduces the composition by playing tom-toms, chimes, cymbal, bass drum, and Burmese gong, setting the stage for Tizol, who plays the melody on valve trombone. Tizol had the strongest classical background of all of Ellington's band members and was renowned for his accuracy and clean playing, but he did not improvise.

Johnny Hodges (1907–1970), Ellington's alto saxophonist, was one of the stalwarts of the band. Along with Benny Carter, Hodges was one of the best alto saxophone players of the swing era. Born in Cambridge, Massachusetts, Hodges played both alto and soprano saxophone. He developed a blues-inflected style that owed a debt to Sidney Bechet, with whom he had studied and performed before joining Ellington in 1928. Except for a brief departure between 1951 and 1955, Hodges remained in the Ellington band for four decades. Nicknamed "Jeep" and "Rabbit," Hodges was considered the leading soloist of the Ellington band in the mid-1930s, and he became its highest-paid member.

Hodges's playing was particularly prominent in many of the small-group recordings made during the late 1930s. A seven-piece group formed from members of the Ellington band made several records, many of which achieved commercial success—for example, the composition "Jeep's Blues" became a jukebox hit. Hodges's ballad performances were said to be aphrodisiacal: The wife of one of the Ellington musicians reputedly warned, "Don't leave me alone around Johnny. When I hear him play, I just want to open up the bedroom door."[16] Other bandleaders acknowledged Hodges's status as a soloist. For example, Hodges and his band mates Cootie Williams and Harry Carney played in the jam session portion of Benny Goodman's Carnegie Hall Concert of 1938.

CHANGES FOR THE BETTER

Toward the end of the 1930s, Ellington made several radical changes. He broke with Irving Mills, who had been his manager and business partner for more than a decade. Mills had also written the lyrics for many of Ellington's compositions, such as "It Don't Mean a Thing (If It Ain't Got That Swing)," "Sophisticated Lady," and "Mood Indigo." Ellington signed with the William Morris Agency. He also left Columbia

The cover of "Shoe Shine Boy" (CD 1, Track 12) displays evocative imagery. It was a musical number in *Hot Chocolates of 1936*—a cabaret revue at one of the famous Harlem clubs for whites, Connie's Inn at Seventh Avenue and 131st Street.

Records and by 1940 was recording for RCA Victor. On the heels of a successful tour of Europe in 1939, Ellington took on several new players and entered what was one of the most intensely fertile periods of his career.

With the addition of tenor saxophonist Ben Webster, Ellington's saxophone section increased to five players. Webster was a big-toned, breathy player from Kansas City who had played with Benny Moten and Andy Kirk in the early 1930s and had played an integral role in the Kansas City scene. When Webster came to New York in 1934, he played with Fletcher Henderson, Cab Calloway, and Benny Carter, and—for a brief period between 1935 and 1936—Ellington's band; he came on board as a full-time member of Ellington's band at the end of 1939. Webster energized the band with his solos on both ballads and swing numbers. "Cottontail," for instance, offers an electrifying display of his solo ability. The harmonic structure of "Cottontail," based on the chords to "I Got Rhythm," provides the vehicle for Webster's solo, which alternates between eighth notes and longer notes and is filled with Webster's trademark devices. Along with Coleman Hawkins and Lester Young, Webster was one of the most important tenor saxophone stylists of the swing era.

Ellington also added Jimmy Blanton on bass in 1939. The virtuosity of this twenty-year-old from Chattanooga, Tennessee, revolutionized jazz bass playing. Creating a driving sense of swing while walking the bass, Blanton was the first bass player to become a proficient soloist in his own right. Taken with Blanton's playing, Ellington recorded a series of duets with the bassist, such as "Pitter Panther Patter," that show Blanton's remarkable agility. In his first studio outing with the full band, Ellington featured Blanton in opening and closing solos on "Jack the Bear."

Finally, Ellington took on a diminutive pianist born in Dayton, Ohio. Initially hired as a second pianist and an assistant arranger, Billy Strayhorn (1915–1967) developed a remarkably close musical relationship with Ellington that lasted nearly three decades. Strayhorn quickly began contributing compositions for the band, including one of the group's theme songs, "Take the A Train." Strayhorn's musical collaborations with Ellington were so intertwined that critics and scholars were not always sure where Ellington's contributions left off and Strayhorn's began. Nicknamed "Sweet Pea," Strayhorn had a background in European classical music and theory. Some of his tunes—such as "Chelsea Bridge" and his bittersweet paean to drinking, "Lush Life"—owed a debt to Debussy. Strayhorn had studied the elements of Ellington's style that contributed to what Strayhorn called the "Ellington effect." He described it this way:

> Each member of the band is to him a distinctive tone color and set of emotions, which he mixes with others equally distinctive to produce a third thing, which I like to call the Ellington effect. Sometimes this mixing happens on paper and frequently right on the bandstand. I have often seen him exchange parts in the middle of a piece because the man and the part weren't the same character.[17]

THE 1940s AND BEYOND

The forties were a mixed time for Ellington and the band. Relatively ignored in the polls during the 1930s, the group now began to achieve national prominence, winning the *Esquire* poll in 1945 and taking the *Down Beat* polls in 1942, 1944, 1946, and 1948. Ellington began to receive handsome royalties for many of his compositions, such as "Don't Get Around Much Anymore," "I'm Beginning to See the Light," and "Do Nothin' Till You Hear from Me." The years also witnessed, however, an increased turnover in players. Sidemen in Ellington's band were beginning to attract offers from competing bands; other players were lost to the wartime draft. Tenor player Ben Webster left in 1943 to lead his own small group. The more modern playing of clarinetist Jimmy Hamilton replaced Barney Bigard. Cootie Williams left Ellington for Benny Goodman's band in 1940 and was replaced by trumpeter, violinist, and singer Ray Nance. Trombonist Juan Tizol joined Harry James's band, and another Ellington trombonist, Joe "Tricky Sam" Nanton, died of a stroke in 1946. Bassist Blanton died of tuberculosis in 1942 at the tragically young age of twenty-three; the young Oscar Pettiford filled the bass chair between 1945 and 1948. Trumpeter Cat Anderson, capable of trumpet screams in the very highest registers, played with the band from 1944 to 1947.

In 1943 Ellington began an annual series of concerts at Carnegie Hall. In addition to featuring his songs and hits, Ellington composed and premiered large-scale concert works. These were often based on themes of African-American culture and history. The first concert on January 23, 1943, included a performance of his *Black, Brown, and Beige: A Tone Parallel to the History of the Negro in America.* This was an ambitious three-movement tone poem that traced the history of African Americans through the story of an African named Boola who is brought to the United States as a slave. Unfortunately, many critics panned the work; as a result, Ellington performed only sections in later concerts, especially "Come Sunday" from the opening "Black" movement. Because critics had called the work "formless," Ellington offered suites in later Carnegie Hall concerts; these shorter musical vignettes better suited Ellington's writing style. In many of the works that followed *Black, Brown, and Beige*—such as "New World a-Comin'," "Liberian Suite," and "Deep South Suite"—we see how Ellington inherited the Harlem Renaissance tradition as he celebrated the history and achievements of African Americans in a concert venue.

By the 1950s, the heyday of the swing era was long gone, and it was becoming increasingly difficult for Ellington to keep his band together. In 1951 his stalwarts Johnny Hodges, drummer Sonny Greer, and trombonist Lawrence Brown all left the band, but Ellington attracted strong replacements. Louie Bellson replaced Greer, and Ellington added a fine young player in the bebop mold, Clark Terry, on trumpet. The departure of his star soloist Johnny Hodges was short-lived; Hodges returned to Ellington in 1955.

In July 1956, the fortunes of the band miraculously reversed themselves. On stage at the Newport Jazz Festival, during a performance of "Diminuendo and Crescendo in Blue," the tenor saxophonist Paul Gonsalves stood up and played twenty-seven electrifying choruses. The response of the crowd was overwhelming: Listeners danced in the aisles, stood on chairs, and cheered. Ellington was in vogue again. With characteristic irony he noted, "I was born in 1956 at the Newport Festival."[18]

The band continued to perform widely, undertaking a State Department–sponsored tour of India and the Middle East. At the end of the decade, Ellington wrote the score for the 1959 Otto Preminger film *Anatomy of a Murder;* the soundtrack won three Grammy awards. He and Strayhorn continued to turn out larger musical suites, notably "Such Sweet Thunder," inspired by Shakespeare and written for the Shakespeare Festival in Stratford, Canada, and "The Queen's Suite," in honor of Queen Elizabeth II. John Steinbeck's novel *Sweet Thursday* inspired the collaboration with Strayhorn on "Suite Thursday," which they wrote for the 1960 Monterey Jazz Festival. The interval of a descending minor sixth musically dominates the work. "A Drum Is a Woman" was a somewhat whimsical history of jazz, narrated by Ellington, in which "Madame Zajj" goes from the Caribbean, to New Orleans, Harlem, and the moon.

Though usually modest about his own piano-playing abilities, Ellington showcased his playing in several small-group recordings in the early 1960s. He cut an album with John Coltrane and recorded *Money Jungle* with Charles Mingus and Max Roach in 1962. Much of Ellington's final work involved religious compositions. For example, San Francisco's Grace Liturgical Church commissioned him to write a liturgical work. His *Concert of Sacred Music,* which incorporated segments of some of his earlier pieces such as *Black, Brown, and Beige* and "New World a-Comin'," premiered in 1965. Ellington performed his *Second Sacred Concert* two years later and performed the third and most introspective of his sacred concerts in 1973, the year before his death.

Ellington's influence and legacy continue to be profound. He had the administrative ability to run a large band for decades. As a pianist, he recorded solos, worked with his large band, and found time to record small-group work. Dozens of his compositions have kept their status as standards of the jazz literature, and their melodic and harmonic structure still attract jazz musicians. As an orchestrator, Ellington created instrumental effects that were dazzling, eerie, and masterly. As a composer of larger works, Ellington elevated the perception of jazz to a music worthy of the concert stage. Some consider him to be the greatest American composer in any category.

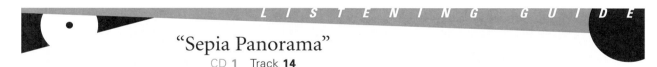

L I S T E N I N G   G U I D E

"Sepia Panorama"
CD **1**   Track **14**

Duke Ellington and His Famous Orchestra: "Sepia Panorama" (Ellington). Victor 26731. New York, July 24, 1940. Wallace Jones, Cootie Williams, trumpets; Rex Stewart, cornet; Joe Nanton, Lawrence Brown, trombones; Juan Tizol, valve trombone; Barney Bigard, clarinet, tenor saxophone; Johnny Hodges, alto saxophone; Ben Webster, tenor saxophone; Harry Carney, baritone saxophone, clarinet; Duke Ellington, arrangement, piano, leader; Fred Guy, guitar; Jimmy Blanton, bass; Sonny Greer, drums.

Exhibiting an arch-form structure much like that of "The Mooche" (see Chapter 4), "Sepia Panorama" is an imaginative composition typical of Ellington's three-minute recordings during the late 1930s and early 1940s. The arch form of "Sepia Panaorama" can be summarized as ABC–D1D2–CBA–tag. The tonal (key) structure also has an arch form: F major, B♭ major, F major. Further, Ellington contrasts dramatic and quiet sections, thus projecting a full "panorama" of expressive devices.

Finally, this piece shows how Jimmy Blanton developed a greater role for the bass: Rather than simply keeping time, he plays prominent solo passages that show off his dexterous technique. Among other innovations, Blanton developed a facility in the higher register of the instrument, which, until then, had been relatively neglected. The higher register is particularly useful for projecting the melody, which was important for solos before routine amplification of the instrument in the latter half of the 1960s.

Section A (F major)—12-bar blues

0:00   The first twelve-bar blues section has an interestingly varied structure. In the first five bars, the whole band presents a theme with a dramatic rising figure.

0:11   An unaccompanied Blanton bass solo answers in measures 6–8.

0:17   In measures 9–10, the saxophones answer Blanton with a syncopated figure emphasizing the bluesy sharp 9th (E♭) of the C7 dominant chord.

0:22   Blanton completes the form with an unaccompanied solo in measures 11–12.

Section B (F major)—8 bars, repeated

0:26   The second section contrasts the first with an eight-bar structure. The first four bars are a trombone solo with saxophone chord accompaniment. These chords are adventurous (B♭13, then E♭9(#11), then D13(#11)) and typical of Ellington's intriguing harmonies.

0:34   In the second four bars, the saxophones accompany answering figures in a solo muted trumpet.

0:44   The section repeats.

Section C (B♭ major)—8 bars

1:02   The whole band with open and aggressive brass accompanies a solo baritone saxophone in a call-and-response format. This more dramatic section recalls Section A.

Section D1 (B♭ major)—12-bar blues

1:19   A duet of Blanton on bass and Ellington on piano. The quieter mood (first heard in Section B) returns. Ellington remains in the high register and uses a combination of blues licks.

1:25   Ellington uses a whole-tone figure at the fourth bar of the section.

        Blanton, rather than just walking in time, creates a duet of equal voices with melodic passages, often with eighth-note triplets.

Section D2 (B♭ major)—12-bar blues

1:45   Ben Webster tenor solo. Webster was one of the premier saxophonists of the swing era. With a sensuous tone and beguiling vibrato, he begins gently and builds his solo to the reprise of section C.

Section C (B♭ major)—8 bars

2:12   Reprise of Section C.

Section B (F major)—8 bars

2:29   Reprise of Section B.

Section A (F major)—12-bar blues

2:47   Reprise of Section A.

Tag B♭7 to F major)—2 bars

3:13   The whole band plays a final tag. Ellington unites the two key centers with a harmonic progression of B♭7 (one bar) to F (one bar) with a final low F on the piano held to ring out.

Questions and Topics for Discussion

1. What are some of the specific features of big-band writing? Cite instrumentation, role of the instrumental sections, and overall form.

2. How did Kansas City provide a foundation for swing? Cite specific bands and aspects of their styles. Among the important bands associated with Kansas City were territory bands. What were they, and how did they function?

3. In what ways was Benny Goodman's nickname, "King of Swing," appropriate? In what ways was it inappropriate?

4. How did the bands of Count Basie and Duke Ellington differ? Further, how do the differences between Ellington and Basie as musicians and bandleaders help account for the different personalities of their bands and music?

Key Terms

Antiphony

Balance

Big band

Call-and-response

Chair

Intonation

Jazz chair

Lead player

Lead trumpet

Library (book)

Rhythm changes

Section

Sideman

Swing

Territory Band

Trading twos (fours, eights)

Walking bass

As the Depression continued, so did the nation's search for diversion. The swing era blossomed with more bands, more stars, more band broadcasts on radio, and more films—particularly musicals. One of them, *Stormy Weather,* contained what was to become the signature song of its star—the very young and beautiful Lena Horne (dancing energetically on this cover of the slow, introspective "torch" song). Bill Robinson (bottom left-hand corner), Fats Waller, and Cab Calloway (in the white suit and hat) also appeared in this film. For the first and only time in its history, jazz would enter the mainstream of popular music.

SWING-ERA BANDS AND STYLISTS

6

THE BASIE, GOODMAN, AND ELLINGTON bands were perhaps the most important of the big-band era, but numerous other groups, both black and white, contributed to the excitement and verve of swing. Many sidemen in the big bands became famous in their own right, and audiences idolized them. Their performing styles formed the roots of jazz music to come. Some of the big-band performers left their original bands to lead their own groups—a few successfully but many less so. Some players, such as Coleman Hawkins, worked largely as "singles"—stars who performed at clubs throughout the country and worked with local rhythm sections. This chapter begins with the most important big bands (besides Basie, Goodman, and Ellington) and concludes with the best-known individual stylists, particularly those who affected subsequent directions in jazz.

Influential Big Bands of the Swing Era

During the 1930s, the hub of the music industry remained in New York, as it had in the 1920s. The record industry was centered there, and radio stations widely broadcast the big bands as they played in popular ballrooms and dance halls. The more successful bands, such as those of Jimmie Lunceford and Cab Calloway, alternated extended performances in the dance halls of Harlem with engagements on the road. Lunceford's group was legendary for its ability to keep up a hectic schedule playing across the country.

CAB CALLOWAY

Cab Calloway (1907–1994) was one of the most popular and colorful bandleaders to emerge during the 1930s and 1940s. His flamboyant vocal style and exuberant scat singing earned him the nickname the "Hi-de-Ho Man." Calloway noted in his biography that his "favorite scat singer has always been Louis Armstrong."[1] Indeed, he followed in Armstrong's footsteps and became famous as an entertainer with a singing style that was infectious, outgoing, and crowd pleasing.

With his band, the Missourians, Calloway took over the house gig at the Cotton Club after Ellington's band departed. The Missourians played at the Cotton Club six months of the year and toured the other half.

Hits such as Calloway's 1931 "Minnie the Moocher" earned the band wide popularity. They also appeared in several films, including *The Big Broadcast* (1932), *The Singing Kid* (1936), and *Stormy Weather* (1943). Calloway's band included several excellent players: He helped launch the careers of tenor saxophonists Ben Webster and Chu Berry, bassist Milt Hinton, and trumpeters Jonah Jones and Dizzy Gillespie.

JIMMIE LUNCEFORD

The Cotton Club also featured another popular big band, led by Jimmie Lunceford (1902–1947). Audiences expected not only a variety of music but a *show,* and Lunceford's band was known for its onstage antics, with the musicians waving their derbies or their horns in the air. (A *derby* is a stiff hat with a round bowl and narrow brim.)

Lunceford studied music in high school in Denver under Wilberforce Whiteman, Paul Whiteman's father, and graduated from Fisk University with a degree in music. He began organizing a band in Memphis in the late 1920s and brought it to New York in 1933, where audiences quickly noted the band's rigorous and rehearsed professionalism.

Although Lunceford's band had fine soloists, the group was better known for its charts. Lunceford hired several top arrangers—pianist Eddie Wilcox, altoist Willie Smith, and trombonist-guitarist Eddie Durham—who contributed several pieces. These included novelty tunes such as "Organ Grinder's Swing" and "The Merry-Go-Round Broke Down," as well as sweet arrangements and hot instrumental numbers in the manner of the influential white band the Casa Loma Orchestra. Lunceford himself wrote an experimental riff piece entitled "Stratosphere."

The Lunceford band got a boost when trumpeter Sy Oliver (1910–1988) began arranging for them in 1934, creating what became known as the Lunceford style. Part of what made the sound distinctive was Oliver's insistence that the rhythm section play in a two-beat style, rather than stating all four beats. Not all the rhythm players liked the Lunceford style, as the band's drummer Jimmie Crawford recalled:

> Sy would say "Drop it in two," and I'd maybe show I didn't agree with him, and so he'd say, "What's wrong with two beats?" and I'd answer, "Well, there are two beats missing, that's all." I felt that if you were really going home in those last ride-out choruses, then you should really go home all the way, full steam and stay in four-four instead of going back into that two-four feel again. Oh yes, Sy and I would have some terrific arguments all right, but then we'd kiss and make up right away.[2]

No band equaled Lunceford's commercial showmanship. He continued directing the group until his death in 1947.

CHICK WEBB

In addition to the Cotton Club, Harlem's Savoy Theater provided a premier jazz spot for listening and dancing during the 1930s. The house band was led by drummer Chick Webb. A childhood accident in Baltimore, where he was born in 1909, had left Webb crippled and hunchbacked, but he became one of the most influential drummers of the early swing period. All the swing-era drummers idolized Webb and were astonished by his four-bar drum breaks in "Clap Hands, Here Comes Charlie" and his solos on temple blocks during "In a Little Spanish Town." Although most of Webb's breaks and fills were brief, he recorded longer drum solos on "Harlem Congo" and "Liza."

Drummer Buddy Rich recalled:

> Chick Webb was startling. He was a tiny man with this big face and big stiff shoulders. He sat way up on a kind of throne and used a twenty-eight-inch bass drum which had special pedals for his feet and he had those old goose-neck cymbal holders. Every beat was like a bell.[3]

Webb recorded in the early 1930s, including a version of "Heebie Jeebies," the song Louis Armstrong had made a hit six years earlier. Webb's version, arranged by Benny Carter, was the last recording of trombonist Jimmy Harrison (1900–1931), who was one of the most significant trombone players of the 1920s and early 1930s (see Chapter 4). He greatly advanced the technique of the instrument. Webb's band of the early thirties also included John Kirby on string bass and tuba, a player who had gotten his start with Fletcher Henderson. Kirby later went on to lead one of the successful small bands of the big-band era.

Webb took on arranger and saxophonist Edgar Sampson, who contributed two compositions that later became anthems of the swing era: "Stompin' at the Savoy" and "Don't Be That Way." Although Webb's band recorded them, these pieces went on to greater fame when Benny Goodman recorded them in 1938.

In the famous Battles of the Bands that took place at the Savoy in the thirties, Webb's loyal audience awarded victories to Webb over such groups as Benny Goodman's and Count Basie's bands. Webb also discovered and launched the career of sixteen-year-old vocalist Ella Fitzgerald, whose recording with Webb of "A-tisket, A-tasket" sold widely. Fitzgerald took over Webb's band after the leader's early death in 1939.

THE CASA LOMA ORCHESTRA

One of the rare bands not to have a leader, the Casa Loma Orchestra functioned as a cooperative. This white group was founded in 1929 from a remnant of a Jean Goldkette band, the Orange Blossoms, that had been based in Detroit. The Casa Loma Orchestra developed an enormous following on college campuses. Many of their up-tempo arrangements forecast the formulas and styles of the mid-thirties swing bands. The key writer and arranger for the Casa Loma Orchestra was banjoist Gene Gifford (1912–1970).

Gifford wrote striking material for the band, particularly "Casa Loma Stomp," in which the call-and-response between the band sections was exciting, exacting, and very well executed. Another particularly fine arrangement from Gifford was "Black Jazz."

MCKINNEY'S COTTON PICKERS

Another important cooperative band was a black, midwestern group formed initially by Jean Goldkette in Ohio and Detroit, McKinney's Cotton Pickers. The Cotton Pickers may have influenced Gifford's work with the Casa Loma Orchestra—the two bands have some striking traits in common, including rhythmic figures. Under the leadership of Don Redman in the late 1920s (after Redman left Fletcher Henderson), Redman and trumpeter John Nesbitt (c. 1900–1935) divided the arranging duties. Nesbitt's arrangements distinguished the band's sound, and he contributed such forward-looking charts as "Put It There" and "Stop Kidding." Like the Casa Loma Orchestra, McKinney's Cotton Pickers presaged many of the stylistic devices of the swing-era orchestra. Later, such superb arrangers and players as Benny Carter, Coleman Hawkins, and Fats Waller would briefly join the group.

TOMMY AND JIMMY DORSEY

The Dorsey brothers were among the most popular swing-era band leaders. Hailing from Shenandoah, Pennsylvania, Tommy (1905–1956) was a trombonist and Jimmy (1904–1957) a saxophonist and clarinetist. The brothers led largely parallel early careers, working their way up the jazz-band pecking order in the 1920s. Eventually both came to work with the Goldkette bands and Paul Whiteman. In 1934 they cofounded the Dorsey Brothers Orchestra, but after a public dispute in 1935, Tommy

Bandleader Jimmy Dorsey in a publicity photo from the 1930s. His brother Tommy, after repeated arguments, left their joint orchestra to form his own band.

I GOT IT BAD
AND THAT AIN'T GOOD

WORDS BY
PAUL WEBSTER

MUSIC BY
DUKE ELLINGTON

Featured by
JIMMY DORSEY
and his Orchestra

ROBBINS MUSIC CORPORATION
799 SEVENTH AVENUE · NEW YORK

left to organize his own group. Each band achieved tremendous popularity during the height of the swing era in the late 1930s. Tommy's band launched the young vocalist Frank Sinatra.

The Dorseys were fine instrumentalists. Jimmy influenced such pioneering saxophonists as Lester Young and Coleman Hawkins. Although less influential as a jazz stylist, Tommy was known for the velvety elegance of his ballad work on trombone. Of the two bands, Tommy's probably featured the more inventive and interesting jazz charts. Among the excellent jazz arrangers associated with the T. Dorsey band was Sy Oliver who had written superb works for both Jimmie Lunceford and Benny Goodman. The Dorsey brothers reunited briefly from 1953 to 1956 and hosted their own television show, on which a young singer named Elvis Presley made his first network appearance.

GLENN MILLER

Glenn Miller's band was one of the most famous of the swing era. Like many of the most acclaimed white groups, it was more strongly rooted in the popular music of the times than in jazz.

Miller (1904–1944) was born in Clarinda, Iowa, and raised in Fort Morgan, Colorado. A trombonist, he played with local orchestras and briefly attended the University of Colorado. In 1924 he joined Ben Pollack's band on the West Coast and eventually journeyed to New York in 1928 with Pollack. Miller remained in New York and, like Benny Goodman and so many others, worked as a freelancer, largely doing studio work. In 1937 he organized his first band but failed to attract much attention. Miller's second group, however, became well known thanks largely to a major booking in 1938 at the Glen Island Casino in New Rochelle, New York, which led to other important gigs and radio broadcasts that gave the band national attention.

In support of the war effort, Miller joined the Air Force in 1942 to form a band to entertain troops. In 1944, Miller flew from England to Paris to see about bookings for the group. Mysteriously, the plane never landed, and no trace of wreckage was found. Miller's plane most likely crashed in the English Channel.

Like the Dorsey brothers' bands, Miller's group is remembered more for its arrangements than its soloists. A taskmaster like Goodman, Miller created ensembles that were known for being very well rehearsed. His most important jazz soloist was probably cornetist Bobby Hackett (1915–1976), a player with an expressive lyricism that recalled the elegance of Bix Beiderbecke. Among Miller's most famous hits were "In the Mood," "Tuxedo Junction," and "String of Pearls." In the latter piece, Hackett fashioned a solo so strong that it has come to be thought of as part of the tune itself. "In the Mood" became one of the most popular pieces of the swing era.

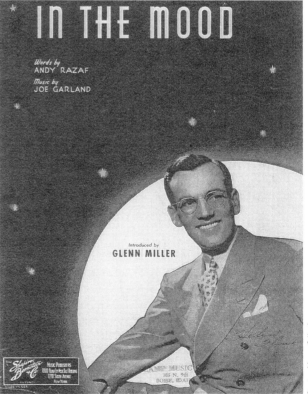

Bandleader Glenn Miller's appearance (1939) reflects the careful polish that went into his music and made it so popular to a wide audience.

Courtesy Morgan Collection

ARTIE SHAW

Artie Shaw was among the most interesting of the white bandleaders to achieve celebrity during the swing era. He was, for instance, the only clarinetist to rival Goodman in popularity, and his many idiosyncrasies brought him as much fame as his accomplishments.

Born in New York City in 1910, Shaw grew up in New Haven, Connecticut. There, he performed early on with the Johnny Cavallaro band, then from 1926 to 1929 moved to Cleveland, where he worked until 1929. Shaw's interest in classical music strongly affected his approach to leading and organizing bands.

In the late 1920s, Shaw relocated to New York, began work as a freelancer, and informally studied jazz with Willie "The Lion" Smith. In 1936, he organized his first band; incredibly, it consisted of a string quartet, Shaw, and a rhythm section. Recording for Brunswick in 1936, Shaw augmented the band with a trumpet, trombone, tenor saxophone, and singer. As might be expected for such an unconventional group, these records were not major sellers. In 1937 Shaw reorganized his group with more conventional instrumentation. His main breakthrough came when he recorded Cole Porter's "Begin the Beguine" in 1938 and created one of the most popular records of the late thirties.

Shaw was something of an iconoclast in the jazz world. He broke the color barrier by briefly employing Billie Holiday as a singer with his band. Touring the South became difficult, however, and Shaw was forced to let the singer go. With eight marriages, Shaw was as celebrated for his love life as for his music; his string of wives included movie stars Ava Gardner and Lana Turner. He had an unpredictable personality that, intentionally or not, made him the focus of the gossip columnists, who reported on his romantic involvements as well as his bands. Shaw often broke up his ensembles, only to return to the music business after a short "retirement."

One of his most respected groups, which included trumpeter Roy Eldridge, was organized in 1944. Their record "Little Jazz" became quite famous. "Lucky Number," arranged by Ray Conniff in 1945, was another of their most interesting records, with a solo by Eldridge. A more unusual and progressive work, "Similau," was arranged by George Russell and recorded in 1949. Shaw continued to work occasionally through the 1980s.

Numerous other bands achieved great popularity in the swing era, including groups led by Benny Carter, Gene Krupa (see later for both), Charlie Barnet (1913–1991), Harry James (1916–1983), Boyd Rayburn (1913–1966), and Bob Crosby (1913–1993). As the swing era waned in the 1940s, other big bands rose to popularity, but such groups never enjoyed the celebrity of the earlier bands. Importantly, these later groups tried to incorporate the breakthroughs of the bebop revolutionaries, a subject taken up in Chapter 7.

Swing-Era Stylists

Here we look at the various styles of the most celebrated swing-era players, composer/arrangers, and vocalists. All contributed greatly to the sound we call "swing." The following is a list of these artists, by their instrument:

▶ Clarinet: Benny Goodman

▶ Saxophone: Coleman Hawkins and Lester Young

▶ Trumpet: Roy Eldridge

▶ Trombone: Jack Teagarden

▶ Piano: Earl Hines, Teddy Wilson, and Art Tatum

▶ Bass: Jimmy Blanton

▶ Drums: Jo Jones and Gene Krupa

▶ Guitar: Charlie Christian

▶ Composing/arranging: Benny Carter

▶ Singing: Billie Holiday and Ella Fitzgerald

BENNY GOODMAN: LYRICAL CLARINET

Of all the jazz clarinet styles, none has ever achieved the popularity of Goodman's easygoing, swinging melodiousness. Goodman's style features a suave, songlike sweetness, an exquisite sense of timing, and an underlying structure marked by melodic and rhythmic accessibility.

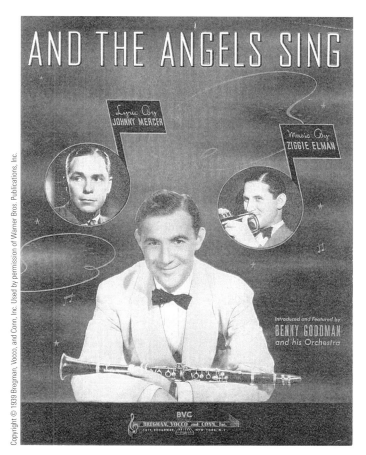

Clarinetist Benny Goodman (CD 1, Track 13) shares the cover with prolific lyricist Johnny Mercer and trumpet player Ziggie Elman.

L I S T E N I N G   G U I D E

"Avalon"
CD **1** Track **13**

The Benny Goodman Quartet: "Avalon" (Jolson-Rose). Victor 25644. July 30, 1937, Hollywood, California.
Benny Goodman, clarinet; Lionel Hampton, vibraphone; Teddy Wilson, piano; Gene Krupa, drums.

In Chapter 5, we listened to the 1937 quartet recording of "Avalon" in its entirety and promised a closer look at Goodman's solo here. One of Goodman's greatest solos, this improvisation reflects the simplicity of Goodman's ideas and his unhurried, sure sense of direction at every moment, a manner that recalls Bix Beiderbecke's style. The exquisitely timed spaces between the phrases ensure that a cool overall tone and sense of effortlessness finely balance Goodman's virtuosity. Here we have organized the table according to various motifs rather than the chronologically ordered structure.

As you listen to the solo, please refer to this transcription by the authors:

First note and principal structural line

1:06 A large-scale voice-leading succession proceeds from the high B♭, the first note of the solo.

1:13 The same pitch is strongly articulated in measures 7–9 and

1:24 18–21, after which it begins a long descent to

1:28   A♭ in measure 23,

1:31   G in measure 25,

1:37   F in measure 30,

1:38   and finally E♭ in measure 32.

Hidden repetition of the B♭–A♭–G–F–E♭ structural line

1:06   The B♭–A♭–G–F–E♭ line occurs on a smaller scale throughout the solo, a technique often called "diminution" or "hidden repetition." These occurrences lend unity to the solo: for example, consider measures 1–2,

1:14   measures 8–9 (though incomplete because the line finishes on F),

1:28   measures 21–24, and

1:37   measures 30–32.

The F–E♭ pitch-pair

1:06–   This portion is harmonically structured by four bars each of B♭7, E♭, B♭7, and E♭. It is unified
1:21   by a large-scale F–E♭–F–E♭ corresponding to each of the chord changes. At each recurrence, Goodman presents the F and E♭ pitches in a fresh melodic light with no hint of mechanical planning. The F–E♭ pitch-pair returns frequently throughout the solo, for example in measures 4–5, 12–15, 24, and 31–32.

Conclusion

Ultimately, the solo is organized around the B♭–A♭–G–F–E♭ line, but this line is never fully stated as an uninterrupted melody. Moreover, the pitch-pair F–E♭, emphasized in the first sixteen bars, can be seen in a new light, as part of the larger scalar pattern. These details highlight the subtlety of Goodman's impeccable technique and show how his smoothness of melodic line is preeminent through the solo.

Goodman's solo in "Avalon" demonstrates several characteristics of Goodman's playing:

► Supple melody characterized by few large leaps within a phrase

► Frequent arpeggiation and use of scale fragments

► Basic eighth-note rhythm

► Limited space between phrases

► Lyrical tone

► Use of the entire range of the instrument

► Avoidance of blues effects

► Cool expression occasionally contrasted by fast vibrato

► Slightly irregular phrase lengths

► Note choices that emphasize the notes of the chord (inside playing)

COLEMAN HAWKINS: ELEVATING THE SAXOPHONE

During the late teens and early 1920s, the front line of clarinet, trombone, and cornet dominated New Orleans– and Chicago-style jazz, relegating the saxophone to be used as a novelty, vaudeville instrument. As the 1920s wore on and the big-band sound evolved, the saxophone grew more and more popular until it became an important reed voice. By the 1930s, Coleman Hawkins, a powerful soloist on the instrument, had made the saxophone a serious improvisational instrument.

Coleman Hawkins, known as "Bean," or "Hawk," was the player most responsible for elevating the tenor saxophone to prominence as a jazz voice. Born in St. Joseph, Missouri, in 1904, Hawkins began playing tenor saxophone at age nine. Three years later he was working professionally for school dances. In 1921 he was living in Kansas City and playing in the Twelfth Street Theater orchestra, where vocalist Mamie Smith heard him and invited him to tour with her group, the Jazz Hounds.

Hawkins's first recordings, with Mamie Smith, date from 1922, but he first attracted national attention during his ten-year association with the Fletcher Henderson Orchestra in New York from 1924 to 1934. His earliest recorded solos with the Henderson Orchestra, on such compositions as "Dicty Blues," had a strong sound but used dated, novelty devices such as slap-tonguing, which produces a rather

Saxophonist Coleman Hawkins (CD 1, Track 15), in the 1940s. A competitive player, always interested in cutting-edge developments, Hawkins performed with many of the younger musicians who were innovating bebop in the early 1940s.

humorous effect on the instrument. Hawkins's style quickly became more authoritative and more legato, particularly after Louis Armstrong's year in Henderson's orchestra exerted its influence. Hawkins's solo in "The Stampede," for example, used call-and-response patterns that may owe a debt to Armstrong.

Hawkins's burgeoning solo style demonstrated a hard propulsive attack, a wide vibrato, and technical virtuosity. Drawing on his skill at the piano, Hawkins developed an improvisational saxophone style rooted in harmonic conception. In contrast to earlier solo styles that tended to paraphrase the original melody of a composition, Hawkins created solos with arpeggiating figures that often followed the chord progression. In addition, Hawkins's sophisticated harmonic knowledge made him fluent in chord substitution, which allowed him to replace the given harmonies of a composition for added effect in his improvisations.

After spending five years in Europe, Hawkins returned to the United States in 1939. His recording of "Body and Soul" from that year is an acknowledged masterpiece. The record solidified Hawkins's standing as the undisputed master of tenor saxophone; for example, in *Down Beat* magazine that year, the general public elected him "Best Tenor Saxophonist."

A dominating force in the 1930s, Hawkins influenced practically all other saxophonists. His contemporaries—Ben Webster, Chu Berry, and Herschel Evans—acknowledged allegiance to Hawkins; later tenor players such as John Coltrane rediscovered his works. In his relentless quest for virtuosity on the instrument, Hawkins constantly sought new modes of expression. In an unusual step, he recorded unaccompanied saxophone solos on his "Hawk Variations" (1945) and "Picasso" (1948). His willingness to absorb and adapt to new styles was evident in his performances with new generations of musicians, Dizzy Gillespie and Thelonious Monk in the 1940s and Max Roach in the 1960s. Hawkins continued to record and perform prolifically until his death in 1969.

An **arpeggiated figure** is a melodic fragment based on the notes of the chord harmony and played in succession. Listen to Track 2 of the Audio Primer CD to hear various arpeggios.

Harmonic substitution replaces the expected or normal chords with different, sometimes more unusual, chords. Listen to Track 6 of the Audio Primer CD.

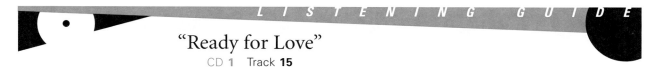

L I S T E N I N G   G U I D E

"Ready for Love"
CD **1**   Track **15**

Coleman Hawkins and His Orchestra: "Ready for Love" (McGhee). Asch 3553. New York,
January 11, 1945. Coleman Hawkins, tenor saxophone; Howard McGhee, composer, trumpet;
Sir Charles Thompson, piano; Edward "Bass" Robinson, bass; Denzil Best, drums.

Hawkins is credited with making the first bebop recordings with Dizzy Gillespie in February 1944, in a session that included "Disorder at the Border" and "Woody n' You." Unfortunately, these historic recordings do not show Hawkins at his best. In early 1945 Hawkins recorded "Ready for Love" with its composer, Howard McGhee, a trumpeter who would later become a member of Charlie Parker's bebop quintet. In this ballad we can hear glimpses of the burgeoning bebop movement as well as enjoy Hawkins's expressive ballad style.

Introduction—2 bars

0:00   In a two-bar chromatic figure, Hawkins on tenor saxophone and Thompson on piano introduce McGhee's melody.

AA—8 bars, repeated

0:05   McGhee plays the eight-bar melody of his tune with a cup-muted trumpet. The harmonic progression of the first three bars is FMA (one bar), D♭MI7 (two beats), G♭9 (two beats), and FMA7 (one bar). The chromatic relation of the G♭ and F chords soon became a standard harmonic device of the bebop era. The prominent E as the major 7th of F major in the third bar of the melody shows an instance of the major-seventh extension becoming a part of the harmonic language of jazz.

The cadence to the F chord at the end of the eight-bar melody uses a chromatic substitute for the dominant: rather than C7 we hear G♭7 as the dominant. (These harmonic innovations became standard practices in the bebop era and will be further discussed in Chapter 7.)

0:25   The melody repeats. We could also interpret the opening F major chord as F minor, which lends an ambiguity to the progression and suggests the use of the F minor harmonies.

B—8 bars

0:45   Thompson plays a piano solo bridge. The harmonic progression of the bridge is even more chromatic:

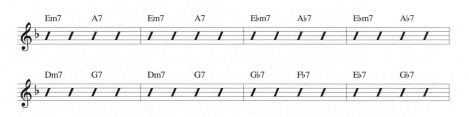

The descending chromatic progression is quite characteristic of bebop.

A—8 bars

1:04   McGhee returns with the final A section.

AABA—Hawkins solo

1:24   In the opening bars of the chorus, articulated F-minor quarter-note chords emphasize the beat before Hawkins enters. Throughout the chorus, interplay between F major and F minor appears. Hawkins's ballad style is in full evidence on this cut. It is robust, yet sensitive; he articulates the harmonies in elegant phrases that often cut across the two- and four-bar structures of the harmonic progression.

2:27   He builds confidently to a high point at the last A section.

2:32   During this last A of the solo, the rhythm cuts off in measure 3 for an extended tenor saxophone cadenza. (A cadenza is a free improvisatory passage without meter.) Note that, on the tonic downbeat concluding the cadenza, the pianist plays an F minor chord.

2:53   As the progression rises (with McGhee doubling on trumpet), the tonality dissolves into F major for the very final chord. Thus the F major–F minor ambiguity is maintained until the very last moment.

In "Ready for Love," we glimpse Hawkins's mature style. Many other players emulated his techniques, as heard in this solo. These techniques include the following:

▶ Sensitive, smoothly articulated melodies

▶ Complex melodic connections based on motivic development and voice leading

▶ Rich, sensuous tone

▶ Loose, free phrasing over the beat, with irregular phrase lengths that remain "vertical," that is, tied to the prevailing harmony

▶ Emotional expression

▶ Large variety of note values

▶ Use of the entire range of the instrument

▶ Improvisation based on the underlying scale/chord structure (inside playing)

LESTER YOUNG: "TELLIN' STORIES" ON THE SAXOPHONE

Probably the only major tenor saxophonist of the time to escape the influence of Hawkins was Lester Willis Young. Billie Holiday claimed to have given him the nickname "Pres" (or "Prez"), short for "president." Gunther Schuller points out that "Lester could not accept Hawkins's essentially staccato, hard-tongued, vertical, chord-anchored approach to the saxophone. His way of hearing music was the way of the blues—and of telling a story in music."[4]

Young, who in the mid-1930s leaped to prominence as a featured soloist with the Count Basie Band, located his influences in white saxophonists Jimmy Dorsey and Frankie Trumbauer. Young cultivated their lighter sound with less vibrato, in contrast to Coleman Hawkins's muscular approach. Reputedly, Young even carried a copy of Trumbauer and Beiderbecke's recording "Singin' the Blues" in his saxophone case. In addition, Young was attracted to Trumbauer's ability to develop an improvisation in a logical and unhurried sequence of events. As Young put it:

> I had to make a decision between Frankie Trumbauer and Jimmy Dorsey—y'dig: I wasn't sure which way I wanted to go, y'dig.... The only people that was tellin' stories that I liked to hear were them.... Ever hear him [Trumbauer] play "Singin' the Blues"? That tricked me right there, that's where I went.[5]

Born in 1909 outside New Orleans in Woodville, Mississippi, Young moved at age eleven to Minneapolis with his father. Young's father formed a minstrel-type band with which Young toured the Midwest, playing carnivals in the Dakotas, Kansas, and Nebraska. A versatile musician, Young played the violin, drums, and alto saxophone before making the tenor his primary instrument. While still in his late teens and early twenties, Young toured with several bands, including King Oliver's group and Walter Page's Blue Devils. In 1933 he settled in Kansas City.

The following year Young joined the band of Count Basie. Young briefly left the band and moved to New York to replace Coleman Hawkins, who had just left Fletcher Henderson to move to Europe. Young's lighter sound and laid-back lyrical style were radically different from Hawkins's approach, however, and were disliked by Henderson's band members. As a result, Young left Henderson and New York, and eventually returned to Kansas City to rejoin Basie's band, a move that would make a significant impact on his career.

Young made his earliest recordings in 1936 with Basie. His solos on "Oh, Lady Be Good" and "Shoe Shine Boy" made an immediate and lasting impact. In his discussion of Young's style, jazz historian Lewis Porter has pointed out many of Young's melodic formulas, which reappear in numerous solos.[6] In addition, Porter shows Young's ability to logically develop a solo through repeated reference to particular melodic ideas—what Young referred to as "tellin' stories." This can be heard in Young's solo on "Shoe Shine Boy" (see the box "Lester Young's Use of Formulas in 'Shoe Shine Boy'").

A **formula** (more popularly called a **lick**) is a worked-out melodic idea that fits a common chord progression. Most improvisers develop formulas for up-tempo pieces because the rapid tempo does not allow time for total spontaneity.

Lester Young's Use of Formulas in "Shoe Shine Boy"

In an extensive analysis of Young's "Shoe Shine Boy" recordings, Lawrence Gushee demonstrates Young's use of formulas to organize a solo.* In the following music example from Gushee, line a shows a basic formula. Lines b through d show how that formula and its variants recur in the same place in relation to the overall AABA song form. In particular, Young always places the formula in measures 5–6 of the tune's A section. Note how the variant in line d departs considerably from the formula's first two occurrences.

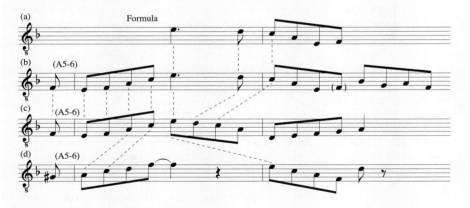

* Lawrence Gushee, "Lester Young's 'Shoe Shine Boy'," in Lewis Porter, *A Lester Young Reader* (Washington and London: Smithsonian Institution Press, 1991), 224–54. Originally published in International Musicological Society, *Report of the Twelfth Congress, Berkeley, 1977*, ed. Daniel Heartz and Bonnie Wade (Kassel: Barenreiter, 1981).

L I S T E N I N G   G U I D E

"Shoe Shine Boy"
CD **1** Track **12**

Jones-Smith Incorporated: "Shoe Shine Boy" (Cahn-Chaplin). Vocalion 3441.
Chicago, November 9, 1936. Carl Smith, trumpet; Lester Young, tenor saxophone;
Count Basie, piano, leader; Walter Page, bass; Jo Jones, drums.

In Chapter 5, we discussed "Shoe Shine Boy" as an example of small-group jazz in the 1930s. The recording is also a fine example of Lester Young's up-tempo saxophone style and use of melodic formulas.

First Chorus—AA sections, 16 bars as 8 + 8

0:00   Count this solo in either a moderate two beats to the bar or a fast four beats.

0:44   Young begins with a two-note motive in syncopation, as if announcing his presence.

0:48   The first use of a melodic formula comes in measures 5–6 of the first A section.

0:52   Second A.

0:56   When these measures (5 and 6) return during the second A, you should be able to hear Young repeating the formula, although not with exactly the same notes. One of the principles of formula use is that in performance the formula will very likely undergo considerable alteration (see the box on Young's use of formulas).

In each of these two A sections, Young begins with a declamatory idea. Afterward, Young returns to his more formulaic playing, as if answering the opening ideas. He "tells his story."

First Chorus—B section, 8 bars

1:00   During the bridge, Young plays a series of planned accents with drummer Jo Jones. (We know they were planned because they also occur on the alternate take.)

First Chorus—A section, 8 bars

1:07   Young ends the first chorus with an idea of alternating between two notes (C and A or C and B♭). The idea of alternating between two notes can be considered another formula and will return.

1:11   Again, measures 5–6 feature a variant of the formula.

Second Chorus—AA sections, 16 bars as 8 + 8

1:15   Young begins his second chorus with another declamatory idea.

1:19   Again, in the fifth and sixth bars, you can hear references to the formula played earlier.

1:22   The second A finds Young developing the two-note repeated idea (now D and A or D and B♭), but now with greater syncopation.

1:27   The second A ends yet again with references to the formula, but this time the reference involves only two notes, E and D.

Second Chorus—B section, 8 bars

1:30   Like the first B section, the second-chorus bridge features accents with drummer Jones. This time, however, Young chooses not to make the accents with Jones but instead builds the bridge to introduce the last A section.

Second Chorus—A section, 8 bars

1:38   Like the other A sections, the final A section of the solo begins with a declamatory idea.

1:42   For a last time, Young alludes to the formula in measures 5–6.

Young, in general, moves among a group of ideas specific to this improvisation and a group of formulas he plays in many of his solos. The result is a refreshing exploration of the "Shoe Shine Boy" harmonic changes that proceeds loosely, yet logically.

Lester Young (CD 1, Tracks 12 and 16), 1939. Notice the tilt of Young's head and the angle at which he holds his saxophone.

Courtesy Frank Driggs Collection

Young's "Shoe Shine Boy" solo shows the following characteristics, all of which influenced the next generation of jazz saxophonists:

▶ Bluesy melodies with rhythmic variety in contrast to eighth-note swing lines

▶ Light, airy tone

▶ Use of space between phrases

▶ Irregular phrase lengths

▶ Melodic connections based on motivic contrast, voice leading, and use of formula

▶ Concentration on the midrange of the instrument

▶ Cool expression

▶ A preference for blues scales and harmonies

Like many of the players associated with Kansas City, Young derived much of his repertory from the blues and compositions written over rhythm changes. One of Young's famous solos is from his composition "Lester Leaps In," based on rhythm changes in B♭ major.

Young remained with Basie until 1940. Playing both tenor and clarinet, he also made several recordings with Billie Holiday, a singer with whom he developed a close bond. After leaving Basie, Young put together several groups of his own, none of which was particularly successful, and he rejoined Basie in 1943. The following year Young won first place in the *Down Beat* poll for tenor saxophonists. Unfortunately, Young was also inducted into the army in 1944, an experience that proved hellish for the thirty-five-year-old tenor player. Arrested for drug use and court-martialed, he spent much of the following year in detention barracks.

After returning to civilian life, Young could not recapture the consistency of his great swing playing, although he made several fine recordings, especially "These Foolish Things" in 1945. Still, he continued to win numerous polls during the forties, and in Leonard Feather's jazz musician poll in 1956, Young won the category of "Greatest Tenor Saxophone Ever." Exacerbated by chronic drinking, Young's health had begun to deteriorate. He died in March 1959, only a few months before the death of his close friend Billie Holiday.

Young's controlled style of playing affected a generation of musicians. Saxophonists who acknowledged a debt to Young included many associated with the later "cool" style of playing, such as Stan Getz, Zoot Sims, Jimmy Giuffre, Al Cohn, Gerry Mulligan, Paul Desmond, and Lee Konitz. At the same time, Young influenced the maturing Charlie Parker, who adapted the flexibility and blues of Young's melodic lines to greater virtuosity. From this mix, Parker decisively influenced the emerging bebop language of the early 1940s (see Chapter 7). Young's stance toward improvisation overturned the dominance of such virtuosos as Louis Armstrong and Coleman Hawkins. In the words of Gunther Schuller, Young's legacy was the launching of "a completely new aesthetic of jazz—for all instruments, not just the tenor saxophone. The essence of his heritage is that he proposed a totally new alternative to the language, grammar, and vocabulary of jazz."[7]

ROY ELDRIDGE: FROM ARMSTRONG TO GILLESPIE

Because the trumpet, as part of the big band, was a major voice in jazz during the swing era, it may be misleading to select one soloist as dominating stylistically. For one thing, Louis Armstrong continued to be the most famous personality in jazz and a major swing-era stylist as well, despite his pioneering work in the 1920s. But if Armstrong's overwhelming presence is discounted, no swing-era player is more significant than Roy Eldridge.

Although Eldridge was hailed as the successor to Louis Armstrong, as well as the predecessor to Dizzy Gillespie, Eldridge evaded Armstrong's influence until he heard the older trumpeter live in 1932. Until then Eldridge had absorbed the playing of trumpeters Rex Stewart and Jabbo Smith. In addition, Eldridge had brought to the trumpet the more harmony-based, vertical approach of Coleman Hawkins.

After 1932 Armstrong exerted a strong influence on swing-style improvisation, but the younger player Eldridge would move beyond him through forward-looking melodic and rhythmic innovations. For example, he fully exploited the three-octave range in the trumpet, and his solos exhibited a fiery vigor and an ability to handle break-neck tempos. His keen awareness of harmony and his instrumental dexterity significantly influenced the pioneers of the subsequent bebop era, especially Dizzy Gillespie.

Born in Pittsburgh in 1911, Eldridge came to New York in 1930. His first recorded solos are from 1935 with the Teddy Hill Band, and he later spent a year as lead trumpeter with the Fletcher Henderson Orchestra. In the late thirties, fronting his own bands, he led a small group at the Three Deuces in Chicago in 1937 and larger bands at various clubs in New York in 1939. His recordings from this period—"Florida Stomp," "After You've Gone," and "Heckler's Hop"—show him completely at ease in rapid playing. He had a penchant for highlighting unusual melodic intervals, and his sinuous melodic lines often encompass two or more octaves within a single phrase.

A **vertical improvisation** is one based on the chord harmonies (stacked vertically), as opposed to the melodic contour (running horizontally).

Eldridge's stature as the leading trumpet soloist of the swing era led to offers from numerous successful white bands, and in 1941 he joined Gene Krupa's band as a featured soloist and, occasionally, as singer. His vocals, along with female vocalist Anita O'Day, were heard on the band's hits "Let Me off Uptown" and "Knock Me a Kiss." Eldridge played ballads and up-tempo numbers equally well, and his performance on Krupa's "Rocking Chair" contains one of his most famous solos.

Flamboyant high-note playing, which comprised more crowd-pleasing antics than successful musical statements, characterized some of Eldridge's work from the 1940s. He also worked with white bandleader Artie Shaw's seventeen-piece band in 1944, but after numerous inevitable racial incidents while touring with the white group, he left after a year to front his own ensembles.

As a trumpet virtuoso, Eldridge thrived in the competitive world of the jam session. In the early forties he played in some of the sessions at Minton's Playhouse, the club that would become the birthplace of the bebop movement. His trumpet battles with Dizzy Gillespie were legendary, and Gillespie frankly acknowledged the musical debt he owed to Eldridge. Thus Eldridge indirectly helped spawn the bebop movement, although he never embraced the newer bebop concepts. While touring Europe with the Benny Goodman band in 1950, Eldridge left to spend a year in Paris. Until he suffered a stroke in 1980, Eldridge led his own groups and performed with Benny Carter, Johnny Hodges, and Coleman Hawkins. He died in 1989.

JACK TEAGARDEN: TROMBONE STYLES

Jack Teagarden (1905–1964) seemingly spanned all periods and styles with his warm, friendly, blues-oriented approach to the instrument. Although he eschewed the rough technique of the early New Orleans players, he became prominently associated with the New Orleans revival of the 1940s, performing often with Louis Armstrong and the fine swing-Dixieland trumpeter Bobby Hackett. His singing was always as relaxed and appealing as his playing. Teagarden based his technique on 1930s swing trombone technique, but he imbued it with a unique personality and feeling for the blues that even avant-garde players respected.

EARL HINES: FLUID AND LINEAR PIANO

Earl Hines established himself as a major talent on piano by performing superbly on the Louis Armstrong Hot Five recordings in the late 1920s (see Chapter 3). He was the musician most responsible for developing a linear, fluid concept of jazz piano; that is, he applied the style of Armstrong's trumpet playing to the keyboard. The dramatic change of style that Hines initiated in the mid-1920s can be appreciated by comparing the earlier Armstrong records, with pianist Lil Hardin, to the later Hot Five selections with Hines. The graceful, easygoing sense of forward movement he contributed to the band predicted the swing style of the 1930s, even while the other sidemen remained entrenched in the New Orleans sound.

Born in Duquesne, Pennsylvania, in 1903, Hines was raised in a musical family. He studied classical piano and played his first gigs in his hometown, which was near Pittsburgh. In 1923 his musical travels brought him to Chicago, where he played with the Carroll Dickerson band and met Louis Armstrong. He performed with Armstrong for several years but decided to continue with his own groups after Armstrong headed off to New York with the Carroll Dickerson band.

Copyright © Bettmann/CORBIS

Earl Hines conducting his orchestra during a 1940 session.

With some earlier experience directing bands, Hines now put together his own group for the Grand Terrace Ballroom. The band eventually grew into a twelve-piece group that used arrangers Cecil Irwin and Jimmy Mundy. (Mundy later became an arranger for Benny Goodman.) Increased celebrity came to Hines when his band began doing radio broadcasts around 1932.

Hines's solo piano recordings from this time—"Blues in Thirds," "I Ain't Got Nobody," and "57 Varieties"—show his superb stride-based piano technique as well as his unparalleled rhythmic creativity. Hines made characteristic use of double-time figures, incorporated occasional left-hand runs, and displayed remarkable independence of the hands. Flights of fancy and liberties with the meter and harmony leave the listener wondering if Hines will land on his feet. Moreover, his improvisations in a group setting contributed to the single-line style of soloing, similar to the linear style of horn players.

Hines's solo approach, with its clean, swinging lines, earned the name "trumpet style" because of its linear melodic emphasis; furthermore, his use of octave tremolos strongly recalled the terminal vibrato of Louis Armstrong's trumpet style. Hines's stunning technique elevated the piano to the level of a lead voice that filled the same role as that of the other solo improvisers.

In the early 1940s Hines directed a band that contributed to the evolution of bebop style. This historically important band included as members Charlie Parker and Billy Eckstine. In the late 1940s Hines rejoined Louis Armstrong, remained until 1951, and continued to perform as a soloist or as a leader of small groups until his death in 1983. Hines was a phenomenal technician whose ability to provide consistently inventive improvisations never diminished. He was indeed one of the finest jazz pianists of all time.

Although Hines's playing never sounded stale, he achieved his greatest distinction during the swing era. He could play with great suaveness, although he tended to be a more rhythmic and adventurous player than Teddy Wilson, who among all others exemplified the smooth swing pianist.

TEDDY WILSON: ELEGANT ENSEMBLE PIANO

Teddy Wilson was probably the most imitated of the swing-era pianists. Earl Hines excelled in both solo piano work and group playing, but Wilson, despite many fine solo efforts, was principally a group pianist. Wilson came to national attention as

Pianist Teddy Wilson (CD 1, Track 13) on the cover of "Goodnight Sweetheart," published in London in 1931. Wilson was probably the most influential swing pianist.

the pianist in Benny Goodman's trio and quartet from 1936 to 1939. His crystalline touch and refined elegance showed an almost classical restraint. Benny Goodman remarked, "My pleasure in playing with Teddy Wilson equalled the pleasure I got out of playing Mozart, and that's saying something."[8]

Born in Austin, Texas, in 1912, Wilson grew up in Alabama, where he studied classical piano and music theory. He learned jazz piano by memorizing works such as Waller's "Handful of Keys" note for note. Wilson eventually forged his own style out of the influences of Earl Hines, Fats Waller, and Art Tatum, but his playing avoided the flamboyance of his mentors. In 1930 Wilson replaced Tatum as the pianist for the Milt Senior Band and soon moved to Chicago. He began playing with Louis Armstrong, Erskine Tate, and Jimmie Noone and occasionally subbed for Earl Hines at the Grand Terrace Ballroom. Through the intercession of John Hammond, Wilson joined Benny Carter's band and moved to New York in 1933. Wilson's earliest recording, dating from 1932, is with Carter's group.

Hammond's advocacy of Wilson laid the groundwork for some of Wilson's most significant musical achievements in the 1930s. For instance, Hammond introduced Wilson to Billie Holiday and set up the famous Brunswick recording series that led to Wilson and Holiday recording numerous sides together. Between 1935 and 1939, Wilson played and wrote these seven-piece arrangements for Holiday and brought together in the recording studio such luminaries as Benny Goodman, Ben Webster, Roy Eldridge, Johnny Hodges, and Lester Young. Much later, Wilson remembered those sessions:

> People have often asked me how I ever managed to get together such a collection of star musicians to accompany Billie Holiday on those records.... They were all big names and it was natural to think it must have cost a fortune to get them together....
>
> I can only explain the mystery by saying that it was only in those sessions that those artists could only play with a group which was at their own level. In their own bands they were the number one soloist, but at my recording sessions they themselves were one of seven top soloists....
>
> So the Teddy Wilson small group sessions were the only chance these men had to play with their peers instead of being the best in the whole band. The result was that nobody really cared about the money they were getting; they were more interested in the excitement of playing with seven men who were all as good as they were.[9]

Hammond also introduced Wilson to Benny Goodman, who was impressed with Wilson's suave pianism. Along with drummer Gene Krupa, Goodman invited Wilson to form the Benny Goodman Trio, the "band-within-a-band" that was featured alongside the Goodman Orchestra. Later, vibraphonist Lionel Hampton joined the small group to create the Benny Goodman Quartet. As noted earlier, Goodman's group became the first important racially mixed band to play and tour publicly.

Because there was no bassist in Goodman's trio and quartet recordings, Wilson contributed significantly to the sound of the group, taking on the equally important roles of accompanist and soloist. Wilson used his left hand in a modified stride style, especially "walking" tenths that provided a linear bass and tenor line on the beat. In addition to using these "walking" tenths, Wilson also used the swing-bass, a stride-derived practice of alternating bass note and midrange chord on every beat.

Although Wilson's right-hand work was rooted in Hines's "trumpet" style of improvisation, Wilson's solos were more restrained and predictable than Hines's flights of fancy. At their best, Wilson's small-group recordings with Goodman's trio and quartet had a "chamber music" quality of improvisation, a balanced conversation among musical peers. This quality can best be heard in Goodman's 1935 landmark recordings of "After You've Gone" and "Body and Soul," as well as on the Goodman quartet version of "Moonglow," recorded the following year, and "Avalon" (see Chapter 5).

After leaving Goodman in 1939, Wilson briefly attempted to lead his own band. In his later career, Wilson continued to perform, fronting his own small groups and performing with Goodman on reunion concerts, touring Russia with Goodman in 1962 and appearing with Goodman at Carnegie Hall twenty years later. He taught jazz piano at Juilliard beginning in 1950 and performed well into the 1980s. Acclaimed as one of the world's great jazz pianists, he died in 1986.

ART TATUM: PIANO TECHNIQUE AT ITS BEST

Art Tatum was certainly one of the most prodigious virtuosos in jazz history. Blind in one eye, and visually impaired in the other, Tatum was trained in the classics in his native Toledo, Ohio, where he was born in 1909. He learned to read music in Braille. He forged a piano style marked with dazzling runs, lightning-fast arpeggios, and an impeccable stride technique derived from Fats Waller. Tatum's repertory drew primarily on popular songs, such as "Tea for Two" and "Willow Weep for Me." While retaining the melody of the tune, he would recast the harmonic structure, substituting more advanced chromatic harmonies for the original chords. As a solo pianist playing with trios, quartets, and larger bands, Tatum made more than 600 recordings that testify to his unerring technique and creative fluency.

Tatum elevated the technique of jazz piano to new heights of excellence, beyond what anyone had thought possible. Although his basic touch was light, his sense of rhythm was extraordinarily secure and provided a swinging foundation to his work that pianists everywhere envied. Moreover, his imaginative treatment of popular melodies and his sense of chordal enrichment influenced and inspired the newly emerging bebop scene of the early 1940s.

Tatum won the admiration of jazz musicians and the public alike for his renditions of light classical pieces in a virtuoso format and at unbelievably fast tempos. His arrangements frequently made use of *rubato* (rhythmically flexible) introductions that moved into up-tempo interpretations based on the rhythms of stride and swing. The arrangements and instrumentation of his trio, which included bassist Slam Stewart and guitarist Tiny Grimes, provided the inspiration for later jazz piano trios, especially those of Nat King Cole and

Virtuoso pianist Art Tatum in a publicity still from the 1940s.

Courtesy Morgan Collection

Oscar Peterson. Moreover, his reharmonizations of popular tunes vastly expanded the vocabulary of jazz harmony. Tatum influenced not only swing-era pianists such as Duke Ellington and Teddy Wilson but also saxophonists Coleman Hawkins and Charlie Parker. In fact, Tatum's virtuosity may very well have been the decisive influence on Parker's emerging bebop style.

Tatum's musical personality had two sides—the popular virtuoso and the after-hours pianist. Listeners often remarked that his best playing took place during sessions that sometimes lasted all night long. This side of Tatum's personality is well represented on "Aunt Hagar's Blues": One of his greatest recordings, it far surpasses most others in depth of expression and structural inventiveness. Tatum expanded the vocabulary of stride and swing piano in solos like this in four significant ways:

1. Timing of Chords: Most stride and swing pianists played octaves, single notes, or perhaps tenths on the first and third beats and three-note or four-note chords on the second and fourth beats, but Tatum sometimes played richly voiced, full chords on all four beats.

2. Runs: While many stride and swing pianists used embellished runs to connect melodic phrases, Tatum used these runs more consistently and elaborately.

3. Rapidity: Swing and stride pianists always featured impressive dexterity and speed, but Tatum's playing was the most rapid.

4. Harmony: While jazz piano had been slowly developing more-sophisticated harmonies, including extended chords and nondiatonic progressions, Tatum was the most harmonically advanced of any of his contemporaries.

In the 1950s, record producer Norman Granz produced a voluminous number of Tatum's recordings that advanced Tatum's career. Sadly, though, Tatum died in 1956, probably because of the effects of alcoholism. Still, we are lucky that his art was documented with exceptionable thoroughness, and it has inspired jazz pianists ever since.

JIMMY BLANTON: BASSIST AS SOLOIST

Jimmy Blanton revolutionized bass playing during his brief tenure with the Duke Ellington band. Born in 1918, he was from a musical family (his mother was a pianist) and was raised in Chattanooga, Tennessee. Although he attended Tennessee State College briefly, his musical interests and ambitions eventually led him to St. Louis in the late 1930s, where he played in the Jeter-Pillars Orchestra and the Fate Marable riverboat bands. Here Duke Ellington discovered Blanton in 1939 and hired him for his orchestra.

Blanton's performances with the Ellington orchestra were exceptional. He recorded numerous pieces in which his virtuosity and ability to carry a solo changed the perceived role of bass players in ensembles. One of the most famous of his pieces was "Jack the Bear." Before Blanton, it was rare to give a solo to a bass player; after Blanton, it became common, as bandleaders grew to expect more from their bassists than routine timekeeping. (Recall from Chapter 5 the discussion of Blanton's playing in "Sepia Panorama," CD 1, Track 14.)

In addition to his fine work with the Ellington group and in small-group settings, Blanton can be heard in an interesting set of piano-bass duos recorded with Ellington.

Sadly, Blanton's playing began to slide in 1941. He was diagnosed with tuberculosis and died in 1942.

JO JONES: MODERNIZING THE DRUMS

In Chapter 5, we discussed how Jo Jones modernized drumming techniques by transferring the timekeeping role from the bass and snare drums to the cymbals, particularly the hi-hat. His feel for time helped popularize the four-beats-to-the-bar orientation of most of the swing bands; he was also well known for his work with brushes. "Shoe Shine Boy" (CD 1, Track 12, discussed earlier in this chapter) is just one example of Jones's fine work.

Born in Chicago in 1911, Jones grew up in Alabama. He worked as a tap dancer in carnival shows before joining Walter Page's Blue Devils in Oklahoma City in the late 1920s. Eventually, he made his way to Kansas City in 1933, where he joined Basie in 1934. After leaving Basie, he toured in 1947 with Jazz at the Philharmonic; in later life, he continued to work in swing-style groups. He died in 1985.

GENE KRUPA: DRUMS WITH DRIVE

Originally from Chicago, Krupa (1909–1973) worked with Red McKenzie and Eddie Condon's Chicagoans in the late 1920s. After performing with numerous bands, his

Courtesy Morgan Collection

Drummer Gene Krupa (CD 1, Track 13).

reputation in the New York studio scene led to an opportunity to join Benny Goodman in late 1934. Krupa became one of Goodman's most important sidemen, and possibly the most idolized. Inevitably, he broke from Goodman in 1938 to form his own band, which included Roy Eldridge and singer Anita O'Day. The Krupa band was among the most popular of the early forties. Later in the decade, Krupa worked with his own groups, performed with Tommy Dorsey, and found time for occasional reunions with Goodman. After breaking up his band in 1951, he performed with Jazz at the Philharmonic tours. In 1954 he founded a percussion school in New York with drummer Cozy Cole.

Gene Krupa was probably the most well-known drummer of the swing era, though his contributions to technique did not equal those of such pioneers as Jo Jones or Kenny Clarke (see Chapter 7). While famous for his showmanship, he was just as often criticized for being heavy-handed and unswinging, with a tendency toward crowd-pleasing antics. Ultimately, however, Krupa's legacy is quite positive—within his limitations, he was able to work with Goodman in creating a band unequaled in its appeal, a band that derived its great energy from Krupa's drive and power.

CHARLIE CHRISTIAN: SHIFT TO ELECTRIC GUITAR

Charlie Christian's legendary career was meteoric and brief. John Hammond, hearing of the guitarist from Oklahoma City, arranged an audition for Christian with Benny Goodman in 1939. Goodman hired him immediately. As a member of Goodman's Sextet, Christian recorded outstanding solos on "Flying Home," "Seven Come Eleven," "Stardust," and "Air Mail Special." In 1941 he was taking part in the ground-breaking jam sessions at Minton's in Harlem (see Chapter 7) and playing nightly sessions with the future architects of the bebop movement, including Dizzy Gillespie and Thelonious Monk. By March 1942, he was dead of tuberculosis at the age of twenty-five.

Born in 1916, Charlie Christian was the first major player to feature electric guitar in jazz ensembles. Indeed, Christian played a fundamental role in the shift to the electric guitar, an instrument available only after 1936, when the Gibson company released its arched-top model. Although the arched-top acoustic guitar—such as the one played earlier in the decade by Eddie Lang—was suitable in the studio where microphones could be strategically placed, it was frequently drowned out in live performance. In the era of the big band, amplification soon became necessary.

With his swinging eighth-note lines, Christian developed an improvisational style with a fluidity akin to that of a horn player. Christian thus made his mark not as a rhythm guitarist, in the manner of Freddie Green's four-to-the-bar style of propelling the Basie band, but as a complete soloist. Although his recordings span a mere two years, they show him to be one of the most fertile improvisers of the era. As a star soloist with the Goodman band, Christian revolutionized jazz guitar playing and became a profound influence on a generation of guitarists. In light of the recordings made toward the end of his life with players of the upcoming bebop movement, it is interesting to speculate on whether Christian would have developed into one of the preeminent voices of the newer bebop idiom.

Christian's solos are remarkably elegant, as definitive of swing as Lester Young's or Benny Goodman's. Charlie Christian's influence was so great that not much happened to change jazz guitar technique until the jazz-rock players of the late 1960s and early 1970s began to restyle the sound. Christian's guitar tone, with slight variations, became the established jazz guitar timbre for more than two decades.

Christian was perfectly poised between swing and bebop. A relaxed sense of swing, perfect voice-leading control, subtle motivic manipulation, variety of phrase length, and imaginative harmonies characterized his style. With his exemplary command of swing improvisation, Charlie Christian was one of the greatest guitar players in jazz history.

BENNY CARTER: COMPOSER AND ARRANGER

Still performing, arranging, composing, and even touring to this day, after eight decades in the music business, Benny Carter personifies the history of jazz. Although an elegant alto saxophone stylist who has also recorded impressively on the trumpet and other instruments, Carter is most noted for his superb arrangements. It is perhaps Carter's misfortune to be so multitalented that he is difficult to categorize.

"All of Me": A Benny Carter Arrangement

Here, we compare the original melody of the popular song "All of Me" to the version in the final chorus of Benny Carter's 1940 arrangement.*

Notice the extensive liberties Carter takes with the melody and the chords. The added syncopations are typical of swing-era arrangers who sought to incorporate the freer rhythms of the improvising soloists into their charts. He completely abandons the rhythmic gesture of dotted quarter, eighth, and half note in measures 1, 3, and 5 of the original. In Carter's first two measures, the opening gesture of B♭–F–D is rhythmically compressed, reversed,

and stated again. Much more syncopated than the original, measures 3 and 5 in Carter's version maintain the identical rhythm to each other. The chromatic triplet in the last beat of measure 4 strikingly sets off the arrival to the G in measure 5. Carter's measures 3 and 5 also include a harmonic substitution from the original, shifting up a half step in the final beat of each.

The final pitches of the original measures 6–7 (A♭–G–F–E♭) appear in Carter's arrangement (circled in our example below) but are there nested within a more rhythmically involved figure.

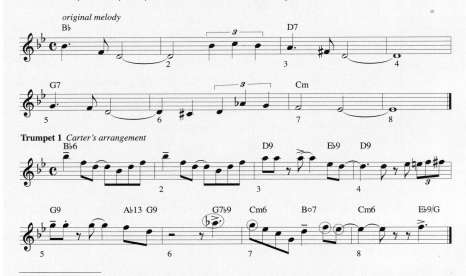

---

* Transcription in Fred Sturm, *Changes Over Time: The Evolution of Jazz Arranging* (Germany: Advance Music, 1995), 21, 40.

Born in 1907 and raised in New York, Carter worked with several local teachers but primarily taught himself. He performed with Earl Hines in the mid-1920s and with Fletcher Henderson from 1930 to 1931. He wrote important arrangements for Henderson, including "Keep a Song in Your Soul" (1930). After a stint as the music director of McKinney's Cotton Pickers, he started his own band in New York in 1932— a band that helped influence the newly emerging swing style. He worked in London as a staff arranger for the BBC from 1936 to 1938 and returned to New York to form a new orchestra at the Savoy ballroom in 1939.

As the swing era began to wane, Carter saw his future in writing and arranging for Hollywood. He moved to Los Angeles in 1942, led some bands, and grew more involved in studio work, which eventually led to his writing for the movie *Stormy Weather* (1943). From 1946 on, he was associated with the Jazz at the Philharmonic tours, while in the 1950s and 1960s he concentrated on arranging and scoring. In the 1970s, he resumed active performing.

Carter is probably one of the two leading alto saxophone stylists of swing, the other being Johnny Hodges of the Duke Ellington band. As an arranger, he helped innovate swing style and was especially well known for his writing for saxophones. Also a songwriter, Carter composed numerous popular tunes, including the standard "When Lights Are Low." (See the box " 'All of Me': A Benny Carter Arrangement.")

BILLIE HOLIDAY: TRAGIC SINGER

Billie Holiday was the touchstone of jazz singing. From Louis Armstrong's model, Holiday cultivated a free sense of rhythm and phrasing, much like an instrumental soloist, and she had an uncanny ability to inhabit and project the lyric of a composition. Despite an untrained voice, "Lady Day," as Lester Young named her, had an unerring sense of pitch. She was perhaps best known for her performances of slow, poignant ballads, frequently of unrequited love; these songs came to mirror her own complex and tragic life. Her later life was marred by failed romances and, ultimately, drug addiction.

Holiday was born in Philadelphia in 1915, but the details of her early life remain murky. We do know that her mother moved to New York and left the young child with family in Baltimore. There, she may have been abused; by her own accounts, Holiday was raped as a child and compelled to work as a prostitute during her early teens. In order to be with her mother, she moved to New York in 1928, and she began working small clubs as a singer in the early thirties. In 1933, John Hammond heard her sing and arranged for her to record with Benny Goodman.

At the peak of her vocal powers, in the 1930s and 1940s, Holiday usually performed with small jazz groups. Her studio recordings with the Teddy Wilson Orchestra from 1935 to 1942 for the Brunswick label are treasures of the swing era, featuring such soloists as Chu Berry, Lester Young, Benny Goodman, and Roy Eldridge (see the earlier discussion of Teddy Wilson in this chapter). Of these recordings, the 1937 version of "A Sailboat in the Moonlight" shows the uncanny musical rapport Holiday had with tenor

Billie Holiday (CD 1, Track 16) and Lionel Hampton (CD 1, Track 13) perform together at Esquire's Fourth Annual All-American Jazz Concert held at the Metropolitan Opera House in New York City, 1944.

saxophonist Lester Young, who weaves his melodic lines around Holiday's vocals in the same relaxed, behind-the-beat manner. Many of the sidemen on "A Sailboat in the Moonlight" were from Basie's band, and Holiday worked with Basie's big band in 1937. Her performances with Artie Shaw in 1938 number among the first instances of a black singer working with a white band.

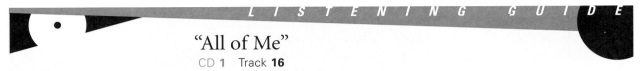

"All of Me"

CD **1** Track **16**

Billie Holiday and Eddie Heywood and His Orchestra: "All of Me" (Simon-Marks).
OKeh 6214. New York, March 21, 1941. Billie Holiday, vocal; Shad Collins, trumpet; Leslie Johnakins,
Eddie Barefield, alto saxophones; Lester Young, tenor saxophone; Eddie Heywood, piano;
John Collins, guitar; Ted Sturgis, bass; Kenny Clarke, drums.

Holiday's performance of "All of Me" provides a good example of Holiday's great work and shows several of her trademarks. The expressivity and plaintive timbre of her voice greatly enhance Holiday's persona and vivid presence. In addition, her reputation as the "jazz singer's singer" derives from one of her greatest strengths—the freedom of her phrasing. This freedom results primarily from delaying the entry of each phrase, a stylistic device now sometimes called *back phrasing*.

Introduction—8 bars

0:00   Heywood's solo piano begins the tastefully arranged introduction. The first three notes are an eighth-note triplet pick-up; count a moderate four beats to the bar, beginning on the fourth note of the introduction (the downbeat, where the left-hand chord enters). The entire band answers the piano with syncopated figures throughout the eight bars.

ABAC—32 bars, presentation of the song

0:18   Holiday presents the tune, which is in thirty-two-bar ABAC form. In this format, the sixteen-bar AB is sometimes called the "first half" and the sixteen-bar AC the "second half."

0:35   The B section ("Take my lips . . .") can be heard as a kind of bridge analogous to the B section in a thirty-two-bar AABA song.

1:23   The last two bars of the song are a solo break for Lester Young on tenor saxophone. The scoring behind Holiday is light, with the drummer using brushes to help keep the mood gentle; the bass player walks. The result is an easygoing fox-trot dance rhythm.

The transcription shows how freely Holiday treats the rhythm and pitches of the melody.

The top line of each score presents the first eight bars of the original tune, while the first and

last choruses of Holiday's performance appear in the second and third lines of each score. Holiday's first chorus (middle line) remains fairly close to the original melody but is consistently back phrased.

Can't you see _____ I'm no good with - out you? _____

The song is constructed around a contraction of the opening motive, F–C–A (measure 1), into E–C#–A (measure 3), and finally into D–C–A (measure 5). These contractions parallel the chord changes F major, A major, and D7.

Lester Young tenor saxophone solo—8 bars

1:27   After the two-bar break ending the previous section, Lester Young's tenor solo begins with an arranged modification of the chord changes. For example, the first two chords are a B♭ major (IV) chord (instead of an F major) progressing to a B♭ minor (iv) chord, then finally to F major. The free-floating quality of Young's solo beautifully complements to Holiday's singing and shows why they worked so well together musically.

AB—8 bars, first half of song

1:46   Holiday returns with the melody, though in modified form. In this, Holiday's final chorus (bottom line of the music example presented in the ABAC section), the pitch A, common to all three appearances of the song's principal motive, is transferred to a higher register and emphasized.

This last chorus is a free paraphrase of the original melody and approaches improvisation, as can be seen in the following analysis:

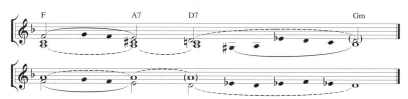

2:16   At the end of this first half, Young answers with a solo break.

AC—8 bars, second half of song

2:20   Holiday finishes the second half of the tune freely, as she did in the first half. The unobtrusive and effective arrangement builds somewhat toward the end, but remains an accompaniment; Holiday continues to hold center stage.

Back phrasing is momentarily delaying the entry of a new phrase, in effect freeing the rhythm of a composition.

Holiday's popular appeal increased. While appearing at New York's Cafe Society in 1939, she recorded "Strange Fruit," a song about lynching in the South. This brave and unusual step for a jazz performer won her critical acclaim as her signature song. (Holiday sometimes claimed to have written the song, but in fact a white male composer, Lewis Allen, wrote it.) She began to focus on dark ballads, exemplified by her own composition "God Bless the Child," as well as "Lover Man," "Gloomy Sunday," and "Don't Explain." Audiences took these works as autobiographical, reflecting her two failed marriages, arrests, incarceration, and drug addiction.

Increasingly, Holiday's arrests and failing health during the 1950s sidelined her career. Although drug abuse ravaged her vocal range and timbre, she could still sing with tortured expression. Her version of the blues song "Fine and Mellow" from the 1957 television show "Sound of Jazz" shows how much she could express with so few notes still available in her range. She died in 1959, only a few months after the death of Lester Young.

Few jazz singers escaped Holiday's influence and her interpretive style. As she herself described it:

> I don't think I'm singing. I feel like I am playing a horn. I try to improvise like Les Young, like Louis Armstrong, or someone else I admire. What comes out is what I feel. I hate straight singing. I have to change a tune to my own way of doing it. That's all I know.[10]

ELLA FITZGERALD: SIXTY YEARS OF SONG

The career of Ella Fitzgerald spanned six decades. Her supreme vocal dexterity, large pitch range, dramatic dynamic contrasts, use of melodic ornaments, and—above all—scat singing made her name synonymous with jazz singing. From the time of her earliest recordings with Chick Webb in the 1930s, her ability to straddle jazz and popular styles made her one of the most beloved performers in jazz.

Fitzgerald was born in Virginia in 1917, but in early childhood she moved to New York. As a teenager, she overcame her basically shy nature by entering local talent contests with dreams of becoming a dancer. It soon became clear that dancing was not her strength but she had tremendous talent as a singer. Chick Webb hired her to work in his band soon after she appeared in a singing contest at the Apollo Theater in 1934. Their recordings of songs such as "A-tisket, A-tasket" and "Undecided" catapulted Fitzgerald to fame.

Fitzgerald led Webb's band for several years following his death in 1939, but later she pursued a solo career. She preferred the backing of a small group, often a quartet or trio, that for four years included her one-time husband, bassist Ray Brown. Some critics find her strongest work to be the "songbooks" recorded with Verve Records between 1956 and 1961, each interpreting the repertory of a particular American popular song composer, including Cole Porter, Rodgers and Hart, Duke Ellington, George and Ira Gershwin, and Harold Arlen.

Fitzgerald's performances on the songbooks treat the melodies in relatively unadorned fashion, but her improvisational skill was unparalleled. Her recording of "You'd Be So Nice to Come Home To" involved a freewheeling improvisation of the melody. Following the first chorus, Fitzgerald fitted the original lyrics to a new improvised line, embellishing and stretching the original melody into a new version, and often trading phrases with an instrumental soloist. Other Fitzgerald works included scat singing that showed an improvisational ability equaling the best instrumental soloists. Fitzgerald's ballad singing has sometimes been criticized for a lack of gravity, but her technique and inventiveness have made her a jazz virtuoso.

Blessed with a long career, Fitzgerald continued to work. Because of complications with diabetes, she began to have difficulty with her eyesight in the 1970s. She also had heart surgery in 1986, but did not stop performing until the early 1990s. She died in 1996.

Pictured on a small-format wartime edition of the "Cow Cow Boogie" published in Belgium (for 7.5 Belgian francs), an exuberant Ella Fitzgerald showcases the Universal picture *Ride 'Em, Cow-Boy.*

Summary of the Features of Swing

The following tables summarize the swing-era features, most of which have been discussed in the last several chapters.

Features of Swing on Piano

RIGHT-HAND TEXTURE

▶ Single-note improvisation much like swing-style, melodic improvisation on other instruments
▶ Less syncopated than ragtime with less pivoting around fixed notes
▶ Looser, greater use of long eighth-note lines
▶ Brilliant runs between phrases
▶ Less aggressive interlock of left hand and right hand (as heard in stride style)

LEFT-HAND TEXTURE

▶ Stride-derived practice of bass as swing bass, but bass notes often in tenths
▶ Use of walking tenths and occasional cross-hand textures
▶ Light, accompanying chords often emphasizing a tenor-voice "thumb line"

HARMONY

▶ Mostly diatonic (based on the chords of the major scale)
▶ Sixth and seventh chords predominating in left hand, with ninth chords occurring from time to time

Features of Swing Improvisation in Ensembles

TIMBRE

▶ More refined and polished than New Orleans/Dixieland
▶ Less use of vibrato
▶ Smoother, lighter saxophone tone
▶ More brilliant trumpet tone
▶ Less use of specific instrumental effects
▶ Instrumental ranges extended upward
▶ Softer attacks and more legato playing
▶ Somewhat less use of blue-note effects

PHRASING

▶ In two-bar or four-bar units, but more varied in later swing styles (ballad playing featured more irregular phrasing)
▶ Not much space between phrases

RHYTHM

▶ More swinging, although less syncopation than in Dixieland
▶ Up-tempo reliance on eighth-note lines
▶ Ballads that feature a greater variety of rhythmic values

THEMATIC CONTINUITY

▶ Less reliance on motive and song embellishment in up-tempo solos, more reliance on voice leading
▶ In ballads, motivic relationships more prominent

CHORD-TO-SCALE RELATIONS

▶ Inside playing
▶ In later swing, more experimentation with extended chord tones within melodic lines

LARGE-SCALE COHERENCE

▶ Voice leading and song paraphrase more often than motivic structure
▶ Gestural balance

FORM AND STRUCTURE

▶ Strophic AABA, ABAC, or blues forms
▶ Tempos ranging from slow to very fast
▶ Improvisations structured by voice leading and motivic relationships

Questions and Topics for Discussion

1. What were some of the important big bands of the swing era besides Ellington, Basie, and Goodman?

2. Can differences of style be detected between the black and white swing-era bands?

3. How did Lester Young's style on tenor saxophone differ from that of Coleman Hawkins?

4. How did swing-era piano style differ from the stride style of the 1920s? Did some pianists retain elements of stride? Who? How did they?

5. Who were some of the important vocalists of the swing era? How did their styles differ?

Key Terms

Arpeggiated figure

Back phrasing

Formula (lick)

Harmonic substitution

Vertical improvisation

The millions of industrial workers who enlisted or were drafted to fight in World War II were, of course, nearly all men. "Rosie the Riveter" was the collective name of the wives, sisters, girlfriends, daughters, and mothers who went to work creating the military hardware that made the United States the "arsenal of democracy." After the war ended, the GIs returned to their factories, and "Rosie" was sent home to have children. A generation later, however, many of Rosie's children, raised on stories of independent women in overalls earning their own paychecks, helped start the women's movement.

THE BEBOP ERA

7

WE THINK OF THE "MODERN JAZZ" ERA as beginning with bebop in the mid-1940s. But what makes bebop "modern," distinguishing it from the preceding swing era? This chapter explores bebop's most significant characteristics:

- General aesthetics grounded in improvisation and solo playing, not in melody, popular song, and arrangement
- The emergence of bebop melodies—"heads"—that stylistically complement the improvisations
- Smaller groups being far more common than big bands
- Musical venues taking place in jazz clubs rather than large dance halls
- Deemphasis on commercial or popular success
- Deemphasis on dancing:
  - ▶ Tempos considerably faster or slower than in swing
  - ▶ Rhythmic pulse less obviously articulated than in swing
- Rise in black consciousness resulting from a new perception of African Americans' contributions to jazz

Many of these points provided the cultural context of jazz for the remainder of the twentieth century. Besides defining a more modern sensibility, these characteristics helped transform jazz from a popular venue to a fine art in many of its more ambitious substyles. Before exploring the characteristics of bebop further, we shall look at the origins of bebop in the 1940s.

Revolution Versus Evolution

The emergence of bebop in the 1940s irrevocably altered the jazz landscape. In contrast to the well-polished big bands of the swing era—many of them incredibly successful— some jazz musicians began gravitating toward smaller groups. Initially they developed their musical ideas in impromptu jam sessions, especially in such after-hours Harlem clubs as Monroe's Uptown House and Minton's Playhouse. By the end of World War II, these cutting-edge musicians had moved downtown to appear at the nightclubs on West Fifty-Second Street. Dozens of clubs—such as the Three Deuces, the Onyx, the Downbeat, the Famous Door, the Spotlite, Kelly's Stables, and the Hickory House—opened their doors on what became known as "The Street." They called the new music *rebop* (eventually to fall into disuse), *bebop*, or just *bop*.

Although many of the architects of bebop—such as Charlie "Yardbird" or "Bird" Parker, John Birks "Dizzy" Gillespie, and Kenny Clarke—began their careers playing in big bands, bebop represented a radical rejection of the musical conventions of the swing era. Instead of elaborate dance halls, bebop players performed in bars and nightclubs. Some of its players seemed indifferent to commercial success as entertainers: They played for listening rather than dancing. Rather than the slick show-business theatrics of the big bands, bebop bands aimed to capture the informal spirit of the jam session. Its groups often comprised only five or six musicians— two or three horn players and a rhythm section of piano, bass, drums. While the big-band arrangers of the swing era carefully inserted improvised solos within longer written arrangements, the smaller bebop bands avoided elaborate charts and emphasized, above all, virtuosic improvisational skill.

Many of the older musicians were perplexed by these new sounds. Bandleader Cab Calloway is said to have derided trumpeter Dizzy Gillespie's playing as "Chinese music." In 1948 trumpeter Louis Armstrong dismissed bebop as an annoying novelty performed by overly competitive musicians. He said:

> All they want to do is show you up, and any old way will do as long as it's different from the way you played it before. So you get all them weird chords which don't mean nothing, and first people get curious about it just because it's new, but soon they get tired of it because it's really no good and you got no melody to remember and no beat to dance to.[1]

Drummer Dave Tough, a "Chicagoan" in the 1920s who later became an important drummer during the swing era, reacted with less hostility but was clearly confused by the music. After first hearing Dizzy Gillespie and Oscar Pettiford's band on Fifty-Second Street, he noted:

> As we walked in, see, these cats snatched up their horns and blew crazy stuff. One would stop all of a sudden and another would start for no reason at all. We never could tell when a solo was supposed to begin or end. Then they all quit at once and walked off the stand. It scared us.[2]

Reactions such as these were not uncommon in the music world, but the fans of traditional jazz were the most disappointed: The music they loved was being called passé, old-fashioned, and—the worst insult of all—unhip. As expected, many champions bemoaned the demise of classic jazz and argued that bebop abandoned

Bebop and **bop** are terms that came about in the 1940s to describe the nervous, energetic style of the younger jazz musicians. The terms probably developed from the nonsense syllables used by scat singers to re-create the characteristic melodic phrases of the new style.

jazz music's most treasured principles. Modernists called these listeners "moldy figs." Arguments between the two sides enlivened much jazz discourse in the late 1940s.

Bebop began in the early 1940s as an "insider's" music—a music for musicians. Despite the efforts of the moldy figs, bebop would become the dominant jazz style by the end of the decade. Among other factors, a wartime tax on dance halls triggered their decline. Small jazz clubs, such as the ones found on Fifty-Second Street, boomed. Younger players, who had fewer outlets for musical employment than the stars of the big bands, joined small groups and experimented with the new musical language.

Bohemianism added an attractive element to the music. Performers and their "hipster" audiences often took on the affectations and inside slang of beboppers. Some of these affectations—such as Dizzy Gillespie's beret, goatee, and horn-rimmed glasses—were benign; others—such as Charlie Parker's heroin addiction—were not.

With bebop, jazz ceased to be a strongly commercial music. Although some musicians, such as Dizzy Gillespie, felt that bebop should try to adapt to dancing, many of its devotees interpreted the music as a political statement, a rejection of all things conformist and mainstream, including a reaction against American racism and segregation. Many players felt that Louis Armstrong and other older musicians conformed to racial stereotypes of black entertainers. Bebop was meant to challenge and defy these stereotypes. Indeed, political activism among some black musicians

Moldy figs was a term used by younger musicians and fans in the late 1940s to describe older jazz fans who clung to the music of the 1920s and 1930s and derided the newer bebop style.

A **hipster** was a young, often white, follower of bebop who affected the dress, speech, and manner of jazz musicians working in the new jazz styles of the late 1940s and early 1950s.

Courtesy Morgan Collection

In 1943, the "zoot-suit" riots—named for the stylized clothing of young Chicanos—erupted in Los Angeles and continued for a week as whites, including soldiers and sailors on leave, attacked Hispanics. A future recording supervisor of jazz for Mercury Records, Norman Granz, organized a concert at the Philharmonic Auditorium in Los Angeles to benefit Mexican youths, and an enduring concert series began. Here is the 1949 program for Jazz at the Philharmonic, picturing, among others, Ron Brown on bass and Shelley Manne on drums. Notice the integrated seating, part of an anti-discrimination clause Granz wrote into all his contracts.

can be traced to the nonconformity of the beboppers. As institutional segregation came under attack in the 1950s and 1960s, black musicians often used their music as a public statement of their political beliefs. Thus the conventions of bebop laid the foundation for modern jazz, both in musical style and in the convictions of its players.

Despite these dramatic, possibly revolutionary, developments, much of the musical style of bebop evolved naturally from swing style. Players carried over to bebop the following features of earlier jazz:

- Improvisation on the following:
  - ▶ Thirty-two–bar popular songs in AABA or ABAC form
  - ▶ Rhythm changes
  - ▶ The blues
- Improvisation based mostly on eighth-note melodic lines
- Characteristic instrumentation of rhythm section plus horns
- Overall performance formats of head-solos-head

Seen in this light, bebop was a natural next step in the musical development of jazz. This should not be surprising, because the musicians who innovated bebop had trained extensively in swing bands. Although many of the revolutionary aspects of bebop were more social than musical, jazz musicians and fans at the time were indeed caught up with what they perceived as the radical newness of its language. In the description of bebop style to follow, we shall emphasize these innovations rather than the older swing elements.

Characteristics of the Bebop Style

The new music that offended or confused older musicians such as Cab Calloway, Louis Armstrong, and Dave Tough differed from earlier jazz in improvisational style, melodic language, and harmonic language. Much of the repertory changed considerably. In typical bebop compositions, the horns played the melody, improvised solos followed, and a reprise of the melody formed the ending. The horns frequently stated the melody in unison or in octaves, creating a starker, leaner sound than the full-voiced chords played by big bands. Bebop groups played at brighter tempos than those of swing bands but played their ballads much more slowly.

Bebop also departed from swing because the newer style did not support dancing as well as the older style. As we have seen, musicians created the jazz of the 1920s and 1930s for dancing. The musicians of the era speak fondly of the energizing give-and-take between the dancers and the bands. The beboppers, however, disassociated jazz from the jitterbugging crowds of the 1930s in an attempt to win respect for their music as an art form. The radical change in tempo also certainly affected dancing. Further, some argue that the swing era had run its course, making the separation of the music from dancing and popular song inevitable. If it were to remain vibrant, jazz needed to evolve. The popular audience, of course, wanted danceable, singable music—a void soon to be filled by rock and roll.

The repertory for the bop-style bands continued to depend on the twelve-bar blues and compositions based on the chords to "I Got Rhythm"—both a legacy of the Kansas City style—as well as the thirty-two–bar AABA or ABAC form in standard popular songs. But an important innovation of the repertory was the *recomposition*

A Recomposition: Dizzy Gillespie's "Groovin' High"

Here is a comparison of the original melody of "Whispering" with Gillespie's recomposition "Groovin' High":

The "Whispering" melody, which is primarily diatonic, almost masks its harmonic progression. In "Groovin' High," Gillespie writes a new melody mostly in eighth notes and with more notes than in the original composition—typical of the bebop melodic language. Gillespie's recomposed melody

▶ Is much more chromatic

▶ Is jagged and angular

▶ Outlines and highlights the harmonic progression through a repeated motive (marked as B)

▶ Has accents that crop up in unexpected places

These are the features of bebop that swing fans sometimes found hard to understand. Gillespie's melody, too, has the typical double-eighth-note figure prevalent in bebop melodies and improvisations (marked as A). This characteristic two-note figure may very well be the source of the word *bebop*.

---

of these popular songs into a bebop framework. In these recompositions, players abandoned the original melody and composed a new one over the harmonic structure of the original. (See the box "A Recomposition: Dizzy Gillespie's 'Groovin' High.'") For the bebop player, recompositions had two advantages:

> A **recomposition** is a new melody composed to fit the harmonic and formal structure of a previously composed popular song.

1. The new melody resembled the bebop improvisations that followed and kept the musical language unified.

2. Performers and record companies did not have to pay song royalties, because they did not use the original melodies.

Many of the significant early works of the bebop era were recompositions:

BEBOP-STYLE TUNE (COMPOSER)	ORIGINAL (COMPOSER)
KoKo (Charlie Parker)	**Cherokee** (Ray Noble)
Hot House (Tadd Dameron)	**What Is This Thing Called Love?** (Cole Porter)
Crazeology (Benny Harris)	**I Got Rhythm** (George Gershwin)
Groovin' High (Dizzy Gillespie)	**Whispering** (Rose-Coburn-Schonberger)

Dizzy Gillespie, one of the founders of the new style, acknowledged the obvious differences in bebop from earlier jazz but was keenly aware of how the music evolved logically from swing. When asked to contrast the newer bebop music with the older style, he cited several differences:

Chords.... And we stressed different accents in the rhythms. But I'm reluctant to say that anything is the difference between our music of the early forties and the music before that, of the thirties. You can get records from the early days and hear guys doing the same things. It just kept changing a little bit more; one guy would play a phrase one way, and another guy would come along and do something else with it.... Charlie Parker was very, very melodic; guys could copy his things quite a bit. [Thelonious] Monk was one of the founders of the movement too, but his playing, my playing, and Charlie Parker's playing were altogether different.[3]

The one characteristic that players most frequently singled out as new was the harmony. As saxophonist Illinois Jacquet pointed out, "The major difference in the new music was the chord changes."[4] The harmonies used by the bebop players sometimes emphasized the upper parts of chords such as ninths, elevenths, and thirteenths. These additions to chords, or extended chord tones, would be contributed not only by the accompanying pianist but also sometimes by the soloist. Hearing the emphasis on these extensions, early critics of the music thought the improvisers were playing "wrong notes."

Music Example 7-1a, the opening of Gillespie's "A Night in Tunisia," shows a prominent use of the seventh, ninth, and thirteenth as arpeggiated chordal extensions. Also prominent in bebop was the so-called flatted fifth, the use of a pitch a tritone away from the root of the chord. The melody of measures 7–8 of "A Night in Tunisia" illustrates the use of the flatted fifth: Here, E♭ is used in conjunction with the A7 chord.

Extended chord tones, sometimes called **tensions,** are notes added to seventh chords to make the harmony richer and more pungent. These tones are usually ninths, elevenths, and thirteenths. Extended chord tones usually resolve to more stable pitches, such as roots, thirds, and fifths.

Music Example 7-1
"A Night in Tunisia."

a. Opening

b. Measures 7–8

Reharmonization was another important new aspect of bebop harmony. Bebop players often inserted new chords and chord progressions into a standard composition: This gave soloists more chords to improvise over. Reharmonization was popular at the jam sessions in Harlem in the early 1940s. "We'd do that kind of thing in 1942 around Minton's a lot," Dizzy Gillespie recalled. "We'd been doing that kind of thing, Monk and I, but it was never documented because no records were being made at the time."[5] Historians have frequently cited pianist Art Tatum's influence on bebop reharmonization because of his extensive harmonic reworkings of popular songs.

Reharmonization refers to the bop practice of inserting different chords into the fundamental chord structure of a well-known song to freshen the interpretation and expand harmonic options for the soloist.

The way rhythm players accompanied soloists also changed. In particular, because of the influence of Kenny Clarke, Max Roach, and others, bebop drummers kept time very differently. While many swing-era drummers marked all four beats of a 4/4 measure with the bass drum, bebop drummers such as Clarke switched to the ride cymbal to maintain the pulse. They used the bass drum for "dropping bombs"— sharp, irregular accents that were far more disruptive than the accents of the swing

Dropping bombs is a term describing how bebop drummers used the bass drum for sharp, irregular accents in the rhythmic accompaniment.

drummers. Bebop drummers used the snare drum to punctuate the musical texture with accents or to maintain a kind of irregular "chattering" as an aside to the principal beat on the ride cymbal.

The faster tempos of the bebop players lay behind some of these changes in drumming. Clarke admitted that he was unable to maintain the breakneck speeds and keep his foot playing the bass drum on all four beats, so he switched the timekeeping role to the ride cymbal. Clarke, nicknamed "Klook" or "Klook-mop" in response to these unpredictable accents, played a fundamental role in developing this new style of drumming.

The faster tempos also brought about changes in piano playing. Bebop pianists abandoned the left-hand striding style that kept steady time. Instead, the pianist broke up the texture with chords, often syncopated, leaving the timekeeping role to the bass and the drummer's ride cymbal. This type of accompanying came to be called *comping*. During their improvisations, the bebop pianists also played lines like those of horn players with the right hand while the left hand accompanied with short, staccato chords.

With the pianist's left hand and drummer's bass drum no longer projecting the pulse, bands relied on their bassists to keep time, usually by "walking" the bass on each beat of the measure. Following the influence of Ellington's bassist Jimmy Blanton (see Chapter 6), bebop bass players played in a more linear fashion instead of merely playing the root notes of each chord. Blanton also influenced such bassists as Oscar Pettiford and Ray Brown, who became renowned for their ability to improvise solos as well as accompany and keep time.

Comping refers to the chordal accompaniment provided by pianists or guitarists in jazz bands. This accompaniment is often syncopated. The term *comp* is probably derived from a contraction of the word *accompany* or *complement*.

The Historical Origins of Bebop

Many factors, both musical and social, contributed to the rise of bebop in the 1940s. In this section we look at the people, places, and political forces that helped create this musical phenomenon. Later, we focus on the specific contributions of several key players in bebop's early development.

THE EARLY FORTIES: JAMMING AT MINTON'S AND MONROE'S

The earliest stirrings of bebop took place in the informal jam sessions in Harlem. In 1940, Minton's Playhouse on West 118th Street hired drummer Kenny Clarke as a bandleader. For the house band, Clarke hired trumpeter Joe Guy, bassist Nick Fenton, and an eccentric pianist named Thelonious Monk. Musicians would stop by Minton's and sit in after they had completed their gigs. The atmosphere was informal, so they could try out ideas, network, and engage in friendly (or not so friendly) competition with the other players. In other words, the jam sessions helped the players make connections, develop new ideas, and establish a rough pecking order of talent. The club, as trumpeter Miles Davis pointed out, was "the music laboratory for bebop."[6]

Guitarist Charlie Christian (Chapter 6), a member of the Benny Goodman band, was a regular participant at Minton's—he even kept a spare amplifier at the club. Thanks to a jazz fan named Jerry Newman who had a portable recorder, some of these sessions were captured and eventually released. The recordings reveal a music in transition. The rhythm section plays with a lighter, more buoyant sound than the steady chugging of swing-era rhythm: Kenny Clarke accents off-beats on the bass and snare drums, and Christian supplies supple guitar lines in which the eighth notes are more evenly spaced than the swing eighths of earlier players.

Pianist Thelonious Monk composed regularly for the band at Minton's. There, he wrote some of his most enduring compositions, including two haunting ballads, "'Round Midnight" and "Ruby My Dear," which showed the unique harmonic sense that characterized Monk's style. Other musicians adopted the Monk tunes heard at Minton's. Trumpeter Cootie Williams used "Epistrophy," which Monk wrote with Kenny Clarke, as his radio theme song in 1942, although he changed the title to "Fly Right." Williams was also the first to record Monk's "'Round Midnight," in 1944. Even when playing standard tunes, Monk often made unusual reharmonizations, especially in introductions. One musician in the audience remembered that Monk "generally started playing strange introductions going off, I thought to outer space, hell knows to where."[7]

Monroe's Uptown House on West 134th Street was another site for jam sessions. Run by pianist Allen Tinney, they normally began at 3:00 A.M. and lasted until morning. The house band included Max Roach, a brilliant drummer who eventually recorded with Charlie Parker. Many new musical ideas came out of these competitive jam sessions. As one participant at Monroe's remembered, "The musicians used to go there and battle like dogs, every night, you know, and just playing for nothing and having a good time."[8] Charlie Parker, in town with the Jay McShann band, was so stunned by the level of musical activity at Monroe's that he left the McShann band and remained in New York:

> At Monroe's I heard sessions with a pianist named Allen Tinney; I'd listen to trumpet men like Lips Page, Roy [Eldridge], Dizzy, and Charlie Shavers outblowing each other all night long. And Don Byas was there, playing everything there was to be played. I heard a trumpet man named Vic Coulson playing things I'd never heard. Vic had the regular band at Monroe's, with George Treadwell also on trumpet, and a tenor man named Pritchett. That was the kind of music that caused me to quit McShann and stay in New York.[9]

The American Federation of Musicians Strike in 1942

Unfortunately, much of the music that marked the transition from swing to bebop in the early 1940s was never documented on studio recordings, because the American Federation of Musicians (AFM) called a strike in August 1942. Protesting the lack of payment to musicians for records played on the radio, the union insisted on a recording ban—with the exception of "V-discs" (Victory discs) produced specifically for the armed forces overseas. Decca settled in September 1943, Columbia and Victor held out another year, and eventually the strike ended. These three record companies held the lion's share of the market before the ban, but several smaller labels sprang up shortly afterward and focused their attention on recording the younger players.

BIG BANDS IN THE EARLY 1940s

If the uptown Harlem clubs like Minton's and Monroe's functioned as the "laboratories" for bebop, the more commercial format of the big band also provided opportunities for many of the newer players to develop and test their ideas. Particularly significant in the early part of the 1940s were the big bands of Earl Hines and, shortly thereafter, Billy Eckstine. These bands included both Charlie Parker and Dizzy Gillespie, so they were especially notable. Because of the record ban, however, most of their music went unrecorded (see the box "The American Federation of Musicians Strike in 1942").

In 1942 Hines recruited Gillespie on trumpet and Parker on tenor saxophone (there was no opening for an alto saxophone player). Outside of Harlem jam sessions, this was the first time Parker and Gillespie had worked together on the bandstand. Also playing trumpet with the Hines band was another player in step with the latest musical developments, "Little" Benny Harris. Harris's composition "Ornithology," a recomposition of the swing standard "How High the Moon," became a bebop classic. The band also featured two outstanding singers who would develop major careers, Sarah Vaughan and Billy Eckstine.

Sarah Vaughan (1924–1990) became a preeminent jazz singer, possibly the greatest to develop in the bebop era. Her leap to the limelight came during the heyday of bop, when she sang with both the Earl Hines and Billy Eckstine big bands in the early 1940s. There, her associations with Parker and Gillespie established her reputation and refined her ability to sing with the looseness and unexpected vocal twists and turns of the newer style. As such, she seems to have concentrated more on jazz singing than did Ella Fitzgerald, who, after leaving the Chick Webb band, became firmly entrenched in a more pop-jazz style. Vaughan also maintained a close connection to the other jazz musicians of her generation.

Billy Eckstine (1914–1993) was a suave baritone vocalist who also played trumpet and valve trombone. In the early 1940s he had a hit with the Hines band in the slightly bawdy blues song "Jelly, Jelly." Persuaded to form his own band, Eckstine left Hines and hired Gillespie as musical director. Gillespie convinced many of the most forward-looking of Hines's musicians to join Eckstine's band, including Parker, pianist John Malachi, and eventually drummer Art Blakey.

The Eckstine band of 1944 has frequently been called the "first bebop big band," but the group did not achieve significant commercial success. Although they played at dance halls in the South, the band's bop-oriented compositions—many written and arranged by Gillespie—kept most people off the dance floor. Parker soon left the band, never having recorded with Eckstine, and Gillespie remained a short time afterward. In April 1944 Gillespie recorded some blues-oriented compositions with Eckstine, including "I Stay in the Mood for You" and "Good Jelly Blues," both cut in the mold of Eckstine's "Jelly, Jelly" hit. At the end of the year Gillespie played on "Blowing the Blues Away," a tenor saxophone "battle" between Gene Ammons and Dexter Gordon. Eckstine, long one of the principal singers in jazz, would continue with a distinguished career as a jazz vocalist.

JAZZ MOVES TO FIFTY-SECOND STREET

Around the middle of the 1940s, the clubs of West Fifty-Second Street became the primary venue for bebop bands. "The Street" comprised two blocks between Fifth Avenue and Broadway. The jazz clubs were tiny, crowded, and often poorly lit—far removed from the elaborate dance halls played by the big bands. In fact, there was no dance floor, merely tables for listening and an area where listeners were not required to buy drinks. During the war an immense concentration of jazz players developed in the city. For the cost of a cover charge, a listener could stroll down The Street and stop in to hear Sidney Bechet, Art Tatum, Coleman Hawkins, or Fats Waller anytime between 9:00 P.M. and 3:00 A.M. Gradually, the newer bebop bands worked their way into Fifty-Second Street.

As Dizzy Gillespie remembered it, the birth of the bebop era came after he left the Eckstine band in 1944. With bassist Oscar Pettiford, Gillespie formed a band to play at the Onyx Club, one of several acts on the bill. Gillespie and Pettiford hired Max Roach on drums and George Wallington on piano; both had been in the house band at Monroe's Uptown House. Gillespie tried to contact Charlie Parker, who had returned to Kansas City after leaving Eckstine, but Parker never received the telegram. When tenor saxophonist Don Byas, a fine player with a big sound reminiscent of Coleman Hawkins, began sitting in with the group, they eventually invited him to join them. With the horns playing in unison, the group's repertory was new and startling:

> In the Onyx Club, we played a lot or original tunes that didn't have titles. We just wrote an introduction and a first chorus. I'd say, "Dee-da-pa-da-n-de-bop...." and we'd go on into it. People, when they'd wanna ask for one of those numbers and didn't know the name, would ask for bebop. And the press picked it up and started calling it bebop. The first time the term *bebop* appeared in print was while we played at the Onyx Club.[10]

The group itself did not record, but much of the band—Gillespie, Pettiford, Roach, and Byas—assembled in the studio in early 1944 under the auspices of Coleman Hawkins for a series of historic recordings. Hawkins, some twenty years into his career, was attempting to stay in the musical vanguard by hiring the more visible young players on the scene. According to many, this attempt resulted in the first bebop recordings. Although half of the six tunes were ballads for Hawkins, the rest were in the newer style: Gillespie's "Woody n' You," Budd Johnson's "Bu-Dee-Daht," and a blues piece called "Disorder at the Border." In these recordings, bebop had an embryonic sound: The ponderous big band, the rhythm section, and many of the solos still seemed weighted down by the conventions of swing. Only Gillespie's energetic start-and-stop solos hinted at the music to come—the music fundamentally indebted to the innovations of Gillespie and Charlie Parker.

The Architects of Bebop

Numerous musicians contributed to the formation of bebop, but none were more significant than Charlie Parker and Dizzy Gillespie. Kenny Clarke, whose role in modifying drum styles also greatly affected bebop, was discussed earlier. Among pianists, the preeminent contributors included Thelonious Monk and Bud Powell.

CHARLIE PARKER

Charlie Parker was probably the greatest, most consistently brilliant jazz saxophonist of all time. Parker's influence on jazz history rivals that of Louis Armstrong: Both generated a major jazz style while radically increasing the level of technical proficiency on their instruments. Parker's improvisations left a mark on almost every subsequent jazz musician.

Born in Kansas City, Kansas, on August 29, 1920, Parker and his family moved across the river to Kansas City, Missouri, seven years later. At first he played baritone and alto horns in his school bands, but he soon turned to the alto saxophone, in 1933. Within two years, he left school to play full-time with a local bandleader known as Lawrence "88" Keyes.

Parker's talent was not immediately apparent. Bassist Gene Ramey described Parker as the "saddest thing in the Keyes band."[11] In the cutthroat world of the Kansas City jam session, Parker learned about competition the hard way. In a radio interview, Parker recalled his first jam session:

> I'd learned how to play the first eight bars of "[Up a] Lazy River," and I knew the complete tune to "Honeysuckle Rose." I didn't never stop to think about there was other keys or nothin' like that. [Laughter] So I took my horn out to this joint where the guys—a bunch of guys I had seen around were—and the first thing they started playing was "Body and Soul," long beat [implied double time] you know, like this. [*Demonstrates.*] . . . So I go to playin' my "Honeysuckle Rose" and [unintelligible], I mean, ain't no form of conglomeration [unintelligible]. They laughed me right off the bandstand.[12]

But Parker was diligent. Known for carrying his horn in a paper bag, the teenager learned a few Lester Young solos note-for-note while studying basic harmony with some of the local guitarists. He joined the band of Buster Smith, a saxophonist who was an early influence on Parker. Then in 1938 he joined the band of Jay McShann, a pianist based in Kansas City, but originally from Oklahoma.

In early 1939, Parker moved to New York for the first time, playing sessions at Monroe's Uptown House and washing dishes at Jimmy's Chicken Shack in order to hear pianist Art Tatum, who often performed there. Undoubtedly, Tatum's sophisticated harmonic sense influenced Parker; further, Tatum's effortless virtuosity and streams of high-speed runs quite likely helped to determine the mature Parker style. In a famous anecdote, Parker credited a guitarist named Biddy Fleet with teaching him more-advanced harmonies: Playing "Cherokee," which would become one of his signature

Charlie Parker (CD 1, Tracks 17 and 18), pictured on the cover of a Gil Fuller transcription of Be-Bop themes including "Oop Bop Sh-Bam" and "Ray's Idea."

tunes, Parker realized that he could emphasize the higher chordal extensions—ninths, elevenths, or thirteenths. These, too, became a feature of his mature style.

In 1940 Parker returned to Kansas City and the McShann band to become one of its musical directors. An amateur recording, probably from 1940, is the first we have of Parker. This recording preserved a solo practice session on "Honeysuckle Rose" followed by "Body and Soul"—significant choices given the story of Parker's first jam session.

Parker cut his first professional recordings informally at a radio station in Wichita, Kansas, on November 30 and December 2, 1940, with the McShann band. These tunes, known as the Wichita transcriptions, revealed the group's Kansas City origins: "Moten Swing," "Honeysuckle Rose," and "Oh, Lady Be Good." In 1941 and 1942, still with the McShann band, Parker made his first studio recordings, including "Swingmatism," "Hootie Blues," "Sepian Bounce," and "The Jumpin' Blues." "Hootie Blues" featured Parker's first important solo—his first statement as a new saxophone stylist.

Parker and the McShann band returned to New York in late 1941 or early 1942 to play at the Savoy. At that time he immersed himself in the New York scene, frequently attended the after-hours sessions at Minton's and Monroe's, and shared the stand with trumpeters Roy Eldridge, Dizzy Gillespie, and Charlie Shavers, as well as saxophonist Don Byas. Drummer Kenny Clarke, who in 1941 considered himself among the newer innovators, was stunned by Parker's playing:

> Bird was playing stuff we'd never heard before. He was into figures I thought I'd invented for drums. He was twice as fast as Lester Young and into harmony Lester hadn't touched. Bird was running the same way we were, but he was way out ahead of us. I don't think he was aware of the changes he had created. It was his way of playing jazz, part of his own experience.[13]

Surrounded by this high level of musical activity, Parker decided to remain in New York, playing in the big bands of Earl Hines and Billy Eckstine. Earning awestruck respect from his fellow musicians, he was rapidly becoming an underground hero. Increasingly during this time, he found himself jamming and sitting in with various groups in the heart of Fifty-Second Street.

Parker's jams with the band of guitarist Tiny Grimes became especially significant. On September 15, 1944, Grimes invited Parker to cut four sides with the band, which included Clyde Hart on piano, Harold "Doc" West on drums, and Jimmy Butts on bass. Parker was featured in all four tunes, including his own composition "Red Cross." In the two takes of "Red Cross" we hear Parker's first recorded solos with rhythm changes. More generally, as Parker's first small-group records featuring him as soloist, we hear the early crystallization of Parker's bebop playing. (Listen to Track 10 of the Audio Primer CD to hear an example of rhythm changes.)

Although the Grimes band was more of a swing than a bop group, Parker plays his solos superbly, presenting several of his trademarks:

▶ A lean, edgy tone

▶ Use of blues inflections

▶ Double-time sixteenth-note runs

▶ Bebop-style licks that were to become the mainstay of the new style

After the Grimes recordings of late 1944, Parker began to work with small groups as his bebop style began to mature. Most significantly, he teamed up with Dizzy Gillespie, and their musical relationship began to flourish. By May 1945 the two were fronting a band at the Three Deuces on Fifty-Second Street, where they remained until July. The group recorded several tunes that became mainstays of the bebop era, including "Groovin' High," "Dizzy Atmosphere," "All the Things You Are," and "Salt Peanuts."

L I S T E N I N G   G U I D E

"Salt Peanuts" (excerpt)
CD **1**   Track **17**

Quintet of the Year: "Salt Peanuts" (Gillespie). Fantasy 6003. Toronto, May 15, 1953. Dizzy Gillespie, trumpet, composer; Charlie Parker, alto saxophone; Bud Powell, piano; Charles Mingus, bass; Max Roach, drums.

"Salt Peanuts" may be the most well-known bebop tune, perhaps because its humorous motivic idea is unforgettable. Gillespie's tune is a crowd pleaser, though Parker adopted it less often because he generally refused to play up to his listeners. Yet, there are instances of Parker performing—and *singing*— "Salt Peanuts" in live versions. This recording is from one of the most famous live jazz performances: a reunion of the two leading personalities of bebop backed by the leading bebop pianist and drummer. At the time, Mingus, a rapidly rising star, was the least-known member of the band.

There are mistakes in this performance of "Salt Peanuts," which merely illustrate what can happen when there is insufficient (or no) rehearsal. Gillespie and Parker had recorded the piece in a classic session of 1945; they attempt to duplicate the arrangement here.

Parker introduces the tune. Some commentators have suggested that Parker's reference to Gillespie as "my worthy constituent" reflected their competition, a patronizing comment on Gillespie's greater success and celebrity.

This well-known performance should be compared with the more recent version by Steve Coleman (CD 2, Track 12).

Introduction, part 1—8 bars

0:11   A driving drum solo begins the tune. The tempo is very fast, typical of many bebop tunes.

Introduction, part 2—8 bars

0:17   The rest of the ensemble enters with the introduction in which the last two bars feature a break with the pianist playing the "Salt Peanuts" (SP) octave motive (heard in the distance). The first four bars hold a G♭7 chord (with a flat fifth) before turning to the tonic F.

AA—8 bars, repeated

0:23   The tune's thematic idea consists of two licks, the second of which is the octave-leaping SP motive. Parker and Gillespie divide the SP motive, with Parker on the lower F and Gillespie on the upper.

B—8 bars

0:35   The bridge features Parker and Gillespie in octaves. The rhythm-changes harmonies are altered to include flat fifths on some of the dominant chords. The second chord change (measures 3–4 of the bridge) is also D minor rather than D7, which would be customary in rhythm changes.

A—8 bars

0:41   The third A section completes the head.

Interlude—8 bars

0:47   Parker and Gillespie play a written line on the A-section changes.

AA—8 bars, repeated

0:53   Parker takes the first lick of the tune himself while Gillespie sings the SP motive as a break. The last time, Gillespie prolongs the SP motive; compare the Steve Coleman performance (CD 2, Track 12), where he largely imitates Gillespie.

B—8 bars

1:06   Parker solos on the bridge.

A—8 bars

1:12   The third A section completes the head with Parker on the tune's first lick and Gillespie singing the SP motive.

Parker's alto saxophone solo—3 AABA choruses

1:19   Parker's solo. Gillespie continues to shout "Salt peanuts" during the first two A sections of the first chorus. Parker seems to be a bit unsure whether to start his solo; Gillespie's shouting may be an attempt to cover up the indecision. Parker ends the first chorus with a held-out middle C (dominant of F major).

1:57   Powell loses his place at the beginning of the bridge in the second chorus. He realizes where he is during the bridge's second half. At the end of Parker's third chorus, another prolonged middle C ushers in Gillespie for an interlude before Gillespie's solo.

Interlude—Irregular

2:35   Gillespie and Parker hint at a line they played in the 1945 performance. The interlude does not come back to them entirely, so they try to coax each other into remembering or playing the line. Roach lays back to see if the horn players find their place. Because they do not, the interlude is irregular rather than the intended eight bars (with the last two as solo break). Listen for the later interlude before Powell's solo, there performed correctly.

Gillespie's trumpet solo—3 AABA choruses

2:43   The trumpet solo here is an impressive statement by Gillespie. The beginning of the second chorus may contain a quotation. Note how he builds to the high Fs at the beginning of his third chorus. In the final chorus, second A section, he alludes to the melody of the introduction.

Interlude

3:59   This time the interlude works. It sets up Powell's piano solo. The last two bars provide a break for Powell—he may have been unaware of this, because he enters tentatively.

Piano solo

4:04   The excerpt fades during the first of Powell's four choruses.

From "Salt Peanuts," we can summarize these characteristic features of both Parker's and Gillespie's up-tempo style:

▶ Angular, irregularly accented melodic lines, mostly comprising eighth-notes

▶ Emotional, intense, and virtuosic expression

▶ Emphasis on middle and upper range of the instrument

▶ Phrases of irregular length

▶ Melodic connections based on subtle voice-leading connections

▶ Use of extended and chromatic chord tones; use of uncommon scales derived from these extended chord harmonies

In addition, these other features distinguish Parker and Gillespie:

▶ Tone. Parker's sound is characterized by a commanding, insistent tone quality. Gillespie's sound is characterized in this up-tempo composition by a lack of vibrato.

▶ Blues-based ideas. Parker uses blue notes and blues expressions frequently. Gillespie here uses very few blues inflections.

On November 26, 1945, Parker supervised his first session as a leader. These recordings for Savoy Records included some of his most important performances as well as the original compositions "Billie's Bounce," "KoKo," "Now's the Time," and "Thriving on a Riff." "KoKo" also featured Dizzy Gillespie on trumpet, but a nervous, nineteen-year-old trumpeter from St. Louis named Miles Davis played the other cuts.

In December 1945 Parker and Gillespie traveled with a band led by Gillespie to the West Coast for an engagement in Hollywood. The gig, at a club called Billy Berg's, was not successful. Gillespie and the band returned to New York within a few months, while Parker stayed on. Reputedly, he pawned his plane ticket to support his heroin habit. His addiction, which he had developed when he was a teenager, caused Parker intense physical and emotional problems. While still in California, Parker entered Camarillo State Hospital in July 1946 and remained there for six months. Following his release and several performances and recordings, Parker returned to New York in April 1947.

The following four years proved to be the most intensely fertile period of Parker's career. He formed his most long-lived working quintet with trumpeter Miles Davis, pianist Duke Jordan, bassist Tommy Potter, and drummer Max Roach, a group that remained together for a year and a half. The band recorded many Parker compositions that became jazz standards. For example, "Scrapple from the Apple" was a kind of double recomposition: The A section used the harmonies from Fats Waller's "Honeysuckle Rose," while the B section took the chords from "I Got Rhythm." "Confirmation" became one of Parker's best known bebop heads. It was also one of his few tunes not based on recomposition over preexisting chord changes. The melody for "Confirmation" was itself tricky to negotiate, a repository of bebop melodic devices.

A recording of "Crazeology" presents Parker at his prime, working with innovative variants to rhythm changes. An unusual chord change to G♭ in the A section forces Parker to rethink how he plays rhythm changes in B♭, because he cannot rely on his established note patterns. As we discussed in Chapter 6, such established patterns are called formulas or, more popularly, licks. Parker excelled at developing formulas for use in up-tempo improvising.

As he gained wider public acceptance and acclaim, Parker undertook several new and interesting projects. He made two European tours, playing Paris in 1949 and Sweden the following year. He recorded in many different settings, including "South of the Border" sessions with Machito's Afro-Cuban band. Most significant was the unusual step of recording with string accompaniment, in which Parker fulfilled a long-held ambition. In *Bird with Strings* Parker played standards in a subdued mood. His recording of "Just Friends" became a classic; it was not only Parker's best-selling record but reputedly was Parker's favorite of his recorded solos.

One of Parker's most significant devices, not new to jazz but one that he developed extensively, was his tendency to quote other music in his solos. The quotations ranged from classical themes to well-known pop tunes, jazz heads, and children's songs. For example, in a solo on "Salt Peanuts" performed in Paris in 1949, Parker quoted the beginning of Igor Stravinsky's *The Rite of Spring*, a famous classical work that had premiered in Paris in 1913. At the other extreme, in a solo on "Just Friends" recorded in 1950, Parker quoted "Pop Goes the Weasel." Both of these performances were live; Parker tended to quote more often in live settings than in studio recordings. Perhaps

The original caption for this photo read: "The show at the new Birdland Restaurant, which opened on Broadway, December 15 [1949], offers music to suit just about every taste. Entertaining at their specialties are (left to right), trumpeter Max Kaminsky, Dixieland style; saxophonist Lester Young, swing; [Oran] "Hot Lips" Page, famed for sweet swing; Charlie Parker on the alto sax, representing bop; and pianist Lennie Tristano, exponent of a new style called 'music of the future.' It marked the first time that these noted musicians, representing completely different schools of modern music, were gathered on the same stage."

Parker chose the live venue because he realized that the joke implied in a quotation would quickly become stale on repeated listening. Of note is the unequaled ingenuity with which Parker wove his quotations into the flow of his solos. Parker's freewheeling quotations greatly influenced later generations of players.

Parker spent his final years in a downward slide both physically and mentally. He suffered from ulcers, became overweight, and drank heavily. When one of his daughters, Pree, died of pneumonia, Parker became severely depressed. In 1954 he twice attempted suicide and voluntarily committed himself to Bellevue Hospital in New York. Parker last performed at a club named for him, Birdland. The performance was disastrous, a visible airing of his feud with pianist Bud Powell. A week later, on March 12, 1955, he died at the apartment of the Baroness Nica de Koeningswarter, a jazz patron who had befriended the saxophonist. His body was so ravaged by years of substance abuse that the examining doctor listed Parker's age as fifty-three. He was only thirty-four.

DIZZY GILLESPIE

Along with Charlie Parker, John Birks "Dizzy" Gillespie (1917–1993) played a crucial role in promoting the new bebop style in the 1940s. "Bird might have been the spirit of the bebop movement," said Miles Davis, "but Dizzy was its 'head and hands,' the one who kept it all together."[14] Despite Gillespie's reputation for clowning around—which early on earned him the nickname "Dizzy"—he was dedicated to his craft as a musician. He made a point of working out experimental harmonies and chord progressions at the piano, often enthusiastically teaching and coaching the other players. Gillespie clearly rejected the stereotype of the untutored, "natural" jazz musician. As he told *Time* magazine in 1949,

> Nowadays we try to work out different rhythms and things that they didn't think about when Louis Armstrong blew. In his day all he did was play strictly from the soul—just strictly from the heart. You got to go forward and progress. We study.[15]

Although his style had originally been influenced by trumpeter Roy Eldridge, Gillespie soon developed an improvisational technique that was much more freewheeling. With his impressive command of the upper register of the trumpet, he punctuated his solos with wild leaps into the "stratosphere." He could play much faster than previous trumpeters, with sinuous chromatic lines in dramatic contrast to the diatonically based solos of swing.

As a composer and an arranger, Gillespie was prolific. Many of his bebop heads became jazz standards in their own right, such as "Groovin'

Dizzy Gillespie (CD 1, Tracks 17 and 18) on the cover of "Lop-Pow" published in 1948 and billed as "Be-Bop (The New Jazz)."

High," "Woody n' You," "Salt Peanuts," and "A Night in Tunisia" (see Music Example 7-1). Written while Gillespie was a member of the Hines band during the early 1940s and originally titled "Interlude," "A Night in Tunisia" was perhaps his most famous piece. Although unusual in its exoticism, it showed many of the hallmarks of the nascent bebop style. The use of the Latin-tinged rhythm in the opening section reflected Gillespie's interests in Afro-Cuban music.

Gillespie was born in Cheraw, South Carolina, on October 21, 1917. Years later, after receiving a scholarship to the Laurinburg Institute in North Carolina, he moved with his family to Philadelphia and there joined a band led by Frankie Fairfax. In 1937 he left Fairfax to move to New York, where he rapidly made his way into the better-known bands, working as the featured soloist with Teddy Hill and, in 1939, Cab Calloway. He was summarily dismissed from Calloway's band in 1941 after the leader mistakenly accused Gillespie of hurling a spitball at Calloway during a performance.

Like Parker, Gillespie frequently participated in the after-hours sessions at Minton's and had been a member of the big bands of Earl Hines and Billy Eckstine. Gillespie soon began to achieve success as an arranger, contributing numbers to the bands of Boyd Raeburn and Woody Herman. After winning the New Star Award in the *Esquire* magazine Jazz Poll in 1944, Gillespie formed the band with bassist Oscar Pettiford that performed at the Onyx Club on Fifty-Second Street (see "Jazz Moves to Fifty-Second Street," p. 180). It was the recordings and performances with Charlie Parker, however, that thrust Gillespie squarely into the front line of the bebop movement. The 1945 performances and recordings of the two principal talents of bebop culminated in the disastrous West Coast trip at the end of the year (discussed earlier).

After his split with Parker, Gillespie returned to the large-group format and led his own big band with increasing commercial success through 1950. On many of their recordings, we hear the successful translation of bebop from small group to big band, including the exciting "Things to Come," a prophetically titled piece written and arranged by Gillespie and Gil Fuller. Gillespie, always attracted to Afro-Cuban elements in jazz, hired conga player Chano Pozo to perform with his band and featured him in a Carnegie Hall concert in 1947. This Afro-Cuban element, which Gillespie felt complemented and expanded the rhythmic resources of jazz, became an important part of Gillespie's work. We hear it, for example, on the Gillespie-Pozo composition "Manteca" as well as on George Russell's "Cubana Be/Cubana Bop."

Compared with Charlie Parker, Gillespie presented a more commercial side to bebop. He insisted that the music be entertaining and lamented its separation from dancing. To the mainstream audience, his stage persona—which included hipster posturing with goatee, glasses, and beret—became at least as well known as his music. However, his many innovations and tireless championing of the music made Gillespie a significant founder and fundamental contributor to the development of bebop. He continued to perform bebop-based jazz with groups both large and small for decades to come as one of the great personalities and elder statesmen of the jazz scene. He died on January 6, 1993.

LISTENING GUIDE

"Bloomdido"
CD **1**   Track **18**

Charlie Parker and His Orchestra: "Bloomdido" (Parker). Mercury-Clef 11058.
New York, June 6, 1950. Dizzy Gillespie, trumpet; Charlie Parker, alto saxophone;
Thelonious Monk, piano; Curley Russell, bass; Buddy Rich, drums.

The Parker-Gillespie recording session of June 6, 1950, was their last together. In contrast to the mid-1940s recordings, it presents the saxophonist in superior audio fidelity. As an added attraction, this session included Thelonious Monk on piano, a rare instance of Monk performing with Parker.

Introduction—9 bars

0:00   Rich plays a bar of solo drums, then Monk enters with a four-bar piano solo answered by a four-bar drum solo to set up the main theme.

Head—12-bar blues, 2 choruses

0:09   *Chorus 1*   Parker and Gillespie play the head twice in octaves. Gillespie's trumpet is muted. The head has a start-and-stop quality typical of bebop melodies, particularly those by Parker; that is, the melody is angular and contains unexpected accents. Although a blues piece, its fast tempo does not allow for bluesy phrasing or blue notes. Parker ends the head unexpectedly on the fourth degree of the scale, usually an unstable note.

0:21   *Chorus 2*

Parker solo—4 choruses

0:34   *Chorus 1*   A classic Parker solo of four choruses with characteristic bebop figures consisting mostly of eighth notes and triplets.

0:47   *Chorus 2*   Note how he builds into the third chorus with a climactic emphasis on the "flat fifth" or F♭ in the key of B♭.

0:59   *Chorus 3*   This third chorus contains more blue notes as well.

1:12   *Chorus 4*   An incomplete reference to the "shave and a haircut" jingle opens the fourth chorus. Throughout Parker's solo, you can hear the band use a classic bebop chord substitution with a iii7-♭iii7/ii7-V7 in measures 8–9 in place of the usual I for measure 8 and V7 for measure 9.

Gillespie solo—3 choruses

1:25   *Chorus 1*   Gillespie plays his three choruses with cup mute. Gillespie ends his first chorus with the characteristic "bebop" phrase.

1:38   *Chorus 2*   The second chorus begins.

1:46   Gillespie plays two unusual descending phrases, first from high B♭ to C, then to C♭.

1:51   *Chorus 3*   The third chorus begins.

1:53   Gillespie plays a long string of faster note values.

1:57   He returns to the previous unusual phrase, but now from high C down to D.

Monk solo—2 choruses

2:03   *Chorus 1*   Monk's style is angular and often humorous. He emphasizes unusual intervals and a percussive touch. The notes sometimes emphasized are not typical chord tones, nor does he run eighth-note lines like most beboppers do.

2:16   *Chorus 2*

Rich solo—2 choruses

2:30   *Chorus 1*   Rich keeps time fairly clearly during his solo, which can be heard as two twelve-bar choruses. Listen to the bass drum in order to keep track of the pulse during the solo.

2:42   *Chorus 2*

Reprise, repeated

2:55   The head is reprised.

3:08   Repeat. The head ends with a falloff on the last note by Parker and Gillespie.

The influential pianist Bud Powell.

Courtesy Morgan Collection

BUD POWELL

Earl "Bud" Powell (1924–1966), generally considered the finest of the bop pianists, transferred Parker's and Gillespie's bebop technique to piano. He gained acclaim for playing up-tempo lines at blistering speed and exercised a profound influence on a generation of pianists. He best codified the "right-hand" bop piano style in which sparse, sharply articulated chords in the left hand punctuated and rhythmically set off linear improvisations in the right. But he was also an immensely capable player in the more two-handed style derived from Art Tatum and the classic stride masters.

A New Yorker, Powell began gigging around town when he was a teenager. He soon began to participate at Minton's, where house pianist Thelonious Monk took an early interest in his development. As the pianist with trumpeter Cootie Williams's band in 1944, Powell made his earliest recordings, which demonstrate Powell's style in transition—equally at home in the traditional swing of Earl Hines as well as in the nascent bebop style. He became a mainstay on Fifty-Second Street, where he played with Gillespie, John Kirby, Don Byas, Dexter Gordon, and others.

Around this time, during a racial incident with a policeman, Powell took a beating, especially to his head. Afterward, he began showing signs of erratic behavior and mental instability and was institutionalized five times between 1945 and 1955. "Bud was always—ever since I've known him—he was a little on the border line," recalled tenor saxophonist Dexter Gordon. "Because he'd go off into things—expressions, telltale things that would let you know he was off."[16] Despite his often moody and withdrawn behavior, Powell's playing astounded his contemporaries.

Powell's performances are well documented by recordings. In January 1947, Powell made his first recording as a leader, with Curley Russell on bass and Max Roach on drums. Powell later recorded frequently with Roach. Although he did not often record with Charlie Parker (they supposedly never got along), Powell joined Parker's first studio session when Parker returned to New York from Los Angeles in May 1947. The group recorded "Donna Lee," "Chasin' the Bird," and "Cheryl."

Powell's trio recordings of 1949, with bassist Ray Brown, showed him to be not only a stunning pianist but also a gifted composer. One of Powell's tunes, "Tempus Fugit," showcased the pianist playing at breakneck speed. Another, a fine solo track called "I'll Keep Loving You," revealed a tender side to his playing and contains references to Art Tatum.

Several of Powell's compositions were elaborate. For example, "Un Poco Loco" was a complex Latin-oriented composition in which Powell soloed over a repeated single-chord vamp and made use of exotic pitches and scales. Another complex piece, "Glass Enclosure," was a disturbing evocation of his time spent in mental asylums, written in four sections. A third example, "Parisian Thoroughfare," was recorded twice in 1951, once with a trio and again as a solo piano feature.

Powell's work during the 1950s was less even. He recorded for Blue Note, Verve, and Victor, but his mental problems, often made worse by drinking, interfered with his playing. He recaptured some of his fiery spirit in the famous concert recorded at Massey Hall, Toronto, on May 15, 1953, in which he performed with Charlie Parker, Dizzy Gillespie, Max Roach, and bassist Charles Mingus—a recording justly acclaimed as reuniting Parker and Gillespie in a "summit meeting" of the top talents in bebop (CD 1, Track 17). Powell moved to Paris in 1959 and recorded with another American expatriate, tenor saxophonist Dexter Gordon. Unfortunately, Powell continued to suffer health problems and was diagnosed with tuberculosis in 1963. He died in 1966.

The quintessential bebop pianist, Powell made a direct impact on the piano styles of Al Haig, Barry Harris, Hank Jones, Tommy Flanagan, and Sonny Clark. Indeed, no pianist who followed Powell could escape his influence. His right-hand-dominated style became the prime technique for nearly all jazz pianists and made Powell the father of modern jazz piano.

THELONIOUS MONK

Thelonious Sphere Monk was an original. Avoiding the virtuosic flamboyance of Art Tatum and the up-tempo facility of Bud Powell, Monk instead created a piano style that struck many of his contemporaries as either erratic and awkward, or just plain odd. But all of Monk's peers considered him one of the prime movers of bebop. "Monk's contribution to the new style of music was mostly harmonic," Dizzy Gillespie said, "but also spiritual."[17]

Although Monk's technique was rooted in the Harlem stride tradition, his solos avoided the energy and virtuosity of the older school. His playing was lean and spare, making abundant use of silence around the notes. A noted characteristic of his playing used clusters and "crushed notes"—a dissonant group of pitches out of which Monk would release all but one or two notes.

Much of Monk's influence on bebop came from his practice of reharmonizing popular standards, a practice evident early in his career. In his introduction to "Sweet Lorraine," as recorded by Jerry Newman at Minton's in 1941, Monk played the melody of the song with an accompaniment that departs radically from the original. Even in this early recording, he displayed much of the wit and quirkiness that would come to be associated with his style. As Miles Davis put it, "Monk had a great

Thelonious Monk (CD 1, Tracks 18 and 19) performing at the Beehive Club, Chicago, 1955.

Photo by Frank Malcolm. Courtesy Frank Driggs Collection.

sense of humor, musically speaking. He was a real innovative musician whose music was ahead of his time.... He showed me more about music composition than anyone else on 52nd Street."[18]

Born in 1917 in Rocky Mount, North Carolina, Monk came to New York with his family when he was four. Largely self-taught, Monk played piano and organ in church. He also acquired some European classical technique in his youth but abandoned it early in favor of his own idiosyncratic jazz style.

As house pianist at Minton's during the early 1940s, Monk was positioned to have his pieces performed frequently by the up-and-coming bebop players. Curiously, however, they rarely asked Monk to record with them. He made his first studio recording with Coleman Hawkins in 1944, but he did not begin to record in earnest for Blue Note Records until 1947. Blue Note's producer, Alfred Lion, was intrigued by Monk's dramatically innovative style, but he insisted on recording fourteen selections before releasing a single 78-rpm record.

Working with both trios and sextets, Monk continued to record for Blue Note Records for the next five years. These recordings highlighted his strengths as a composer. His poignant ballads "'Round Midnight," "Ruby My Dear," and "Monk's Mood" featured a rich harmonic vocabulary. A medium tempo number, "In Walked Bud," was a tribute to pianist Bud Powell that outlined both the melody and harmony of Irving Berlin's "Blue Skies" in an effective recomposition. Some of his melodies, such as those in his blues pieces "Straight No Chaser" and "Criss Cross," seemed to shift the beat around by using motives repeated in different parts of the measure.

Monk's distinctive approach to jazz dramatically foreshadowed the minimalism and abstract objectivity that were to become fashionable in the West from the 1950s on. Monk's performances draw us into a conscious awareness of each note and ask us to judge it, to place it in its context, and to enjoy its unique occurrence at that particular moment. In his decision to revamp traditional jazz piano values, Monk addressed the problem of how to imbue each pitch—out of the few pitches available—with special significance and still create good music. Hence, Monk did not rely on dazzling the listener with flashy, previously worked-out licks.

L I S T E N I N G   G U I D E

"Four in One"
CD **1**   Track **19**

Thelonious Monk Quintet: "Four in One" (Monk). Blue Note 1589. New York, July 23, 1951. Monk, piano; Sahib Shihab, alto saxophone; Milt Jackson, vibraphone; Al McKibbon, bass; Art Blakey, drums.

"Four in One" is a characteristic Monk composition. This piece also shows off to excellent advantage Monk's idiosyncratic piano playing in a group setting.

Introduction—8 bars

0:00   Piano solo. Blakey taps the hi-hat lightly on the second and fourth beats of each bar. The third and fourth bars contain the syncopated whole-tone runs from the tune's A section.

AABA Head—First two A sections

0:12   The entire band plays the melody first in unison then moves quickly to notes occasionally harmonized in seconds and thirds. During the third and fourth bars, listen for syncopated and repeated whole-tone runs in thirds.

0:20   The eight-bar A section ends humorously with a "bebop" figure. In a piano voicing below the alto saxophone melody, Monk adds a lowered major ninth—a "wrong-note" D—a ninth below an E♭ melody note in an E♭ major chord.

0:24   The A section repeats.

AABA Head—B section (bridge)

0:37   The eight-bar bridge begins with the vibraphone and alto sax on the melody. The II–V harmonic patterns are conventional for the first two bars, then move up a half-step for the third bar and back down for the fourth bar.

The second four-bar group begins as if it were a transposition of the first group, but instead of following the pattern, it turns to Monk-style humorous "wrong-note" chords for measures 6–7. The downbeat chord of measure 6 is especially sharp:

A dominant-seventh harmony at the end of the bridge sets up the return to the A section.

AABA head—Final A section

0:49   Repeat of the A section.

Monk piano solo—One AABA chorus

1:02   As the solo begins, Monk refers to the head's melodic motives.

1:34   At the downbeat of the sixth bar of the bridge, Monk repeats the sharply dissonant chord from the B section of the head. He ends the bridge with a paraphrase of the head, which continues during the first two bars of the last A section.

1:41   During the whole-tone sequence of measures 3–4 of the last A, however, Monk develops an alternate higher-register whole-tone syncopation. The solo is remarkable in its imaginative references to the head.

Shihab alto solo—First half of chorus (AA)

1:51   Shihab has a Parker-like quality to his tone, lines, and bebop phrasing.

2:04   At the start of the second A, he refers directly to the melody.

Jackson vibraphone solo—Second half of chorus (BA)

2:15   Entering at the bridge of the tune, Jackson continues the pattern of clear melodic references. His final A section is freer.

2:17–2:21   Monk's accompaniment ranges in the B section from single notes in octaves

2:23–2:39   to dense chords.

2:30–2:35   He then moves on to parallel tenths in the final A section.

Reprise of the head

2:39   The head repeats almost exactly. As a brief coda, Monk plays a witty "bebop" cutoff in measure 7 of the last A.

Monk's trademarks, heard in such pieces as "Four in One," include the following:

▶ Unusual rhythmic irregularities in the melodic line

▶ Use of the whole-tone scale

▶ A conventional large-scale form (AABA with eight-bar sections) that, because of its predictability, sets off the more personal, stylistic elements

▶ From time to time, intriguing harmonies that break the conventional "rules" of jazz harmony

▶ A whimsical effect created by the contrast between Monk's personal idioms and bebop norms

Although Monk would eventually leave a legacy of jazz standards, he was slow to achieve recognition as a performing artist. During the 1950s he recorded with such musicians as Sonny Rollins and Gigi Gryce, and he continued to innovate rhythmically. His solo from "Bag's Groove" with the Miles Davis All Stars in 1954 was a tour de force of the techniques of metric displacement—Monk deliberately repeats motives in different parts of the measure, in effect "turning the beat around."

In the latter part of the decade, Monk gained visibility and praise from his masterly album *Brilliant Corners* and his celebrated 1957 engagement at the Five Spot in New York with saxophonist John Coltrane. In 1959, at New York's Town Hall, he appeared in a concert that featured his compositions with big band. By 1964, his visibility and reputation had increased so much that *Time* magazine pictured him on its cover. Interestingly, his solo piano recording from that same year, *Solo Monk,* revealed Monk's indebtedness to the Harlem stride school.

Although Monk continued to perform and record into the mid-1970s, he spent his last years living in seclusion at the home of his patron, Baroness Pannonica de Koenigswarter. He died in 1982.

Slightly outside the mainstream bop tradition, Monk's playing nevertheless enormously influenced several generations of pianists. For example, Herbie Nichols and Elmo Hope both owed a debt to Monk during the 1950s; Andrew Hill, Randy Weston, and Chick Corea all took something from Monk's style. Some aspects of Monk's style prefigure the "free jazz" that burst on the scene in the late 1950s. Although Monk was relatively neglected during his lifetime, devoted players and groups have kept his music alive. For instance, the jazz group Sphere (taking Monk's middle name) formed in the early 1980s to perform Monk's compositions.

Other Bebop Artists

Apart from Parker, Gillespie, Powell, and Monk, many other players contributed in various ways to bebop. Here we look at two artists who provided innovations on trombone and tenor saxophone, respectively: J. J. Johnson and Dexter Gordon.

J. J. JOHNSON

Although common enough in all types of jazz ensembles, the trombone has never enjoyed the popularity of the other horns. The up-tempo single-note lines pervasive in jazz wind styles are difficult to execute on the trombone because of the slide mechanism. Because this is especially true for the low register, agile trombone playing usually occurs in the upper register. The difficulties of the slide mechanism have occasionally led trombonists to switch to valve trombone, which is fingered like a trumpet. (Because the trombone is pitched an octave lower than the trumpet, valve trombone can be readily learned by trumpet players as well.)

J. J. Johnson (1924–2001) shook up jazz trombone playing in the late 1940s, although his technical developments followed logically from the work of the swing players. Johnson emphasized the high register and astonished everyone with boplike lines—at the time thought to be impossible on the trombone—that were reminiscent of Parker and Gillespie.

After working with big bands in the 1940s, Johnson made a series of important records with smaller groups in the late 1940s and early 1950s. Eventually he teamed up with fellow trombonist Kai Winding (1922–1983) to jointly lead a two-trombone quintet in 1954. With a distinguished career that continued into the 1990s, Johnson became well established as both a trombonist and a composer.

DEXTER GORDON

Despite the dominance of the alto saxophone during the bebop period due to Charlie Parker's overwhelming influence, significant bebop tenor saxophonists emerged during the 1940s. Chief among them was Dexter Gordon, whose career lasted into the 1980s. Gordon's bebop playing was confident and extroverted, offering a rich, muscular, and warm sound on the tenor. He also often played with humor, picking up Charlie Parker's habit of quoting melodies from other pieces within his improvisations. Initially influenced by such Basie regulars as Herschel Evans, Gordon's relaxed, behind-the-beat phrasing owed a special debt to Lester Young.

Gordon was born in Los Angeles in 1923. When still a teenager, he became a member of Lionel Hampton's group and shared the bandstand with saxophonist Illinois Jacquet, an early role model for Gordon. In 1944 Gordon joined the Billy Eckstine band, which was staffed with many of the fiery young bebop players of the day. Shortly after, Gordon was featured in a saxophone "duel" with Gene Ammons on Eckstine's "Blowin' the Blues Away." This was the first of many saxophone "duels" for Gordon; his 1947 recording "The Chase" pitted Gordon against another important bebop tenor player, Wardell Gray (1921–1955).

Like so many others of the bebop era, Gordon was plagued by heroin. Despite incarceration and parole in the 1950s, Gordon continued to evolve as a player. He had an immense influence on two upcoming tenor players—John Coltrane and Sonny Rollins. The influence was reciprocal: Coltrane's hard-edged sound attracted Gordon, and in the late 1970s he took up soprano saxophone, which was largely popularized by Coltrane. Gordon also displayed a talent for theater: He provided the music for, played for, and acted in the 1960 Jack Gelber play *The Connection*.

Prior to moving to Europe, Gordon recorded for Blue Note, issuing *Go*, *Gettin' Around*, and *A Swingin' Affair*. Gordon then lived in Copenhagen from 1962 to 1977. He played frequently at the Club Montmartre and toured, recorded, and taught. When he returned to the United States in 1978, the *Down Beat* Readers' Poll pronounced him "musician of the year." He also received that title in 1980. Gordon starred in the 1986 movie *'Round Midnight,* in which he played an expatriate jazz musician living in Paris, and was nominated for an Academy Award. Gordon died in 1990.

Bop-Style Big Bands in the Late 1940s

As we have seen, the bebop revolution emphasized the small ensemble. Further, the late 1940s witnessed the demise of many celebrated big bands. Despite all this, bebop proved attractive to some of the large bands. Dizzy Gillespie's big band was probably the first to commit completely to the new music. Other large ensembles soon followed and built much of their repertory along bebop lines. Some bands achieved even more popularity than Gillespie's band.

WOODY HERMAN

Woody Herman (1913–1987), a white clarinetist from Milwaukee, brought the bebop sounds to a wider audience and probably achieved the greatest commercial success in this style. Primetime radio shows, sponsored by Old Gold cigarettes and "Wild Root" hair tonic, broadcast Herman and his band. These broadcasts—largely

Bandleader and clarinetist Woody Herman on the cover of "Early Autumn." This number featured saxophonist Stan Getz (see Chapter 8).

EARLY AUTUMN

Words by JOHNNY MERCER · Original Music by RALPH BURNS and WOODY HERMAN

Introduced and Recorded by WOODY HERMAN on Mars Records

CROMWELL MUSIC, INC.
New York 19, N.Y.

PRICE
40¢

CHAPTER **7** THE BEBOP ERA

unavailable to the black bands—made Herman's band the first bebop-oriented music that many people in the United States heard.

Herman started his group in the mid-1930s, and in 1945 "Herman's Herd" earned a jukebox hit with "Caldonia." This novelty tune made deliberate and humorous use of the "hip" language that was emerging from the clubs on Fifty-Second Street. Largely a head arrangement, "Caldonia" featured a celebrated five-trumpet unison passage, written by trumpeter Neal Hefti, that had obviously originated in the solo lines of Gillespie. The band's rhythm section—Ralph Burns on piano, Chubby Jackson on bass, Billy Bauer on guitar, and Dave Tough on drums—created a furious drive on the up-tempo arrangements of "Northwest Passage" and "Apple Honey."

Herman reformed his band in 1947 into a group known as the "Second Herd." The band boasted several rising stars, including tenor saxophonists Stan Getz and Zoot Sims, both of whom based their distinctive sounds on that of Lester Young. In contrast to the normal saxophone section of two altos, two tenors, and one baritone, Herman's band featured the three tenors and one baritone. Known as the "Four Brothers" after a Jimmy Giuffre composition of the same name, the section was renowned for its clean, swinging ensemble sound. (See the box "Swing Bands in the Bebop Era.")

CLAUDE THORNHILL

Less successful commercially, but thoroughly committed to the new bebop music, was the band of pianist Claude Thornhill (1909–1965). Like Woody Herman and Gene Krupa, Thornhill's career began during the swing era of the mid-1930s (he even recorded with Billie Holiday in 1938), but he devoted his recordings of 1947–1948 to big-band arrangements of bebop compositions by Charlie Parker and others. The arrangements were unusual and original. Thornhill's arranger, Canadian Gil Evans (1912–1988), was influenced by the French Impressionist composers as well as by jazz, and he experimented with coloristic sounds and instruments not often heard in a big band: French horn, tuba, and bass clarinet. The absence of vibrato in the horns gave the band a stark, moody sound. For Thornhill, Gil Evans arranged Parker's compositions "Yardbird Suite," "Anthropology," and "Donna Lee." (The authorship of "Donna Lee" was credited to Charlie Parker, although it was probably composed by Miles Davis.)

Swing Bands in the Bebop Era

The big bands that made it through the end of the 1940s all seemed to jump on the bebop bandwagon. Swing drummer Gene Krupa and his band redid "Lemon Drop," written by bebop pianist George Wallington and popularized by Woody Herman in 1948. In Krupa's 1949 version, "Lemon Drop" trombonist Frank Rosolino supplied a bebop scat vocal in the style of Dizzy Gillespie. Krupa's staff arranger, Gerry Mulligan, created a hit for Krupa with his bop-oriented "Disc Jockey Jump." The more commercial bebop recordings of Herman and Krupa did much to popularize the music among white audiences. As we saw in Chapter 5, even Benny Goodman briefly tried his hand at leading a bop-style group in the late 1940s.

Despite the use of bebop compositions, some listeners still found the spirit of Thornhill's band at odds with the small groups of Fifty-Second Street. Miles Davis, who would collaborate with Gil Evans in the following years, noted, "I didn't really like what Thornhill did with Gil's arrangement of 'Donna Lee,' though. It was too slow and mannered for my taste. But I could hear the possibilities in Gil's arranging and writing on other things."[19]

Miles Davis and many of Thornhill's players—Gil Evans, baritone saxophonist and arranger Gerry Mulligan, and alto saxophonist Lee Konitz—eventually reacted against and rejected the prevailing bebop style. The result was known in the following decade as "cool" jazz, which we explore in the next chapter, on the jazz of the 1950s.

See the following table for a summary of bebop characteristics.

Bebop-Era Melodic Features

TIMBRE

▶ Tougher, edgier sound than swing, often raspy
▶ Little use of vibrato except on ballads
▶ Little use of instrumental effects
▶ Strong attacks combined with legato lines
▶ Little use of blue-note effects on up-tempo pieces
▶ Instrumental ranges extended upward, especially for brass

PHRASING

▶ Highly irregular, perhaps to offset symmetrical AABA forms
▶ Little space between phrases

RHYTHM

▶ Great reliance on eighth-note lines in up-tempo pieces
▶ Ballads featuring more rhythmic variety

THEMATIC CONTINUITY

▶ Voice leading almost exclusively in up-tempo pieces
▶ Motivic relationships less obvious, except on ballads

CHORD-SCALE RELATIONS

▶ Inside, but based on more-complex scales that include extended chord tones

LARGE-SCALE COHERENCE

▶ Voice leading
▶ Occasional reliance on use of climax followed by relaxation
▶ Balance of gesture

Questions and Topics for Discussion

1. What are some of the differences between bebop and swing? What are some of their similarities? In what ways are the differences revolutionary or evolutionary?

2. How was Charlie Parker the consummate bebop musician? Refer to aspects of his life and music.

3. How did the lives of Dizzy Gillespie and Thelonious Monk differ from Charlie Parker's life? Refer to big bands, compositions, attitudes toward music, and personal history.

4. How did the repertory of bebop change from that of swing? What aspects of the repertory stayed the same?

5. Is it appropriate to regard bebop as the beginning of "modern jazz"? Cite both musical and sociological factors in arguing your case.

Key Terms

Bebop/bop

Comping

Dropping bombs

Extended chord tones (tensions)

Hipster

Formula/lick

Moldy fig

Recomposition

Reharmonization

Encouraged by advertisements such as this one featuring Hopalong Cassidy on a 1950 Motorola television, mainstream America grew entranced with the new medium.

THE FIFTIES AND NEW JAZZ SUBSTYLES

THE CONTROVERSIES surrounding bebop in the 1940s led to a profoundly different jazz environment in the 1950s. No longer was it possible to speak of "jazz" and expect everyone to understand the meaning. It became necessary to indicate the *kind* of jazz, for the music now included a variety of substyles, the most important being "hard bop" and "cool." Hard bop developed from bebop, whereas cool developed, in part, as a reaction against bebop. In addition, Dixieland continued to flourish everywhere, thanks to a revival in the early 1940s. Finally, popular performers such as Ella Fitzgerald and Frank Sinatra who had roots in the swing bands of the 1930s or early 1940s retained many of the elements of swing from the big-band era.

Tracking general trends in such a complex jazz world is difficult. However, there was one point of view that musicians in the vanguard shared at the time—modernism. According to this view, jazz must develop, even "progress." This was not an entirely new idea. As far back as the 1930s, jazz musicians thought of themselves as technically and artistically more advanced than the "rough" and "naive" early players. But in the 1950s many musicians, propelled by the changes of the late 1940s, came to consider jazz one of the fine arts, a category that embraced the principle of progressive development and mandated change. If jazz was to remain *art,* the artist and the music had to move forward in a constant, conscious evolution. Thus the advancing of jazz, as we shall see, became an important goal for many of its players and writers.

Jazz and the New Substyles

The decade of the 1950s witnessed a flowering of jazz styles as the music splintered in several directions. We shall examine two general trends and one or two subgenres of each:

- ■ Cool jazz
  - ▶ Third-stream music
  - ▶ Modal jazz
- ■ Hard bop
  - ▶ Funky or soul jazz

Third-stream music blends jazz with European concert music. In many instances, third-stream composers create concert works that allow for improvisation within larger-scale structures influenced by both jazz and concert music.

As with all categories, these are not hard-and-fast distinctions. For example, some third-stream music is not "cool." And in the 1960s, modal jazz is often linked more closely with hard bop than with cool jazz. Generally, jazz critics and record executives, rather than the musicians themselves, coined these labels.

The cool jazz style, which was associated with the West Coast, rejected some of the significant features of bebop and pursued different aesthetic principles. Miles Davis, Gerry Mulligan, Chet Baker, Dave Brubeck, the Modern Jazz Quartet, and others emphasized the following:

- ▶ Restraint
- ▶ Lyricism
- ▶ Musical space
- ▶ Counterpoint
- ▶ Quieter dynamic range

Counterpoint is the use of simultaneously sounding musical lines. Music that has counterpoint is often called polyphonic (see Chapter 1).

In contrast to the breathtaking pace of some of the bebop players, many of the cool players concentrated on relaxed tempos. Tenor saxophonists such as Stan Getz, Zoot Sims, Jimmy Giuffre, and Al Cohn—all members of Woody Herman's "Four Brothers" saxophone section during the late 1940s—emulated Lester Young's light

Technological Advances in the 1950s

The decade of the 1950s profited from two technological advances in recording. By the end of the 1940s magnetic-tape recording had replaced the more limited and cumbersome metal discs. Tape recording offered several advantages:

- ▶ Performance editing (splicing together different parts to create a performance with fewer errors)
- ▶ Overdubbing (adding new parts to a previously recorded performance)

- ▶ Longer performance times, which encouraged the creation of longer compositions specifically for listening
- ▶ Live recording, when tape machines became more portable

Along with tape recording, the long-playing disc (LP) contributed greatly to the evolution of jazz. LPs first became commercially available when Columbia released its 33⅓ rpm recordings in 1948.

LPs were made with polyvinyl chloride (hence the nickname "vinyl" for records), which allowed more than twice the number of grooves on each side of the record than the 78 rpm did. The new "microgroove" records thus allowed more playing time per side—up to around twenty-five minutes (versus the previous three or four). LPs and magnetic tape freed musicians to record in longer segments and to approximate live performances more closely than ever before.

sound along with his relaxation, control, and wit. Composers Charles Mingus, George Russell, Gunther Schuller, J. J. Johnson, and Pete Rugolo frequently focused on larger, ambitious works, such as suites and multimovement compositions. Cool jazz groups took different sizes, although after Miles Davis's nine-piece group made its highly influential recordings for Capitol Records in 1949 and 1950, several eight- to ten-piece groups arose. Note that the players did not always embrace the term *cool jazz*, because it implied a lack of passion and emotional depth.

Although cool jazz was undoubtedly a brand new direction for the music, many players were committed to perpetuating bebop. These players forged a style that came to be known as hard bop. Interestingly, many of them came to New York from the urban centers of Detroit and Philadelphia. The hard bop groups varied in size, but their instrumentation often kept the standard bebop quintet of a rhythm section with piano, bass, drums, and two horns, typically a tenor saxophone and a trumpet. Many of these groups favored thirty-two–bar compositions and a straight-ahead improvisation full of intensity, speed, and volume.

In addition, the repertory of hard bop groups often included music that wedded the traditions of bebop to the simpler, earthier blues, creating a style sometimes known as funky jazz, gospel jazz, or, in the 1960s, soul jazz. Strongly influenced by currents in black music, funky/soul jazz took much of its inspiration from gospel music, blues, and rhythm and blues, as in the music of gospel singer Mahalia Jackson and blues singer/pianist Ray Charles. Leaning toward the popular-music side of jazz, funky/soul jazz used a bluesy harmonic style; catchy, earthy melodies; and, often, the call-and-response formulas of the black churches.

New jazz venues—concerts especially—arose during the 1950s. Annual jazz festivals sprang up and allowed the music to reach large audiences. The first international jazz festival opened in Nice, France, in 1948; in the United States, the famous Newport Jazz Festival, directed by George Wein, began in Newport, Rhode Island, in 1954. These festivals had enormous power to help or revive performers' careers. One legendary jazz story tells how Duke Ellington's 1956 performance at Newport jump-started Ellington's flagging career. In addition to jazz festivals, students on college campuses in the 1950s sponsored jazz concerts that helped such groups as the Dave Brubeck Quartet and the Modern Jazz Quartet gain visibility and popularity. Finally, jazz received a boost from the new recording technology, which allowed artists to record at length (see the box "Technological Advances in the 1950s" for more).

Cool jazz was a reaction to bebop. It embraced the values of increased compositional complexity, slower tempos, and at times less emotional involvement.

Hard bop drew on the speed, intensity, and power of bebop and sometimes married bop to gospel and blues-influenced music.

Funky jazz or **soul jazz** represented an equal wedding of rhythm and blues or gospel styles with the traditional jazz ensemble and was in many ways an outgrowth of hard bop.

On the cover of this sheet music republished with the revival of his popularity at the 1956 Newport Jazz Festival, Duke Ellington seems to be sharing the lighthearted irony of his song's title.

Cool Stylists

Many artists contributed to the cool jazz style. One of the most influential was Miles Davis, with his groundbreaking pieces later collected as the album *Birth of the Cool*. Other artists and groups who played major roles include Gerry Mulligan, Chet Baker, the Modern Jazz Quartet, Dave Brubeck, Stan Getz, and Lennie Tristano.

MILES DAVIS AND BIRTH OF THE COOL

A series of influential recordings for Capitol Records in 1949–1950, later released as *Birth of the Cool*, helped set the tone of jazz for the decade to come. Through three studio sessions, trumpeter Miles Davis led a nine-piece group in startling arrangements that represented a drastic shift for Davis. Since coming to New York in 1944, he had been recording and performing consistently with bebop players, particularly Charlie Parker. In contrast to the freewheeling, loose, intense improvisations of Parker's quintet, the *Birth of the Cool* sessions exhibited careful arranging, musical restraint, and lyricism.

The young Miles Davis (CD 1, Track 20 and CD 2, Track 5) signed this Fontana publicity postcard for a fan in Belgium.

Courtesy Morgan Collection

Davis capitalized on the "cool" elements of his style, which had begun to emerge in his earlier recordings: He focused his trumpet in the middle register, played with less virtuosic bravura, and used more "space," or rests between phrases. Given his natural inclination toward the "cool," Davis admired the arrangements Gil Evans had created for the Claude Thornhill band. He decided to emulate Thornhill's sound with fewer instruments. The result was his nonet, which had three rhythm players (on piano, bass, and drums) and six horns. The horns were grouped in pairs of high and low ranges: trumpet/trombone, French horn/tuba, and alto saxophone/baritone saxophone. Significantly, there was no tenor saxophone, an unusual omission for a medium-sized band. Even more striking was the use of French horn and tuba, instruments more common to the European classical tradition than to jazz but part of Evans's earlier arrangements for Thornhill.

In 1948 Davis's nonet booked a two-week performance at New York's Royal Roost, where they alternated sets with Count Basie. With their unusual instrumentation, the nonet played to lukewarm reviews and were no longer working when they entered the studio in 1949. Over fifteen months they recorded twelve sides, initially released on 78s. Only in 1954 would eight of the twelve compositions appear on a 10-inch LP and all twelve be released in 1957 as *Birth of the Cool*.

Gil Evans was not the only arranger for the group. Baritone saxophonist Gerry Mulligan, pianist John Lewis, and trumpeter Johnny Carisi all contributed charts and compositions. Many of the arrangements, such as Carisi's "Israel," featured the horns in counterpoint, creating a web of parts moving independently. Others, such as "Budo" (a slightly revised version of Bud Powell's "Hallucinations"), paid tribute to bop, but the nonet version purged the music of its demonic energy. The harmonies were lush, the writing often dense. Gil Evans's arrangement of "Moon Dreams" was a slow, dreamy work, completely composed and with no improvisation. In some works, arrangers abandoned the nearly universal jazz practice of playing compositions in eight-bar sections; for example, the first A section of Evans's "Godchild" arrangement is seventeen-and-a-half bars.

LISTENING GUIDE

"Jeru"
CD **1** Track **20**

Miles Davis and His Orchestra: "Jeru" (Mulligan). Capitol M-11026. New York, January 21, 1949.
Miles Davis, trumpet and leader; Kai Winding, trombone; Junior Collins, French horn; Bill Barber, tuba;
Lee Konitz, alto saxophone; Gerry Mulligan, baritone saxophone, composer-arranger;
Al Haig, piano; Joe Schulman, bass; Max Roach, drums.

Gerry Mulligan's "Jeru" is a fine example of the *Birth of the Cool* recordings. The piece features a complex formal structure that in many ways anticipates third-stream practice.

Head—AA section, 16 bars

0:00   No introduction; the head is in AABA form. The whole band plays and repeats the eight-bar A section.

Head—B section, 12 bars with measures 4–8 in 3/4

0:21   Prefiguring third-stream ideas, the bridge is irregular: twelve bars with the meter changing from 4/4 to 3/4 in measures 4–8, then back to 4/4 for measures 9–12.

0:30   The baritone saxophone has the lead for the last four bars of the bridge.

Head—A section, 9 bars
0:36   The return of the A section features a one-bar extension of the form leading to the Davis trumpet solo.

Davis trumpet solo—AABA, 32 bars
0:48   Davis's solo, a regular 8–8–8–8, drops the complexities of the sectional groupings.

AA—Band alternates with Mulligan baritone solo, irregular 16 bars
1:31   When the band reenters, the arrangement features a section that is in stop time, syncopated to sound like 3/4. It is most easily counted in 4/4 with the fourth bar as a 2/4 bar (as shown here).

1:35   Mulligan solos through measures 5–8 in 4/4.

1:41   The format repeats for the second A.

BA—Last part of Mulligan solo, 16 bars
1:51   For the bridge and final A of Mulligan's solo, the form is straightforward: two eight-bar sections.

Out-chorus AABA—Irregular as 8–8–12, final A extended with coda
2:13   The two A sections from the head are dramatically recomposed for the climactic out-chorus.

2:35   The twelve-bar B section is similar to its earlier presentation, with measures 4–8 in 3/4. Measures 9–12 of the bridge are also recomposed to be more polyphonic.

2:50   The final A section uses the out-chorus theme but is extended with a coda. The final chord uses a dissonant voicing, with the baritone on the major seventh of the E♭MA7 chord.

Many of the players on *Birth of the Cool* were strongly associated with cool jazz throughout their later careers. Alto saxophonist Lee Konitz, a student of pianist Lennie Tristano, brought a light, airy, vibratoless sound to the horn. He went on to record as a leader. Baritone saxophonist Gerry Mulligan gained increasing fame during the decade for his pianoless quartet with Chet Baker (discussed in the next section). Pianist John Lewis, a veteran of Dizzy Gillespie's band, gained prominence with the Modern Jazz Quartet. In the late 1950s, Gil Evans collaborated again with Miles Davis on the significant Columbia recordings *Miles Ahead, Porgy and Bess,* and *Sketches of Spain.*

The *Birth of the Cool* recordings had an enormous influence. Their emphasis on subtlety and their balance of composition and improvisation provided an alternative model to bebop. Jazz critic Nat Hentoff described the influence of *Birth of the Cool* as follows:

> These records were comparable in their impact on a new generation of jazz musicians to the Louis Armstrong Hot Five and Hot Seven records of the 1920s, some of the Duke Ellington and Basie records of the Thirties, and the records made by Parker and his associates in the early and middle Forties.[1]

GERRY MULLIGAN AND CHET BAKER

Mulligan's importance in creating the *Birth of the Cool* sessions has sometimes been undervalued. Not only did he play baritone saxophone and compose "Jeru," "Venus de Milo," and "Rocker," he also arranged "Darn That Dream" and "Godchild." After completing the *Birth of the Cool* recordings, Mulligan hitchhiked to California and began playing and arranging on the West Coast. Although born in New York in 1927, from the time he arrived in California, Mulligan was associated with West Coast jazz.

Gerry Mulligan (CD 1, Track 20) in a publicity photograph.

After leading a ten-piece group in a recording modeled on the *Birth of the Cool* instrumentation, Mulligan formed his most famous group while performing on Monday nights at a Los Angeles club called The Haig. The quartet featured Mulligan on baritone saxophone, Chet Baker on trumpet, Bob Whitlock on bass, and Chico Hamilton on drums. Instrumentation that lacked an instrument that played chords, such as a piano, was unusual. The group developed an airy open sound based on ingenious counterpoint of the baritone saxophone and trumpet—a technique that allowed the horn players to weave spontaneous lines and create call-and-response patterns. Without piano, the group exhibited a sparseness that operated at low volume.

The quartet quickly found success. They recorded their first hit, "My Funny Valentine," in 1952. In this piece, listeners could hear the plaintive and fragile trumpet style of Chet Baker (1929–1988). Baker, who hailed from Oklahoma, was only twenty-two years old at the time of the recording and earlier that year had performed on a tour of southern California with Charlie Parker. Tall and photogenic (producers considered him for movie roles before his heroin habit proved too consuming), Baker played extremely quietly, with a delicate lyricism. Listeners and critics compared the trumpet playing of Baker to that of Miles Davis, although Baker played with a softer tone. Baker's vocal style closely resembled that of his trumpet: quiet, relaxed, with a shade of vibrato at the end of a phrase.

With the success of the band and his newly won recognition in the polls of *Down Beat* and *Metronome,* Baker left the band over a financial disagreement with Mulligan. He continued to perform throughout the 1950s and recorded frequently, often with West Coast pianist Russ Freeman. After spending four months on drug-related charges at Riker's Island prison in New York City, Baker moved to Europe in 1959. His heroin addiction continued to plague him, however, and he was arrested repeatedly in Europe. He achieved something of a comeback in the 1970s and 1980s but died tragically in Amsterdam after falling from a window.

When Baker left the group in 1954, Mulligan continued to lead his own bands, a tentet as well as newer versions of his quartet. His performance at the Salle Pleyel in Paris featured trombonist Bob Brookmeyer; a later version of the quartet included saxophonist Zoot Sims. After leading the thirteen-piece Concert Jazz Band in the late 1950s and early 1960s, he continued to work as a sideman, playing with Dave Brubeck from 1968 to 1972. Mulligan also composed several film scores. In his later years, he became one of the most popular artists on the jazz concert scene. He died in 1996.

Besides Duke Ellington's baritone saxophonist Harry Carney, Mulligan was probably the most important baritone saxophonist in jazz. Moreover, Mulligan took the baritone out of the big band and placed it in a small-group setting. During the 1950s, only Serge Chaloff and Pepper Adams rivaled Mulligan on the instrument.

THE MODERN JAZZ QUARTET

Ironically, the group known as one of the leading exponents of cool jazz started out by playing bebop with Dizzy Gillespie. The original members of the Modern Jazz Quartet—pianist John Lewis, drummer Kenny Clarke, bassist Ray Brown, and vibraphonist Milt Jackson—came together in Gillespie's big band in 1946. Five years later they began recording as the Milt Jackson Quartet. After Percy Heath (b. 1923) replaced Ray Brown on the bass, they issued their first records as the Modern Jazz Quartet on Prestige Records. Connie Kay (1923–1994) became the drummer after Kenny Clarke left the group.

The Modern Jazz Quartet (MJQ) became celebrated for their polished, refined performances. Like many jazz groups of the 1950s, the MJQ attempted to avoid the stigma of the disreputable jazz musician and to bring greater respectability to jazz

The Modern Jazz Quartet in the mid-1950s. Left to right: Percy Heath, Connie Kay, John Lewis, Milt Jackson.

Courtesy Frank Driggs Collection

performances. In formal tuxedos, they performed with the serious demeanor of the classical musician—and filled concert halls.

Milt Jackson (1923–1999) and John Lewis (1920–2001) were the fire and ice of the band. Jackson, the primary soloist, played an exuberant, swinging, blues-based vibraphone above the subtle accompaniments and countermelodies of pianist Lewis. In a style that often featured single-line counterpoint rather than the chordal punctuation typical of bebop pianists, Lewis's simplicity and restraint on the piano contrasted well with Jackson's ebullience.

The band was known not only for improvisation but also for sophisticated arrangements and compositions. John Lewis was the primary architect. He often sought to merge elements of jazz with those inspired by European classical techniques—as the title of their album *Blues on Bach* suggests. For example, counterpoint figured in Lewis's accompaniments, and he based some of his compositions, such as "Vendome," "Concorde," "Versailles," and "Three Windows," on the baroque technique of the fugue.

Lewis consciously attempted to develop extended compositions and forms—to move away from the thirty-two–bar frameworks that were the mainstay of jazz. As he noted in an address in 1958:

> The audience for jazz can be widened if we strengthen our work with structure. If there is more of a reason for what's going on, there'll be more overall sense, and therefore, more interest for the listener. I do not think, however, that the sections in this "structured jazz"—both the improvised and written sections—should take on too much complexity. The total effect must be within the mind's ability to appreciate through the ear.[2]

One of the best examples of Lewis's interest in this "structured jazz" can be heard in his "Django," a tribute to European jazz guitarist Django Reinhardt. The piece alternates a plaintive twenty-bar lament in F minor with a medium-tempo bluesy section.

Even more ambitious were collaborations with composer Gunther Schuller, who had coined the term *third stream* to describe the confluence of the independent streams of jazz and European classical music. The MJQ made a recording entitled *Third Stream Music* with the Beaux Arts String Quartet and performed Schuller's *Concertino for Jazz Quartet and Orchestra* with the Stuttgart Symphony.

The MJQ broke up in 1974 because Milt Jackson wanted to pursue a solo career, but it reunited in 1981 to seek concert bookings. They continued to perform together for different tours through the 1990s.

DAVE BRUBECK

One of the most commercially successful jazz musicians of the 1950s and 1960s was pianist and composer Dave Brubeck (b. 1920). Brubeck's quartet, with alto saxophonist Paul Desmond, came together in 1951 and gained visibility through concerts on college campuses. In turn, Brubeck brought academic respectability to jazz by performing and recording at such schools as Oberlin College, Ohio University, and the University of Michigan during a time when the music was considered inappropriate for campus concerts. (Jazz had long been performed on campus, but usually only at parties.) Brubeck's success led to his appearance on the cover of *Time* magazine in 1954. Moreover, he consistently won the *Down Beat* popularity polls

A **fugue** is a baroque form characterized by continuous counterpoint based on a principal melodic idea called the **subject**. At the beginning of a typical fugue, in a section known as the exposition, each voice (or part) in the texture begins by stating the subject.

Courtesy Morgan Collection

The cover of the Dave Brubeck classic. Left to right: Paul Desmond, composer, on saxophone; Joe Morello on drums; Eugene Wright on bass; and Dave Brubeck on the piano. Based in California, far from New York's Fifty-Second Street, Brubeck was especially popular on college campuses.

throughout the fifties and sixties. However, critics vilified him for music they considered heavy-handed and unswinging.

While a student at Mills College during the mid-1940s, Brubeck studied composition with French composer Darius Milhaud, famous as a member of *Les Six,* a group of French composers. Some of Milhaud's compositions from the 1920s made use of jazz elements. Under this influence, Brubeck embraced a style of composition and improvisation that drew upon the European preoccupation with form. Many of Brubeck's compositions resonated with the contrapuntal techniques learned from his teacher.

In 1946 Brubeck organized an octet with like-minded students to create jazz works with a European sensibility; the titles included "Rondo," "Prelude," and "Fugue on Bop Themes." Brubeck's arrangement of "Just the Way You Look Tonight" wove together the main theme and the bridge of the composition, a contrapuntal experiment rarely heard in jazz arranging. Although the Brubeck octet was far less influential than Miles Davis's nonet from *Birth of the Cool,* the two groups had some interesting features in common: The groups were similarly sized, and the arrangements juxtaposed written and improvised sections with considerable counterpoint.

The quartet with Paul Desmond was the group that made Brubeck famous. Originally from San Francisco, Desmond (1924–1977) played alto saxophone with a liquid, creamy sound. Consistently inventive and lyrical, Desmond rarely played a wasted note. In 1959 Desmond penned the group's most famous composition, "Take Five," a catchy, bluesy melody in 5/4, a meter rarely explored in jazz. (Drummer Max Roach was one of the few jazz musicians to have used 5/4 prior to Brubeck's band.)

By the time "Take Five" was recorded on Brubeck's 1959 album, *Time Out,* Brubeck's famous quartet had taken shape: Brubeck on piano, Desmond on alto, Joe Morello (b. 1928) on drums, and Eugene Wright (b. 1923) on bass. The group was celebrated for its exploration of unusual meters. Brubeck wrote "Blue Rondo à la Turk" in a 9/8 meter that he subdivided into groupings of 2 + 2 + 2 + 3.

"Blue Rondo à la Turk" deftly combines cool jazz and European styles into a third-stream mixture. The cool jazz elements include the following:

▶ An overall cool ambience and fairly unemotional playing

▶ A light, airy saxophone tone reminiscent of Lester Young on tenor

▶ A simple, clear swing beat with a walking bass

▶ Few flashy displays of technical prowess

▶ Little use of the slides, blue notes, and other expressive effects of blues playing (although a blues form is used)

The third-stream aspects of the performance include these:

▶ A detailed formal plan inspired by the classical rondo

▶ Clever use of a compound meter

Although many third-stream experiments sound contrived and dated, "Blue Rondo à la Turk" sparkles, largely because of its rhythmic drive and its beautifully contrasting blues improvisations. The piece is an admirable mixture of the experimental and the conventional, both of which are carefully planned and impeccably performed.

Although Brubeck became well known as a jazz pianist, his principal interest was composition. Not surprisingly, he disbanded his group in 1967 to devote more time to composing. He has since written ballets, an oratorio, cantatas, and other music for jazz groups and orchestras, while occasionally performing and recording with jazz groups. In recent years, he has intensified his touring schedule and recorded with his sons, keyboardist Darius Brubeck, trombonist and electric bassist Chris Brubeck, and drummer Danny Brubeck.

STAN GETZ

Like Desmond, many of the cool saxophonists avoided the influence of Charlie Parker. Instead, they looked back to tenor saxophonist Lester "Prez" Young for a lighter, airier sound and a more relaxed approach. As tenor saxophonist Stan Getz noted in his aptly named composition, they sought "Prezervation."

Earlier, we mentioned that many prominent disciples of Lester Young were white players who formed the saxophone section known as the "Four Brothers" from Woody Herman's Herd of the late 1940s. They included tenor saxophonists Stan Getz, Zoot Sims, Al Cohn, and Jimmy Giuffre. Of these, Getz won the most praise. Born in Philadelphia in 1927, Getz came to Herman's band in 1947 after having made his first recording at age sixteen with Jack Teagarden and having played with both Stan Kenton and Benny Goodman.

Getz was certainly capable of playing virtuosic bebop—his 1949 recording of "Crazy Chords" traveled through the blues in all twelve keys at a hair-raising tempo—but he had a distinctive tone that shone beautifully in ballads. His sound was breathy and relaxed, with evident vibrato, yet surprisingly strong and centered. Getz's solo feature in Woody Herman's 1948 "Early Autumn" established him as a formidable lyrical improviser. Soon after, Getz left Herman to lead small groups. Although problems with drug addiction led him to live in Scandinavia for much of the late 1950s, he returned to the United States in 1961.

The young Stan Getz on the cover of a jazz samba collection.

Once back in the United States, Getz embarked on several projects. His 1961 album, *Focus,* featured daring string arrangements by Eddie Sauter that overtly merged jazz with elements of classical music. Several of his recordings combined Brazilian rhythms with jazz—or "bossa nova." The most famous of these was "The Girl from Ipanema," sung by Brazilian vocalist Astrud Gilberto. This became a hit that brought Getz much commercial popularity. His landmark record, *Jazz Samba* (1962), contributed significantly to the bossa nova craze and catapulted his name into public consciousness. Rarely did another post-1950s mainstream jazz musician, with the possible exception of Cannonball Adderley, achieve Getz's commercial success.

When the popularity of bossa nova began to ebb in the late 1960s, Getz continued to perform widely, often with many of the best-known names in jazz, including Chick Corea and Bill Evans. Other important collaborations toward the end of his career included work with pianists Joanne Brackeen and Andy LaVerne. Getz died in 1991.

Bossa nova was a Latin jazz style developed in the late-1950s and early-1960s from Brazilian rhythms. Of all the jazz players with bossa nova hits, Stan Getz was the most prominent.

LENNIE TRISTANO

Although he never reached the level of popularity and commercial success that some of the other cool jazz players did, pianist Lennie Tristano earned widespread acclaim from jazz critics and musicians. Tristano (1919–1978), a blind pianist born in Chicago, founded an informal school of musicians. Among his students were saxophonists Lee Konitz and Warne Marsh and guitarist Billy Bauer. Konitz and Marsh recorded more frequently and received more visibility than Tristano himself did.

Tristano's playing exhibited virtuosic cool precision. He sounded relaxed even at breakneck tempos, tossing off long, even streams of eighth notes with surprising syncopations and cross-rhythms. Many of his improvisations also made use of the locked-hands style of Milt Buckner and George Shearing. (See glossary and listen to Track 9 of the 🅟 Audio Primer CD.) Although some performers found Tristano's playing overly intellectual and precise, he nevertheless fashioned a viable alternative for bebop ensemble playing and improvisation.

In contrast to the fiery bebop drumming of Max Roach or Roy Haynes, Tristano usually insisted that his drummer use brushes to accompany the soloists quietly. (Listen to Track 35 of the 🅟 Audio Primer CD to hear brushes.) Often making use of the eighth-note musical language of bebop, Tristano managed to avoid many of bebop's clichés. He preferred instead to explore contrapuntal textures and fiendishly difficult unison figures.

Upon moving to New York in 1946, Tristano quickly gained critical recognition when *Metronome* magazine named him its "Musician of the Year" for 1947. Tristano's 1949 sextet recordings—with his students Konitz, Marsh, and Bauer, along with bassist Arnold Fishkin and various drummers—showed Tristano's distinctly modern outlook. For example, while opening with a standard chord progression, "Tautology" unfolded in surprising harmonic twists. Tristano wrote the melody in a rigorous contrapuntal style that encompassed all twelve notes of the chromatic scale.

Some of Tristano's compositions were even more exploratory. Anticipating the "free jazz" movement by a decade, his 1949 recordings of "Intuition" and "Digression" were collective improvisations without preset melodies, meters, or harmonic progressions. In the mid-1950s, Tristano investigated the possibilities of overdubbing. His "Turkish Mambo" boasted three separate piano tracks in which he created left-hand patterns of five, six, or seven beats, all conflicting with each other and all beneath a right-hand improvisation.

Tristano's influence as a teacher was legendary. His students studied and learned the classic solos of jazz masters such as Louis Armstrong, Earl Hines, Lester Young, Charlie Parker, and Bud Powell. An admirer of the contrapuntal organization of J. S. Bach, Tristano had his students perform arrangements of Bach's *Inventions*.

Alto saxophonist Lee Konitz (b. 1927) became the best-known player of the Tristano circle. Konitz cultivated a light, airy tone on the alto, using almost no vibrato. Like many other cool saxophonists, his sound and style rejected the intimidating speed and edgy timbre of Charlie Parker. Instead, Konitz brought to the alto the dry timbre of Lester Young's tenor sound, in the manner of Paul Desmond. In addition to playing with Tristano, Konitz performed with the Claude Thornhill band and joined several Thornhill alumni in Miles Davis's *Birth of the Cool* recordings. He also won the *Metronome* poll for 1954 (as did Tristano and Tristano's student Billy Bauer), and he performed with the Metronome All-Star Band the following year.

The 1950 version of the Metronome All-Star band included—along with Konitz, Tristano, and Bauer—trumpeter Dizzy Gillespie, drummer Max Roach, clarinetist Buddy DeFranco, trombonist Kai Winding, tenor saxophonist Stan Getz, and baritone saxophonist Serge Chaloff. Their recording of Tristano's "No Figs," a complex and difficult work, was particularly successful. Tristano wrote this recomposition of "Back Home in Indiana" in triplets and sixteenth notes, creating a dense harmonic web for the horns, guitar, and piano. Konitz's solo, with his characteristic legato, smooth, and light tone, remained in the upper register of the horn. Tristano's blisteringly fast solo, in quadruple time, was all the more astonishing for his harmonizations in a block-chord style.

Konitz redefined his approach in the mid-1950s, offering a simpler, more concentrated style. Despite his cool label, he also played down-home blues, as in "Cork 'n' Bib," from his 1956 *Inside Hi-Fi* record. As late as 1975 he rejoined fellow Tristano student Warne Marsh for a recording entitled *Jazz Exchange*. His subsequent bands, particularly his nonet modeled on *Birth of the Cool* instrumentation, have continued to perpetuate the cool jazz tradition.

Jazz on the West Coast

The musical aesthetic of cool jazz, a deliberate alternative to bebop, became a touchstone for many bands and performers of the 1950s. This was particularly true for players on the West Coast. Shelly Manne, a highly visible drummer at the time, acknowledged the importance of Miles Davis and described some of the important characteristics of the West Coast music scene during the 1950s:

> I think the main influence on West Coast Jazz, if one record could be an influence, was the album Miles Davis made called *Birth of the Cool*. That kind of writing and playing was closer to what we were trying to do, closer to the way a lot of us felt, out on the west coast.... It had a lot to do not only with just improvisation and swing. It was the main character of the music we liked—the chance for the composer to be challenged too. To write some new kind of material for jazz musicians where the solos and the improvisation became part of the whole and you couldn't tell where the writing ended and the improvisation began.[3]

The term *West Coast jazz* has often been used interchangeably with *cool jazz,* although they are not necessarily synonymous. Not all cool jazz players lived in California, and not all West Coast players played cool jazz. Nevertheless, several jazz players in and around Los Angeles were considered important figures. Many of them had been affiliated with the postwar bands of Woody Herman and of Stan Kenton and had settled in California. They earned their living performing in the studio music industry and at jazz clubs such as the Lighthouse and The Haig.

West Coast jazz embodied many of the principles of cool jazz as performed by a group of players centered in California.

The big band of pianist Stan Kenton was, for some, "the starting point for West Coast jazz."[4] Kenton's band earned immense popularity during the late 1940s as well as intense condemnation from critics who considered it unswinging, bombastic, and pretentious. "Let's face it," shrilled one critic, "this is the loudest band ever."[5] In trying to avoid any of the old associations of jazz with dance music, Kenton (1911–1979) championed what he called "progressive jazz," named after his 1949 twenty-piece band. Kenton envisioned concert works, and he and staff arrangers Pete Rugolo, Bill Holman, and Bill Russo wrote arrangements with such titles as "Artistry in Rhythm," "Artistry in Bolero," "Fantasy," and "Opus in Pastels."

Although Kenton's arrangements often emphasized improvisations less than written compositional structures, his band included significant soloists strongly associated with jazz on the West Coast, for example, Lee Konitz, Art Pepper, Stan Getz, Zoot Sims, and Bud Shank. Alto and baritone saxophonist Art Pepper (1925–1982) was the leading soloist of the Kenton band between 1946 and 1951. One of the "hotter" players of the cool West Coast style, he played with an intense fiery passion. Pepper's career suffered from his drug addiction and incarceration, which he chronicled in painful detail in his autobiography *Straight Life.*

The West Coast cool players and bands that emerged during the decade emphasized written arrangements, compositional structures, restrained dynamics, and unusual instrumentation. Miles Davis's *Birth of the Cool* nonet—with a single representative of each instrument rather than big-band sections—became the model for many octets, nonets, and tentets that arose in California during the decade. Composer, arranger, and trumpeter Shorty Rogers (b. 1924) adopted this instrumental technique for recordings with his group Shorty and His Giants. Rogers used five lead instruments on "Popo," a twelve-bar blues that would become his theme song, and six lead instruments on "Pirouette." Rogers, who had played and written for Woody Herman and Stan Kenton, devised intricate, contrapuntal orchestrations for his music.

Much of West Coast cool jazz emphasized subdued dynamics, with the drummer providing an understated accompaniment. Shelly Manne (1920–1984), a drummer working with his own groups and in a trio with pianist André Previn, was known for his elegant and supportive brush work. In his 1953 recording "Mallets," we can hear Manne using mallets on the drums in a dialogue with the horns. Instead of aggressively driving the band, drums for Manne played a different role, one that made them an equal melodic partner with the horns:

> I have always felt that the drums have great melodic potential.... If a drummer must play an extended solo, he should think more about melodic lines than rudiment lines.... On some of my records, the writers have written definitive "melodic" lines for the drums to play, and if these lines were left out, it would be like one of the horns dropping out.[6]

Another West Coast drummer with an even more subdued approach was Chico Hamilton (b. 1921), who played quietly not only when accompanying soloists but also when performing his delicate and subtle drum solos. Hamilton's group exhibited another trait of several groups on the West Coast—the use of unusual combinations of instruments. Hamilton's quintet included a guitarist, bass player, drummer, cellist, and saxophonist who doubled on flute. At the time, cello and flute were rarely encountered in jazz. In the 1960s, Hamilton changed his style and became a more driving player.

Perhaps the most unusual instrumental combinations were recorded by saxophonist Jimmy Giuffre (b. 1921), who had replaced Zoot Sims in the Woody Herman "Four Brothers" saxophone section. Giuffre began his career as a cool tenor saxophonist in the Lester Young tradition, but he was a restless experimenter. As noted earlier, Giuffre had written Herman's hit "Four Brothers" with its unusual saxophone choir of three tenors plus baritone. On his 1956 album *The Jimmy Giuffre Clarinet,* he featured a work for solo clarinet; a work for clarinet and celesta; a work for flute, alto flute, bass flute, clarinet, and drums (with Shelly Manne playing drums with his fingers); and an arrangement of the well-known standard "My Funny Valentine" for clarinet, oboe, bassoon, English horn, and bass.

The most radical recording of the West Coast cool players may have been Giuffre's 1955 *Tangents in Jazz.* On it, Giuffre sought to free the bass and drums from their traditional timekeeping roles by composing individual, contrapuntal parts for them. This vision represented a strong experimental stance, particularly to those who considered a swinging pulse—as provided by the bass and drums—to be one of the most fundamental aspects of jazz. In answer to the question, "What is this music?" the liner notes replied:

> Jazz, with a non-pulsating beat. The beat is implicit but not explicit; in other words, acknowledged but unsounded. The two horns are the dominant but not domineering voices. The bass usually functions somewhat like a baritone sax. The drums play an important but non-conflicting role.[7]

Third-Stream Music

Many of the features associated with West Coast jazz were not confined to California. The emphasis on compositional structures and counterpoint, the understated role of the rhythm section, and the inclusion of instruments more typical of European classical music than jazz (such as the French horn or cello) were part of an aesthetic that suggested a new synthesis. To composer and jazz historian Gunther Schuller, who had himself played French horn on the *Birth of the Cool* sessions, this fusion seemed part of an inevitable trend. In a 1957 lecture at Brandeis University, Schuller labeled this trend "third-stream music," representing the merging of the two streams of jazz and classical music into a unique third stream.

Certainly, the blend of jazz and the concert tradition was not new, as can be seen in works ranging from Scott Joplin's ragtime opera *Treemonisha* to George Gershwin's *Rhapsody in Blue* to Duke Ellington's *Black, Brown, and Beige.* But Schuller's term *third stream* captured a renewed interest in the synthesis that the changing artistic consciousness of the musicians themselves had sparked during the decade. Thus, as pointed out earlier, many jazz composers in the 1950s—Dave Brubeck in his "Blue Rondo à la Turk" and John Lewis in his "Versailles"—borrowed the compositional forms and procedures of European classical music. Some jazz composers—Jimmy Giuffre in his 1953 "Fugue" and Robert Graettinger in the ambitious four-movement work *City of Glass* that he wrote for Stan Kenton—also explored atonality, a twentieth-century classical technique that abandons tonal centers.

Atonality avoids the standard chords, scales, harmonies, and keys of tonality. It is sometimes associated with free jazz, a style of music that began to flourish in the 1960s.

Gunther Schuller (b. 1925) also composed third-stream works that united complex compositions and improvisation. One of his most notable was *Concertino for Jazz Quartet and Orchestra,* which was performed by the Modern Jazz Quartet. Schuller's "Transformation" explored a conflict between the classical and jazz elements. This work, like others of Schuller's, merged twelve-tone compositional technique (pioneered by Viennese composer Arnold Schoenberg) and rhythmic asymmetry (found in the music of Russian composer Igor Stravinsky) with jazz improvisation.

The soloist on "Transformation" was pianist Bill Evans, who also recorded some memorable works with composer George Russell (b. 1923). Russell featured Evans on *Concerto for Billy the Kid,* inspired by the classical concerto, which normally pits the soloist against the ensemble. In this work, Russell used the harmonic progression from the jazz standard "I'll Remember April." As early as 1949 Russell had explored the combination of jazz and classical music with his "A Bird in Igor's Yard," the title wittily acknowledging both Charlie "Yardbird" Parker and Igor Stravinsky.

Besides embracing rhythm and formal experimentation, atonality, and serialism, the third-stream idea inspired an important music theory that would affect jazz composition and performance. In the 1950s, George Russell devised what he called "The Lydian Chromatic Concept of Tonal Organization." Since then, he has based many of his works on the theory, which came to apply to improvisation as well. As Russell conceived it, the Lydian Concept supplies objective musical laws; once they are understood, the artist creates within those laws:

> I approach music like an architect. First with an idea in mind. The overall idea is manifested into a blueprint. The architect uses bricks and I use notes, rhythms, and different modes of music. By modes I don't mean modes in a simplistic musical sense but modes of behavior, tonal behavior, rhythmic behavior, psychological behavior, timbre behavior. I translate them and build my house. The orchestration is like the paint, the decorative factor.[8]

Third-stream music has never provided a full-blown direction for jazz artists, and some have argued that it is tangential to jazz. Nevertheless, the works of the 1950s reflect an earnest desire to investigate different and extended forms. From its genesis in ragtime and the blues, jazz had evolved rapidly, particularly in the sphere of instrumental technique, harmony, and rhythm. Yet jazz forms had remained relatively static. Much of early jazz was limited to the sixteen-bar sections of ragtime (derived from the march) and the twelve-bar blues; later, players often confined themselves to twelve-bar blues and thirty-two–bar song forms. Those composers writing third-stream music offered jazz challenging new ideas in the one realm—the formal—that had so far remained unchanged.

Piano Stylists

In Chapter 7, we explored pianist Bud Powell's astounding single-line improvisations and sparse left-hand accompaniments, which greatly influenced the bebop pianists of the day. Other pianists, however, developed alternative styles. The quintet of blind pianist George Shearing was known for its distinctive sound resulting from Shearing's locked-hands or block-chord style (see Music Example 8-1). Earlier, Milt Buckner, the pianist for Lionel Hampton, had used this method of rendering melodies. In Shearing's quintet, the vibraphone doubled the upper note of the piano, while the

In **twelve-tone composition,** as it was originally conceived, all twelve pitches of the chromatic scale are arranged into ordered "sets." A "set" is also called a *tone row* or *series.* The order of the notes in the row governs the flow of the melody and harmony in a piece. Works written with the twelve-tone procedure and its variants are often called *serial,* standing for series. Twelve-tone composition was pioneered by Viennese composer Arnold Schoenberg in the 1920s.

guitar doubled the pianist's lower note, providing an elegant and sophisticated sound. With its five notes contained within the octave, locked-hands style emulated big-band writing for saxophone sections.

Music Example 8-1
Locked-hands style.

Shearing's somewhat commercial ensemble sound was immensely popular. His most famous composition was the hit "Lullaby of Birdland," written in 1952 and titled after the New York jazz club named after Charlie Parker.

Shearing was born in 1919 in London, where he trained as a classical pianist. He developed an extensive repertory, learning to read music through Braille notation, and picking up jazz from the recordings of Earl Hines, Fats Waller, Teddy Wilson, and Art Tatum. After immigrating to the United States in 1947, he came under the influence of some of the bebop players, especially Bud Powell and Hank Jones. Yet throughout his career Shearing never lost touch with his roots in traditional jazz piano.

Pianist Erroll Garner (1921–1977), on the other hand, had no formal musical education, was completely self-taught, and did not read music. Originally from

Locked-hands style is a mode of performance in which the pianist plays a four-note chord in the right hand and doubles the top note with the left hand an octave below. The hands move together in a "locked" rhythmic pattern as they follow the same rhythm. This style is also called **block-chord** or **full-chord style**. (Listen to Track 9 of the Audio Primer CD for an example of locked-hands style.)

Erroll Garner on the cover of his 1956 composition "Dreamy." His most famous composition is the jazz-pop ballad "Misty."

Pittsburgh, his early influences were fellow Pittsburgh pianists Dodo Marmarosa and Billy Strayhorn. Although Garner was a mainstay on Fifty-Second Street in the mid-1940s and even recorded with Charlie Parker on the West Coast in 1947, he stood apart from the mainstream bebop tradition.

Garner cultivated a highly distinctive solo piano style in which the left hand kept a quarter-note pulse, playing four chords to the bar. His insistent style often pushed or anticipated a bar's downbeat with the preceding upbeat. Against the left hand, Garner's right hand often played full chords that dragged "behind" the beat. He often led off compositions by playing an extended, involved, and often witty introduction. In ballads, such as his famous "Misty" (also recorded by singer Johnny Mathis), he made use of full, thick chords, creating a dense, orchestral texture. Garner's 1955 trio recording *Concert by the Sea* became one of the best-selling jazz records of the 1950s.

Pianist Oscar Peterson's prodigious technique made him particularly suited to inherit the mantle of virtuoso Art Tatum. Encouraged and mentored by Tatum himself, Peterson concentrated on fast boplike lines and blues lines in an energetic style. Frequently in his solos, Peterson would burst into right-hand glissandos, a chorus in locked-hands style, left-hand stride piano, or walking tenths. He recorded with countless players throughout his career—Ben Webster, Lester Young, Dizzy Gillespie, Stan Getz, Ella Fitzgerald, and Milt Jackson—and his own piano trio was extremely successful during the 1950s and 1960s.

Peterson grew up in Montreal, where he was born in 1925 and where jazz concert promoter Norman Granz heard him play and brought him to the United States. After an important appearance in 1949 at Carnegie Hall, Peterson toured with Granz's Jazz at the Philharmonic series. He then formed his own trio with piano, bass, and guitar, an instrumentation popularized by Nat King Cole and Art Tatum. With bassist Ray Brown and guitarist Herb Ellis, Peterson wowed audiences and critics, playing blues and sophisticated, complex arrangements of standards such as "Love for Sale" and "Swinging on a Star." In 1959 drummer Ed Thigpen replaced guitarist Ellis and remained in the group for six years.

In his later years, Peterson's playing was sometimes more dazzling than creative, although some of his solo piano recordings, such as *Tracks,* showed Peterson at his most harmonically advanced and exploratory. One of the most popular jazz musicians of our time, Peterson has continued to perform and record, despite suffering a stroke.

Vocalists

The 1950s was an important time for vocalists as well as instrumentalists. With its intrinsic focus on melody, singing provided a respite from the hectic instrumental pyrotechnics of bebop. During the 1940s, many popular singers established themselves with solo careers as heirs to the big bands. These singers' careers flourished into the 1950s and beyond.

In general, four main characteristics identify jazz singing:

▶ Loose phrasing, often becoming back phrasing

▶ Use of blue notes and occasional blues inflections

▶ Free melodic embellishment

▶ A repertory of songs preferred by jazz musicians

In **back phrasing,** the singer delays phrases of the song relative to their normal rhythmic placement as written. Occurring most often in ballads, it generally conveys a loose feeling, as if the singer were delivering the song spontaneously.

Of the four main characteristics of jazz singing, the first is by far the most important. Back phrasing has influenced the performance of all American popular music, including rock. Although many jazz singers are talented at scat singing, this technique does not necessarily occur in the best jazz singing. For example, Billie Holiday—the standard against which all jazz singing is measured—was not a scat singer.

JOE WILLIAMS

One of the most important jazz singers was Joe Williams (1918–1999). Although his career had already begun, he achieved major success in the 1950s. Virtually no other singer has so successfully bridged jazz and blues.

After working with Coleman Hawkins and others, Williams attracted attention as a replacement for Jimmy Rushing in the Count Basie band of the 1950s. He left Basie in 1961 to pursue a solo career, at the same time enlarging and enriching his style. His big, rich, smooth tone established a virtual genre of its own in jazz singing. Williams's lengthy solo career led to a Grammy Award in 1984 for best jazz vocalist, and his recording career continued up to 1995 with his final album, *Feel the Spirit.*

VOCALESE: EDDIE JEFFERSON AND LAMBERT, HENDRICKS, AND ROSS

In contrast to the career of Joe Williams, Eddie Jefferson (1918–1979) just lately has been recognized as an important jazz vocalist, an original artist who established an alternative singing style strongly dissociated from the Billie Holiday–Ella Fitzgerald mainstream. Jefferson was interested not only in improvising vocally but also in composing lyrics to fit existing instrumental solos, a technique called vocalese. To provide a change of pace from these carefully worked-out settings, Jefferson also mixed scat singing into his performances.

Jefferson's performance strength lay in his tremendous vocal agility. His flexible falsetto never seemed to strain or bury the lyric. Unlike the regular four-bar phrases usually found in popular songs, the jazz solos he set usually featured complex phrasing. Despite the difficulty of setting lyrics to freely wandering instrumental lines, Jefferson often found felicitous solutions that incorporated intriguing rhyme schemes.

The jazz vocal group began in the 1950s and continues to attract artists today. Vocal ensembles were certainly not new; after all, Bing Crosby and his Rhythm Boys were an important feature of the Paul Whiteman Orchestra in the 1920s. Featured groups, such as the popular Andrews Sisters who sang in harmony with band backups, continued through the swing era. But the 1950s witnessed a different kind of vocal ensemble, one allied more with the jazz tradition than with rendering popular songs in close harmony. In the latter half of the decade, a pioneering vocal group broke onto the scene. This trio—Jon Hendricks, Dave Lambert, and Annie Ross—mixed three distinct styles:

▶ Imitation of big band textures and arrangements

▶ Vocalese

▶ Traditional scat

Vocalese is the technique of setting lyrics to existing jazz solos. Eddie Jefferson was probably the most important pioneer of this technique, although the practice can be traced to the late 1920s.

This extremely inventive group provided much inspiration for such contemporary singing ensembles as the Manhattan Transfer and the New York Voices.

FRANK SINATRA

No survey of vocalists in the 1950s can ignore the overwhelming importance of Frank Sinatra (1915–1998), whose active career lasted well into the 1990s (see the box "Frank Sinatra"). Although a popular icon, he has rightfully been included in the ranks of the jazz singers for his exceptionally free phrasing, swinging big-band recordings; his identification with outstanding songs; and his ability to convey the meaning and emotional content of a lyric. Given these attributes, his domination of the pop-vocal market for five decades, and the respect many jazz musicians have given him, Sinatra's importance remains indisputable. We place him in this chapter because he established many of the essential attributes of his persona during the 1950s.

In some ways Sinatra belied the image of the cool 1950s. He projected a macho persona—the girl-chasing, booze-loving, tough guy who hobnobbed not only with the elite Kennedy family but also with gangsters. Nonetheless, much of Sinatra's work from the 1950s and 1960s captured the essence of jazz singing: loose phrasing, direct expression, and the ability to make a song his own.

Along with most of the singers discussed in this section, Sinatra had his roots in the big-band era. In the 1940s, he achieved teen idol status, bringing screaming fans to their feet much in the way that Elvis Presley would do in the 1950s and the Beatles in the 1960s. Compared with the other singers of his generation and style, he perhaps remained closest to the Billie Holiday ideal of the jazz-pop vocalist.

Frank Sinatra

Frank Sinatra's career spanned over 50 years, beginning with his earliest hits in the 1940s with the Tommy Dorsey Orchestra. Notice that the publisher of "Paper Doll" hoped to capitalize on the hit recording by the Mills Brothers. Soon, nothing more than a picture of Frank Sinatra on the cover could help sell a song. By the end of his life, his signature song had become "My Way," published in 1969.

Hard Bop and Funky/Soul Jazz

For some players and listeners, cool jazz was overly cerebral and devoid of energy and emotion. The complexity of Lennie Tristano's piano playing, the airy counterpoint of Gerry Mulligan and the Chet Baker Quartet, the smoky atmosphere of Sinatra with strings, the compositional experiments of the Dave Brubeck Quartet, and the concert hall settings of the tuxedo-clad Modern Jazz Quartet all seemed to abandon the elemental fire and passionate core of the jazz tradition. The compositional sophistication of many of the West Coast players and third-stream composers too frequently seemed an attempt to align with the European classical tradition—a pretentious striving for the cachet of "high art."

In contrast, the hard bop players continued to extend the bebop tradition with its emphasis on improvisation, thirty-two–bar formal structures, and straight-ahead swinging. The bands of Art Blakey and the Jazz Messengers, Horace Silver, and Charles Mingus; the Clifford Brown–Max Roach Quintet; and Miles Davis were representative of the driving hard bop bands. Further, some of the compositions of these bands made use of the simpler, earthier style known as funky (or soul) jazz.

ART BLAKEY AND THE JAZZ MESSENGERS

Drummer Art Blakey, born in Pittsburgh in 1919, recorded the album *Hard Bop*, which gave its name to the 1950s resurgence of forceful, swinging jazz. Blakey became one of the leading exponents of the hard bop tradition. Never cool, Blakey's drumming was aggressive, strong, and loud. His group, the Jazz Messengers, remained active from the 1950s until Blakey's death in 1990.

Blakey began his career with pianist Mary Lou Williams and Fletcher Henderson, but in the mid-1940s he played drums for the Billy Eckstine band, from

Art Blakey (CD 1, Tracks 19–21) performing with characteristic energy in a publicity shot from the 1950s.

Courtesy Morgan Collection

where he quickly moved to the center of the growing bebop movement. He played with Eckstine from 1944 to 1947, sharing the stage with Charlie Parker, Dizzy Gillespie, Dexter Gordon, and Miles Davis. Blakey organized his first group in 1947, a rehearsal band called the Seventeen Messengers, and later that year recorded with an octet called the Jazz Messengers.

In 1955 he formed another group, with pianist Horace Silver, that kept the name Jazz Messengers; this was the group that helped propel Blakey to fame. The quintet—with tenor saxophonist Hank Mobley, trumpeter Kenny Dorham, and bassist Doug Watkins—recorded three albums before Silver left the group. Blakey continued to lead the Messengers. With its classic quintet instrumentation (even after the group added a trombone in the early sixties to become a sextet) and its emphasis on aggressive soloing accompanied by Blakey's powerful drumming, it was the quintessential hard bop group. The band's personnel shifted over time, and Blakey staffed the group with young players, many of whom—such as trumpeters Donald Byrd, Freddie Hubbard, Lee Morgan, and Chuck Mangione; saxophonists Johnny Griffin, Jackie McLean, and Wayne Shorter; and pianists Cedar Walton, Bobby Timmons, and Keith Jarrett—would go on to develop successful careers on their own.

Blakey gave ample room to his players as both soloists and composers. Some of them contributed jazz compositions that would become standards of the jazz repertory. In the late 1950s Blakey's pianist, Bobby Timmons, composed several tunes representative of funky/soul jazz. His "Moanin'" made use of call-and-response formulas and the "Amen" harmonic church cadence (also known as a plagal cadence). Other Timmons compositions were similarly earthy, especially his "Dis Here" and "Dat Dere." Tenor saxophonist Bennie Golson contributed "Whisper Not," a minor-key work that employed stop time. Golson's "I Remember Clifford" was a plaintive and posthumous tribute to trumpeter Clifford Brown, who played with Blakey in 1954.

Dizzy Gillespie called Blakey "The Fire" of jazz drumming. Blakey, who had visited Africa in the late 1940s, derived some of his techniques from African drumming—using an elbow on the tom-tom to alter its pitch or playing on the side of the drum. His impact on jazz drumming was tremendous, and many of his techniques came to identify his style: the precise clicking of the hi-hat on the second and fourth beats of the measure, the tom-tom roll, and Blakey's shuffle pattern, sometimes even called the "Blakey Shuffle." Blakey was also one of the first drummers to use polyrhythms extensively, playing even eighth notes against triplets on the cymbal. (Listen to Tracks 26–35 of the 🅟 Audio Primer CD to hear a sampling of drum sounds.)

Between 1954 and 1964 Blakey recorded with five different groups of Jazz Messengers. Freddie Hubbard replaced the impassioned trumpeter Lee Morgan in 1961. Morgan and Hubbard, both born in 1938, were strongly influenced by hard bop trumpeter Clifford Brown. Tenor saxophonist Wayne Shorter replaced Blakey's earlier players Bennie Golson and Hank Mobley. Shorter joined the group in 1959 and remained for five years, becoming its musical director and altering the group's sound somewhat to accommodate his innovative compositions such as "Ping Pong." After Hubbard and Shorter joined him, Blakey enlarged his group from a quintet to a sextet to include trombonist Curtis Fuller and pianist Cedar Walton; they played from 1961 to 1964. Until his death, Blakey continued to tour with his classic quintet-sextet instrumentation while keeping alive the hard bop tradition.

A **plagal cadence**, sometimes called a "church" cadence or "Amen cadence," contains the harmonic progression IV–I (instead of the more common progression V–I). It is often used at the ends of hymns with the concluding "Amen." Plagal cadences were featured frequently in funky/soul jazz.

A **shuffle** is the 4/4 rhythmic pattern shown here. The drummer usually plays a shuffle on the ride cymbal accompanied by a walking bass:

LISTENING GUIDE

"Moanin'"

CD **1** Track **21**

Art Blakey and the Jazz Messengers: "Moanin'" (Timmons), from *Moanin'*. Blue Note
Reissue CDP 7 46516 2. New York, October 30, 1958. Lee Morgan, trumpet; Benny Golson, tenor
saxophone; Bobby Timmons, composer, piano; Jymie Merritt, bass; Art Blakey, drums.

"Moanin'" is a fine example of gospel jazz. The melody features a written-out call-and-response that can be heard as an "Amen" or "Yes, Lord." (In Lambert, Hendricks & Ross's arrangement, the "Yes, Lord" was sung.) In gospel jazz, we can sometimes interpret bluesy pieces such as "Moanin'" as major *or* minor. For example, the first time through the bridge, Timmons plays a clear F minor harmony at measure 4 (0:37); other times, the chord played sounds closer to F major. Note also the plagal cadence from measures 3–4 of the bridge, which echoes the A section and further helps infuse the tune with a gospel and blues feel. (Recall that we pointed out the major-minor ambiguity of certain jazz tunes in the discussion of Howard McGhee's "Ready for Love" in Chapter 6.) With its expressive blues inflections and considerable passion, Morgan's solo is especially memorable.

Head—First A section, 8 bars after 3-beat pick-up

0:00 Pianist Timmons states the head with no introduction. The band answers with the two-note "Amen" (or "Yes, Lord") motive:

Head—Second A section, 8 bars

0:15 For this second time through the A section, the trumpet and tenor state the call. The pianist, drums, and bass take over the response.

Head—Bridge, 8 bars

0:31 The bridge goes into straight time with the trumpet and tenor on the melody—a perfect example of a *release*, an older term for the B section. The elegant chromatic chord progression of the bridge unleashes the tension built up in the repetitive A section:

Notice that the plagal cadence of measures 3–4 echoes the A section.

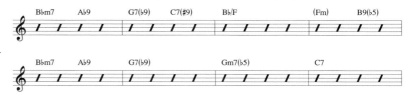

Head—Final A section, 8 bars

0:44 The pianist returns with the call, while the rest of the band, led by the trumpet and tenor, take the response.

Morgan trumpet solo—Two choruses

1:00 Morgan's solo begins with half-valve inflections and catchy funky riffs. The half-valve inflections are the almost "squeaky," "bent" sounds. Blakey's drumming keeps a constant back beat, emphasizing beats two and four.

1:15 In the second A section of the first chorus, Morgan incorporates "double-tonguing," a technique that allows him to repeat the same note rapidly. The double-tonguing idea returns twice.

2:55 Double-tonguing wraps up the solo.

Golson tenor solo—Two choruses

3:04 Golson picks up the end of Morgan's solo to launch his own and begins simply with variants of phrases strung together quite logically.

4:03 The beginning of his second chorus displays a move to the higher register that signals greater activity to come. The solo in fact becomes quite modernist in its second chorus: The bluesy runs and use of the high register sometimes seem to run outside the chord changes in ways that sound like the work of John Coltrane.

Timmons piano solo—Two choruses

5:04 Timmons begins his solo with blues phrases and riffs. The repetitive nature of the riffs and their occasional two-note textures in the right hand link the solo to the blues tradition. Meanwhile, the left hand plays simple punctuating chords.

6:03 In his second chorus, Timmons incorporates dramatic piano glissandos to create an internal call-and-response: These dramatic glissandos contrast effectively with the simpler blues riffs that Timmons uses as answers.

6:47 The solo builds to an emotional climax and texture involving repeated chords and the highest register of the piano.

Merritt bass solo—One chorus

7:03 Timmons accompanies lightly. Blakey still emphasizes beats two and four but simplifies and lightens the drum texture so that the bass can be more easily heard.

Repeat of the head—AABA, 32 bars

8:00 Here the band returns to the same format presented at the beginning of the tune. Timmons states the call, then the rest of the band gives the response for the first A; the trumpet and tenor take the call for the second A; the whole band plays the bridge; Timmons takes the call for the final A.

Coda

8:58 The band repeats the opening four bars of the bridge three times, each time louder than before. The third time, Timmons takes a cadenza based on blues riffs to end the tune. The harmonic progression of the final cadenza is a plagal cadence.

HORACE SILVER

Pianist Horace Silver left the Jazz Messengers in 1956 to lead his own quintet. Silver, who was one of the most imaginative of the major funky jazz players of the 1950s, became one of its most important and prolific composers as well. Although Silver was born in Norwalk, Connecticut, in 1928, his family was from the former Portuguese colony of Cape Verde, off the coast of northern Africa. As a child, he was exposed to

Cape Verdean folk music by his father, who encouraged Silver to adopt the idiom to jazz. Although bebop pianist Bud Powell influenced him early on, Silver's piano playing by comparison became less technical, simpler, more tuneful, and bluesier. In reacting against the bop players, Silver learned to play with fewer notes, emphasizing instead a few funky figures and favoring tremolos and crushed notes separated by generous space.

Many of Silver's compositions were infectious and catchy, such as his "Song for My Father," a Latin-tinged work dominated by a simple tonic-and-fifth bass motive. Silver wrote numerous blues compositions: His "Opus de Funk" and "Señor Blues" were recorded by dozens of other artists. In typical hard bop fashion, the trumpet and tenor saxophone generally stated the melody in Silver's compositions; however, his works often involved more than just a string of solos following the head. Many made extensive use of fixed introductions, written "shout" choruses, connecting passages, and mixed rhythmic forms. In "Nica's Dream," for example, Silver changed the accompaniment pattern within the song itself, providing a Latin-oriented backup to the A section and a swinging walking bass for the B section. Some of Silver's compositions were even more complex: "The Outlaw," from a 1958 recording entitled *Further Explorations,* used a fifty-four–bar theme made up of four sections of 13 + 13 + 10 + 18 measures. In summary, Silver helped solidify the hard bop and funky tradition, codifying its instrumentation and providing some of its most memorable compositions.

CHARLES MINGUS

Bassist and composer Charles Mingus attained legendary status for both his uncompromising view of the jazz tradition and his innovative approach to the art form. As a bassist, he developed a flawless technique, extending the accomplishments of Duke Ellington's bassist, Jimmy Blanton. As a composer, Mingus became increasingly visible and important throughout the 1950s and 1960s. He wrote works that encompassed numerous influences, especially the music of Ellington and the soulful expressiveness of the black church.

The scope of Mingus's music was enormous, embracing the whole of jazz—from historical references to the New Orleans tradition to a forward-looking use of collective improvisation that provided an important precedent for free jazz. Much of Mingus's work paid homage to the blues and gospel music, but it also included inventive instrumentation, tempo changes, and stop time. Although he began composing and arranging conventionally—writing a careful score with worked-out parts—his later techniques of dictating from the keyboard recalled the head-arrangement procedures of early jazz and its spirit of collective improvisation.

Originally from Arizona, where he was born in 1922, Mingus was raised in the Watts section of Los Angeles,

Bassist Charles Mingus (CD 1, Track 22) in a publicity still from the 1960s.

Courtesy Morgan Collection

where he paid his dues as a bass player and sideman with both swing and bop groups, working with Louis Armstrong, clarinetist Barney Bigard, and vibraphonist Lionel Hampton. As a member of vibraphonist Red Norvo's trio, along with guitarist Tal Farlow, Mingus became nationally known. The group, which had no drummer, was celebrated for its ability to play fiendishly rapid tempos; he contributed "Mingus Fingers" to the band's book. The sole black player in the trio, Mingus left Norvo's group when he was excluded from a television performance for being black. After moving to New York, he took part in the Jazz Composers' Workshop, contributing compositions along with Teo Macero and Teddy Charles.

Mingus founded his own workshop in 1955, putting together a group to feature his compositions. The group numbered from four to eleven players. Dissatisfied with printed musical notation, Mingus dictated from the piano the parts and lines he wanted his sidemen to play. Considering his "workshop" to be just that, he sometimes shouted instructions to his players on the bandstand or interrupted compositions in midstream to correct one of his musicians or castigate the audience. He made reference to New Orleans pianist Jelly Roll Morton in "Jelly Roll Soul" and to gospel music in "Wednesday Night Prayer Meeting" and "Better Git It in Your Soul"; he paid tribute to Charlie Parker in "Bird Calls" and to Lester Young in "Goodbye Pork Pie Hat." "Nostalgia in Times Square" was an altered twelve-bar blues, originally written for the John Cassavetes film *Shadows*.

Some of Mingus's compositions were quite complex. "Fables of Faubus"—a denunciation of Arkansas Governor Orville Faubus, who attempted to ignore de-segregation—had a seventy-one–bar theme written in four sections that incorporated tempo changes within the solos. Mingus's most ambitious composition was "The Black Saint and the Sinner Lady," a complicated four-movement work recorded in 1963. It evoked Ellington in Jaki Byard's piano introduction to the second movement and in the plunger trombone work of Quentin Jackson, which recalled Ellington's "jungle music" from the Cotton Club. "Black Saint" was also highly experimental, interweaving sections with changing tempos or without tempo. Mingus also used overdubbing on the recording.

Overdubbing or multitracking is a recording studio technique that was generally available by the 1950s. Recording tape has several parallel "tracks" that enable musicians to record additional performance parts at later times. The added part is called an *overdub*. By wearing headphones, the players follow and "play to" the previously recorded tracks. In current recording studios, computer-controlled equipment and digital technology permit virtually unlimited overdubbing and editing of recorded parts.

L I S T E N I N G   G U I D E

"Hora Decubitus"
CD **1**   Track **22**

Charles Mingus and His Orchestra: "Hora Decubitus" (Mingus), from *Mingus, Mingus, Mingus, Mingus, Mingus.* Impulse AS-9234-2. New York, September 20, 1963. Charles Mingus: bass, director; Eddie Preston, Richard Williams, trumpets; Britt Woodman, trombone; Don Butterfleld, tuba; Eric Dolphy, Dick Haffer, Booker Ervin, Jerome Richardson, woodwinds; Jaki Byard, piano; Walter Perkins, drums.

"Hora Decubitus" is a hybrid work, adroitly straddling traditional and free jazz. Throughout the performance, Mingus maintains control of the ensemble through forceful, interesting bass lines.

The following analysis shows that the fundamental idea of the piece is a mixture of various lines in counterpoint. These are introduced gradually, slowly building a complex group sound. (In discussing its form here, we anticipate some of the stylistic attributes of free jazz described more fully in Chapter 9.)

Introduction—Mingus's solo bass, 12 bars

0:00   Alternating octaves here reveal Mingus's strength and sense of forward momentum. Mingus sets the tempo, harmony, and mood for the blues choruses that follow.

Head—Chorus 1

0:12 A rifflike blues tune played on the baritone saxophone. Although the rhythmic and melodic character of the tune is traditional, it borders on atonality.

Head—Chorus 2

0:24 The baritone continues to play the theme, joined now by the other saxophones sometimes playing in unison but occasionally splitting into different parts.

Head—Chorus 3

0:37 A trombone is added, playing a counter-riff that often seems to clash with the saxophones, who meanwhile repeat their second chorus.

Head—Chorus 4

0:50 An alto saxophone separates from the reed section to add still another part, while the trombone and remaining saxophones repeat what they had played in the preceding chorus.

Head—Chorus 5 (final chorus of head)

1:02 A trumpet player joins the others with still another riff in counterpoint with the ongoing parts. This set of contrasting and competing lines remains traditional in its blues-riff orientation as well as in the marvelous cacophony of everyone playing together.

Ervin tenor saxophone solo—4 choruses

1:15 At first reminiscent of gospel jazz, Ervin's solo finishes with the fleet, atonal runs that are somewhat more typical of free jazz. As accompaniment, the orchestra enters from time to time with background figures derived from the opening riffs of the head.

1:51 On Ervin's last chorus, Mingus pushes the beat so forcefully that he seems almost ahead of the pulse.

Dolphy alto saxophone solo—4 choruses

2:03 After beginning with the more "outside" melodic lines of free jazz, Dolphy returns to a more typical blues line, though many of his pitches still purposely avoid the chord changes.

2:40 Mingus briefly quotes his opening introductory statement in the middle of Dolphy's solo as if trying to forge together the disparate sections of the work. The other instruments freely enter with riffs and sharp punctuations as if to comment on Dolphy's solo.

Williams trumpet solo—4 choruses

2:56 A few bebop licks can still be heard from time to time. The passionate cries Williams injects into the solo are both expressive and appropriate.

Return of the head—3 choruses

3:40 Some of the opening riffs are heard but are exchanged here, that is, played by different groups of instruments. The alto saxophones "lay out" (don't play) during the second chorus. During the third chorus, the ensemble plays the main riff tune in unison, which lends a feeling of finality to the performance.

Tag

4:16 Here are two chords that may be heard as echoing the IV–I "Amen" cadence heard in church music. On the first of these chords, the instruments freely interpolate runs and fills in the manner of a cadenza. The second chord is not so heavily scored, and as it dies out Mingus plays the last few notes himself, thus recalling his solo introduction.

Mingus wrote about his career in a highly creative and sometimes fanciful autobiography, *Beneath the Underdog* (1971). He rarely performed between 1966 and 1969 but was granted a Guggenheim Fellowship in 1971. During his final years, he suffered from Lou Gehrig's disease and was confined to a wheelchair. In the mid-1970s, Mingus collaborated with pop singer Joni Mitchell for her album *Mingus,* a tribute to the bassist. After his death in 1979, his family found portions of a score for a two-hour work entitled "Epitaph." Gunther Schuller completed the partial score and recorded it in 1989.

Charles Mingus was one of the very few bassists in jazz to contribute directly to the formation of a jazz substyle and a new way of thinking about music. Today, the Mingus Big Band is a renowned large jazz ensemble. Under the direction of his widow, Sue, the group continues to explore the dimensions of Mingus's original and challenging music.

CLIFFORD BROWN–MAX ROACH QUINTET

Many of the trumpeters of the 1950s followed Miles Davis and Chet Baker by cultivating a lyrical, restrained style in the medium range of the instrument. Others, though, kept alive the bebop tradition of Dizzy Gillespie and Fats Navarro. Clifford Brown was perhaps the finest trumpet player of the 1950s, perpetuating the running eighth-note style of Gillespie, but with a personal, intimate sound that was arguably warmer than the older player's style. Brown's playing emphasized clean technique, a vast variety of articulations, and a satisfying, logical progression to his solos that usually avoided the gratuitous, showy high notes of Gillespie. Brown had a slightly percussive attack and negotiated impossibly fast tempos with ease.

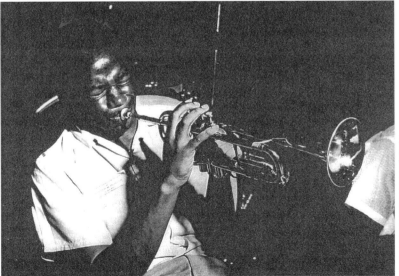

Trumpeter Clifford Brown (CD 2, Track 1).

Photo by John Krantz. Courtesy Morgan Collection.

Max Roach and Modern Drumming

Roach had become one of the leading innovative drummers of the bebop generation, performing and recording with Gillespie and Charlie Parker in the 1940s. He became a member of Parker's longest-lived quintet and was also heard on eight of the twelve tracks of Miles Davis's *Birth of the Cool*. With other bebop drummers such as Kenny Clarke, Roach was instrumental in transferring the pulse from the bass drum and hi-hat to the ride cymbal. He developed a conversational style of accompanying improvisers, creating a dialogue with the soloists and accenting with the bass and snare drums. Roach's technique provided a foundation for modern jazz drumming. By giving separate roles to each hand and foot, Roach's style helped establish what came to be called "coordinated independence."

Brown won the *Down Beat* "New Star" award in 1954. However, his career ended two years later—one of the great tragedies in jazz. As a result, Brown's recorded output is relatively small, although it establishes him as one of the greatest of all trumpet players. Originally from Wilmington, Delaware, where he was born in 1930, he worked mostly around Philadelphia and New York. In 1953 he toured Europe with Lionel Hampton's band, making several records there.

Brown's most important legacy was his participation in the Clifford Brown–Max Roach Quintet with drummer Max Roach (b. 1924). (See the box "Max Roach and Modern Drumming.") Roach and Brown formed their cooperative quintet in 1954. The band, along with Brown on trumpet and Roach on drums, included bassist George Morrow, pianist Richie Powell (the brother of bebop pianist Bud Powell), and saxophonist Harold Land. (Sonny Rollins replaced Land in 1955.) The group was one of the most brilliant in jazz, lasting until Brown's death in 1956 in an automobile accident that also killed pianist Richie Powell.

Along with jazz standards, the group recorded many of Brown's originals, some of which showed his effortless ability to negotiate difficult chord progressions. For example, "Joy Spring"—one of his most famous tunes—was a thirty-two–bar AABA composition with a twist: The second A section modulated a half-step from F to G♭. After a modulating bridge, the final A section returned to F. Other fine Brown originals include "Sweet Clifford," "Daahoud," and "Sandu."

A publicity photograph of Dizzy Gillespie (CD 1, Tracks 17 and 18) and Max Roach (CD 1, Track 20 and CD 2, Track 1) in the 1960s.

Photo by Carol Friedman. Courtesy Morgan Collection.

"Powell's Prances"

CD **2** Track **1**

Clifford Brown–Max Roach Quintet: "Powell's Prances" (Powell). EmArcy 36070. New York,
January 4, 1956. Clifford Brown, trumpet; Sonny Rollins, tenor saxophone; Richie Powell, piano,
composer-arranger; George Morrow, bass; Max Roach, drums.

"Powell's Prances" is a fine example of the Roach-Brown quintet. This up-tempo, swinging number with an unusual structure typifies the sound of the band. The bluesy quality of the piece derives from its shift to the subdominant harmony during the B section of the ABA form. It is a minor mode composition in the tradition of earlier bop works such as Bud Powell's "Tempus Fugit."

Head—24 bars as ABA

0:00   After a short drum-fill introduction, the head begins. It is in C minor with an up-tempo, driving sound. The trumpet and tenor play the melody in octaves. The unusual form of the head is ABA, with each section having eight bars. The middle eight bars are in stop time and feature a harmonic shift to the subdominant, F minor.

Brown trumpet solo—2 choruses

0:22   The variety of Brown's articulations is evident on the solo. The clarity of each note derives from Brown's ability to tongue at a rapid tempo. Brown begins his second chorus by emphasizing and repeating the sixth of the C minor harmony, A.

Rollins tenor saxophone solo—2 choruses

1:00   Rollins contrasts his solo with Brown's by including passages of longer note values. Listen to how he develops a motivic idea in the second chorus, bridging the end of the first A section and the beginning of the B section. His solo closes with a blues-based idea, using ♭5–4 (G♭–F).

Powell piano solo—2 choruses

1:38   Powell's solo concentrates on developing simple blueslike riffs in the piano's midrange. It moves out of the range only briefly for a short contrast.

Roach drum solo—2 choruses

2:15   Roach begins his solo by echoing and developing the rhythm at the end of Powell's final riff. Roach maintains the energy and drive of the preceding solos. Notice that he avoids playing the cymbals during his solo, concentrating instead on the snare drum, bass drum, and tom-toms.

Reprise of the 24-bar head as ABC

2:48   After the solos, the head returns but is not literally restated. A new section (C) replaces the final A section, with the piano and horns playing a passage in unison that arpeggiates numerous chords and sounds like an exercise.

Coda

3:08   The C section of the head has introduced a coda consisting of a dramatic series of out-of-time chords prolonged over drum fills. These chords are unusually dissonant, beginning with a C major triad with a D♭ in the bass.

SONNY ROLLINS

A star with the Brown-Roach quintet, Sonny Rollins was one of the leading tenor saxophonists of the 1950s. Rollins's playing boasted rhythmic imagination, harmonic ingenuity, and a strong, muscular sound. He achieved his big, dramatic tone by infusing the traditional, full-throated eloquence of Coleman Hawkins with the edgy raspiness sometimes heard in Charlie Parker.

Rollins was born in 1930 in New York and raised in the same neighborhood that produced Coleman Hawkins, Bud Powell, and Thelonious Monk. Rollins was a teenager while bebop was taking hold as the dominant jazz style. In fact, he made one of his first recordings in 1949 with bebop pianist Bud Powell. This recording displays Rollins's sound and inventiveness and makes clear his ties to the New York bebop world.

During the 1950s, Rollins recorded and performed with many significant players and groups, including J. J. Johnson, Art Blakey, Thelonious Monk, and the Modern Jazz Quartet. He formed an association with Miles Davis that continued throughout the decade and brought Rollins to the forefront not only as an exceptional improviser but also as a composer. To a Davis recording session for Prestige in 1954, Rollins contributed three compositions that were to become jazz standards: "Oleo," based on rhythm changes; "Doxy"; and "Airegin," a minor-key romp whose title was a thinly disguised tribute to Nigeria. Rollins's sense of humor resonated throughout his playing and his occasionally idiosyncratic choice of repertory, such as his 1957 album *Way out West*, which boasted "I'm an Old Cowhand" and "Wagon Wheels" in a pianoless trio of saxophone, bass, and drums.

Rollins was passionately committed to his musical progress; he even traveled to Chicago in 1950 to study percussion and enhance his rhythmic flexibility. Highly self-critical, he took three extended sabbaticals during which he stopped performing in public. The first of these, which began in November 1954, ended a year later when he joined the Clifford Brown–Max Roach Quintet, where he remained until 1957. During his tenure with the quintet, Rollins earned prestige for his technical proficiency and the fertility of his musical ideas.

Evident in such songs as "I'll Remember April" and "Powell's Prances," Rollins's style includes the following characteristics:

▶ A wide variety of melodies, from bop lines to floating phrases slightly reminiscent of cool jazz

▶ Melodic connections based on voice leading and motivic development, some of which are quite subtle

▶ Varied melodic rhythms

▶ Highly irregular phrase lengths, from single notes to long bop phrases

▶ Rich tone with occasional raspiness

▶ Use of space between phrases

▶ Use of entire range of instrument

▶ Full range of emotional expression

▶ Mostly "inside" playing, with chord-scale relationships based on the bop practice of using extended chords and altered scales

Sonny Rollins and Improvisation

Rollins's ability to thread motives through his solos was especially memorable on his performance of "Blue Seven." This cut, from *Saxophone Colossus,* exemplified logical development in improvisation. In a well-known article entitled "Sonny Rollins and the Challenge of Thematic Improvisation," Gunther Schuller singled out this solo—a mysterious twelve-bar blues based on the interval of a tritone—as representing a breakthrough in improvisational technique.* For Schuller, this solo contained an unprecedented display of interrelated themes and motives, making the solo a unified and coherent whole. Not all other critics agreed: In a response to Schuller, jazz historian Lawrence Gushee suggested that Schuller's analysis was an oversimplification of Rollins's style, one that ignored many other disparate aspects of Rollins's improvisational approach. Still, Rollins's penchant for motivic improvisation is such that he often preferred tunes with strong, simple melodies he could easily allude to, for example, his recording of "Surrey with the Fringe on Top" or his own "St. Thomas."

---

* Gunther Schuller, "Sonny Rollins and the Challenge of Thematic Improvisation," *The Jazz Review* (November 1958): 6–11; reprinted in Schuller's *Musings: The Musical Worlds of Gunther Schuller* (New York and Oxford: Oxford University Press, 1986), 86–97.

During the latter half of the 1950s, Rollins continued to record as a leader. His tune "Valse Hot" was one of the first bebop compositions in 3/4 meter. In 1956 Rollins recorded *Saxophone Colossus*—a quartet recording hailed by critics as a milestone. It included the sunny calypso tune "St. Thomas," the first of several compositions in that vein by Rollins. His performance of "You Don't Know What Love Is," earlier recorded by Billie Holiday, was elegiac and profound.

Perhaps as a result of Schuller's laudatory article (discussed in the box "Sonny Rollins and Improvisation"), the ever self-critical Rollins took another sabbatical between 1959 and 1961. During his self-imposed retirement, his late-night practice sessions on the Williamsburg Bridge over the East River became legendary. When he returned to performing, he made reference to his nocturnal habit in an album titled *The Bridge,* which included guitarist Jim Hall.

In the early 1960s, Rollins continued to expand musically with projects that encompassed both the old and the new. For the latter, Rollins attempted to come to grips with the free jazz movement of Ornette Coleman. He collaborated with several musicians who had been associated with Coleman, including trumpeter Don Cherry, drummer Billy Higgins, and pianist Paul Bley. Yet he also recorded with his idol Coleman Hawkins in an album entitled *Sonny Meets Hawk.* Picking up on a practice Hawkins had embraced in the 1940s, Rollins experimented with performing unaccompanied saxophone solos.

Several years after Rollins provided the soundtrack to the 1965 Michael Caine movie *Alfie,* Rollins took yet another sabbatical; upon his return he concentrated on playing in a slightly more commercial vein. Influenced by jazz trends in the late 1960s and early 1970s, he brought the electric piano into his groups and began emphasizing rock and funk rhythms and often doubled on soprano saxophone. Currently, Rollins remains one of the most honored players in jazz, appearing in prestigious venues throughout the world, both as a guest and with his own groups.

Miles Davis in the 1950s

Earlier in this chapter, we explored Miles Davis's seminal contributions to cool jazz. But there was much more to his career; in fact, Miles Davis was to become one of the most profoundly influential figures in the history of jazz. Lasting over four decades, his career was marked by an uncanny ability to explore and develop new styles. Davis was consistently on the cutting edge of musical developments:

▶ Bebop in the late 1940s

▶ Cool jazz in the early 1950s

▶ Hard bop in the mid 1950s

▶ Modal jazz the later 1950s and 1960s

▶ Jazz-rock fusion in the 1970s

▶ MIDI sequencing and sampling in the 1980s

Never content with relying on earlier successful formulas, Davis hired the best young players, who continued to challenge him. As one of his former sidemen noted, Davis was a "star-maker": Many of the most important jazz performers in the later twentieth century at one time had played in his band.

Though nurtured on bebop, Davis did not follow Dizzy Gillespie in developing fireworks in the trumpet's higher register. His playing was usually lyrical and spare, though still impassioned despite often being centered in the middle range of the instrument. He cited trumpeter Freddie Webster as an early influence; Webster played in an unfussy style without much vibrato.

Davis was born in Hilton, Illinois (near St. Louis), on May 25, 1926, and began playing professionally as a teenager. A pivotal event occurred when he was eighteen. The Billy Eckstine band, with Charlie Parker, Dizzy Gillespie, and Sarah Vaughan, came to town, and Davis was asked to sit in. In his autobiography, Davis wrote, "[Hearing the band] changed my life. I decided right then and there that I had to leave St. Louis and live in New York City where all these musicians were."[9] For the remainder of his life, Davis claimed that he was always attempting to recapture the awesome musical experience of that St. Louis performance.

Davis arrived in New York in fall 1944, ostensibly to study at the Juilliard School of Music, but he was more interested in pursuing bebop opportunities with Charlie Parker. The following year, at age nineteen, Davis achieved his first remarkable success: He recorded for Savoy as part of Parker's first session as a leader. That session, on November 26, 1945, was in fact Davis's second recording session; though brilliant for Parker, this recording was not entirely successful for the young trumpeter. Davis's playing on "Billie's Bounce" and "Now's the Time" revealed him to be almost out of his depth with the group. Because Davis was unable to perform the virtuosic "KoKo" with Parker, Dizzy Gillespie played the cut.

Davis continued to improve and develop his own voice. Critics began to speak of Davis as representing a new generation of trumpeters with a warmer, softer, mellower sound than Gillespie's. He performed with Parker through 1949, becoming a member of his working quintet. He contributed compositions such as "Donna Lee" (though the tune is attributed to Parker) and hired Parker to play tenor saxophone for his own Savoy session with the originals "Milestones," "Little Willie Leaps," "Sippin' at Bells," and "Half Nelson." Davis's compositions were in the bebop tradition, and they offered slightly more complexity: For example, "Sippin' at Bells" was a twelve-bar blues with eighteen chord changes.

Despite Davis's long association with Parker, the alto saxophonist was unpredictable and often difficult to work with. On December 23, 1948, Davis's irritation with what he considered Parker's lack of professionalism came to a head. Davis stormed off the bandstand of the Royal Roost claiming, "Bird makes you feel about one foot high."[10] No longer part of the Davis quintet, Parker struck out on his own.

While working on the *Birth of the Cool* sessions, Davis traveled to Paris to perform at the Festival de Jazz in 1949, which earned him increased visibility and critical attention. When he returned to the States, Davis, like many other jazz players of his generation, succumbed to heroin addiction. Although he won the *Metronome* Critics Poll each year between 1951 and 1953, some of Davis's performances for Prestige suffered from technical problems that can probably be traced to his addiction. Some writers even began to consider his best work behind him.

Fortunately, Davis overcame his addiction in 1954 and in the same year recorded several brilliant performances. His recording for Prestige with J. J. Johnson on trombone, Lucky Thompson on tenor saxophone, Horace Silver on piano, Percy Heath on bass, and Kenny Clarke on drums included "Blue 'n' Boogie" (a Dizzy Gillespie composition) and Richard Carpenter's "Walkin'." Both were blues compositions firmly rooted in the bebop tradition. Hailed for his early involvement in cool jazz on the *Birth of the Cool* sessions, Davis now returned to his bebop roots, providing some of the finest hard bop music of the decade. Davis discussed the difference:

> *Birth of the Cool* had . . . mainly come out of what Duke Ellington and Billy Strayhorn had already done; it just made the music "whiter," so that white people could digest it better. And then the other records I made, like "Walkin'" and "Blue 'n' Boogie"—which the critics called hard bop—had only gone back to the blues and some of the things that Bird and Dizzy had done. It was great music, well played and everything, but the musical ideas and concepts had mostly been already done; it just had a little more space in it.[11]

Davis continued to record other jazz classics that year. Two months after the "Walkin'" session, in June 1954, Davis took the same rhythm section, added Sonny Rollins on tenor saxophone, and recorded three Rollins originals: "Airegin," "Doxy," and "Oleo." The A section of "Oleo" included Rollins's start-and-stop melody based on a three-note motive, and it was played in unison by the horns without piano. On Christmas Eve, Davis assembled pianist Thelonious Monk and vibraphonist Milt Jackson and recorded six sides, including two takes each of Jackson's "Bags' Groove" and Gershwin's "The Man I Love." The session was notorious: Monk was reputedly furious over Davis's request that Monk not play behind Davis's solos. Davis's playing showed a mastery of timing and a depth in his economical style.

The 1954 recordings helped revive Davis's career, as did his performance on Thelonious Monk's "'Round Midnight" at the Newport Jazz Festival the following year. In this piece he enraptured the audience with a wistful solo in which he used a harmon mute (listen to Track 14 of the 🎵 Audio Primer CD). Davis was becoming a hot commodity. Signing with Columbia Records, he put together a quintet that featured some rising stars: tenor saxophonist John Coltrane, pianist Red Garland, bassist Paul Chambers, and drummer Philly Joe Jones. The group combined poignant ballads, often performed with Davis on muted trumpet, along with fiercely intense swing. Ever interested in the use of space and openness in his music, Davis asked

A **harmon mute** is a hollow metal mute that, when placed in the bell of the trumpet, gives the sound a distant, brooding quality. Miles Davis's use of the harmon mute from 1954 onward helped popularize its use.

pianist Garland to listen and learn from Chicago pianist Ahmad Jamal, whose strategic use of silence Davis admired.

In addition to his rise in popularity, Davis found notoriety. Critics and audiences noted his prickly personality, his unwillingness to announce compositions, and his disappearance from the bandstand when other soloists were playing. Yet this almost surly behavior helped Davis become a cult figure, noted for his mystique. He was also laconic and temperamental. In a flash of anger in 1956, he raised his voice too soon after a throat operation, thereby permanently reducing his voice to a whisper.

In 1958 alto saxophonist Julian "Cannonball" Adderley joined the band, making it a sextet. The two saxophonists, Coltrane and Adderley, had markedly different styles: Coltrane's playing was rigorous, technical, and exploratory; Adderley's was traditional, rooted in the blues and bebop. The sextet's recording *Milestones* began to show a new musical direction for Davis, particularly on the title tune. Coltrane commented:

> I found Miles in the midst of another stage of his musical development. There was one time in his past that he devoted to multichorded structures. He was interested in chords for their own sake. But now it seemed that he was moving in the opposite direction to the use of fewer and fewer chord changes in songs.[12]

What Is Modal Jazz?

Modal jazz loosely describes a body of music that originated in the late 1950s and 1960s. Jazz historians typically refer to Miles Davis's recordings on *Kind of Blue* (and Davis's earlier 1958 composition "Milestones"), as well as the music of John Coltrane's classic quartet (1960–1964), as important points of departure for modal jazz.

Modal jazz gets its name from the idea that modes (particular scales) provide improvisers with the appropriate pitches to use in their solos over individual chords. In the liner notes to *Kind of Blue,* pianist Bill Evans indicates that each chord is associated with a particular scale. These scales are the modes, including the Ionian, Dorian, Phrygian, Lydian, Mixolydian, Aeolian, and Locrian.

However, the term *modal jazz* often leads to confusion, because many of the qualities attributed to modal jazz do not necessarily have to do with the use of modes. In fact, as critics of the term point out, improvisers do not always restrict themselves to the pitches of the mode in their solos.* In addition, the term often refers to a composition or accompaniment that makes use of one or more of the following techniques:

▶ Slow-moving harmonic rhythm, in which a single chord may last for four, eight, sixteen, or more measures

▶ Use of pedal points (focal bass pitches over which the harmonies may shift)

▶ Absence or suppression of standard functional harmonic patterns, such as V–I or ii–V–I

▶ Chords or melodies that make use of the interval of a perfect fourth

As this list suggests, many of the features associated with modal jazz concern composition and accompaniment rather than improvisation. Accounts of modal jazz, however, often do not distinguish among these three related yet distinct ideas. After Miles Davis and John Coltrane, such performers as Herbie Hancock, Wayne Shorter, and McCoy Tyner were considered important exponents of modal jazz.†

* See Barry Kernfeld, "Adderley, Coltrane, and Davis at the Twilight of Bebop: The Search for Melodic Coherence" (Ph.D. diss., Cornell University, 1981).

† For more on the problems and ambiguities of the term *modal jazz,* see Keith Waters, "What Is Modal Jazz?" *Jazz Educators Journal* 33, no. 1 (July 2000): 53–55.

Modal jazz refers to a body of music that makes use of one or more of the following characteristics: modal scales for improvising, slow harmonic rhythm, pedal points, and the absence or suppression of functional harmonic relationships. Significant early examples of modal jazz come from Miles Davis's recording *Kind of Blue* (1959) and the recordings of John Coltrane's classic quartet (1960–1964). Listen to CD 2, Track 4 for the first movement of Coltrane's album *A Love Supreme*. See also the boxes "Coltrane's Modal Compositions" (in Chapter 9) and "What Is Modal Jazz?"

Coltrane was referring to a move to "modal" jazz. Instead of the complex chord progressions of bebop and hard bop, Davis's compositions incorporated fewer chords. Significantly, the improvisations over these chords were often based on a single scale. (See the box "What Is Modal Jazz?") The decisive shift toward modal jazz was evident in Davis's 1959 recording *Kind of Blue,* an album universally acclaimed as one of the most significant in the history of jazz. All the elements of Davis's mature style—his deep lyricism, economy, and searching—crystallized on this record. The introspective nature of much of the record was inspired by Davis's pianist, Bill Evans—a lyrical player who brought an impressionistic transparency to the music.

Evans wrote the liner notes to the album: "Miles conceived these settings only hours before the recording dates and arrived with sketches that indicated to the group what was to be played."[13] On the surface, one of the songs, "So What," was a normal thirty-two–bar AABA composition. But each of the eight-bar A sections was based on a single chord and scale, while the eight-bar B section transposed the original chord and scale up a half-step.

Many of the other tunes on *Kind of Blue,* such as "Flamenco Sketches," "Blue in Green," and "All Blues," have become jazz standards. The album is one of the best-selling jazz records of all time.

Although Davis has undergone various style changes throughout his career, the following list summarizes his cool/early modern playing:

▶ Sensitive melodic lines with frequent blues inflections

▶ Irregular phrase length

▶ Wide range of note values

▶ Use of space between phrases

▶ Concentration on midrange of trumpet

▶ Full but reticent tone (especially obvious in his playing with harmon mute)

▶ Melodic connections based on motives and large-scale gestures

▶ Sensitive yet cool expression

▶ Little reliance on previously composed licks

▶ "Inside" playing, using conservative chord-scale associations

During the late 1950s, Davis also revived his collaboration with arranger Gil Evans, with whom he had worked in the *Birth of the Cool* sessions a decade before. The pair turned out three recordings, noted for their lush instrumentation beneath Davis's searing sound. Davis also began to use flugelhorn, which is like a trumpet but has a larger bore and a much mellower timbre. The first of these collaborations, the album *Miles Ahead,* featured Davis as soloist with a nineteen-piece orchestra. More remarkable was their 1958 recording of *Porgy and Bess,* in which Davis put his definitive stamp on Gershwin's compositions, such as "Summertime." The concerto ideal—soloist with accompanying orchestra—reached its culmination in *Sketches of Spain,* which actually featured an arrangement of a guitar concerto, the *Concierto de Aranjuez* by Joaquin Rodrigo.

By the end of the 1950s, Davis had established himself as one of the leading figures in jazz, exploring new directions for improvised ensemble music. We shall return to his seminal band in our discussion of the music of the 1960s in Chapter 10.

Cool and Hard Bop Melodic Styles

QUALITY	COOL	HARD BOP
Timbre	▶ Softer, smoother, more relaxed ▶ Midrange of instruments emphasized ▶ Almost no use of blue-note effects ▶ Soft attacks and legato	▶ Beboplike hard-edged, brittle, insistent ▶ Use of upper registers ▶ Blue-note effects, blues riffs ▶ Wide variety of attacks and articulations
Phrasing	▶ Irregular, like bebop ▶ Much use of space between phrases	▶ Slightly more regular than bebop phrasing ▶ Return to two- and four-bar units in funky/soul jazz
Rhythm	▶ Much greater variety than bop in up-tempo and medium tempo pieces	▶ More syncopated ▶ Trend toward simpler blues patterns ▶ More variety than bebop
Thematic continuity	▶ Balanced between motivic and voice leading	▶ Motives sometimes emphasized over voice leading
Chord-scale relations	▶ Inside, often with extended chord tones heard in bop	▶ Inside, often based on blues scale
Large-scale coherence	▶ Motivic structure and voice leading ▶ Balance of gesture	▶ Motivic, especially in funky/soul jazz, use of climax-release, and gestural balance

Questions and Topics for Discussion

1. What new jazz substyles developed in the 1950s? Which performers were associated with which substyle?

2. How was cool jazz distinguished from bebop? Was the separation always distinct?

3. Why is cool jazz sometimes called West Coast jazz?

4. What aspects of the jazz tradition were modified or experimented on by third-stream musicians? Who were some of the important third-stream musicians?

5. Who were the principal hard bop musicians? How did their music differ from cool jazz and third-stream music?

6. How did Miles Davis transcend some of the standard 1950s substyle boundaries?

Key Terms

Atonality

Bossa nova

Back phrasing

Cool jazz

Counterpoint

Fugue

Funky jazz (soul jazz)

Hard bop

Harmon mute

Locked-hands (block or full-chord) style

LP

Overdubbing

Modal jazz

Overdubbing

Plagal cadence

Shuffle

Subject

Third-stream music

Twelve-tone composition

Vocalese

West Coast jazz

I HAVE A DREAM

DR. MARTIN LUTHER KING

★ ★ ★ APPEARING AT THE ★ ★ ★

SOUTHERN BAPTIST CHURCH

APRIL 4th - 1968

MEMPHIS, TENNESSEE

The fight for civil rights was the hallmark of the 1950s and 1960s. Dr. Martin Luther King, Jr. (1929–1968) was at the forefront of nonviolent protest against segregation. This poster advertises his last speech, given at a rally in support of striking garbage collectors; later that evening James Earl Ray shot and killed King as he stood on his motel balcony.

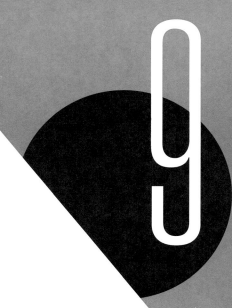

THE SIXTIES AVANT-GARDE

THE STYLISTIC INNOVATIONS in jazz during the 1950s led directly to the formation of a controversial avant-garde in the 1960s. Heated debates arose, recalling the vitriolic exchanges between the beboppers and the moldy figs during the 1940s. The principal issue in the 1960s (as in the 1940s) was disagreement between innovators and populists: Innovators felt that the music must progress, while populists thought that the music should attract and please a mass audience. Even today, these controversies remain far from settled. In many respects these issues mirror the general tension in the West between popular and fine art. What ultimately validates an art form? Acceptance by a large audience (the popular) or the originality resulting from cutting-edge experimentation (the avant-garde)?

Given that this issue had been around a while, what made the 1960s "free jazz" of the avant-garde so controversial? The principal reason was that the avant-gardists radically rejected aspects of the jazz tradition that many players and listeners considered fundamental. Improvisation still remained, but other elements were drastically altered—changes that made the music seem incoherent to some. These changes included the following:

▶ Absence of a steady pulse or meter. The 4/4 swing feel, often considered essential to the jazz tradition, was frequently abandoned.

▶ Absence of a predetermined harmonic structure. For the avant-garde soloists, improvisations did not have to be bound by an underlying harmonic progression. Horn soloists sometimes resorted to a *nontempered* intonation

Free jazz, the **avant-garde**, and the **New Thing** are terms used to describe the 1960s jazz substyle that overturned many of the traditional elements of jazz.

Nontempered intonation is the use of pitches unrestricted by the "equal-tempered," twelve-note chromatic scale. For example, a nontempered pitch might be a note between D and E♭. Pitches between the tempered notes of the chromatic scale are sometimes called **microtones**.

that could conflict with a pianist or guitarist comping the changes. Many groups did away with the instruments that normally provided harmonic support, such as piano or guitar.

▶ Altered role for rhythm-section instruments. Avant-garde bassists and drummers no longer performed their typical timekeeping roles but instead often participated in collective improvisation.

▶ Freer formal structures. Before the 1960s, musical structures were based on smaller groupings of four, eight, and sixteen measures, helping listeners orient themselves within the form. The avant-garde players eschewed this regularity in composing and improvising.

▶ Use of atypical or extended sounds. The avant-garde soloists cultivated new timbres and sounds. Percussion became more prominent; saxophonists and trumpeters explored the highest registers and incorporated shrieks and wailing.

Avant-Garde Jazz and Black Activism

As the avant-garde jazz movement expanded during the 1960s, it became intimately connected to and nurtured by black nationalism and militant protest. As pointed out earlier, an increase in black ethnic pride has paralleled the history of jazz. This increase was rooted in the Harlem Renaissance and, before that, in the writings of W. E. B. Du Bois and others. Du Bois's concept of the "talented tenth"—the elite of the black population, whose achievements could inspire and "uplift" blacks as a

Voices of Discontent

In part as a result of blacks' frustrations in their attempt to gain equality with whites, much social and racial turbulence erupted in the 1960s. Black separatism became an important force in the African-American community, as many intellectuals sought to distance themselves from what they considered to be the unyielding white power structure. These efforts were often accompanied by conscious attempts to incorporate Afrocentrism into art and everyday life: African names and clothing as well as Afro hairstyles became more common.

Despite the Supreme Court rulings of the 1950s and the 1964 Civil Rights Act, the 1960s did not see the expected improvement in the relationship between the races. In fact, the separation of whites and blacks increased through the creation

of the black ghettos in U.S. inner cities during this time. The ghettos were created largely by "white flight" to the suburbs, which left blacks in decaying city centers without jobs or opportunity. Long frustrated at the ingrained racism of white society, black people grew angry at the crime, housing conditions, poverty, and lack of opportunity in the inner city. This anger fueled greater militancy on the part of many. The phrase "Black power" was coined by activist Stokely Carmichael in response to the intransigence of white society. At the same time, the Black Panther Party was formed to promote a

volatile mix of race, sex, and Maoist revolution [that] coalesced in a new violent cultural figure—a photogenic caricature of black masculinity, which the New Left loved for its seditious outrageousness and "authenticity" and

which would haunt the public's understanding of young black males for the next 30 years.*

Given such tension, small events could trigger major explosions. Eventually rioting erupted in such important urban centers as Newark, New Jersey, the Watts section of Los Angeles, and Detroit.

Musicians aroused by political concerns also became involved in the general turbulence of the black population. Early on, in the 1940s and 1950s, jazz musicians had focused on the importance of black contributions to music. In the 1960s, LeRoi Jones—who later changed his name to Amiri Baraka—made an influential contribution to American social history by writing *Blues People* (1963). In this book,

* Charles Johnson, "A Soul's Jagged Arc," *The New York Times Magazine,* January 3, 1999, 16.

whole—helped spur the growth of a black intelligentsia. The Harlem Renaissance was an early realization of Du Bois's vision (see Chapter 4). Later, the bebop musicians of the 1940s upheld the importance of black achievement when they sought to distance themselves from what they perceived as the subservience of older black entertainers to the white mainstream.

In the 1950s, growing activism among blacks, including the brilliant legal tactics of Thurgood Marshall, led to important court victories in which societal barriers to equality were overturned. For example, the Supreme Court decision in *Brown v. Board of Education* struck a major blow against segregation in the South. Further protests against segregation, including the "Freedom" demonstrations of the early 1960s, eventually led to the passage of the Civil Rights Act of 1964, which officially outlawed

Copyright © Bettmann/CORBIS

The original New York City newspaper caption read: "Noted jazz trumpeter Miles Davis (left) is led into court for arraignment here, August 26th [1959]. Davis, thirty-two, was arrested for felonious assault and disorderly conduct after allegedly grappling with a policeman outside the Birdland Jazz Emporium on Broadway. Police said that Davis suffered a head laceration when a detective hit him with a blackjack. The trouble reportedly happened when patrolman Gerald Kilduff ordered the trumpeter to clear the sidewalk. Police said that Davis refused to move and that the jazz musician wrested a nightstick from the patrolman when Kilduff took Davis by the arm to lead him to the police station."

he claimed that jazz and American popular music in general was essentially black. Baraka argued that the blues defined blacks as Americans—that is, it made them American Negroes rather than displaced Africans working in a new land. The blues, once matured, later defined jazz:

> When Negroes began to master more and more "European" instruments and began to think musically in terms of their timbres, as opposed to, or in conjunction with, the voice, blues began to change, and the era of jazz was at hand.[†]

---

† LeRoi Jones, *Blues People* (New York: William Morrow, 1963), 70.

In the 1960s, then, the onset of black militancy and separatism espoused by Malcolm X and the Black Panthers was paralleled by angry claims that although jazz was a form of black music, its economic rewards flowed to whites, its imitators. These views were forcefully argued in 1970 by Frank Kofsky in *Black Nationalism and the Revolution in Music,* in which he stated the following:

> Whites can learn to play jazz... but for most whites... this new accomplishment will ordinarily come later in life than if they had been raised in the traditions of the ethnic group that they now seek to emulate; and in most cases the "second language" thus acquired will always be a touch more stiff and stilted for the "outsider" than for the "insider."[‡]

Kofsky also claimed:

> The number of white musicians who have made a permanent contribution to the tradition of jazz... is astonishingly small. More than likely, one could count them on one's fingers.... It is probably safe to state that there have been more black innovators of consequence on any *two* instruments we might choose at random—trumpet and trombone, say— than there have been whites on all instruments put together.[**]

Kofsky also proclaimed his view of the essential economic injustice of jazz. He quoted tenor saxophonist Archie Shepp at length, including Shepp's succinct summary of their views: "You own the music and we make it."[††]

---

‡ Frank Kofsky, *Black Nationalism and the Revolution in Music* (New York: Pathfinder Press, 1970), 17.

** Ibid., 19.

†† Ibid., 26.

discrimination. Leaders such as Martin Luther King, Jr., were instrumental in these efforts. Unfortunately, the legal end to segregation and discrimination did not lead to acceptance of blacks into the dominant society. Black militancy in the 1960s was a direct result of these developments.

This revolution in black activism anticipated a wider rebellion within middle-class society as well. Inspired by the Beat movement of the 1950s, many young people in the following decade rebelled against what they considered unthinking conformity and social duty. This rebellion took special aim at the war in Vietnam, which many people, young and old, considered pointless and unwinnable. The smaller but more visible group called "flower children" embraced the hippie lifestyle and derided their parents' sexual timidity as "uptight." "Do your own thing" became a catchphrase.

The 1960s have rightly been considered pivotal in the history of U.S. society and of the West as a whole. This era of generational and racial rebellion was reflected by musical substyles in jazz that were as uncompromising as the attitudes of its foremost musicians.

ARCHIE SHEPP

Archie Shepp (b. 1937) was one of the most vocal and articulate of the avant-garde musicians championing the cause of blacks. His album, *Fire Music* (1965), featured the piece "Malcolm, Malcolm, *Semper* Malcolm," a tribute to black leader Malcolm X. Shepp studied dramatic literature at Goddard College, where he earned his bachelor of arts in 1959. Originally an alto player, he switched to tenor through the inspiration of John Coltrane, with whom he eventually performed. He also worked with Cecil Taylor, Bill Dixon, Roswell Rudd, and others.

Shepp thought that free jazz ought to be a political medium. His calls for justice for blacks have not wavered through the years. In 1999 he pointed out that Jewish survivors of the Holocaust were seeking monetary compensation: "What if our people asked for compensation for all the years of slave labour?"[1]

Shepp performed on Coltrane's important free jazz album, *Ascension* (1965). In addition to *Fire Music,* Shepp recorded several other important albums in the 1960s, including *Four for Trane* (1964). Eloquent in his defense of black nationalist principles, Shepp became an educator, teaching at the State University of New York at Buffalo and the University of Massachusetts at Amherst.

ALBERT AYLER

Another important contributor to the scene, Albert Ayler (1936–1970), brought a fiercely independent style and a plethora of avant-garde techniques to the tenor saxophone. Like Shepp, Ayler worked with Cecil Taylor. *Ghosts* and *Spiritual Unity* (both 1964) were two of his most important albums. His works encompassed shrieks, cries, wails, multiphonics, and other techniques that can be summed up as a "sound"-oriented approach to the instrument rather than anything one could notate easily. Unfortunately, the jazz world would lose this innovator all too soon. In 1970 Ayler disappeared for almost three weeks before his body was found in New York's East River. The circumstances surrounding his death are sketchy, but the official verdict was death by drowning.

Ayler's "Ghosts" had followed the first wave of the avant-garde jazz recordings by artists Ornette Coleman and Cecil Taylor. Many of the avant-garde tenor saxophonists of the 1960s, such as Ayler and Pharoah Sanders, drew much of their initial inspiration from John Coltrane. For his part, Coltrane keenly supported these players, even helping both Ayler and Sanders obtain record contracts from Impulse Records.

"Ghosts" is from Ayler's most productive period: He recorded four albums during 1964. Ayler uses the entire range of the tenor saxophone during his solo. Gary Peacock is on bass, and Sunny Murray is on drums. There is no piano, which is typical of many free jazz recordings of the 1960s.

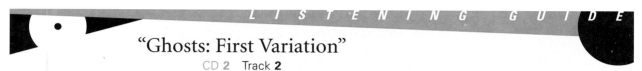

"Ghosts: First Variation"
CD **2**   Track **2**

Albert Ayler Trio: "Ghosts: First Variation" (Ayler), from *Spiritual Journey*. ESP 1002. New York, July 10, 1964. Albert Ayler, tenor saxophone; Gary Peacock, bass; Sunny Murray, drums.

Like many of the avant-garde recordings, the improvisation to "Ghosts" makes listening particularly challenging. What is unusual, however, is the simplicity of its melody. Drawn to this simplicity, Ayler recorded at least five different versions of "Ghosts." "I'd like to play something—like the beginning of 'Ghosts'—that people can hum," he acknowledged. "And I want to play songs that I used to sing when I was real small. Folk melodies that all people would understand."[2]

The group follows the traditional "melody-solos-melody" format, but following the statement of the melody, members engage in free collective improvisation. The players abandon a regular pulse, an underlying tonal center or harmonic progression, and a predetermined formal structure.

Ayler plays extremely freely, developing a repertory of extended tenor saxophone techniques, overblowing notes and distorting pitches. Peacock's solo displays his clean technique; his sound and facility on the instrument are reminiscent of bassist Scott LaFaro (heard with Bill Evans on "Peri's Scope," CD 2, Track 6). Murray's earlier work with Cecil Taylor contributes to the "arhythmic" approach to the drums heard here. Murray often played with a stripped-down drum set, using only cymbal, snare drum, and bass drum.

8-bar intro

0:00   Ayler plays an introductory melody alone, using both fixed and indeterminate pitches.

Melody—Three 8-bar phrases

0:11   Bass and drums enter, accompanying Ayler beneath the melody. This melody is primarily diatonic and hummable, quite similar to Sonny Rollins's lyrical calypso melody "St. Thomas."

0:21   Two folklike eight-bar ideas closely related to the melody appear, setting up a clear tonal center.

Ayler's tenor saxophone solo

0:44   In the first thirty seconds of the solo, Ayler vaguely recalls the melody: The pitches are often indeterminate, but the phrasing seems to echo the starting and stopping places of the melody. Careful listening reveals the use of some of the motives from the melody.

1:16   The pacing of Ayler's solo creates an arc, reaching a high point of intensity before winding down at the end of the solo. Ayler uses several avant-garde techniques here, including multiphonics, cries, shrieks, and wails. The accompaniments by Murray on drums and Peacock on bass do not keep time for Ayler but contribute freely, interjecting and commenting on Ayler's ideas.

Peacock's bass solo

2:49   In this solo, the time is still very free: Note that Murray's drumming is at times very spare, emphasizing the cymbals while commenting on Peacock's lines.

Melody returns

4:12   The entire group returns to the melody, including the introductory melody that Ayler played by himself at the beginning of the composition. Ayler plays both follow-up eight-bar melodies and repeats the last.

BLACK ACTIVISM AND THE AVANT-GARDE TODAY

The struggle for equality and recognition of black achievement continues today, as it probably will for some time. Among the influential younger musicians who have sought greater black recognition and advocated multiculturalism is clarinetist Don Byron (b. 1958). He has gained a reputation for combining jazz with Jewish klezmer music in addition to other crossover experimentation. Recently, he confronted racial stereotypes with his album *Nu Blaxploitation* (1998). Byron leads a band called Existential Dred, a name that neatly evokes contemporary angst, the *Dred Scott* Supreme Court decision of 1857, and Byron's own dreadlocks hairstyle. His album *Music for Six Musicians* (1995) featured a piece called "Shelby Steele Would Be Mowing Your Lawn." (Steele is a black scholar who has written against affirmative action programs.)

Although social statement remains an important form of the black avant-garde, its message seems less urgent thirty years later. Nonetheless, the black nationalist movement continues to focus attention on the essential black contribution to jazz. Some feel, however, that this focus has gone too far, that a kind of reverse racism has resulted, with white contributions to the music undervalued and fine white players overlooked. For example the argument of the essential blackness of jazz has been countered recently by Gene Lee's *Cats of Any Color* (1995) and Richard Sudhalter's *Lost Chords: White Musicians and Their Contributions to Jazz, 1915–1945* (1999). These books argue that jazz is an American music whose innovators have been largely black but to which whites have contributed significantly and that without whites and their input, jazz would not be the rich music it is.

In any case, the jazz avant-garde of the 1960s pioneered forceful political statements that heightened awareness of and emphasis on the African heritage of jazz. The general atmosphere of the 1960s, both in the black community and in society more generally, provided a sympathetic backdrop for musical revolution. In the rest of this chapter, we continue to explore the principal avant-garde artists of the 1960s. In Chapter 10, we finish our discussion of the 1960s by examining Miles Davis's later career as well as the substyles that retained closer identification with bebop on the one hand and the continuation of the funky jazz (or soul jazz) movement on the other.

Ornette Coleman and Free Jazz

With the arrival of alto saxophonist Ornette Coleman on the New York scene in 1959, avant-garde jazz—also called "free jazz" or the "New Thing"—received its strongest initial boost. In fact, "free jazz" received its name from the 1960 Coleman album of the same name. A cover painting by abstract expressionist Jackson Pollock reinforced its avant-garde statement. Coleman, who played a plastic alto saxophone, polarized the jazz community in New York in the late 1950s: Some hailed him as a genius while others denounced him as a charlatan.

Coleman's music was controversial. His quartet—with trumpeter Don Cherry, bassist Charlie Haden, and drummer Billy Higgins (replaced by Ed Blackwell in 1960)—had no chordal instruments such as the piano. While some listeners dismissed his music as a radical rejection of the jazz tradition, those who praised him considered his music an extension of historical practice. Among Coleman's earliest champions was pianist John Lewis of the Modern Jazz Quartet, who had heard Coleman's group in California:

> I've never heard anything like Ornette Coleman and Don Cherry before. Ornette is, in a sense, an extension of Charlie Parker—the first I've heard. This is the real need... to extend the basic ideas of Bird until they're not playing an imitation but actually something new.[3]

With his pianoless quartet in the late 1950s, Ornette Coleman (CD 2, Track 3) was one of the key figures of early avant-garde jazz.

As his album titles *Change of the Century* and *The Shape of Jazz to Come* suggested, Coleman's music was new. The improvised solos were not necessarily tied to traditional harmonic progressions but instead were based on loose and shifting tonal centers. Without any harmonic accompaniment, the soloists could move freely to different harmonic areas, although Haden's bass lines sometimes retained the pieces' original forms.

Coleman was an astonishingly prolific composer whose tuneful, sometimes cheerful compositions were written to be interpreted freely. Coleman noted:

> I don't tell the members of the group what to do. I want them to play what they hear in the piece themselves. I let everyone express himself just as he wants to. The musicians have complete freedom, and so, of course, our final results depend entirely on the musicianship, emotional make-up, and taste of the individual members.[4]

Unlike traditional jazz improvisation, in which the soloist and the accompaniment often follow a repeating thirty-two–bar structure, Coleman's work sometimes abandoned this form. Most of Coleman's compositions, however, retained the large-scale organization of melodic statement–improvisations–melodic statement associated with more conventional jazz.

Coleman was born in Fort Worth, Texas, in 1930. After beginning his career performing in rhythm-and-blues (R&B) bands in the mid-1940s, he briefly moved to New Orleans in 1948, working mostly in nonmusical jobs, then returned to Fort Worth. Joining the R&B band of Pee Wee Crayton, Coleman traveled to Los Angeles, where he settled in 1954 after being fired by Crayton. He then worked for a while as an elevator operator—a job that allowed him to read and study music theory while parked on the tenth floor. Participating in Los Angeles jam sessions, he occasionally encountered scorn from other musicians, but he also found like-minded players interested in his music and in his freer approach to improvisation.

In 1958 Coleman signed with Contemporary Records and recorded two albums for the label. His first, *Something Else!!!! The Music of Ornette Coleman,* was cut in 1958 and featured a conventional rhythm section with drummer Billy Higgins and pianist Walter Norris; the second, *Tomorrow Is the Question,* was recorded the following year and abandoned the use of piano.

The forms for Coleman's early compositions were frequently conventional, following the structure of the twelve-bar blues and the thirty-two–bar AABA song form. Of his irregular pieces, "Mind and Time" used a ten-bar form, while "Giggin'" was a thirteen-bar blues. However, Coleman's unique contribution was his ability to veer into different tonal directions, dissociating himself from a fixed harmonic scheme in his solos. Although Coleman's albums for Contemporary were less radical than his work to come, they show how his music was beginning to evolve toward complete freedom from syntactic constraints.

After signing with Atlantic Records in 1959, Coleman recorded *The Shape of Jazz to Come* and *Change of the Century* with his own quartet, comprising Cherry, Haden, and Higgins. Coleman's approach to the alto saxophone was unique: He emulated the human voice, using bent pitches and unusual intonation. "There are some intervals," he stated, "that carry that human quality if you play them in the right pitch. You can reach into the human sound of a voice on your horn if you're actually hearing and trying to express the warmth of a human voice."[5] Coleman's unusual intonation and motivic playing was often embedded in a relatively simple rhythmic language, creating, as one writer put it, "a touch of folksong naiveté."[6]

These features summarize Coleman's style:

▶ Fragmented, angular melodies instead of the long, spun out eighth-note phrases of bebop

▶ Melodic connections based on motivic structure and large-scale gestures and more abstract relations among sets of pitches

▶ Little if any use of conventional harmony and voice leading, but solos often establish loose, shifting tonal centers

▶ Variety of melodic rhythm but avoidance of even-note phrases

▶ Nasal, insistent tone

▶ Rhythm loosely connected to background pulse

▶ Concentration on middle and upper range of instrument

▶ Passionate expression

▶ Deviations from standard intonation

As tightly controlled as Coleman's playing was, his pitch structure and rhythmic fluidity created an impression of spontaneous expression. Coleman combined a sensuous, linear approach to the instrument with a strikingly original sound, created in part by his unique, well-controlled intonation. Although harmony in the conventional sense of chord changes did not often factor in Coleman's music, harmony in the larger sense of related intervals and control always appeared. Without conventional harmony, Coleman shaped large-scale form by establishing loose, shifting tonal centers and through musical gestures such as dynamic climax, melodic contour, and sectionalization. All in all, Coleman succeeded in allying passionate expression to rigorous linear structure; his playing was emotional, powerful, and thoroughly individual.

Pianist John Lewis of the Modern Jazz Quartet was an early ardent supporter of Coleman, arranging for him and Don Cherry to attend the Lenox Jazz School in Massachusetts in 1959. Shortly after, Coleman and his group came to New York for their legendary gig at the Five Spot. Despite the acclaim of Lewis and famous others such as Gunther Schuller and Leonard Bernstein, the group experienced derision by some of the older established players. For example, trumpeter Roy Eldridge claimed, "He's putting everybody on. They start with a nice lead-off figure, but then they go off into outer space. They disregard the chords and they play odd numbers of bars. I can't follow them."[7]

In December 1960, Coleman took the unprecedented step of bringing together eight players (two quartets) in a composition titled *Free Jazz*. Coleman had expanded his quartet—Cherry, Haden, and Blackwell—with Higgins, bassist Scott LaFaro, and bass clarinetist Eric Dolphy. The group recorded two takes, lasting thirty-six minutes, which combined solo improvisation, collective improvisation, and prearranged ensemble passages.

To many listeners, *Free Jazz* was daunting: It seemed formless and chaotic, a radical rejection of all jazz conventions. Careful listeners, however, heard within its collective freedom a musical conversation in which motives and ideas were stated, then drawn out, reinterpreted, and developed by other players. The role of the rhythm-section players seemed predetermined as well: Haden and Blackwell maintained the fundamental rhythmic pulse, while LaFaro and Higgins played against the time.[8] Coleman's written ensemble passages were used as transitions between the improvised sections.

In some ways, *Free Jazz* profoundly influenced the emerging jazz avant-garde. It suggested new sets of relationships among improvisers and allowed the rhythm section to jettison routine timekeeping. Both the use of collective improvisation based on freely improvised motives and the abandonment of cycling harmonic-metric forms redefined the possibilities of group interaction. Other players, such as pianist Cecil Taylor, may also have been experimenting with freely improvised music, but Coleman's greater visibility forced many players to reevaluate their own approach to the inherited practices of the jazz tradition.

By 1962, Coleman had temporarily withdrawn from public performance; he returned in 1965, playing not only saxophone but also trumpet and violin in a trio with drummer Charles Moffett and bassist David Izenzon. An even more radical player than Haden, Izenzon contradicted the pulse at times, provided melodic commentary, and often used the bow. Coleman brought an intensely percussive, furious, driving approach to the violin, while he centered his trumpet playing in the instrument's higher register, alternating rapid runs with smeared notes and strong accents. Approaching new instruments in an unorthodox manner, Coleman continued to generate controversy among musicians and listeners, although his European tour in 1965 had an important impact on the avant-garde overseas. On his recording from Stockholm, *Live at the Golden Circle,* Coleman's alto saxophone solos remained highly organized motivically, as can be heard in his compositions "Dee Dee" and "European Echoes."

Ornette Coleman's Chamber and Orchestral Compositions

While in England, Coleman premiered a chamber music work, *Sounds and Forms for Wind Quintet,* that showed his ability to create extended compositional structures. His interest in contemporary concert music and the third stream were further revealed by an appearance on Gunther Schuller's album *Jazz Abstractions* in 1960; Coleman was the alto saxophone soloist in "Abstractions," a serial work by Schuller for alto, string quartet, two double basses, guitar, and percussion.

Continuing in a third-stream vein, Coleman in 1967 wrote *Sounds and Forms for Wind Quintet,* performing trumpet interludes between each of the ten movements. This work helped Coleman win the prestigious Guggenheim Award for composition; he was the first jazz composer to be so honored.

Several years later, in 1971, Coleman completed a large-scale work for orchestra entitled *Skies of America,* with movements that included "Foreigner in a Free Land" and "The Men Who Live in the White House." This work was revived at Lincoln Center by the New York Philharmonic in 1997.

In 1997 Lincoln Center presented an entire evening dedicated to Coleman—*Civilization: A Harmolodic Celebration*—that featured performances of his group, Prime Time, and reunited Coleman with Charlie Haden and Billy Higgins. Among the other guests were Lou Reed and Laurie Anderson. (See the box "Ornette Coleman's Chamber and Orchestral Compositions.")

Coleman's work in the 1970s and 1980s has been influenced by what he calls *Harmolodic Theory,* a term first discussed in the liner notes to *Skies of America.* Coleman noted that harmolodics presented "melody, harmony, and the instrumentation of the movement of forms." Later, he wrote that they "had to do with using the melody, the harmony, and the rhythm all equal."[9] Gunther Schuller suggested that harmolodics relates to the use of similar melodic material in different clefs and keys, producing a texture of predominantly parallel motion, although Schuller freely admitted that it was unclear how this idea related directly to Coleman's own compositional technique. The term is characteristic, Schuller noted, of Coleman's obscure and often contradictory pronouncements on music.[10] Despite Coleman's own writing on the subject, the theory remains vague.

During the early 1970s, Coleman worked sporadically, sometimes insisting on fees for records and appearances too large for a jazz musician of his celebrity and audience appeal. He preferred to remain underemployed and underrecorded rather than sacrifice his artistic principles.

Coleman regained the jazz limelight during the mid-1970s, combining his free style with funk rhythms and reemerging as an important and innovative player. Coleman formed the group Prime Time to incorporate these changes in his style and in his interests. As with his earlier music, much of the improvisational material was not governed by conventional harmonic structure. This time, however, Coleman used electric instruments.

Prime Time began as a quintet, with two electric guitarists and an electric bassist; it was later expanded to a sextet, with the addition of a second drummer. The group featured an interesting amalgam of rhythm and blues, free jazz, and other influences, including Moroccan music. Against an unusual combination of rock and funk backbeats (heavy emphases on beats 2 and 4) alongside rhythm-and-blues vamps, Coleman improvised atonally, often using microtonal pitches. Clearly, Coleman was attempting to broaden his status as an avant-garde figure and reconnect with his rhythm-and-blues origins.

Harmolodics is a theory of music devised by Ornette Coleman. Although its meaning is vague, harmolodics has provided the theoretical motivation behind Coleman's work since the 1970s.

Coleman achieved a wider degree of recognition after touring and recording with fusion guitarist Pat Metheny between 1985 and 1986. He recorded with Metheny on the 1985 album *Song X*. In 1987 Coleman recorded *In All Languages*, in which his original 1959 quartet including Don Cherry, Charlie Haden, and Billy Higgins was juxtaposed with his Prime Time electric ensemble. This album, now considered a Coleman classic, was reissued on CD by Verve/Harmolodic in 1997. It provides a remarkable summary of Coleman's distinguished career.

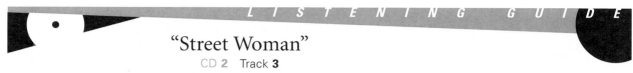

L I S T E N I N G   G U I D E

"Street Woman"

CD **2**   Track **3**

Ornette Coleman: "Street Woman" (Coleman), from *Science Fiction*. Original issue Columbia KC31061. Reissued on Sony SRCS 9372. New York, September 9–13, 1971. Don Cherry, pocket trumpet; Ornette Coleman, alto saxophone; Charlie Haden, bass; Billy Higgins, drums.

"Street Woman" shows the joyful, up-tempo sound of Coleman's best-known quartet. Like so many of Coleman's pieces, "Street Woman" projects a basic tonal center (in this case, G), although it avoids standard chord progressions. The motivic tightness of the melody is remarkable: After the opening three figures present their abrupt flourishes, the remainder of the melody releases the built-up tension with descending three-note ideas. These three-note descents are either two steps or a step and a third.

Head—First time through

0:00   The following music example shows the melodic basis of "Street Woman" in nine numbered melodic figures:

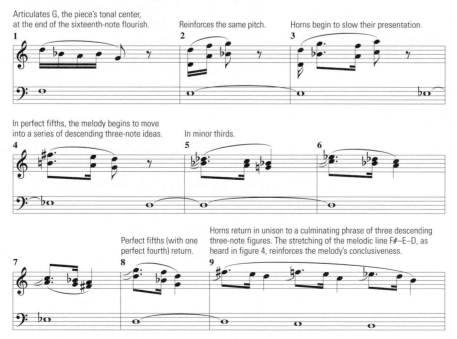

▶   Note the pattern of intervals in the horns' presentation underlying the nine figures: *unison, sixths, perfect fifths, minor thirds, perfect fifths, unison.*

▶ An outline of the bass line is shown in the lower staff throughout the example. Haden's bass accompaniment consists largely of rapid alternations between single-pitch octaves. He follows the horns through the figures of the melody, while his bass line imparts a sense of harmonic movement to the head without detailing specific chords.

Head—Second time through

0:15 The principal melody is repeated in virtually the same manner.

Coleman alto saxophone solo

0:31 This solo begins with a flourish up to high G that recalls melodic figure 2. He largely works with pitches from the G major scale, then deviates, then returns to the basic G pitch center, which he articulates in numerous ways.

1:28 Coleman returns to the high G
and in a passionate statement several
1:56 times toward the end of his solo.

Haden gradually assumes a walking bass as accompaniment, although he will return to octaves at times.

Haden bass solo

2:07 Haden works with the idea of keeping one pitch constant and moving the other.

2:46 Later he moves into a freer statement that ushers in Cherry's pocket trumpet solo.

Cherry pocket trumpet solo

3:11 Cherry presents ideas that recall strongly the figures of the head, particularly melodic figure 1. His solo begins energetically, with a flurry of notes. Haden returns to the octave idea of the head.

3:35 Cherry's lines become more lyrical and tonal, emphasizing G minor.

4:02 Cherry ends his solo with an almost classical F#–G (leading-tone-to-tonic) phrase.

Head—Return

4:07 The head is played twice, as it was heard at the beginning of the performance.

Coda

4:41 Melodic figure 1 is repeated three times with a follow-up high G. Haden closes the bass line on E♭, avoiding the traditional cadence to the tonic G.

By the 1990s, Coleman was accepted as one of the elder representatives of the jazz avant-garde. He was inducted into the French Order of Arts and Letters in 1997 and was elected to the American Academy of Arts and Letters the same year.

John Coltrane

In the twelve years from 1955, when he joined Miles Davis's quintet, to his death in 1967, John Coltrane, initially an obscure and often criticized tenor player, became the leading saxophonist of his generation and one of the most important jazz artists of the 1960s. His influence was profound. He was consistently devoted to his craft, to technical proficiency, to musical exploration, and to endless practicing and studying.

His album titles, such as *A Love Supreme* and *Om*, revealed the connection of his music to his religious beliefs and spiritual quest. Fans and listeners heard his extended solos as reaching for the ineffable. Particularly with his quartet of 1960–1965, Coltrane became the symbol of the improvising musician as exploratory seeker. Even in his later, successful years, Coltrane remained uncompromising in his musical ideals and overall goals.

OVERVIEW OF COLTRANE'S CAREER

Although Coltrane underwent many changes and transformations in his sound and style, his career encompasses three general periods:

▶ 1955–1960: Hard bop and "sheets of sound"

▶ 1960–1965: Classic quartet and modal compositions

▶ 1965–1967: Avant-garde

The career of John Coltrane (CD 2, Track 4) was marked by a restless search for musical growth and the transcendental.

Courtesy Morgan Collection

In the first period, he and Sonny Rollins competed to be the premier tenor saxophonist in jazz. At that time Coltrane was often described as a hard bop player with an edgy sound. Jazz critic Ira Gitler coined the phrase *sheets of sound* to describe his rapid-fire execution, irregular groupings of notes, unusual phrasing, and technique of inserting several harmonies over a single chord. Coltrane's 1959 composition "Giant Steps" was a tour de force of improvisation over rapid and unusual harmonic shifts, which showed off his dazzling ability to execute difficult sequences of chord changes.

Coltrane launched his second period by bringing together his well-known and long-lived quartet, which included McCoy Tyner on piano, Jimmy Garrison on bass, and Elvin Jones on drums. The repertory of the quartet emphasized modal composition, often with particular attention to minor modes such as the Dorian. The group's extended improvisations, such as in their performance of "My Favorite Things," featured fewer and slower-moving harmonies. The quartet's modal approach reached its zenith in the December 10, 1964, recording *A Love Supreme*, a four-movement suite (listen to CD 2, Track 4, to hear one of these movements).

Coltrane's third and final period spanned the last two years of his life, when he became increasingly involved in the jazz avant-garde. His album *Ascension*, which used several young, radical musicians, provided a significant document of the free jazz movement.

Sheets of sound, an expression coined by jazz critic Ira Gitler, describes a method of playing that features extremely fast notes with irregular phrase groupings. Sometimes, unusual harmonies are introduced over the given chord change. This method originated with John Coltrane.

EARLY YEARS

Born in Hamlet, North Carolina, on September 23, 1926, and raised in High Point, North Carolina, Coltrane played alto horn, clarinet, and then, as a teenager, the alto saxophone. Initially influenced by Ellington's Johnny Hodges, he eventually came under the inescapable spell of Charlie Parker. After moving to Philadelphia, he studied at several local music schools, then joined the U.S. Navy band and was stationed in Hawaii between 1945 and 1946. The following year, while on tour in California with the King Kolax band, Coltrane met Charlie Parker, recently released from Camarillo State Hospital. Coltrane attended Parker's February 19 recording session for Dial—which included pianist Erroll Garner—and later took part in a jam session with the altoist.

In 1948 Coltrane joined the band of Eddie "Cleanhead" Vinson. It was at that time that Coltrane took up the tenor saxophone, which opened up a range of possibilities:

> When I bought a tenor to go with Eddie Vinson's band, a wider area of listening opened up for me. I found I was able to be more varied in my musical interests. On alto, Bird had been my whole influence, but on tenor I found there was no one man whose ideas were so dominant as Charlie's were on alto. Therefore, I drew from all the men I heard during this period, beginning with Lester [Young], and believe me, I've picked up something from them all, including several who have never recorded. The reason I like Lester so was that I could feel that line, that simplicity.... There were a lot of things that [Coleman] Hawkins was doing that I knew I'd have to learn somewhere along the line. I felt the same way about Ben Webster.... The first time I heard Hawk, I was fascinated by his arpeggios and the way he played. I got a copy of his "Body and Soul" and listened real hard to what he was doing.[11]

This quotation reveals Coltrane's ability to absorb a huge array of influences. Throughout his career, he remained profoundly interested in the musical developments of his colleagues and was extremely supportive of many of the younger musicians. In addition to his appetite for music, unfortunately, Coltrane displayed an inclination toward substance abuse. He began using heroin in the late 1940s, and he frequently drank and ate obsessively. He remained addicted to heroin for nearly ten years.

Coltrane joined Dizzy Gillespie's band in 1949, when Gillespie hired members of Vinson's band. Coltrane's first commercial recording was made with Gillespie. During this time, Coltrane continued to study and absorb the styles of other tenor saxophonists, particularly bop pioneers Dexter Gordon and Wardell Gray, as well as Sonny Stitt, a bop altoist who also doubled on tenor.

Taking on a staggering variety of gigs as a sideman, Coltrane appeared in the R&B bands of Earl Bostic, as well as Gay Crosse and His Good Humor Six. In 1954 he joined the band of one

Dizzy Gillespie (CD 1, Tracks 17 and 18), shown here with Adam Clayton Powell. For many years Powell represented New York's Harlem in Congress, where he was especially effective in helping to create the "Great Society" programs that attempted to generate economic and social opportunities for blacks and the poor.

of his earliest idols, alto saxophonist Johnny Hodges. Coltrane appreciated Hodges's musical sincerity and confidence, and noted that "I liked every tune in the book."[12] Unfortunately, Coltrane's problems with drugs and alcohol caused him to leave the band the same year. He returned to Philadelphia to recuperate. Although he had already accumulated numerous professional experiences, his most significant ones were yet to come.

HARD BOP WITH MILES DAVIS

Flush with success from his 1955 appearance at the Newport Jazz Festival, Miles Davis formed a working quintet that year, hiring Coltrane on tenor. Although Davis had been using tenor saxophonist Sonny Rollins, Rollins had moved to Chicago, taking the first of his extended sabbaticals from performing. Davis's drummer, Philly Joe Jones, and pianist Red Garland—both Philadelphians—persuaded Davis to hire Coltrane, who was then working with organist Jimmy Smith. In September 1955, on the same night he married his fiancée, Naima Grubbs, Coltrane played his first performance with Davis.

"When Coltrane joined Miles Davis's quintet in 1955," writes Thomas Owens, "he formed a musical alliance that would have a great impact on the evolution of jazz."[13] Coltrane's years with Davis were indeed formative. Although critics were initially hostile to Coltrane's aggressive technique and steely tone, his virtuosity was dazzling. Phrases frequently began with an upward glissando, moving to a longer-held vibratoless pitch.

Despite his technical advances, Coltrane's drug habit, along with that of Philly Joe Jones, was causing problems on the bandstand. Miles Davis's biographer, Jack Chambers, recounts the story of Coltrane's falling asleep on stage during an entire set. Present was a record executive intent on signing him to a major record label; after seeing his condition, he left without talking to Coltrane.[14]

The year 1957 was pivotal in Coltrane's career. Davis, exasperated by his behavior, fired him. Shaken, Coltrane managed to get off heroin and quit drinking alcohol. During the spring and summer he worked with pianist Thelonious Monk; later that fall, the two teamed up for a famous engagement at New York's Five Spot. Monk gave Coltrane further freedom to experiment, with extended solos often backed by only bass and drums. In Coltrane's words, Monk was "a musical architect of the highest order.... I felt I learned from him in every way—through the senses, theoretically, technically."[15] Coltrane also claimed that Monk was the first to show him how to produce two or three notes simultaneously on the tenor saxophone.

Around this time, Coltrane also recorded his first album as a leader. On the LP *Coltrane,* his version of

Publicity photo by Frank Lindner. Courtesy Morgan Collection.

Saxophonist Sonny Rollins (CD 2, Track 1) preceded Coltrane in the Miles Davis Quintet. Jazz writers and analysts singled out Rollins's musically inventive and thematically coherent solos.

"Violets for Your Furs"—a song earlier recorded by Billie Holliday—showed the depth of tone and emotion that Coltrane could summon on ballads. For these slower, more sensitive solos, he frequently balanced melodic paraphrase with florid runs.

Other Coltrane improvisations showed a turn to the long, sixteenth-note phrases and patterns that were to become a distinctive part of his style. Some of Coltrane's hard bop compositions, such as "Moment's Notice" from his 1957 recording *Blue Train,* contained unusual and quick-moving harmonic twists.

As his technique and approach to the instrument continued to evolve, Coltrane rejoined Davis in 1958. Gitler's description "sheets of sound" was an apt description for Coltrane's torrid scalar passages. In addition, Coltrane made conscious use of unusual and irregular phrasing:

> I found there were a certain number of chord progressions to play in a given time, and sometimes what I played didn't work out in eighth notes, sixteenth notes, or triplets. I had to put the notes in uneven groups like fives and sevens in order to get them all in.[16]

Similarly, Coltrane was candid about harmonic experimentation, sometimes superimposing extra chords on the tunes' basic changes. His solo in "Straight, No Chaser" (from Miles Davis's *Milestones*) contained unusual harmonic substitutions. Referring to Davis's music, Coltrane said, "Due to the direct and free-flowing lines in his music, I found it easy to apply the harmonic ideas that I had. I could stack up chords—say, on a C7, I sometimes superimposed an E♭7, up to an F♯7, down to an F. That way I could play three chords on one."[17]

Harmonic superimposition is the technique of adding chords on top of the harmonies already present in a song. It adds harmonic complexity.

Davis's modal music supplied the ideal repertory for Coltrane's experiments in harmonic superimposition. Davis's "So What," from *Kind of Blue,* allowed Coltrane to "stack" harmonies over the given D Dorian and E♭ Dorian modalities. In the spring of 1959, the same time he recorded *Kind of Blue* with Davis, Coltrane took his own group into the studio and recorded one of his most famous works, "Giant Steps." This imaginative tune used the harmonic patterns of hard bop, but reworked them into a large-scale format with fast key changes linked by major thirds. In this tour de force, Coltrane showed his mastery of bebop harmonies and unusual progressions in a driving, up-tempo format.

COLTRANE'S CLASSIC QUARTET

In 1960 Coltrane took the decisive step of leaving the Davis sextet and forming his own quartet, which opened at the Jazz Gallery in May. At first the personnel was unstable. Coltrane initially tried pianist Steve Kuhn, bassist Steve Davis, and drummer Pete LaRoca, but he quickly replaced Kuhn with Philadelphian McCoy Tyner, a hard-driving, percussive pianist who had earlier been a member of the Art Farmer–Benny Golson Jazztet.

In Tyner (b. 1938), Coltrane found a pianist in sympathy with his own modal interests. Tyner's sound was based on chords built in fourths. In backing up Coltrane, he frequently intoned a bass-register open fifth in his left hand, operating as a kind of drone that created a tonal center. This open-fifth drone focused the tonality, leaving Coltrane free to depart from and return to the tonal center within his improvisations. Tyner's own solos projected an extremely forceful and clipped staccato touch on improvised lines, which sometimes culminated in thunderous tremolos. On his earliest recordings—including his own *Inception* and *Reaching Fourths*—Tyner played his staccato and even eighth-note lines in a hard bop idiom, skillfully negotiating each harmony. However, during his five years with Coltrane, he interpreted the harmonies more freely, ranging both inside and outside the tonal centers, often through *pentatonic scales.*

Renowned for his powerful touch and almost demonic energy, Tyner has remained one of the most popular pianists in jazz. He continues to work with his own groups, including a big band, and has appeared as a special guest both live and on recordings with other major artists.

Like Tyner, Coltrane's drummer, Elvin Jones, was also a fiery, intense player. Born in Pontiac, Michigan, in 1927, Jones came from a musical family that included his equally renowned brothers, trumpeter Thad Jones (1923–1986) and pianist Hank Jones (b. 1918). Before joining Coltrane, Elvin Jones had recorded with Miles Davis, Art Farmer, J. J. Johnson, and Sonny Rollins. Jones's years with Coltrane brought him fame, not only for his complex polyrhythms but also for sheer physical endurance. In the context of the band's extended improvisations, Jones generated unbelievable energy and drive as both a powerful timekeeper and a complementary voice to Coltrane's own style. Their performances often included extended duets without piano or bass accompaniment. The level of energy generated by Jones's playing brought about an increased participation for the drummer relative to the bassist and pianist. Jones was aware of this role. In discussing his playing with Coltrane, he said:

Pianist McCoy Tyner (CD 2, Track 4), whose powerful playing and modal harmonies were built in fourths, complemented John Coltrane's extended solos.

> I always realize I'm not the soloist, that John is, and I'm merely the support for him. It may sound like a duet or duel at times, but it's still a support I'm lending him, a complementary thing.... It's being done in the same context of the earlier style, only this is just another step forward in the relationship between the rhythm section and the soloist. It's much freer—John realizes he has this close support, and, therefore, he can move further ahead; he can venture out as far as he wants without worrying about getting away from everybody and having the feeling he's out in the middle of a lake by himself.[18]

A **pentatonic scale (set)** is a five-note set that avoids the interval of a tritone and can be arranged as a series of perfect fourths or perfect fifths. The black notes of the keyboard form one such scale.

Coltrane's classic quartet was rounded out by bassist Jimmy Garrison (1934–1976), who joined at the end of 1961. Like its other members, Garrison had played and recorded with numerous hard bop musicians in the late fifties. Garrison had even performed with Ornette Coleman on *Ornette on Tenor.* Less technically oriented than Tyner and Jones, Garrison was a thoroughly solid player who often relied on drones and fixed patterns in addition to the more customary walking lines when he was accompanying soloists. In his own solos, Garrison featured unusual bass techniques, sometimes strumming the bass with three-note chords in a quasi-flamenco style.

Although the quartet became one of the premier groups in jazz, Coltrane personally continued to expand his musical interests and influences by studying the music and scales of Africa, India, and the Mideast. He also took up the soprano

Coltrane's Modal Compositions

The Coltrane quartet built much of its repertory on a modal foundation. Instead of negotiating a set of changes, modal jazz players often piled up chords, sometimes in fourths, freely chosen from the modal scale. The relationship of their melodies to the chords could also be quite free, often extending chromatically beyond that modal scale. In Coltrane's performance of "My Favorite Things," for example, the song's original harmonic progression was simplified to single modal areas during the solos, which the Coltrane quartet then stretched to the breaking point.

Another important tune in the quartet's repertory was Coltrane's "Impressions," which bore an interesting resemblance to Miles Davis's "So What." The pieces had identical thirty-two–bar AABA forms and modal areas: D Dorian for the A sections and E♭ Dorian for the B section. The E♭ Dorian bridge was largely a transposition of the A section—again, resembling "So What."

As Coltrane continued to explore the outer limits of modality, he also incorporated a shift in his improvisational language. In place of the hard bop formulas carefully integrated into his earlier solos (for example, "Giant Steps"), Coltrane more and more worked from short motivic ideas, which he would explore through repetition with extensive, sometimes obsessive variation. As Coltrane worked through the variants of these "motivic cells," the effect

> **Motivic (thematic) cells**
> are short melodic ideas subject to variation and development.

on the listener was hypnotic, often recalling the incantational atmosphere created by some Eastern musical styles. In part, this effect derived from Coltrane's deep interest in the music of Asia and the Near East.

---

saxophone, which provided further inspiration and new paths to explore. Coltrane featured the soprano on some of his best-known performances, including the well-known "My Favorite Things," recorded in 1960. (See the box "Coltrane's Modal Compositions.")

During 1961 and 1962, Coltrane's quartet was frequently expanded to a quintet, incorporating Eric Dolphy on flute and bass clarinet. (Dolphy also arranged and conducted the big band on Coltrane's 1961 *Africa/Brass.*) Dolphy's influence on Coltrane's group was liberating. Dolphy's extended improvisations on such compositions as "India," based on the G Mixolydian mode, triggered hostility from music critics, some of whom attacked what they perceived as Coltrane's move toward free jazz. *Down Beat* editor John Tynan dismissed the music as "anti-jazz":

> At Hollywood's Renaissance club recently, I listened to a horrifying demonstration of what appears to be a growing anti-jazz trend exemplified by these foremost proponents [Coltrane and Dolphy] of what is termed avant-garde music. I heard a good rhythm section . . . go to waste behind the nihilistic exercises of the two horns. . . . Coltrane and Dolphy seem intent on deliberately destroying [swing]. . . . They seem bent on pursuing an anarchistic course in their music that can but be termed anti-jazz.[19]

On the other hand, Coltrane's 1964 recording *A Love Supreme* was enormously successful; selling a half a million copies in its first year, it was hailed as a masterpiece. *A Love Supreme* represented the crystallization of the musical ideas Coltrane had developed since he had formed his quartet: modal improvisation, extended pedal points, and the "motivic cell" approach to solos. Moved by Coltrane's fervor and intensity, audiences received the recording as a profound, courageous statement of a man seeking musical and spiritual truth. *A Love Supreme* is a suite in four movements: "Acknowledgement," "Resolution," "Pursuance," and "Psalm."

An **ostinato** is a repeated melodic or harmonic idea that forms the basis for a section or an entire composition.

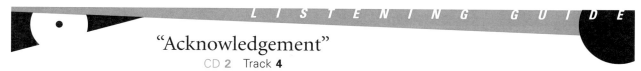

"Acknowledgement"
CD **2** Track **4**

John Coltrane: "Acknowledgement," from *A Love Supreme* (Coltrane), from the album of the same name. Impulse A-77. Englewood Cliffs, New Jersey, December 9, 1964. John Coltrane, tenor saxophone; McCoy Tyner, piano; Jimmy Garrison, bass; Elvin Jones, drums.

The following schema illustrates the sections of "Acknowledgement."

Intro	I	II	III	IV	V
Cadenza	Add bass Add drums Add piano	Tenor solo	Transposed motives	Vocal	Drop vocals Drop piano Drop drums Bass solo ending

Introduction

0:00   The piece begins with a sparsely accompanied, out-of-tempo cadenza.

I—Layered background texture

0:32   The bass begins a four-note ostinato that establishes the tempo, beat, and modal center F Dorian on the motive, F–A♭–F–B♭. This ostinato provides the thematic material, that is, its motivic cell.

At the drummer joins the bass, playing a relatively simple beat that grows more complex and insistent as the piece intensifies.

Tyner on piano follows with chords that reinforce the modal center. The rhythmic backdrop is complete.

II—Tenor saxophone solo

1:04   This solo is an immediate improvisation rather than a head statement. It centers on a few notes in F Dorian but begins to veer off the mode, which is perceived as a point of harmonic stability to which he returns.

1:44   The solo gradually becomes more elaborate and intense as Coltrane varies and explores the numerous rhythms and patterns he can make with the first few notes.

3:52   Here the solo achieves its greatest intensity, highlighting Coltrane's preference for the high notes of the tenor, as if he were reaching for unplayable notes to express the inexpressible.

II continued—Piano and bass

4:14   Coltrane begins to develop a three-note idea here. Tyner and Garrison sometimes follow Coltrane's harmonic excursions but just as often react freely to them, as if to illuminate rather than track his musical path.

III—Transposed motives

4:56 Coltrane transposes the motive to all twelve keys before returning to state it in unison with the bass—as shown here:

IV—Vocal

6:07 Coltrane and Garrison chant "a love supreme" along with the bass motive in a reprise of the four-note ostinato with added lyric. The transposing-motives section followed by the vocal provides a recapitulation of this minimal, but cogent, thematic material.

V—Instruments drop out; motive transposed to E♭

6:37 In the midst of the vocal section, the motive and general modal center abruptly drops down a whole step to E♭. One by one, the vocals, the piano, and the drums drop out, disassembling the background texture erected at the beginning of the piece, to leave the bass to finish alone.

As the next movement, "Resolution," begins, the bass continues to solo in E♭ Dorian. Thus the shift to E♭ Dorian provides a connecting link between the two movements and underscores Coltrane's conception of the album as an extended work rather than a collection of separate pieces.

Each part of the suite is equally compelling. (See the Listening Guide for more on "Acknowledgement.") "Resolution" proceeds with an eight-measure theme over a single harmony. Tyner's piano solo is a powerful statement that demonstrates his ability to create a sense of harmonic evolution over a single modal center. The third movement, "Pursuance," is a twelve-bar blues in B♭ minor, played over a blisteringly fast tempo. "Psalm" returns to the out-of-tempo playing of the opening, with Jones doubling on timpani. Coltrane biographer Lewis Porter has shown that the saxophone melody is in fact a wordless recitation to Coltrane's poem included in the liner notes to the album.[20]

The following points summarize Coltrane's mature modal jazz style:

▶ Free melody, usually not formed into square phrases

▶ Melodic connections based on development of motivic cells rather than voice leading, which was more prominent in his bop-oriented work

▶ Widely varying melodic rhythm, from long emotion-charged pitches to fast "sheets of sound"

▶ Concentration on upper range and extreme upper range of instrument

▶ Passionate expression

▶ Full, rich tone with raspy edge

▶ "Outside" playing, often featuring free chord-scale relationships

A Love Supreme, possibly Coltrane's most popular record, exemplifies his deeply felt spiritual commitment and confirms his intense religious faith.

COLTRANE AND THE AVANT-GARDE

Despite his musical advances and the great success of *A Love Supreme,* Coltrane was still interested in exploring new worlds. He had been supportive of the avant-garde players and took a strong interest in their expansion of musical resources. One of Coltrane's influences was tenor saxophonist Albert Ayler; another was Sun Ra's saxophonist John Gilmore, who provided a model for Coltrane's use of motivic cells. Among Coltrane's newly developing musical gestures were sounds that imitated human cries, an increased use of *multiphonics,* and an ability to create a "dialogue" within his solos by alternating different registers of the horn.

Coltrane's 1965 album *Ascension* unveiled a strong move to the jazz avant-garde. This was not completely surprising: The loose modal improvisation in *A Love Supreme* and other albums had foreshadowed Coltrane's evolution into free jazz. Although Ornette Coleman had been advocating jazz without tonal centers since the late 1950s, Coltrane had not rushed to embrace the controversial new style, but had instead progressed naturally to it.

In addition to his regular quartet, Coltrane's group on *Ascension* was augmented by a second bassist (Art Davis), two trumpeters (Dewey Johnson and Freddie Hubbard), two alto saxophonists (Marion Brown and John Tchicai), and two other tenor saxophonists (Pharoah Sanders and Archie Shepp). The group recorded two takes of the composition "Ascension." In its use of collective group improvisation it bore a superficial resemblance to Ornette Coleman's 1960 double quartet recording *Free Jazz,* but *Ascension* was much denser and more dissonant. For example, the relative transparency of Coleman's *Free Jazz* arose from a looser exchange of motivic ideas passed around among the soloists, while Coltrane's *Ascension* often relied on dense blocks of sound created by the seven horn players, generating what writer Ekkehard Jost called "sound fields."[21]

Multiphonics is a technique of producing more than one note at a time on a wind instrument. Using nonstandard fingering and appropriate embouchure, the player splits the air stream into two or more parts, thus producing a multinote "chordal" effect. The technique is difficult to control, may be strident, and is generally associated with avant-garde playing.

Sound fields result when coinciding melodic lines fuse into an indistinguishable web or mass of sound with irregular accentuation within each line.

Ascension used both group improvisation and individual solos. Despite its freedom and spontaneity, it contained some predetermined material, which helped provide overall direction. Throughout the eight collective improvisational sections, the group loosely invoked different modes. Additionally, the melodic idea in the first collective improvisation section—stated by Coltrane—was a motive comprising the same intervals as the motivic cell of "Acknowledgement" had.

Coltrane continued to align himself with the avant-garde. Saxophonist Pharoah Sanders joined the group in the fall of 1965, as did a second drummer, Rashied Ali. Coltrane's 1965 recordings *Om* and *Kulu se Mama* moved closer to totally free improvisation and away from the modal improvisations of previous years. Unhappy with the group's new directions, both Jones and Tyner left the band by the end of 1965. Coltrane's wife, harpist and pianist Alice Coltrane, replaced Tyner. Among Coltrane's final recordings were *Interstellar Space* (a duet with Rashied Ali) and *Expression*. Coltrane died of liver cancer on July 17, 1967, at age forty.

A case can be made that since the 1950s only Miles Davis has exerted a more powerful influence on jazz than John Coltrane has. Coltrane's intensity, technical skill, spirituality, and continual search for new sounds remain an inspiration to all jazz musicians. His legendary status was enhanced by his unfortunate early death, probably brought on by the effects of excessive drinking. Uniting non-Western musical models and modal jazz with his original mastery of bebop, John Coltrane created some of the most personal, powerful, and exciting jazz of the 1950s and 1960s.

Courtesy Morgan Collection

Cecil Taylor's dissonant, athletic pianism was and remains fiercely uncompromising.

Cecil Taylor

Because much of the free jazz of the 1960s—such as Ornette Coleman's seminal quartet and the music of Albert Ayler—did not include piano, it is interesting that one of the foremost proponents of free jazz, Cecil Taylor, was a pianist. Taylor's piano style was dissonant and athletic. His power, energy, and unlimited drive produced a fascinating and sometimes foreboding wall of dense sound blocks. Taylor's study of timpani as a youth may have influenced his rhythmic conception, because his keyboard concept was as much rhythmic as melodic, with rapid-fire clusters of hands, fists, forearms, and elbows. Throughout his career, Taylor has remained a controversial and fiercely uncompromising figure.

Taylor drew his wide-ranging musical ideas from both jazz and the European concert tradition. Among jazz pianists, he was initially attracted to the dense harmonies of Dave Brubeck and the linear clarity of Lennie Tristano before turning to Duke Ellington, Thelonious Monk, and Horace Silver. He was also inspired by the European composers Igor Stravinsky and Béla Bartók. Thus much of Taylor's music invoked the aesthetic of the European avant-garde alongside that of traditional jazz.

Born in 1929, Taylor was raised in the Corona section of Queens, New York, and began studying piano at age five. In 1952 he moved to Boston to attend the New England Conservatory of Music, where he studied piano and theory. At the conservatory, Taylor focused on the music of European composers, while exploring Ellington, Monk, and Silver on his own. He continued as a student for three years, but then left, bothered by the school's lack of attention to jazz and popular music.

Only gradually did Taylor reject convention and arrive at his mature style: His recordings prior to 1960 are considerably closer to the jazz mainstream than his later ones are. His first album as a leader was *Jazz Advance,* a trio and quartet recording from December 1955, with Steve Lacy on soprano saxophone, Buell Niedlinger on bass, and Dennis Charles on drums. The quartet still adhered to chorus structures; for example, Duke Ellington's "Azure" was given a fairly conventional reading, although both Taylor and Niedlinger occasionally wandered outside the harmonic structure. In other pre-1960 recordings, Taylor's harmonic language was often dissonant, but he continued to explore standards—Cole Porter's "Love for Sale" and "I Love Paris," for example. As a pianist, he maintained the usual technique of right-hand melody accompanied by left-hand chords.

In 1957 Taylor's engagement at the Five Spot and appearance at the Newport Jazz Festival enhanced his visibility. Unfortunately, commercial success was slow in coming, so Taylor had to work as a cook and dishwasher to support himself.

On his two Candid albums from 1960 and 1961, *Air* and *Lazy Afternoon,* Taylor's performances became decidedly less traditional. He clearly was redefining his overall approach and innovating a new conception of jazz piano. Joined by Archie Shepp, Niedlinger, and Charles, Taylor performed passages in dynamic free rhythm. Because of *Air* and *Lazy Afternoon,* Taylor won the *Down Beat* "New Star" award for pianists. Ironically, at the time he was unemployed.

Taylor's Unit Structures

The title track from *Unit Structures* was sectional and highly organized; it showed Taylor's independence from the jazz mainstream. The work was conceived in five large sections, entitled "Anacrusis," "Plain 1," "Area 1," "Plain 2," and "Area 2." Following "Anacrusis," which lasted less than a minute, "Plain 1" comprised fifteen differentiated "units"—brief sections lasting anywhere from about five to forty seconds. Some of the material in these units was precomposed, with the instruments introduced in varying combinations. At times the horns played in a loose unison; at other times the instruments interacted polyphonically, with fluctuating tempos.

Included in the work were primary and subsidiary themes that were later reprised.

The complex organization of *Unit Structures* showed Taylor rejecting not only the traditional harmonic and rhythmic principles of the jazz mainstream but also its usual methods for generating form. It was a radical repudiation of both the repeating chorus structure of traditional jazz and the "head-solos-head" organization that long dominated the music. In place of traditional methods of determining form, in *Unit Structures* we find the following:

▶ Various "unit sections" providing an overall large-scale shape

▶ Predetermined motivic or textural ideas replacing conventional harmonic progressions

▶ A separation and independence of sections, which undermined traditional progression and development

Along with saxophonist Jimmy Lyons, who successfully translated some of Charlie Parker's bebop rhetoric into a free jazz context, *Unit Structures* also featured Ken McIntyre on bass clarinet and oboe. The inclusion of instruments not associated with the jazz mainstream was also typical of Taylor's approach.

Because Taylor's evolving stylistic direction began to conflict with the traditional role of the drummer as timekeeper, Taylor replaced Dennis Charles with Sunny Murray (b. 1937). Murray, who remained with Taylor until 1964, tended to avoid steady meter, instead projecting a fluid and kinetic style that matched Taylor's free approach to the keyboard.

In 1966 Taylor recorded two albums for Blue Note, *Unit Structures* and *Conquistador,* with two bassists—Henry Grimes and Alan Silva—and drummer Andrew Cyrille, who worked with Taylor for the decade 1965–1975. Like his predecessor Sunny Murray, Cyrille conformed readily to full-group improvisation while downplaying pulse and meter. (See the box "Taylor's *Unit Structures.*")

Taylor won increased recognition during the 1970s. He taught at the University of Wisconsin–Madison and at Antioch College in Ohio, where he recorded his solo piano album *Indent.* During the decade he was awarded a Guggenheim Fellowship and an honorary doctorate from his old school, the New England Conservatory of Music. Taylor also performed for Jimmy Carter's 1979 White House Jazz Day. His solo piano recording, *Silent Tongues,* won the 1974 *Down Beat* "Jazz Album of the Year" in its international critics poll. In discussing his composition "Abyss" from *Silent Tongues,* Taylor pointed out the plan at work in his conception of the different registers of the piano:

> Just in the keyboard element I can, if I want to, have four or five bodies of sound existing in a duality of dimension. In other words, I might decide to have three or four different voices or choirs existing and moving with different weight propelling their ongoing motion . . . so that one can have—say that two or three octaves below middle C is the area of the abyss, and the middle range is the surface of the earth, the astral being the upper range—you have three constituted bodies also outlined by a specific range, a specific function of how the innards of these groups relate to themselves and then to each other. You have, therefore, what starts out as a linear voice becoming within itself like horizontal because of the plurality of exchange between the voices.[22]

Taylor has continued to record and perform with his ensemble, the Cecil Taylor Unit, whose membership has remained somewhat fluid. Alto saxophonist Jimmy Lyons, who began playing with Taylor in 1960, was still with the group in 1978 for their recording *Idut,* which also included trumpeter Raphé Malik, violinist Ramsey Ameen, bassist Sirone, and drummer Ronald Shannon Jackson.

Over the decades, audiences have found Taylor's music difficult or impenetrable. As one writer observed, an initial unprepared encounter with Taylor's music usually causes complete confusion.[23] Nevertheless, even the unprepared respond to the music's intensity and energy.

Chicago: AACM, the Art Ensemble of Chicago, and Anthony Braxton

By the later 1920s, the so-called Second City of Chicago was eclipsed by New York as the country's jazz center. Nevertheless, Chicago's jazz scene has remained active and was especially influential during the 1950s. Tenor saxophonist Sonny Rollins took the first of his extended sabbaticals there in 1955. Saxophonist Johnny Griffin, pianist Ahmad Jamal, and Sun Ra's band were based in the city. Additionally, several young

Memphis jazz players came to Chicago to study, including pianist Harold Mabern, saxophonist George Coleman, trumpeter Booker Little, and alto saxophonist Frank Strozier. Drummer Walter Perkins's group, MJT + 3, employed at different times many Chicago-based players, including pianist Muhal Richard Abrams. Abrams became instrumental in creating the Association for the Advancement of Creative Musicians (AACM), a school and cooperative on the South Side that became the center of Chicago's avant-garde jazz scene.

Although Abrams began as a hard bop pianist, he gradually turned his attention toward free jazz, forming the Experimental Band in 1961, a rehearsal group that met weekly. By 1965, the band evolved into the AACM, an organization that sponsored concerts and performances, and—most importantly—fostered self-determination for musicians. In allowing musicians to be independent of commercial promoters and agents, it promoted artistic and creative goals. Later, the group also produced radio shows and brought jazz education to inner-city schools.

The liner notes to alto saxophonist Joseph Jarman's recording *As If It Were the Seasons* (1968) described the aims of the organization:

> The Association for the Advancement of Creative Musicians, a non-profit organization chartered by the State of Illinois, was formed... when a group of Musicians and Composers in the Chicago area saw an emergent need to expose and showcase original Music which, under the existing establishment (promoters, agents, etc.) was not receiving its just due. A prime direction of our Association has been to provide an atmosphere conducive to serious Music and the performance of new, unrecorded compositions. The Music presented by the various groups in our Association is jazz-oriented.[24]

The music was indeed jazz oriented. It was particularly indebted to the free jazz movement, as Jarman's tribute "Ornette" suggested, but it was also new in other ways. Jarman's own background in drama inspired him to add extramusical, theatrical elements to the performances. On Jarman's "Non-cognitive Aspects to the City" (from his recording *Song For*), he recited his own spoken poetry following a prelude consisting of fragmented melodic ideas and a drum solo.

Along with poetry and social statement, much of the music of the AACM explored timbre, tone color, nontempered intonation, collective improvisation, and the use of unusual instruments. It also relied on humor and surprise. Trumpeter Lester Bowie's earliest experiences were with R&B bands and the tent shows of an itinerant carnival troupe, experiences he brought to bear on his work with the AACM. His album *Numbers 1 and 2* used gongs, police sirens, and nonsense syllables sung in falsetto. In it, after someone yells "Ring the bell, man," a cowbell is played furiously. In search of freedom, the AACM players were clearly seeking a release from the conventions of traditional jazz. As Bowie noted in the liner notes to *Numbers 1 and 2*:

> Jazz, at first apart from this struggle for renewal in the western world, has come to face these "freedoms." But there is only one true freedom for us, and that is what this music seeks. The signs of the revolution permeate most of jazz today, and in Chicago there are young musicians who, desiring freedom, are beginning to know how it is created.[25]

Bowie's *Numbers 1 and 2* was made with saxophonists Jarman and Roscoe Mitchell and bassist Malachi Favors, who together formed the four principals of the

Art Ensemble of Chicago. Pursuing the path begun by the early AACM recordings, the Art Ensemble of Chicago relied heavily not only on free, collective improvisation but also on theater: They incorporated dramatic sketches, poetry, costumes and makeup, dance, pantomime, comedy, and parody in their performances. The group moved to Paris in 1969, recording albums for the French label BYG, including several film scores.

Rejecting specialists' roles as performers, the members of the Art Ensemble of Chicago each played several instruments. When they moved to Europe, the group took about 500 instruments with them. On recordings such as *A Jackson in Your House,* the group mixed comical pastiche—mock Dixieland and swing—with sound explorations and free improvisations that were in part a rejection of the showy virtuosity of bebop. The recordings the group made during their eighteen months overseas revealed the varied instruments, many of them percussion, handled by the performers. A list of their instruments compiled by Ekkehard Jost shows this breadth:

* Lester Bowie: flugelhorn, trumpet, cowhorn, bass drum

* Roscoe Mitchell: soprano, alto, and bass saxophone, clarinet, flute, cymbals, gongs, conga drums, steel drum, logs, bells, siren, whistles

* Joseph Jarman: soprano, alto, and tenor saxophones, clarinet, oboe, bassoon, flutes, marimba, vibraphone, guitar, conga drums, bells, gongs, whistles, sirens

* Malachi Favors: double bass, Fender bass, banjo, zither, log drum, other percussion instruments[26]

The group added drummer Don Moye, whose first recording with the band was on the soundtrack to *Les Stances à Sophie.* Moye increased the huge arsenal of percussion instruments and joined the others in wearing African hats, costumes, and makeup. The group continued to record after resettling in the United States in 1971, although the players also began to concentrate on their own projects. Their recordings for ECM records included *Nice Guys* and *Urban Bushman,* the latter a double-LP live recording that showed the dramatic breadth of the group. The group has continued to work together—involved in tours and projects that take them throughout the world—and have stayed together for more than thirty years.

Whereas the Art Ensemble of Chicago celebrated African elements in their music and theater, the music of another Chicagoan tilted toward European formal organization. Alto saxophonist Anthony Braxton (b. 1945) joined the AACM in 1966. Braxton's earliest influences were cool jazz altoists Paul Desmond and Lee Konitz, but after joining the AACM he began studying Ornette Coleman and John Coltrane, seeking in part to translate Coltrane's raw expressiveness to the alto. He also studied the techniques of avant-garde concert-music composers such as John Cage and Karlheinz Stockhausen.

Along with Leroy Jenkins and Leo Smith, Braxton formed the Creative Construction Company in 1967. The group explored free improvisational methods on Braxton's *Three Compositions,* recorded the following year. In 1968 Braxton made *For Alto,* his first unaccompanied alto saxophone recording. Following in the footsteps of the Art Ensemble of Chicago, the Creative Construction Company traveled to Paris in 1969. The group was not particularly well received—in part, thought Braxton, because they lacked a rhythm section.

However, Braxton later teamed up with the stellar rhythm section of pianist Chick Corea, bassist Dave Holland, and drummer Barry Altschul. The new group, Circle, recorded a concert in Paris for ECM records in February 1971. Braxton's improvisations were masterpieces of free interaction, weaving together multiphonics, unusual sonic and timbral resources, and pointillism. When Corea broke up the group in 1971, Braxton formed his own band, combining the rhythm section of Circle with Kenny Wheeler on trumpet. Braxton's later recordings for Arista records in the 1970s—*New York Fall 1974, Five Pieces 1975,* and *For Trio*—incorporated echoes of bebop, combined notated and improvised music, and brought together free collective improvisation, individual solos, and written ensemble passages.

As a result of his many activities, Braxton became one of the leading figures of the avant-garde. In addition to his jazz work, Braxton has written for band and large orchestra, sometimes with elements of theatricality that recall the early work of the AACM. His compositions often avoid conventional titles and use instead geometric designs, arrangements of numbers and letters, and human and animal figures. Braxton has served as a member of the faculty of Wesleyan University in Middletown, Connecticut, for many years.

Other Avant-Garde Stylists

BLACK ARTISTS GROUP AND THE WORLD SAXOPHONE QUARTET

Inspired by artistic independence, self-sufficiency, and many of the ideals of black nationalism—the same goals that helped launch the AACM—other cities formed creative arts organizations that embraced the avant-garde. A particularly successful group of free jazz players in St. Louis formed a cooperative organization in 1968, the Black Artists Group (BAG). Like the AACM, the BAG tutored young musicians, sponsored musical and multimedia performances, and received support from government and state grants. Although the BAG folded in 1972, three of its former members—alto saxophonists Oliver Lake and Julius Hemphill and baritone saxophonist Hamiet Bluiett—formed the World Saxophone Quartet (WSQ) in 1976. The fourth member was a Californian, tenor saxophonist David Murray.

The WSQ was unique—a versatile ensemble that turned the absence of a rhythm section to their advantage. Although the players were influenced by the free jazz of Ornette Coleman and Albert Ayler, they also relied heavily on both composed music and traditional styles of improvisation. The four saxophonists produced a remarkable cross section of twentieth-century music, incorporating elements of bebop, swing, and collective improvisation into an eclectic mix that ranged from the sound of the Ellington saxophone section to that of Stravinsky-style ballet. Their album *Live in Zurich* demonstrated their diversity, combining swing and mambo in "Hattie Wall," bebop in "Funny Paper," and French classical saxophone quartet music in "Touchic." For improvisational sections, one or two saxophones would create an ostinato figure over which another improvised.

Bluiett's muscular, sometimes raucous baritone provided the underpinning for the group. Of the two alto saxophonists, Lake was initially influenced by bebop altoist Jackie McLean, but later rejected the predictability of the style. Hemphill maintained a cleaner, purer alto sound. Murray was strongly eclectic, able to draw upon the entire history of tenor saxophone playing.

A long-lived group, the World Saxophone Quartet has continued to perform in recent years. They are highly effective in concert, with marked variety of programming and a lighthearted, engaging stage manner. Recent projects of the WSQ have included other musicians, especially drummers and African percussionists.

SUN RA

A unique jazz personality, Sun Ra led a legendary big band called the Myth-Science Solar Arkestra—one among several of its varied, but similar names. Established in the mid-1950s, the Arkestra played "intergalactic music" that painted "pictures of infinity." It also contained numerous musicians loyal to Sun Ra, the music, and its uniquely mystical ambience. With the players and audiences chanting "Space is the Place," the band's performances were transcendental. As his reputation continues to grow, Sun Ra has emerged as one of the most colorful and discussed pioneers of the avant-garde.

Sun Ra has made wide-ranging contributions to the avant-garde. He was one of the first jazz performers to use electric keyboards and synthesizers and was one of the few big-band leaders to encourage extensive free improvisation. The group was especially creative with percussion, exploring a large palette of sound colors with timpani, celesta, bells, chimes, and other instruments less often heard in jazz. The emphasis on unusual timbre extended to nonpercussive instruments as well: Sun Ra's saxophonists doubled on such instruments as piccolo, oboe, bassoon, and bass clarinet. As alto saxophonist Marion Brown noted, "Sun Ra plays the piano, but his real instrument is the orchestra."[27] In many ways, Sun Ra, with both idiosyncratic arranging techniques and the long-term tenure of many of his players, was something of an avant-garde Duke Ellington.

Sun Ra, however, remained an underground phenomenon, never achieving the mainstream success of Ellington. He was born Herman Blount in Birmingham, Alabama, in 1914 and moved to Chicago in the mid-1940s, working as the arranger-pianist Le Sony'r Ra in a variety theater. Between 1946 and 1947 he played piano for bandleader Fletcher Henderson. He then formed his own band; among his musicians were tenor saxophonist John Gilmore, who became a long-standing associate and who would later influence John Coltrane. His first recordings from the mid-1950s with the Myth-Science Solar Arkestra (*Sun Song* and *Sound of Joy*) merged Ellington-like ensemble colors with an idiosyncratic hard bop orientation. They featured unusual sounds, such as the timpani solos in "A Street

Courtesy Morgan Collection

Shown here at an electric keyboard and clad in exotic garb, avant-garde bandleader Sun Ra was one of the few big-band leaders to allow free improvisation.

from Hell." The band also included timpani on "A Call for All Demons," which hilariously combined atonal improvising with a mambo beat.

The Arkestra relocated from Chicago to New York in 1960. Once settled, the group continued to rehearse prodigiously, with all of the band members becoming multi-instrumentalists, especially on percussion. As the band moved decisively toward free jazz, the players collectively improvised, often over a background of dense percussion. Indeed, some compositions focused primarily on percussion.

In general, improvised solos in the Arkestra often used modal or tonal centers rather than standard harmonic progressions. On some of the recordings from the 1960s, such as *The Heliocentric Worlds of Sun Ra*, there seemed to be no prewritten music; only the general formal outline was predetermined, invoked by cues from Sun Ra.

In the 1970s, the Arkestra relocated again—this time to Philadelphia—and began using the city as a base for concert performance. Their 1976 appearance on the television show "Saturday Night Live" increased the band's exposure. Since then, the group has also performed works of Duke Ellington, Fletcher Henderson, and Thelonious Monk.

The use of microtonal melodies and electronic effects enhanced the space-age aura of Sun Ra's music, as did his flowing robes and headdresses. Sun Ra's live performances recalled the "happenings" of the 1960s, complete with the psychedelic paraphernalia. Sun Ra died in 1993.

ERIC DOLPHY

Perhaps no saxophonist has managed the borderline between hard bop and free jazz as convincingly as Eric Dolphy has. In parlance that was new at the time, Dolphy was equally convincing at playing both "inside" and "outside." That is, he could move "outside" the harmonic progressions—with pitches not part of the given chord or mode—then deftly return "inside" to take up the harmonies. Dolphy's album titles, *Outward Bound* and *Out to Lunch*, punned on the notion of "outside" playing.

Dolphy, who was born in Los Angeles in 1928, performed on alto saxophone, flute, and bass clarinet. On alto, Dolphy developed an original sound, characterized by wide intervallic leaps, unusual phrasing, and the use of glissandi, smears, and untempered intonation. In contrast to more conventional players, Dolphy's rhythmic conception tended to be freer, that is, less tied to the beat. His influences ranged from Ornette Coleman to African and Indian music. He even attempted, he said, to imitate the music of birds.[28] His flute playing was more traditional; Dolphy often turned to the more pastoral instrument for jazz standards, as he did in his recording of "You Don't Know What Love Is" from *Last Date* (1964).

As his work with John Coltrane on "India" (from *Impressions*) and with Ornette Coleman on *Free Jazz* revealed, Dolphy was an outstanding virtuoso on bass clarinet, helping to generate interest in an instrument fairly new to jazz settings. In addition to these recordings and his own, Dolphy appeared on several other significant albums with bassist Charles Mingus, trumpeter Booker Little, and arranger Oliver Nelson.

Dolphy's made his first important musical alliance when he joined the quartet of Chico Hamilton in 1958. He recorded *Gongs East* with Hamilton, a West Coast drummer (discussed in Chapter 8), whose ensemble was notable for including a cellist. After moving to New York in 1959, Dolphy began to work with Charles

Mingus; this association lasted until Dolphy's untimely death in 1964. Together, Dolphy and Mingus recorded an astounding duet, "What Love," in which the two players floated in and out of tempo, creating a conversation between Mingus's bass and Dolphy's bass clarinet that mimicked human speech. Dolphy's alto solo on Mingus's "Hora Decubitis" bordered on free jazz (see Chapter 8 and CD 1, Track 22): The solo at times ignored and at other times projected the harmonic progression of the twelve-bar blues.

Dolphy's work on Ornette Coleman's trailblazing *Free Jazz* solidified his reputation as a major presence in the jazz avant-garde; even so, he never abandoned more traditional settings. Amazingly, on the same day that he recorded *Free Jazz*— December 21, 1960—Dolphy also recorded his own album *Far Cry*, with a standard rhythm section consisting of Ron Carter on bass, Jaki Byard on piano, and Roy Haynes on drums. Several of the compositions paid tribute to Parker, such as Byard's "Ode to Charlie Parker" and the twelve-bar blues "Mrs. Parker of K. C." On "Mrs. Parker," the rhythm section experimented with breaking up the time for the first chorus of each solo, creating rhythmic and harmonic conflicts before moving into a 4/4 swing. Dolphy's unaccompanied alto solo on the popular standard "Tenderly" showed his ability to underscore and outline the harmonies of the tune. (See the box "Eric Dolphy and Booker Little.")

As discussed earlier, Dolphy's alliance with the John Coltrane Quartet between 1961 and 1962 was controversial, eliciting the negative label of "anti-jazz" from critics who thought the solos too long, anarchistic, and unswinging. Of course, Coltrane had a more positive view: He insisted that Dolphy's inclusion in the group "had a broadening effect on us. There are a lot of things we try now that we never tried before. We're playing things that are freer than before."[29] Dolphy recorded *Live at the Village Vanguard* and *Impressions* with Coltrane and toured Europe with the group at the end of 1961.

Dolphy was also involved in third-stream and twentieth-century concert music; for example, he performed on Gunther Schuller's 1960 recording *Abstractions*.

Eric Dolphy and Booker Little

Far Cry featured Booker Little, a trumpeter who maintained a close musical relationship with Dolphy until Little's tragic death in 1961 at age twenty-three. A hard bop player from Memphis, Little began his career as a devotee of Clifford Brown. He recorded his first albums with the Max Roach Quintet before he was twenty years old. Roach even recorded some of Little's compositions with a pianoless quintet that included Ray Draper on tuba. Little's "Larry LaRue," from Roach's *Words, Not Deeds*, was harmonically complex, with the melody—scored for trumpet, tenor saxophone, and tuba— frequently moving in parallel motion, a com-

positional technique that Little often brought to his writing. Little's playing was technically polished, lyrical, and creative.

Dolphy took part in Little's own recording for Candid records, *Out Front*. The two also collaborated on a gig at the Five Spot, which was recorded and released in a series of albums that included Mal Waldron on piano, Richard Davis on bass, and Ed Blackwell on drums. On the Five Spot recordings, the influence of Dolphy on Little is clear, as Little often adopted Dolphy's flurry-of-notes approach. Little's compositions employed complex and unusual forms.

His interest in the European avant-garde led to a performance of Edgard Varèse's *Density 21.5* for unaccompanied flute at the Ojai Music Festival in California. After touring Europe with Mingus in 1964, Dolphy elected to remain abroad rather than return to the United States. Shortly after, he died in Berlin from a heart attack brought on by diabetes.

Although critics often focused on the radical elements in Dolphy's playing, his musical collaborators considered Dolphy's breadth enormous and maintained that he was in complete control of all the musical elements. Pianist Jaki Byard remembered:

> Eric's freedom in playing and writing is never chaos. He always makes sense, and those critics who call him disorganized should first have the chords and the overall forms of his tunes written out for them before they make that kind of accusation. Eric is very well organized, but it's not the kind of organization that is immediately apparent to people who are accustomed to more conventional ideas of form.[30]

The jazz avant-garde of the 1960s, like the jazz styles of earlier eras, has inspired numerous artists and innovative approaches in our own day. After consideration of the more mainstream musical currents of the 1960s in Chapter 10 and the pop-fusion jazz of the late 1960s and 1970s in Chapter 11, we shall return to the avant-garde to examine its legacy.

Free Jazz Styles

TIMBRE

- ▶ Emphasis often on hard-edged, tough sound
- ▶ Use of entire range of instrument but upper range more prominent
- ▶ Wide variety of attacks and articulations
- ▶ Vocal sounds—cries, shrieks, etc.—used
- ▶ Extended techniques such as multiphonics on individual instruments emphasized

PHRASING

- ▶ Extremely irregular

RHYTHM

- ▶ Free use of extreme rhythms, from held notes to "sheets of sound" effects
- ▶ Syncopations
- ▶ Often lack of steady pulse

THEMATIC CONTINUITY

- ▶ Usually motivic

CHORD-SCALE RELATIONS

- ▶ Outside playing, if a tonal center exists at all

LARGE-SCALE COHERENCE

- ▶ Gestural, motivic, sometimes based on set theoretical principles

Questions and Topics for Discussion

1. How did the 1960s avant-garde overturn traditional practices in jazz? Cite factors that include instruments, repertory, melody, harmony, and rhythm.

2. How did the social movements that called for integration and the greater acceptance of blacks into mainstream society affect avant-garde jazz works? Can the word *freedom* be applied to both musical and political relationships? How?

3. Who were the principal musicians of the jazz avant-garde? How did these musicians differ in terms of their level of political involvement? Was this evident in their music?

4. What were John Coltrane's three stylistic periods? In a brief biographical outline, show how his musical evolution paralleled his spiritual and professional life.

5. How did free jazz resemble the New Orleans and Chicago Dixieland jazz of the 1920s?

Key Terms

Free jazz (avant-garde, New Thing)

Harmolodics

Harmonic superimposition

microtones

Motivic (thematic) cells

Multiphonics

Nontempered intonation

Ostinato

Pentatonic scale (set)

Sheets of sound

Sound fields

The Vietnam War and the space race between the United States and the former Soviet Union dominated headlines in the 1960s. In October 1957, the Soviets had launched *Sputnik I*—the first satellite in space—and in April 1961 sent a capsule carrying Yuri Gagarin—the first man in space. Spurred by President John Kennedy, NASA intensified its efforts, and on July 20, 1969, Neil Armstrong landed the *Apollo 11* module on the moon. Meanwhile, 58,000 U.S. service personnel died in the Vietnam War between 1961 and 1973. Here, in an interesting conjunction of the two themes, Neil Armstrong greets troops in Vietnam on Christmas 1969. The soldier in the crowd is waving a copy of the *Moon Flight Atlas,* which Armstrong signed.

MAINSTREAM JAZZ IN THE 1960s

10

IN THIS CHAPTER, we follow the evolution of the relatively mainstream jazz styles from the 1950s into the 1960s. No artist had a greater impact on the development of jazz in these decades than Miles Davis.

Miles Davis in the Sixties

Davis flowed on a flood tide of activity into the the 1960s, garnering immense critical success as his band evolved into one of the most notable groups in jazz. As we saw in Chapter 8, his hard bop quintet and sextet in the late 1950s featured the dynamic saxophonists John Coltrane and Cannonball Adderley. On the collaborations *Porgy and Bess* and *Sketches of Spain*, Davis's spare lyricism acted as a foil to arranger Gil Evans's lush orchestrations and dense harmonies. Finally, Davis's 1959 recording *Kind of Blue*, spurred by the poetic pianism of Bill Evans, set the standard for modal improvisation.

For the next several years, Davis's group underwent several changes of personnel. Coltrane's departure in 1960 was an enormous loss for Davis. After trying saxophonist Sonny Stitt, whose alto style was closely derived from Charlie Parker's, and tenor player Jimmy Heath, Davis eventually hired Hank Mobley on tenor. With Art Blakey and Horace Silver, Mobley (1930–1986) had helped to found the Jazz Messengers. He performed with Davis from 1961 to 1962, then continued his distinguished career through the 1960s and beyond. On Davis's recording *Someday My Prince Will Come*, Mobley displayed a more conventional rhythmic and harmonic sensibility than his predecessor had, avoiding Coltrane's searching intensity and "sheets of sound" technique.

Along with Mobley, Davis used Jamaican pianist Wynton Kelly (1931–1971). Kelly's improvisations displayed a sparkling sense of swing, heard especially on twelve-bar blues compositions such as "No Blues," from *Miles Davis at Carnegie Hall* (1961). Although his harmonies were typically less lush and dense than those of Bill Evans, in ballads such as "Old Folks" from *Someday My Prince Will Come* some Evans-style voicings could be heard beneath Davis's poignant, muted trumpet. These two sides to Kelly—his exuberant, joyful swing and his sophisticated harmonic sense—earned him high praise from Davis, who described his work as "a combination of Red Garland and Bill Evans."[1] Davis also praised Kelly's accompanying ability: His rhythmically subtle and creative comping anticipated and complemented the soloist.

In the early 1960s, Davis was only in his mid-thirties, but he found himself in the odd position of seeming to be old-fashioned. Ornette Coleman, Cecil Taylor, and Eric Dolphy were stirring up the jazz world with their challenging and controversial innovations. At the same time that Coleman was launching his radical *Free Jazz,* Davis's repertory remained rooted in thirty-two–bar standards, twelve-bar blues, and ballads. Davis's rhythm section of Kelly on piano, Jimmy Cobb on drums, and Paul Chambers on bass was a fine, swinging unit, but the group projected a conventional hard bop approach.

A Ron Carter (CD 2, Track 5) publicity shot from CTI Records.

This soon changed. In 1963 Davis formed the nucleus of a group that would stay together for the next five years. His most dramatic move was to revitalize his rhythm section by taking on younger players. On piano, he hired twenty-three-year-old Herbie Hancock, who had been working with trumpeter Donald Byrd and recording under his own name as a leader for Blue Note. Ron Carter, an accomplished classical and jazz bassist, left trumpeter Art Farmer to join Davis. Davis's most astonishing choice was an incredibly young drummer from Boston, Tony Williams, who joined the group at age seventeen. Despite his youth, Williams already showed flawless technique, consistent creativity, and fierce drive. Even on their earliest recordings, the new Davis rhythm section was stunning. Hancock, Carter, and Williams interacted at nearly telepathic levels, bringing fresh, free interpretations to Davis's traditional repertory.

Given the group's unparalleled polish and technical aplomb, listeners often missed their high level of creativity. On one of their earliest recordings—Victor Feldman's "Joshua," from *Seven Steps to Heaven*—the rhythm section shifted seamlessly between the 4/4 meter of the A section and 3/4 meter of the B section. When playing jazz standards during their live performances from 1963 to 1964, the rhythm section experimented further, superimposing different meters above the standard meter of the composition. On ballad performances, such as "My Funny Valentine" and "Stella By Starlight," the three players rapidly shifted moods and tempos, freely interpreting the harmonic structure to create what sounded like a multimovement suite. Drummer Tony Williams would lay out (stop playing) for stretches at a time, return playing the tempo, then move effortlessly into double time. The group negotiated blistering tempos, propelled by Williams's intense drumming.

Williams's interest in the jazz avant-garde had a major impact on the group, as Hancock later acknowledged:

> Tony Williams turned me on to different rhythms, overlapping this and that. Tony was really into Paul Bley, Gary Peacock . . . Ornette [Coleman]—like I never paid that much attention to Ornette when he first came out, but Tony got me interested in Ornette and got me to the point where I could get into it.[2]

Although the rhythm section was in place, Davis was unable to settle quickly on a tenor saxophone player. The recordings from 1963 and1964 featured George Coleman, a strong, assertive player from Memphis who was too conservative for Davis's musical conception. On Tony Williams's recommendation, Coleman was replaced by Sam Rivers, whom Williams had known in Boston. Rivers remained for a short time, appearing on the recording *Miles in Tokyo*. Finally, in the fall of 1964, Davis hired the saxophonist he had been after for several years, Wayne Shorter. With this final addition, Davis's group was set. "Getting Wayne made me feel real good," remembered Davis, "because with him I just knew some great music was going to happen. And it did; it happened real soon."[3]

Davis had been trying to lure Shorter into his band since 1960, but Shorter was reluctant to leave Art Blakey's Jazz Messengers. When he finally joined Davis, Shorter began contributing numerous compositions, significantly altering the sound and approach of the group. On tenor, he owed his tone quality and musical ideas in part to Coltrane, although Shorter's melodies were more oblique and filled with space.

With Davis, Shorter, Hancock, Carter, and Williams on board, the group was now stabilized. They tended to emphasize popular standards in live performance and Shorter's compositions in the studio. An outstanding example of their live work is *The Complete Live at the Plugged Nickel,* which, although recorded in December 1965, was not released in the United States until the 1990s. On it we can hear the Davis quintet pushing the envelope on the performance of well-known jazz and popular standards. For example, on "Stella By Starlight," recorded in the first set of December 23, Davis's solo maintains the form of the tune, but just barely. Hancock deviates radically from the changes of the song and Williams goes into double, then quadruple time. On the song's C section, a consistency of motivic reference establishes that the band is in fact following the form. Shorter's solo, which follows Davis's, is even more abstract.

Shorter's compositions were also unusual. Avoiding the standard harmonic clichés of the hard bop idiom, he instead explored unusual voicings and progressions. The melodic lines of his compositions lay sometimes outside the bop tradition, too; for example, "E.S.P." (from the album of the same name) and "Masquallero" (from *Nefertiti*) emphasized the ambiguous interval of a perfect fourth. Shorter's composition "Nefertiti" was made even more radical by its reversal of the roles of horn soloists and rhythm section: The trumpet and saxophone merely restated the slow-moving sixteen-bar melody throughout, providing a static obbligato, while the "accompanying instruments"—the piano, bass, and drums—improvised beneath, providing the active role. "Footprints," a well-known tune from *Miles Smiles,* was a minor blues composition in 3/4, which alternated with several bars in fast 4/4. Later in the piece, Williams and Carter maintained a complex 4-against-3 pulse.

"E.S.P."

CD **2** Track **5**

Miles Davis Quintet: "E.S.P." (Shorter), from *E.S.P.* Columbia CS 9150.
Los Angeles, January 20, 1965. Miles Davis, trumpet; Wayne Shorter, composer, tenor saxophone;
Herbie Hancock, piano; Ron Carter, bass; Tony Williams, drums.

"E.S.P." has a straightforward, thirty-two–bar, ABAC form, although it is difficult to follow during the solos by Shorter, Davis, and Hancock because the chord changes are opaque and the quintet avoids articulating the form clearly. As such, it is a concentrated example of the sound of Davis's 1960s quintet, with its open, freewheeling character. Yet, in contrast to the free jazz discussed in Chapter 9, the piece does indeed follow a given set of changes, which are constantly elaborated.

Head—32 bars, 1 chorus, in ABAC

0:00   Davis and Shorter state the up-tempo head in unison. The basic identity of the tune is the perfect fourth, as shown by the pitch sequence of the head's opening phrase: C–G–D–G–C–G–D–C–G. (Use of the perfect fourth is also common in modal compositions.) The B and C sections of the head are quite similar melodically, with an alteration at the end of the C section for the cadence. The tune also ends with two fourths: a downward E♭–B♭ followed by an upward A–D.

Shorter tenor solo—2 choruses

0:29   Shorter's fine tenor solo begins obliquely, putting space in unusual places. Tony Williams keeps time on the ride cymbal, while playing inventive fills that complement Shorter's ideas.

1:03   The second chorus, measures 9–11, alludes to the head with an arpeggiation that spans the range of the tenor from high to low.

Davis trumpet solo—6 choruses + 4 bars

1:23   This is an extremely dexterous solo by Davis, who sometimes has been accused of lacking technical facility. With great agility, he builds to several climaxes. Williams and Hancock accompany him brilliantly, rarely articulating the formal boundaries of the tune but always remaining in step with Davis's emotional story. Davis builds to several satisfying climaxes as the group stretches the form to the breaking point.

Hancock piano solo—2 choruses (beginning in the 4th bar)

4:04   Hancock's solo is typically excellent. In the left hand, he often uses three-note chords that are voiced in fourths, or a three-note chord built with a tritone between the lower two notes and perfect fourth between the upper two.

4:40–4:45   Listen for the interplay between Hancock and bassist Ron Carter; Hancock plays a bass note in answer to Carter's emphasized low note.

Reprise of the ABAC head—1 chorus

4:54   The tune is stated as in the opening, with a prolonged final chord.

Although Shorter wrote the majority of compositions for the quintet, all of the members contributed tunes. Most of them maintained a conventional role for the rhythm section, keeping a 4/4 swing feel with walking bass. But often Hancock would stop backing the trumpet or saxophone solos for long stretches of time, which rendered the harmony ambiguous and brought about the group's distinctive open sound. In his own solos, Hancock often omitted the punctuating chords in his left hand entirely, playing only long right-hand melodic lines.

Hancock must have been surprised when, at a Davis recording session toward the end of 1967, he was confronted with an unknown instrument:

> I walked into the studio and I didn't see any acoustic piano. I saw this little box sitting there, this little toy, so I said, "Miles, where's the piano?" He said . . . "I want you to play this.". . . So I tested it and I heard this sound—this big mellow sound coming out. . . . I liked it right away.[4]

The instrument was a Fender Rhodes electric piano. Davis had been intrigued by the electric piano ever since hearing Josef Zawinul play a Wurlitzer electric piano in the Cannonball Adderley band. Davis's first recording with Fender Rhodes was the 1968 release *Miles in the Sky,* and his continued use of the instrument signaled the onset of an inexorable trend. Thereafter, Davis continued to bring about a gradual shift in jazz to rhythms influenced by rock, pop, and soul music. For Davis fans finally acclimated to the innovations of the 1963–1968 quintet, this newer rock-influenced music was difficult to swallow, but for Davis, it was only the beginning. With this move to rock and funk came a shift to electric instruments. These became more and more common on Davis's records, although he continued to use acoustic bass, both on *Miles in the Sky* and the following *Filles de Kilimanjaro.* The latter album also included pianist Chick Corea on electric keyboard.

Davis's *In a Silent Way* was even more radical, presenting music that was both harmonically and rhythmically far simpler than Davis's previous work. The riff-oriented album featured three electric keyboardists—Herbie Hancock, Chick Corea, and Josef Zawinul—as well as British guitarist John McLaughlin. In place of the usual recorded performances of individual compositions, *In a Silent Way* was assembled by producer Teo Macero, who edited the studio sessions to create two compositions, each of which took up the entire side of an LP. "In a Silent Way/It's About That Time" was a medley, with the opening drumless section providing a four-minute introduction that was spliced in again at the end to provide a frame for the entire work.

In addition to experimentation in the studio, Davis continued to perform live with his quintet. Although Shorter remained, the rhythm section was interested in moving on and gave notice. Hancock was replaced by pianist Chick Corea, Ron Carter by British bassist Dave Holland, and Tony Williams by Jack DeJohnette. At the same time, Davis was increasingly drawn to the popular

Joe Zawinul (CD 2, Track 9) signed this promotional postcard for a fan in Switzerland.

rock and soul music of James Brown, Jimi Hendrix, and Sly and the Family Stone, as well as Cannonball Adderley's soul jazz hit, "Mercy, Mercy, Mercy."

Davis's next studio recording, *Bitches Brew,* was pivotal. From here on, his music centered on rock-based rhythms and completely abandoned the 4/4 swing feel that had defined his music for twenty-five years. The compositions amalgamated rock and soul influences; a steady, insistent rock or funk beat underscored the freewheeling improvisations by Davis or bass clarinetist Bennie Maupin. Davis also augmented the group's personnel, often including three drummers and a percussionist to create a densely textured and layered rhythmic foundation. For many of the compositions, Davis provided only a general sketch consisting of melodic ideas and a tonal center. The recording sold well, although most of the tracks were long and uncompromising. With *Bitches Brew,* Davis created a significant landmark on the road to the jazz-rock fusion of the 1970s. We shall complete Davis's story in Chapter 11, which is devoted to fusion.

Pianists

As we have seen, several keyboard artists made their mark in the jazz world of the 1960s. Here we look at Bill Evans, Herbie Hancock, Chick Corea, and Keith Jarrett.

BILL EVANS

Courtesy Morgan Collection

Pianist Bill Evans (CD 2, Track 6) was a lyrical, poetic player whose improvisations also elasticized the underlying meter.

When Miles Davis's *Kind of Blue* was released in 1959, his listeners were introduced to a young, recently established pianist whose identity at the keyboard was in its own way as individual as Thelonious Monk's. Bill Evans's pianism—his dense, impressionistic voicings, his dreamy, introspective moodiness, his singing lyricism—appeared fresh and original. Despite its apparent uniqueness, Evans's style was rooted in the work of Lennie Tristano, Bud Powell, and Horace Silver, as suggested by Evans's early recordings, which were considerably more centered in the bebop mainstream than his later recordings were. The refined harmonic language of George Shearing also contributed to Evans's stylistic heritage.

Born in 1929, Evans was from Plainfield, New Jersey. As a teenager, he listened to swing and bop, and he occasionally played piano in local bands. Following high school, Evans attended Southeastern Louisiana University with a scholarship for classical piano—an interesting choice of school for a future jazz musician from the Northeast. After Southeastern Louisiana, Evans was drafted, served in the army, then moved to New York in 1956. He attended the Mannes College of Music for a semester and recorded his own albums *New Jazz Conceptions* (1956) and *Everybody Digs Bill Evans* (1958).

Evans also played on several recordings with jazz composer George Russell in the 1950s. Working with Russell allowed Evans to show off the various facets of his approach to improvisation. For example, on Russell's tribute to Evans, *Concerto for Billy the Kid*, Evans played long, chromatic lines over the chord progression to "I'll Remember April." Occasionally, Evans verged on atonality, as on "New York, New York."

Evans joined Miles Davis's sextet in 1958, performing on Davis's *Jazz at the Plaza* and the profoundly influential *Kind of Blue*. As with so many other sidemen, Evans found that his stint with Davis incisively enhanced his visibility and reputation; he was to remain at the forefront of jazz piano for the remainder of his career.

Evans drastically redefined postbop piano. He was praised for the poetic beauty of his playing, which was enhanced by his sensitivity to dynamic shadings. His ballad performances exhibited a rich harmonic vocabulary, often whispered at remarkably soft dynamic levels. On solo piano recordings such as "I Loves You Porgy" and "People," Evans brought to the fore sophisticated voice-leading techniques, creating a contrapuntal texture by moving the inner voices of chords. On ballads as well, Evans frequently reharmonized the chord progressions with compelling originality. Even Evans's posture at the piano—hunched over the keyboard, listening intently to each and every note—seemed to symbolize his elusive quest for musical transcendence.

Evans generally avoided working with larger groups, preferring the trio format of piano, bass, and drums. Sophisticated listeners heard an unprecedented level of interaction among the members of the group, particularly because of Evans's uncanny ability to develop long, even phrases that stretched across bar lines and *elasticized* the meter by avoiding strongly emphasized downbeats. To superficial listeners, Evans's style was merely pretty, but beneath the elegant veneer were a sensibility and formal control that number among the very best in jazz.

Evans preferred sidemen who could interact with him rather than merely provide accompaniment. His bassists were usually virtuoso soloists in their own right, who often played in the upper registers of the instrument. They frequently emerged from a subsidiary role to musically comment on and converse with Evans's solo lines. Evans's drummers often did the same thing, preferring to complement and punctuate the phrasing of the piano and bass rather than merely keep time.

Evans's landmark trio was formed in 1959. It consisted of an unusually sensitive and coloristic drummer, Paul Motian, and a superb twenty-three-year-old bassist, Scott LaFaro, who, despite his youth, had already performed with Chet Baker, Sonny Rollins, Barney Kessel, and Benny Goodman. This trio set the standard for Evans's future groups. Its performance of "Autumn Leaves," from the Riverside album *Portrait in Jazz*, showed off the group's most characteristic features. During the introduction, the trio projected a meter at odds with the 4/4 rhythm to follow. Evans's solo lines moved between eighth notes and triplets, with phrasing that was often irregular. These phrases were sometimes separated by dramatic pauses that were themselves punctuated by Motian's drumming and LaFaro's countermelodies. With all the members contributing to the musical conversation, the trio frequently broke up the sense of regular metric flow.

An **elastic meter** is created when the soloist or rhythm section masks the strong metric downbeats. The meter seems to be stretched beyond its normal parameters. This illusion is often created by playing unusually long phrases that move the melodic emphasis off the expected downbeats that occur at the beginning of each measure.

Metric displacement is a technique whereby the soloist implies or states a rhythm in the melody line that seems to go against the underlying basic rhythm of the piece. It also can be achieved by placing melodic phrases irregularly against the underlying rhythm.

Evans particularly sought to explore sophisticated aspects of *metric and rhythmic displacement* in his playing. He expressed this concern in an interview with pianist Marian McPartland for her radio show, "Piano Jazz":

> As far as the jazz playing goes, I think the rhythmic construction of the thing has evolved quite a bit. Now, I don't know how obvious that would be to the listener, but the displacement of phrases and . . . the way phrases follow one another and their placement against the meter . . . is something that I've worked on rather hard and it's something I believe in.[5]

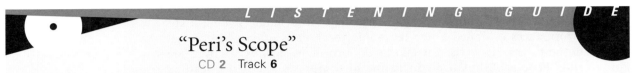

"Peri's Scope"
CD **2**   Track **6**

Bill Evans Trio: "Peri's Scope" (Evans), from *Portrait in Jazz*. Riverside RLP-1162. New York, December 28, 1959. Bill Evans, piano; Scott LaFaro, bass; Paul Motian, drums.

Metric displacement was a feature not only of Evans's improvisation but also of his compositions. For example, in measures 13–16 of "Peri's Scope," the melody contradicts the 4/4 meter by implying a 3/4 meter.

Head—Irregular 24 bars

0:00   The performance begins at the top of the head without introduction.

0:15   Beginning in measure 13, the superimposed 3/4 rhythm becomes part of the tune, as shown here:

The 3/4 rhythm is itself grouped as dotted quarter note + dotted quarter note. The cross-rhythm continues for four 4/4 bars.

0:29   Here there is a two-bar break for Evans to set up his solo.

Evans piano solo—4 choruses

0:31   Evans begins his solo developing a two-note idea before moving to longer lines. Listen for Evans's dynamic shadings during his eighth-note ideas and for the interplay between Evans's left-hand chordal punctuation and Motian's snare drum accents.

2:14–2:37   Evans moves away from single hornlike melodies to chordal textures.

Restatement of head

2:37   Evans's solo flows directly into the restatement of the head. The 3/4 cross-rhythm returns from measures 13–16. The performance ends directly without coda.

Like many other jazz musicians, Evans wrote numerous compositions, many of which have become jazz standards. He was particularly fond of waltz time (3/4), which was not often heard in traditional jazz performances, and he composed many jazz waltzes, including the popular "Waltz for Debby." When not performing originals, Evans tended to draw his repertory from the golden era of U.S. popular song—roughly 1920 to 1950—which featured compositions by Irving Berlin, George Gershwin, Rodgers and Hart, Harold Arlen, and others.

Evans suffered a severe musical and personal blow when Scott LaFaro died in a car accident in July 1961. Although only twenty-five at the time, LaFaro had come close to revolutionizing the role of the bass within the context of the jazz trio. (He had also taken part in the groundbreaking *Free Jazz* sessions with Ornette Coleman.) LaFaro's immediate replacement was Chuck Israels. Later bassists included Eddie Gomez, an imposing virtuoso who appeared on Evans's 1968 *Live in Montreux* album, which won a Grammy award.

Evans also made recordings without his trio. For example, his unique 1963 recording *Conversations with Myself* included solo piano tracks on which Evans overdubbed himself, often in three layers consisting of a bass line, mid-range accompanying chords, and upper solo and melodic lines. On his version of "'Round Midnight" from that album, Evans used colorful arpeggios, making clear his debt to classical music, particularly the French composers Claude Debussy and Maurice Ravel. Evans's interest in European concert music was even more evident on the record *Bill Evans Trio with Symphony Orchestra* (1965), on which he performed jazz arrangements of classical works by Gabriel Fauré, Alexander Scriabin, Sergei Rachmaninoff, and others. Evans also recorded with larger jazz groups. For example, the album *Crosscurrents* (1977) included Lee Konitz on alto and Warne Marsh on tenor saxophones.

Evans's solo piano albums—such as *Alone* (1968) and *Alone (Again)* (1975)— usually emphasized American popular standards. Evans preferred slow, dreamy ballads, though occasional faster tempos provided variety. In these solo piano improvisations, Evans developed a distinctive piano texture of right-hand melodic lines above a thin—often three-note—texture in his left hand. The left-hand voicings often consisted of a bass pitch along with the third and seventh of the harmony. This kind of voicing in his solo style contrasted with his chordal approach when performing with bass players: In the latter circumstances, Evans usually allowed the bassist to take the chordal roots, while adding ambiguous three-note voicings in the mid-range.

Evans recorded two duo albums with a remarkably compatible guitarist, Jim Hall (b. 1930), entitled *Undercurrent* (1959) and *Intermodulation* (1966). Hall, who achieved recognition through working with both Evans and Sonny Rollins, became one of the premier guitar stylists of the 1960s. Earlier, he had worked with Jimmy Giuffre in Los Angeles. The wonderful sensitivity of his playing closely echoed Evans's style, making Hall the pianist's "alter ego" on guitar. Hall has maintained a distinguished and active career. In recent years, he has also experimented with writing for orchestra.

Evans's work in his later trios, with bassist Eddie Gomez and Marty Morrell, or in his final trio, with bassist Marc Johnson and drummer Joe LaBarbera, maintained the same high standard, although the pianist sought to refine his approach and take more chances. Evans also wrote new material while exploring previously untapped veins in the jazz repertory. For example, he recorded Herbie Hancock's "Dolphin Dance" as well as "Up With the Lark" by country singer Bobbie Gentry, the latter being a particularly imaginative choice for a jazz reading. Evans remained committed to some compositions for decades: He first recorded "Some Other Time" in a 1958 recording session; the same composition appeared on his 1975 duet album with singer Tony Bennett.

Rhythmically and harmonically, Evans profoundly affected the major pianists of the 1960s. Interestingly, many of these pianists—such as Herbie Hancock, Chick Corea, and Keith Jarrett—also worked as sidemen for Miles Davis. From Evans they learned sophisticated techniques of rhythmic and metric displacement. Significantly, too, they appropriated some of Evans's characteristic harmonic voicings, such as a three-note chord voiced as a major third atop a minor second. Evans's "So What" voicing used on *Kind of Blue* (open fourths with top notes separated by a major third) was also imitated. These harmonies had an ambiguous, open sound, appropriate for modal playing.

Unfortunately, Evans died at age fifty-one in 1980, succumbing to years of drug and alcohol abuse. Regardless of his early death, Evans was arguably the most influential postbebop pianist of the 1960s.

The sixties witnessed the coming of age of three of the most important jazz pianists of the latter half of the twentieth century. Traces of Bill Evans's approach to the keyboard can be heard in the work of Herbie Hancock, Chick Corea, and Keith Jarrett, but each is also a remarkably innovative player in his own right, with distinct styles as well as varying musical interests.

HERBIE HANCOCK

From 1963 to 1968, Herbie Hancock formed part of Miles Davis's legendary quintet. With performances that were consistently creative, fresh, and versatile, he remained one of the most sought-after pianists for studio recordings throughout the 1960s.

Courtesy Morgan Collection

A signed Herbie Hancock (CD 2, Tracks 5 and 7) publicity photograph. Hancock's own Blue Note recordings and his work with the Miles Davis Quintet left many listeners unprepared for his phenomenal success in jazz-rock fusion in the 1970s.

Born in 1940 in Chicago, Hancock was a child prodigy. At age eleven, he performed the first movement of a Mozart piano concerto with the Chicago Symphony Orchestra in a young people's concert. An early jazz influence was pianist Oscar Peterson.

After graduating from Grinnell College, Hancock found himself in demand as a pianist in Chicago. Joining the quintet of trumpeter Donald Byrd, Hancock moved to New York in the early 1960s. On his early Blue Note recordings with Byrd, he assimilated a vast array of styles, from the blues-based approach of funky jazz to the harmonic sophistication and refined lyricism of Bill Evans. He even experimented with classically based compositional principles, which he learned while a music composition major at Grinnell.

Hancock recorded his first album as a leader for Blue Note in 1962: *Takin' Off*. He wrote all the tunes for the session, which included veteran tenor saxophonist Dexter Gordon and trumpeter Freddie Hubbard, whose own experiences ranged from Art Blakey and the Jazz Messengers to Ornette Coleman's *Free Jazz*. With its characteristic two horns and rhythm section, *Takin' Off* was a typical hard bop LP, but Hancock's catchy, bluesy composition "Watermelon Man" became a popular hit, making it to the Top 100 of the popular music charts. The composition became even more popular when recorded by Mongo Santamaria in the mid-1960s; it was recorded yet again by the big bands of Woody Herman and Maynard Ferguson. Between 1962 and 1963, Hancock also appeared with saxophonist Eric Dolphy, who induced Hancock to play more freely.

As a member of the Miles Davis Quintet, Hancock joined drummer Tony Williams and bassist Ron Carter to create the most influential and innovative rhythm section of the 1960s. When Hancock improvised, the uncanny sense of communication among the three players enhanced the inventiveness of his solos.

Although part of the Davis quintet, Hancock continued to record as a leader for Blue Note. By embracing more open-ended improvisations, fewer chord changes, and subtle metric displacements, Hancock moved away from the standard hard bop feel of his first recordings. On *Empyrean Isles,* for example, "One Finger Snap" was an unusually structured, twenty-measure tune: Its opening four bars used all twelve pitches of the chromatic scale, while Freddie Hubbard improvised the remaining sixteen bars. The most radical composition, "The Egg," incorporated passages of free improvisation.

Hancock's "Dolphin Dance" from *Maiden Voyage* became well known. Its melody grew out of the opening four-note motive, while the complex harmonic progression featured shifting chords over *pedal points* in the bass. Ballads such as "Dolphin Dance" most fully revealed the connection to Bill Evans in Hancock's style. Yet, Hancock's projection of Evans's harmonic palette was enhanced by his more ambitious textural and tonal sense. Evans responded to his trio but tended to think like a soloist, whereas Hancock seemed to listen to and anticipate his accompaniment more perceptively than Evans did. Evans worked with a sense of absolute stylistic command, whereas Hancock always seemed to be reaching, trying to stretch his harmonic concept to the very limit.

This continual searching perhaps led to Hancock's eventual disillusionment with the modern modal style, which he thought had become too abstract and not responsive enough to the audience. In the early 1970s, he found a release in the repetition, heavy beat, and electronic orientation of jazz-rock funk.

Before Hancock's plunge into fusion, however, and before departing from Davis's touring band, Hancock recorded several important acoustic albums during the 1960s. On both *Speak Like a Child* and *The Prisoner,* the size of the group was augmented to include bass trombone, alto flute, and trumpet. The coloristic writing for the horns evoked the work of arranger Gil Evans. With *Fat Albert Rotunda,* originally written for the animated Bill Cosby television show "The Fat Albert Animated Special," a pronounced shift took place: Hancock performed on a Fender Rhodes electric piano. Most significantly, several of the compositions, such as "Wiggle Waggle," were simple, funky, riff-based tunes.

Hancock turned exclusively to electric keyboards with his sextet of 1971–1973, playing synthesizer and even featuring a second synthesist, Patrick Gleason, along with bassist Buster Williams, drummer Billy Hart, reed player Bennie Maupin, and trombonist Julian Priester. With its electronic sounds, the group seemed to evoke the "space music" of Sun Ra in extended improvisations such as "Ostinato," a riff in 15/8 meter from the album *Mwandishi.* Hancock's phenomenal commercial success coincided with his 1973 fusion album *Head Hunters* (see Chapter 11).

A **chromatic scale** is a scale with all twelve notes of the Western musical system, for example, all the adjacent notes on the piano. There are twelve notes in an octave, which create a chromatic scale.

A **pedal point** is a repeated bass note or drone played to accompany a melody. Harmonies may also shift over pedal points.

CHICK COREA

Like Hancock, Chick Corea is a significant composer as well as pianist. Less subtle than Hancock as a player, Corea developed a steely, percussive touch, particularly on his early recordings, where the influence of John Coltrane's pianist, McCoy Tyner, strongly appeared.

Corea was born in 1938 in Chelsea, Massachusetts. Raised in a musical atmosphere—his father was a gigging musician—Corea as a teenager transcribed solos by bop pianists Bud Powell and Horace Silver. Corea received early professional experience in the Afro-Cuban bands of Willie Bobo and Mongo Santamaria; not surprisingly, much of his later work reflected Latin and Afro-Cuban music. Corea's first recording as a leader came in 1966, when he made *Tones for Joan's Bones,* named after a composition that Corea had recorded earlier with trumpeter Blue Mitchell.

Corea could be sensitive and lush, as his playing on Stan Getz's *Sweet Rain* made clear, but his hard-driving, staccato style was especially influential. Like McCoy Tyner, Corea favored pentatonic scales and harmonies based on open fourths. These stylistic attributes came to infuse both his improvisations and his compositions.

On his second recording, *Now He Sings, Now He Sobs,* Corea appeared with a trio that included Czech bassist Miroslav Vitous and drummer Roy Haynes. The trio was energetic, overtly dramatic, and highly inter-active, a distinctly different sensibility from the quiet introspection of the Bill Evans Trio. Corea composed all the tunes for the album. Both "Matrix" and "Steps" were twelve-bar blues, but Corea took an unusual approach toward the classic form by avoiding the customary 4 + 4 + 4 phrasing in his solos. Rather, Corea would spin out lines in which the usual arrival points of the form were disguised and the harmonies rendered more ambiguously. It was a tribute to Corea's skill that his orientation toward the classic blues did not sound awkward but was fully integrated into his overall approach to improvisation.

In 1968 Corea replaced Herbie Hancock in Miles Davis's group, where he was quickly swept into the jazz-rock experiments of the late 1960s. Despite his initial reluctance to play anything other than acoustic piano with the group, he often performed on the Fender Rhodes electric piano. "At first, Miles kind of pushed the Fender piano in front of me against my will," Corea admitted, "and I resisted. But then I started liking it, especially being able to turn up the volume and combat the drummer."[6]

Corea left Davis two years later, along with bassist Dave Holland, and returned for a while to acoustic piano. The album *Song of Singing* featured an acoustic trio that strongly reflected the jazz avant-garde. With bassist Holland and drummer Barry Altschul, the trio

Courtesy Morgan Collection

A driving pianist and inventive composer, Chick Corea (CD 2, Track 8) gradually moved toward electric keyboards during his work with Miles Davis in the late 1960s. His group Return to Forever was one of the celebrated fusion groups of the 1970s.

experimented with free improvisations that frequently avoided predetermined chordal structures. The music reflected the influence of both pianist Paul Bley's work and that of Ornette Coleman.

In 1971 Corea augmented his group with the alto/soprano saxophonist Anthony Braxton. The quartet, called Circle, recorded a concert in Paris (issued by ECM Records) that was largely given over to free improvisation. Nonetheless, its ties to the tradition appeared in their performance of "There Is No Greater Love," which shifted in and out of free playing, at times moving into a traditional 4/4 swing feel with walking bass. The tension between traditional and free playing also arose in Corea's two solo piano albums recorded in the early 1970s, *Piano Improvisations,* volumes 1 and 2. The first side of each recording reflected a marked lyrical simplicity, while the second side incorporated free atonal playing.

Corea returned to electric keyboards in the early 1970s and soon became one of the key figures in the jazz fusion movement. We shall resume his story in Chapter 11.

KEITH JARRETT AND ECM RECORDS

Like Herbie Hancock and Chick Corea, Keith Jarrett is a significant and innovative pianist whose career began in the 1960s. Although Jarrett made some recordings on electric piano—particularly during his tenure with Miles Davis between 1969 and 1971—he has dedicated himself almost exclusively to the acoustic instrument as the vehicle for his widely heralded, virtuosic performances. Jarrett's playing is eclectic, bringing to the piano not only elements of traditional jazz but also free jazz and traces of classical, folk, and gospel music. Like Hancock and Corea, Jarrett was inspired by the lyricism of Bill Evans. In addition, Jarrett owed a strong debt to the freer, open-ended playing of pianist Paul Bley, as well as John Coates, a pianist Jarrett heard growing up in Pennsylvania, who similarly blended gospel and folk elements into a jazz style. Moreover, Jarrett cultivated a legato, classically based touch on the piano, a technique that has served him well in widely publicized performances and recordings of works in the European concert tradition.

Born in Allentown, Pennsylvania, in 1945, Jarrett began playing at age three; by seven he was already composing and improvising. He moved to Boston after receiving a scholarship from the Berklee College of Music in 1962. Although he attended Berklee only a year, he remained in Boston, playing gigs with Roland Kirk and Tony Scott. After moving to New York in 1965, he and his wife were nearly penniless until Art Blakey heard him at a jam session. Jarrett joined Blakey's band and recorded the album *Buttercorn Lady* with the group in 1966, which included trumpeter Chuck Mangione. In this traditional hard bop ensemble, Jarrett exhibited his virtuosic technique and even experimented with avant-garde concepts, such as playing inside the piano—strumming the strings—during Mangione's ballad "Recuerdo."

As a member of the Charles Lloyd Quartet between 1966 and 1969, Jarrett received full rein to explore his experimental tendencies and eclectic musical interests. Lloyd was a West Coast tenor saxophonist and flutist who had performed with Chico Hamilton and Cannonball Adderley in the early 1960s. Lloyd's quartet, which included Jarrett, drummer Jack DeJohnette, and bassist Cecil McBee (later replaced by Ron McClure), was astonishingly successful. At the height of the 1960s "flower power" era, Lloyd's followers consisted of not only jazz fans but also teenagers who thronged to hear the group at rock music venues such as the Fillmore Auditorium in San Francisco. Lloyd was something of a guru to the flower children. "I play love vibrations," he insisted in the liner notes to the aptly titled record *Love-In.* "Love, totality—like bringing everyone together in a joyous dance."[7]

John Coltrane's quartet strongly influenced Lloyd and his band. For instance, on the band's first recording, *Dream Weaver,* "Autumn Sequence" (which served as an introduction to "Autumn Leaves") incorporated an extended modal vamp. But Lloyd's group was also wildly eclectic, merging elements of traditional jazz, free jazz, gospel, and R&B. Lloyd's Latin-tinged composition "Forest Flower" became his best-known composition.

Jarrett's performances with Lloyd's quartet dazzled audiences and critics. Even on jazz standards such as "East of the Sun," from *Forest Flower,* Jarrett's solo moved the band from traditional 4/4 swing into completely free improvisation—with sections reminiscent of Cecil Taylor—before returning to a subdued ending. Elsewhere, Jarrett's gospel and rock-oriented approach set the tone in simple blues compositions, such as "Island Blues" from *The Flowering.*

After leaving Lloyd, Jarrett played electric piano and organ during his eighteen months with Miles Davis. Jarrett rarely performed on electric instruments after that. One exception was his inspired electric piano work on Freddie Hubbard's recording *Sky Dive.*

Ignoring the jazz-rock electric fusion trends of the 1970s, Jarrett recorded more than a dozen albums between 1971 and 1976 with a quartet consisting of tenor saxophonist Dewey Redman, bassist Charlie Haden, and drummer Paul Motian. The choice of sidemen itself revealed much about Jarrett's interest in the free jazz of Ornette Coleman as well as the lyricism of Bill Evans; both Redman and Haden had played with Coleman, while Motian had been Evans's drummer in the early 1960s. Much of the quartet's work seemed inspired by Ornette Coleman, although it was sometimes rooted in a more definite harmonic structure.

The eclecticism of Jarrett's work grew especially pronounced in the 1970s. Throughout the quartet recordings, Jarrett drew on the whole tradition of piano improvisation, including traditional jazz. For example, a ragtime-inspired solo piano composition entitled "Pardon My Rags" appeared on *The Mourning of a Star.* Jarrett's 1972 recording *Expectations* included free improvisations and gospel-tinged works, along with pieces for string orchestra and piano. The sound of the quartet owed much to the rich tenor saxophone sound of Dewey Redman. Interestingly, Jarrett also played soprano saxophone on the recordings, as well as organ and percussion.

In contrast to most contemporary jazz pianists, Jarrett explored solo piano performance extensively. His first such album, *Facing You,* was a studio recording; with eight different originals, the album exhibited Jarrett's fine technique and legato touch. By 1973, Jarrett began performing live solo concerts, which generally comprised extended, freely improvised works. Many of these lasted an entire side (or longer) of an LP and often began rhapsodically, out of tempo, before launching into an extended ostinato over which Jarrett would improvise.

Solo Concerts and the *Köln Concert,* both recorded for ECM Records, included some of his most acclaimed improvisations, which ranged from rock, gospel, and folk to atonal free playing. (See the Box "ECM Records.") Jarrett's approach to the keyboard was nearly orgiastic; at times he would stand, grimace, and writhe, and he sometimes sang along with his melodies or moaned between phrases. Jarrett has been taken to task for both his emotional extravagance and his lack of editing. For example, his recording *Sun Bear Concerts* is a ten-record set assembled from five different concerts in Japan.

ECM Records

An important label that issued Jarrett recordings and became one of the most prominent exponents of nonfusion music during the 1970s and 1980s was ECM Records. Founded in Cologne, Germany, in 1969 by Manfred Eicher, ECM released albums by U.S. jazz artists such as pianists Keith Jarrett, Paul Bley, and Chick Corea, as well as vibraphonist Gary Burton and guitarist Pat Metheny. Additionally, the label sponsored European jazz players such as Norwegian saxophonist Jan Garbarek and bassist Eberhard Weber.

Some jazz critics and jazz musicians dismissed ECM's music as atmospheric "Euro-jazz"—sterile, moody, cerebral, introspective, and overly refined—a precursor to the New Age music that arose in the 1980s on labels such as Windham Hill. Nevertheless, the ECM label maintained consistently high standards of musicianship in recordings admired for their engineering and high technical quality. Many of the ECM artists were distinguished by a pronounced allegiance to European classical music and aesthetics. For example, "Mirrors," from Jarrett's recording *Arbour Zena,* incorporated a string ensemble, using the orchestra for accompaniment beneath the improvisations of Jarrett on piano and of Jan Garbarek on saxophone.

The ECM label also released recordings best characterized as free jazz. One of the most significant was bassist Dave Holland's 1972 recording *Conference of the Birds,* which featured saxophonist Sam Rivers, who was largely associated with free jazz. Far from having a single distinctive sound, ECM has represented a wide array of jazz performers and styles. Among its most successful records were Keith Jarrett's recordings of live solo piano recitals.

Some of Jarrett's work in the 1970s was tangential to the jazz mainstream. For example, his album *In the Light* included compositions for string orchestra, brass quintet, and string quartet; *The Celestial Hawk* was a three-movement work for piano and orchestra, recorded at Carnegie Hall in 1980, in which Jarrett performed with the Syracuse Symphony Orchestra. Jarrett has also recorded the music of European composers as diverse as J. S. Bach and Dmitri Shostakovich.

Since the 1980s, Jarrett has largely returned to comparatively straight-ahead jazz. His trio with bassist Gary Peacock and drummer Jack DeJohnette has been devoted to recording the standard jazz repertory with chorus structures, chord changes, and regular meter. Within this traditional format, Jarrett's debt to Bill Evans is even more apparent than in his earlier work, both in his performances of harmonically lush ballads and through the techniques of rhythmic displacement pioneered by Evans in the sixties. Though partially incapacitated with chronic fatigue syndrome in the late 1990s, Jarrett continues as a major force in jazz piano.

Funky/Soul Jazz

The funky jazz tunes recorded in the 1950s by such groups as Art Blakey's Jazz Messengers and the Horace Silver Quintet were infectious blues-based works steeped in the gospel tradition. As noted in Chapter 8, the gospel singing of Mahalia Jackson and the blues-based and gospel music of Ray Charles provided two significant influences for funky jazz. During the 1960s, funky jazz continued to attract musicians who preferred more direct communication with audiences than either cool jazz or

Singer/pianist Ray Charles. Charles's earthy, blues-based music influenced many of the funky/soul jazz players.

Courtesy Morgan Collection

free jazz could provide. The term *soul jazz* came about after 1960; it was initially used by Riverside Records to promote the Cannonball Adderley Quintet.

CANNONBALL ADDERLEY

Julian "Cannonball" Adderley (1928–1975) was a superb alto saxophonist from Tampa, Florida. After moving to New York and appearing in various venues, his growing prominence led to an invitation to join Miles Davis's group in 1957, where he remained until 1959. Adderley was a major factor in the success of Davis's important *Milestones* and *Kind of Blue* albums, in which he helped balance the lyricism of Davis and the emotional intensity of Coltrane. After leaving Davis, Adderley formed his own group with his younger brother, cornetist Nat Adderley (b. 1931).

The Adderley group specialized in both bebop and funky/soul jazz. The latter included such well-known tunes as Nat Adderley's "Work Song," which featured call-and-response between the rhythm section and the horns in imitation of a chain gang. Once the melody was stated, though, the rhythm section reverted to a 4/4 swing with walking bass. In 1966 Adderley's popular hit "Mercy, Mercy, Mercy," written by Austrian pianist Josef Zawinul, incorporated a funky rock beat throughout. In his work with Adderley's group, Zawinul was one of the earliest jazz players to play the electric piano (partly inspiring Miles Davis's later use of the instrument). Zawinul's other compositions recorded with Adderley, such as "Country Preacher," typified the gospel themes of funky/soul jazz.

THE BLUES IN FUNKY/SOUL JAZZ

In stark contrast to the avant-garde wing of jazz, some of the funky/soul jazz of the 1960s was commercially quite successful. After his 1963 hit "Watermelon Man," which reached the Top 100 of the popular music charts, Hancock later recalled that on his subsequent albums he tried to include at least one tune with the even eighth notes of funky/soul jazz.[8] Also in 1963, hard bop trumpeter Lee Morgan recorded a successful hit with "The Sidewinder," a catchy, instrumental blues with a funky/soul-jazz feel.

The twelve-bar blues was the mainstay of much funky/soul jazz, particularly the music played by the jazz organists who sprang up during the late 1950s. Although Fats Waller recorded wonderful jazz solos on the pipe organ in the late twenties, musicians generally thought that the organ was not well-suited to jazz, because the attack of the notes was extremely smooth and lacked the bite usually heard in jazz phrasing. Beginning in 1935, the Hammond company manufactured an electronic organ, which was portable and lighter than the traditional pipe organ (usually only found in churches because of its huge size and weight). The electronic organ was soon used by jazz musicians Glenn Hardman and Milt Buckner, although the instrument remained relatively uncommon in jazz settings until the mid-1950s. Meanwhile, by the fifties the electronic organ had become a mainstay in black churches and the backbone of modern gospel music. As a result of its practicality and popularity, the electronic organ soon found its way into black neighborhood clubs, where it was often heard in a trio setting with saxophone and drums. Instead of using a bass player, the organist could play bass lines with either the feet or the left hand.

JIMMY SMITH AND JAZZ ORGANISTS

One of the most influential jazz organists to emerge in the late 1950s was Jimmy Smith, who was born in Norristown, Pennsylvania, in 1925. Although he began his career as a pianist, he formed his first organ trio in 1955. His New York debut took place at the Cafe Bohemia the following year, but his international career lifted off after a performance at the Newport Jazz Festival in 1957. Even the titles of Smith's albums, such as *The Sermon* and *Prayer Meetin'*, emphasized the gospel origins of the music.

Smith's approach to the organ set the standard for the instrument. Although Smith used bebop tunes on his earliest albums, he gravitated toward the blues, combining blistering right-hand runs against bass lines played by his left hand and feet. He made abundant use of idiomatic organ sounds, working the volume pedal to create *swells* in the style of the gospel church organists, or sustaining a single high note above rapid-fire, sixteenth-note lines.

Smith influenced virtually all subsequent jazz organists. Many, such as Brother Jack McDuff, Richard "Groove" Holmes, and Jimmy McGriff, maintained Smith's strutting approach to the blues. Don Patterson, who had recorded and performed with altoist Sonny Stitt, switched from piano to organ after hearing Jimmy Smith play, but he remained more tied to the bebop tradition than Smith did.

Courtesy Morgan Collection

Jimmy Smith, organist, in a smooth publicity pose.

A **swell** is the rapid change in volume that can be created by pushing down on or releasing the volume pedal on an electronic or conventional organ.

Many jazz organists favored the muscular tenor players, some of whom began their careers playing in R&B bands. Tenor saxophonist Stanley Turrentine (1934–2000) played with Ray Charles before recording with Jimmy Smith and Turrentine's wife, organist Shirley Scott. Houston Person, another full-throated tenor player, recorded with organists Groove Holmes and Charles Earland.

GUITARISTS

Organists also showcased their guitarists, many of whom were strongly rooted in the blues. Kenny Burrell had a mellow guitar sound; although he played fluently, he often preferred simple, singable lines, as heard on Jimmy Smith's recording, *Midnight Special*. George Benson created a major impact with his 1976 album *Breezin'*, which became quite popular thanks to the hit recording of "This Masquerade." Benson had begun his career with organist Jack McDuff, whose bluesy orientation strongly influenced the guitarist:

> That was a value I learned in Jack McDuff's band, the value of playing everything with a little blues touch. You know, adding a bended note here and there, a little cry over there, a little glissando here. It really helped to give me a concept, something to build on.

Benson also acknowledged how jazz organists helped highlight guitarists:

> I think that's what really helped the guitar to come to the front... as far as jazz music is concerned, because there was never any real, dynamic guitar playing, except for exceptional guys like Wes Montgomery, and even he came by way of the organ at first. And Kenny Burrell and just a couple of others, but I think the organ gave the guitar a form.... It featured the guitar so much. Guys could really test themselves, and night after night they had to come with some interesting solos, so it was a good format for guitar players.[9]

Blue Note Records

Two of the leading hard bop groups of the 1950s, the Horace Silver Quintet and Art Blakey's Jazz Messengers, recorded primarily for Blue Note Records. Blue Note was established in 1939, where it developed a reputation for interest not only in newer music but also in recording fine jazz players who had not gained popular appeal. For example, during the 1940s its catalog included jazz elder statesmen James P. Johnson and Sidney Bechet as well as bebop pioneer Thelonious Monk. In the 1950s, the label earned a reputation for its high standards in recording the finest hard bop players and bands. Much of the label's success was due to the vision of its founder, Alfred Lion, as well as recording engineer Rudy Van Gelder, who supervised many of the sessions.

Blue Note continued as a major force in jazz recording during the sixties; as in the fifties, the groups that recorded on the label helped keep alive the mainstream legacy. In the midst of the free jazz upheaval, the Blue Note bands—usually standard quartets, quintets, and sextets—maintained the hard bop tradition and sometimes adapted to newer musical developments, such as modal improvisation.

Wes Montgomery (1923–1968) may have performed with organ trios, but he worked principally with mainstream jazz groups. Montgomery became known in the fifties from several albums recorded for Riverside. He later played with John Coltrane. During the mid-1960s, Montgomery became one of the best-known jazz guitarists with hit pop-jazz records, such as *Goin' Out of My Head* (1965) and *A Day in the Life* (1967).

The Hard Bop Legacy

During the 1960s, many jazz artists continued the tradition of hard bop. Here we look at some of these key players. Many mainstream jazz musicians recorded with Blue Note Records, which had built a reputation since the 1930s for promoting fine jazz (see the box "Blue Note Records").

LEE MORGAN AND FREDDIE HUBBARD

Many of the artists who recorded on Blue Note in the 1960s began their careers with the Art Blakey and Horace Silver bands. Trumpeter Lee Morgan, born in Philadelphia in 1938, played with Blakey's Jazz Messengers between 1958 and 1961 and returned briefly in 1964 and 1965. He also participated in John Coltrane's 1957 *Blue Train* recording. Morgan was heavily influenced by Clifford Brown, with a swaggering and virtuosic style, confidently in control of all registers of the horn.

Morgan had a major hit, "The Sidewinder," in 1963; he wrote other important compositions as well. His album *Cornbread,* which included Hank Mobley on tenor and Jackie McLean on alto, contained a beautiful Latin-based composition, "Ceora." The twelve-bar blues, "Our Man Higgins," also from *Cornbread* and dedicated to drummer Billy Higgins, contained an unusual twist: The opening choruses of each solo used the whole-tone scale before returning to the standard twelve-bar blues chord changes. Morgan experimented with other tangents in modern jazz as well. For example, the title track from his *Search for the New Land,* with guitarist Grant Green, explored modal improvisation. Morgan died in 1972, murdered by his lover at a gig.

Morgan was replaced in the Jazz Messengers by trumpeter Freddie Hubbard (b. 1938), an equally fiery player whose tone was slightly mellower. Interestingly, Hubbard participated in several important free jazz recordings, including Coleman's *Free Jazz,* Coltrane's *Ascension,* and recordings with Eric Dolphy between 1960 and 1964. Nonetheless, Hubbard's own Blue Note albums made during the early 1960s, *Goin' Up* and *Hub Tones,* showed him to be a fundamentally more

Courtesy Morgan Collection

Trumpeter Lee Morgan (CD 1, Track 21) was one of the many significant players to work with Art Blakey's Jazz Messengers. On his recordings for Blue Note Records, his own compositions touched on hard bop, funky/soul jazz, and modal jazz.

traditional player than the avant-garde musicians. *Hub Cap,* recorded in 1961, kept the same instrumentation as Blakey's Messengers, combining three horns (trumpet, trombone, and tenor) with a rhythm section of piano, bass, and drums.

Hubbard's work as a sideman on two of Herbie Hancock's Blue Note recordings, *Maiden Voyage* and *Empyrean Isles,* contained some of his finest work. After 1970, Hubbard turned to more commercially promising music, recording jazz-rock fusion and funk.

WAYNE SHORTER

Hubbard's band mate in Blakey's Messengers was tenor saxophonist Wayne Shorter. Shorter was born in 1933 in Newark, New Jersey. After earning a bachelor's degree in music education from New York University in 1956, Shorter worked with Horace Silver and Maynard Ferguson. Beginning in 1959, Shorter served as music director for the Jazz Messengers until his defection to Miles Davis in 1964.

Shorter's early Blue Note recordings were in the hard bop mainstream, but as both tenor player and composer, he was attracted to the exploratory and experimental. On the title track of his 1964 album *Speak No Evil,* the melody emphasized the interval of a perfect fourth over slow-moving modal harmonies in the A section. In addition to modal compositions, Shorter experimented with a funky/soul-jazz rhythmic feel on the title track to his quartet recording *Adam's Apple,* and he moved decisively toward free jazz playing on *The All Seeing Eye.* In recent years, Shorter has been writing for orchestra, often with pieces that feature himself as soloist. His work with the fusion group Weather Report is discussed in Chapter 11.

JOE HENDERSON

Another significant tenor saxophonist to emerge in the sixties was Joe Henderson, born in 1937 in Lima, Ohio. Henderson was a member of the Horace Silver Quintet between 1964 and 1966, appearing on Silver's best-known tune, "Song for My Father." On tenor, Henderson combined Coltrane's intensity with Sonny Rollins's motivic approach to improvisation.

In 1963 Henderson made his first recording for Blue Note, *Page One,* which included bebop trumpeter Kenny Dorham. The album featured Dorham's "Blue Bossa," which became a jazz standard, as well as Henderson's own Latin-based "Recorda Me."

Henderson's subsequent recordings for Blue Note blended traditional hard bop instrumentation with modally based compositions, such as his 1966 *Mode for Joe.* This album included Blakey alumni Curtis Fuller on trombone and Lee Morgan on trumpet, along with Joe Chambers, one of the finest yet most underrated drummers of the decade. Henderson produced some of his most creative pieces working as a sideman; for example, he played open-ended modal improvisations on McCoy Tyner's *The Real McCoy* and on Herbie Hancock's *The Prisoner.*

Henderson died in 2001.

OTHER BLUE NOTE ARTISTS

Under the influence of John Coltrane's and Miles Davis's groups, many other Blue Note artists in the 1960s moved into modal composition and improvisation. Organist Larry Young (1940–1978) abandoned the funky/soul-jazz orientation of the organ; his *Unity,* with Joe Henderson and trumpeter Woody Shaw (b. 1944), responded strongly to Coltrane's modal innovations. The recordings of vibraphonist Bobby Hutcherson (b. 1941) featured some of Davis's and Coltrane's sidemen, such as pianists McCoy Tyner and Herbie Hancock and bassist Ron Carter, with the latter two on Hutcherson's *Components.* Pianist Andrew Hill (b. 1937), a devotee of Thelonious Monk, recorded modal jazz and free jazz on his *Point of Departure,* made with Eric Dolphy and Joe Henderson; Henderson also performed on Hill's *Black Fire.*

Thus the Blue Note label not only kept alive the hard bop tradition but also adapted to the innovations of the decade. In addition, the label recorded many of the most important exponents of funky/soul jazz, including guitarist Grant Green and organist Jimmy Smith. Although the bulk of its recordings represented the jazz mainstream, Blue Note was not totally averse to controversy: The label also issued some of the freest jazz of the decade, Cecil Taylor's *Unit Structures.*

Questions and Topics for Discussion

1. What was Miles Davis's response to the free jazz revolution of the 1950s?

2. Which principal jazz pianists matured in the 1960s? Compare and contrast their styles.

3. What factors led to the rise of funky/soul jazz? In developing your answer, discuss the importance and history of the Hammond electronic organ.

4. How did the bebop style of the 1940s continue to develop through the 1950s and 1960s? What was this continuation called, and who were the principal musicians involved?

Key Terms

Chromatic scale
Elastic meter
Metric displacement
Pedal point
Swell

What kind of computers will be needed tomorrow?

...nowl-
...come
...ping
...them.

...puters
...a sec-
...in the

...t. The
...g giv-
...every

day. They point to the eventual need for faster speeds and greater capacities. After years of dealing in millionths of a second, IBM scientists now talk of billionths of a second.

How do they hope to achieve such speeds? By tapping completely new principles for the operation of computer circuits. IBM scientists and engineers, for example, are developing computer circuits and high-speed memories of thin magnetic films of metal. They also are

investigating the application to computers of tunnel diodes, and of cryogenic circuits which function at temperatures approaching absolute zero.

From these research directions will come new generations of computers. IBM is exploring them all now, to assure businessmen and scientists that computer technology will be ready for new generations of information-handling problems.

IBM

A is for Apple.

It's the first thing you should know about personal computers.

The era of the personal computer is here. Apple will challenge your imagination for years to come. Thousands of uses, from finances to fun and games. For information, call toll-free (800) 538-9696.* Or write:

apple computer

*In California, call (408) 996-1010.   10260 Bandley Dr., Cupertino, California 95014.

The 1970s witnessed the entrance of the personal computer into U.S. society. Above right, in a 1961 advertisement that shows the former size of computers, IBM wonders what kind of computer people will need in the future. Immediately above is one of the answers—the Apple computer of 1978.

JAZZ-ROCK, JAZZ-FUNK FUSION

11

THE DEVELOPMENT of jazz-rock and jazz-funk fusion during the seventies remains controversial. Fusion involved the incorporation of rock, soul, and funk elements into jazz, and it drastically altered the musical directions taken in the postbop era. The key elements of jazz-rock and jazz-funk include the following:

- Replacement of the 4/4 swing feel with rock or funk rhythms
- Harmonies and progressions that were usually simpler and often characterized by a slow harmonic change or use of long vamps
- Electric and electronic instruments as the norm; specifically:
  - ▶ Replacement of the acoustic bass with the electric bass guitar
  - ▶ Replacement of the piano with electric piano and synthesizers (so that "pianists" became "keyboardists")
  - ▶ Rise to prominence of the electric guitar as perhaps the most characteristic instrument of the fusion ensemble
- Intense amplification and use of electronic effects

An important element in fusion was the addition of the synthesizer to the ensemble. As synthesizers underwent development in the seventies and became less expensive and more convenient to play (smaller and more portable), the typical fusion ensemble became more likely to adopt them. (See the box "Synthesizers" for more.)

Jazz-rock, **jazz-funk**, or **fusion** is a form of jazz that combines elements of rock (or R&B funk) and jazz.

293

Synthesizers

Synthesizers were originally developed for musical use in the early 1950s. Unlike acoustic instruments, the synthesizer produced sound electronically: In analog synthesizers, an oscillator supplies a voltage to an amplifier, from which it is routed to a speaker. The earliest models pioneered by RCA, Bell Laboratories, and European companies were cumbersome: They did not have attached keyboards and were unsuitable for live performance.

In the sixties, manufacturers produced the first synthesizers that allowed keyboardists to conveniently control and manipulate the sound during live performances. During the seventies, synthesizers became cheaper and more compact, leading to the familiar sight of the rock band multikeyboardist surrounded by stacks of electric pianos,

synthesizers, mixers, and other gear. The Minimoog was perhaps the first widely used synthesizer, a standard keyboard accessory in rock bands and fusion groups in the early seventies.

The mid-seventies witnessed the dual breakthroughs of polyphonic and digital synthesizers. Polyphonic models enabled the keyboardist to play chords. Digital synthesizers were even more flexible: Their numerical translations of complex sound waves allowed for the creation of a greater number of timbres or sound qualities for each note.

In addition to synthesizers, *samplers* were gradually developed: When acoustic instrumental sounds (or in fact any kinds of sounds) are recorded and reproduced for musical use, the practice is known as *sampling*.

Sampling is the practice of recording sounds for musical use in playback. Any kind of sound can be sampled, from a note on an acoustic instrument, to natural sounds, to a passage of music already recorded. For playback, the sound is usually activated by computer or by pressing a key on a keyboard. **Sound modules** play back prerecorded samples, which can be digitally stored in a computer for playback. **Samplers** are used both to sample and to play back sounds.

Curiously, even early jazz synthesizer solos reflected the instrument's potential. The synthesizer was then at the forefront of the developing jazz-rock and jazz-funk styles. Musicians were intrigued by the expressive qualities of the new instrument, and many imaginative solos were created.

In addition to adopting the new timbre of the synthesizer, jazz musicians began modifying the role of the electric guitar. The traditional mellow timbre of the hollow-body electric guitar had been defined by such players as Charlie Christian in the late 1930s and maintained in jazz through the sixties. In fusion, this sound was superseded by the steely, cutting timbre, the sustained notes, and often the distortion obtained from the solid-body electric guitar. (Listen to Tracks 39 and 40 of the Audio Primer CD to compare these sounds.) A common form of distortion was created by intentional feedback. Musicians such as Jimi Hendrix in the rock world showed how feedback could be controlled and used as a musical quality.

Feedback is a distorted effect created when the sound coming from a speaker is picked up by the electronic sensing device of an instrument (or a microphone) and routed back to the speaker. As this process multiplies, harsh electronic wails are created. Feedback commonly (and annoyingly) occurs in PA systems when the microphones pick up the sound coming from the speakers.

The radical changes of instrumental timbre associated with fusion were accompanied by changes in the roles of the players themselves. In particular, the concept of solo accompaniment was radically modified: Instead of the improvised comping of the pianist or guitarist, the group often relied on repeated vamps or ostinato figures.

For the most part, seventies jazz fusion can be broken down into either jazz-rock or jazz-funk. The latter term, though less common, was often more accurate, because the music incorporated elements of R&B and funk more often than rock.

In a very general sense, differences between rock and funk are perhaps best understood by their rhythmic underpinning. Music Example 11-1 compares a rock drum pattern with a funk drum pattern.

The funk drum pattern is more complex, because it is based on a sixteenth-note subdivision and incorporates more syncopation, while the rock rhythm is based on an eighth-note subdivision. Hence, funk music is more likely to be syncopated and

Music Example 11-1
A rock drum pattern and a funk drum pattern.

rhythmically complex; rock music is generally less syncopated and often characterized by the use of "straight" or "even" eighth notes. Both drum patterns incorporate a heavy use of backbeats, almost always played on the snare drum.

The first experiments in fusion took place in the late sixties. Much of the impetus for and early development of the style came from Miles Davis and his sidemen. Davis's watershed albums *In a Silent Way* and *Bitches Brew,* both from 1969, helped introduce both electric keyboards and rock/R&B rhythms and harmonies to the jazz audience.

The first wave of popular jazz-rock groups in the early seventies—Mahavishnu Orchestra, Weather Report, Return to Forever, and Herbie Hancock's Headhunters—were formed by former Miles Davis sidemen. These groups earned extensive critical and popular acclaim. Using electronic instruments and the rhythmic grooves of rock and funk, these new groups displayed first-rate improvisational skills and strongly defined compositional structures. Recordings by these groups sold well, too, surpassing many of the musicians' expectations for commercial success. For the first time since the swing era, a form of jazz had become popular again.

Despite the potential of these early fusion groups, two trends occurred that helped, as musician/critic Bill Laswell described, "assassinate the promise of fusion"[1] during the second half of the seventies. The first negative trend was an overreliance on flashy but largely empty technique. Some of the fusion players relied on faster and faster playing in their improvisations. As guitarist Al DiMeola candidly admitted, "I really wanted to become the fastest guitarist in the world. Just like the track stars want to become the fastest runner in the world."[2]

The second negative trend in fusion's evolution was its commercialization. Whereas a typical jazz record might sell 10,000 to 20,000 copies, some of the most popular fusion records sold more than a million. To tap into this market, record companies put subtle—and sometimes not so subtle—pressure on musicians to simplify their music. The more commercially oriented fusion products gravitated toward slickly packaged, danceable, ingratiating music, with catchy melodic hooks replacing the substance of an improvisational or compositional core.

Because of these commercial trends, fusion musicians soon began to earn withering critical scorn for "selling out." For example, in a telling interview with keyboardist George Duke in 1977, *Down Beat* interviewer Lee Underwood soundly reprimanded Duke for his commercial leanings: "There are some artists who shoot for immortality," Underwood pontificated, "not just for a heated swimming pool and a house in the Hollywood hills."[3]

Although some fusion artists continue to break new ground, one of the legacies of fusion—"smooth jazz"—is unabashedly oriented toward extensive radio airplay

Backbeats are heavy emphases on beats 2 and 4, as played by the drummer (usually) on the snare drum. (Other drums or the hi-hat can be used for quieter backbeats.) Backbeats can be added to a 4/4 swing rhythm as well. Backbeats increase danceability by clarifying the rhythm and adding to the visceral excitement of the music.

Smooth jazz is a popular form of fusion jazz that is common today. It combines rock or funk grooves with an electronic ambience to create an "easy listening" feel. Although improvisation may be present, the pleasant quality of the groove and melody are its dominant features.

(see Chapter 12). Although it can be argued that smooth jazz is simply satisfying popular demand—much like the cookie-cutter swing tunes of the late 1930s—it can also be argued that latter-day fusion has not fulfilled its earlier artistic promise. Its detractors disdainfully refer to the music as lite jazz, hot-tub jazz, or fuzak (a combination of fusion + Muzak).

The Appeal of Rock and Funk

Many jazz musicians developed a fascination with rock and soul music as these styles developed during the sixties. These types of music were popular with youth to an unprecedented degree and largely embodied the rebellion of the sixties against the mores and values of the previous generation. The new generation of jazz musicians— often naturally rebellious—grew up listening to rock and funk; it was natural for them to incorporate these elements into their experimentation with jazz.

Soul and, later, funk developed out of rhythm and blues, which itself was the offspring of the so-called race records of prewar African-American music. The rhythm and blues of the 1940s embraced a danceable style with a heavy beat and often syncopated rhythms. As the sounds of the swing-era big bands faded away and bebop proved to be uncommercial, rhythm and blues filled the demand for popular music among black audiences.

The soul and funk groups of the sixties and early seventies strongly influenced the development of fusion. The band of singer James Brown, the self-proclaimed "hardest working man in show business," featured horns, electric guitar, electric bass, and drums. Brown's hits such as "Papa's Got a Brand New Bag" and "I Feel Good" made prominent use of harmonies heard in jazz, such as ninth chords. Brown's music was also rhythmically complex, with a strong backbeat and highly syncopated, rhythmically interlocking parts for the bass, guitar, and drums. The dense interplay of the rhythm section instruments in funk suggested a way for upcoming jazz-fusion players to integrate their jazz-oriented harmonies with syncopated rhythms.

Herbie Hancock made the connection between Brown's funk rhythms and the new jazz fusions explicit:

> In the popular forms like funk, which I've been trying to get into, the attention is on the interplay of rhythm between the different instruments. The part the Clavinet plays has to fit with the part the drums play and the line that the bass plays and the line that the guitar plays. It's almost like African drummers where seven drummers play different parts. They all play together and it sounds like one part. To sustain that is really hard.[4]

Slap bass is a technique in which the bass player percussively hits the low strings of the instrument while picking melodies on the higher ones. This style was created by Larry Graham and subsequently imitated by jazz, funk, and popular bass players.

Another influential soul band, particularly admired by Miles Davis and Herbie Hancock, was the group Sly and the Family Stone, whose hits in the late sixties and early seventies included "There's a Riot Going On," "I Want to Take You Higher," and "Everyday People." The group's electric bassist was Larry Graham, who developed a technique of thumping the low strings while plucking the higher strings, creating a percussive funky sound. This style was picked up by other funk players and by fusion electric bassists such as Stanley Clarke, Alphonso Johnson, Marcus Miller, and Jaco Pastorius, who made the "slapping and popping" sound an important component of their playing.

In addition to soul and funk, rock also made an impact on the development of fusion. Rock, which came of age in the 1950s, developed out of a complicated mix of 1940s R&B, country and folk music, and Delta and electric blues, among other elements. With the "British Invasion" of the mid-1960s, groups such as the Beatles and the Rolling Stones earned phenomenal popularity by covering compositions by African-American blues and R&B artists such as Chuck Berry, Muddy Waters, and Robert Johnson.

After first performing in the United States in 1964, the Beatles became cultural icons impossible to ignore. In 1966 jazz drummer Art Taylor conducted a series of interviews with jazz musicians in his book *Notes and Tones,* asking each of the jazz musicians interviewed what they thought of the Beatles.[5] Intense opinions about them, pro and con, also arose in George Simon's interviews with big-band leaders Count Basie, Woody Herman, Stan Kenton, and Artie Shaw in Simon's book *The Big Bands.*[6] Eventually, many of the jazz stalwarts gave in to pressure from the record companies and other musicians to incorporate rock tunes into their records and performances. On the recording *Ellington '66,* Duke Ellington recorded versions of the Beatles' compositions "All My Loving" and "I Want to Hold Your Hand." Count Basie recorded *Basie's Beatle Bag,* consisting entirely of Beatles compositions. Jazz guitarist Wes Montgomery's albums *Michelle* and *A Day in the Life* were titled after the Beatles compositions included on each record. Woody Herman's late sixties group played the Fillmore auditoriums and recorded rock songs such as the Doors' "Light My Fire."

Despite such experimentation, covering popular rock tunes in a jazz setting proved to be relatively infertile. As fusion developed, the music retained the rhythms, harmonic concepts, and electric ambience of rock music but used these elements to support improvisation. Covering hit tunes became far less common.

Early fusion artists expressed admiration for the solos of rock guitarist Jimi Hendrix. Hendrix was a self-taught guitar virtuoso who used feedback, distortion, and electronic devices in his extended and flamboyant solos. His hit "Purple Haze" (the title based on a nickname for the hallucinogenic drug LSD) prominently featured a sharp ninth chord, a harmony frequently found in jazz settings. Hendrix took part in two of the most famous rock music festivals of the late sixties—the Monterey Pop Festival and Woodstock. His psychedelic performance of "The Star-Spangled Banner" at Woodstock is one of the most compelling and famous moments in the film of the concert. He also had an interest in jazz. For example, he recorded with fusion guitarist John McLaughlin and organist Larry Young late in his career, and he had several discussions with Miles Davis about recording an album, which sadly never materialized. Hendrix died in 1970 from a drug overdose.

Other rock-oriented bands of the late sixties and early seventies managed to fuse jazz with rock while appealing to a wider public. Blood, Sweat, and Tears thrived on a formula of horns and jazz-based solos to augment their rock compositions, which featured the soul-based singing of David Clayton-Thomas. The group penned a string of Top 40 hits, as did the band Chicago, which used similar instrumentation. Some experimental rock groups, such as the British bands Soft Machine and King Crimson, featured even more extended improvisation. Jazz artists Chick Corea and Gary Burton both acknowledged the influence of King Crimson on their work.

The Fusion Music of Miles Davis

In a remarkable jazz life in which he was always at or near the center of the action, Davis managed to pioneer jazz development yet again with his groundbreaking work in fusion. His watershed albums *In a Silent Way* and *Bitches Brew* were important for their adoption of electric keyboards, rock-based rhythms, dense percussion textures, and simplified harmonic foundations often based on repeated ostinato figures. As we shall soon discuss, Davis's sidemen on these recordings formed the first wave of the major fusion groups in the early seventies.

Davis never turned back. For the rest of his career, he continued to explore creative, improvised music within rock, funk, and computer-controlled synthesizer frameworks. In doing so, he gained an even higher degree of popularity and commercial success. After releasing *Bitches Brew*, Davis began playing at rock music venues, such as the Fillmore East in New York and the Fillmore West in San Francisco. In this astute professional move, Davis tapped into a wider audience by opening for rock acts such as the Grateful Dead, the Band, Santana, and Crosby, Stills, and Nash. (See the box "Miles Davis in the Early 1970s.")

Davis stopped performing between 1975 and 1981 because of declining health. He had developed problems from cocaine addiction; further, he had an arthritic hip and stomach ulcers exacerbated by alcoholism. He returned from seclusion with the 1981 album *The Man With the Horn*, which included saxophonist (not pianist) Bill Evans, bassist Marcus Miller, drummer Al Foster, and guitarist Mike Stern, whose

Miles Davis in the Early 1970s

With his move to fusion and accompanying popularity, jazz traditionalists such as singer Betty Carter accused Davis of selling out by cashing in on a popular trend: "It's all about money. . . . They [Davis, Herbie Hancock, and Donald Byrd] have a 'reasonable' excuse for the why of what they're doing, but the only excuse is money."[*]

Nevertheless, a review of Davis's early 1970s recordings shows just how uncompromising and uncommercial much of his music actually was. In contrast to the well-rehearsed, high-octane precision of fusion groups like the Mahavishnu Orchestra and Return to Forever, or to the dance-floor grooves of Herbie Hancock, Davis's groups often performed dissonant, atmospheric, seemingly free-form medleys stitched

together loosely by a rock or funk beat. With a band consisting of keyboardists Chick Corea and Keith Jarrett, drummer Jack DeJohnette, bassist Dave Holland, and saxophonist Steve Grossman, Davis gave his musicians plenty of improvising space. As a result, many of the pieces seemed to rewrite themselves each night: "Friday Miles" (named for the night the group performed), from his 1970 recording *At Fillmore*, combined versions of "Pharoah's Dance," "Sanctuary," "Bitches Brew," "Miles Runs the Voodoo Down," "I Fall in Love Too Easily," and "The Theme." The record-side length of each composition on the double album was created by splicing together chosen segments of longer, live performances.

In the live performances themselves, Davis developed a musical system to signal

the group to segue into another piece, as Enrico Merlin shows here:

> I have discovered three types of what I call "coded phrases" corresponding to particular characteristics of the relative piece:
> 1. The first notes of the tune
> 2. The bass vamp
> 3. The voicings of the harmonic progressions
>
> For example, in the case of "It's About That Time" the coded phrase is taken from the voicings of the descending chord progressions played by the electric piano.[†]

Merlin's observations have been corroborated by musicians who played with

[*] Linda Prince, "Betty Carter: Bebopper Breathes Fire," *Down Beat,* May 3, 1979, p. 14.

[†] Enrico Merlin, "Code MD: Coded Phrases in the First 'Electric Period,'" 1996 [Online]; available at http://wam.umd.edu/~losinp/music/code_md.html.

heavy-metal, Hendrix-like solos jazz critics loved to hate. In the 1980s Davis continued to show his flair for hiring some of the rising young stars of jazz by picking up guitarist John Scofield in 1982. Scofield inspired Davis to return to his blues roots: The trumpeter featured a twelve-bar blues on "It Gets Better" from *Star People.*

As in the past, these newer sidemen continued with prominent careers after their association with Davis. Guitarists Stern and Scofield are among the important guitarists of today; Miller flourished with an accomplished career as a bassist, synthesist, and producer, and Bill Evans has remained in the forefront as a saxophonist.

Although Davis continued to tour and perform, he turned more often to the studio for his albums rather than recording live as he had in the early seventies. For example, Davis created a landmark album in 1985—*Tutu*—which was named after Archbishop Desmond Tutu, winner of the Nobel Peace Prize for his work in ending apartheid in South Africa. *Tutu* made extensive use of studio technology; the tracks were arranged and the synthesizers were programmed by Davis's former bass player, Marcus Miller, with the help of Jason Miles. The album was constructed by introducing layers of synthesized drum tracks, percussion, and keyboards. The funk grooves and catchy melodic ideas provided a foundation over which Davis later added his trumpet solos.

Despite the slick studio technology on *Tutu*, Davis's playing was unmistakable. For instance, over the funky vamp on "Splatch," Davis displayed his trademark muted trumpet—the same subtlety of phrasing and the same start-and-stop ideas that had characterized his playing for four decades. Despite the sometimes radical change of

Courtesy Morgan Collection

A promotional button from WPLJ Radio advertises a Miles Davis 1982 concert in New York City.

Davis during this period. Interestingly, Merlin notes that Davis developed the medley concept before he turned to fusion. For example, with his acoustic bands of the mid-1960s, Davis would often begin the next piece while the previous piece was ending.

Captivated by the guitar playing of Jimi Hendrix, Davis began incorporating guitar into his ensembles in the seventies, at times recording with two and sometimes even three guitarists. He soon dispensed with acoustic bass by hiring Michael Henderson, an electric bassist who had played R&B and soul in the Motown studios with songwriter/vocalist Stevie Wonder. Henderson provided the anchor for Davis's group, establishing the tonal center and two- or four-bar ostinato riffs for the soloists to improvise over. Al Foster was often the drummer called on to set the groove with Henderson.

In contrast to the funk-based rhythm sections, Davis's horn lineup was more in keeping with his bands of the past. For his saxophonist, Davis often used a player strongly influenced by John Coltrane, such as Dave Liebman, Gary Bartz, or Sonny Fortune. Usually these players played soprano saxophone. Davis himself played both trumpet and organ. Like the rock guitarists and keyboardists of the era, he often used a wah-wah pedal on trumpet. During live performances, Davis would stalk the stage, often directing the musicians from the organ with cues that were sometimes overt, sometimes imperceptible.

A **wah-wah pedal** is a pitch-frequency filter operated by the foot that is usually used by guitarists or electric keyboardists. When the pedal is depressed, the note or chord being held makes a "wah" sound. (An acoustic "wah" sound can be achieved by brass players using their left hands or mutes over the bells of their instruments.) The up-and-down movement of the pedal creates the repeated "wah-wah" effect.

musical circumstances, his style was remarkably consistent throughout his career. Trombonist and composer J. J. Johnson sums up this point neatly:

> Miles is doing his natural thing. He's just putting in today's setting, on his own terms. If you put Miles and his new group in the studio and record them on separate mikes and then you cut the band track and you just played the trumpet track, you know what you'd have? The same old Miles. What's new is the frame of reference.[7]

On his final albums, Davis continued to experiment with studio technology. His work from the late eighties featured sampled, electronically derived soundscapes—much like Miller's work on *Tutu*—over which Davis added trumpet improvisations. Davis died of a stroke on September 28, 1991, at age sixty-five. His last recording, *doo bop,* was released posthumously and incorporated hip-hop grooves and rap. He had been an integral part of the jazz scene for more than four decades, always moving and changing. Interestingly, nearly half of his career was dedicated to fusion music after he helped spark the trend in the late sixties.

Speaking of Davis's role in incorporating aspects of R&B, rock, and funk music into the jazz idiom, pianist Ramsey Lewis noted:

> It was not until the late sixties when Miles Davis gave his stamp of approval by incorporating some of these ideas into his albums that musicians accepted the fact that rock rhythms and influences other than the traditional ones could be integrated with jazz.... Davis extended the harmonic concept, employed polyrhythmic patterns, added electronic instruments and devices to his trumpet along with his highly unique and creative ability, and set the pace for what has come to be known as fusion music.[8]

Other Fusion Pioneers

Miles Davis was not the only prominent jazz musician responding to rock and funk in the sixties. Jazz guitarist Larry Coryell (b. 1943) was one of the earliest musicians to incorporate rock, blues, and even country elements into his jazz playing. Like some of the other young players in the mid-sixties, he took a wildly eclectic approach. Coryell later remembered, "We were saying, We love Wes [Montgomery], but we also love Bob Dylan. We love Coltrane but we also love the Beatles. We love Miles but we also love the Rolling Stones."[9]

In 1966 Coryell was part of the Free Spirits; the following year, he joined the Gary Burton Quartet, recording the albums *Duster* and *Lofty Fake Anagram* with Burton. Most of Coryell's solo from "Walter L." (from *Gary Burton in Concert*) could have come from a late-sixties rock band. Coryell used blues-based licks, playing with sustain and distortion that approached feedback in one spot. Coryell's performance with guitarist John McLaughlin on Coryell's 1970 recording *Spaces* provided one of the high points of early fusion guitar. In the seventies, Coryell formed the group Eleventh House, but his playing was eclipsed by emerging fusion guitarists such as McLaughlin.

Another early form of jazz-rock fusion was played by The Fourth Way, a San Francisco–based band led by New Zealand pianist Mike Nock (b. 1940). Nock was one of the first players to make extensive use of electric keyboards, playing a Fender Rhodes electric piano, synthesizers, and using devices such as the wah-wah pedal on the three albums the group recorded between 1968 and 1971.

Courtesy Morgan Collection

Guitarist Larry Coryell was one of the first guitarists to bring a rock-based approach into a jazz idiom.

The late sixties also witnessed the formation of an important band called Dreams. Among its players were many of the upcoming stars of the fusion movement, including drummer Billy Cobham (b. 1944); tenor saxophonist Mike Brecker (b. 1949); Mike's brother, trumpeter Randy Brecker (b. 1945); and guitarist John Abercrombie (b. 1944). Abercrombie's use of feedback and distortion on "Try Me," from the 1970 recording *Dreams*, showed the attraction of high-energy rock guitar playing.

CTI Records

Another important development in the early seventies was the founding of CTI Records, named after record producer Creed Taylor. Many sixties-era jazz musicians who were on the verge of moving into fusion were still maintaining a postbop approach on their records for this label. These included drummer Billy Cobham, pianists Chick Corea and Herbie Hancock, guitarist George Benson, and saxophonist Joe Farrell. Despite its fine roster, however, CTI's critical reception was often mixed, largely because of Taylor's frequent practice of overdubbing string or orchestral accompaniments. Taylor also supposedly discouraged drummers from using brushes, so that on many of the slower ballads the listener was treated to the unusual sound of the drummer keeping time with sticks. On the best of the CTI Recordings, such as Milt Jackson's *Sunflower* and George Benson's *White Rabbit*, the quality of the improvisations made up for the string accompaniments.

LIFETIME

One of the most important early fusion bands was Lifetime, a dynamic trio formed by Tony Williams, the drummer who had earned tremendous acclaim with Miles Davis in the sixties. Originally from Boston, Williams had been a drumming prodigy, playing regularly around the city by age fifteen. In 1963, at age seventeen, Williams recorded in New York with saxophonist Jackie McLean (for Blue Note) and was soon asked to join Miles Davis's quintet. Williams's style changed along with Davis's: for example, on Davis's 1969 album *In a Silent Way*, Williams kept up a steady, regular rhythm, abandoning the explosive, unpredictable playing that had previously been his trademark with the Davis quintet.

In a Silent Way included an astounding British guitarist who had arrived in the United States only two weeks before. John McLaughlin, born in Yorkshire in 1942, had played in British rock and jazz groups during the fifties and sixties and had participated in studio sessions with pop singers Tom Jones, Petula Clark, and David Bowie. McLaughlin's 1969 album *Extrapolation,* recorded while he was still living in England, demonstrated the guitarist's remarkably fast execution in an acoustic jazz format. Instead of the syncopated phrasing of traditional jazz guitarists, McLaughlin's playing was even, hard, and cutting. He occasionally used bent pitches in the manner of rock guitarists.

Invited by Williams, McLaughlin left Britain to come to the United States and join Lifetime. The group began as a trio; along with Williams on drums and McLaughlin on guitar was organist Larry Young. Lifetime not only was indebted to the jazz tradition but also drew inspiration from jam-oriented rock bands such as Jimi Hendrix and Cream. On the title track from the Lifetime recording *Emergency!*, the group alternated a repeated four-bar figure with a half-tempo improvisation by McLaughlin. "Spectrum" probably best showcased the hybrid approach of the group: It moved from a Hendrix-like rock vamp to improvisational sections with a 4/4 swing feel, with walking bass played by Young on the organ. The rapid unison line of "Spectrum," played by guitar and organ, foreshadowed McLaughlin's later work with the Mahavishnu Orchestra.

Blending jazz and rock rhythms and held together by Williams's high-energy "take no prisoners" style of drumming, Lifetime never achieved a wide popularity. The group's raucous energy, propelled by the distortion and sheer volume of the guitar and organ, was too extreme for mainstream jazz fans, while its often dissonant and extended improvisations proved too esoteric for mainstream rock fans. Lifetime's second album, *Turn It Over,* was even more explicitly rock-based: It included bassist Jack Bruce of Cream on three of the tracks.

Tony Williams's work with Miles Davis and Lifetime earned him almost legendary status among jazz drummers of the eighties and nineties. He continued with a variety of projects involving both jazz and rock, including reunions with the Miles Davis rhythm section of Herbie Hancock and Ron Carter in a group known as V. S. O. P. He also performed with some up-and-coming younger players such as Mulgrew Miller and Donald Harrison. The jazz world was greatly saddened by his early death from heart failure at age fifty-one in 1997. His final albums, *Wilderness* and *Young At Heart,* are interestingly varied: The former includes experiments with merging the classical and jazz worlds, while the latter is a piano trio record featuring Mulgrew Miller and bassist Ira Coleman. Later in 1997, Williams was elected to the *Down Beat* Hall of Fame.

A **bent pitch** is achieved by pushing against the guitar's string on the fretboard, thus "bending" it. The resulting effect is a tiny glissando or slide from one frequency to a slightly higher one.

MAHAVISHNU ORCHESTRA

Lifetime was short-lived—the group broke up in 1971—but the hard-driving energy of the music was something fresh. John McLaughlin was emerging as one of the important guitarists on the jazz scene. McLaughlin and Larry Coryell were perhaps the two musicians most responsible for bringing the sound of rock guitar into the jazz idiom.

McLaughlin's concept of jazz-rock guitar included elements of non-Western musical traditions, especially classical Indian styles, along with the blues licks typical of the fifties and sixties R&B guitar playing. During this time, McLaughlin adopted as his guru Sri Chimnoy; accordingly, the titles of McLaughlin's solo albums *Devotion* and *My Goal's Beyond* reflected his newly formed spiritual interests. On *Devotion*, McLaughlin hired two of Jimi Hendrix's sidemen, drummer Buddy Miles and bassist Billy Cox; *My Goal's Beyond* used two Indian musicians, Badal Roy and Mahalakshmi, along with jazz players such as saxophonist Dave Liebman, bassist Charlie Haden, and drummer-percussionist Airto Moreira. One side of *My Goal's Beyond* was merely solo acoustic guitar.

After Lifetime broke up, McLaughlin began to assemble one of the first, and most important, fusion bands of the seventies. The Mahavishnu Orchestra was named by McLaughlin's guru. McLaughlin hired drummer Billy Cobham, who had played with Horace Silver and the band Dreams, Czech keyboardist Jan Hammer, who had been a member of Sarah Vaughan's trio, Irish bassist Rick Laird, and violinist Jerry Goodman, who had been a member of the rock group The Flock.

The success of the Mahavishnu Orchestra was phenomenal. Their 1971 recording *The Inner Mounting Flame* reached number 89 on the *Billboard* chart; the following year their second album, *Birds of Fire,* reached an astounding 15 on *Billboard*. (The *Billboard* chart records the top 200 selling albums on a weekly basis; jazz albums have rarely shown up even at the bottom of the chart.) Like that of Miles Davis, the Mahavishnu Orchestra's popularity enabled them to play concerts and tour on the rock music circuit. In contrast to the loose, often ethereal jazz-rock improvisations played by Miles Davis, however, the Mahavishnu Orchestra was tightly rehearsed. The group played dazzling unison figures, complex meters (such as 7/8 or 5/16), ostinato figures—sometimes indebted to Indian music—and rock rhythms pounded out at a ferocious velocity by drummer Billy Cobham, who used a drum set with double bass drums, one played by each foot. On *double-necked guitar,* using wah-wah pedal and other electronic devices, McLaughlin tore through rapid-fire sixteenth-note solo passages, bending notes and using distortion at deafening volume. (Listen to Track 41 on the 🅟 Audio Primer CD to hear jazz-rock guitar with wah-wah pedal.)

Not all of the compositions played by the Mahavishnu Orchestra relied on high-octane, blisteringly fast playing. For example, "A Lotus on Irish Streams," from *The Inner Mounting Flame,* and "Open Country Joy," from *Birds of Fire,* are pastoral, acoustic reveries. Much of the band's impact derived from the dramatic juxtaposition of acoustic works such as these with high-energy electric compositions.

All in all, as more than one writer has observed, the Mahavishnu Orchestra's recordings "remain benchmarks for ensemble cohesion and inspired jazz-rock improvisation."[10] The group seemed to awaken new possibilities at a time when

A **double-necked guitar** has two necks. Sometimes the second neck has twelve strings rather than the usual six.

many jazz musicians were excited by the potential of jazz-rock. Keyboardist George Duke recalled:

> When fusion was first happening, it was the most interesting music I had heard in my life. It reached its peak with the Mahavishnu Orchestra. . . . But it seemed like after that everybody was copying each other and getting too technically oriented, playing so many notes and scales that the feeling was going out of the music.[11]

The group disbanded in 1973. McLaughlin formed a second Mahavishnu Orchestra in 1974. The short-lived, eleven-piece group included Jean-Luc Ponty, a highly talented French violinist who went on to create his own fusion recordings during the seventies and eighties, including the albums *Imaginary Voyage* and *Enigmatic Ocean*. After the Mahavishnu Orchestra broke up, much of McLaughlin's work abandoned the fusion directions he had helped chart. He concentrated on acoustic guitar, playing with the Indian-based group Shakti and later in an acoustic guitar trio with Paco de Lucia and Al DiMeola.

HERBIE HANCOCK AND HEAD HUNTERS

With his work as a member of the breakthrough Miles Davis quintet between 1963 and 1968 and with his own Blue Note recordings, Herbie Hancock distinguished himself as one of the most important jazz pianists and composers of the sixties. Hancock was Davis's first sideman to use the Fender Rhodes electric piano, on the album *Miles in the Sky*. After leaving Davis's band, Hancock continued to use electric piano on his recordings *Crossings, Mwandishi*, and *Sextant*. Hancock's group for these recordings—usually a sextet—was booked into rock music venues such as the Fillmore, but their spacey, open-ended improvisations proved unsuccessful, and Hancock was forced to disband the group in 1973.

Before abandoning the rock circuit, however, Hancock had the significant experience of opening for the R&B pop group the Pointer Sisters at the Troubadour club in Los Angeles. Hancock was impressed by the direct audience appeal of the Pointer Sisters. He began to think about taking his music in a direction that had more popular appeal, one rooted in the funk and R&B styles of James Brown, Stevie Wonder, and especially Sly and the Family Stone. Introduced to Nichiren Shoshu Buddhism by his bassist, Buster Williams, Hancock experienced a revelation while chanting:

> My mind wandered to an old desire I had to be on one of Sly Stone's records. It was actually a secret desire of mine for years—I wanted to know how he got that funky sound. Then a completely new thought entered my mind: Why not Sly Stone on one of my records? My immediate response was: "Oh, no, I can't do that." So I asked myself why not. The answer came to me: pure jazz snobbism.[12]

Although Hancock never recorded with Stone, he did achieve a breakthrough into popular culture with his phenomenally successful album *Head Hunters*. The album reached number 13 on the *Billboard* chart, then eventually went platinum. With the exception of reed player Benny Maupin, who was with his earlier group, all the members of Hancock's new quintet had been steeped in funk music. His intent, Hancock claimed, was to hire not jazz musicians who could play funk, but funk musicians who could play jazz. *Head Hunters* made extensive use of overdubs and

The **Mellotron** is an electronic instrument that was used for string-ensemble effects in the seventies. An early, analog sound module, the Mellotron produces notes by activating short tape recordings of a string ensemble playing each note of the scale. When a key is depressed, the tape recording of the particular note corresponding to the key plays.

Arp synthesizers were among the first synthesizers made specifically for live performance.

studio technology, including tape loops. In addition to playing the Fender Rhodes electric piano, Hancock also played Arp synthesizers, the Mellotron, and other electronic keyboards.

Hancock's solo on "Chameleon" established him as one of the finest live performers on synthesizer. Much of the success of Hancock's *Head Hunters* album was due in fact to "Chameleon," which became a hit largely because of its syncopated, danceable two-measure bass riff and catchy melody. (See the box "Herbie Hancock's Synthesizer Solo on 'Chameleon.'")

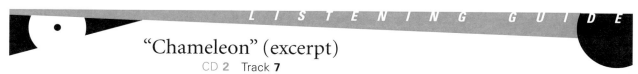

L I S T E N I N G   G U I D E

"Chameleon" (excerpt)

CD **2**   Track **7**

The Herbie Hancock Group: "Chameleon" (Hancock), from *Head Hunters*. Columbia KC 32731. San Francisco, 1973. Herbie Hancock, keyboards; Bennie Maupin, soprano saxophone, tenor saxophone, saxello, bass clarinet, alto flute; Paul Jackson, electric bass and marimbula; Harvey Mason, drums; Bill Summers, percussion.

Because of its infectious funk groove, "Chameleon" was an enormously successful hit for Hancock, earning him a huge crossover audience. Most of the composition is based on a simple riff in the bass texture, played by the synthesizer.

Opening Riff

0:00   The piece begins with a repeated funk riff played on the synthesizer. This riff forms the backbone of the entire composition. The riff is played twice by itself.

0:12   The other instruments are gradually added to the texture, one by one. The drums begin against four statements of the riff.

0:31   A guitarlike synthesizer sound plays a simple, rhythmic line.

0:51   The clavinet, a percussive keyboard instrument, is now added to the texture. Hancock plays a funky rhythmic accompaniment on the clavinet.

Melody—Repeated 8 times, then altered

1:29   The tenor saxophone, doubled by a synthesizer, states the catchy melody over the accompanimental texture. The melody repeats four times and is based on the B♭ minor pentatonic scale (B♭, D♭, E♭, F, A♭, B♭).

2:15   The melody is stated four more times.

2:53   The first half of the melody is altered, beginning with a descending gesture. The second half of the melody remains the same. The opening synthesizer riff stops and plays in unison with the final statement of the descending gesture.

3:24   The drums play a break, bringing about the return of the synthesizer riff.

3:28   The synthesizer riff returns. Again, as at the beginning, the bass and the clavinet are added to the texture.

Synthesizer Solo

4:04   The synthesizer solo begins. (See box "Herbie Hancock's Synthesizer Solo on 'Chameleon.'")

5:55   Listen here for Hancock's repeated riff.

7:05   The tenor saxophone/synthesizer melody returns, now stated along with Hancock's synthesizer solo.

On *Head Hunters*, Hancock revived his earlier hit "Watermelon Man," a composition recorded more than ten years earlier on his first album. On the updated version, percussionist Bill Summers plays an Africanlike rhythm by blowing on a beer bottle. Although Hancock was later criticized for "selling out," not all of the compositions on *Head Hunters* were overtly commercial. "Sly," a homage to Sly Stone, included several drastic tempo changes and featured daring improvisations by both Hancock and saxophonist Benny Maupin.

Herbie Hancock's Synthesizer Solo on "Chameleon"

The synthesizer performs most advantageously when its unique timbral qualities are imaginatively exploited. Hancock's solo succeeds because it does what cannot be done on any other instrument, particularly the segments with the modulated sounds and the portamenti (slides between notes).

Hancock's synthesizer solo is so effective partly because of the beautiful balance among three distinct elements: free blues lines, repeated funky riffs, and nonpitched sounds. Unlike the controlled voice leading and motivic structure that tend to unify bop and traditional jazz solos, the funky jazz-rock solo tends to be sectional, that is, to feature a single idea until it settles in.

The bass line establishes the harmonic orientation of the piece by alternating B♭7 and E♭7—the standard I and IV harmonies of the B-flat blues. Hancock's solo responds to these blues harmonies with an emphasis on the B-flat blues scale.

Hancock begins his solo with several very funky blues licks, generously separated by space. The repeating pattern of measures 38–43 is gradually transformed by the addition of modulated sound. As "noise," this passage cannot be transcribed exactly into notes on the staff; hence, only the rhythm is suggested for the most part. Noise or unpitched sound of this sort is usually produced by frequency or amplitude modulation of the signal.

Compositional subtlety and extended improvisation gradually faded from Hancock's later recordings. The group's next project, *Thrust*, used repetitive funk and dance rhythms, although Hancock's composition "Butterfly" was haunting and evocative, reminiscent of some of his earlier impressionistic recordings for Blue Note in the sixties. Hancock's subsequent recordings were marketed squarely as commercial products, placing strong dance grooves in the forefront. Hancock's *Manchild* was

Modulation of a sound wave occurs when the sound is modified by being fed through another wave.

In **amplitude modulation**, the amplitude (the range of loud and soft) of the wave is modified by another wave.

In **frequency modulation**, the frequency (the range of high and low) of the wave is modified by another wave. Both of these techniques produce sounds vastly different from the original.

This modulated section is the first of two such passages that are similarly syncopated. The continuous dotted quarter notes of this section effect a fascinating cross-rhythm with the underlying 4/4 meter.

The drummer moves to the bell of the ride cymbal to complement the funky patterns beginning in measure 102. The repetitions help to drive the solo forward, but not at the expense of its funky earthiness.

Hancock's pattern beginning in measure 116 shows a 3/4 rhythm superimposed on the basic underlying 4/4 of the bass line and rhythm section. Such a polyrhythm begins to create a sense of polymeter, because the rhythms are maintained for a considerable length of time and are clearly delineated.

Polymeter is the juxtaposition of two or more musical lines in different meters at the same time.

(continued on the following page)

aimed at the burgeoning seventies disco market; nevertheless, he found space for an impressive acoustic piano solo on "Hang Up Your Hangups."

In response to the sometimes hostile comments from jazz critics, Hancock insisted that his dance music recorded in the seventies and eighties was not jazz:

> Jazz fusion is another idiom. It uses elements of jazz and elements of popular forms, but it established its own idiom. I'm not concerned with changing that idiom, or changing disco. I want to play the music I'm playing and still have it be dance music. Making some music that is fun to dance to and really nice to listen to, some music that has emotion in it.... It's funny because many of the elements are simpler than before. For example, a lot of the music happening today has simpler chord structures and simpler harmonies than in the past. The complexity is now in the textures and in keeping the groove going.[13]

Hancock's biggest success came with "Rockit," from the 1983 album *Future Shock,* which stayed on the pop music charts for more than a year and became a classic MTV video. Musically and commercially successful, Hancock's work within fusion

Herbie Hancock's Synthesizer Solo on "Chameleon"
(continued)

Beginning in measure 134, the rhythmic component of the modulated sound becomes very complex: The 4:5 notation signifies that four notes are played in the time of five beats. This rhythm interlocks with the 4/4 meter in such a way that the pattern begins first on the downbeat, then on the second beat, and so on. In addition to the overall 4:5 polyrhythm, each large pulse is subdivided into three or four smaller note values, thus generating a multilevel polyrhythmic texture.

When Hancock chooses to step out of the blues scale, he usually does so with a patterned riff. A strikingly effective deviation from the blues scale occurs toward the end of the solo (measures 156–162), where Hancock gradually bends the pitch of the synthesizer (probably using a left-hand control device such as a pitch-bend wheel) a half-step higher, thus simulating the upward blue-note bend on a larger scale. The bounce back to the correct intonation comes across as the large-scale resolution of the inflected blue note.

and funk-based styles numbers among the most important of any jazz artist in the seventies and eighties.

Despite success in the pop-funk market, Hancock frequently returned to an acoustic jazz format, playing in a hard bop idiom with the V. S. O. P. ("Very Special One-Time Performance") Quintet. The group reunited Hancock with his former band mates from the Miles Davis Quintet—bassist Ron Carter, drummer Tony Williams, and saxophonist Wayne Shorter—and included trumpeter Freddie Hubbard. Hancock also returned to the hard bop and modal idiom in recordings with trumpeters Wynton Marsalis and Wallace Roney. On his 1996 album, *The New Standard*, Hancock performed jazz arrangements of pop hits by the Beatles and others, succeeding where many earlier attempts to cover such tunes failed.

On the 1998 album *Gershwin's World*, Hancock teamed up with an impressive array of players from the jazz, popular, and classical fields, such as jazz pianist Chick Corea, classical soprano Kathleen Battle, the Orpheus Chamber Ensemble, and pop musicians Stevie Wonder and Joni Mitchell. We shall return to Hancock and this album in Chapter 12, because it both embodies the eclecticism of the 1990s and hints at a possible direction for jazz in the twenty-first century.

The solo reaches its climax with the return of the full band, in call-and-response exchanges with Hancock. Here, Hancock plays solo breaks that blend the ubiquitous blues licks into chromatic scale segments. This procedure winds up the solo in a logical and satisfying manner.

CHICK COREA AND RETURN TO FOREVER

Herbie Hancock's replacement in the Miles Davis Quintet was Chick Corea, who joined Davis in the fall of 1968. In summer 1970, Corea gave notice to Davis in order to pursue his own projects and an interest in what he called musical "abstraction." His recordings *Song of Singing* and *Circle: The Paris Concert* made extensive use of free improvisation. The next year, however, Corea became interested in communicating with a wider audience, as Hancock had. His two solo piano albums, *Piano Improvisations,* volumes 1 and 2, showed Corea in a transitional stage: The first side of each contained songs marked by relatively simple forms, structures, and lyrical melodies, while the second side of both albums were free atonal improvisations.

With Corea's group Return to Forever, the pianist abandoned free playing, moving decisively toward airy, Brazilian-influenced music. He hired bassist Stanley Clarke, saxophonist and flutist Joe Farrell, drummer Airto Moreira (who often went by his first name only), and Airto's wife, singer Flora Purim. The group made two recordings, *Return to Forever* and *Light as a Feather,* which highlighted Corea's sophisticated compositions. Some of these—such as "Spain" and "La Fiesta"—were playful references to Spanish music. "Spain," in fact, opened with a solo piano introduction that borrowed material from composer Joaquin Rodrigo's *Concierto de Aranjuez*—a melody which was used earlier on the Miles Davis/Gil Evans collaboration *Sketches of Spain.* Both Airto and Purim were Brazilian, and the group played Brazilian sambas and Latin-influenced rhythms with astonishing clarity and freedom. Corea's tunes caught on. "It seemed like after we made that record," saxophonist Joe Farrell related about *Light as a Feather,* "Everybody and their brother started playing sambas and songs with melodies. It became very popular."[14]

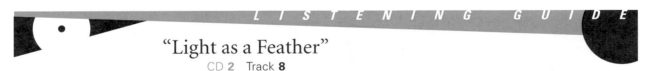

LISTENING GUIDE

"Light as a Feather"
CD 2 Track 8

Chick Corea and Return to Forever: "Light as a Feather" (Purim-Clarke), from *Light as a Feather.*
Polydor PD 5525. London, October, 1972. Chick Corea, electric piano; Stanley Clarke, electric bass; Flora
Purim, vocal; Joe Farrell, tenor saxophone and flute; Airto Moreira, drums and percussion.

"Light as a Feather" is a Latin-oriented example of early seventies jazz-rock. Recorded without over-dubbing, except perhaps for a few percussion instruments, it could be performed live without much change in its sound or impact.

The work has a more complex structure than the AABA or ABAC form typical of older jazz standards. As shown in the following guide to the performance, section I presents the song as a head. It can be broken down into smaller sections, s1–s1–alternating chords interlude–s2, where s1 and s2 are the first and second parts of the song itself.

Section I—Head; subsection s1 (repeated)

0:00   The first part of the song (s1), beginning with the words *clear days,* is stated twice, followed by a freer vocal melisma (notes sung on one syllable) of *ah.* The vocal melody is doubled in the flute an octave higher.

Section I—Head; alternating-chords interlude

1:14   A calm, almost static passage with alternating chords. This passage serves to delineate sections of the performance.

Section I—Head; subsection s2

1:28   The second part of the song (s2) begins with the lyric *there's a place*. The vocal is not doubled by the flute.

1:55   The song climaxes on the word *free,* the exact moment that Corea uses the wah-wah pedal for intensity. The saxophone and electric piano solos each build to climaxes that can be identified by the use of this device.

Section II—Electric piano solo, part 1

2:03   Corea's solo starts out sparsely, with interjections between phrases by bassist Clarke, and this continues for eighteen bars. The drummer continues with the light, even-eighths beat heard in the head.

2:36   Corea's phrases become much more rhythmic.

Section II—Electric piano solo, part 2

2:51   The drummer changes to a new pattern along with a fast walking bass. Corea's solo is characteristically driving, with chordal rhythmic attacks in unusual places.

4:16   The solo winds down with the wah-wah pedal.

Section II—Alternating-chords interlude

4:49   The alternating-chords interlude returns to introduce the saxophone solo.

Section II—Saxophone solo, part 1

4:57   Saxophonist Joe Farrell plays short, lyrical lines at first, using a good deal of space in his solo.

5:22   The accompaniment becomes more funky and forceful here. Farrell begins to play longer lines.

5:52–5:58   Listen for his move to playing outside of the chord changes.

Section II—Saxophone solo, part 2

6:02   The entire group moves into a samba feel. Listen for the bass and drums playing this groove, making the rhythm seem twice as fast as the music heard previously. Corea's comping on the electric piano is highly syncopated.

7:01–7:06   Corea plays a Latin-style accompanimental line in octaves here.

End of saxophone solo

7:19   The saxophone solo reaches its climax at the same time that Corea uses the wah-wah pedal on the electric piano. The solo ends with effects played in the highest range of the horn.

Section II—Bass solo, parts 1 and 2

7:39   The bass solo shows Clarke's adept, facile playing.

8:03   The bass solo moves to a double-time feel here, with precise, virtuosic lines played with Brazilian percussion accompaniment.

Piano solo and interlude

9:13   Following the bass solo, Corea plays a brief solo that leads to the return of the s1 and alternating-chords sections.

Return of vocal

9:40   The vocal returns here with s2 ("There's a place...").

10:21   The song concludes with s1.

Return to Forever: The Masters.

Chick Corea, Stanley Clarke, Lenny White and Al DiMeola have created a music that presents staggering technical demands, emphasizes interplay between musicians, and insists on constant originality.

They've developed a style which is increasingly imitated. But there's no doubt who the masters are. Return to Forever. "Romantic Warrior." A radically original album on Columbia Records.

RETURN TO FOREVER
ROMANTIC WARRIOR
including:
Medieval Overture/Sorceress
Majestic Dance / The Magician
Duel Of The Jester And The Tyrant
(Part I & Part II)

The members of the Return to Forever (CD 2, Track 8) band were Chick Corea, Stanley Clarke, Lenny White, and Al DiMeola; here is an advertisement for their album *Romantic Warrior* from Columbia Records in 1976.

The title "Light as a Feather" characterizes the album as a whole. The lightness is achieved by the relative lack of bass drum in the rhythm section. Instead, the bass—itself never too heavy—dominates the lower frequencies. The amplified acoustic bass here offers a delicate sound, more akin to an unamplified bass than the heavier electric bass guitar usually heard in jazz-rock. The prominent Latin rhythms and the lively character of the performances imbue the work with a feeling of joy and exhilaration throughout.

Corea reorganized Return to Forever in 1973, converting the group into an electric quartet. Only Stanley Clarke remained from the earlier band, but he switched from amplified acoustic bass to electric bass. Lenny White, who had performed on Miles Davis's *Bitches Brew,* was the drummer. The electric guitarist on *Hymn to the Seventh Galaxy,* the first album of the revamped Return to Forever, was Bill Connors, but he was soon replaced by Al DiMeola. As for the repertory and overall style of the group, Corea drew upon his own experiences playing with Miles Davis, but he was equally inspired by John McLaughlin's Mahavishnu Orchestra. "John's band, more than my experience with Miles," Corea admitted, "led me to want to turn the volume up and write music that was more dramatic and made your hair move."[15]

Like the Mahavishnu Orchestra, Return to Forever excelled in playing exciting, impressive unison lines at breathtaking speed. Corea performed not only on electric piano but also on Moog and Arp synthesizers, clavinet, and organ. As heard on "Vulcan Worlds," from the album *Where Have I Known You Before,* Clarke was one of the fastest and most facile electric bassists around. Adept at both improvising and accompanying, he made effective use of the slap-and-pop techniques of funk bass. *Where Have I Known You Before* also contained occasional solo interludes on acoustic piano, with the free-flowing harmonies of the title cut sounding like an homage to Bill Evans's "Peace Piece." At its best, Return to Forever's music was compositionally sophisticated: The group effectively blended complex forms, meter and tempo changes, and well-written ensemble passages with dynamic and virtuosic improvisation.

The group's follow-up recordings, *No Mystery* and *Romantic Warrior,* pursued the path begun with the earlier albums, although some of the compositions became shorter and contained less improvisation. It is possible that the group and its record company were aiming for selections suitable for commercial radio airplay. On these recordings, the group experimented with numerous subgenres of jazz-rock, rock, and funk; hence, there were funk grooves ("Sophistifunk" and "Jungle Waterfall"), "art-rock" orchestral effects ("Romantic Warrior"), and even heavy metal ("Excerpt from the First Movement to Heavy Metal").

Corea broke up the electric group in 1975. Bassist Stanley Clarke (b. 1951) worked sporadically with Corea during the remainder of the decade but also issued a series of commercially oriented recordings under his own name. Among them, "School Days" was a successful hit; even more popular was "Sweet Baby," a collaboration between Clarke and keyboardist George Duke that made the Top 20 in 1981.

Like Clarke, guitarist Al DiMeola (b. 1954) continued as one of the most successful names in fusion. He released a series of albums in the Return to Forever mold, most notably *Elegant Gypsy* and *Casino*. These emphasized DiMeola's brilliant though flashy technique and were testaments to his desire to become "the fastest guitarist in the world." Among later projects, DiMeola played in an acoustic guitar trio with John McLaughlin and Paco de Lucia and experimented with synthesizer textures as accompaniment to the acoustic guitar.

Corea went on to create a larger, more orchestral version of the Return to Forever concept by making use of strings and horns. A series of "thematic" albums followed in the second half of the seventies. *Mad Hatter*, with its Alice in Wonderland motif, included lesser efforts such as the "Trial of the Queen of Hearts," distinguished by the repeated phrase "Who stole the tarts, was it the Queen of Hearts." On one cut, however, Corea returned to a postbop, acoustic jazz format, playing in a straight-ahead swinging quartet context on "Humpty-Dumpty" with drummer Steve Gadd, saxophonist Joe Farrell, and bassist Eddie Gomez. Similarly, *MusicMagic* featured dazzling solos as well as

Stanley Clarke (CD 2, Track 8) in an early promotional photograph. Clarke made the switch to electric bass as a member of Return to Forever when Corea turned the group electric.

Courtesy Morgan Collection

stunning, complicated written ensemble passages for horns with simpler pop-style tunes sung by Corea's wife, Gayle Moran, and bassist Stanley Clarke. One of Corea's most dramatic and sparkling improvisations was played over a Latin-based rhythm on "Armando's Rhumba" (from *My Spanish Heart*), played with bassist Stanley Clarke and violinist Jean-Luc Ponty.

Like Hancock, Corea's subsequent career in the 1980s and nineties included work in both electric and acoustic formats. His group, Chick Corea's Elektric Band, with bassist John Pattitucci and drummer Dave Weckl, set the standard for fusion playing in the 1980s. Corea also returned to the acoustic trio format on two recordings: *Trio Music* (featuring the music of Thelonious Monk) and *Live in Europe*. The trio reunited Corea with bassist Miroslav Vitous and drummer Roy Haynes, who had performed on Corea's 1968 recording *Now He Sings, Now He Sobs*.

Corea's compositional inventiveness and brilliance has led him to undertake musical projects that combine extensive written composition with improvisation, such as *Three Quartets* and his *Sextet* recording. In the 1990s Corea returned to his earlier musical roots, recording a tribute to Bud Powell and performing with his group Origins.

WEATHER REPORT

One of the longest-lasting and best-known fusion groups, Weather Report first formed in 1970. They recorded fifteen albums in their fifteen-year history. The group underwent numerous personnel changes, with only founding members keyboardist Josef Zawinul and saxophonist Wayne Shorter—both of whom worked with Miles Davis in the sixties—remaining through the band's tenure. In addition to changes in personnel, Weather Report also undertook several changes in musical direction. They began as an acoustic group that used collective improvisation that was sometimes metrically free. However, by their third album, 1973's *Sweetnighter*, keyboardist and composer Zawinul was moving the group in a direction toward more strongly defined compositional structures and more rock- and funk-based rhythms and grooves. They reached the high point of their popularity when electric bassist Jaco Pastorius joined the band and they recorded their hit composition "Birdland," from the album *Heavy Weather*.

Born in Austria in 1932, Zawinul was raised in Vienna and studied at the Vienna Conservatory. Arriving in the United States in 1959, he worked early on with band-leader Maynard Ferguson and singer Dinah Washington. But it was his ten-year stint, from 1961 to 1970, with alto saxophonist Cannonball Adderley that gave Zawinul national exposure. Foreshadowing his later interest in synthesizers and fusion, Zawinul played electric piano with Adderley during the late sixties. His use of the instrument

A 1979 publicity photo of Weather Report (CD 2, Track 9): Joe Zawinul, Wayne Shorter, Peter Erskine, and Jaco Pastorius.

Courtesy Morgan Collection

helped bring its sound into the jazz idiom. (Zawinul was not first to promote the electric piano in jazz, however: Ray Charles and Sun Ra had performed on electric keyboards in the late fifties, and Earl Hines had both performed and recorded on a "Storytone" electric piano as early as 1940.)

Showing a natural talent for pop-jazz crossover, Zawinul wrote the Adderley band's prominent soul jazz hit, "Mercy, Mercy, Mercy." On this cut, Zawinul played the Wurlitzer electric piano; on the group's other big hit, "Country Preacher," he played a Fender Rhodes. In the latter performance, he altered the tone bars to give the instrument a more percussive sound. In 1969 Miles Davis paid the distinct compliment of recording Zawinul's composition "In a Silent Way," while hiring him to play electric piano alongside Chick Corea and Herbie Hancock. On the recording, Davis simplified the piece's harmonic progression. Zawinul, who described "In a Silent Way" as a tone poem recalling the Austrian hills of his childhood, rerecorded the composition on his own album, *Concerto Retitled,* the following year.

In 1970 Zawinul and Wayne Shorter formed Weather Report with Czech bassist Miroslav Vitous. The quintet was initially filled out by drummer Alphonse Mouzon and percussionist Airto Moreira. With Zawinul on electric piano and Shorter primarily on soprano saxophone, Weather Report's first two albums, *Weather Report* and *I Sing the Body Electric,* emphasized mood, color, and collective improvisation. On these early albums, the group frequently abandoned traditional distinctions between soloist and accompanist. Bassist Vitous not only provided support but also played melodically. Similarly, Zawinul rarely relied on traditional chordal accompaniment behind soloists but instead interjected lines and chords freely.

By *Sweetnighter,* the group had moved toward danceable grooves underlying the solos. In "Boogie Woogie Waltz," for example, the group maintained a consistent 3/4 rock beat beneath Shorter's oblique saxophone lines and Zawinul's Fender Rhodes's parts, colored by the sound of the wah-wah pedal. The composition also showed new directions that the group would continue to explore: the use of electric bass (on the piece, both electric and acoustic bass are heard) and a short, catchy four-measure melody that is repeated. The latter highlighted Zawinul's ability to write brief melodic ideas as song hooks.

Sweetnighter was the first of Weather Report's recordings on which Zawinul also played synthesizer. He would soon become one of the premier synthesists in fusion, mining the vast compositional and coloristic possibilities of the instrument. By the group's next album, *Mysterious Traveller,* Zawinul was behind a stack of Moog and Arp synthesizers as well as electric piano augmented by wah-wah pedal, *phase shifter,* and *echoplex.* With electric bassist Alphonso Johnson replacing Miroslav Vitous, the group also took a decisive turn toward funk rhythms and grooves. Johnson, who played fretless electric bass, laid down a syncopated, funky, repeated figure on "Cucumber Slumber"; as on Hancock's "Chameleon," the bass figure dominated the groove.

Beginning with the 1976 album *Black Market,* electric bassist Jaco Pastorius joined the band. Pastorius redefined electric bass playing with ripping, staccato funk accompaniments; fast, clean solos; interjections of surprising harmonics and entire chords; and a liquid sound that often incorporated vibrato at the ends of phrases. Born in Morristown, Pennsylvania, in 1951, Pastorius began his career playing in local soul and jazz bands. He made the trio recording *Bright Size Life* with guitarist Pat Metheny, but it was his own 1975 recording *Jaco Pastorius* that showcased his

A **phase shifter** is an electronic device that alters the sound of an instrument by altering the wave shape. The resulting sound has a bubbling or slightly hard-edged quality.

An **echoplex** unit is a commercial electronic device popular in the late sixties and seventies that could be used to add echo to a sound. The rate of speed of the echo could be altered so that the delay effect could be slight or more pronounced.

remarkable abilities. On "Donna Lee," accompanied only by percussion, Pastorius glided effortlessly through the melody of the bebop classic, then followed with an astounding solo; on "Come On, Come Over," with vocals by soul singers Sam and Dave, Pastorius's percussive accompaniment revealed new and exciting approaches to funk bass playing.

With Weather Report, Pastorius's outgoing exuberance brought more and more fans to the band's live performances, which generally showcased the bassist in a solo feature that combined Jimi Hendrix's "Purple Haze" and "Third Stone from the Sun" with "Donna Lee" and the Beatles tune "Blackbird." Pastorius was "an electrifying performer and a great musician," noted Zawinul. "Before Jaco came along we were perceived as a kind of esoteric jazz group . . . but after Jaco joined the band we started selling out concert halls everywhere."[16]

Pastorius was a talented composer, too, writing "Teen Town" and "Havana" for the Weather Report's best-selling album, *Heavy Weather*. Largely on the popularity of Zawinul's composition "Birdland," *Heavy Weather* reached 30 on the *Billboard* chart and became a gold record, selling more than 500,000 copies. The tune was later recorded by bandleader Maynard Ferguson and, with added vocals, by Manhattan Transfer. "A Remark You Made," also from *Heavy Weather*, was a hauntingly evocative ballad featuring Wayne Shorter on tenor saxophone.

L I S T E N I N G   G U I D E

"Birdland"
CD **2**   Track **9**

Weather Report: "Birdland" (Zawinul), from *Heavy Weather*. Columbia PC 34418. North Hollywood, California, 1977. Josef Zawinul, composer, keyboards; Wayne Shorter, soprano and tenor saxophone; Jaco Pastorius, bass, mandocello, vocals; Alejandro Acuna, drums; Manalo Badrena, tambourine.

As do many of Zawinul's fusion compositions, "Birdland" comprises tightly connected sections of brief, singable melodies. The piece is a marvel of ingenuity, with its varied sections uniting in an imaginative and well-crafted whole.

As the following table shows, the piece exhibits a complex structure with numerous sections of unpredictable length, rather than the usual eight-bar units of AABA formats.

Introduction—12 measures

0:00   A four-bar synthesizer bass line is heard three times.

Part I—AAB, 24 measures

0:18   A four-bar main thematic idea (A), played by bassist Jaco Pastorius, is added to the four-bar vamp. The idea is played four times: twice in a lower register, then twice in a higher register; an eight-bar B section idea completes Part I with a saxophone added.

G Pedal—4 measures

0:55   A transition pedal point that reaffirms the G tonality.

Part II—20 measures

1:02   The piano introduces a new four-bar vamp idea. At the end of the third statement of the vamp, a new bass line enters that recalls the earlier bass line, but in augmentation (longer note values).

Part III—9 measures

1:32   A saxophone melody is joined to the next section to create this unusual nine-bar unit.

Transition—9 measures

1:46   The saxophone melody deconstructs into call-and-response funky figures among various timbres.

Part IV—24 measures

1:59   A new four-bar vamp idea appears that implies a III–VI–II–V–I "turnaround" chord pattern.

Transition—8 measures

2:36   Recalling the earlier G pedal, this transition emphasizes G. During the second four bars of the eight-bar section, a backbeat (in part syncopated) is added in the snare and continues into the next section.

Synthesizer solo—12 measures

2:49   The synthesizer solo grows out of the bass line almost imperceptibly. The harmonic focus continues to be on a G pedal.

Saxophone solo—14 measures

3:07   The static G of the last two sections beautifully sets up the background for the saxophone solo: The synthesizers create a two-bar vamp of chords moving down in half-step chromatic motion. This is the climax of the performance. Shorter's saxophone solo shows the group's ability to interweave written and improvised sections seamlessly.

Transition—4 measures

3:29   The texture is again radically simplified for contrast with the preceding section: The G pedal returns.

Reprise of Part I—24 measures

3:35   Over the simplified texture of the preceding section, the melody from Part I returns. As it proceeds, the original bass line is added, then the B section returns with heightened energy.

Reprise of Part II—8 measures, modified

4:11   The four-bar vamp from Part II returns in a modified form.

Reprise of Part IV—Fade-out

4:23   The material from Part IV returns with a long fade-out combining added texture and improvisation.

5:00–5:56   Sparsely at first, Zawinul adds a synthesizer solo to the texture, which gradually becomes more active.

A handclap is added as a backbeat, increasing the energy and adding a jam-session aura during the fade.

On some subsequent Weather Report albums of the late seventies—as with other promising fusion bands, such as the Brecker Brothers—the group turned to formulaic disco rhythms. Their 1978 album *Mr. Gone,* with Peter Erskine on drums, received negative reviews. *Mr. Gone* earned only a one-star "poor" rating in *Down Beat;* according to the critic, Weather Report had abandoned its creative moorings:

> It seems that the general Weather Report idea is to fill each composition with a mechanical bass ostinato, dense synthesized chording, and funky, cluttered drumming.... Where earlier Weather Report albums possessed a sense of adventure, *Mr. Gone* is coated with the sterility of a too completely pre-conceived project.[17]

The review generated enormous controversy, and the group angrily responded to the criticisms in a *Down Beat* interview the following month.

Nevertheless, the group remained enormously popular. In 1980 Weather Report won the reader's poll category in *Down Beat* for the ninth year in a row. Pastorius left the group in 1982, forming his own group, Word of Mouth, which recorded two albums. Unfortunately, alcohol and cocaine addiction brought about severe personal problems for Pastorius, who died after a barroom fight in 1987.

After Pastorius left, Weather Report persisted, creating several albums—*Procession* (1983), *Domino Theory* (1984), *Sportin' Life* (1985), and their final recording, *This Is This* (1986). After the group broke up in 1986, Zawinul formed Weather Update, a short-lived group that played Weather Report compositions; in 1988 he put together the Zawinul Syndicate with guitarist Scott Henderson.

The Zawinul Syndicate has continued to explore musical styles that blend different cultures. For example, Zawinul's album *Stories of the Danube* (1996) unites orchestral music and jazz in a tapestry linked thematically by the Danube and the cultures influenced by the river. In 1998 the band toured the world and released a two-CD set documenting an event called *World Tour.* Zawinul has also been involved in staging multicultural festivals throughout the world.

As mentioned in Chapter 10, Wayne Shorter has also pursued a variety of projects. For example, he recorded an interesting duo record with Herbie Hancock in 1997, *1+1.* Other projects include large-scale orchestral works that sometimes feature Shorter on saxophone.

Despite the varied directions of Shorter and Zawinul in the 1990s, Weather Report remains their legacy from the seventies and eighties. During the fifteen years they kept the band together, Weather Report explored a remarkable abundance of compositional styles and approaches. As Stuart Nicholson summarizes:

> Despite being routinely described as a "jazz-rock" band, their stylistic outlook was extremely broad, perhaps the most inclusive in jazz. Their range extended from classical influences such as the French Impressionists to free jazz, from World music to bebop, from big-band music to chamber music, from collective improvisation to tightly written formal structures, from modal vamps to elaborately conceived harmonic forms, from structures with no apparent meter to straight-ahead swing.... Both Zawinul and Shorter created a large body of work that, outside of Duke Ellington, numbers among the most diverse and imaginative in jazz.[18]

PAT METHENY

Guitarist Pat Metheny was one of the most original and popular fusion artists to emerge in the mid-seventies. Much of his work avoided the cutting, hard-rock sound favored by other fusion guitarists such as John McLaughlin. Instead, Metheny preferred bright, lyrical, and often gentle timbres.

Metheny's distinctive sound was created by his use of electronic devices, such as *chorus reverberation, digital delay,* and phase shifters. He used them not for distortion and power effects, but rather to give his instrument a fatter, richer sound. In addition, Metheny shunned the pyrotechnics of other fusion guitarists, such as John McLaughlin and Al DiMeola. "I'm not," he made clear, "drawn to the athletic approach to the music." Rather, Metheny saw his lyricism as part of the midwestern melodic tradition of Lester Young and Kansas City: "Even today I think of what I'm playing as sort of a Kansas City style, evolved or modernized. It's that melodic, lyrical thing."[19]

Pat Metheny in the 1970s.

Courtesy Morgan Collection

Metheny was born in Lee's Summit, Missouri, in 1954. A musical prodigy, he taught guitar at the University of Miami at age seventeen. Two years later he was invited by vibraphonist Gary Burton to join the faculty at the Berklee College of Music in Boston. Metheny continued his association with Burton by recording and performing in the vibraphonist's quartet.

Metheny's first album, *Bright Size Life,* was released in 1976. Created with bassist Jaco Pastorius and drummer Bob Moses, it showed Metheny's penchant for clear melodic lines with an occasional country twang. "Unity Village" was a quiet solo guitar piece, on which Metheny overdubbed himself. Elsewhere, he displayed his affinity for the music of Ornette Coleman—whom Metheny called "one of the most melodic musicians ever"[20]—by recording two of Coleman's compositions in a medley, "Round Trip/Broadway Blues."

After *Bright Size Life,* Metheny put together a quartet for touring, consisting of drummer Danny Gottlieb, electric bassist Mark Egan, and keyboardist Lyle Mays. The group built a national reputation by playing one-nighters throughout the country. *Watercolors,* his next album, was followed by the lyrical *The Pat Metheny Group* in 1978. The moody, gentle "Phase Dance," from the latter album, featured simple, spacious, diatonic harmonies, with pianist Lyle Mays capturing the folksy quality sometimes heard in Keith Jarrett's playing.

Metheny's next several albums explored a variety of genres. For example, in contrast to his earlier work, *American Garage* was more rock-oriented and was dedicated to the garage bands across the country. "Heartland"—one of Metheny's many compositions recalling his midwestern roots—had a decidedly country flavor. Metheny brought Brazilian percussionist Nana Vasconcelos into his group for *As Falls Wichita, So Falls Wichita Falls,* but the dreamy ostinatos featured on many of that album's compositions caused some to dismiss the recording as musically thin—

Chorus reverberation is an electronic effect that guitarists use to "fatten" or fill out sounds. The sound signal is enriched through the addition of reverb (echo) and a chorus-effect (that is, added frequencies complement the sound, giving the effect of several voices or tones sounding at once).

Digital delay is an electronic effect that creates an echo or secondary sound, so that a guitarist can, in effect, play several parts at once.

a cross between Muzak and New Age. For his album *Offramp*, Metheny made use of what was then the most sophisticated synthesizer, the Synclavier.

Metheny also performed in acoustic jazz settings. His recording *80/81* included Ornette Coleman's former bassist Charlie Haden, along with drummer Jack DeJohnette and saxophonists Michael Brecker and Dewey Redman. The group engaged in open-ended improvisation on Ornette Coleman's "Turnaround." On *Rejoicing*—recorded with bassist Charlie Haden and another Coleman alumnus, drummer Billy Higgins—Metheny featured three of Coleman's compositions. On *Song X*, Metheny finally recorded with Ornette Coleman himself. The record was an uncompromising enterprise that both enhanced Metheny's status in the jazz world and brought Coleman to a larger listening public.

On subsequent recordings, Metheny merged his neoromantic streak with Brazilian elements, as on the 1987 album *Still Life Talking*, which won a Grammy award, and on *Letter from Home* (1989), which brought to the fore another aspect of Metheny's music, the use of wordless vocals. Metheny also provided some of the music to the soundtrack for the 1985 film *The Falcon and the Snowman*.

By the late 1990s, Metheny—by now an eminent and respected elder statesman for fusion—was involved in several related projects that built on his previous work and reputation and that sometimes involved nonfusion concepts as well. In 1999, for example, he released albums with his longtime hero, guitarist Jim Hall, and saxophonist Dave Liebman. In a recent article, Metheny summed up his beliefs:

> I made a commitment to focus on and bring into sound the ideas I heard in my head that might not have existed until my time, to try to represent in music the things that were particular to the spiritual, cultural and technological potentials that seemed to be actively available to me in the shaping of my own personal esthetic values.[21]

This statement may serve as a general credo for the ideals of jazz-rock fusion. At its best, it is a happy marriage of rock, funk, technology, and jazz. Despite reactions against fusion on the part of some musicians (see Chapter 12), its basic philosophy has provided an important direction for jazz in the twenty-first century.

Jazz-Rock, Jazz-Funk Styles

TIMBRE

- ▶ Electronic; either
  - Very hard-edged, raucous
  - Smooth, vague
- ▶ Upper instrumental ranges emphasized
- ▶ Use of blue note effects, particularly in funky substyles
- ▶ Ambience of rock with many electric and electronic instruments in addition to more traditional instruments
- ▶ High volume in many forms

PHRASING

- ▶ Highly irregular in improvisation, but thematic heads often composed in two- and four-bar units

RHYTHM

- ▶ Wide variety of rhythmic values, but eighth notes emphasized in up-tempo improvising
- ▶ Highly energetic
- ▶ Very relaxed; sometimes out of tempo

THEMATIC CONTINUITY

- ▶ Motivic

CHORD-SCALE RELATIONS

- ▶ Inside, although can become outside in high-energy modal rock performances
- ▶ Blues scale usages in funky styles

LARGE-SCALE COHERENCE

- ▶ Motivic

Questions and Topics for Discussion

1. What are the principal differences between rock and funk?

2. What changes in rhythm and instrumentation did fusion bring to jazz? Describe the new instrument that the fusion bands of the 1970s began to use.

3. How did the performance and sound of the electric guitar change in the fusion bands, compared with electric guitar in earlier jazz groups?

4. How does the keyboardist's accompaniment in a fusion band generally differ from that of a pianist in an acoustic jazz group?

5. How can Miles Davis's career be seen as a virtual history of jazz from the late 1940s to the 1970s?

6. What were some of the most significant fusion bands? Who were their key musicians?

Key Terms

Amplitude modulation
Arp synthesizer
Backbeats
Bent pitch
Chorus reverbation
Digital delay
Double-necked guitar
Echoplex
Feedback
Frequency modulation
Jazz-rock (jazz-funk, fusion)
Mellotron
Modulation
Phase shifter
Polymeter
Samplers
Sampling
Slap bass
Smooth jazz
Sound modules
Wah-wah pedal

With CDs, MP3, streaming audio, MIDI technology, and programmable disks, never has music—recorded and live—been more widely and instantly available to so many people. At the dawn of the twenty-first century, the potential for creativity and invention appears just as boundless as it was a hundred years ago. Although the previous century may well have been the American century, the next promises to be global—perfectly in sync with jazz trends.

JAZZ SINCE THE 1980s

ALTHOUGH THE SEVENTIES was the decade of fusion, numerous nonfusion artists and substyles prospered then: Dixieland and traditional jazz (Doc Cheatham, Preservation Hall), swing-based styles (Count Basie, Benny Carter), bebop (Johnny Griffin, Phil Woods, Art Blakey), big bands (Toshiko Akiyoshi and Thad Jones/Mel Lewis), and free jazz (Ornette Coleman, Lester Bowie). Fusion gained the most attention, however, by attracting many of the younger players and by generating the most controversy among the media and jazz fans.

The proliferation of nonfusion jazz styles in the seventies is no surprise: Musical styles launched in the course of jazz history almost never disappear. As a result, the history of jazz should be seen not as a linear progression from style to style—with each new style displacing the previous one—but as a profusion, with styles added as younger musicians tinker with, build on, or simplify the work of more-established artists. Hence, jazz history is a rich overlapping of improvisational approaches—a general succession from artist to artist, not from style to style.

Still, because fusion was the big story of the seventies, the eighties has rightly been seen as a return to jazz traditionalism: a revival of the acoustic formats and postbop approaches that were forged in the late fifties and sixties. For many of the younger players of the eighties, this return to traditionalism meant a reconnection to the roots of jazz, roots sometimes neglected by the fusion players of the seventies. For some, such as Wynton Marsalis, this traditional stance became ideological: Marsalis has positioned himself as a forceful, influential, and articulate spokesperson in support of the traditional aesthetic. Traditional values continue to be extremely popular as the twenty-first century begins.

As with other jazz styles since the eighties, fusion has not dropped from the scene; indeed, smooth jazz, fusion's commercial legacy, remains quite popular, with such well-known artists as Kenny G generating interest and impressive record sales. Further, many commercial radio stations are entirely devoted to the smooth jazz format. In the case of 1970s fusion, there have been three spin-offs: the popular-music connection, the recent jazz avant-garde, and world-beat popular musics. Similarly, the 1960s avant-garde also can be seen as having three legacies: a continuation of an acoustic avant-garde scene, an electronic avant-garde scene (intersecting with a legacy of fusion), and a world-music connection. These legacies are in many cases called "crossover" because they combine jazz (or jazz values) with the styles and musics of other cultures.

To summarize, we can think of contemporary jazz as:

- Traditionalist or Mainstream
- A legacy of 1970s fusion:
  - ▶ Popular-music connections, electronic or smooth jazz
  - ▶ Electronic avant-garde
  - ▶ Crossover to "world-beat" popular music
- A legacy of 1960s avant-garde:
  - ▶ Acoustic avant-garde
  - ▶ Electronic avant-garde
  - ▶ Crossover to world-music cultures

The rest of this chapter discusses these three trends in further detail, beginning with an overview of the traditionalists and their return to jazz "classicism."

Classicism and the Jazz Repertory Movement

Jazz since the eighties has witnessed an exploding interest in the history of jazz. This mini-renaissance has had two key results:

1. Increases in the re-creation and live performance of the older jazz music

2. Complete works of older jazz artists reissued on digital compact discs (CDs)

The live performance of earlier jazz—usually in concert hall settings—is called the "jazz repertory movement."

To introduce the repertory movement and its widespread implications for jazz in the twenty-first century, we shall describe the notable appearance of complete-works jazz recordings on CD, a movement parallel to and thematically linked with the repertory movement.

COMPLETE JAZZ-RECORDING REISSUES

After the LP was introduced in the late 1940s, record companies began to learn that profiting from the highlights of their *back catalog* was simpler and cheaper than developing and promoting unknown artists was. However, many of the major labels, such as Columbia and RCA, initially failed to capitalize on this idea. Instead, smaller independents—such as Riverside and Original Jazz Library (OJL)—reissued this

Crossover music combines jazz or jazz values with other styles and musics of other cultures.

The **jazz repertory movement** refers to ensembles devoted to the re-creation and performance of historically significant jazz artists and their work. Just as classical music has an accepted repertory of great works, the jazz repertory movement is trying to establish an official canon for jazz.

A **back catalog** includes the complete recordings that a company holds in its vaults or claims the rights to by having purchased other record labels. Many of these recordings are out of print or were never issued in their original form.

material, often by drawing on collectors who had meticulously preserved the original 78 recordings. When the major labels realized the profits that could be made by issuing this material, they began their own reissue series, beginning in the late fifties and early sixties and continuing through today.

The digital CD replaced the analog LP as the commercial record format of the 1980s and 1990s. Record companies realized they could sell the same albums that they had issued in the fifties, sixties, and seventies to a new generation of listeners (and in many cases to the same audience who had purchased the LPs originally and now wanted the same material on CD). Also, the development of digital sound *remastering* enabled companies to reissue with superior sound quality much of the material on 78s.

Hence, the 1980s and 1990s witnessed an explosion of CD reissues. *Down Beat* magazine, for example, began a column devoted entirely to reissues. What used to be a difficult collector's task—tracking down every recording made by a particular artist—has became much simpler. Current CD reissues comprise not only studio recordings but also live work.

*Complet*e reissues in jazz arguably began with Charlie Parker, whose collected Savoy studio recordings appeared in 1978 (on LP). The company decided to include every scrap of recorded material, no matter how insignificant. Sometimes excerpts were only a few seconds long, with the recording cut off by Parker, the recording engineer, or producer following a *false start,* technical problem, or other blatant error. No matter—every flub was issued, available for scrutiny. This completist philosophy was subsequently extended to Parker's other two record companies, Dial and Verve, as well as to live performances of Parker, often captured on amateur equipment in informal settings.

Complete issues work fairly well for jazz of the 78-rpm era and perhaps the early LP era, but it is more controversial when modern studio sessions are anthologized. For example, *The Miles Davis Quintet 1965–68: The Complete Studio Recordings* contains fascinating material, but the integrity of the original albums is destroyed, because the cuts (and outtakes) are all issued in chronological order. This arbitrary reordering of the material has created further problems. For example, only a portion of Davis's album *Filles de Kilimanjaro* is included in the reissue, because the personnel of the band changed while the recording was under way.

This type of reissue disregards the *album* as an aesthetic entity worked up by artist and producer. An album is carefully prepared by an artist who may exclude outtakes and weaker cuts and carefully choose the order of presentation. Still, for those interested in Davis, it is probably better to have this material available for study, despite the problems created by the reissue.

The completist philosophy also has implications for the general direction of jazz. This practice marks a phase of jazz in which the past has overtaken the present in importance. As such, it marks a turning point for jazz by promoting an art form that is less alive, less immediate, and more self-conscious than jazz has ever been before. Historically, European concert music reached a similar point around the end of the nineteenth century and the beginning of the twentieth century, when listeners and many professional performers deemphasized contemporary music and made earlier compositions the focus of their repertory. Some have argued that this point marked a downturn in the immediacy and vitality of European concert music. Interestingly, this turn to the past in classical music may have created the opportunity for the success of jazz: The West was ready for something new, a spontaneous art form that could

Remastering is the digital enhancement of an original recording's sound quality; it includes such techniques as filtering out extraneous noise and boosting certain frequencies.

A **complete reissue** duplicates any recorded material—including errors, outtakes, and technical problems—that the issuing record company can locate.

A **false start** is an incorrect start of a performance: A musician begins playing a measure or two, then, realizing a mistake, stops abruptly.

mirror the increased rhythmic pace and speed of industrialization and communication in the new century.

A refocusing of interest on the jazz past is evident not only in the huge number of CD reissues but also in the repertory movement itself. These practices are mutually related: CD reissues stimulate interest in an artist and lead to more concert performances, while the repertory ensembles stimulate more reissues. Thus, much attention in jazz has been refocused on what has been accomplished, not on what is happening now. It remains to be seen how this preoccupation will affect the second century of jazz.

LIVE PERFORMANCE

The appearance of a book in 1984 by Grover Sales called *Jazz: America's Classical Music* speaks of the impetus of the jazz repertory movement. The idea of jazz as American classical music is not new. Indeed, the U.S. violinist Misha Elman claimed as far back as 1922 that in Europe jazz had "become known as the American classical music."[1] But the difference between current times and the 1920s is that older jazz has now become the preoccupation of major performance organizations, whereas before it was not.

Interestingly, this practice was predicted by stride pianist and composer James P. Johnson in 1947, when he wrote that "jazz musicians of the future will have to be able to play all different kinds of jazz—in all its treatments—just like the classical musician who, in one concert, might range from Bach to Copland."[2]

The idea that jazz should be appreciated and studied alongside the history of Western concert music has generated controversy. Some have argued that such a practice demeans jazz—that by calling it "classical," we are somehow evaluating it through aesthetic and formal criteria developed for European music. Others have countered by claiming that jazz must be appreciated on the same level as European music but not judged by the same aesthetic criteria.

These concerns have helped spark the jazz repertory movement, which is devoted to re-creating older jazz styles and the masterpieces of earlier eras. For example, the Lincoln Center Jazz Orchestra in New York has performed much of the music of major jazz figures at their Jazz at Lincoln Center concerts. Composer and conductor Gunther Schuller has also played a pivotal role in transcribing, performing, and promoting the music of Scott Joplin, Jelly Roll Morton, Duke Ellington, and others. By publishing transcriptions and edited editions of important jazz artists, recent jazz scholarship also supports this historical focus.

A key issue has arisen regarding the performance of jazz repertory: Should a repertory ensemble duplicate recorded performances that were based on improvisation, or does this oppose the jazz spirit? It can be argued that because a recording "freezes" or codifies certain solos, they have become so identified with the pieces that it is a disservice not to duplicate them. And we could respond that if John Coltrane himself were performing in concert, he would not duplicate his own well-known solo from an earlier recording.

Certainly, one common idea about jazz performers is that they improvise all of their solo material. However, by studying alternate takes recorded by the early jazz bands, scholars have shown that performers played some solos more or less identically on each take. A musician always bases his or her improvisation on some notion of the overall shape of the solo; despite variations in individual notes or phrases, this notion usually stays the same. At this point in jazz history, the issue of literal versus imitative duplication of improvisation remains unresolved in practice. Depending on the band, the individual musicians, and the jazz style, repertory ensembles follow a variety of performance techniques ranging from a literal duplication of well-known records to much more informal practices based on the spirit of the earlier music.

Of the nation's repertory jazz ensembles, the three most influential are the Lincoln Center Jazz Orchestra (associated with Jazz at Lincoln Center), the Carnegie Hall Jazz Band in New York, and the Smithsonian Jazz Masterworks Orchestra in Washington, D.C. Jon Faddis has directed the Carnegie Hall Jazz Band since its inception in 1992. Although it is technically a repertory orchestra, the group has premiered numerous new works. Nor does Faddis want to perform older music exactly as it was played previously; as he points out, "One of our goals is to try and do the classical jazz repertoire in our own way."[3] Faddis (b. 1953) has long been a highly respected player on the scene—as a lead trumpeter, high-note specialist, and soloist. He has also associated with many important artists, including the Thad Jones–Mel Lewis band and Dizzy Gillespie.

The Smithsonian Jazz Masterworks Orchestra was founded by Gunther Schuller and David Baker, a jazz trombonist who has taught at Indiana University for many years. It is associated with the National Museum of American History, where it was established in 1990 by an act of Congress. Baker generally uses a twenty-year benchmark in choosing works for programming—that is, any music played should be at least twenty years old so that its historical importance and musical value are reasonably clear.

The best known repertory organization is Jazz at Lincoln Center. The director, Wynton Marsalis, is undoubtedly the most visible jazz artist today. The program has enjoyed astounding success: Beginning with three concerts in 1987, the program soon became a department at Lincoln Center, then in 1996 it became a full-fledged member of the arts consortium, equal in stature to the New York Philharmonic and the Metropolitan Opera. In 1998 Jazz at Lincoln Center announced the creation of a new concert space that will include an 1,100-seat auditorium, as well as office suites and rehearsal rooms.

Jazz at Lincoln Center has benefited immensely from the work of its former executive director, Rob Gibson, and writers Stanley Crouch and Albert Murray, but no one has been more important to its success than Marsalis, who has sought to identify and promote a canon of jazz masterpieces. In making Jazz at Lincoln Center an expression of his musical personality and interests, Marsalis is perhaps the primary spokesperson for the traditionalist point of view.

WYNTON MARSALIS

Wynton Marsalis embodies many of the jazz traditionalist values of the eighties and nineties. Many jazz musicians have cited him as one of the main catalysts responsible for the resurgence of jazz since the eighties. Born in New Orleans in 1961, Marsalis at an early age showed extraordinary talent as a trumpeter, in both the European classical tradition and jazz. His father, Ellis Marsalis, is a professional jazz pianist and prominent educator, while his older brother Branford is a prominent saxophonist.

A 1989 photograph of Wynton Marsalis (CD 2, Track 10) by Ken Frankling. Despite his many Grammy awards for jazz and classical music, Wynton Marsalis may be most widely known for his work promoting music education and his commentary on the Ken Burns *Jazz* series on PBS.

Wynton Marsalis's talent became clear at an early age. For example, at fourteen he performed the Haydn Trumpet Concerto with the New Orleans Philharmonic Orchestra. He attended the Juilliard School of Music briefly, but dropped out to join Art Blakey's Jazz Messengers in 1980. He subsequently toured with Miles Davis's brilliant 1960s rhythm section of Herbie Hancock, Ron Carter, and Tony Williams. This association led to his first album as a leader, *Wynton Marsalis* (1981). In 1984 Marsalis became the first musician to win Grammy awards in both classical and jazz categories.

In 1991 Marsalis was appointed as artistic director of Jazz at Lincoln Center. He has filled this position capably, helping to bring about a greater appreciation of the music. In the latter regard, Marsalis was featured prominently in the Ken Burns multiepisode documentary *Jazz* (2000), which was first broadcast on PBS in January 2001. Largely through the influence of Marsalis, the greats of the jazz past, in particular Louis Armstrong, dominated the Burns film. Not everyone has agreed with Marsalis's protraditionalist point of view, yet there is no denying the positive effect he is having on the appreciation of jazz.

In spite of his rise to prominence as a trumpet player, Marsalis has been focusing more and more on composition. His earliest pieces followed a postbop and modal style; however, he disavowed this direction as his interests began to turn to earlier jazz. For example, in 1987 he wrote a song called "In the Afterglow," which appeared on the album *Marsalis Standard Time,* volume 1. About this tune, Marsalis comments:

> That was the first time I wrote something with a certain type of traditional [chord] progression. Before that, I would write stuff that was modal, with no chords on it. But "In the Afterglow" got me to try to break out of writing the typical type of New York–scene tune and trying to experiment with form, with modulations, with developing themes in different keys, with different grooves.... That's when my [composed] music really started to evolve.[4]

After this point, Marsalis began to incorporate earlier jazz traditions into his music, as the 1989 album *The Majesty of the Blues* testified. His jazz-roots evolution continued with such albums as *Soul Gestures in Southern Blue* (1991), *Blue Interlude* (1992), and *In This House, On This Morning* (1994), the last a large-scale work based on a traditional Baptist church service.

Marsalis's extended oratorio, *Blood on the Fields,* was his first composition for large ensemble and included a libretto by Marsalis. It premiered in 1994 and in 1997 became the first jazz composition to win the Pulitzer Prize for music. The work examines American slavery and its aftermath. An important result of

Marsalis's award is that the Pulitzer Prize in music is now offered for important, large-scale works of any musical genre, whereas the Pulitzer had previously been restricted to concert music.

Despite the honor accorded *Blood on the Fields*, the work received a mixed reception. For example, some critics thought that it had stilted lyrics and that it gave a ponderous overall impression. The piece also generated good reviews and a sufficiently enthusiastic audience response to support an international tour. Above all, the work reveals Marsalis's ambitions to create large-scale pieces in the Duke Ellington tradition. Indeed, Marsalis credits Ellington's *Black, Brown, and Beige* as a precedent for his composition and has frequently cited Ellington as his primary compositional inspiration.

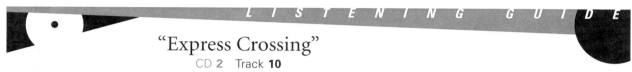

L I S T E N I N G   G U I D E

"Express Crossing"
CD **2**   Track **10**

Jazz at Lincoln Center: "Express Crossing" (Marsalis), from *Jazz: Six Syncopated Movements* (1993), *They Came To Swing*. Columbia CK 66379, 1994. New York, January 14, 1993. Wynton Marsalis, composer and trumpet; Marcus Printup, trumpet; Wycliffe Gordon, Ronald Westray, trombones; Todd Williams, tenor saxophone; Wes Anderson, alto saxophone; Kent Jordan, piccolo; Victor Goines, baritone saxophone; Eric Reed, piano; Reginald Veal, bass; Herlin Riley, drums; Robert Sadin, conductor.

"Express Crossing" is from the larger dance work *Jazz: Six Syncopated Movements,* written for the New York City Ballet. The live performance analyzed here is highly spirited and reveals a composer with a fertile imagination that blends influences ranging from early jazz to Ellington to contemporary modernism. The piece can be compared, for example, with Ellington's "Daybreak Express" (1933), a well-known jazz depiction of a train. Though Marsalis is at heart a traditionalist, this piece can be called postmodern in its blending of disparate styles.

Section I—AA, irregular 8 bars repeated, at tempo I

0:00   After three dissonant chords serving to "start the train," the rhythm begins in a rhythmically complex first section in F major. For the first two bars, the trombones play on-the-beat quarter notes, but an eighth rest at the top of the third bar pushes the quarter notes off the beat. The fourth bar is a 9/8 bar, which serves to bring the quarter notes back "on the beat." (Compare Robert Sadin's comment in the main discussion.)

For the last part of the first A, the alto and tenor saxophones trade rapid quintuplets followed by a "train whistle" honk in the tenor to end the part. Despite the rhythmic irregularities, the basic feel of part A is that of an eight-bar thematic statement.

0:15   The part A is then repeated.

Section II—B, irregular 9 bars, at tempo I

0:27   The B part maintains the up-tempo drive of section I. Its nine bars are punctuated by a 7/8 fourth bar and 7/8 ninth bar. Again, the odd bars serve to turn the beat around.

Section III—C, 4 bars in 4/4, at tempo II

0:40   The tempo changes abruptly for four bars. Amidst train whistles and honks, the piccolo occasionally interjects the chromatic idea heard in the A section. There is also a new syncopated motive played in lower register trumpets, and alto and baritone saxophones.

Section IV—D, 32 bars in 4/4 as 16+16, at tempo I

0:48 A return to the hectic tempo of sections I and II. The sixteenth-note idea is developed in the piccolo, alto, and tenor into a perpetual motion of sixteenth notes. The bass walks in double time. The brass punctuate with sharp chords and occasionally sustain longer chords with glissandi and "fall-offs." The last two bars of the first half feature a break with wah-wah chords in the brass.

1:10 The wah-wah chords continue into the second sixteen bars, as the sixteenth notes in the winds return. The harmonies of the D section are based on the Dixieland classic, "Tiger Rag."

Section V—D, 32 bars in 4/4, at tempo I; Marsalis trumpet solo

1:33 Using the "Tiger Rag" chord progression of part D, Marsalis offers a virtuosic muted trumpet solo. Interestingly, the solo is based on bebop-style chromatic lines. The ensemble backs Marsalis with punctuated chords.

1:52–1:54 Bars 15–16 are a break for Marsalis.

2:14–2:16 Bars 31–32 are also a break for the ensemble to introduce the next section.

Section VI—D, 32 bars in 4/4, at tempo I

2:17 The ensemble returns for a written-out piccolo solo that alternates in turn with Marsalis's (now open) trumpet, honks, brass punctuation and wah-wah chords, and a short bass solo. The final two bars again serve as a break for the ensemble to introduce the next section.

Interlude—3 bars in 2/4 and 1 bar in 4/4, at tempo I

3:01 The piano repeats the quintuplet runs first heard in the alto and tenor at the end of section I. The D bass note at the end of the interlude signals the new key.

Section VII—E, 22 bars in 4/4 + 1 extra beat, at tempo I

3:04 This new section changes key from F major to D major and is largely a duet featuring counterpoint between Marsalis's muted trumpet and the flute. The rhythm continues, and the ensemble punctuates with chords. The last two bars (+ 1 beat) are a break for the ensemble that combines hints of D major and the original key of F major.

Section VIII—A, 4 bars in 4/4, at tempo I

3:35 This section recalls the opening A material, combined with the running sixteen-note idea in the flutes. The trombones, alternating notes, speed up the rhythm of the alternation. The alto and tenor alternate the quintuplets at the end of the section. This section is in G, however, rather than F of the original part A.

Section IX—F, 32 bars in 4/4 at tempo III; 2 beats clipped from last bar

3:46 The mood completely changes as this section features new material in a slower 4/4 swing tempo. The key of G remains from the preceding section. The "Tiger Rag" layout remains roughly as the thirty-two bars divided into a 16+16, although the chords are modified.

Section X—A, irregular 8 bars

4:45 In a reprise of section I, A returns. The last couple of beats are clipped from the alto-tenor quintuplet alteration. The piece ends abruptly.

Marsalis goes beyond traditionalism, however, in works such as "Express Crossing." This piece is a quintessentially *postmodern* work, an imaginative collage of elements that spans twentieth-century jazz and concert music. These elements include the following:

► Modernist dissonance

► Modernist irregular time signatures

► Modernist tempo changes

► Dixieland harmonic progressions

► Train simulations that recall early jazz and boogie-woogie blues

► Bebop-style improvisation

Robert Sadin, who conducted the piece, compares it to composer Igor Stravinsky's *Pulcinella,* a work that similarly weaves in earlier musical elements. Sadin summarizes the impact of "Express Crossing":

> Conducting "Express Crossing" for me was an experience very similar in feeling to conducting Stravinsky's *Pulcinella.* Although Wynton's borrowings are less literal than Stravinsky's, there is a kindred sense of respecting and at the same time revisiting and even refreshing the past.
>
> The blending of elements of Ellington's train music, of Kansas City shuffle, with a sense of the unexpected rhythmic flavor is very characteristic of Wynton (the irregular meters at the beginning, which have the effect of turning the beat around). All of this makes for a very exhilarating musical experience.
>
> Characteristic of Marsalis is that although with the exception of a few solos (and the rhythm section, of course), the music is entirely written out, and yet the players are expected to bring a great deal of personal color and imagination to their parts while also executing the not inconsiderable technical difficulties.[5]

Marsalis's expectation that individual musicians will contribute "personal color and imagination to their parts" recalls the bandleading techniques of Duke Ellington. Clearly, Ellington has provided Marsalis with a potent role model. In a *New York Times* article celebrating the Duke Ellington centennial in 1999, Marsalis described what he admires most about how Ellington handled his own career. The description seems to apply to Marsalis as well:

> After his [Ellington's] initial fame, he could easily have escaped into the art world of the "serious composer" and created some very interesting and tongue-twisting theories about harmony and what-not. He could have retreated to the university to rail bitterly against the establishment while creating a distinguished body of work that ran people out of the concert hall. Or he could have become a tired imitator of pop trends, which have proved to be the creative graveyard for so many jazz musicians. He didn't.[6]

Nor has Marsalis. He seems to be patterning both his jazz career and his musical values after Ellington. With the international platform provided by Jazz at Lincoln Center and its ties to public television and other important forums, it is likely that Wynton Marsalis—as both a composer and performer—will continue to be one of the most significant jazz artists in the decades to come.

Postmodernism is an attitude toward art and culture that has become common since the 1970s. It disavows some of the cerebral, audience-distancing tenets of modernism and replaces them with a free-wheeling conception of culture. Some postmodernist practices do the following:

► Blend styles and cultures

► Forgo structural unity as a necessity for art

► Incorporate older styles and genres

► Project an ironic, even cynical conception of art and expression

► Break down barriers between popular and fine art

THE BLAKEY ALUMNI

In addition to the repertory movement, there has been a significant resurgence of tradition-minded players since the fusion developments of the 1970s. The traditionalists have in many ways rejected fusion in either its commercial or avant-garde legacies. Some traditionalists, such as Marsalis, have returned to classic jazz for their inspiration. Most of the others look back to the bebop or hard bop of the 1950s. Marsalis first gained national recognition as a member of the Art Blakey Quintet; many keepers of the hard bop flame since 1980 also include those who first gained attention playing with Blakey.

Even in the 1950s, drummer Art Blakey showed a knack for hiring musicians who would go on to form important groups of their own and establish a major presence in jazz. The finest players from Blakey's early bands included Horace Silver, Kenny Dorham, Wayne Shorter, Benny Golson, Hank Mobley, Lee Morgan, Freddie Hubbard, and Cedar Walton. Retaining his traditional hard bop orientation and instrumentation through the 1980s, Blakey was something of a university for up-and-coming jazz players, providing them with a rich environment for musical growth. Membership in Blakey's band constantly shifted, but it allowed his later sidemen to trace their lineage back to the hard bop roots of the fifties and sixties. Blakey's sidemen—in particular, "Blakey's class of 1980–89"[7]—played a significant role in the hard bop renaissance of the 1980s and 1990s.

During his stint with Blakey from 1980 to 1982, Wynton Marsalis and his brother Branford helped elevate the group's visibility. After they departed, they were replaced by nineteen-year-old trumpeter Terence Blanchard and saxophonist Donald Harrison.

Also working as a team through the 1980s, Blanchard and Harrison recorded five albums as co-leaders. Their re-creation of the music performed at the Five Spot in 1961 by Eric Dolphy and Booker Little, *Eric Dolphy and Booker Little Remembered*, provides a fascinating example of jazz repertory in a small-group format. After these recordings, the two took separate paths. For example, Blanchard created *The Heart Speaks*, which was nominated for a Grammy in 1996. He has also maintained an active career as a film composer: His score for *Mo' Better Blues* was nominated for a Grammy in 1990. On the other hand, Harrison has lately been working with merging mainstream jazz with funk, which he calls "nouveau swing."

Blanchard was replaced in Blakey's band by Wallace Roney, whose often spare and thoughtful playing contrasted with many of the busier hard bop trumpeters. Roney went on to record with Tony Williams's quintet in 1986, playing on Williams's recordings *Foreign Intrigue, Civilization, Angel Street,* and *Native Heart.* Roney's visibility was enhanced considerably after he was chosen to perform with Miles Davis at a tribute sponsored by the Montreux Jazz Festival in July 1991. Roney has also recorded with Herbie Hancock and Chick Corea, turning in a brilliant performance on Corea's *Remembering Bud Powell* album. Finally, Roney has collaborated with his wife, jazz pianist Geri Allen.

Alto saxophonist Bobby Watson (b. 1953)—from Lawrence, Kansas—served as music director for Blakey from 1977 to 1981. Watson earned a music degree from the University of Miami then went to New York in 1976. In addition to working with Blakey, he has performed with drummer Max Roach and singers Joe Williams and Lou Rawls. Like Terence Blanchard, Watson has also composed music for films, such as his original score to *A Bronx Tale.* In the past two decades, Watson has recorded more than a dozen albums as a leader.

Other Traditionalists

Tradition-minded musicians abound today. Although it is impossible to compare and contrast all of the most important artists, the following table surveys some of the most notable ones.

SAXOPHONISTS		
NAME	INFLUENCES	LIFE AND WORK
Joe Lovano (b. 1952) Tenor saxophone	John Coltrane	▶ Often works in a trio led by Paul Motian (drums) and Bill Frisell (guitar). ▶ Collaborated with Gunther Schuller on *Rush Hour* (1995), an album featuring elements of third-stream music.
Joshua Redman (b. 1969) Tenor saxophone	Son of saxophonist Dewey Redman	▶ Successful records have led to some criticism for playing "accessible" music.
James Carter (b. 1969) All saxophones and bass clarinet	Mixes both traditional and free jazz elements	▶ Mixes "inside" and "outside" playing in a popular blend. ▶ Anything-goes approach shows influence of postmodernism.
Phil Woods (b. 1931) Alto saxophone	Charlie Parker	▶ Since 1974 has worked in a quartet that included bassist Steve Gilmore and drummer Bill Goodwin.
Charles McPherson (b. 1939) Alto saxophone	Charlie Parker, Eric Dolphy	▶ First worked with Charles Mingus. ▶ Album *Manhattan Nocturne* (1998) displays inspiration in the mainstream tradition.
TRUMPETERS		
NAME	INFLUENCES	LIFE AND WORK
Tom Harrell (b. 1946)	Bebop with more modern harmonies	▶ Worked with Stan Kenton, Woody Herman, and Horace Silver through the 1970s before moving to New York. ▶ *Play of Light* (1982) established him as a significant composer/arranger/leader.
Nicolas Peyton (b. 1973)	Fats Navarro, Clifford Brown	▶ Won Grammy for his collaboration with trumpeter Doc Cheatham (nearly seven decades his senior) in 1998. ▶ Regular soloist at Jazz at Lincoln Center.
Roy Hargrove (b. 1969)	Clifford Jordan, Jackie McLean, Slide Hampton, Jon Faddis, Freddie Hubbard	▶ First championed by Wynton Marsalis. ▶ Traditionalist, with an interest in world music.
Ryan Kisor (b. 1973)	Bebop	▶ Won Monk Competition in 1990. ▶ Worked with various bands over the decade and as a solo recording artist, showing proficiency in many different styles.

Other Traditionalists

(continued)

PIANISTS		
NAME	INFLUENCES	LIFE AND WORK
Kenny Barron (b. 1943)	Thelonious Monk, McCoy Tyner	▶ Performed with various groups as a sideman from the 1960s through the 1980s. ▶ Founder/member of the group Sphere, honoring Thelonious Monk and his music. ▶ Jazz educator at Rutgers University since 1973.
Marcus Roberts (b. 1963)	Early jazz pianists from Jelly Roll Morton through stride and bop stylists	▶ Championed by Wynton Marsalis, with whom he recorded/performed from 1985 to 1991. ▶ Has developed jazz interpretations of Scott Joplin's ragtime works, Gershwin's *Rhapsody in Blue,* and James P. Johnson's *Yamekraw.*
Cyrus Chestnut (b. 1963)	Gospel	▶ Noted for blending jazz improvisation with gospel stylings and rhythms.
Stephen Scott (b. 1969)	Thelonious Monk	▶ Worked as accompanist for Betty Carter.
Jackie Terrasson (b. 1965)	Bill Evans	▶ Worked as accompanist for Betty Carter. ▶ Likes to work in trio format pioneered by Bill Evans.
Brad Mehldau (b. 1970)	Bill Evans, Kenny Werner	▶ Melds jazz and European classical traditions. ▶ Draws on harmonies and arrangements in Evans's style.
Eliane Elias (b. 1960)	Brazilian jazz	▶ Mixes Brazilian rhythms and harmonies with traditional jazz repertory.

OTHER INSTRUMENTS		
NAME	INFLUENCES	LIFE AND WORK
Joey DeFrancesco (b. 1971) Organ	Jimmy Smith, Groove Holmes, Jimmy McGriff	▶ Discovered at age sixteen by Miles Davis, with whom he toured and recorded. ▶ Plays in hard bop and funky-jazz style.
Steve Turre (b. 1948) Trombone and conch shells	Eclectic	▶ Originally with rock band Santana in 1970. ▶ Has recorded with many leading jazz musicians and bands.
Mike Whitfield (b. 1967) Guitar	George Benson	▶ Worked with a variety of bands/styles, from pop-fusion to traditional postbop.

Other Traditionalists

(continued)

VOCALISTS		
NAME	INFLUENCES	LIFE AND WORK
Betty Carter (1929–1998)	Bebop	▶ Major vocal stylist since the 1940s. ▶ Mentor to dozens of young musicians.
Bobby McFerrin (b. 1950)	Jazz, opera, pop, rock	▶ Widely versatile, able to produce many vocal sounds. ▶ Multitracks elaborate arrangements of standards and his own compositions.
Cassandra Wilson (b. 1955)	Sixties rock, postbop jazz	▶ Popular singer who has recorded works not normally associated with jazz, including songs by country legend Hank Williams and by the pop group the Monkees.
Diana Krall (b. 1965)	Nat Cole	▶ Canadian-born singer in straight-ahead repertory from American popular song.
Kevin Mahogany (b. 1958)	Blues	▶ Worked on a number of film soundtracks for Clint Eastwood.
Kurt Elling (b. 1967)	Mark Murphy, Tony Bennett, pop-jazz standards	▶ Known for "ranting" style in which he improvises lyrics.

Watson and Harrison are not alone among the fine altoists who have worked with Blakey. For instance, Kenny Garrett is one of the most accomplished players on the scene. In addition to Blakey, Garrett has also performed with the Mercer Ellington Orchestra, Freddie Hubbard, and Miles Davis. Born in 1961, Garrett worked with Davis through the late eighties for some five years and served as Davis's personal assistant.

Many fine pianists have also been associated with Blakey. Among the pre-eminent is James Williams (b. 1951), who, like Bobby Watson, was with Blakey from 1977 to 1981. Originally from Memphis, Williams began piano at age thirteen, playing R&B and gospel. He taught at the Berklee College of Music from 1974 to 1977, and he has worked with Alan Dawson, Joe Henderson, Woody Shaw, Milt Jackson, and Clark Terry.

Another significant pianist who played with Blakey is Mulgrew Miller, from Greenwood, Mississippi, where he was born in 1955. Miller's playing is strongly assertive and follows the hard bop tradition; moreover, his style has amassed an astonishing variety of modern piano influences, from McCoy Tyner to Chick Corea and Herbie Hancock. In addition to playing with Blakey from 1983 to 1986, Miller has recorded with Branford Marsalis, Freddie Hubbard, Bobby Hutcherson, Kenny Garrett, Wallace Roney, Joe Chambers, and Cassandra Wilson.

BIG BANDS

Many of the big bands today are known as *ghost bands,* groups that tour and sometimes record even though the founders who established the band are no longer alive. There is a long tradition of ghost bands. The most important early ghost band was the one associated with Glenn Miller (discussed in Chapter 6), which continued for many years under such leaders as Ray McKinley.

Of the current ghost bands, perhaps the most important is the Count Basie Orchestra, which has been led by such fine talents as Thad Jones, Frank Foster, and more recently Grover Mitchell. Some of the surviving players who worked with Basie himself are members. The band continues to emphasize the enormous Basie book built up over the decades, but new material has been added, too. Another important ghost band featuring the works of Duke Ellington was led by Ellington's son, Mercer Ellington, until his death in 1996.

A fascinating big band that unites a creative modern unit, a traditional ghost band, and a repertory ensemble is the Mingus Dynasty, which continues the tradition of the bassist and composer (see Chapter 8). Interestingly, Mingus himself never led a big band.

The Mingus Dynasty is directed by Sue Mingus, the bass player's widow. Because Mingus did not himself amass a standard big-band book, the players often contribute arrangements. Andy McKee, the band's bassist and one of its musical directors, points out:

> [Mingus] expected musicians to find their own paths through his work. That spirit of improvisation and freedom is entirely characteristic of Mingus's method. This often will determine who will work out well in the band and who won't. A player may be a tremendous musician but needs more structure to frame his work. This band needs musicians who know how to frame themselves. That's my understanding of how Mingus's original groups worked.[8]

A surprisingly long-lived unit, the Either/Orchestra, has been established on the jazz scene since 1985. Composed mostly of Boston-area musicians, many of whom attended Berklee and the New England Conservatory of Music, the band is largely organized by its leader, saxophonist Russ Gershon, but its current members usually contribute charts.

Toshiko Akiyoshi has been one of the most successful big-band composers in jazz for many years. She was born in China in 1929 and began studying jazz in Japan in 1947. Encouraged by Oscar Peterson, she studied at Boston's Berklee College of Music during the late 1950s and worked briefly with bassist Charles Mingus. In 1973 she and reed player Lew Tabackin started a big band in Los Angeles, which became one of the most successful groups of the early eighties. Her

Courtesy Morgan Collection

A young Toshiko Akiyoshi.

writing style can be traced to Gil Evans and Thad Jones; it incorporates considerable modernism and occasional influences of Japanese music.

While Akiyoshi has been associated with a post-bebop musical vocabulary, composer-arranger Carla Bley (b. 1938) has ventured memorably into the avant-garde. She has written for George Russell, Jimmy Giuffre, and Charlie Haden's Liberation Music Orchestra. She is perhaps best known for *Escalator over the Hill,* a jazz opera completed in 1971.

One of the most visible of current big bands is led by composer-arranger Maria Schneider. Born in 1960 in Windom, Minnesota, Schneider studied at the University of Minnesota and the Eastman School of Music. She led the Maria Schneider Jazz Orchestra at New York's Visiones club during the 1990s. After graduating from Eastman, Schneider studied with composer and trombonist Bob Brookmeyer. In 1985 she became Gil Evans's assistant and in 1988 started her first band.

Steeped in the tradition of composer/arranger Gil Evans, bandleader Maria Schneider is renowned for her subtle and sophisticated compositions.

Schneider's first album, *Evanescence* (1994), established her reputation as innovative yet steeped in the tradition of Gil Evans and other arranger-composers such as Brookmeyer. Schneider's second album, *Coming About* (1996), was even more successful; her third album, *Allegresse,* was released in 2000. Schneider brings to her work a sophisticated compositional palette derived from jazz and Western concert music, and she creates an excellent balance between composition and improvisation.

Schneider is one of the distinctive new voices in jazz composition. Her approach to modal harmony is shown here in Music Example 12-1, the theme and harmonies from "Green Piece."

a. The diatonic eight-bar theme.

b. Harmonization for two flugelhorns and four trombones.

Music Example 12-1
"Green Piece" (Maria Schneider), theme and harmonies.

c. Harmonization for four trumpets and two trombones.

About this excerpt, which occurs at measure 62 of the score, Schneider notes the following:

> The basic melody of "Green Piece" is gentle and sweet. It's in F Ionian about a Pedal F. At m. 62, I jolt the listener into a more chromatic world, opening his ears to expect much transformation of this melody. I created this sudden change by using contrary motion between two opposing elements, triads or quartal structures on top, and fifths in the bass. Here, the melody is restated in F, but with dark harmonic color underneath, introducing shifting modes like F Phrygian, E minor, E♭ Lydian, D♭ Lydian augmented, etc. Most of the movement in the parts is stepwise. The reeds hang on to the idea of the original F pedal by answering each phrase with an F in the middle to high register.[9]

The Popular Connection

Another side to jazz is the development of several popular forms stemming from advances in digital technology. Since the 1980s, smooth jazz and acid jazz have carried on the legacy of fusion. Meanwhile, other popular interests have arisen as well, such as the retro fad neo-swing, which reflects an interest in a largely acoustic sound.

DIGITAL TECHNOLOGY

In the early 1980s, the jazz-fusion music of the 1970s began to adopt new technology. In particular, synthesizers became largely digital, and analog instruments took on a vintage status. Synthesizers were combined with the increasingly popular personal computer. The convenience of storing data on the computer increased the variety, complexity, and interaction of the digitally synthesized sounds. Computer memory also enabled the mixing of multiple tracks of digitally produced sound, simulating a multitrack tape recorder. The technology that enabled computers to "talk" to the synthesizers became known as MIDI, for Musical Instrument Digital Interface.

MIDI technology is a major part of the work of jazz-pop and avant-garde artists. In general, the widespread use of electronics and MIDI often distinguishes these artists from the traditionalists discussed earlier in this chapter, who tend to rely on acoustic instruments. For example, MIDI-controlled synthesizers and samplers may wholly or in part provide a background texture for the principal voices or instruments in an ensemble; or percussionists or other players may enhance the MIDI textures by interacting with preprogrammed synthesizer textures. This kind of work may take place in both live and recorded performances but is obviously easier to control in the recording studio. Smooth jazz has made extensive use of MIDI technology. Some computer-synthesizer technologies more complex and sophisticated than MIDI are also in use.

MIDI is an acronym for Musical Instrument Digital Interface. This standard language allows computers to control synthesizers or samplers.

SMOOTH JAZZ

Smooth jazz has been called "the jazz of the '90s"[10] by its advocates, while its detractors describe it as "smooth like a lobotomy flattens out the ridges on a brain."[11] None can deny its extreme popularity. Radio stations that broadcast the format are among the most listened to in a given metropolitan area. In this sense, smooth jazz can be compared with the wildly popular swing music of the late 1930s and early forties: For perhaps the second time in its history, a jazz style can be looked on as a type of mainstream U.S. popular music.

Many artists have provided consistently interesting performances of popular-jazz fusion. For example, the work of Grover Washington, Jr. (1943–1999), could be considered as a form of smooth jazz, although it was often quite adventurous and unusually well-crafted.

Growing up in Buffalo, New York, Washington performed with rhythm and blues groups as a teenager. He also worked in military service bands and in organ trios, the latter leading to mastery of the funky/soul-jazz styles created in the 1950s and 1960s. His first record as a leader was *Inner City Blues* (1971). Many of his records were quite successful, and he emerged as one of the leading stars of pop-jazz and one of its best overall musicians. He also worked in more mainstream venues, exhibiting his excellence and versatility.

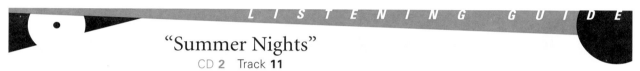

LISTENING GUIDE

"Summer Nights"
CD **2** Track **11**

Grover Washington, Jr.: "Summer Nights" (Miller), from *Strawberry Moon.*
Columbia Records/CBS 40510. West Orange, New Jersey, 1987. Grover Washington, Jr., soprano
saxophone; Marcus Miller, composer-producer, bass guitar; Tyrone Brown, synthesist
(with additional programming by Jason Miles); Darryl Washington, timbales.

"Summer Nights" is a fine example of imaginative synthesizer textures and ideas wedded to a smooth jazz groove. Washington enhances Miller's evocative and moody textures with a beautiful performance of the original melody and effective solo statements.

The textures heard on this performance were composed and programmed by Miller (with assistance from Jason Miles). Any acoustically produced sounds, such as the timbales, Washington's soprano saxophone, and possibly Brown's bass, were added as overdubs.

Despite the complex form of the piece, its basic idea is straightforward and historically typical of jazz performances: introduction, head, solo, head, coda. The thematic material consists of an easily recognizable melody, but rather than an AABA form, the melody spans an eight-bar A section, an eight-bar B section that largely includes just the synthesizers (and is adapted to the introduction, interludes, and coda), and a contrasting six-bar C section with greater harmonic activity. These three sections (A, B, and C) are mixed and varied to create the final form of the piece.

Introduction—Out-of-tempo chords + 16-bar groove as 8 + 8 (B section material)

0:00   Moody, string-sound chords with added flutelike timbres begin the introduction before the percussion sounds come in to create the groove. There is a prominent backbeat with a snare drum sound. The bass line, along with the percussion groove, sets up a modal texture in D minor.

0:23   The string and flute sounds return to the texture in the second eight bars of the introduction. The introduction builds to a small climax with an E♭7 chord on the last two beats to usher in Washington's first statement of the melody.

Statement of melody—AA section, 16 bars as 8 + 8

0:39   Washington states the melody, which begins with a signature motive: a syncopated, descending D minor triad, A–F–D. In the eight-bar tune, there are blues references, with Washington bending a flat five with suitable accompanying harmonies. The A section is repeated with an added stringlike texture.

Interlude—B section, 8 bars

1:13   In place of the usual bridge with contrasting harmonies, Miller creates an eight-bar unit of D minor modal harmony with the synthesized textures. This material was used for the introduction. Chords are deemphasized in the B section; a cymbal crash marks its beginning.

Restatement of the melody—AA' section, 16 bars as 8 + 8

1:29   The A-section material returns with echoes of the main thematic idea answering the saxophone. At the end of the second A (the repeat), the harmony changes slightly before cadencing.

Interlude—B section, 4 bars

2:03   Here we have a second interlude as an extension of the A-section cadence.

C section—6 bars

2:11   A contrasting section that begins with a two-beat harmonic rhythm to contrast the modal emphasis on D minor heard so far. The melody as played by Washington climaxes before a return to the A section.

A section—8 bars

2:24   Repeat of the A section.

Interlude—B section, 8 bars

2:40   In this interlude, Miller adds a more sustained texture in the last four bars to contrast the drier sound of the first four bars.

Washington solo—AAAC as 8 + 8 + 8 + 6

2:57   For the first twenty-four bars, Washington improvises over the A section. In the six-bar C section, Washington builds the solo beautifully to climax in the altissimo (highest) register.

Reprise of A section—8 bars

3:59   Return of the A section.

Synthesizer solo interlude—B section, 8 bars

4:16   An improvised solo statement on the synthesizer (a "synthesizer lead") as a contrast to the previous B sections that featured only grooves.

AA section—16 bars as 8 + 8

4:33   More A-section reprises with an added call-and-response between Washington and the synthesizer lead on the second A.

Coda as 8 + 8 + 8; Tag as 4 + 1

5:06   Washington improvises over D minor for the coda. Rather than the expected fade-out, a four-bar tag leads up to a final chord.

Other Pop Jazz Stars

The following table summarizes the careers of popular fusion stars other than the ones already discussed in the text.

NAME	FAME	LIFE AND WORK
Chuck Mangione (b. 1940)	Trumpet	▶ "Feels So Good" (1978) his major hit, featuring a pleasant pop-fusion groove.
Bill Frisell (b. 1951)	Guitar	▶ Use of electronic effects. ▶ Eclectic style, as shown by his country music crossover in his album *Nashville* (1997), which won the *Down Beat* Jazz Critic's Jazz Album of the Year award in 1998.
The Yellowjackets	Fusion band	▶ Popular, long-lived fusion band together since the early 1980s. ▶ Plays in both electronic and acoustic styles.
Medeski Martin & Wood	Fusion band	▶ Popular funk-fusion group, particularly on college campuses. ▶ Exhibits a fascinating blend of styles that is sometimes reminiscent of film music.
John Scofield (b. 1951)	Guitar	▶ Worked with Miles Davis in the seventies.
Phish	Rock band	▶ Heavily into improvisation, in the tradition of the Grateful Dead.
Kenny G (b. 1956)	Saxophone	▶ Probably the most popular of all the pop-jazz artists.
David Sanborn (b. 1945)	Saxophone	▶ Has worked with Stevie Wonder.

Other extremely popular smooth jazz artists include Kenny G, who is perhaps the most commercially successful, Charlie Hunter, Earl Klugh, Al Jarreau, Hubert Laws, and David Sanborn. Of these, Sanborn is probably the most interesting. He has worked as a sideman with Stevie Wonder and Bob James and appeared on late-night television talk shows; his 1982 album, *Voyeur,* was a gold record. With a style rooted in the bebop masters, such as Charlie Parker, and the R&B saxophone styles of Stanley Turrentine and Arnette Cobb, Sanborn has established himself as a preeminent pop-jazz presence.

ACID JAZZ

A style that had a major impact on the jazz world in the early- to mid-1990s is known as *acid jazz,* a fusion of jazz and hip-hop. Groups with hits include Buckshot LeFonque (featuring Branford Marsalis—the group's name comes from a nickname for Cannonball Adderley), Incognito, and Us3. Nurtured on the rap and hip-hop of the

Acid jazz is a fusion style that incorporates sampling of older jazz recording, rap, and hip-hop grooves and techniques.

1980s, the young musicians in these bands were inspired to sample jazz tracks and vamps to form the basis of their new sound.

One of the biggest acid jazz hits to date was Us3's "Cantaloop (Flip Fantasia)," from the album *Hand on the Torch.* This single consisted of a rap over samples from Herbie Hancock's "Cantaloupe Island"; it reached the Top 20 pop charts in 1994. For the remainder of the album, raps and electronic efforts were introduced over samples from classic jazz recordings in an intriguing collage. "It's Like That," for example, included the riff of Charlie Parker's "Cool Blues" alternating with the theme of the movie *Alfie,* by Sonny Rollins. Substantial portions of the tracks included improvisation. Despite this success and others like it, by the late 1990s the future of acid jazz was unclear, with many of the earlier groups no longer producing records.

THE MASS MARKET: RADIO AND THE INTERNET

The various types of pop-jazz share an important goal: attracting a mass market. Hence, pop-jazz must generate extensive radio airplay to boost record sales and draw in listeners for live performance. Not surprisingly, some radio stations interested in jazz conduct in-depth studies of their listeners' preferences in order to better understand what the public wants to hear. In this process, the program director of Seattle's KPLU, Joey Cohn, made an unsettling discovery, as Charles Levin notes here:

> Cohn's research breaks down jazz into six modes: lyrical, instrumental, driving improvisation, contemporary rhythms, vintage, swinging singers and blues. On the ratings scale, "driving improvisation was at the bottom of the list," [KXJZ Music Director Gary] Vercelli says. "'Driving improvisation' was driving a lot of our audience away."[12]

Cohn's classifications have little to do with jazz history or stylistic congruity: They depend entirely on split-second reactions from listeners with little or no knowledge of jazz. With some radio stations testing market reactions to jazz so carefully, it seems likely that radio play for jazz will continue to feature smooth jazz and the most popular crossover styles. Radio play for a larger spectrum of jazz styles may continue to decline.

Another potentially significant development in the realm of electronics has been the use of the Internet for selling music and for live broadcasts. The MP3 digital music format allows recorded music to be transferred and stored for reuse, although controversies have arisen regarding appropriate compensation for artists and record companies. Jazz clubs such as the Blue Note and Knitting Factory in New York are also broadcasting shows from their Web sites. The practice of archival broadcasts has arisen as well: A venue can create a video of a performance for later broadcast over the Internet. The long-established Montreux Jazz Festival in Switzerland, for example, has been experimented with this practice.

NEO-SWING

In a recent remarkable development, the big-band swing sound has returned. The music has become quite popular, especially among teenagers and young people in their twenties, who have become enthusiastic about the jitterbug and the older ballroom dances. Their enthusiasm stems in part from nostalgia for the glamor of the 1930s and 1940s; for example, retro clothing styles play a big part in the revival.

The music is reminiscent of 1940s jump-style swing, which itself was a precursor to rock and roll, rather than the more sedate, smoother sounds of many of the 1930s big bands.

Although the relationship of neo-swing to jazz remains controversial, the music offers a distinctive change of pace from the ubiquitous electronic ambience of popular music. Its largely acoustic sound is modernized through amplification, in which the bass and drums are much more prominent than they were in traditional swing. This emphasis on a heavy beat—the drummer emphasizing backbeats on the snare—along with the blues and occasional band choreography help the music connect to the 1940s and 1950s R&B scene as well. Because the music is easy to dance to, it helps attract younger audiences to the clubs. Older swing tunes are revived in the process and, according to journalists' reports, interest in traditional 1930s jazz recordings has been whetted among much of the audience.

A particularly successful neo-swing artist is guitarist Brian Setzer. In the later 1990s, the Brian Setzer Orchestra, a big band with standard instrumentation, was enormously popular—one of its CDs, *The Dirty Boogie* (1998), sold in double platinum figures (four million CDs). Their live performances have attracted as many as 4,000 people.

The Avant-Garde, Crossover, World Music, and Jazz to Come

Although it seems safe to say that the principal styles of jazz—from Dixieland to swing to hard bop to fusion—will continue to have their fans and proponents, jazz will itself continue to develop in the years to come. It seems likely that future developments will see change regarding such issues as the following:

- Crossover with other musical styles and cultures, including:
    - Popular music (such as neo-swing)
    - Non-Western music cultures
    - Concert music (third-stream experimentation)
- Greater participation of women
- Greater participation of artists from countries other than the United States

We shall conclude this chapter by looking at where these trends might go. We shall also mention some of the most significant artists in each area.

JAZZ AND FEMINISM

A glance back through this book shows that jazz has been a music dominated by men. Apart from talented pianists and composer-arrangers such as Lil Hardin and Mary Lou Williams, women have largely participated in jazz as vocalists. One important consequence of feminism in the 1960s and 1970s has been a remarkable increase in the number of women with jazz careers. Among the important artists of our time, we have spoken of pianist Eliane Elias and composer-arrangers Toshiko Akiyoshi, Carla Bley, and Maria Schneider. Among others are violinist Regina Carter; drummers Terri Lyne Carrington, Susie Ibarra, and Cindy Blackmon; pianists Geri Allen and Renee Rosnes; alto saxophonist Virginia Mayhew; and trumpeter Ingrid Jensen. The Kennedy Center in Washington, D.C., sponsors a

Women in Jazz festival in honor of Mary Lou Williams to showcase the many fine women artists at work today.

For example, Renee Rosnes (b. 1962) has been especially prominent among the pianists. Originally from Saskatchewan, she has worked with Joe Henderson, Wayne Shorter, James Moody, the Carnegie Hall Jazz Band, and the Lincoln Center Jazz Orchestra. Pianist Geri Allen (b. 1957) is comfortable in both traditional and avant-garde settings, and in both traditional piano trios and larger ensembles. She has also worked extensively with synthesizers and electronic media. Allen has taught jazz piano at the New England Conservatory and has recorded and performed extensively, playing with bassist Charlie Haden, drummer Paul Motian, Ornette Coleman, and vocalist Betty Carter.

Pioneer Jane Ira Bloom (b. 1955) has been one of the first women to carve a major jazz career on an instrument other than piano. As a soprano saxophonist, she has worked in numerous venues, most recently in a quartet. As a composer, she has worked on projects with NASA and the innovative dance company Pilobolus.

The big band Diva (with the slogan "No Man's Band") contains all women. It includes the well-regarded trumpeter Ingrid Jensen and drummer/leader Sherrie Maricle. The group has been getting much attention and many gigs.

JAZZ ABROAD

Superb non-Americans have been involved in jazz virtually since its beginning. If ragtime may be considered a form of jazz, the history of jazz in Europe extends back to the teens, when fine ragtime was performed and recorded there by Europeans as well as Americans. In the 1930s, Django Reinhardt from France became one of the most outstanding and important guitarists. Associated with Reinhardt and the Hot Club of France was French violinist Stephane Grappelli, a superb performer who enjoyed a career extending from the late 1920s until his death in 1997. The life and work of artists from countries other than the United States, such as John McLaughlin, Josef Zawinul, and Oscar Peterson, have greatly affected the development of jazz.

CROSSOVER, POSTMODERNISM, AND WORLD MUSIC

Crossover is the practice of mixing musical styles and cultures. As first seen in the concert jazz of the 1920s and thethird-stream practices of the 1950s, crossover can mix different styles within a given culture—for example, bluegrass and classical music—or it can mix entirely different cultures, such as traditional Japanese music and bebop.

Both the neo-swing and fusion movements can be likened to *crossover,* or blending one music style with another in order to attract listeners of the other style. Because jazz combined aspects of the European and African traditions, one could argue that the original jazz crossover was jazz itself. Forms of jazz have almost always maintained crossover connections to popular music, a connection most commonly forged through vocal and dance music. As jazz splintered into numerous substyles in the late 1940s and 1950s, some substyles such as funky/soul jazz retained a tie to instrumental popular music. Much of today's vocal jazz continues to maintain crossover connections to popular music.

Beyond the vocal connection, numerous jazz artists are experimenting with the song repertory of the early 1960s and later as a means of expanding the traditional jazz focus on the great popular standards of 1920–1950. Artists are experimenting with tunes by numerous rock groups, including the Beatles; the Grateful Dead; Sly and the Family Stone; Crosby, Stills, Nash & Young; and the Doors. John Zorn (discussed later) has featured the music of pop songwriter Burt Bacharach. Herbie Hancock recently issued a record called *The New Standard.*

Another original crossover music, Latin jazz, has been evident since the 1923 recordings of Jelly Roll Morton. It most likely had a significant impact on the formation of the early New Orleans jazz style. Dizzy Gillespie and Charlie Parker worked with Latin jazz in the earliest days of bebop. The Latin connection has continued unabated since then. The exceptional Latin jazz percussionist Tito Puente was a presence on the scene for many years. He died in 2000. Today the thriving Latin jazz scene includes many fine artists, such as saxophonist-clarinetist Paquito D'Rivera.

Crossover experiments will likely continue to affect jazz in the near future. For example, even mainstream artists, such as Wayne Shorter and guitarist Jim Hall, are experimenting with writing for orchestra. The development of jazz depends on its capacity for absorbing and integrating new music.

Crossover has been linked to world-music styles since the 1980s at least. Among the most interesting artists are Fred Ho, a baritone saxophonist who unites Asian music sensibilities with jazz; pianist Randy Weston, who created a fine blending of African music and jazz in his album *The Spirits of Our Ancestors* (1991), and pianist Horace Tapscott, who founded the Pan African Peoples Arkestra in Los Angeles.

Crossover that ambitiously attempts to link disparate styles and cultures can be likened to postmodernism, which John Zorn virtually personifies in his musical approach. Zorn has emerged as one of the most intriguing figures of the downtown New York scene. Probably more important as a composer and conceptual artist than as an altoist, this prolific musician has worked in numerous media, from his quartet Masada, which shows a blending of Ornette Coleman and klezmer music, to commissions for the New York Philharmonic.

Zorn was born in New York City in 1953. As a child, he became interested in music and studied flute; at age twelve he was already beginning to compose. He was soon attracted to the concert-music avant-garde, largely through the work of Charles Ives, Anton Webern, Alban Berg, Iannis Xenakis, and Karlheinz Stockhausen. During musical studies at Webster College in St. Louis, Zorn became interested in jazz, and, partly through the inspiration of Anthony Braxton, he began to study alto saxophone. After leaving Webster College, Zorn returned to New York to experiment with combining improvisation and composition. A period of gestation followed that included composing many works and

Contemporary Jazz Musicians in Other Countries

The following table highlights just a few of the outstanding jazz musicians not from the United States who have claimed considerable attention and reputation since the 1980s.

SAXOPHONISTS	
▶ **Jan Garbarek**	(Norway)
▶ **Evan Parker**	(England)

TRUMPETERS	
▶ **Hugh Masekela**	(South Africa)
▶ **Valery Ponomarev**	(Russia)
▶ **Arturo Sandoval**	(Cuba)

PIANISTS	
▶ **Eliane Elias**	(Brazil)
▶ **Abdullah Ibrahim**, a.k.a. **Dollar Brand**	(South Africa)
▶ **Adam Makowicz**	(Poland)
▶ **Michel Petrucciani**	(France)
▶ **Gonzalo Rubalcaba**	(Cuba)
▶ **Tete Montoliu**	(Spain)

GUITARISTS	
▶ **John McLaughlin**	(England)

BASSISTS	
▶ **Dave Holland**	(England)
▶ **George Mraz**	(Czechoslovakia)
▶ **Niels-Henning Orsted Pedersen**	(Denmark)
▶ **Miroslav Vitous**	(Czechoslovakia)

DRUMMERS/PERCUSSIONISTS	
▶ **Trilok Gurtu**	(India)
▶ **Airto Moreira**	(Brazil)

SINGER-SONGWRITERS	
▶ **Gilberto Gil**	(Brazil)
▶ **Milton Nascimento**	(Brazil)
▶ **Flora Purim**	(Brazil)

John Zorn directing a performance in London, England, in 1989.

appearing on both his own jazz albums and those of others. Beginning around 1984, Zorn started to become better known. He began to experiment with game concepts in his composing, in a manner reminiscent of John Cage or Xenakis: Rules are set up for the elaboration of pieces in which the outcomes are unpredictable. In addition to his performance and composition, he composed film scores. In 1987 he formed his group, Naked City, which included Joey Baron on drums, Wayne Horvitz on keyboards, Fred Frith on bass, and Bill Frisell on guitar.

The Knitting Factory in New York was for many years Zorn's home base, and the venue marked the composer's fortieth birthday with a month-long celebration. As Zorn's reputation spread, he became involved in numerous ventures. Although it is difficult to pin down his style, an important quality is its postmodern sensibility of stylistic juxtaposition. Segments of medieval Gregorian chant might segue into a distorted heavy-metal timbre, then into a more conventional jazzlike swing within minutes. In a surprising 1997 project, for example, Zorn produced an evening devoted to the music of popular songwriter Burt Bacharach. Zorn's eclecticism virtually defines postmodernism in jazz.

Dave Douglas (b. 1963), who has worked extensively with Zorn, is one of the most interesting crossover trumpet players today. Always involved in a large number of projects, he has recorded extensively, with CDs as both leader and sideman approaching 100 by the late nineties. Douglas is from Montclair, New Jersey, and studied at the Berklee College of Music, the New England Conservatory of Music, and New York University. In the late 1990s, he was working with Zorn in the group Masada. His numerous projects have included experiments with electronics, Romanian folk music and other Eastern European traditions, the twentieth-century styles of Webern and Stravinsky, and Lebanese music. Truly difficult to categorize, Douglas is one of the most adventurous players on the scene.

James "Blood" Ulmer (b. 1942) is a guitarist who played with Ornette Coleman's band Prime Time. Before Ulmer began playing and studying with Coleman in 1973, he was associated with blues and organ groups. Inspired by Coleman's ideas about music, in the late 1970s Ulmer led his own group, which combined funk, avant-garde jazz, and hard rock. The combination of elements have taxed the ability of jazz critics to label Ulmer's music, which has been described as "avant-garde fusion," "jazz-funk," "futuristic jazz-funk," and even "harmelodic diatonic funk." Ulmer's sound on guitar makes extensive use of distortion. After appearing on Arthur Blythe's 1978 *Lennox Avenue Breakdown,* Ulmer was signed to Columbia Records, playing the musical role, in one critic's words, of both "spacey conceptualist and post-Hendrix funkster."[13] Ulmer's 1982 album *Black Rock* marks a shift away from improvised structures and toward predetermined compositional ideas. In 1983 Ulmer formed the group Odyssey, which consisted of electric guitar, violin, and drums.

Ronald Shannon Jackson (b. 1940) worked as the drummer for "Blood" Ulmer; like Ulmer, Jackson also worked closely with Ornette Coleman, playing on the first two Prime Time albums. Jackson's band, the Decoding Society, similarly merges funk, rock, and avant-garde into combinations creatively described as "No-Wave," "funk-jazz," and "punk-jazz." The recordings by the Decoding Society, such as their first album, *Eye on You* (1981), shows a pronounced emphasis on interlocking rhythmic parts beneath edgy improvisation. On *De-Code Yourself,* the group performs a blistering version of Dizzy Gillespie's classic "Be-bop" in an astonishing forty-nine seconds. The Decoding Society provides a unique glimpse into the world of decidedly noncommercial fusion music.

Anthony Davis (b. 1951) blends jazz with concert music. In particular, he has written several operas, including *X,* which is based on the life of black leader Malcolm X. Premiering in 1985 in Philadelphia, the work—in its use of tailgate trombone and Coltrane-like sheets of sound—made extensive use of jazz elements. Other Davis pieces also refer to African-American history, such as his solo piano work entitled "Middle Passage," named after the harrowing slave-ship voyages from Africa.

Early in his career, Davis worked with many of the free jazz performers associated with the AACM of Chicago, such as George Lewis, Leo Smith, and LeRoy Jenkins. More recently, Davis has only occasionally performed or recorded as a jazz pianist: He was heard as a sideman on a 1988 recording by trombonist Ray Anderson entitled *Blues Bred in the Bone.* Within his dual role as composer and jazz artist, Davis clearly sees himself as part of a greater historical lineage of jazz composer/pianists. In the liner notes for *Lady of the Mirrors,* Davis wrote:

> I consider myself fortunate to be part of a long and vital tradition of composer-pianists in creative music. From Scott Joplin to Cow-Cow Davenport, to Jelly Roll Morton, James P. Johnson, Duke Ellington, Fats Waller, Thelonious Monk, Bud Powell, and Cecil Taylor, this is a tradition which has always been at the fulcrum of change and evolution in our music.[14]

George Lewis is another eclectic figure. Like Davis, he has performed extensively as a jazz improviser, while also writing composed music. Born in Chicago in 1952, Lewis began study at Chicago's AACM in 1971 with Muhal Richard Abrams. While a member of AACM in 1976, Lewis performed with two wildly disparate performers—the venerable Count Basie Orchestra and the iconoclastic free jazz saxophonist Anthony Braxton. Lewis's interest in electronic music gradually increased. He has created compositions for acoustic and electronic media indebted to nonjazz composers such as John Cage and Karlheinz Stockhausen. Like Davis, some of Lewis's composed works combine aspects of concert music and jazz, such as his *Shadowgraph* series nos. 1–3, written for a standard jazz ensemble. He has taught computer music at the University of San Diego, California.

Steve Coleman's M-Base concept has attracted a number of players. Coleman (CD 2, Track 12) has explored a variety of crossovers since the 1980s.

Courtesy Steve Coleman/Sooya Arts

Steve Lacy (b. 1934) was one of the principal soprano saxophonists of the 1990s. He has spent much time living in Europe because of its openness to the avant-garde. Lacy has been known for his free jazz associations, although lately he has been favoring music that combines free improvisation with composed constraints. Lacy's résumé boasts an enormous discography, with experience ranging from work with free jazz musicians Ornette Coleman and Cecil Taylor to the classical world and collaborations with staged dance. Lacy received a MacArthur Fellowship in 1992 and published *Findings: My Experience with the Soprano Saxophone* in 1994.

Saxophonist Steve Coleman (b. 1956) is experimenting with combining jazz with rap, funk, and rock grooves. He has been interested in such crossovers at least since the early eighties, when he organized his Five Elements band. He underscores his commitment to crossover when he says, "I'd like to have all those elements in the music, something for people who want to dance, something for people who are intellectual and want to find some abstract meaning, and something for people who just want to forget their troubles."[15]

Coleman has been closely associated with what he calls the M-Base concept, which stands for "Macro-Basic Array of Structured Extemporization." According to Coleman, M-Base should not be considered a stylistic label; it is a "way of thinking about creating music, not the music itself."[16] Coleman has been deeply influenced by non-Western musics, particularly African music and meter. Coleman's ideas have taken hold on a loose-knit community of jazz musicians; among those affiliated with the M-Base concept are saxophonists Greg Osby and Gary Thomas, trombonist Robin Eubanks, keyboardists Geri Allen and Renee Rosnes, and vocalist Cassandra Wilson.

However esoteric his philosophy, much of Coleman's crossover conception is rooted in jazz tradition. For example, in addition to original compositions, he performs jazz standards of the bebop period, such as "Salt Peanuts."

LISTENING GUIDE

"Salt Peanuts"
CD **2**   Track **12**

Steve Coleman and Five Elements: "Salt Peanuts" (Gillespie), from *Def Trance Beat (Modalities of Rhythm)*. RCA-BMG 63181-2. Brooklyn, New York, 1994. Steve Coleman, alto saxophone, leader; Andy Milne, piano; Reggie Washington, electric bass; Gene Lake, drums and percussion.

A prime example of Coleman's crossover approach is found in his version of "Salt Peanuts," recorded in 1994. Coleman's reinterpretation of the classic Gillespie tune pays homage to the bebop tradition. Yet a comparison with the Gillespie-Parker version (CD 1, Track 17) reveals startling differences, particularly in rhythm. Coleman's 1994 version imbues the composition with driving rock rhythms played by the drums; the use of electric bass further removes it from the bebop tradition.

Most notably, Coleman alters the meter of the composition, pushing the overall metric feel somewhat off-kilter. In Gillespie's version, "Salt Peanuts" comprises thirty-two bars of 4/4 rhythm changes. In contrast, Coleman's version truncates the final measure of each four-bar group, shortening it to 2/4 meter. Following the brief introduction played by Coleman alone, the band comes in at a tempo in which the half note equals about 170 beats per minute. This pulse can be understood as follows: Each four-bar section of the tune can be counted as four half notes, followed by three half notes, as illustrated here:

This metric reinterpretation poses significant challenges for the improviser. In the recording, the group sounds tightly rehearsed, with predetermined ensemble passages as well as improvised sections. Both the original AABA form and F tonal center are retained throughout.

Introduction

0:00   Coleman plays the introductory riff on saxophone alone.

Melody—AABA

0:06   The group plays the melody of the entire AABA form. Note the driving rhythms on drums and the electric bass.

0:17   The B section begins.

Written ensemble + 16-bar drum solo

0:27   Coleman plays the written-ensemble passage of the tune, and the drummer follows with a sixteen-bar drum solo.

Stop time melody

0:38   Two bars of the melody are followed by two bars of silence. The "Salt Peanuts" (SP) motive is omitted.

Coleman solo, then "mop-mop" figure

0:59   A brief improvisation by Coleman leads to the repeated-note "mop-mop" figure (from the original arrangement as played by Parker and Gillespie), first by Coleman, then by the drummer.

Milne piano solo

1:09   Milne's piano solo develops motives over two choruses, alternating between short rhythmic ideas and longer linear runs.

1:28–1:30   Drum break takes place between the first and second choruses.

Coleman solo

1:48   The beginning of Coleman's aggressive and energetic solo overlaps with the end of the piano solo. Although the drummer plays very actively with Coleman, during much of the solo the drummer keeps the half-note beat audible on the cymbal.

Coleman's 2nd chorus into B

2:29   During the end of Coleman's second chorus, he begins a repeated figure (from the original arrangement) as if to announce the end of his solo. He plays the figure five times, follows with the B section of the composition, then plays the figure two more times.

Reprise of AABA

2:51   The group returns to the melody of "Salt Peanuts." This time, the band stops while Coleman plays the SP motive.

Coda

3:11   The group plays the brief coda to the tune, again taken from the original arrangement.

DIRECTIONS FOR CROSSOVER JAZZ

We will close this overview of recent crossover developments in jazz with brief discussions of two fascinating records that appeared in 1998 and 1999 and that presage the possible directions for the twenty-first century. One is by an almost legendary older artist, pianist Herbie Hancock, and the other is by Tim Hagans, who has been a visible trumpeter on the New York scene for many years. Both albums are eclectic, heavily produced, and as such embody crossover to electronic media as well as traditional performance.

Herbie Hancock's 1998 album *Gershwin's World* combines Hancock's interests and accomplishments: the postbop jazz of the sixties, his funk hits of the seventies and eighties, and his long-abiding interest in classical music. For example, some of the tracks are mostly improvised postbop jazz ("Cottontail"), some combine live performance (with touches of African music) and MIDI technology ("Here Come De Honey Man"), some are pop oriented ("St. Louis Blues" with Stevie Wonder), some combine world-music grooves ("Overture"), and some are European classical works given a jazz interpretation (Ravel's *Concerto for Piano and Orchestra in G*). In this last performance, Hancock improvises much of his solo against the original orchestral score as performed by the Orpheus Chamber Ensemble.

Gershwin's World was a top-selling jazz album and eventually won two Grammy awards. In a *New York Times* article on the album, Hancock said, "Anything I can do to be a force to encourage multiculturalism is what I want to do."[17] It is clear that Hancock's future work will maintain a similar eclectic combination of musical styles and cultures as well as incorporate both electronic and acoustic media.

Tim Hagans (b. 1954) has emerged as one of the most highly respected trumpeters on the New York scene. A native of Dayton, Ohio, Hagans paid his dues in the Stan Kenton and Woody Herman bands. He once lived in Sweden, where he directed the Norrbotten Big Band, he taught at Berklee, and he has worked with some of the most visible groups on the scene, including the Maria Schneider band and the Yellowjackets.

In an album released in 1999, *Animation • Imagination,* Hagans and producer Bob Belden combine the free jazz spirit of the 1960s and electronic fusion sounds of the 1970s with up-to-date studio techniques and grooves derived from hip-hop and rap. The record contains many selections entirely produced by interacting with and overdubbing preproduced electronic tracks. Totally unlike *Gershwin's World*, *Animation • Imagination* is uncompromising in its exploration of effects and electronics and does not necessarily seek broad-range appeal within a multiplicity of styles.

Courtesy Tim Hagans

Trumpeter Tim Hagans (CD 2, Track 13) is exploring world-music crossovers with his latest work.

"Far West"
CD **2** Track **13**

Tim Hagans: "Far West" (Hays), from *Animation • Imagination*. Blue Note 7243 4 95198 2 4. New York,
May 6, 1998. Tim Hagans, trumpet; Kevin Hays, composer, Fender Rhodes electric piano, programming;
Scott Kinsey, synthesizers; Ira Coleman, bass; Billy Kilson, drums; Alfred Lion, narration.

"Far West" is a typically interesting track from *Animation • Imagination*. It combines synthesized textures, sampled sounds, and live improvisation.

Introduction—4-bar groove

0:00   A hip-hop groove begins the track with tabla samples added to the drum texture.

Section I—8 bars

0:09   An acoustic bass line with additional synthesizer textures is added. In the second four bars, these synthesizer and electric piano textures are elaborated.

Section II—16 bars as 8 + 8

0:26   The North-Indian vocal sample defines what might be called the head. The eight-bar unit is repeated. The electric piano employs wah-wah pedal textures.

Section III—Extended trumpet solo

1:05   Hagans enters with sustained notes in the high register over swirling electronic textures for eight bars.

1:19   The vocal sample returns twice between Hagans's solo. After the second return, his solo becomes more active, and drum work on the snare increasingly answers the solo's repeated figures.

Section IV—Electric piano solo

3:48   The electric piano is in the forefront of the texture.

4:14   The vocal sample returns.

Section V—Trumpet returns with rhythmic breakdown

4:24   Hagans returns for the climactic electronic breakdown of the rhythm sounds. The vocal sample is also treated electronically. Hagans continues to solo over the thick textures.

5:05   The backbeat rhythm returns as the textures blend together for a climax with a slow fade-out.

Tag

5:53   Alfred Lion, the founder of Blue Note Records, is sampled for a short vocal tag. (The clipped ending of the sample occurs in the original.)

Gershwin's World and *Animation • Imagination* present alternative visions for jazz in its second century. *Gershwin's World* is extremely popular as well as beautifully crafted and imaginative, displaying a huge stylistic and cultural palette that in no way panders to the audience in hopes of increased sales. The album emphasizes a multiplicity of crossover combinations. It is also a *tribute* record—a genre that has become more and more common in jazz. Alternatively, *Animation • Imagination,* by a relatively unknown but well-established musician, aggressively projects a consistent musical vision, colored by electronics and original compositions with avant-garde free playing.

The exciting musical directions and points of view heard in *Gershwin's World* and *Animation • Imagination* ecertainly differ from most of the jazz produced in the twentieth century. As such, they may anticipate directions for the music in its second century, while the older, long-established jazz styles will likely continue to attract audiences.

The Future of Jazz

A comparison of the first fifty years of jazz with the second reveals an intriguing difference, one that may have implications for the future of the music. Without question, the first fifty years featured three artists of indisputable greatness and incomparable influence on the development of the music: Louis Armstrong, Duke Ellington, and Charlie Parker. In addition to these three, the first fifty years of jazz included such legendary giants of the music as James P. Johnson, Jelly Roll Morton, Earl Hines, Sidney Bechet, Lester Young, Coleman Hawkins, Benny Goodman, Thelonious Monk, Dizzy Gillespie, and Clifford Brown.

What about the second fifty years? John Coltrane and Miles Davis have certainly influenced jazz in long-lasting and far-reaching ways. Arguably, no artists have yet emerged comparable to Coltrane and Davis since 1970, with the possible exception of Wynton Marsalis. Additionally, the jazz world in the nineties was saddened by the deaths of major artists such as Miles Davis, Dizzy Gillespie, Art Blakey, Sarah Vaughan, Gerry Mulligan, Betty Carter, Joe Williams, and Stan Getz. Some critics claim that there are simply no artists of remotely comparable stature.

Examining the jazz section of any well-stocked record store reveals the imbalance of major artists between the first and second halves of the century: The number of available CDs by players no longer living dwarfs the work of contemporary artists. In this respect, jazz-record departments resemble more and more classical-record departments. Many, if not most, of the major younger jazz artists receiving attention today are traditionalists of some sort. Thus, the end of the first century of jazz may be the first time in its history that middle-aged and older players epitomize the avant-garde, while the younger players disavow the new and attempt to refurbish the old. Given this state of affairs, can it be possible that jazz is dying?

The other side can be argued as well: The dearth of decisively influential new artists may be part of a larger historical process. When measured by record sales, attendance at festivals and clubs, interest among scholars, and the creation of repertory ensembles, jazz is thriving. With music in general, and with jazz in particular, a splintering of the market seems an almost necessary by-product of the information age.

With so many disparate substyles and audiences for radically different kinds of music, the emergence in jazz of a dominant figure comparable to Parker, Ellington, Armstrong, Coltrane, or Davis does not seem likely: There are simply too many different tastes to satisfy. A paradox, which has become a cliché of our times, is that as the information age homogenizes culture throughout the world, numerous subcultures have sprung into healthy and even aggressive existence as if in retaliation.

Jazz is no exception. Its many competing substyles reveal the urgency of its message and its ability to reach audiences throughout the world.

Thus as jazz begins its second century, its vital signs are mostly positive. Activity throughout the jazz community remains vigorous, as it draws from its own historical tradition, non-Western cultures, electronics, the high-culture avant-garde, and the many formats of popular music. With the easy-listening grooves of Kenny G, the postmodern eclecticism of John Zorn, the popular and blues infusions by Stevie Wonder, the neo-traditionalism of Wynton Marsalis, and the straight-ahead swinging of Charles McPherson, jazz remains vibrant in its stylistic multiplicity and continuing world-class appeal. If the history of the music in the last half century is any indication, jazz will continue the same complex and paradoxical course begun one hundred years ago. At the same time that new substyles continue to spin off from the center of jazz, reissues of classic jazz will consolidate a greater appreciation of its history and deeper understanding of its evolution. The outlook is indeed exciting on all fronts.

Questions and Topics for Discussion

1. Why is it important not to think of the history of jazz as one style succeeding or supplanting another? Cite contemporary artists mentioned throughout the chapter to argue the point that the history of jazz is not rigidly linear.

2. How can the 1980s be described as a reaction against fusion?

3. How has the jazz repertory movement changed the large-scale cultural perspective on jazz?

4. What approach to jazz does Wynton Marsalis personify? How does he personify it? In considering this issue, refer to his life, his role in the jazz repertory movement, and in particular his work as a composer.

5. What traditional prejudices have restricted the role of women in jazz? How have some of these prejudices been overcome in the last two or three decades?

6. Is jazz a worldwide phenomenon? Cite artists from the 1920s to the present to make your case.

7. Is jazz, most broadly conceived, increasing or declining in either importance or popularity? Cite cultural trends to support your view. Part of your answer may depend on what you consider to be jazz. Another important consideration may be record sales: They measure popularity, but do they measure importance?

8. How do Herbie Hancock's *Gershwin's World* and Tim Hagans's *Animation • Imagination* suggest possibilities for the future of jazz? Which possibility do you prefer? Can you think of any possibilities not discussed in the text?

Key Terms

Acid jazz
Back catalog
Complete reissue
Crossover
Crossover music
False start
Ghost bands
Jazz repertory
    movement
MIDI
Postmodernism
Remastering

NOTES

Chapter 1

1. Olly Wilson, "The Significance of the Relationship Between Afro-American Music and West African Music," *Black Perspective in Music* 2, no. 1 (Spring 1974): 16.

2. Robert Farris Thompson, "Kongo Influences on African-American Artistic Culture," in *Africanisms in American Culture,* ed. Joseph E. Holloway (Bloomington: Indiana University Press, 1990), 149–50.

3. Quoted in Robert L. Hall, "African Religious Retentions in Florida," in *Africanisms in American Culture*, ed. Joseph E. Holloway (Bloomington: Indiana University Press, 1990), 108.

4. See Sterling Stuckey, *Slave Culture: Nationalist Theory and the Foundations of Black America* (New York: Oxford University Press, 1987).

5. Marshall Stearns, *The Story of Jazz* (New York: Oxford University Press, 1958), 19.

6. William Francis Allen, Charles Pickard Ware, and Lucy McKim Garrison, *Slave Songs of the United States* (New York: Peter Smith, 1951; orig. pub., New York: A. Simpson, 1867; reprint, New York: Dover, 1997), vi.

7. A. M. Jones, "Blue Notes and Hot Rhythm," *African Music Society Newsletter* 1 (June 1951): 10. See also Jones's "African Rhythm," *Africa* 24, no. 1 (January 1954): 39; and *Studies in African Music* (New York: Oxford University Press, 1959).

8. Allan P. Merriam, "African Music," in *Continuity and Change in African Cultures,* ed. William R. Bascom and Melville Herskovits (Chicago: University of Chicago Press, 1959), 76–80; Paul Oliver, *Savannah Syncopators: African Retentions in the Blues* (New York: Stein and Day, 1970), 60.

9. Bruno Nettl, *Folk and Traditional Music of the Western Continents* (Englewood Cliffs, NJ: 1973), 185.

10. R. Nathaniel Dett, Introduction to *In the Bottoms: Characteristic Suite* (Chicago: Clayton F. Summy, 1913).

11. Thomas L. Riis, *Just Before Jazz: Black Musical Theater in New York, 1890–1915* (Washington, DC: Smithsonian Institution Press, 1989), 5–6.

12. Frederick James Smith, "Irving Berlin and Modern Ragtime," *New York Dramatic Mirror*, January 14, 1914, p. 38.

13. Edward A. Berlin, *Ragtime: A Musical and Cultural History* (Berkeley: University of California Press, 1980), 12.

14. See Berlin, *Ragtime*, esp. pp. 147–170.

15. Blues lyrics quoted in Paul Oliver, *Aspects of the Blues Tradition* (New York: Oak Publications, 1970), 18.

16. W. C. Handy and Arna Bontemps, *Father of the Blues* (New York: Macmillan, 1941; reprint, New York: Collier Books, 1970), 13.

Chapter 2

1. Gunther Schuller, *Early Jazz: Its Roots and Musical Development* (New York: Oxford University Press, 1968), 359–72.

2. Walter Kingsley, *New York Sun*, August 5, 1917.

3. Kathy J. Ogren, *The Jazz Revolution: Twenties America and the Meaning of Jazz* (New York: Oxford University Press, 1989), 102.

4. Lawrence Gushee, "How the Creole Band Came to Be," *Black Music Research Journal* 8, no. 1 (1988): 85.

5. Lawrence Gushee, liner notes to *Steppin' on the Gas: Rags to Jazz 1913–1927*, New World Records 269.

6. Alan Lomax, *Mister Jelly Roll: The Fortunes of Jelly Roll Morton, New Orleans Creole and "Inventor" of Jazz* (New York: Pantheon Books, 1950), 109. See also 2nd ed. (Berkeley: University of California Press, 1973).

7. Pops Foster, as told to Tom Stoddard, *Pops Foster: The Autobiography of a New Orleans Jazzman* (Berkeley: University of California Press, 1971), 18–19.

8. Nat Shapiro and Nat Hentoff, eds., *Hear Me Talkin' to Ya: The Story of Jazz as Told by the Men Who Made It* (New York: Rinehart, 1955; reprint, Dover, 1966), 22.

9. See William J. Schafer, with Richard B. Allen, *Brass Bands and New Orleans Jazz* (Baton Rouge: Louisiana State University Press, 1977), 8. Lewis Porter discusses the relationship of the brass band instrumentation to frontline Dixieland instrumentation in Lewis Porter, Michael Ullman, and Edward Hazell, *Jazz: From Its Origins to the Present* (Englewood Cliffs, NJ: Prentice-Hall, 1993), 18.

10. Baby Dodds, as told to Larry Gara, *The Baby Dodds Story* (Baton Rouge: Louisiana State University Press, 1992), 17–18.

11. Christopher Washburne, "The Clave of Jazz: A Caribbean Contribution to the Rhythmic Foundation of an African-American Music," *Black Music Research Journal* 17, no. 1 (Spring 1997): 75.

12. Dodds, *Baby Dodds Story*, 106.

13. Quoted in Donald M. Marquis, *In Search of Buddy Bolden* (Baton Rouge: Louisiana State University Press, 1978), 105.

14. Martin Williams, *Jazz Masters of New Orleans* (New York: Macmillan, 1967), 1.

15. Lomax, *Mr. Jelly Roll*, 93.

16. Ibid., 109.

17. Ernest Ansermet, *Revue Romande*, October 19, 1919; reprinted in John Chilton, *Sidney Bechet: The Wizard of Jazz* (New York: Oxford University Press, 1987), 40. Also in Robert Walser, *Keeping Time: Readings in Jazz History* (New York: Oxford University Press, 1999), 11.

18. Jelly Roll Morton, Library of Congress Recording, Riverside 9001-12.

19. Transcription from Schuller, *Early Jazz*, 163.

20. Lomax, *Mr. Jelly Roll*, 79.

21. Martin Williams, *The Jazz Tradition*, 2nd ed. (New York: Oxford University Press, 1983), 55. See also 1st ed., 1970.

22. Frederick Ramsey, Jr., and Charles Edward Smith, eds., *Jazzmen* (New York: Harcourt, Brace, 1939), 51.

23. William Howland Kenney, *Chicago Jazz: A Cultural History, 1904–1930* (New York: Oxford University Press, 1993), 42.

24. Shapiro and Hentoff, *Hear Me Talkin' to Ya*, 49.

25. Ibid., 45.

26. Sally Placksin, *American Women in Jazz: 1900 to the Present: Their Words, Lives, and Music* (New York: Seaview Books, 1982), 60–61.

27. Kenney, *Chicago Jazz*, 12.

Chapter 3

1. William Howland Kenney, *Chicago Jazz: A Cultural History, 1904–1930* (New York: Oxford University Press, 1993), 9.

2. Ibid., 45.

3. Lawrence Gushee, liner notes to King Oliver, *King Oliver's Jazz Band—1923*, Columbia P2 12744.

4. Kenney, *Chicago Jazz*, 104.

5. Edmond Souchon, "King Oliver: A Very Personal Memoir," in *Jazz Panorama*, ed. Martin Williams (New York: Collier, 1964), 27–29.

6. Gushee, liner notes to King Oliver, *King Oliver's Jazz Band—1923*.

7. Transcription by Lewis Porter, *Jazz: From Its Origins to the Present* (Englewood Cliffs, NJ: Prentice-Hall, 1993), 47.

8. Richard Hadlock, *Jazz Masters of the Twenties* (New York: Collier, 1974), 15.

9. Max Kaminsky, with V. E. Hughes, *My Life in Jazz* (New York: Harper & Row, 1963), 39–41.

10. Nat Shapiro and Nat Hentoff, eds., *Hear Me Talkin' to Ya: The Story of Jazz as Told by the Men Who Made It* (New York: Rinehart, 1955; reprint, Dover, 1966), 120.

11. Hadlock, *Jazz Masters*, 80–81.

Chapter 4

1. Gunnard Askland, "Interpretations in Jazz: A Conference with Duke Ellington," *Etude* (March 1947): 134.

2. Many of the ideas in this section are influenced by Samuel A. Floyd, Jr., "Music in the Harlem Renaissance: An Overview," in *Black Music in the Harlem Renaissance,* ed. Samuel A. Floyd, Jr. (New York; Westport, CT: Greenwood Press, 1990), 1–27.

3. Nathan Irvin Huggins, *Harlem Renaissance* (New York: Oxford University Press, 1971), 5.

4. See Nathan Irvin Huggins, "Interview with Eubie Blake," in *Voices from the Harlem Renaissance,* ed. Nathan Huggins (New York: Oxford University Press, 1976), 339–40.

5. Robert Bartlett Haas, ed., *William Grant Still and the Fusion of Cultures in American Music* (Los Angeles: Black Sparrow Press, 1975), 134.

6. Floyd, "Music in the Harlem Renaissance," 21.

7. Willie "The Lion" Smith, with George Hoefer, *Music on My Mind: The Memoirs of an American Pianist* (New York: Burdge & Co., 1954; reprint, New York: Da Capo Press, 1984), 66–67. *Authors' note:* "The Charleston" in the quotation is correct, but the preferred title is "Charleston."

8. Tom Davin, "Conversations with James P. Johnson," *Jazz Review* 2, no. 6 (July 1959), 12.

9. Richard Hadlock, *Jazz Masters of the Twenties* (New York: Da Capo Press, 1988), 153.

10. James T. Maher and Jeffrey Sultanof, "Pre-Swing Era Big Bands and Jazz Composing and Arranging," in *The Oxford Companion to Jazz,* ed. Bill Kirchner (Oxford: Oxford University Press, 2000), 264.

11. Hadlock, *Jazz Masters,* 212.

12. Duke Ellington, *Music Is My Mistress* (New York: Da Capo Press, 1976), 419.

13. Nat Shapiro and Nat Hentoff, eds., *Hear Me Talkin' to Ya: The Story of Jazz as Told by the Men Who Made It* (New York: Rinehart, 1955; reprint, Dover, 1966), 231.

14. Mark Tucker, *Ellington: The Early Years* (Urbana: University of Illinois Press, 1991), 201.

15. Gunther Schuller, *The Swing Era: The Development of Jazz 1930–1945* (New York: Oxford University Press, 1989), 48

16. Tucker, *Ellington,* 201.

17. John Edward Hasse, *Beyond Category: The Life and Genius of Duke Ellington* (New York: Simon & Schuster, 1993), 92.

Chapter 5

1. James Lincoln Collier, *Benny Goodman and the Swing Era* (New York: Oxford University Press, 1989), 5.

2. "Who Started Swing?" *Metronome* (August 1936): 11.

3. George T. Simon, *The Big Bands*, rev. ed. (New York: Macmillan, 1974), 4.

4. Transcription adapted from Fred Sturm, *Changes over Time: The Evolution of Jazz Arranging* (Rottenburg, Germany: Advance Music, 1995), 65.

5. Ross Russell, *Jazz Style in Kansas City and the Southwest* (Berkeley: University of California Press, 1971), 72.

6. Nathan W. Pearson, Jr., *Goin' to Kansas City* (Urbana: University of Illinois Press, 1987), 67.

7. Pearson, *Goin' to Kansas City,* 119.

8. John Hammond, "Count Basie Marks 20th Anniversary," *Down Beat,* November 2, 1955, p. 11.

9. Teddy Wilson, with Arie Ligthart and Humphrey van Loo, *Teddy Wilson Talks Jazz* (London: Cassell, 1996), 33, 82.

10. Count Basie, as told to Albert Murray, *Good Morning Blues—The Autobiography of Count Basie* (New York: Random House, 1985), 382.

11. Benny Goodman and Irving Kolodin, *The Kingdom of Swing* (New York: Frederick Ungar, 1961), 140.

12. Goodman and Kolodin, *Kingdom of Swing,* 198–99.

13. John Edward Hasse, *Beyond Category: The Life and Genius of Duke Ellington* (New York: Simon & Schuster, 1993).

14. Haase, *Beyond Category,* 215.

15. James Lincoln Collier, *Duke Ellington* (New York: Oxford University Press, 1987), 130.

16. Gary Giddins, "Notes on the Music," in the liner notes for *Giants of Jazz: Johnny Hodges,* Time-Life Records TL-J19, 1981, p. 47.

17. Billy Strayhorn, "The Ellington Effect," *Down Beat,* November 5, 1952, p. 4.

18. Derek Jewell, *Duke: A Portrait of Duke Ellington* (New York: Norton, 1977), 110.

Chapter 6

1. Cab Calloway and Bryant Rollins, *Of Minnie the Moocher and Me* (New York: Crowell, 1976), 112.

2. George T. Simon, *The Big Bands,* 4th ed. (New York: Schirmer Books, 1982), 331–32.

3. Whitney Balliett, *Super Drummer: A Profile of Buddy Rich* (Indianapolis, IN: Bobbs-Merrill, 1968), 83.

4. Gunther Schuller, *The Swing Era: The Development of Jazz 1930–1945* (New York: Oxford University Press, 1989), 548.

5. Nat Hentoff, "Pres," *Down Beat,* March 7, 1956, p. 9.

6. See Lewis Porter's study in *Lester Young* (Boston: Twayne, 1985), especially chap. 4 (pp. 56–88). Also pp. 175–180.

7. Schuller, *Swing Era,* 547.

8. Teddy Wilson, with Arie Ligthart and Humphrey van Loo, foreword to *Teddy Wilson Talks Jazz* (London: Cassell, 1996), ix.

9. Wilson, *Teddy Wilson Talks Jazz,* 23–24.

10. Nat Shapiro and Nat Hentoff, eds., *Hear Me Talkin' to Ya: The Story of Jazz as Told by the Men Who Made It* (New York: Rinehart, 1955; reprint, Dover, 1966), 201.

Chapter 7

1. "'Bop Will Kill Business Unless It Kills Itself First'— Louis Armstrong," *Down Beat,* April 7, 1948, p. 2.

2. Marshall Stearns, *The Story of Jazz* (New York: Oxford University Press, 1958), 159.

3. Ira Gitler, *Jazz Masters of the Forties* (New York: Da Capo Press, 1983), 26–27.

4. Dizzy Gillespie with Al Fraser, *To Be or Not… to Bop* (Garden City, NY: Doubleday, 1979), 146.

5. Ibid., 135.

6. Miles Davis, with Quincy Troupe, *Miles: The Autobiography* (New York: Simon & Schuster, 1989), 54.

7. Danny Barker, *A Life in Jazz* (New York: Oxford University Press, 1986), 171–72.

8. Budd Johnson, quoted in Gillespie, *To Be,* 218.

9. Gitler, *Jazz Masters,* 22.

10. Gillespie, *To Be,* 208.

11. "My Memories of Bird Parker," *Melody Maker,* May 28, 1955. Reprinted in Carl Woideck, *The Charlie Parker Companion* (Schirmer Books, 1998), 136.

12. "Interview: Charlie Parker, Marshall Stearns, John Maher, and Chan Parker," in Woideck, *Charlie Parker Companion,* 93.

13. Ross Russell, *Bird Lives: The High Life and Hard Times of Charlie (Yardbird) Parker* (New York: Charterhouse, 1973; reprint, New York: Da Capo Press, 1996), 138. For more on Parker's solo, see Henry Martin, *Charlie Parker and Thematic Improvisation* (Lanham, MD: Scarecrow Press, 1996).

14. Davis, *Miles,* 64.

15. "Louie the First," *Time* 53 (February 21, 1949): 52.

16. Gitler, *Jazz Masters,* 120.

17. Gillespie, *To Be,* 137.

18. Davis, *Miles,* 80–81.

19. Davis, *Miles,* 104.

Chapter 8

1. Jack Chambers, *Milestones 1: The Music and Times of Miles Davis to 1960* (Toronto: University of Toronto Press, 1983), 129.

2. John Lewis, *The World of Music* (Information Bulletin No. 4, International Music Council, UNESCO House, Paris, May 1958).

3. Chambers, *Milestones 1,* 131.

4. Ted Gioia, *West Coast Jazz* (New York: Oxford University Press, 1992), 143.

5. "What's Wrong with Kenton?" *Metronome* 64, no. 2 (February 1948): 32.

6. Shelly Manne, "Shelly Manne Offers His Concept of Jazz Drums," *Down Beat,* December 14, 1955, p. 9.

7. Liner notes to Jimmy Guiffre, *Tangents in Jazz,* Capitol T634.

8. As quoted in Gil Goldstein, *Jazz Composers Companion* (New York: Consolidated Music Publishers, 1981), 128.

9. Miles Davis, with Quincy Troupe, *Miles: The Autobiography* (New York: Simon & Schuster, 1989), 9.

10. Ross Russell, *Bird Lives: The High Life and Hard Times of Charlie (Yardbird) Parker* (New York: Charterhouse, 1973; reprint, New York: Da Capo Press, 1996), 267.

11. Davis, *Miles,* 219.

12. John Coltrane, in collaboration with Don DeMichael, "Coltrane on Coltrane," *Down Beat,* September 29, 1960, p. 27.

13. Liner notes to Miles Davis, *Kind of Blue,* Columbia CK 64935.

Chapter 9

1. Jerry D'Souza, "Richard Davis—Philosophy of the Spiritual," *Coda Magazine* 285 (May–June 1999): 11.

2. Ekkehard Jost, *Free Jazz* (New York: Da Capo Press, 1981), 127.

3. Nat Hentoff, *The Jazz Life* (New York: Dial Press, 1961), 238.

4. Ornette Coleman, liner notes to Ornette Coleman, *Change of the Century,* Atlantic 1327.

5. Hentoff, *Jazz Life,* 241.

6. Jost, *Free Jazz,* 54.

7. Hentoff, *Jazz Life,* 228.

8. Jost, *Free Jazz,* 59.

9. John Litweiler, *The Freedom Principle: Jazz After 1958* (New York: Morrow, 1984), 55.

10. Gunther Schuller, "Coleman, Ornette," in *The New Grove Dictionary of Jazz,* ed. Barry Kernfeld (New York: St. Martin's Press, 1994), 230. For example, see Coleman's explanation of harmolodics in *Down Beat,* July 1983, pp. 54–55.

11. John Coltrane, in collaboration with Don DeMichael, "Coltrane on Coltrane," *Down Beat,* September 29, 1960, p. 26.

12. Ibid.

13. Thomas Owens, *Bebop: The Music and the Players* (New York: Oxford University Press, 1995), 94.

14. Jack Chambers, *Milestones 1: The Music and Times of Miles Davis to 1960* (Toronto: University of Toronto Press, 1983), 249.

15. Coltrane, "Coltrane on Coltrane," 27.

16. Ibid.

17. Ibid.

18. Joe Hunt, *52nd Street Beat: Modern Jazz Drummers 1945–1965* (New Albany, IN: Jamey Aeborsold Jazz, n.d.), 44.

19. Quoted in Don DeMichael, "John Coltrane and Eric Dolphy Answer the Jazz Critics," *Down Beat,* April 12, 1962, p. 20. Originally published in a *Down Beat* review of November 23, 1961.

20. Lewis Porter, "John Coltrane's *A Love Supreme:* Jazz Improvisation as Composition," *Journal of the American Musicological Association* 38, no. 3 (1983): 593–621.

21. Jost, *Free Jazz,* 89.

22. J. B. Figi, "Cecil Taylor: African Code, Black Methodology," *Down Beat,* April 10, 1975, pp. 14, 31.

23. Quoted in Jost, *Free Jazz,* 83.

24. Liner notes to Joseph Jarman, *As If It Were the Seasons,* Delmark 410.

25. Liner notes to Lester Bowie, *Numbers 1 and 2,* Nessa N-1.

26. Jost, *Free Jazz,* 177.

27. Ibid., 190.

28. DeMichael, "John Coltrane and Eric Dolphy," 21.

29. Ibid., 21–22.

30. Liner notes to Eric Dolphy, *Far Cry with Booker Little,* Prestige 7747.

Chapter 10

1. Miles Davis, with Quincy Troupe, *Miles: The Autobiography* (New York: Simon & Schuster, 1989), 241.

2. R. Townley, "Hancock Plugs In," *Down Beat,* October 24, 1974, p. 15.

3. Davis, *Miles,* 270.

4. Townley, "Hancock Plugs In," 14.

5. On Track 2, at 1:02, of Marian McPartland, *Piano Jazz,* with guest Bill Evans, The Jazz Alliance TJA-12004.

6. Conrad Silvert, "Chick Corea's Changes: A Return to Forever Is Not Forever," *Rolling Stone,* July 15, 1976, p. 24.

7. Liner notes to Charles Lloyd, *Charles Lloyd: Love-In,* Atlantic SC 1481.

8. Ben Sidran, *Talking Jazz: An Oral History, Expanded Edition* (New York: Da Capo Press, 1995), 268.

9. Ibid., 324, 327.

Chapter 11

1. Bill Laswell, foreword to *Jazz-Rock: A History,* by Stuart Nicholson (New York: Schirmer Books, 1998), x.

2. Bill Milkowski, liner notes to Al DiMeola, *Electric Rendezvous,* Sony/Columbia 468216-2.

3. Lee Underwood, "George Duke: Plugged-In Prankster," *Down Beat,* March 10, 1977, p. 34.

4. Bret Primack, "Herbie Hancock: Chameleon in His Disco Phase," *Down Beat,* May 17, 1979, p. 42.

5. Art Taylor, *Notes and Tones: Musician-to-Musician Interviews* (Liège, Belgium: Taylor, 1977; reprint, New York: Da Capo Press, 1993).

6. George T. Simon, *The Big Bands,* 4th ed. (New York: Macmillan, 1981).

7. Liner notes to *Miles Davis at Fillmore,* Columbia CG 30038.

8. Julie Coryell and Laura Friedman, preface to *Jazz-Rock Fusion: The People, The Music* (New York: Delacorte Press, 1978), x.

9. Bill Milkowski, "Larry Coryell: Back to the Roots," *Down Beat,* May 1984, p. 16.

10. Mark Gridley, *Jazz Styles: History and Analysis,* 5th ed. (Englewood Cliffs, NJ: Prentice-Hall, 1994), 337.

11. Scott Yanow, "George Duke: Dukin' out the Hits," *Down Beat,* November 1984, p. 17.

12. Len Lyons, *The Great Jazz Pianists: Speaking of Their Lives and Their Music* (New York: Da Capo, 1989), 276.

13. Primack, "Herbie Hancock," 42

14. Coryell and Friedman, *Jazz-Rock Fusion,* 239.

15. Josef Woodward, "Chick Corea: Piano Dreams Come True," *Down Beat,* September 1988, p. 19.

16. Bill Milkowski, *Jaco: The Extraordinary and Tragic Life of Jaco Pastorius, "The World's Greatest Bass Player"* (San Francisco: Miller Freeman Books, 1995), 73.

17. Review of *Mr. Gone, Down Beat,* January 11, 1979, p. 22.

18. Stuart Nicholson, *Jazz-Rock: A History* (New York: Schirmer Books, 1998), 181.

19. Fred Borque, "Pat Metheny: Musings on Neo-Fusion," *Down Beat,* March 22, 1979, pp. 13–15.

20. Nicholson, *Jazz-Rock,* 240.

21. Pat Metheney, "In Search of Sound," *Down Beat,* February 1998, p. 19.

Chapter 12

1. Ann Douglas, *Terrible Honesty: Mongrel Manhattan in the 1920s* (New York: Farrar, Straus, Giroux, 1995), 352.

2. James P. Johnson, "I Like Anything That's Good," *The Jazz Record* (April 1947): 14.

3. Dave Hellend, "Repertory Big Bands," *Down Beat,* January 1997, p. 35.

4. Howard Reich, "Wynton Marsalis," *Down Beat,* December 1997, p. 34.

5. Robert Sadin, personal communication, May 20, 1999.

6. Wynton Marsalis, "Ellington at 100: Reveling in Life's Majesty," *New York Times,* January 17, 1999, Arts and Leisure section.

7. Stuart Nicholson, *Jazz: The 1980s Resurgence* (New York: Da Capo Press, 1990), 227.

8. John McDonough, "Doin' 'em Proud," *Down Beat,* January 1997, p. 20.

9. Maria Schneider, personal communication, June 10, 1999.

10. Radio emcee Don Burns of smooth jazz station KTWV of Los Angeles, as quoted in Eliot Tiegel, "Smooth Moves on the Air," *Down Beat,* December 1996, p. 10.

11. Record producer Michael Cuscuna, as quoted in Eliot Tiegel, "Smooth Moves on the Air," *Down Beat,* December 1996, p. 10.

12. Charles Levin, "Reconfiguring the Public Radio Puzzle," *Down Beat,* April 1999, p. 44.

13. Stuart Nicholson, *Jazz-Rock: A History* (New York: Schirmer Books, 1998), 312.

14. Liner notes to Anthony Davis, *Lady of the Mirrors,* India Navigation IN 1047.

15. Nicholson, *Jazz Resurgence,* 258.

16. Steve Coleman [Internet home page], available from www.m-base.com/mbase.htm/.

17. David Hadju, "Rhapsody in Black and White: Herbie Hancock Finds a Soul Mate in George Gershwin," *The New York Times Magazine,* October 28, 1998, p. 52.

GLOSSARY

AABA song form   A musical form that comprises an eight-bar theme (A) played twice. A contrasting melody (B) follows, also usually eight bars long, before the A theme returns. Quite often the second and third A sections will vary slightly.

ABAC song form   A musical form in which each section is usually eight bars and has three themes (A, B, and C). Musicians often speak of the "first half" of the tune (AB) and the "second half" (AC).

Acid jazz   A fusion style that incorporates sampling of older jazz recordings, rap, and hip-hop grooves and techniques.

Amplitude modulation   Sound modulation in which the amplitude (the range of loud and soft) of the wave is modified by another wave, producing a sound vastly different from the original. *See also* **modulation** and **frequency modulation**.

Antiphony   The trading of melodic figures between two different sections of the band; the formal musical term for **call-and-response**.

Arpeggiated figure   A melodic fragment based on the notes of the chord harmony and played in succession.

Arp synthesizers   Among the first synthesizers made specifically for live performance.

Arranger   The person who plans the form of a band's performance and often notates the parts for the different instruments. *See also* **head arrangement**.

Atonality   A description of music that avoids the standard chords, scales, harmonies, and keys of **tonality**. It is sometimes associated with free jazz, which flourished in the 1960s.

Avant-garde   *See* **Free jazz**

Backbeats   Heavy emphases on beats 2 and 4, as played by the drummer, usually on the snare drum. (Other drums or the hi-hat can be used for quieter backbeats.) Backbeats can be added to a 4/4 swing rhythm as well. Backbeats increase danceability by clarifying the rhythm and adding to the visceral excitement of the music.

Back-beat (change-step)   A stride piano technique in which the performer breaks up the regular striding left hand with its normal alternation of bass note and mid-register chord—that is, 1-2-1-2 ("1" refers to a bass note and "2" refers to a chord). Instead, the left hand plays a more complex pattern such as 1-1-2-1/ 1-2-1-2 or 1-2-2-1/2-2-1-2/1-2-1-2, which is called a back-beat (not to be confused with **backbeats**). Listen to Track 5 of the 🎵 Audio Primer CD.

Back catalog   All the recordings that a company holds in its vaults—or claims the rights to by having purchased other record labels. Many of these recordings are out of print or were never issued.

Back phrasing   A musical technique in which the singer momentarily delays the entry of a new phrase, in effect freeing the rhythm of a composition. Occurring most often in ballads, it generally conveys a loose feeling, as if the singer were delivering the song spontaneously.

Balance   The ability of a section to blend. In a well-balanced section, none of the players will be too soft or too loud relative to the others.

Banjo   A stringed, strummed instrument that often provided the chords in New Orleans and Chicago-style (Dixieland) jazz.

Bass   A low-pitched stringed instrument and one of the members of the **rhythm section** in a jazz band. Listen to Track 43 of the 🎵 Audio Primer CD to hear an acoustic bass.

Bebop (bop)   A nervous, energetic style of jazz that developed in the 1940s. The terms probably developed from the nonsense syllables used by scat singers to re-create the characteristic melodic phrases of the new style.

Bent pitch   A small glissando or slide from one frequency to a slightly higher one, achieved by pushing against the guitar's string on the fretboard, thus "bending" it.

Big band   A large jazz ensemble typically including three to four trumpets, three to four trombones, four to five reeds (saxophones and doublings), and rhythm (typically piano, bass, guitar, and drums).

Block-chord style   *See* **Locked-hands style**

Blue note   A bent, slurred, or "worried" note. Most often occurs on the third of the scale, but any note can be made "blue" by varying its intonation in a blues or jazz performance.

Blues   An African-American folk music that appeared around 1900 and exerted influence on jazz and various forms of U.S. popular music.

Blues form   A basic twelve-bar chord progression that may be varied depending on the blues or jazz style. The basic progression is shown in Music Example 1-6. Its fundamental harmonies are I (4 bars), IV (2 bars), I (2 bars), V (1 bar), IV (1 bar), I (2 bars). Listen to Track 11 of the Audio Primer CD for a modern version of blues form.

Blues scale   A form of scale that incorporates the principal notes used in the blues. Most often, 1–♭3–4–♯4–5–♭7. Listen to the second scale played on Track 1 of the Audio Primer CD. See Chapter 1 for a blues scale in music notation.

Bossa nova   A Latin jazz style that developed from Brazilian music in the late 1950s and early 1960s. Stan Getz was prominent among jazz players with bossa nova hits.

Break   A short pause in a band's playing—usually one or two bars—to feature a soloist. Often a band will play in **stop time** while the soloist improvises breaks between the band's chords.

Cadence   The closing strain of a phrase, section, or movement. Also a term used for a common closing chord progression.

Cakewalk   A dance involving an exaggerated walking step. In exhibitions of cakewalking, the most talented couple won a cake at the end of the evening. The cakewalk may have been an imitation of the way members of white "high society" comported themselves.

Call-and-response   A musical procedure in which a single voice or instrument states a melodic phrase—the *call*—and a group of voices or instruments follows with a responding or completing phrase—the *response*.

Chair   Each part of a section, as in first trumpet chair, first trombone chair, and so on.

Change step   *See* **Back-beat**

Chicago jazz   A type of New Orleans–style jazz created by Chicago musicians in the 1920s.

Chorus   Each time the performers execute or work through the form of a song, it is called a chorus—for example, once through a twelve-bar blues or once through a thirty-two-bar song.

Chorus reverberation   An electronic effect that guitarists use to "fatten" or fill out sounds. The sound signal is enriched through the addition of reverb (echo) and a chorus-effect (that is, added frequencies complement the sound, giving the effect of several voices or tones sounding at once).

Chromatic scale   A scale with all twelve notes of the Western musical system, for example, all the adjacent notes on the piano. There are twelve notes in an octave, which create a chromatic scale.

Clarinet   A single-reed woodwind instrument. Listen to Tracks 20–21 of the Audio Primer CD to hear the sound of the clarinet.

Comping   The chordal accompaniment provided by pianists or guitarists in jazz bands. This accompaniment is often syncopated. The term *comp* is probably derived from a contraction of the word *accompany* or *complement*.

Complete reissue   The duplication of an artist's or group's entire available body of recorded material—including errors, outtakes, and technical problems.

Cool jazz   A reaction against bebop that involved more-complex compositions, slower tempos, and sometimes less emotional involvement.

Cornet   A medium-range brass instrument much like a trumpet but with a larger bore and hence a mellower sound. Heard mostly in New Orleans and Chicago jazz in the 1920s where, like the trumpet, it was a **lead instrument**.

Countermelody   A separate line that runs in counterpoint to the main melody. Like an **obbligato,** a countermelody is a secondary melody that accompanies the main melody. A countermelody, however, is generally heard on the trombone or in a lower voice, has fewer notes than the obbligato, and is often improvised. Another word for countermelody is *counterline*. Listen to Track 7 of the ⏺ Audio Primer CD to hear a countermelody.

Counterpoint   The use of simultaneously sounding musical lines. *See also* **Polyphony.**

Creoles of Color   People of mixed black and white ancestry, often from New Orleans. Until the late nineteenth century, they enjoyed more freedom and were better educated than the general black population. Musicians from this group generally had classical training and could read musical scores.

Crossover   The practice of mixing musical styles and cultures. As first seen in the concert jazz of the 1920s and the third-stream practices of the 1950s, crossover can include different styles from a given culture—for example, bluegrass and classical music—or it can involve music from entirely different cultures, such as traditional Japanese music and bebop.

Crossover music   Music that combines jazz or jazz values with other styles and music of other cultures.

Cross-rhythms   The performance of simultaneous and contrasting rhythms, such as patterns with duple and triple groupings. Superimposing one rhythmic pattern on another causes a cross-rhythm to develop.

Digital delay   An electronic effect that creates an echo or secondary sound so that a guitarist can, in effect, play several parts at once.

Dixieland   *See* **New Orleans jazz**

Double drumming   An early jazz technique of placing the snare and bass drum close together so that players could hit both drums quickly.

Double-necked guitar   A guitar that has two necks. Sometimes the second neck has twelve strings rather than the usual six.

Dropping bombs   A technique in which bebop drummers used the bass drum to make sharp, irregular accents in the rhythmic accompaniment.

Drums   The backbone of the jazz rhythm section. Usually a drum kit consists of snare drum, bass drum, several tomtoms, and various cymbals. Listen to Tracks 26–35 of the ⏺ Audio Primer CD to hear a range of drum sounds.

Echoplex   A commercial electronic device that adds echo to a sound. The rate of speed of the echo can be altered to make the delay effect slight or more pronounced. This device was popular in the late 1960s and 1970s.

Elastic meter   A rhythmic effect created when the soloist or rhythm section masks the strong metric downbeats so that the meter seems to be stretched. This illusion is often created when musicians play unusually long phrases that move the melodic emphasis off the expected downbeats that occur at the beginning of each measure.

Exposition   The beginning of a typical **fugue.**

Extended chord tones (tensions)   Notes added to seventh chords to make the harmony richer and more pungent. These tones are usually ninths, elevenths, and thirteenths. Extended chord tones will usually resolve to more-stable pitches, such as roots, thirds, and fifths.

False start   An incorrect start of a performance—a musician begins playing a measure or two, then, realizing the mistake, stops abruptly.

Feedback   A distorted effect created when the sound coming from a speaker is picked up by an electronic sensing device such as a microphone and routed again back to the speaker. As this process multiplies, harsh electronic wails are created.

Formula   A worked-out melodic idea that fits a common chord progression. Most improvisers develop formulas for up-tempo improvisation especially, because the rapid tempo does not allow time for total spontaneity. A formula is more popularly known as a *lick*.

Free jazz   The 1960s jazz substyle that overturned many of the traditional elements of the music. Also called *avant-garde* and the *New Thing*.

Frequency modulation   Sound modulation in which the frequency (the range of high and low) of the wave is modified by another wave, producing a sound vastly different from the original. *See also* **amplitude modulation** and **modulation.**

Front line   The lead (melody) instruments in early jazz bands. The front line usually included trumpet (or cornet), trombone, and clarinet. (Use of saxophone was a later development.) *See also* **lead instrument.**

Fugue A baroque form characterized by continuous counterpoint based on a principal melodic idea called the **subject.** At the beginning of a typical fugue, in a section known as the **exposition,** each voice (or part) begins by stating the subject.

Full-chord style *See* **Locked-hands style**

Funky jazz (soul jazz) A style that combines elements of gospel music and R&B with jazz. It began to emerge in the 1950s as an outgrowth of hard bop and became quite popular in the 1960s.

Fusion *See* **Jazz-rock**

Ghost bands Groups whose founding leaders have died but who continue to travel and work under new direction.

Glissando A technique whereby notes are slurred directly from one to another, producing a continuous rise or fall in pitch.

Guitar A string instrument played as either a **lead instrument** (through picking) or a rhythm instrument (through chord strumming). It can be acoustic or amplified. Listen to Tracks 36–42 of the Audio Primer CD to hear examples of acoustic and electric guitar in different settings.

Hard bop A jazz movement of the 1950s that drew on the speed, intensity, and power of bebop and sometimes married bop to gospel and blues-influenced music.

Harlem Renaissance A period—roughly 1921 to 1929—of outstanding artistic activity among African Americans. The movement was centered in Harlem, in New York City.

Harmolodics A theory of music devised by Ornette Coleman.

Harmon mute A hollow metal mute that, when placed in the bell of the trumpet, gives its sound a distant, brooding quality. Miles Davis's use of the harmon mute from 1954 onward helped popularize its use.

Harmonic substitution The technique of replacing an expected chord with a more unusual one. Listen to Track 6 of the Audio Primer CD to hear examples of harmonic substitution.

Harmonic superimposition The technique of adding chords on top of the harmonies already present in a song, thereby adding harmonic complexity.

Head arrangement A musical plan and form worked up verbally by the players in rehearsal or on the bandstand.

Hipster A young, often white, follower of jazz who affected the dress, speech, and manner of jazz musicians working in the new jazz styles of the late 1940s and early 1950s.

Hot bands Jazz bands that featured fast tempos and dramatic solo and group performances, usually with more improvisation than **sweet bands** had.

Inside playing The jazz technique of playing melodic lines that favor the principal notes of the harmonies. *See also* **outside playing.** Listen to Track 8 of the Audio Primer CD to hear examples of inside and outside playing.

Intonation The ability of an musician to reproduce a given pitch. Musicians with good intonation are said to be playing "in tune." That is, the players know how to make small adjustments in the pitch of their instruments as they play so that they match the pitches of the other players in the section.

Jazz chair A player hired especially for improvisational fluency; spoken of as the jazz chair of a given section. For example, Bix Beiderbecke occupied the jazz trumpet chair in the Paul Whiteman band, as did Bubber Miley in the Ellington band.

Jazz-funk *See* **Jazz-rock**

Jazz repertory movement A movement since the 1980s in which ensembles devoted themselves to the re-creation and performance of historically significant jazz artists and their work. Just as classical music has an accepted repertory of great works, the jazz repertory movement is trying to establish an official canon for jazz.

Jazz-rock A form of jazz that combines elements of rock (or R&B funk) and jazz. Also called *jazz-funk* or *fusion*.

Lead instrument The instrument carrying the principal part, usually the melody. In a section of instruments of the same type, the lead instrument usually plays the highest part as the "leader" of the section.

Lead player The player in a section who usually takes the melody or top part and occupies the first chair of the section. The lead player usually plays slightly more loudly than the other players in the section.

Lead trumpet The lead chair or first trumpet player of the trumpet section. This player needs to be dominating and capable of precision, power, and control of the high register. A big band is particularly dependent on the lead trumpet.

Legato   The technique of playing notes smoothly in a connected manner. The opposite of legato is **staccato**.

Library (book)   A band's collection of arrangements or pieces. These are usually songs but may also include larger-scale works. A library is necessary for big bands, but smaller groups may have one.

Lick   *See* **Formula**

Locked-hands style   A mode of performance in which the pianist plays a four-note chord in the right hand and doubles the top note with the left hand an octave below. The hands move together in a "locked" rhythmic pattern as they follow the same rhythm. This style is also called *block-chord* or *full-chord style*. Listen to Track 9 of the 🎧 Audio Primer CD to hear an example of locked-hands style.

LP   A long-playing record that typically plays at 33⅓ rpm (revolutions per minute). LPs first became commercially available in 1948. LPs were made with polyvinyl chloride (hence the nickname "vinyl" for records) and allowed up to about twenty-five minutes of music per side.

Mellotron   An electronic instrument used for string-ensemble effects in the 1970s. An early, analog sound module, the Mellotron produces notes by activating short tape recordings of a string ensemble playing each note of the scale. When a key is depressed, the tape recording of the chosen note plays.

Meter   A rhythmic pattern arising from regular groupings of two or three beats. These define, respectively, duple or triple meter. Most music has meter.

Metric displacement   A technique whereby the soloist implies or states in the melody a rhythm that seems to go against the underlying basic meter of the piece. It also can be achieved by placing melodic phrases irregularly against the underlying meter.

Metronomic sense   A steady rhythmic pulse, often associated with drums and with music from Africa.

Microtones   Pitches between the tempered notes of the chromatic scale. Used in **nontempered intonation**.

MIDI   An acronym for *Musical Instrument Digital Interface*. This standard language allows computers to control synthesizers or samplers.

Minstrelsy   A form of U.S. musical theater and variety show that flourished in the nineteenth century. Traveling troupes performed songs, dances, and skits based on caricatures of African Americans. Performed by both blacks and whites in blackface, minstrelsy is often considered the first distinctively U.S. musical genre.

Modal jazz   A body of music that makes use of one or more of the following characteristics: modal scales for improvising, slow harmonic rhythm, pedal points, and the absence or suppression of functional harmonic relationships.

Modulation   Changing a sound by feeding one sound wave through another. *See also* **amplitude modulation** and **frequency modulation**.

Moldy figs   A term used by younger musicians and fans in the 1940s to describe older jazz fans who clung to the music of the 1920s and 1930s and derided the newer bebop style.

Motive (motivic material)   A short melodic fragment used as the basis for improvisation or development.

Motivic cells   Short melodic ideas subject to variation and development. Also called *thematic cells.*

Multiphonics   A technique of producing more than one note at a time on a wind instrument. Using non-standard fingering and appropriate embouchure, the player splits the air stream into two or more parts, thus producing a multinote "chordal" effect. The technique is difficult to control, may be strident, and is generally associated with avant-garde playing.

Multitracking   *See* **Overdubbing**

Mutes   Devices played in or over the bells of brass instruments to alter their tone. Different mutes create different kinds of effects, but a muted brass tone will usually be less brilliant than the "open" horn.

New Orleans jazz   The jazz style that originated in New Orleans and flourished in the late 1910s and 1920s. Often called *Dixieland*. The New Orleans jazz band often had a front line (of trumpet or cornet, trombone, and clarinet) accompanied by a rhythm section (of piano, guitar or banjo, bass, and drums).

New Thing   *See* **Free jazz**

Nontempered intonation   The use of pitches unrestricted by the "equal-tempered," twelve-note chromatic scale. For example, a nontempered pitch might be a note between D and E♭. *See* **microtones**.

Obbligato   A complementary melodic part, played at the same time as the main melody. In jazz, the obbligato part is usually improvised. In early jazz, obbligato parts were often florid, usually played by the clarinet, and sometimes improvised.

Ostinato A repeated melodic or harmonic idea that forms the basis for a section or an entire composition.

Out-chorus The final, usually highly exuberant chorus of a jazz performance. Also called *shout chorus*.

Outside playing The jazz technique of playing notes that depart from (or are "outside") the chords of a given piece. *See also* **inside playing**. Listen to Track 8 of the 🅟 Audio Primer CD to hear examples of inside and outside playing.

Overdubbing A recording-studio technique that was generally available by the 1950s. The recording tape has several parallel tracks that enable musicians to record additional performance parts at later times. The added part is called an *overdub*. By wearing headphones, the players follow and "play to" the previously recorded tracks. Also called *multitracking*.

Partial (overtone) A series of higher notes that occurs when a note is sounded and that contributes to the timbre of the original pitch. These higher notes are based on mathematical relationships to the original note, known as the *fundamental*.

Pedal point A sustained or repeated bass note or drone played to accompany a melody.

Pedal tone *See* **Pedal point**

Pentatonic scale A five-note set that avoids the interval of a tritone and can be arranged as a series of perfect fourths or perfect fifths. The black notes of the keyboard form one such pentatonic scale. Also called *pentatonic set*.

Phase shifter An electronic device that alters the sound of an instrument by altering the sound wave's shape. The resulting sound has a bubbling or slightly hard-edged quality.

Piano The principal Western keyboard instrument. In jazz it functions as a solo instrument and as part of the rhythm section (usually with bass and drums and sometimes added guitar or banjo). The piano trio (with bass and drums or bass and guitar) is a common small jazz ensemble that features the piano.

Piano rolls Cylinders of rolled paper punched with holes. When fed through a properly equipped player piano, the holes activate hammers that play the piano automatically.

Plagal cadence A type of cadence that contains the harmonic progression IV–I (instead of the more common progression V–I). Sometimes called a "church" cadence or "Amen cadence," it is often used at the ends of hymns with the concluding "Amen." Plagal cadences were featured frequently in funky/soul jazz.

Player piano A piano equipped with a mechanism that allows it to play piano rolls.

Plunger A type of mute derived from a plumber's sink plunger. The rubber cup of the plunger is held against the bell of the instrument and manipulated with the left hand to alter the horn's tone quality.

Polymeter The simultaneous juxtaposition of two or more musical lines in different meters.

Polyphony Distinct, simultaneous musical parts. Another name for a polyphonic texture is **counterpoint**.

Postmodernism An attitude toward art and culture that has become common since the 1970s. It disavows some of the cerebral, audience-distancing tenets of modernism and replaces them with a freewheeling conception of culture.

Prolonged note A note that is held across a harmonic change. More abstractly, we conceive of notes that are not actually being played as holding through chord changes to connect stepwise to later notes in a solo. Prolongation helps build continuity in a solo.

Race record An early recording, usually of jazz or blues and typically performed by and marketed to African Americans.

Ragtime An African-American musical genre that flourished from the late 1890s through the mid-1910s and is based on constant syncopation in the right hand often accompanied by a steady march bass in the left hand. Associated now primarily with piano music, ragtime was originally a method of performance that included syncopated songs, music for various ensembles, and arrangements of nonragtime music. Scott Joplin was ragtime's most famous composer.

Recomposition The composition of a new melody to fit the harmonic and formal structure of a previously composed popular song.

Reharmonization The bop practice of inserting different chords into the fundamental chord structure of a well-known song to freshen the interpretation and expand harmonic options for the soloist.

Remastering   The digital enhancement of an original recording's sound quality. It includes such techniques as filtering out extraneous noise and boosting certain frequencies.

Rent party   An informal gathering in the 1920s, held to help raise money to pay the rent or buy groceries. At these parties, musicians would often gather and perform, sometimes in competition with one another.

Rhythm changes   The harmonies of the George and Ira Gershwin song "I Got Rhythm" (1930). (The final 2-bar tag of the original song is omitted, so that a symmetrical 32-bar AABA plan results.) The bridge in rhythm changes consists of 2-bar harmonies following a circle-of-fifths pattern that returns to the tonic. For example, if rhythm changes are performed in B♭, the harmonies of the 8-bar bridge are D7 (2 bars), G7 (2 bars), C7 (2 bars), and F7 (2 bars). The F7, as the dominant of the tonic B♭, leads back to the A section. Extremely popular since the 1930s, rhythm changes are still commonly used by jazz musicians for improvisation and composition. Listen to Track 10 of the 🅟 Audio Primer CD to hear an example of rhythm changes.

Rhythm section   A part of a jazz band that provides the rhythmic pulse, harmonies, and bass line. It may include any of the following: bass, drums, piano, or guitar. Early jazz bands sometimes included banjo and tuba in place of the guitar and bass.

Riff   A short melodic idea, usually one to two bars long, that is repeated as the core idea of a musical passage. Sometimes different band sections trade riffs in a call-and-response format. Usually rhythmic and simple, the riff also can provide an effective background for an improvising soloist.

Ring shout   A rhythmic dance performed in a circular figure, originally derived from African religious practice. Worshipers moved in a counterclockwise direction while singing spirituals and accompanying themselves by clapping and stamping. Some historians describe the ring shout as contributing the essence of African song, dance, and spirit to African-American music.

Samplers   Electronic devices used both to sample and to play back sounds.

Sampling   The practice of recording sounds for musical use in playback. Any kind of sound can be sampled, from a note on an acoustic instrument, to natural sounds, to a passage of music already recorded. For playback, the sound is usually activated by computer or by pressing a key on a keyboard. *See also* **samplers** and **sound modules**.

Saxophone   A single-reed instrument made of brass that is common in all jazz styles except New Orleans (Dixieland). The saxophone comes in many sizes and ranges. Listen to Tracks 16–19 of the 🅟 Audio Primer CD to hear the four most common saxophones.

Scat singing   A jazz vocal style in which the soloist improvises using made-up or "nonsense" syllables.

Section   A group of related instruments in a big band; three trumpets and three trombones might form the brass section.

Sheets of sound   An expression coined by jazz critic Ira Gitler to describe John Coltrane's method of playing that features extremely fast notes with irregular phrase groupings. Sometimes, unusual harmonies are introduced over the given chord change.

Shout chorus   *See* **Out-chorus**

Shuffle   A 4/4 rhythmic pattern in which each beat is represented by the drummer playing a dotted-eighth and sixteenth note, usually on the ride cymbal.

Sideman   A player who is not a lead player or featured soloist.

Slap bass   A technique in which the bass player percussively hits the low strings of the electric bass while picking melodies on the higher ones. This style was created by Larry Graham and subsequently imitated by jazz, funk, and popular bass players.

Slash notation   A method of showing the harmonies (or "chord changes") in jazz and popular music. Each slash in a measure denotes a beat. The arranger places chords over the slashes to show the beats on which the harmonies change. (See Music Example 1-1 for an example.)

Smooth jazz   A popular form of fusion jazz that combines rock or funk grooves with an electronic ambience to create an "easy listening" feel. While improvisation may be present, the pleasant, mood-music quality of the groove and melody dominates.

Song plugger   In the 1920s someone who performed a song, usually at a music store, to encourage people to buy the sheet music.

Soul jazz   *See* **Funky jazz**

Sound fields   A musical effect created when coinciding melodic lines fuse into a indistinguishable web or mass of sound with irregular accentuation within each line.

Sound modules   Electronic devices that play back pre-recorded samples. *See also* **Sampling**.

Speakeasy   A Prohibition-era nightclub in which liquor was sold illegally.

Spirituals   African-American songs that arose in the nineteenth century and consisted of religious lyrics with folk melodies. They were often harmonized for vocal choir.

Staccato   The technique of playing short notes with distinct spaces between them. The opposite of staccato is **legato**.

Step connection   The principal means of stringing together the melodic and harmonic elements. The steps are often based on the scale determined by the key of the piece. This is a key element in **voice leading**.

Stock arrangement (stock)   An arrangement created and sold by a publishing company to bandleaders. Bands played stock arrangements to keep up with the latest hit songs.

Stop time   The punctuation of distinct beats, often to accommodate a soloist's improvisations between the band's chords.

Stride piano   A school of jazz piano playing based on a moving left-hand accompaniment alternating bass notes and chords with appropriate right-hand figuration pulling or tugging at the left hand.

Strophic form   A song form based on a series of verses (or strophes), each sung to the same repeated tune. Typically, folk songs have strophes of sixteen or thirty-two bars; these are repeated for each new lyrical verse. Each strophe is usually called a **chorus** in jazz.

Subject   The prinicipal melodic idea of a piece, such as a **fugue**.

Suite   A European classical musical work that has several sections, each with distinctive melodies and moods. The sections may or may not be related thematically. Often, composers will extract the most popular or most effective sections from extended works, such as opera and ballets, to create a suite for concert performance.

Sweet bands   Bands that played relatively less-syncopated, slower pieces, such as ballads and popular songs. *See also* **hot bands**.

Swell   The rapid change in volume that can be created by pushing down on or releasing the volume pedal of an electronic or conventional organ.

Swing   Generic term for the jazz and much popular music of the mid-1930s through the mid-1940s.

Syncopation   The unexpected accenting of a "weaker" melody note or offbeat. Syncopation displaces the accent, or emphasis, from an expected to an unexpected position. For example, because the first and third beats are usually emphasized in each bar of a 4/4 piece, emphasizing the second beat would be syncopation. In general, syncopation involves unexpected accents occurring within a regular pulse stream. For an illustration, see Music Example 1-3, third measure, and listen to Track 4 of the Audio Primer CD. The Joplin phrase is played first as it was written (with syncopation), then without.

Tag   A short, codalike section added to the end of a composition to give it closure.

Tailgate trombone   The New Orleans style of playing trombone with chromatic glissandos. The trombonist would play in the back—on the tailgate—of the New Orleans advertising wagons when the bands traveled during the day to advertise their upcoming dances. Listen to Track 25 of the Audio Primer CD to hear an example of tailgate trombone.

Tensions   *See* **Extended chord tones**

Terminal vibrato   A vibrato added to the end of a sustained note.

Territory band   In the swing era, a band that played and toured a region around a major city that served as a home base.

Texture   The density of musical sound, as determined by the instruments (or voices) heard, the number of instruments, and the number of notes or sounds being played by them. Textures are often described as thick (many notes heard) or thin (few notes).

Thematic cells   *See* **Motivic cells**

Third-stream music   A blend of jazz and European concert music. In many instances, third-stream composers create concert works that allow for improvisation within larger-scale structures influenced by both jazz and concert music.

Tonality   A Western musical system in which pieces are organized according to harmony within some key or with respect to some central pitch.

Trading twos, trading fours, or trading eights   Improvisational jazz formats common since the swing era. In trading fours, for example, each soloist improvises for four bars before the next soloist takes over for four bars. Any number of soloists may participate, but most typically two to four do. Trading solos is often used to create climactic moments in performances.

Transcribe   To write in standard, European music notation what the transcriber hears when listening to a piece of music. *See also* **transcription**.

Transcription   The notated version of a piece of music. Transcriptions of the same piece of music can vary widely, depending on the quality of the original sound source, the skill of the **transcriber**, and what the transcriber chooses to include in the notation.

Trombone   A lower brass instrument that changes pitch by means of a slide. (There is also a less common valve trombone that works largely like a lower-pitched trumpet.) In New Orleans jazz, it typically provides **countermelodies** to the trumpet lead. Big bands often feature sections of three or four trombones. It is also an important jazz solo instrument. Listen to Tracks 22–25 of the Audio Primer CD to hear examples of trombone playing.

Tuba   A low brass instrument that sometimes provided the bass part in New Orleans and Chicago-style (Dixieland) jazz. Uncommon in later jazz styles.

Twelve-tone composition   A twentieth-century procedure pioneered by Viennese composer Arnold Schoenberg in the 1920s. In twelve-tone composition, as it was originally conceived, all twelve pitches of the chromatic scale are arranged into an ordered "set," also called a *tone row* or *series*. The order of the notes in the row governs the flow of the melody and harmony in a piece. Works written with the twelve-tone procedure and its variants are often called *serial,* standing for series.

Vertical improvisation   An improvisation based on the chord harmonies (stacked vertically), as opposed to the melolodic contour (running horizontally).

Vibrato   A method of varying the pitch frequency of a note, producing a wavering sound. A vibrato brings a note to life. Heard mostly on wind instruments, strings, and vocals.

Vocalese   The technique of setting lyrics to existing jazz solos. Eddie Jefferson was probably the most important pioneer of this technique.

Voice leading   A means of making logical melodic and harmonic sequences within an improvised solo. **Step connection**, a key element in voice leading, is the principal means of stringing together the melodic and harmonic elements. The steps are often based on the scale determined by the key of the piece.

Wah-wah pedal   A pitch-frequency filter, operated by the foot, that is usually used by guitarists or electric keyboardists. When the pedal is depressed, the note or chord being held makes a "wah" sound. (An acoustic "wah" sound can be achieved by brass players using their left hands or mutes over the bells of their instruments.) The up-and-down movement of the pedal creates the repeated "wah-wah" effect.

Walking bass   A musical technique in which the bass player articulates all four beats in a 4/4 bar. The bass lines often follow simple scale patterns, avoiding too many disruptive leaps between notes. The walking bass is quite common in jazz, heard in all styles since becoming firmly established during the swing era. Listen to Track 43 of the Audio Primer CD to hear a walking bass.

West Coast jazz   A jazz style from the 1950s that embodied many of the principles of cool jazz as performed by a group of players centered in California.

Whole-tone scale   A scale with whole steps only and thus no dominant, making it impossible to form major or minor triads. A whole-tone scale starts on a note and proceeds up or down by whole step only. There are only two whole-tone scales: C–D–E–F#–G#–B♭ and D♭–E♭–F–G–A–B. Notice that they share no notes. This scale was common among French composers, including Claude Debussy.

SELECTED READINGS

Allen, William Francis, Charles Pickard Ware, and Lucy McKim Garrison. *Slave Songs of the United States.* New York: Peter Smith, 1951. Orig. pub. New York: A. Smith, 1867. Reprint, New York: Dover, 1997.

Armstrong, Louis. *Satchmo: My Life in New Orleans.* New York: Prentice-Hall, 1954. Reprint, New York: Da Capo Press, 1986.

———. *Swing That Music.* New York: Longmans, Green, 1936.

Balliett, Whitney. *Jelly Roll, Jabbo, and Fats: Nineteen Portraits in Jazz.* New York: Oxford University Press, 1983.

Barker, Danny. *A Life in Jazz.* New York: Oxford University Press, 1986.

Basie, Count, as told to Albert Murray. *Good Morning Blues: The Autobiography of Count Basie.* New York: Random House, 1985.

Bechet, Sidney. *Treat It Gentle: An Autobiography.* New York: Hill and Wang, 1960. Reprint, New York: Da Capo Press, 1978.

Berlin, Edward A. *Ragtime: A Musical and Cultural History.* Berkeley: University of California Press, 1980.

Bethell, Tom. *George Lewis: A Jazzman from New Orleans.* Berkeley: University of California Press, 1977.

Borque, Fred. "Pat Metheny: Musings on Neo-Fusion." *Down Beat,* March 22, 1979, pp. 13 ff.

Brown, Theodore Dennis. "A History and Analysis of Jazz Drumming to 1942." Ph.D. diss., University of Michigan, 1976.

Calloway, Cab, and Bryant Rollins. *Of Minnie the Moocher and Me.* New York: Crowell, 1976.

Carr, Ian. *Miles Davis: A Biography.* New York: Morrow, 1982.

Carver, Reginald, and Lenny Bernstein. *Jazz Profiles: The Spirit of the Nineties.* New York: Billboard Books, 1998.

Chambers, Jack. *Milestones 1: The Music and Times of Miles Davis to 1960.* Toronto: University of Toronto Press, 1983.

———. *Milestones 2: The Music and Times of Miles Davis since 1960.* Toronto: University of Toronto Press, 1985.

Charters, Samuel, and Leonard Kunstadt. *Jazz: A History of the New York Scene.* Garden City, NY: Doubleday, 1962. Reprint, New York: Da Capo Press, 1981.

Chase, Gilbert. *America's Music: From the Pilgrims to the Present.* 3rd ed. rev. Urbana: University of Illinois Press, 1987.

Chilton, John. *Sidney Bechet: The Wizard of Jazz.* New York: Oxford University Press, 1987.

———. *Who's Who of Jazz: Storyville to Swing Street.* 4th ed. New York: Da Capo Press, 1985.

Collier, James Lincoln. *Benny Goodman and the Swing Era.* New York: Oxford University Press, 1989.

———. *Duke Ellington.* New York: Oxford University Press, 1987.

———. *Louis Armstrong: An American Genius.* New York: Oxford University Press, 1983.

Coltrane, John, in collaboration with Don DeMicheal. "Coltrane on Coltrane." *Down Beat,* September 29, 1960, pp. 26–27.

Coryell, Julie, and Laura Friedman. *Jazz-Rock Fusion: The People, The Music.* New York: Delacorte Press, 1978.

Dance, Stanley. *The World of Earl Hines.* New York: Scribner, 1977. Reprint, New York: Da Capo Press, 1979.

————. *The World of Swing.* New York: Scribner, 1974. Reprint, New York: Da Capo Press, 1979.

Davis, Miles, and Quincy Troupe. *Miles: The Autobiography.* New York: Simon & Schuster, 1989.

DeMichael, Don. "John Coltrane and Eric Dolphy Answer the Jazz Critics." *Down Beat,* April 12, 1962, pp. 20 ff.

DeVeaux, Scott. "Bebop and the Recording Industry: The 1942 AFM Recording Ban Reconsidered." *Journal of the American Musicological Society* 41, no. 1 (1988): 126–65.

————. *The Birth of Bebop: A Social and Musical History.* Berkeley: University of California Press, 1997.

Dodds, Baby, as told to Larry Gara. *The Baby Dodds Story.* Rev. ed. Baton Rouge: Lousiana State University Press, 1992.

Douglas, Ann. *Terrible Honesty: Mongrel Manhattan in the 1920s.* New York: Farrar, Straus, Giroux, 1995.

Ellington, Duke. *Music Is My Mistress.* Garden City, NY: Doubleday, 1973. Reprint, New York: Da Capo Press, 1976.

Floyd, Samuel A., Jr. "Music in the Harlem Renaissance: An Overview." In *Black Music in the Harlem Renaissance,* ed. Samuel A. Floyd, Jr. New York: Greenwood Press, 1990.

Foster, Pops, as told to Tom Stoddard. *Pops Foster: The Autobiography of a New Orleans Jazzman.* Berkeley: University of California Press, 1971.

Gillespie, Dizzy, with Al Fraser. *To Be or Not . . . to Bop.* Garden City, NY: Doubleday, 1979. Reprint, New York: Da Capo Press, 1985.

Gioia, Ted. *West Coast Jazz.* New York: Oxford University Press, 1992.

Gitler, Ira. *Jazz Masters of the Forties.* New York: Macmillan, 1966. Reprint, New York: Da Capo Press, 1983.

————. *Swing to Bop: An Oral History of the Transition in Jazz in the 1940s.* New York: Oxford University Press, 1985.

Goldstein, Gil. *Jazz Composers Companion.* New York: Consolidated Music Publishers, 1981.

Goodman, Benny, and Irving Kolodin. *The Kingdom of Swing.* New York: Stackpole, 1939. Reprint, New York: Frederick Ungar, 1961.

Gridley, Mark. *Jazz Styles: History and Analysis.* 5th ed. Englewood Cliffs, NJ: Prentice-Hall, 1994.

Gushee, Lawrence. "How the Creole Band Came to Be." *Black Music Research Journal* 8, no. 1 (1988): 85–100.

————. "Lester Young's 'Shoe Shine Boy.'" In *A Lester Young Reader,* edited by Lewis Porter, 224–54. Washington, DC: Smithsonian Institution Press, 1991. Originally published as International Musicological Society, *Report of the Twelfth Congress, Berkeley, 1977,* edited by Daniel Heartz and Bonnie Wade. Kassel, Germany: Barenreiter, 1981.

————. Liner notes to King Oliver, *King Oliver's Jazz Band—1923.* Columbia P2 12744.

————. Liner notes to *Steppin' on the Gas: Rags to Jazz 1913–1927.* New World Records 269.

Hadlock, Richard. *Jazz Masters of the Twenties.* (New York: Macmillan, 1965. Reprint, New York: Da Capo Press, 1988.

Hall, Robert L. "African Religious Retentions in Florida." In *Africanisms in American Culture,* edited by Joseph E. Holloway. Bloomington: Indiana University Press, 1990.

Handy, W. C., and Arna Bontemps. *Father of the Blues.* New York: Macmillan, 1941. Reprint, New York: Da Capo Press, 1991.

Hasse, John. *Beyond Category: The Life and Genius of Duke Ellington.* New York: Simon & Schuster, 1993.

————, ed. *Ragtime: Its History, Composers, and Music.* New York: Schirmer Books, 1985.

Hentoff, Nat. *The Jazz Life.* New York: Dial Press, 1961.

Hodeir, André. *Jazz: Its Evolution and Essence.* New York: Grove, 1956. Reprint, New York: Da Capo Press, 1976.

Howlett, Felicity. "An Introduction to Art Tatum's Performance Approaches: Composition, Improvisation, and Melodic Variation." Ph.D. diss., Cornell University, 1983.

Huggins, Nathan Irvin. *Harlem Renaissance.* New York: Oxford University Press, 1971.

———. "Interview with Eubie Blake." In *Voices from the Harlem Renaissance*, edited by Nathan Huggins. New York: Oxford University Press, 1976.

Hunt, Joe. *52nd Street Beat: Modern Jazz Drummers 1945–1965*. New Albany, IN: Jamey Aeborsold Jazz, n.d.

Jewell, Derek. *Duke: A Portrait of Duke Ellington*. New York: Norton, 1977.

Jones, A. M. "African Rhythm." *Africa* 24, no. 1 (January 1954): 39.

———. "Blue Notes and Hot Rhythm." *African Music Society Newsletter* 1 (June 1951): 10.

———. *Studies in African Music*. New York: Oxford University Press, 1959.

Jones, LeRoi. *Blues People*. New York: Morrow, 1963.

———. "The Jazz Avant Garde." *Metronome* 78, no. 9 (September 1961): 9 ff.

Jost, Ekkehard. *Free Jazz*. Graz, Austria: Universal Edition, 1974. Reprint, New York: Da Capo Press, 1981.

Kaminsky, Max, with V. E. Hughes. *My Life in Jazz*. New York: Harper & Row, 1963.

Kenney, William Howland. *Chicago Jazz: A Cultural History, 1904–1930*. New York: Oxford University Press, 1993.

Kernfeld, Barry, ed. *The New Grove Dictionary of Jazz*. New York: St. Martin's Press, 1994.

Kirchner, Bill, ed. *The Oxford Companion to Jazz*. New York: Oxford University Press, 2000.

Kofsky, Frank. *Black Nationalism and the Revolution in Music*. New York: Pathfinder Press, 1970.

Levine, Lawrence. *Black Culture and Black Consciousness: Afro-American Folk Thought from Slavery to Freedom*. New York: Oxford University Press, 1977.

Lewis, John. *The World of Music*. Information Bulletin No. 4 of the International Music Council, Unesco House, Paris, May 1958.

Litweiler, John. *The Freedom Principle: Jazz After 1958*. New York: Morrow, 1984.

Lomax, Alan. *Mister Jelly Roll: The Fortunes of Jelly Roll Morton, New Orleans Creole and "Inventor" of Jazz*. 2nd ed. Berkeley: University of California Press, 1973.

Lyons, Len. *The Great Jazz Pianists: Speaking of Their Lives and Their Music*. New York: Da Capo Press, 1989.

Marquis, Donald M. *In Search of Buddy Bolden, First Man of Jazz*. Baton Rouge: Louisiana State University Press, 1978.

Martin, Henry. *Charlie Parker and Thematic Improvisation*. Lanham, MD: Scarecrow Press, 1996.

———. *Enjoying Jazz*. New York: Schirmer Books, 1986.

Merriam, Allan P. "African Music." In *Continuity and Change in African Cultures*, edited by William R. Bascom and Melville Herskovits. Chicago: University of Chicago Press, 1959.

Milkowski, Bill. *Jaco: The Extraordinary and Tragic Life of Jaco Pastorius, "The World's Greatest Bass Player."* San Francisco: Miller Freeman Books, 1995.

Murphy, Jeanette Robinson. "The Survival of African Music in America." In *The Negro and His Folk-Lore*, edited by Bruce Jackson. Austin: University of Texas Press, 1967.

Nettl, Bruno. *Folk and Traditional Music of the Western Continents*. 3rd ed. Englewood Cliffs, NJ: Prentice-Hall, 1990.

Nicholson, Stuart. *Jazz-Rock: A History*. New York: Schirmer Books, 1998.

———. *Jazz: The 1980s Resurgence*. New York: Da Capo Press, 1990.

Ogren, Kathy J. *The Jazz Revolution: Twenties America and the Meaning of Jazz*. Oxford University Press, 1989.

Oliver, Paul. *Blues Fell This Morning: The Meaning of the Blues*. 2nd ed. New York: Cambridge University Press, 1990.

———. *Savannah Syncopators: African Retentions in the Blues*. New York: Stein & Day, 1970.

Owens, Thomas. *Bebop: The Music and the Players*. New York: Oxford University Press, 1995.

Pearson, Nathan W., Jr. *Goin' to Kansas City*. Urbana: University of Illinois Press, 1987.

Placksin, Sally. *American Women in Jazz, 1900 to the Present: Their Words, Lives, and Music*. New York: Seaview Books, 1982.

Porter, Lewis. *John Coltrane: His Life and Music*. Ann Arbor: University of Michigan Press, 1998.

———. *Lester Young*. Boston: Twayne, 1985.

Porter, Lewis, with Michael Ullman and Edward Hazell. *Jazz: From Its Origins to the Present.* Englewood Cliffs, NJ: Prentice-Hall, 1993.

Ramsey, Frederick, Jr., and Charles Edward Smith, eds. *Jazzmen.* New York: Harcourt, Brace, 1939. Reprint, 1977.

Riis, Thomas L. *Just Before Jazz: Black Musical Theater in New York, 1890–1915.* Washington, DC: Smithsonian Institution Press, 1989.

Russell, Ross. *Bird Lives: The High Life and Hard Times of Charlie (Yardbird) Parker.* New York: Charterhouse, 1973. Reprint, New York: Da Capo Press, 1996.

———. *Jazz Style in Kansas City and the Southwest.* Berkeley: University of California Press, 1971.

Schafer, William J., with Richard B. Allen. *Brass Bands and New Orleans Jazz.* Baton Rouge: Louisiana State University Press, 1977.

Schuller, Gunther. *Early Jazz: Its Roots and Musical Development.* New York: Oxford University Press, 1968.

———. "Sonny Rollins and the Challenge of Thematic Improvisation." *Jazz Review,* November 1958, pp. 6–11. Reprinted in *Musings: The Musical Worlds of Gunther Schuller,* by Gunther Schuller. New York: Oxford University Press, 1986.

———. *The Swing Era: The Development of Jazz 1930–1945.* New York: Oxford University Press, 1989.

Shapiro, Nat, and Nat Hentoff, eds. *Hear Me Talkin' to Ya: The Story of Jazz as Told by the Men Who Made It.* New York: Rinehart, 1955. Reprint, New York: Dover, 1966.

Sidran, Ben. *Talking Jazz: An Oral History.* New York: Da Capo Press, 1995.

Simon, George T. *The Big Bands.* Rev. ed. New York: Collier Books, 1974.

Smith, Willie "The Lion," with George Hoefer. *Music on My Mind: The Memoirs of an American Pianist.* Garden City, NY: Doubleday, 1964. Reprint, New York: Da Capo Press, 1984.

Southern, Eileen. *The Music of Black Americans.* 2nd ed. New York: Norton, 1983.

Stearns, Marshall. *The Story of Jazz.* New York: Oxford University Press, 1958. Reprint, 1970.

Stewart, Rex. *Jazz Masters of the Thirties.* New York: Macmillan, 1972. Reprint, New York: Da Capo Press, 1982.

Strayhorn, Billy. "The Ellington Effect." *Down Beat,* November 5, 1952, pp. 4 ff.

Stuckey, Sterling. *Slave Culture: Nationalist Theory and the Foundations of Black America.* New York: Oxford University Press, 1987.

Sturm, Fred. *Changes Over Time: The Evolution of Jazz Arranging.* Rottenburg, Germany: Advance Music, 1995.

Tallmadge, William. "Blue Notes and Blue Tonality." *The Black Perspective in Music* 12, no. 2 (Fall 1984): 155–64.

Taylor, Art. *Notes and Tones: Musician-to-Musican Interviews.* Liège, Belgium: Taylor, 1977. Reprint, New York: Da Capo Press, 1993.

Thomas, J. C. *Chasin' the Trane: The Music and Mystique of John Coltrane.* Garden City, NY: Doubleday, 1975. Reprint, New York: Da Capo Press, 1976.

Thompson, Robert Farris. "Kongo Influences on African-American Artistic Culture." In *Africanisms in American Culture,* edited by Joseph E. Holloway. Bloomington: Indiana University Press, 1990.

Tucker, Mark. *Ellington: The Early Years.* Champaign: University of Illinois Press, 1991.

———, ed. *The Duke Ellington Reader.* New York: Oxford University Press, 1993.

Washburne, Christopher. "The Clave of Jazz: A Caribbean Contribution to the Rhythmic Foundation of an African-American Music." *Black Music Research Journal* 17, no. 1 (Spring 1997): 75 ff.

Williams, Martin. *The Art of Jazz: Essays on the Nature and Development of Jazz.* New York: Oxford University Press, 1959. Reprint, New York: Da Capo Press, 1979.

———. *Jazz Masters of New Orleans.* New York: Macmillan, 1967. Reprint, New York: Da Capo Press, 1979.

Wilson, Olly. "The Significance of the Relationship Between Afro-American Music and West African Music." *Black Perspective in Music* 2, no. 1 (Spring 1974): 3–22.

Wilson, Teddy, with Arie Ligthart and Humphrey van Loo. *Teddy Wilson Talks Jazz.* London: Cassell, 1996.

SELECTED DISCOGRAPHY

Chapter 1

The Greatest in Country Blues. Vol. 1. 1201 Music 70022.

The Greatest Ragtime of the Century. Biograph BCD 103.

Robert Johnson. King of the Delta Blues. Columbia/Legacy CK 65746.

Joplin, Scott. *Scott Joplin: His Greatest Hits.* Richard Zimmerman, piano. Legacy International CD 316.

Ragtime to Jazz. Vol. 1: 1912–1919. Timeless Records CBC 1-035 Jazz.

Ragtime. Vol. 1: 1897–1919. Jazz Archives No. 120 159052.

Smith, Bessie. *The Essential Bessie Smith.* Columbia/Legacy C2K 64922.

Chapter 2

Note: There are three widely available series of recordings reissued as CDs that encompass most of the artists of the 1920s and 1930s, as well as many artists of the 1940s:

The Best of Jazz: A good introductory series, in which each CD is devoted to a given artist and includes many of the artist's best or best-known recordings.

The Chronological Classics: This series contains hundreds of CDs that treat the major jazz artists' work in chronological order. CD covers are color-coded to make identification easier. A drawback to the series is that it does not include alternate takes, but only principal (master) recordings.

Média 7 Masters of Jazz: Like the Chronological Classics in that major artists' work is presented in chronological order, but with a critical difference: Every known recording is included. That is, these CDs contain all takes from each recording session, live recording (irrespective of recording quality), and radio/TV broadcasts. In instances where previous reissues have already exhaustively covered an artist in question for a given period, the series purposely avoids duplication.

Bechet, Sidney. *The Best of Sidney Bechet.* Blue Note CDP 7243 8 28891 2 0.

Morton, Jelly Roll. *Jelly Roll Morton and His Red Hot Peppers.* Vol. 1. Jazz Archives No. 110 158942.

Chapter 3

Armstrong, Louis. *Louis Armstrong and His Orchestra 1929–1930.* Chronological Classics 557.

———. *Louis Armstrong: The 25 Greatest Hot Fives and Hot Sevens.* ASV CD AJA 5171.

Beiderbecke, Bix. *Jazz Me Blues.* AAD JHR 73517.

Jazz the World Forgot: Jazz Classics of the 1920s. Yazoo (Shanachie Entertainment Corporation) 2024.

Oliver, King. *King Oliver's Creole Jazz Band 1923–1924.* Retrieval RTR 79007 Jazz.

Chapter 4

Ellington, Duke. *The Best of Early Ellington.* Decca GRD-660.

Henderson, Fletcher. *Tidal Wave—The Original Decca Recordings.* Decca GRD-643.

Johnson, James P. *An Introduction to James P. Johnson—His Best Recordings 1921–1944.* The Best of Jazz 4035.

Waller, Fats. *Turn on the Heat—The Fats Waller Piano Solos.* Bluebird 2482-2-RB.

Chapter 5

Basie, Count. *Count Basie: The Complete Decca Recordings.* Decca GRD-3-611.

Duke Ellington. *In a Mellotone.* RCA 07863 51364-2.

Goodman, Benny. *Benny Goodman: Sixteen Classic Performances.* Camden (BMG) CAMCD 192.

The Real Kansas City of the '20s, '30s, and '40s. Columbia/Legacy (Sony) CK 64855.

Chapter 6

Carter, Benny. *Benny Carter.* Vol. 3. Média 7 MJCD 39.

Fitzgerald, Ella. *The Jazz Sides.* Verve 314 527 655-2.

Hawkins, Coleman. *In the Groove, 1926–1939.* Indigo Records IGOCD 2037.

Hines, Earl. *An Introduction to Earl Hines—His Best Recordings 1927–1942.* The Best of Jazz 4047.

Holiday, Billie. *Greatest Hits.* Columbia/Legacy CK 65757.

Tatum, Art. *The Quintessence.* Frémeaux & Associés FA 217.

Wilson, Teddy. *An Introduction to Teddy Wilson—His Best Recordings 1935–1945.* The Best of Jazz 4044.

Young, Lester. *Lester Young.* Vol. 1, 1936–1942. Blue Moon BMCD 1001.

Chapter 7

Gillespie, Dizzy. *Dizzy Gillespie 1940–1946.* Jazz Archives No. 99 158182.

Monk, Thelonious. *The Best of Thelonious Monk—The Blue Note Years.* Blue Note CDP 7 95636 2.

Parker, Charlie. *The Complete Savoy and Dial Studio Recordings.* Savoy 92911-2.

————. *Complete Live Sessions on Savoy.* Savoy Jazz SVY-17021-24.

Powell, Bud. *The Complete 1946–1949.* Roost/Blue Note/Verve Swing Masters. Definitive Records DRCD 11145.

Chapter 8

Blakey, Art, and the Jazz Messengers. *Moanin'.* Blue Note 7243 4 95324 2 7.

————. *Ugetsu.* Original Jazz Classics OJCCD 090-2.

Brown, Clifford, and Max Roach. *Brown and Roach, Inc.* EmArcy 814 644-2.

Brubeck, Dave. *Time Out.* Columbia CK 65122.

Davis, Miles. *Birth of the Cool.* Capitol CDP 7243 4 94550 2 3.

————. *Kind of Blue.* Columbia CK 64935.

Giuffre, Jimmy. *Free Fall.* Columbia 65446.

Modern Jazz Quartet. *Concorde.* Original Jazz Classics OJCCD 002-2.

Chapter 9

Coleman, Ornette. *Change of the Century.* Atlantic 7 81341-2.

————. *The Shape of Jazz to Come.* Atlantic 1317-2.

Coltrane, John. *Giant Steps.* Atlantic 1311-2.

————. *A Love Supreme.* Impulse! GRD 155.

Dolphy, Eric. *Out to Lunch!* Blue Note CDP 7 46524-2.

Taylor, Cecil. *Unit Structures.* Blue Note CDP 7 84237 2.

Chapter 10

Adderley, Cannonball. *Mercy, Mercy, Mercy.* Capitol CDP 7 72438 29915 2 6.

Davis, Miles. *ESP.* Columbia CK 65683.

————. *Nefertiti.* Columbia CK 65681.

Evans, Bill. *Portrait in Jazz.* Original Jazz Classics OJCCD 088-2.

Jarrett, Keith. *Arbour Zena.* ECM 1070.

Getz, Stan. *Getz/Gilberto.* Verve UDCD 607.

Hancock, Herbie. *Maiden Voyage.* Blue Note CDP 46339 2.

Henderson, Joe. *Inner Urge.* Blue Note CDP 7 84189 2.

Hubbard, Freddie. *Hub Tones.* Blue Note CDP 84115 2.

Lloyd, Charles. *Forest Flower.* Soundtrack. Atlantic/Rhino 71746.

Tyner, McCoy. *The Real McCoy.* Blue Note 7243 4 97807 2 9.

Chapter 11

Hancock, Herbie. *Headhunters.* Columbia CK 65123.

Corea, Chick. *Light as a Feather.* Verve 314 557 115-2.

Coryell, Larry. *Spaces.* Vanguard VMD79345.

Mahavishnu Orchestra. *The Inner Mounting Flame.* Columbia CK UDCD 744.

Weather Report. *Heavy Weather.* Columbia CK 65108.

———. *Weather Report.* Columbia CK 48824.

Williams, Tony, and Lifetime. *Emergency!* Verve 314 539 117-2.

Chapter 12

Hagans, Tim. *Animation/Imagination.* Blue Note 7243 4 95198 2 4.

Hancock, Herbie. *Gershwin's World.* Verve 314 557 797-2.

Lincoln Center Jazz Orchestra. *Portraits by Ellington.* Columbia CK 53145.

Marsalis, Wynton. *Jump Start and Jazz.* Sony SK 62998.

Medeski Martin, and Wood. *Last Chance to Dance Trance (Perhaps).* Gramavision GCD 79520.

Redman, Joshua. *Freedom in the Groove.* Warner Brothers 9 46330-2.

Schneider, Maria. *Evanescence.* Enja ENJ-8048 2.

Washington, Grover. *Strawberry Moon.* Columbia Records CK 40510.

Zorn, John. *Spy versus Spy—The Music of Ornette Coleman.* Elektra/Musician 9 60844-2.

INDEX

AUDIO PRIMER CD TRACKS

PART ONE — BASICS

1 **Scales.** Major, blues, acoustic (or melodic minor, ascending form), octatonic (or diminished), whole-tone.

2 **Arpeggios.** Various seventh chords.

3 **Melody without chords, then with chords.**

4 **Syncopation.** First four bars of Scott Joplin's "The Entertainer" as written (with syncopation), then the same four bars with the syncopation removed.

5 **Back-beat or change step.** A stride left-hand chord progression is played twice; the first time without a back-beat, the second time with a back-beat.

6 **Harmonic substitution.** A ii7–V7–I progression stated simply, then gradually embellished with extensions and tritone substitutions.

7 **Counterline/countermelody with guitar and piano.** Two blues choruses: The first chorus is performed without a counterline; the second chorus includes a counterline in the piano.

8 **Inside/outside melodic lines with guitar and piano.** A ii7–V7–I progression is played twice: First the guitarist plays inside over the chords, then he plays outside over the chords.

9 **Locked hands.** A brief demonstration of this technique.

10 **Rhythm changes with piano, bass, and drums.** A 32-bar chorus of rhythm changes.

11 **Blues changes with piano, bass, and drums.** Demonstration of blues chord changes.

PART TWO — JAZZ INSTRUMENTS AND PERFORMANCE EFFECTS

Trumpet
12 Open
13 Cup mute
14 Harmon mute without stem (Miles Davis sound)
15 Harmon mute with stem (wah-wah effect)

Saxophone Family
16 Soprano
17 Alto
18 Tenor
19 Baritone

Clarinet
20 Swing clarinet sound
21 Obbligato part in Dixieland setting

Trombone
22 Open
23 Cup mute
24 Growl effect
25 Glissando and tailgate effect

Drum Set
26 Snare
27 High tom
28 Low tom
29 Bass
30 Ride cymbal (swing beat)
31 Hi-hat with chick sound (foot pedal)
32 Hi-hat with swing beat; combine foot/hand
33 Sample crash cymbals
34 All drums/cymbals together in swing groove
35 All drums/cymbals with brushes in swing groove

Acoustic and Electric Guitar
36 Acoustic chords: comping
37 Acoustic melody
38 Acoustic bossa nova style
39 Early electric sound
40 Jazz-rock (fusion) sound
41 Jazz-rock with wah-wah pedal
42 Phasing, echo, and other effects

Acoustic Bass
43 Walking bass

PART THREE — BUILDING THE JAZZ BAND THROUGH SIX BLUES CHORUSES

Bass, Drums, Piano, Trumpet, and Tenor Saxophone

44 *First chorus:* Bass and drums playing alone in a swing walking style.

45 *Second chorus:* Add piano comping.

46 *Third chorus:* Trumpet solo breaks on bars 1–2, 5–6, and 9–10.

47 *Fourth chorus:* Trumpet and saxophone trade twos. Example of antiphony or call-and-response.

48 *Fifth chorus:* Tenor saxophone solo accompanied by three-quarter-note stop time.

49 *Sixth chorus:* Tenor saxophone solo accompanied by trumpet playing a background riff.

Musicians: Keith Waters (1, 2, 3, 6, 9, and all ensemble work), piano; Henry Martin (4 and 5), piano; Ron Miles, trumpet; Rich Chiaraluce, clarinet and soprano, alto, and tenor saxophones; Mark Harris, baritone saxophone; Joe Hall, trombone; Bill Kopper, guitar; Ken Walker, bass; and Todd Reid, drums.

Recorded February 12 and 13, 2001, at the Career Education Center, Denver, Colorado. Engineer: Joe Hall. Assistant engineers: Ty Blosser, Jerry Wright, and John Romero. Produced by Henry Martin and Keith Waters.